THE BRITISH CONFEDERATE

THE BRITISH CONFEDERATE

Archibald Campbell,
Marquess of Argyll, 1607–1661

Allan I. Macinnes

JOHN DONALD

First published in Great Britain in 2011 by
John Donald, an imprint of Birlinn Ltd

West Newington House
10 Newington Road
Edinburgh
EH9 1QS

www.birlinn.co.uk

ISBN 978 1 904607 96 0

British Library Cataloguing-in-Publication Data
A catalogue record for this book is available on request
from the British Library

Typeset in Minion by
Koinonia, Manchester
Printed and bound in Britain by
MPG Books, Bodmin, Cornwall

To Dougie and Susan

Contents

Acknowledgements

The immensely stressful activity of political biography requires unstinting support and assistance, which has readily been forthcoming from a variety of individuals and institutions. This book is the culmination of twenty years of research on the house of Argyll (1603–1761), funded for the first seven years by Major Research Grants from the British Academy that sponsored access to Inveraray Castle in Argyllshire, Dumfries House in Ayrshire and at Buckminster, Grantham in Lincolnshire. For permission to work at Inveraray Castle, I am immensely indebted to the Trustees of the 10th Duke of Argyll and to the advice and acumen of the former chief executive of the ClanCampbell, Alastair Campbell of Airds. I must also thank the same Trustees and the Scottish National Portrait Gallery in Edinburgh for permission to reproduce the paintings of Archibald Campbell as Lord Lorne, 8th Earl and Marquess of Argyll. I am also grateful for the permissions for archival research at Dumfries House and Mount Stuart from the late Marquess of Bute, and at Buckminster from the Tollemache family. In collating this material, I had the privilege of working with three diligent research assistants: Fiona MacDonald, Fiona Watson and, above all, Linda Fryer, for whose aid in structuring and systematically organising the sources I shall be eternally grateful. My work on the Loudoun Scottish Collection and related papers at the Huntington Library in California was facilitated by three research fellowships in 1993, 2002 and 2005, as it also was by generous assistance from Roy Ritchie (W.M. Keck Foundation Director of Research) and Mary Robertson (William A. Moffet Chief Curator of Manuscripts). In having first a sabbatical and then a relatively light teaching load in the last three years to aid writing up, I must thank my colleagues at the University of Strathclyde and in particular the head of department, Richard Finlay, who was instrumental in bringing me to this 'useful place of learning' in 2007. My researches have been further aided by helpful assistance from staff in Rigsarkivet in Copenhagen and Newberry Library in Chicago, the Folger Library in Washington D.C. and the New York Public Library in the United States. George MacKenzie as Keeper of the Records and his staff in the National Archives of Scotland have been particularly helpful, as have the staff in that other Edinburgh institution, the National Library of Scotland, as have those in the British Library and The National Archives in London. I have been very well served by staff at the Bodleian in Oxford and at the university archives in Aberdeen, Glasgow, Edinburgh, Hull and St Andrews, as I have in Duke at Durham in North Carolina. I also appreciate the assistance I have received in the city and local archives in Aberdeen, Berwick-upon-Tweed, Dundee, Glasgow, Newcastle and Westminster. Special mention in this context must be given to the sterling support and historical insights received from Murdo MacDonald, now retired as archivist to the Argyll and Bute District.

Much intellectual sustenance has been derived from my former graduate students at Aberdeen, namely Kirsteen MacKenzie, Barry Robertson, David Menarry, Aonghus MacCoinnich and Tom McInally. I should also like to thank my undergraduate students at Glasgow, Aberdeen, Chicago and Strathclyde who helped shape my ideas on the Marquess of Argyll and the Covenanting Movement. I owe a special thanks to Alexia Grosjean, John Scally and David Scott for making important archival material available to me. I have also received illuminating insights on the Marquess of Argyll from John Young, Steve Murdoch, John Adamson, John Morrison and Keith Brown. I must also thank the usual suspects for their comradeship, contentiousness and conversation, namely Sarah Barber, Ciaran Brady, Mike Broers, Ali Cathcart, Steven Ellis, Tim Harris, Peter Lake, Patrick Little, Catriona MacDonald, Roger Mason, Esther Mijers, Edward Opalinski, Jason Peacey, Steve Pincus, Thomas Riis, Jean-Frédéric Schaub, Kevin Sharpe and last, but by no means least, Art Williamson.

Much needed spiritual sustenance continues to be provided in St Margaret's in the Gallowgate from my fellow hill walker Emsley Nimmo, Dean of Aberdeen and Orkney, and in the Stead Inn, Potterton from the lads in the local appreciation society for Scotch single malt whisky. I must thank John and Val Tuckwell for their continuing encouragement to embark upon and complete this political biography. I also thank the academic managing editor, Mairi Sutherland, for her encouragement, understanding and forbearance. I should further like to thank Jacqueline Young for her assiduous, constructive and sympathetic copy editing. Finally, I should like to thank my family in both Scotland and Denmark for their love and support, and especially my wife Tine Wanning.

The sins of omission and commission in the production of this book are solely mine.

Abbreviations and Conventions

Abbreviations

ABDA	Argyll and Bute District Archives, Lochgilphead
ACA	Aberdeen City Archives
ACL	*Aberdeen Council Letters, 1552–1681*, L.B. Taylor ed., 6 vols (Oxford, 1942–61)
AHR	*American Historical Review*
APS	*Acts of the Parliament of Scotland*, T. Thomson and C. Innes eds, 12 vols (Edinburgh, 1814–72)
AUL	Aberdeen University Library
BBT	*The Black Book of Taymouth*, C. Innes ed. (Edinburgh, 1855)
Balfour, *HW*	Sir James Balfour, *Historical Works*, J. Haig ed., 4 vols (Edinburgh, 1824–25)
BL	British Library, London
BOU	Bodleian Library, Oxford University
Burnet, *Memoirs*	Gilbert Burnet, *The Memoirs of the Lives and Actions of James and William, Dukes of Hamilton and Castleherald* (London, 1838)
CAL	*Correspondence of Sir Robert Kerr, First Earl of Ancrum and his Son William, Third Earl of Lothian*, D. Laing ed., 2 vols (Edinburgh, 1875)
Clarendon, *History*	Edward [Hyde], Earl of Clarendon, *The History of the Rebellion and Civil Wars in England* (Oxford, 1843)
CSCL	*Correspondence of the Scots Commissioners in London, 1644–1646*, H.W. Meikle ed. (Edinburgh, 1907)
CSP, Domestic	*Calendar of State Papers Domestic Series, of the Reign of Charles I*, 17 vols, J. Bruce and W.D. Hamilton (eds) (London, 1858–82)
CSP, Scotland	*Calendar of State Papers, Scotland*, vols 11–12 (1593–97), A.I. Cameron and M.S. Giuseppi eds (Edinburgh, 1936 and 1952)

CSP, Venetian	*Calendar of State Papers and Manuscripts relating to English Affairs existing in the Archives and Collections of Venice, and in other Libraries of Northern Italy* A.B. Hinds ed. (London, 1913–23)
DCA	Dundee City Archives
DH	Dumfries House, Cumnock, Ayrshire [all material has now been relocated to Mount Stuart House, Isle of Bute]
DNB	*Dictionary of National Biography*
DR	Rigsarkivet, Copenhagen, Denmark
EHR	*English Historical Review*
EUL	Edinburgh University Library
GCA	Glasgow City Archives
Gordon, *Distemper*	Patrick Gordon of Ruthven, *A Short Abridgement of Britane's Distemper from the Yeare of God MDCXXXIX to MDCXLIX* (Aberdeen, 1844)
Gordon, *HSA*	James Gordon, *History of Scots Affairs from MDXXXVII to MDCXLI*, J. Robertson ed., 3 vols (Aberdeen, 1841)
HJ	*Historical Journal*
HL	Huntington Library, San Marino, California
HMC	Historical Manuscripts Commission
ICA	Inveraray Castle Archives, Inveraray, Argyllshire
IHS	*Irish Historical Studies*
LJB	*The Letters and Journals of Robert Baillie A.M., Principal of the University of Glasgow, 1637–1662*, D. Laing ed., 3 vols (Edinburgh, 1841–42)
MHG	*Memoirs of Henry Guthry, Late Bishop of Dunkeld: Containing an Impartial Relation of the Affairs of Scotland, Civil and Ecclesiastical, from the Year 1637, to the Death of King Charles* (Glasgow, 1747)
MM	*Memorials of Montrose and his Times*, M. Napier ed., 2 vols (Edinburgh, 1848–50)
MMM	*Memoirs of the Marquis of Montrose*, M. Napier ed., 2 vols (Edinburgh, 1856)
Montereul	*The Diplomatic Correspondence of Jean De Montereul and the Brothers De Bellievre, French Ambassadors in England and Scotland 1645–48*, J.G. Fotheringham ed., 2 vols (Edinburgh, 1898–99)
NAS	National Archives of Scotland, Edinburgh
Nicoll, *Diary*	John Nicoll, *A Diary of Public Transactions and Other Occurrences, Chiefly in Scotland, from January 1650 to June 1667*, D. Laing ed. (Edinburgh, 1836)

NLS	National Library of Scotland, Edinburgh
Rosehaugh, *Memoirs*	Sir George Mackenzie of Rosehaugh, *Memoirs of the Affairs of Scotland from the Restoration of King Charles II, A.D. MDCLX* (Edinburgh, 1821)
Rothes, *Relation*	John Leslie, Earl of Rothes, *A Relation of Proceedings Concerning the Affairs of the Kirk of Scotland from August 1637 to July 1638*, J. Nairne ed. (Edinburgh, 1830)
RPCS	*Registers of the Privy Council of Scotland*, first series, 14 vols, D. Masson ed. (Edinburgh, 1877–98); second series, 8 volumes, D. Masson and P.H. Brown eds (Edinburgh, 1899–1908)
RSCHS	*Records of the Scottish Church History Society*
SHR	*Scottish Historical Review*
SNPG	Scottish National Portrait Gallery, Edinburgh
Spalding, *Troubles*	John Spalding, *The History of the Troubles and Memorable Transactions in Scotland and England, 1624–45*, J. Skene ed., 2 vols (Edinburgh, 1828–29)
SPT	*A Collection of the State Papers of John Thurloe, Esq. Secretary, First to the Council of State, and afterwards to the Two Protectors, Oliver & Richard Cromwell*, J. Birch ed., 7 vols (London, 1742)
SR	Riksarkivet, Stockholm, Sweden
SRRL	*The Earl of Stirling's Register of Royal Letters, Relative to the Affairs of Scotland and Nova Scotia from 1615 to 1635*, C. Rogers ed., 2 vols (Edinburgh, 1885)
TFA	Tollemache Family Archives, Buckminster, Grantham, Lincolnshire
TGSI	*Transactions of the Gaelic Society of Inverness*
TKUA	Tyske Kancellis Udenrigske Afdeling
TNA	The National Archives, London
Turner, *Memoirs*	Sir James Turner, *Memoirs of His Own Life and Times, 1632–70*, T. Thomson ed. (Edinburgh, 1829)
TWA	Tyne and Wear Archives, Newcastle
Wariston Diary I	*Diary of Sir Archibald Johnston of Wariston, 1632–39*, J.M. Paul ed. (Edinburgh, 1911)
Wariston Diary II	*Fragment of the Diary of Sir Archibald Johnston of Wariston, 1639*, G.M. Paul ed. (Edinburgh, 1896)
Whitelock, *Memorials*	*Memorials of English Affairs from the Beginning of the Reign of Charles the First to the Happy Restoration of King Charles the Second*, 4 vols (Oxford, 1853)
Wishart, *Memoirs*	George Wishart, *The Memoirs of James, Marquis of*

Montrose, 1639–1650, A.D. Murdoch and H.F.M. Simpson eds (London, 1893)

Wodrow, *Sufferings*   Robert Wodrow, *The History of the Sufferings of the Church of Scotland from the Restoration to the Revolution*, 2 vols (Edinburgh, 1721–22)

Conventions

Coinage: All values are principally in £ Scots. From 1603, the exchange rates between Scotland and England were standardised at 12:1 – thus, £12 Scots was equivalent to £1 sterling. The merk is two-thirds of a pound.

Dating: From 1600, the new year in Scotland commenced on 1 January, not on 25 March as in England. However, Scotland and England adhered to *old style* dating whereas *new style*, which was eleven days in advance, prevailed in continental Europe.

List of Illustrations

ONE

Introduction

The life and times of Archibald Campbell, 8th Earl and only Marquess of Argyll, were marked by upheavals, convulsions and revolution. His childhood occurred in the wake of regal union in 1603, when James VI of Scotland succeeded to the English throne and instituted the Stuarts as a British dynasty. He attained adulthood during the authoritarian rule of Charles I, against which the Scots revolted, expressing their opposition through the National Covenant of 1638, which formally launched the Covenanting Movement. In the Kirk, Presbyterianism, that is rule through a hierarchy of courts, replaced the control by bishops which came to be known as Episcopalianism. In the State, the Covenanters accomplished a revolution that fundamentally limited monarchical powers by 1641. Over the next two years, the Covenanters exported their ideology, practices and aspirations to Ireland and England, most notably by the Solemn League and Covenant of 1643. Civil wars for all three kingdoms followed, with Oliver Cromwell coming to power first in England and Ireland, then in Scotland by military might. The Commonwealth, established in the wake of the regicide of Charles I in 1649, absorbed Scotland in 1651, before giving way three years later to the Protectorate which, in turn, was pushed aside for the Restoration of Charles II in 1660. Argyll was executed in the following year, as the foremost Scottish revolutionary and purported collaborator with Cromwell.

The future Marquess of Argyll was probably born in Inveraray Castle, the principal Argyllshire stronghold of the chiefs of ClanCampbell. But we do not know exactly when. He certainly entered the world after 1598 and no later than 1607. While portraiture can be used to support the former date (see Plate 9) it can also more convincingly suggest (see Chapter 2) that Archibald Campbell reached his majority in 1628 (see Plate 8), which affirms the later birth date. His mother, Anna Douglas, daughter of the 8th Earl of Morton, died on 3 May 1607, but not necessarily in childbirth. Her only surviving son was perhaps born around the outset of that year, which would have made him sixteen years of age when, as a squint-eyed, non-graduating student, he won the silver medal for archery at the University of St Andrews in 1623. We certainly know when and how he died. On placing his head on the block of the execution device incongruously known as 'the Maiden', Argyll was guillotined for treason on the High Street of Edinburgh on 27 May 1661.[1] Conscious that his political career had been controversial and that his reputation had suffered from false aspersions that he supported the regicide and resisted the restoration of Charles II, he insisted from the scaffold that he was a Covenanter by conviction not convenience:

> I entered not upon the work of reformation with any design of advance for myself, or prejudice to the King and his government.[2]

Comparative Significance

From his birth to his death Argyll was a complex character, cautious yet volatile, never far from intrigue and as prone to polarise as to conciliate. Clear guiding principles ran his life. First and foremost he was born to become the chief of ClanCampbell, the most ruthless and territorially acquisitive clan in the *Gàidhealtachd* (Scottish Gaeldom). Second, he became a committed and pious Presbyterian which, third, propelled him to the leadership of the radical mainstream of the Covenanting Movement. Fourth, as clan considerations prevented him completing his formal education through a continental grand tour, he lacked the cultural polish of his contemporaries among Scottish magnates. But he more than compensated by his theoretical and practical grasp of politics and statecraft that was grounded in the classical teachings of Aristotle and the Stoics with which he was first imbued at St Andrews[3] – teaching that made him sceptical about, rather than deferential to, absolutism or authoritarian monarchy. Fifth, the political stage on which he chose to operate was British. He was not prepared to restrict himself to Scottish any more than to Highland dramas and crises.

Underestimating Argyll's British significance has been a feature of his entries in both the original *DNB* and the new *Oxford DNB*. This British deficit was compounded by the apologetic stance in the only previous biography of

---

1 J. Willcock, *The Great Marquess: Life and Times of Archibald, 8th Earl, and 1st (and only) Marquess of Argyll* (Edinburgh and London, 1903), pp. 10–12, argues convincingly for a birth date in March or early April 1607. The death of the Countess of Argyll around mid-day was commemorated in Alexander Julius, *In Illlustrissimam Dominam Annam Duglasiam, Comitissam Argatheliae* (Edinburgh, 1607).

2 Rosehaugh, *Memoirs*, pp. 41–2; [Archibald Campbell], My Lord Marquis of Argyle, *His Speech upon the Scaffold, 27 May 1661: As it was spoken by himself, and written in Short-hand by one that was present* (Edinburgh, 1661); BL, Scotch Sermons etc 1659–1664, Egerton MS 2215, ff.62–4.

3 University of St Andrews Acta Rectorum 4, p. 181

substance on the Marquess, that by John Willcock in 1903.[4] In defending the integrity, influence and intellect of Argyll, Willcock was responding to an ongoing historiographic tradition which has rarely assessed the Marquess on his political merits, preferring to concentrate on his perceived deficiencies rather than his proven prowess. Historians no less than contemporaries have too frequently judged Argyll adversely in comparison to his enemies, opponents and rivals (see Chapter 2). There have been relatively recent biographies of varied quality on James Hamilton, 3rd Marquess and 1st Duke of Hamilton, on James Graham, 5th Earl and 1st Marquess of Montrose, and on Randall MacDonnell, 2nd Earl and 1st Marquess of Antrim.[5] Respectively they stand to Argyll as his foremost opponent, his inveterate enemy and his territorial rival. In contrast to the Marquess, all had continental experience as travellers, soldiers or diplomats. But they all lacked Argyll's political nous, his political timing and his political craft.

Hamilton was Argyll's principal Scottish opponent both within and without the Covenanting Movement. Where Hamilton oscillated between acting as a conservative Covenanter or as a pragmatic Royalist, Argyll remained committed to the radical mainstream of the Movement. For his part, Hamilton recognised the revolutionary potential of Argyll when he warned Charles I, in November 1638, that the then 8th Earl, who had still formally to declare himself a Covenanter, must be watched, 'for it feares me he will proufe the dangerousest man in this state';[6] and so it proved for the cause of this ill-fated king and his Royalist cause, albeit another eight years were to elapse before Charles came to the summative judgement that Argyll was 'very civil and cunning'.[7] The much-acclaimed campaigning brilliance of Montrose has tended to be accompanied by the denigration of Argyll both as a commander and as a warrior. Notwithstanding the glorious reputation accorded his Royalist campaigns in the 1640s, Montrose attained no worthwhile political accomplishments. Within Gaeldom, Argyll's reputation has certainly suffered from the adverse press generated principally by poets of ClanDonald in Scotland and Ireland, whose polemical

---

4 Willcock, *The Great Marquess, passim.* As well as the detailed portrayal by T.F. Henderson in the *DNB*, vol. 8, L. Stephen ed. (London, 1886), pp. 319–29, David Stevenson has also provided a constructive, if attenuated, reappraisal in the *Oxford DNB*, http://www.oxforddnb.com. articles/4/4772-article.html (subscription database).

5 H.L. Rubinstein, *Captain Luckless: James, First Duke of Hamilton, 1606–1649* (Edinburgh and London, 1975); E.J. Cowan, *Montrose: For Covenant and King* (London, 1977); J.H. Ohlmeyer, *Civil War and Restoration in the Three Stuart Kingdoms: The Career of Randal MacDonnell, Marquis of Antrim* (Cambridge, 1993).

6 NAS, Hamilton Papers, GD 406/1/326.

7 *Charles I in 1646: Letters of King Charles I to Queen Henrietta Maria*, J. Bruce ed. (London, 1856), p. 49.

stridency was in inverse proportion to their clan's declining political influence. Since the fall of their Lordship of the Isles in the late fifteenth century, the ClanDonald had fragmented and become embroiled in feuds primarily to the advantage of the ClanCampbell. Attempts to unite this fragmented clan around Antrim at the outbreak of the civil wars were mere political posturing. Antrim's brokering of an alliance between the Confederation of Irish Catholics and the Scottish Royalists certainly led to the stunning guerrilla warfare waged by his kinsman, Alasdair MacColla, in association with Montrose. Their campaign in 1644–45 exposed Argyll's lack of valour and his deficient generalship. But the Marquess was the main political orchestrator who had the Covenanting forces outmanoeuvre and eventually crush MacColla and Montrose. Antrim was left a political bystander in the affairs of the three kingdoms.

While Argyll has been the subject of but one previous biography, there is a veritable growth industry on the life and times of both Charles I and Oliver Cromwell, his main British sparring partners.[8] Charles I was an authoritarian king with absolutist aspirations. His reign was marked by political ineptitude, patent untrustworthiness and a wilful incapacity to accept counsel that favoured conciliation and compromise. Nevertheless, his dignified refusal to become entangled in a show trial, his majestic bearing on the scaffold and his uncompromising support for Episcopalianism made him a martyr for Stuart monarchy. A cult of kingly sacrifice, based on the twin pillars of justice and piety, was soon developed through *Eikon Basilike*, the purported meditations of Charles I as he awaited execution, and later through the apologetic writings of Anglican clergy. The cult of Charles the martyr spread to Scotland to become part of the Episcopalian tradition, a cult which glossed over his marked intransigence, his warmongering and his diplomatic isolation.[9]

Notwithstanding the regicide of 1649, Cromwell's political standing has endured as a man of destiny, a strong ruler and a statesman of international repute. Despite a tendency towards glory-hunting, a penchant for bloody ruthlessness towards his enemies and an abiding conviction of his own rightness, Cromwell remains an English national hero in a belligerent line that stretches

---

8 See respective *Oxford DNB* entries, J. Morrill, 'Cromwell, Oliver (1599–1658)': http://www. oxforddnb.com/articles/6/6765-article.html, and M.A. Kishlansky and J. Morrill, 'Charles I (1600–1640)': http://www.oxforddnb.com/view/article/5143

9 [John Gauden] *Eikon Basilike: The Portraiture of His Sacred Maiestie in his Solitudes and Sufferings* (London, 1649); Peter Heylyn, *A Short View of the Life and Reign of King Charles (the Second Monarch of Great Britain) from his Birth to his Burial* (London, 1658); Arthur Wilson, *The History of Great Britain Being the Life and Reign of King James the First, Relating to What Passed from his First Access to the Crown, till his Death* (London, 1653); J. Peacey, 'Reporting a Revolution: a Failed Propaganda Campaign' in J. Peacey ed., *The Regicides and the Execution of Charles I* (Basingstoke 2001), pp. 161–80.

back from Edward I through Henry V and Elizabeth Tudor, and on to Winston Churchill and Margaret Thatcher. He is thus lauded as a soldier, politician and statesman who 'towered above his age'.[10] Argyll can be deemed second only to Cromwell as a British statesman of the mid-seventeenth century. Less vilified and less celebrated, Argyll exercised as pronounced a polarising influence in all three kingdoms. Cromwell deemed his exclusive brand of English patriotism to be divinely warranted. Argyll was no less devout but more inclusive in his patriotism as he pursued his unique, non-anglocentric calling as a Gaelic chief, Scottish magnate and British statesman. Cromwell had determined the political agenda of the three kingdoms for less than a decade prior to his death in 1658. From 1638 until he was beheaded twenty-three years later, Argyll personified the Scottish corrective to the Stuarts as an authoritarian British monarchy. Yet, Argyll has no accepted place in any Scottish pantheon of heroes. He remains an enigmatic figure, his reputation sullied by calumny, distortion and neglect rather than glorified or commemorated with respect and honour. His contribution to the British Revolution of the mid-seventeenth century continues to be underplayed. Nevertheless, without Argyll, the revolt against Charles I would not have retained its radical edge in England as it had in Scotland.

Paradoxical Identities

Charles I, Cromwell and Argyll have added political significance in that they personified different and rival perspectives on what constituted British identity in the seventeenth century. These perspectives should be viewed as normative in that they are prescriptive not just descriptive, being grounded in myth, providence, prophecy and the humanist scholarship of the Renaissance.

The Britannic perspective favoured by the early Stuarts since the Union of the Crowns in 1603 advocated full integration of England and Scotland, failing which James VI and I promoted common foreign, frontier and colonial policies. More controversially, Charles I sought administrative, social, economic and religious uniformity throughout the British Isles. However authoritarian this prescription, it had the merits of an inclusive British agenda centred on the royal court. Nevertheless, in England the Gothic perspective, whose most celebrated exponent was Cromwell, elevated parliamentary statute and common law over the privileges of governance reserved as the prerogative powers of the Stuart monarchy. While the Gothic agenda was propagated as the defence of civil and religious liberties, these liberties were exclusive to the English. Accordingly, any union with Scotland, as with Ireland, was to be based on subordination and absorption. The Scottish perspective – as indeed the Irish equivalent – was based on liberation theology. For the Irish, their prevailing Roman Catholicism was

10 B. Warden, *Roundhead Reputations* (London, 2001), p. 225.

their confessional counter to notions of civility as imposed by the English and, simultaneously, their validation that Ireland was a free, not a dependent, kingdom within the Stuart's British dominions. For the Scots, Calvinism as received at the Reformation of 1560–67 enhanced the rights of resistance vested in their commonwealth since the Wars of Independence in the late thirteenth and early fourteenth centuries. These rights in a religious context were advocated first by John Knox and George Buchanan in defiance of monarchy. Subsequently, they were reinforced in the later sixteenth century by the ideological resistance to monarchy that emanated within France from the Protestant Huguenots during the Wars of Religion, and from Dutch Calvinists who preferred republicanism to rule by the Spanish Habsburgs. At the same time, proponents of the Scottish perspective sought a virtuous commonwealth that should be open to wider federative arrangements within and beyond the British Isles. These arrangements were deemed necessary to counter universal monarchy as pursued by the Spanish and Austrian Habsburgs in association with the papacy.[11]

The notion of a virtuous commonwealth that was bound by divine warrant to resist ungodly, imperial and papal monarchy at home and abroad was firmed up by federal theology or covenanting. This theology, which had a particular appeal not only to Scottish Presbyterians but to evangelical Protestants from Transylvania to New England, emphasised the contractual relationship between God and man, rather than the stark Calvinist reliance on election by divine decree. Predestination and, thereby, man's ultimate dependence on divine grace was not denied. The true believer proved his or her election by covenanting with God, not by exercising free will to choose his or her salvation. Divine grace moved man to covenant. But once man had so banded himself to God he was assured of election. At its most potent, in moving individuals and nations to demonstrate their faith through purposeful works as well as graceful living, the covenant could be interpreted as a divine band between God and the people of Scotland. Such a band carried political as well as religious imperatives. As evident from the promulgation of the National Covenant in 1638, the Scots constructed constitutional arrangements that were 'no wayes repugnant' to the will of God and that required binding limitations on the monarchy in both Kirk and State. As manifest by the Solemn League and Covenant in 1643, these imperatives were exportable.[12]

Argyll was not just a participant but an active player in these momentous British events of the mid-seventeenth century. The Marquess was the principal architect of the Scottish Moment, when the Covenanters dominated the British

---

11 A.I. Macinnes, *The British Revolution, 1629–1660* (Basingstoke, 2005), pp. 8–39.

12 *A Source Book of Scottish History, vol. III (1567–1707)* , W.C. Dickinson and G. Donaldson eds (London and Edinburgh, 1961), pp. 95–104, 122–5.

political agenda from 1638 to 1645.[13] As a radical Covenanter, he consistently advocated a federative arrangement for Scotland and England as more just and equitable than either regal union or political incorporation. Such an arrangement can be viewed as an association or confederation of executive powers authorised by the Scottish Estates and the English Parliament that did not involve either the subordination or the merger of these separate constitutional assemblies. This visionary standpoint marked him out as the leading British confederate during the 1640s. He was also the principal broker for the patriotic accommodation, which attempted to restore Charles II as King of Great Britain and Ireland in 1650–51. However, there is a central paradox about his Scotto-British standpoint. A confederate could also be viewed by his contemporaries as a conspirator or collaborator; a perspective that undoubtedly bedevilled Argyll's endeavours to reconfigure British politics. At the same time, Argyll's political reputation has undoubtedly suffered from the association of confederacy with conspiracy in all three kingdoms during the 1640s.

The British paradox of Argyll as a confederate and a conspirator was forcibly articulated in 1648 by Clement Walker, a polemicist for the Presbyterian faction within the English Parliamentarians. He considered Argyll, notwithstanding his public image as a Covenanting stalwart and bulwark of Presbyterianism in Scotland, to be 'joined in confederacy' with the Independent faction among the Parliamentarians led by Oliver Cromwell. Having laid out the factional differences between the Presbyterians and Independents in England, Walker devoted a lengthy appendix to demonstrating that Argyll was 'an Apostate Covenanter, whose ambition and avarice hath ruined the KING, Church and State, or three flourishing Kingdomes'. Argyll was the chief political promoter of the Solemn League and Covenant, which upheld Presbyterianism in all three kingdoms. Yet he subsequently aligned himself with the Independents as Protestant sectaries and schismatics who individually and collectively sought salvation outwith a national church. In the process, Argyll and his faction – in reality the radical mainstream of the Covenanting Movement – were deemed 'the chiefe Malignants, Incendiaries and evill Instruments, who have been the Ruiners of these three flourishing Kingdomes and the Authors of the bloodshed in all of them'. According to Walker, the paradox central to Argyll's political career was to be explained by his pursuit of public ends for private advantage. His political commitment to Covenanting masked his intent to make territorial acquisitions in Scotland and Ireland. His professed piety was likewise for purely personal advancement in ensuring that the Presbyterian ministers supported the harassment and ruin of his enemies. Writing prior to the regicide, Walker sought to

---

13 A.I. Macinnes, 'The Scottish Moment, 1638–1645' in J. Adamson ed., *The English Civil War: Conflicts and Contexts, 1640–49* (London, 2009), pp. 125–52.

demonstrate that Argyll was a more malevolent influence than Cromwell in the British Isles. How was this so?

First, in 1640–41, Argyll had conspired with his confederates to make Scotland a republic or free state along Dutch lines. Second, in 1642, he began his confederacy in England by showing Parliamentarians how to mobilise funds by taxes, voluntary contributions and forced loans to wage war against Charles I. Third, he was simultaneously despatching embassies to Cardinal Armand-Jean de Richelieu to bring France into his confederacy under the guise of revitalising the Franco-Scottish 'Auld Alliance'. Fourth, the main point of his conspiracy was to cast off monarchy in Scotland, if necessary by provoking civil war in 1644–45. Fifth, finding English Presbyterians prepared to make peace with Charles I, he abandoned them for Cromwell. In the process, he was instrumental in having Charles I handed over to the Independents eight months after the king had sought refuge with the Covenanting Army in England in May 1646. Sixth, by 1648 he was encouraging Cromwell to move towards a republic in England. Accordingly, he obstructed the endeavours of James, Duke of Hamilton, 'a Professor of the true Protestant Religion' and leader of the conservative Covenanters, to facilitate the restoration of monarchical power through a Britannic Engagement. Seventh, after the Engagement came to grief militarily in England, Argyll solicited Cromwell's assistance to effect an internal revolution that would not only entrench his radical regime in power, but also turn Scotland into a sectarian dependency, 'a Province to the Kingdome of the Saints' that Cromwell was determined to accomplish in England. Reissues of Walker's appendix in the wake of the regicide of 1649, and again following the execution of the Marquess in 1661, helped ensure that Argyll's reputation was also tainted with collaboration in the 1650s. Yet in that decade, his relationship with Oliver Cromwell was primarily marked by mutual distrust.[14]

Notwithstanding Walker's strictures on confederacy, Argyll, as the foremost promoter of a federative Britain, was steeped in the virtuous Scottish tradition of a godly commonwealth resisting ungodly monarchy. By the same token, he died as a committed Covenanter convinced that he ranked with the godly rather than with the reprobate as the openly profane, or with those who paid only lip-service to religion. Accordingly, he used his speech on the scaffold neither to justify his political conduct nor to rebut calumnies or condemn his opponents. For he was assured of his own salvation:

---

14 Clement Walker, *Relations and Observations, Historicall and Politick, upon the Parliament, begun anno Dom. 1640: Divided into II Books: 1. The Mystery of the Two Iunto's, Presbyterian and Independent. 2. The History of Independency, &c. Together with an Appendix, Touching the Proceedings of the Independent Faction in Scotland* (London, 1648). This appendix consisted of 16 pages.

I bless him that hath taken away the sting of my sufferings; I may say that my charter is seal'd this day; for the Lord hath said to me, Son, be of good cheer, thy sins are forgiven thee.[15]

Wider Dimensions

In death as in life, Argyll was driven by the helpful and the chastising hand of providence as God revealed his divine purposes to his people. Such divine revelation, which was rooted in Judaic-Christian tradition, cut across the confessional divide opened up by the Reformation throughout and beyond the British Isles. As a religious counter to classical auguries of fortune and fate, belief in providence affirmed God's plan for the universe, whether applied generally to nations or specifically to individuals. God's majesty, evident through His manifest conferral of blessings and punishments, motivated mankind regardless of social standing or economic resources to strive collectively for grace and seek individual assurance of salvation. In the Reformed tradition, the wholesale striving of a nation to live gracefully indicated their providential calling as a chosen people. At the same time, Protestant pulpits throughout the Stuart's dominions carried the prophetic warning that national apostasy, just like individual backsliding, assured heavenly vengeance.[16] Divine revelation did not stand apart from but interacted with clanship, nobility and statesmanship. This interaction was particularly evident in Argyll's response to wider influences shaping Scottish and British politics – notably, the Thirty Years War, apocalyptic expectations and secular prophecy.

The Thirty Years war nominally dates from the Bohemian crisis in 1618. The overturning of the endeavours of Frederick, the Elector Palatine – who was married to Elizabeth, daughter of James VI and I – to secure election as King of Bohemia and prevent the Austrian Habsburg, Archduke Ferdinand, becoming Holy Roman Emperor, initiated a general European conflagration that was not concluded until the Peace of Westphalia in 1648. Arraigned against the particular interest of the Elector Palatine and his supporters among the German princes and their political estates were the Austrian and Spanish Habsburgs supported by the papacy. While this was certainly portrayed by contemporaries as the forces of Protestantism resisting the Counter-Reformation and Catholic absolutism, the Protestant alliance of Calvinists and Lutherans was uneasy and unstable despite support from the Dutch Republic or United Provinces and

---

15 Rosehaugh, *Memoirs*, pp. 41–6; Wodrow, *Sufferings*, I, p. 55.
16 R. Eisen, *Gersonides on Providence, Covenant, and the Chosen People: A Study in Medieval Jewish Philosophy and Biblical Commentary* (New York, 1994), pp. 1–3, 169–83; R. Gillespie, *Devoted People: Belief and Religion in Early Modern Ireland* (Manchester, 1997), pp. 40–62; A. Walsham, *Providence in Early Modern England* (Oxford, 1999), pp. 281–325.

the monarchies of Great Britain, Denmark-Norway and Sweden. Confessional allegiance was further breached when Catholic France, under the direction of Cardinal Richelieu – the supreme exponent of *politique* who acted for reasons of state – brokered an alliance with the United Provinces and Sweden in 1635. This alliance not only prevented the attainment of Habsburg hegemony in Europe, but also took a benign stance towards the emergence of the Covenanting Movement in Scotland three years later.[17]

The release of Scottish forces serving with the Swedes and the Dutch gave a professional backbone and a cutting edge to the Covenanting forces that engaged with Charles I in the Bishops' Wars of 1639–40. The key to their release was Alexander Leslie, a field-marshal in Swedish service who became the supreme commander of the Covenanting forces that were to intervene in Ireland and England in the course of the 1640s. General Leslie (later 1st Earl of Leven) had also served with Hamilton when the latter commanded the British expeditionary forces that fleetingly participated with the Swedes in the main continental theatre of the war in 1631–32. However, Hamilton was too dilatory in attempting to secure Leslie's services, even though this military veteran had returned to Scotland on family business as the National Covenant was being subscribed in 1638. Unlike Hamilton, Argyll was not a veteran of the Thirty Years War. But he was able to draw on real and fictitious ties of kinship to secure Leslie's service for the Covenanting Movement. Argyll exploited ties of fosterage which linked together the clan elite from childhood and built up lasting associations with Lowland families of nobles and gentry. Alexander Leslie, from Balgonie in Fife, was foster-brother to Sirs Colin, Robert and John Campbell, successive lairds of Glenorchy. All were close and trusted kinsman of Argyll, who had also sent his own four-year-old son Archibald, the future 9th Earl, to be fostered with Sir Colin Campbell from 1633 to 1639.[18]

The devastation and social dislocation brought about by the Thirty Years War, combined with the intensive religious rivalries of forces fighting the Anti-Christ, heightened a European sense that the end of days was imminent, from which Scotland was not immune. Letters home from the front reinforced notions of an impending apocalypse as defined through the prophetic revelations which concluded the New Testament. Eschatological expectations also

---

17 Macinnes, *The British Revolution*, pp. 119–25; A. Grosjean, *An Unofficial Alliance: Scotland and Sweden 1569–1654* (Leiden and Boston, 2003), pp. 165–90.

18 S. Murdoch, *Network North: Scottish Kin, Commerical and Covert Associations in Northern Europe 1603–1746* (Leiden and Boston, 2006), pp. 38–48; *BBT*, pp. xviii–xxii; NAS, Breadalbane MSS, GD 112/1/496; ICA, Argyll Letters (1633–39), A36/43, /48–9. A secondary tie, binding Leslie to the Covenanting Movement derives from the marriage of his son Alexander to Margaret, daughter of John Leslie, 6th Earl of Rothes, initially prominent as a Covenanting leader before being eclipsed by Argyll in 1639.

stimulated reform projects driven by confessional confederation that would prepare for the millennium and the second coming of Christ.[19] Prominent in these endeavours was an expatriate Scot, John Durie from Edinburgh. Having been educated in the United Provinces and France, Durie began his career as pastor to the British mercantile community at Elbing in Prussia in 1624. There he was drawn into the extensive, intellectual network of Samuel Hartlib, a merchant, pietist and educationalist with an encyclopaedic mind, who relocated to England from 1628. Inspired by the Hartlib circle, in which he became a major figure, Durie dedicated his life to an irenicist accommodation between the Lutheran, Calvinist and other Reformed traditions. Throughout the 1630s, he strove unflinchingly to gather support for confessional confederation among Protestants by chronically underfunded, peripatetic endeavours in Germany, Poland-Lithuania and Sweden. As his promotion of confessional confederation was also targeted against Habsburg imperialism, Durie and his backers held firm to the prospect that the exiled family of Elizabeth Stuart, the 'Winter Queen' of Bohemia, could be restored to the Palatinate from which they had been ousted at the outset of the Thirty Years' War.[20]

Durie's most supportive backing in Scotland came from a group of academics and intellectual clerics, known as the Aberdeen Doctors, who favoured episcopacy. However, his claims to speak for 'the British Churches' carried little weight with Scottish Presbyterians, who were militantly opposed to the hegemonic Anglican agenda then being promoted by Charles I and rigorously pursued by William Laud, as Archbishop of Canterbury, in all three Stuart kingdoms. Indeed, with the emergence of the Covenanting Movement, Scottish Presbyterians were intent not on irenicism but on a godly redefinition of the political agenda through permanent checks on prerogative rule in Kirk and State. In terms of apocalyptic expectation the Scots gave precedence to the conversion of the Jews who, unlike Roman Catholics and Muslims, were not viewed as irredeemable followers of the Anti-Christ.[21] However, the Covenanters under the radical leadership of Argyll did seek to replace regal union with a federative

---

19 D. Horsbroch, 'Wish You Were Here? Scottish Reactions to "Postcards" home from the "Germane Warres"' in S. Murdoch ed., *Scotland and the Thirty Years' War, 1618–1648* (Leiden and Boston, 2001), pp. 245–69; A.H. Williamson, *Apocalypse Then: Prophecy and the Making of the Modern World* (Westport CT, 2008), pp. 101–4.

20 Macinnes, *The British Revolution*, pp. 5–6, 71–2; A. Milton, '"The Universal Peacemaker"? John Dury and the Politics of irenicism in England ' in M. Greengrass, M. Leslie and T. Raylor eds, *Samuel Hartlib and Universal Reformation* (Cambridge, 1994), pp. 1–25; John Dury, *A Summary Discourse concerning the work of peace ecclesiastical, how it may concurre with the aim of a civill confederation amongst Protestants. Presented to the consideration of my lord ambassador Sir T. Row at Hamburg 1639* (Cambridge, 1641).

21 Williamson, *Apocalypse Then*, pp. 136–9, 146–8; *LJB*, III, p. 371.

union, based on confessional confederation not just with England, but also with the United Provinces and Sweden. The Solemn League and Covenant between the Scottish Covenanters and the English Parliamentarians in 1643 gave tangible expression of these endeavours. As Argyll made clear in a celebrated speech to the Grand Committee of both the Lords and the Commons in the English Parliament in June 1646, British Union based on confessional confederation was not only indispensible to prevent division between Covenanters and Parliamentarians but vital for a lasting peace with Charles I. Argyll, in the interest of godliness, also contemplated moving beyond confederation: 'The work of Reformation in these Kingdomes, is so great a work, as no age nor history can parallel since Chirsts daies.' Accordingly, he wished to merge Scotland and England into a British commonwealth 'all under one King, one in Religion, yea one in Covenant'.[22]

The act of covenanting provided Argyll and his radical associates with the political will to effect British revolution. No less potent, though lacking public endorsement from Presbyterian ministers, was the popular appeal of secular prophecy as propagated through almanacs, tracts, engravings, chapbooks and oral tradition. Predictions were the essence of secular prophecy, which ranged from astrology through second sight, the discerning of omens and other portentous signs to horoscopes. In studying the heavens, a broad distinction can be maintained between general interpretations of current conditions from such portents as comets and eclipses, and specific interpretations of future private and public developments based on individual astral readings.[23]

Notwithstanding his eminence as a physicist and astronomer, Johannes Kepler, a pioneer of the laws of motion, was lauded more for his general prediction of the European conflagration that became the Thirty Years War, a prediction that coincided with the regal union of 1603, when James VI and I sought to bring specific predictions about British destiny into play for his dynastic advantage. James initially sponsored the reprinting in Edinburgh in 1604 of assertions by an anonymous English apologist that the miraculous and happy union between England and Scotland would prove expeditious and profitable to both nations, and stop unnecessary wars. This endeavour to convince the Scottish Estates to participate, without equivocation, in the creation of 'the moste opulent, strong and entire Empire of the worlde', capable of transatlantic confrontation with Spain and the papacy, was made redundant by the failure of the English Parliament to support political incorporation in 1607. Nonetheless,

---

22　[Archibald Campbell], *A Speech By the Marquesse of Argile, to the Honourable Lords and Commons in Parliament. 25 June 1646* (London, 1646).

23　P. Curry, *Prophecy and Power: Astrology in Early Modern England* (Princeton, 1989), pp. 3–15; H. Rusche, 'Prophecies and Propaganda, 1641 to 1651', *EHR*, 84 (1969), pp. 752–70.

James remained determined to demonstrate that secular prophecy had run its course with his accession to the English throne as the peaceful fulfilment of British unification, not only predicted by wizards such as Merlin and Thomas the Rhymer, and by chroniclers such as Bede. British Union was also endorsed from French and Danish sources. This text, which was printed in 1617 both in Latin verse and Scots metre, gained notable British currency throughout the 1640s.[24]

But such secular prophecy, which was deliberately opaque and ambiguous, was recyclable, readily customised and easily adapted to the sweeping political and religious changes that characterised the British Isles in the mid-seventeenth century. For the prophecies favouring union and concerted action against the papal Anti-Christ could also be reinterpreted to uphold Covenanting claims against the absentee Stuart monarchy, to secure Scottish deliverance from dependence on England and to impose British unification from the north. A manuscript newsletter from Newcastle, written variously by a gentleman or alderman to a friend in London on 8 September 1640, when the north of England was occupied by the Covenanting Army, copies the insolent discourse of the common Scottish soldiers. Not only did they routinely disparage the Royalist war effort and, indeed, the martial prowess of the English nation but, in their cups, they justified their conquest as the fulfilment of prophecy. Particularly remarkable was their recitation of verses translated from Latin into Scots, attributed to Merlin and applied to the course of the Bishops' Wars: 'They beleeve it noe lesse then Gospell.' These verses were in fact textual variants drawn from *The Whole Prophecies* printed in Edinburgh and dedicated to King James of Great Britain in 1617. Especial weighting was given to the lines asserting that England faced forcible flattening, sudden death and ruination, having been betrayed from within as well as besieged by the Scots. Irish plotting and Welsh menaces were compounded by French hostility and Dutch alienation, which foretold greater griefs to come.[25]

Prophesying underscored the commitment of the Covenanting Movement to secure recognition from the Crown and the English Parliament of the political independence of Scotland; recognition that was duly attained by the Treaty of London in August 1641. Conversely, prophesying from a Scottish perspective on reformation rather than conquest also facilitated the refashioning of the regal union into British confederation, the substance of the Solemn League and Covenant of 1643. Nonetheless, prophecy that foretold a return to peace

---

24 Anon., *The Miraculous and Happie Union of England & Scotland* (Edinburgh, 1604); *The Whole Prophecies of Scotland, England, France, Ireland and Denmarke* (Edinburgh, 1617).

25 HL, Bridgewater and Ellesmere MSS, EL 7859; BL, Trumbull Papers, vol. CXCI, Add.MSS 72,432 ff.122–3.

in the British Isles after the cathartic impact of war on all three kingdoms instigated from the north could be utilised also from the Gothic perspective of Cromwell and the regicides. English triumph over internal foes as well as external enemies justified the occupation of Scotland after the forcible conquest of Ireland by 1651.[26]

Throughout his adult life, Argyll was mindful of secular prophecy, especially that from oral Gaelic tradition. On 14 March 1633, the then Lord Lorne made a contractual arrangement with Captain David Alexander, a skipper from Anstruther in Fife. The latter's ship, the *Unitie*, was commissioned to seek an island rumoured to be beyond the Hebrides in the Atlantic Ocean, 'which hes not heretofore beine discovered nor planted'. In promoting this venture, which was to commence no later than 20 April and conclude by 1 August, Lorne was inspired partly by the contemporaneous voyages of discovery to promote British colonising in the Americas, and partly by the enduring Gaelic tradition of *Tir nan Og* (Land of the Ever Young), the Gaelic equivalent to the Viking Valhalla. Lorne advanced £8,000 for wages, freight and victuals, with a promise of a further £4,000 on receipt of a 'trew report' of the location and topography of the island and whether it was inhabited on discovery. His total expenditure of £12,000 (£1,000 sterling) was not recouped even though Lorne had taken out the additional assurance of placing a kinsman, Captain William Campbell, as an adviser on the ship, with instructions to disembark at Canna or other convenient Hebridean island on the return voyage in order that he may report independently and speedily.[27]

It reputedly made no difference to Argyll whether he was the foremost earl or the most recent marquess in the Scottish peerage. But he supposedly welcomed his elevation in rank in 1641 because Highland seers had foretold that if the *MacChailein Mor*, the soubriquet of the chief of ClanCampbell, was 'rede heired and squint eyed', he would be the last Earl of Argyll. However, there was an associated prophecy: so long as *MacChailein Mor* continued faithful to his prince, so long should the Campbells flourish in grandeur, 'but how sonne they tooke armes against there soueraine, then sould that familie be extinguished

---

26 [Matthew Walbancke], *Sundry Strange Prophecies of Merline, Bede, Becket and Others* (London, 1652); Macinnes, *The British Revolution*, pp. 29–39.

27 ICA, Argyll Transcripts, vol. IX (1629–37), no.442; Willcock, *The Great Marquess*, pp. 24–5. Argyll remained open to potentially lucrative, maritime opportunities. During the course of Scottish negotiations for confederal union with England in 1641 and 1643, Argyll took the time to secure a warrant from Charles I, subsequently ratified by the Scottish Estates, that allowed him exclusive right of recovery from the wrecked treasure ships of the Spanish Armada sunk near Tobermory on the Isle of Mull in 1588 (ICA, Argyll Transcripts, vol. XII (1639–49), no.181; ABDA, Argyll Papers, 40.07).

and come to noght'.[28] This latter prophecy cannot be held to have made Argyll reluctant to wage war against Charles I in all three kingdoms during the 1640s. Yet Argyll, who was increasingly the subject of omens portending his bloody end, could not but be conscious of the recirculation of this prophetic theme during the 1650s. The Marquess was castigated for his acquisitive, ruthless and brutal conduct in the previous decade. His eventual execution was also foretold. Indeed, his forlorn endeavour to throw himself upon the mercy of Charles II after the Restoration can in part be attributed to his attempt to evade this prophecy.[29] However, the prediction that he would be hanged was not carried out to the letter. How much satisfaction Argyll derived from the altering of his sentence to beheading remains an open question!

28 Gordon, *Distemper*, p. 57.
29 [C.C.], *Ane Brief Explanation of the Life, or A Prophicy [sic] of the Death of the Marquis of Argyle, with diverse verse thereupon* (Edinburgh, 1686); Willcock, *The Great Marquess*, pp. 301–2.

TWO

Forging Reputations

One major problem confronts any political biography of Argyll. While much has been written about him, little appears to have been written by him; a rather ironic situation for a man eventually held to account for a few supportive letters to General George Monck (later Duke of Albemarle) as the commander of the Cromwellian forces in Scotland during the 1650s. This relative lack of correspondence can only be attributed in part to the vagaries affecting the survival of records since the seventeenth century. Argyll had a well-honed sense of political accountability and personal liability. He was acutely aware of the need to avoid self-incrimination as can be gleaned from one letter that has survived from July 1640, when Argyll was commander of the Covenanting forces suppressing Royalist resistance in the north-east of Scotland. In the process he deliberately confused public policy with family feuding. His order to his kinsman and military aide, Dougall Campbell, then heir to Inverawe, to forcibly remove livestock from estates owned by James Ogilvie, Lord Ogilvie, was the cover for further punitive reprisals to be inflicted upon the future 2nd Earl of Airlie's house of Forther in the Braes of Angus.

> And albeit ye should be the longer in following me [to Strathardale] yeit ye shall not faill to stay and demoleishe my Lord Ogilveis hous of Forther. Sie how ye can cast off the Irone greattis & windows & take doun the roof. And iff ye find it wilbe langsame ye shall fyire it weill that so it may be destroyed. But ye neid not to latt know that ye have directione from me to fyir it, onlie ye may say that ye have warrand to demoleishe it and that to make ye work short ye will fyr it.[1]

Fortunately, Argyll was a meticulous keeper of detailed financial accounts, as befitting a man who laid out vast sums of money in support of the Covenanting Movement. He also was not averse to securing a favourable political press for his speeches and actions as a British confederate. However, his *Instructions to His Son*, purportedly written up in prison while awaiting trial and execution,

1 ICA, Argyll Letters (1638–85), A36/120.

are not authentic statements of his political ideology, but anodyne aphorisms on public and private life attributed to, but not actually authored by, Argyll. Accordingly, the document talks in platitudes about monarchy and aristocratic duty rather than deal with Argyll's commitment to a godly commonwealth, inspired by George Buchanan, Scotland's leading civic humanist in the sixteenth century. Buchanan's two major works – *De Iure Regnis apud Scotus dialogus* (1579) and *Rerum Scoticarum Historia* (1582) – upheld rights of resistance vested in the Scottish commonwealth and advocated elective rather than hereditary kingship, much to the annoyance of his former pupil James VI and I and all subsequent members of the Stuart dynasty. These works were deemed in the Restoration era, particularly by those who recanted their engagement with the Covenanting Movement, as incendiary and the chief inspiration for revolution under the radical leadership of Argyll.[2]

As a political operator, Argyll relied less on correspondence and written instructions than on the placement of reliable agents in all four of the Scottish Estates. Thus, his main collaborator in the estate of the nobility was his kinsman, John Campbell, 1st Earl of Loudoun, who, as Chancellor of Scotland, was the highest ranking Covenanter in public office. Argyll maintained his guiding influence on the younger nobility through William Ker, 3rd Earl of Lothian, who had secured his title through marriage to Argyll's niece, Anne. His closest political adviser as well as his confederate from the estate of the gentry was the hyper-active lawyer, Sir Archibald Johnston of Wariston, a leading ideologue and a joint author of the National Covenant for Scotland in 1638 and the Solemn League and Covenant for Britain in 1643. In the estate of the burgesses, Argyll relied on his former tutor, Robert Barclay, perennial provost of Irvine in Ayrshire. Although he remained close to the principal ideologues among the Presbyterian ministry – notably Alexander Henderson, Samuel Rutherford and Robert Douglas – his most dependable contact in the estate of the clergy was Robert Baillie, minister of Kilwinning in Ayrshire and later Principal of Glasgow University. While Argyll shuttled between Scotland and England and made occasional forays to Ireland during the 1640s, his main power base remained in Edinburgh or in the councils of the Covenanting Army. However, his four agents – Loudon, Wariston, Barclay and Baillie – were prominent as resident Scottish commissioners in England for much of that decade, serving as indispensible links between Argyll and the English Parliamentarians. Simultaneously, Lothian supported Argyll in the field and in the corridors of power, not only as a military commander all three kingdoms, but as a diplomat and intelligence gatherer in continental Europe.

2 Duke University NC, Special Collections, Sir James Turner Papers: Tracts Critical and Historical, Buchanan Revised, pp. 1–2, 5–9, 11, 13, 15, 18–19,134, 196–7.

Covenanting Martyr?

Baillie, in particular, was to provide the most sympathetic account of Argyll, 'a notable instrument' as a wise political operator and as a committed Covenanter. Argyll was the consummate political manager of the affairs of the Kirk as well as the State. He was notably resistant to clerical intrusions in parliamentary proceedings in particular and civil affairs in general. While he sought support from the pulpit, he did not countenance theocracy. Ultimately, political power rested in the parliaments of nobles, gentry and burgesses that constituted the Scottish Estates. The rule of the clergy in the Presbyterian hierarchy of courts – from kirk sessions in the parishes to presbyteries and synods in the districts and regions, and on to the national general assemblies – was moderated by the presence of members of the lay estates as elders. Baillie did recognise that Argyll's 'irreconcilable discords' with Hamilton on the direction of the Covenanting Movement had threatened to tear Britain asunder in the 1640s. However, he also defended Argyll against contemporaneous charges of pusillanimous behaviour and outright cowardice when confronted by Montrose in battle and by other opponents offering duels during the 1640s. Argyll's military conduct was deemed politically pragmatic, and he was reputedly averse to duelling because it was ungodly. Baillie parted political company with Argyll in the early 1650s when the Marquess moved his support from the more accommodating Resolutioners to the uncompromising Protestors in the struggle for the soul of Presbyterianism during the Cromwellian occupation of Scotland. This shift, along with his failure to support the patriotic rising initiated by William Cunningham, 9th Earl of Glencairn in 1653–54, lost him the high regard in which he was held in all three kingdoms and reputedly earned him 'the people's great hatred' in Scotland. Yet, Baillie never lost sight of Argyll's enormous financial contribution to the Covenanting Movement, as he had accumulated extensive debt and exhausted his personal fortune in sustaining the cause in all three kingdoms. For Baillie, Argyll was unquestionably 'the greatest subject' of Charles II at the Restoration, and 'was the best and most excellent man our State of a long tyme had enjoyed'. His dignified conduct during his trial and execution redeemed his public standing. His death 'was much regrated by many, and by none insulted over'.[3]

The first among Baillie's contemporary political commentators to question the motives and probity of Argyll was James Gordon, parson of Rothiemay in Aberdeenshire, a lukewarm Covenanter more committed to geography and cartography. Never averse to the use of historical hindsight in revising his account of the emergence of the Covenanting Movement between 1637 and

---

3 *LJB*, I, pp. 145–7, 192–3, 303–4, 378–9, 393–4; II, pp. 63–4, 72–3, 94–6, 262–3, 376, 383; III, pp. 35–6, 109, 249–51, 287–8, 387, 418, 465–7.

1641, Gordon claimed that Argyll was primarily motivated to oppose Charles I on account of jealousy, particularly his aversion to the influence exercised at the royal court by Hamilton. Argyll, in turn, confirmed well founded concerns about his acquisitiveness at court by using his Covenanting leadership primarily to further his territorial ambitions as chief of ClanCampbell at the expense of his Royalist opponents. However, the parson of Rothiemay admitted that Argyll was universally perceived as the *major potestas* who gave 'being, lyfe and motione' to the firm establishment of the Covenanting Movement in power in Scotland by 1641.[4] A noted patron of the parson's scientific endeavours was Sir John Scott of Scotstarvit, well versed in the acquisitive opportunities of office holding and an occasional dabbler in colonial ventures. Notwithstanding his willingness to disparage the opportunism, mendacity and corruption of Scottish politicians holding public office between 1550 and 1650, Scotstarvit was conspic-uously silent in not traducing the commitment and honesty of the Marquess. He merely noted with regret that the deep-seated hatred between the followers of Argyll and those of Hamilton within Scotland 'hath been a prey and a conquest to the English nation'.[5]

Argyll's reputation as a 'pillar of the Covenant' was first qualified then traduced by John Spalding, an Aberdeen lawyer more noted for his survival instincts than his political commitment. Prior to the outbreak of civil war in Scotland in 1644, Spalding deemed Argyll a forceful leader but crafty operator who was prepared to dispense with the advice and consent of nobles and other leading statesmen that did not accord with his interpretation of public service. His willingness to carry out cruel and inhumane acts led him to behave not just oppressively, but tyrannically, towards his Royalist opponents, particularly in the north-east. But he remained reluctant to engage them in the field, prefer-ring to distress and wreck their estates for his own private advantage.[6] Whereas Spalding was a trimmer who revised his manuscript as Scotland moved from Covenanting revolution to monarchical restoration, Sir James Balfour of Denmylne, Lord Lyon King at Arms to both Charles I and Charles II, was a more dispassionate commentator who preferred to report rather than edito-rialise Argyll's prominence within the Covenanting Movement. Accordingly, Argyll was complimented for his short and pithy harangues to the Scottish Estates, for being a stickler for correct procedures in Kirk and State, for his exercise of 'exact discipline' in terrifying those who stood against the National Covenant, and for his occasional acts of clemency. The Lord Lyon did not demur when Argyll was commended by the Scottish Estates 'for acquitting himself

---

4 Gordon, *HSA*, I, p. 96; II, pp. 171–3, 234; II, 132–3, 182.
5 Sir John Scot [of Scotstarvit], *The Staggering State of the Scottish Statesmen* (1754), p. 3
6 Spalding, *Troubles*, I, pp. 91, 217, 228, 288 and II, pp. 39, 71, 184–5, 205, 215, 233, 245, 263.

lyke a good and faithful patriot' in promoting British confederation through the Solemn League and Covenant. He noted Argyll's frequent and unrequited pleas to the Scottish Estates to be reimbursed for his extensive expenditure on behalf of the Covenanting cause. Only once did he record the Marquess being upbraided for giving vent to his frustrations, that those who accused him of meddling with public funds to his own advantage at the conclusion of the civil war in Scotland were 'basse calumniators'. The Lord Lyon did become more markedly hostile to Argyll in 1649 in claiming that the Marquess, Loudoun and Wariston were but minions of the Kirk. He also recalled the less than honourable conduct of the Marquess in avoiding a duel in 1648, which also entailed the recycling of student gossip that Argyll was infamous for his daily oppressions. The Lord Lyon moved against Argyll not for any purported association with the regicide but on account of his association with the radical regime which came to power in the wake of the Britannic Engagement of 1648, a regime intent on social as well as political revolution. However, once Argyll distanced himself from the financial ambitions of the clergy and became the leading proponent of the patriotic accommodation to restore Charles II as King of Great Britain and Ireland, the Lord Lyon reverted to his preferred role of commentator rather than critic. The Marquess was particularly commended for his endeavours to negotiate purposefully 'to stop the shedding of more Christian blood' as English troops loyal to Oliver Cromwell occupied Scotland.[7]

A more succinct, but rounded appreciation of Argyll's character and political merits was provided by the soldier and scholar Patrick Gordon of Ruthven. A noted protagonist of Argyll during the 1640s, Ruthven was understandably less effusive than Principal Baillie. Nonetheless, he manifestly had an intimate understanding and a no less balanced perspective on the Marquess, whose 'many good and laudable partes' were subverted by the 'iniquitie of the tyme'. Argyll was essentially led astray from his cautious, wary and thrifty disposition by personal ambition for 'supreame and absolut rule'. As the most eminent and greatest of the Covenanting revolutionaries, Argyll was palpably susceptible to Machiavellian politics which, by his practices in power, 'he seemed perfectly to have studied'. Ruthven contrasted Argyll's private and public personas. One the one hand, he was 'of homely carriage, gentle, myld, and effable, gratious and courteous to speak too'. He was also generous and understanding, yet naturally apprehensive and austere. On the other hand, though tainted 'with a loftie and unsatiable ambition', Argyll 'proued the deepest statesman, the most craftie, subtill, and over-reacheing politician, that this age could produce'.[8]

---

7 Balfour, *HW*, II, pp. 380–1; and III, pp. 42, 80, 153, 159, 199, 221, 272–3, 295, 319–20, 377, 391, 395–6, 411–12, 417–8; and IV, pp. 2, 86, 169–70, 173–4, 186, 220, 223, 242, 247, 316–7, 350.

8 Gordon , *Distemper*, pp. 56–7.

The Edinburgh lawyer and diarist John Nicoll commented in 1660 that Argyll had been 'a prince and chief commander in the land' for the past twenty-three years, but faced timely prosecution at the Restoration for 'his many horrible' acts over this period. His indictment for high treason demonstrated how God cast down the mighty.[9] A more charitable Presbyterian perspective was provided by Alexander Brodie of Brodie. Closely tied to Argyll in the 1650s not so much by ties of kinship or political clientage as by Christian fellowship, Brodie was not averse to expressing his misgivings about the deep resentments harboured by the Marquess and the 'keeping in his mind injuries, and offences and prejudices'. Nonetheless, he felt a profound sense of loss following Argyll's execution in 1661;[10] a loss shared by the Covenanting remnant that refused to conform to Episcopalianism at the Restoration. Thus, for James Kirkton, the Marquess was 'to die a sacrifice to royal jealousy and revenge'. Argyll had adhered to the radical fundamentals of Covenanting when they no longer constituted the political mainstream in the 1650s. He had kept his authority while most of the former leadership of the Movement was marginalised during the Cromwellian occupation. Notwithstanding a great deal of envy, he remained 'very wise and politick' although, as Kirkton affirmed, 'he was by many reckoned either subtile or false!' As the Covenanting cause shifted from a movement of power to that of protest in the Restoration era, Argyll came to be viewed by preachers in outlawed conventicles in hill and field as a godly patriot sacrificed on the altar of absolute monarchy.[11]

As the perspectives of Argyll from Baillie to Kirkton were not published until the eighteenth and nineteenth centuries, the propaganda emanating from the later Covenanting Movement that made him a martyr for 'his zeal and activity for the work of God' largely went unchallenged within Presbyterian circles. Writing in 1665 from exile in Holland, John Brown, as 'a well wisher to the good old cause', affirmed that Argyll had been an enemy to monarchy for the twenty-three years from the signing of the National Covenant in 1638 to his trial and execution in 1661, 'when a great prince falleth'. Accordingly, he had been 'an active friend for the interests of Christ'. As 'an ornament' to Scotland, the charges against him were groundless in law, whether divine or civil. Far from acting treasonably in his dealings with the Cromwellian regime, he was doing what he thought best for a country that had been conquered and subdued in

---

9 Nicoll, *Diary*, pp. 308–9, 321–2.

10 *The Diary of Alexander Brodie of Brodie, 1652–1680 & of his son, James Brodie of Brodie, 1680–1685*, D. Laing ed. (Aberdeen, 1863), pp. 147, 251.

11 James Kirkton, *The Secret and True History of the Church of Scotland from the Restoration to the year 1678*, C.K. Sharpe ed. (Edinburgh, 1817), pp. 69–70.

order to 'prevent its utter ruin and destruction'.[12] The imprimatur of martyrdom was duly affirmed by Robert Wodrow, minister of Eastwood in Renfrewshire, the seemingly indefatigable chronicler of the sufferings endured by the later Covenanting Movement. Thus Argyll was deemed 'a person of extraordinary Piety, remarkable Wisdom & Prudence, great Gravity and Authority and singular Usefulness'. His irregular trial and execution had vindicated him from the reproaches of his enemies:

> He was the great Promoter and Support of the covenanted work of Reformation during his life, and steadfast in witnessing to it at his Death.[13]

However, the godly patriot of Covenanting tradition ran up against an ongoing Royalist polemic that tarnished Argyll with insurrection, civil war and usurpation. Vehement, intemperate and highly partisan imprints, in Latin, French and English, carried the greater national and international weighting that prevailed until the mid-eighteenth century.

Royalist Villain

The first, well published Royalist denigrator of Argyll was George Wishart, who served as chaplain and secretary to Montrose, with whom he went into continental exile in 1646. Wishart eventually returned to Scotland to become Bishop of Edinburgh after the Restoration. Wishart had been removed from his ministry in St Andrews by the Covenanting Movement in 1638. Having moved to Newcastle, he was subsequently imprisoned by the Covenanters there and in Edinburgh from October 1644. He was only released from prison following Montrose's victory at Kilsyth in August 1645. Accordingly, he did not witness the campaigns of Montrose and MacColla in the Highlands and the north-east of Scotland. His association with Montrose was marked by defeat at Philiphaugh in September 1645, then exile twelve months later, followed by disappointment and despair when Montrose's abortive return to Scotland led to his capture and execution in 1650. Wishart did not come back for Montrose's last campaign. His first commentary on the civil wars, issued in Latin, probably from The Hague in late 1647, covered Montrose's military activities from 1644 to 1646. Given that he was only an eye-witness to defeat, his account was essentially a manifesto for the Royalist's cause in Scotland and, above all, a personal vindication for Montrose. Wishart wrote with the full compliance and co-operation of his hero. In the process Argyll was vilified. This first commentary was republished in

---

12 [John Brown], *An Apologeticall Relation of the Particular Sufferings of the Faithfull Ministers & Professours of the Church of Scotland since August 1660* (Rotterdam, 1665).

13 Wodrow, *Sufferings*, I, pp. 42, 56.

Paris and Amsterdam over the next two years. Unauthorised freelance translations in English seem to have circulated in London from 1649. Wishart around 1652 composed a supplementary Latin account of Montrose's fruitless diplomatic negotiations and of events in Scotland from 1647 to 1650, which was not translated into English until 1720. Wishart in exile had no first-hand experience of how Scottish affairs were then conducted. Yet his works, which were circulated extensively in print and manuscript before the Restoration, became the accepted texts for dismissing Argyll as a dangerous fanatic intent on personal aggrandisement, and not a martyr to any motive other than selfishness.

For Wishart, the Marquess of Argyll, a craven man of a 'crafty but cowardly disposition' who preferred flight to fight, had no redeeming features. As enemies to the Royalists, the gentry of the ClanCampbell 'were stout and gallant men, well worthy of a better chief and a juster cause', given the willingness of Argyll to abandon them to their slaughter. Notwithstanding their criticisms that Argyll's leadership had failed, 'through want of care or courage', the house of Hamilton and their associates had colluded with his designs to subvert the monarchy in Scotland. Argyll and his Argathelians constituted a seditious confederacy intent on tyranny, which Montrose alone stood against. By 1648, Argyll had entered 'an accursed compact' with Cromwell to root out monarchy throughout Britain. Wishart took little consolation from the 'characteristic duplicity' of Charles II, who ruined both Montrose and Argyll, having sacrificed the former through an abortive expedition deprived of foreign assistance in 1650, and having the latter brought to trial and executed eleven years later.[14]

The Royalist backlash was furthered in 1658, by Sir William Sandersone. As a courtier, he was appalled that the Covenanters had made diplomatic overtures to foreign powers from 1639. He also resented and distrusted Covenanting intervention in Ireland from 1642, and especially in England from 1644. The intent was clearly to export revolution:

> For Subjects to make foreign Confederacies without their Soveraignes assent, to invade the Territories of their undoubted King, to go about by force to change the Laws and Religion established, is a grosse Treason without all contradiction.

He drew heavily on Wishart for his appraisal of Argyll's conduct up to and during the Scottish civil war as oppressive, treacherous, cruel, tyrannical,

14 George Wishart, *De Rebus Auspiciis Serenissimi, & Potentissimi Caroli Dei Gratia Magnae Britanniae, Franciae & Hiberniae Regis, &c. sub imperio illustrissimi Jacobi Montisrosarum Marchionis . . . Supremi Scotiae Gubernatoris anno MDCXLIV, & duobus sequentibus praeclare gestis, Commentarius* (The Hague, 1647), pp. 81–2, 118; Wishart, *Memoirs*, pp. xxix–xli, 77, 80, 83–5, 106–7, 180, 205, 218, 251, 291.

corrupt and cowardly; conduct which made him hated by his own Highlanders. The Marquess was further indicted for his confederacy with Cromwell and the Independents, which paved the way for the regicide.[15]

By the time of Argyll's execution in 1661, the debate on his character and conduct had been given a further twist by a Scottish émigré, Robert Monteith of Salmonet, whose historical writings in French were not translated into English until 1735. Monteith certainly had first-hand knowledge of the troubles of Great Britain from the Scottish coronation of Charles I in 1633 to the patriotic accommodation of Covenanters and Royalists in favour of Charles II in 1650. He duly shifted the focus away from Montrose towards Hamilton as the main victim of Argyll's political machinations. Argyll's defeat by the manifestly more valiant Montrose in 1645 diminished his credit among his own followers, but this was attributed as much to ineptitude as to cowardice. His defeat was no more than a temporary setback. After the failure of the Britannic Engagement, Argyll made no effort to save Hamilton as the leader of that abortive Scottish venture from a judiciously dubious execution. In March 1649, the regicides had determined that Hamilton should stand trial under his English title, as 2nd Earl of Cambridge. Argyll purportedly compounded this self-serving act – he had 'no mind to have a competitor in Scotland' – by stalling Covenanting commitment to the patriotic accommodation in order to give Cromwell time to ravage Ireland and secure the Commonwealth in England.[16]

The Royalist perspective was given renewed impetus by the memoirs of Henry Guthry. Although not published in his lifetime, a manuscript copy was certainly circulating in the 1660s after Guthry, a former Presbyterian minister who had signed the Covenants, became Bishop of Dunkeld. Guthry, who was intent on laying to rest his Covenanting past, wrote to eulogise Montrose. Argyll, though recognised as the foremost Covenanter, was castigated as a scheming, miserly and vindictive opportunist who was usually first in flight when faced by mortal combat. Albeit Argyll was deemed to have exercised political mastery over Hamilton until 1648, the Britannic Engagement was undermined by Argyll's covert dealings with Oliver Cromwell. Without a shred of evidence beyond gossip and hearsay, Guthry claimed that Cromwell had taken Argyll and other leading Covenanters into his confidence about his future designs for Charles I,

15 Sir William Sandersone, *A Compleat History of the Life and Raigne of King Charles I* (London, 1658), pp. 277, 287, 793–5, 1075–6. Argyll was not entirely an unalloyed villain within Royalist circles. In his brief cataloguing of Royalist martyrs published in the wake of the Restoration, William Winstanley (*The Loyall Martyrology* (London, 1665), pp. 46–7) certainly cited Montrose's martial prowess at the expense of Argyll. Yet the chief of ClanCampbell was not cited among the 'dregs of treachery' in his accompanying brief catalogue of the regicides

16 Robert Monteith of Salmonet, *The History of the Troubles of Great Britain* (London, 1735), pp. 197, 501, 510, 512–13.

receiving in turn their assent to the regicide.[17]

A switch in focus away from Montrose towards the rehabilitation of the house of Hamilton was effected by Gilbert Burnet. This Scottish exile's memoirs of James, the 1st Duke and his brother William, initially as Earl of Lanark then as 2nd Duke, were first published in 1677. The future Bishop of Salisbury was no friend of Presbyterianism, although his maternal uncle was Johnston of Wariston, the principal political agent and confidant of Argyll. Burnet recorded the growing estrangement and then outright enmity between Argyll and the Hamilton brothers from 1641, on account of the Marquess being 'so backward in all motions for the king's service'. The main purpose of these memoirs was to exonerate the Hamilton brothers from the failure of the Britannic Engagement, which they engineered with considerable political cunning, using their conservative contacts and clients to outmanoeuvre Argyll and his radical associates. But the miscarriage of the hastily executed and hapless Engagement could not solely be attributed to the internal opposition mounted by Argyll. Nevertheless, Burnet excused their abortive expedition on the grounds that the Covenanting troops under their command were raw and undisciplined, inadequately equipped and constantly harassed from their entry into England until their defeat at Preston in September 1648. Hamilton was only blamed for too readily accepting errant advice from more senior officers. Burnet's rather restrained criticism of Argyll was thrown over with the posthumous publication of his own voluminous memoirs from 1724. In his description of Argyll, commendation soon gave way to condemnation:

> a more solemn sort of a man, grave and sober; free of all scandalous vices, of an invincible calmness of temper and a pretender to a degree of piety: but he was a deep dissembler, and great oppressor in all his private dealings, and he was noted for a defect in his courage on all occasions where danger met him. This had one of its usual effects on him, for he was cruel in cold blood: he was much set on raising his own family to be a sort of king in the highlands.[18]

In response to Burnet, William Dugdale, who was primarily concerned with drawing an analogy between the civil wars of the mid-seventeenth century and

---

17 *MHG*, pp. 73, 76, 94, 102, 118–19, 127–9, 149, 172–4, 178–9, 193–4, 234, 252–3, 261, 270–2, 276, 290, 294, 298; Duke University Special Collections, Sir James Turner Papers, 'Some Animadversions on Bishop Guthries Memoirs', pp. 1, 6, 7–13, 14. Guthry's memoirs were first published in London in 1702.

18 Burnet, *Memoirs*, pp. 239, 260, 335–78; and [Gilbert Burnet] *Bishop Burnet's History of His Own Time*, W. Legge, 1st Earl of Dartmouth, P. Yorke, 1st Earl of Hardwick and A. Onslow eds, 6 vols (Oxford, 1833), I, p. 49.

the French Wars of Religion in the later sixteenth century, presented a more prevaricating picture of Hamilton in 1681. The Duke had purportedly sought to stave off his trial and execution by offering a ransom of £100,000 sterling for his life and intimating to the regicides that he would join with Argyll in Scotland to serve their interests. Argyll's refusal to collaborate, 'resolving that none should share with him in so Glorious a Work', expedited Hamilton's trial and execution in 1649. Dugdale was less given to irony and more to outrage when outlining the Covenanting aims to secure a negotiated peace in tripartite negotiations with Charles I and the English Parliamentarians at Uxbridge in 1644–45. For the Covenanters, under the leadership of Argyll, were reportedly intent on Scottish imperialism by claiming 'the Supreme Command of Ireland to be put into their Hands: As also to have a share in the Government of England'.[19]

A further hostile attack on the Covenanters was made by John Neilson, primarily because of their association with the English Parliamentarians during the civil wars. Hamilton was again castigated for prevarication and for being duped by the Covenanting leadership. This rather oblique criticism of Argyll was sharpened up when Neilson attacked the Covenanters for their 'Injustice and Impiety' and, above all, for their preference 'to petition with the Sword in their hands'.[20] Their British aspirations were further disparaged by the belated publication in 1705 of the selective reminiscences of Sir Edwald Walker, who had been Secretary of War to Charles I and Clerk of the Council to Charles II. Walker focused his criticisms of Argyll on his involvement with the patriotic accommodation. During 1650, the Marquess attempted to obstruct the participation of Royalists, restrict their importation of arms from abroad and sabotage their attempts to mobilise support from sympathetic Ulster Scots. Argyll and his inner radical circle were set on retaining 'the sole Administration of Affairs'. They were less intent on restoring Charles II than on pursuing 'their work of Reformation by the most severe and rigid Rule both in Church and State' which, if accomplished, would have reduced the Royalist party in all the king's dominions to 'a far more miserable Condition both for their Consciences and Estates' than under Cromwell.[21]

The most weighty, if not the definitive, Royalist contribution was actually made in the three years prior to Walker's reminiscences, with the long delayed publication of *The History of the Rebellion* by Edward Hyde, who had set aside

---

19 William Dugdale, *A Short View of the Late Troubles in England* (London, 1681), pp. 389, 645.
20 John Neilson, *An Impartial Collection of the Great Affairs of State, from the beginning of the Scotch Rebellion in the year MDCXXXIX to the Murther of King Charles I*, 2 vols (London, 1682–83), I, pp. 1, 3–4; II, p. 209.
21 Sir Edwald Walker, *Historical Discourses upon Several Occasions* (London, 1705), pp. 161–3, 188, 193–4.

his initial sympathies with the English Parliamentarians to become a staunch adviser of Charles I from 1642. Although his moderating influence fell out of favour with Charles I as the civil war was lost, Hyde became a close adviser of the Prince of Wales, the future Charles II, from 1646 and remained so throughout enforced exile. At the Restoration he was ennobled as 1st Earl of Clarendon and reinstated to prominence and for a time to political pre-eminence in the royal counsels as Lord Chancellor of England. The publication of his work also served a contemporary polemic purpose. For in 1703–04, radical opponents of political incorporation with England in the Scottish Estates had attempted to impose fundamental limitations on monarchy inspired by the revolutionary attainments of the Covenanting Movement under the direction of Argyll in 1640–41. These attempted limitations had outraged Clarendon's grand-daughter, Queen Anne.[22] His momentous work was a stark warning against radical constitutional upheavals.

Clarendon felt obliged to severely censure the actions of many who had not the least thought of disloyalty or infidelity. But he directed his particular ire at those who, 'with the most deliberate impiety, prosecuted their design to ruin and destroy the crown'. He certainly did not spare the Marquess of Argyll. Initially, Clarendon made much of the prophetic warning given at Court to Charles I by Archibald Campbell, 7th Earl of Argyll on the emergence of the Covenanting Movement in Scotland. The 7th Earl claimed that his estranged son, then Lord Lorne, 'is a man of craft, subtilty and falsehood, and can love no man; and if ever he finds it in his power to do you mischief, he will be sure to do it'. Clarendon readily came to realise over the next two decades that without mentioning the Marquess of Argyll 'there can hardly be any mention of Scotland'. With respect to Argyll's principal Scottish rivals, Clarendon considered Montrose was all but consumed by jealousy and detestation of Argyll who, notwithstanding his consistent tyranny towards his enemies, 'wanted nothing but honesty and courage to be a very extraordinary man'. Hamilton lacked the necessary ruthlessness to marginalise the Marquess in the Covenanting leadership. In shaping the British aspirations of the Covenanting Movement, Clarendon considered Argyll to be 'purely Presbyterian' in matters of religion, but in relation to issues of state and the conduct of the civil wars, 'perfectly Independent'. Argyll's alleged partiality towards Cromwell and his associates made him a willing subverter of the Britannic Engagement and no more than a lukewarm promoter of the patriotic accommodation. Clarendon was especially unforgiving of Argyll's dissembling conduct towards Charles II, although he was instrumental in having the Prince of Wales crowned as King of Great Britain and Ireland at Scone in Perthshire

22 A.I. Macinnes, *Union and Empire: The Making of the United Kingdom in 1707* (Cambridge, 2007), pp. 258–66.

at the outset of 1651. Castigated as the creature of Cromwell, Argyll's desire to retain power in Scotland had to be tempered by the groundswell of support in favour of the monarchy. Clarendon, however, was unable to prove directly or circumstantially that Argyll actively colluded with Cromwell either in the regicide or, when his 'empire seemed not be so absolute' during the 1650s, to prevent the restoration of Charles II in all three kingdoms. But he did admit that Charles II in 1660 bore considerable malice towards Presbyterianism and to the house of Argyll from his brief sojourn in Scotland during the patriotic accommodation.[23]

Although Clarendon glossed over Argyll's trial and execution, and declaimed the Marquess as 'a man universally odious to the whole nation', he did offer a judicious summation of his political influence within and beyond Scotland:

> Without doubt he was a person of extraordinary cunning, well bred; and though, by the ill-placing of his eyes, he did not appear with any great advantage at first sight, yet he reconciled even those who had aversion to him very strangely by a little conversation . . . His wit was pregnant and his humour gay and pleasant, except when he liked not the company or the argument . . . When the other faction prevailed, in which there were likewise crafty managers, and that his counsels were commonly rejected, he carried himself so, that they who hated him most were willing to compound with him.[24]

With the work of Clarendon bolstering the writings of Wishart and Burnet, the Scottish antiquarian George Craufurd affirmed confidently in 1726 that Argyll was not just a violent and assertive Covenanter. He was also 'a grand villain' who was 'most Justly Execute' as the Covenanting ringleader in the murder of Charles I and many other political opponents.[25]

Blurring the Lens

That the reputation of the Marquess of Argyll was predominantly negative can also be attributed to the oral circulation of poetry in Gaelic and Scots, and even to the visual arts in terms of portraiture. The vilification of the house of Argyll had long been part of Gaelic tradition, particularly by classical bards and vernacular poets associated with the diverse branches of the MacDonalds and the

23 Clarendon, *History*, pp. 52, 473, 540–1, 642–3, 678, 705–8, 737–8, 741, 746–7, 750–1, 758–9, 1022–3, 1112.

24 *Ibid.*, pp. 1022, 1113.

25 George Craufurd, *The Lives and Characters of the Officers of the Crown, and of the State in Scotland, from the Beginning of the Reign of King David I to the Union of the Two Kingdoms* (London, 1726), p. 189.

Macleans, the main victims of the territorial aggrandisement of the ClanCampbell since the fifteenth century.[26] Thus, Iain Lom alias John MacDonald from
Keppoch rejoiced in the impending execution of the Marquess of Argyll:

> 'N am rùsgadh a choileir
> Théid an ceann deth o cholainn –
> Glòir agus moladh do'n Ardrigh –
> Le maighean sgorshuileach smachdail
> Dh'fhàgas giallan gum mheartainn,
> Dhuineas fiaras a 'Mharcuis mhì-chàirdeail.

[When his collar is torn off, his head will be severed from his body – all
glory and praise to the king on high – by a sharp-eyed austere Maiden that
leaves jaws powerless, and will close forever the malevolent Marquess'
squint].[27]

Although Gaelic poetry had limited circulation outwith the Highlands and
Islands, the Scots language was no less unrelenting in tarnishing reputations.
There was, however, a greater degree of ambivalence towards Argyll in Scots
than in Gaelic poetry.

There are several versions of the ballad 'The Bonnie House of Airlie', which
deals with Argyll's destruction in July 1640 of the seat of James Ogilvie, 1st Earl
of Airlie, in his absence. It was in the same campaign that Argyll gave instructions to Campbell of Inverawe to burn the house of Airlie's son and heir, James,
Lord Ogilvie in Forther on the Braes of Angus (see above). As these ballads
were not collected for publication until the nineteenth century, it is difficult to
determine the exact date of their composition. All ballads deem Argyll to be
taking revenge on Airlie, usually within the context of Covenanting reprisals
against the Royalist house of Airlie, but also in terms of a territorial feud. Argyll
had lands in the shire of Angus in close proximity to those of Airlie. The ballad
clearly propagates the fairly accurate view that Argyll turned public policy
to private advantage, and is very much in keeping with contemporary claims
that Argyll was the 'first who raised fyre in Scotland' in the conflicts between
Covenanters and Royalist.[28]

---

26 A.I. Macinnes, 'Seventeenth Century Scotland: The Undervalued Gaelic Perspective' in C.
Byrne, M. Harry and P. O'Siadhail eds, *Celtic Languages and Celtic Peoples* (Halifax, N.S., 1992),
pp. 535–54.

27 *Orain Iain Luim: Songs of John MacDonald, Bard of Keppoch*, A.M. MacKenzie ed. (Edinburgh,
1973), pp. 78–9. When Archibald Campbell, 9th Earl of Argyll was also executed in 1685, Iain
Lom again rejoiced that the Maiden had earlier, in 1661, taken the crookedness out of the
Marquess of Argyll – Thug i 'm fiabhras a Marcus Earr'-Ghàidheal (*Ibid.*, pp. 180–1).

28 Gordon, *HSA*, II, p. 234

However, there is less common ground in describing further personal motives for the reprisals. Argyll is stated in all versions to have made improper sexual advances to the lady of the house. It is even hinted in the version most hostile to Argyll that he had been her former suitor and would not have sacked the castle if she had accepted his hand in marriage. Lady Ogilvie is named as Margaret in another version. However, neither Airlie nor his son Lord Ogilvie were married to a Margaret, which is a name held in common by the Earl's aunt, sister and daughter. There is no extant record that Argyll was ever a suitor for any Margaret from the house of Airlie. More pertinently, the fullest and probably original version describes Argyll as both 'great' and 'fause' (false), but a later version, almost certainly adapted after his execution, frequently just cites him as 'gley'd', that is squint-eyed.[29] Yet not all Scots poetry disparaged Argyll. A ballad on the surrender of Dumbarton Castle in August 1639 eulogises him for not only sparing the Royalist garrison but also granting honourable terms for their unmolested departure. Verses on the death of Marquess in 1661 elegise 'Argyll the great' as a virtuous Covenanting martyr. Notwithstanding his 'weevering temper', he was a stalwart of the Protestant Reformation, a judicious shaper of public policy and the veritable 'pillar of the state', yet the greatest subject in Scotland to challenge monarchy.[30]

The ambivalence of poetry is replicated in the portraiture. Of the ten known portraits of Archibald Campbell, five relating to his time as Marquess of Argyll can be attributed to the school of David Scougall.[31] But only one, the most iconic and enduringly influential (see Plate 1), painted probably in the mid-1650s, has definitively been ascribed to that artist from around 1720. All the portraits of the Scougall school are of the bust and have the Marquess looking penetratingly at the viewer with dark blue eyes tinged with grey. All portray a similar style of dress. He wears a black, enclosed head band from which locks of his auburn hair fall down onto a broad white square collar tied by tassels to a black tunic. The prominent, aquiline nose associated with leading members of the house of Argyll is clearly defined. Curled lips can be interpreted as a visual pun on the Campbell name, which is derived in Scottish Gaelic from *cam beul*, literally twisted mouth. But this feature more than hints at the arrogance of power and is, in turn, enhanced by a pencil-thin moustache over the upper lip and a

29 *Scottish Ballads and Songs: Historical and Traditional*, J. Maidment ed., 2 vols (Edinburgh, 1868), I, pp. 271–9; Willcock, *The Great Marquess*, pp. 349–51.

30 *Scottish Ballads and Songs*, I, pp. 331–2; NLS, Wodrow MSS, quarto xxxv, fo.89; and folio xxxii, fo.17.

31 All these portraits have been classified by SNPG. I am grateful for the assistance of Deborah Hunter for locating them in the photo library of SNPG. The original of Plate 1, catalogued as S.Ph.II.8–4, is at Newbattle Abbey, the seat of the Earls, later Marquesses, of Lothian. There is also a photograph of the original catalogued as PG 1408/ David Scougall.

short, triangulated goatee beard under the lower lip. Scougall and his school have uniformly painted the Marquess with a three-quarter length face from the right, which highlights rather than disguises a pronounced squint in his left eye. In sum, the impression is given of an authoritarian, rather severe and humourless statesman whose confessional commitment is undoubtedly Presbyterian. The portraiture clearly demonstrates why the soubriquet *Gilleasbuig Gruamach* (Archibald the Grim) was passed on to the Marquess from his father the 7th Earl of Argyll. But there is also grudging respect for a politician of stature who clearly has the accumulated experience of a man of power. It is not portraiture of a man worn down by the cares of office, unduly apprehensive about his future or prematurely aged by his financial burdens. These paintings stand in striking contrast to the contemporaneous portrayal of Argyll as 'the old Marquess' by the London diarist John Evelyn in May 1656.[32]

However, there are five other quite different portraits of Archibald Campbell. Three or four relate to his time as Lord Lorne prior to 1638, and one or two relate to that as 8th Earl of Argyll. All these portraits have their subject bareheaded, with eyes looking beyond rather than directly at the viewer. The earliest reputed portrait has rather tenuously been attributed to Scougall's celebrated predecessor from Aberdeen, George Jamesone.[33] But the attribution of this bust portrait and its inscription as the 'Marquis of Argyll' were added by an art gallery prior to the First World War to enhance its sale rather than establish its provenance. The painting is rather anachronistic (see Plate 9). It is dated to 1627, yet Archibald Campbell did not become Marquess for another fourteen years. The sitter is stated to be twenty-nine, which would have placed Lorne's birth in 1598, probably nine years too early. The sitter also seems to have prematurely aged. He has a moustache that is almost handle-bar, and a full goatee beard which falls below his chin. The nose is not distinctively Campbell. There is no hint of a curled lip, and a squint, if any, is in his right eye. Although the portrait appears to mark Lorne's first visit to the court of Charles I, his dress style is distinctively Jacobean, a period which ended two years before the portrait is stated to have been painted. The portrait, which seems more reliant on customised stereotypes rather than original creations, has also be linked with 'Adam de Colone', a jobbing painter at the court of James VI and I just after the regal union.

32 *The Diary of John Evelyn, Esq., F.R.S., from 1641 to 1705–6*, W. Bray ed. (London, 1890), pp. 248, 251.
33 This portrait (Plate 9) has been catalogued by the SNPG as S.Ph.II.8–9. In the frontispiece to Willcock, *The Great Marquess*, there is a portrait reproduced from the original in Newbattle Abbey that purports to be Lord Lorne, probably at the time of his marriage. However, the clean shaven, young man in ceremonial dress is not the future 8th Earl and Marquess as groom to Margaret Douglas, daughter of William, 9th earl of Morton in 1626, but that of his son Archibald, the future 9th Earl of Argyll, probably at the time of his marriage to Margaret Stewart, daughter of James, 4th Earl of Moray in 1650.

Adam of Cologne is not to be confused with another German painter, Schunemann, who worked for a considerable period in Scotland and has been identified as painting one of two, almost identical, portraits of Lorne.[34] These are the only full-length portraits of Archibald Campbell and the only paintings that have the subject facing left. Schunemann's painting (see Plate 8), which conforms to the Court portraiture of Charles I, identifies the subject as Lord Lorne and is dated to 1630. Lorne holds a broad hat in his left hand and a sword of office in his right. This sword must relate to his admission to the Scottish Privy Council in June 1628, after he reached his majority. Although the sword has also been identified with his post as master of the royal household in Scotland, Lorne did not attain this post in his own right until February 1633.[35] The full-length figure reveals a well proportioned if rather slight man of around medium height: 5 ft 5 in to 5 ft 7 in (1.65–1.70 cm) who, unlike the diminutive Charles I, did not require built-up shoes to enhance his stature. Lorne has a similar, if more restrained moustache and a narrower goatee beard than in the 1627 portrait, but a slight trace of a squint has been restored to the left eye. The almost identical picture, which differs in dress only in the angle of the sword and minor collar details, has Lorne looking slightly younger and more assured. However, this portrait is also inscribed anachronistically as 'the Marquis of Argyll', which suggests that its provenance was not 1628, the year of his sword-wielding majority, but actually later than 1630, and may even commemorate his appointment as master of the household. It seems to represent a subsequent touching-up to flatter a subject who was becoming a more assured councillor and occasional courtier.

Jamesone, who painted Margaret Douglas, the future Marchioness of Argyll, in a gentle and pensive mood around 1634,[36] has again been linked, convincingly but not conclusively, with another bust portrait in more martial array. This portrait was actually painted on wood panelling found in the House of Argyll's Lowland stronghold of Castle Campbell in Clackmannanshire (see Plate 7). There may be echoes of the portraiture of the Thirty Years War, or even that of the civil wars for the three kingdoms in the 1640s. But this ceremonial composition was probably occasioned by the royal visit of Charles I to Scotland for his coronation in 1633, when Lord Lorne featured as a leading Scottish magnate,

34 J. Holloway, *Patrons and Painters: Art in Scotland 1650–1760* (Edinburgh, 1989), p. 24. The SNPG has catalogued these two portraits as S.Ph.II.8-7 (for Plate 8) and as S.Ph.II.8-13. It has not been possible to provide an illustration of the second portrait (copy after Schunemann) as the Scottish National Portrait Gallery, despite repeated requests, was unable to secure permission to publish from either the unknown owner or the estate administrator. This portrait was to be found in Drumlanrig Castle, Dumfriesshire, the seat of the Dukes of Buccleuch, and the other version (Plate 8) in Newbattle Abbey.

35 *RPCS*, second series, II (1627–28), p. 91; and V (1633–35), pp. 49–50

36 D. Thompson, *The Life and Art of George Jamesone* (Oxford, 1974), pp. 102–3.

PLATE I

The Marquess as a committed Presbyterian and as an authoritarian,
rather severe and humourless statesman, by David Scougall, c.1655

PLATE 2
The Marquess as a scowling
and austere statesman, by
an apprentice from the
Scougall school copying
David Scougall, post-1655

PLATE 3
The Marquess as a more
bland statesman, by
an apprentice from the
Scougall school copying
David Scougall, post-1655

PLATE 4
The Marquess as a less severe statesman, attributed to both
David Scougall and George Jameson but almost certainly by an
apprentice from the Scougall school, post-1655

PLATE 5
The Marquess as an arrogant and sinister statesman, by an
unknown artist probably from the Scougall school and familiar with
the works of both David Scougall and George Jameson, c.1661

PLATE 6
The 8th Earl as a leading Covenanter and man of
power and purpose, by George Jameson, c.1639

PLATE 7
Lord Lorne as leading magnate, by unknown artist, possibly but not conclusively
by George Jameson for the coronation visit of Charles I, c.1633

PLATE 8

Lord Lorne as courtier and royal councillor, by the
German painter Schunemann, c.1630

PLATE 9

Lord Lorne, rather anachronistically as a courtier in terms of
date and title, by unknown artist, tenuously linked to George Jameson
but more plausibly to the jobbing painter Adam de Colone, c.1627

rather than by the Bishops' Wars of 1639–40, when the 8th Earl of Argyll was as prominent a Covenanter in the field as in political circles. The image conveyed is not so much a man of action as a rather melancholic stoic. The Campbell nose is slightly underplayed. There is a well trimmed moustache but no beard, and it is difficult to tell whether there is a squint in the right or the left eye. There is no hint of a twisted mouth. Jamesone can, however, be more assuredly identified with the most strikingly sympathetic portrait of Archibald Campbell as a man of power and purpose, dressed reservedly as a leading Covenanter rather than flamboyantly as a courtier (see Plate 6). Accordingly, the sitting would seem to date not before but after the emergence of the Covenanting Movement, when the 8th Earl established himself as the foremost radical by the outbreak of the Bishops' Wars in 1639.[37] The strong facial features and sombre countenance suggest a statesman whose political horizons ranged beyond Scotland. Again there is no trace of sneer or arrogant curl of the lips, but there is more than a slight squint in his left eye. His nose is more hooked than in other portraits. A fulsome goatee beard has been restored to the tip of his chin to complement a moustache that is rather unkempt. The overarching impression is that of determination, commitment and authority rather than arrogance, menace or malice.

Because of these inconsistencies in portraiture we must be wary of accepting the Scougall school as painting free from polemic. David Scougall was a member of an Episcopalian family from the north-east of Scotland. His cousin Patrick became Bishop of Aberdeen following the Restoration. His one attributed portrait was certainly painted in the last decade of Argyll's life, when the Marquess' political star was on the wane. The first portrait that can actually be attributed to Scougall was that of Argyll's daughter Jean, as Countess of Lothian, in 1654.[38] So Scougall's portrait of the Marquess would seem to have been painted after this date, when Argyll was in his late forties or early fifties. Of the four other paintings attributed to the Scougall school, three are less severe in their representation of Argyll in terms of portraying his squint or his twisted mouth. One appears to be a man in his late forties rather than early fifties. This painting (see Plate 4) has been attributed to both Scougall and Jamesone. But the latter had died in 1643 and the figure lacks the stature of his portrayal of the then 8th Earl as a man of destiny. As this work was almost certainly a test-piece by an apprentice, it would suggest a date of around 1655 for the Scougall original. Two of the other paintings can also be attributed to ongoing work by apprentices copying Scougall's finished picture, probably before the Restoration. One has a fuller face (see Plate 3), a shorter collar and elongated tassels.

---

37 *Ibid.*, p. 113. The SNPG has catalogued these two portraits respectively as S.Ph.II.8-12 for Plate 7 and S.Ph.II.8-14 for Plate 6. Both are held in Inveraray Castle, Argyllshire.

38 Holloway, *Patrons and Painters*, p. 14

The other (see Plate 2) has the merest hint of a sneer and a squint in the right eye as well as the left. The sitter is represented as scowling and austere, but not arrogant and sinister, unlike the remaining portrait (see Plate 5).[39]

Here a younger version of the Scougall bust has pronounced curling of the lips, a marked squint in his left eye and a suggestion of a squint in his right. His moustache is fuller but poorly groomed. The aquiline shape of the nose is exaggerated. The overall impression is of a ruthlessly exploitive politician, untrustworthy and vindictive and perhaps shading towards the vampiric. There does not appear to be too great a difference in age from the Jamesone picture of c. 1639 (see Plate 6). But if this unflattering picture was an authentic portrayal of Argyll later in that decade, it sits uneasily with his political position as the dominant figure in the radical mainstream of the Covenanting Movement. At the same time, if actually painted in the late 1640s, it seems rather early for Scougall. This leaves one other possibility: that it was a painting by someone familiar with both the works of Jamesone and Scougall and who produced a customised, but posthumous, portrait of Argyll to suggest his complicity with the regicides in 1649 and justify his execution as a Cromwellian collaborator in 1661. However, the one stumbling block to this hypothesis is the question of who would commission such a picture? There was no national rogues' gallery established after the Restoration. Nevertheless, the painting does appear polemically motivated. Given Argyll's public stature, even in his latter years, accentuating his negative characteristics would only have been feasible after his execution.[40]

Enlightened Scepticism

Argyll's rehabilitation as a British statesman began with the philosophical speculation of David Hume. A leading figure of the Enlightenment in Scotland, Hume was clearly influenced by Wodrow and the Covenanting tradition in declaring that Argyll could not, 'by any equitable construction' be held to account for treason. Hume was readily prepared to admit that Argyll 'was universally known to have been the chief instrument of past disorders and civil wars'. But his compliance with the Cromwellian Occupation of Scotland was 'a crime common to him with the whole nation'. Notwithstanding the judicial irregularities of his trial, the Marquess faced execution 'with great constancy and courage'.[41] James Macpherson, who found fame and notoriety for his rich

39 The four portraits attributed to the Scougall school have been catalogued respectively by the SNPG as S.Ph.II.8-8 for Plate 4; as PG 583/ artist unknown for Plate 3; as S.Ph.II.8-1 for Plate 2; and S.Ph.II.8-15 for Plate 5. All but Plate 3 have been associated with the collection of the Dukes of Argyll in Inveraray Castle.

40 I am indebted to Dr John Morrison, History of Art, School of Divinity, History and Philosophy, University of Aberdeen, for advice on the portraiture of Argyll.

41 David Hume, *The History of Great Britain*, 2 vols (Edinburgh, 1754 and 1758), II, p. 141.

embellishment of Gaelic oral tradition that sparked off the 'Ossianic controversy', was also a historian immersed in archival sources. His characterisation of Argyll as being 'artful' with 'insinuating talents' was drawn from Clarendon. Notwithstanding his 'delinquency', Argyll was sacrificed in a politically expedient trial. But Macpherson too readily accepted Wishart's negative portrayal in claiming that Argyll's 'misfortunes were the less regretted, for his barbarity and insolence to Montrose'.[42]

The balancing of reason and emotion that characterised the Enlightenment was exemplified in the historical writing of the Edinburgh lawyer Malcolm Laing, who considered the political pretexts for the trial and execution of Argyll as 'judicial murder'. Laing contended that Argyll was driven to rebel by the willingness of Charles I to countenance plans devised by his estranged father (the 7th Earl) in tandem with the Marquess of Antrim, 'to invade him and deprive him of a large part of his estate'. Laing considered Argyll to have been 'a better patriot than a subject, more attached to the national religion than to the interests of the Crown'. He summed up the character of the Marquess:

> His ambition was regulated by habitual prudence, penetration, experience and consummate address; but his sagacity was not always exempt from enthusiasm; his prudence was apt to degenerate into craft, and the apprehensions which his subtle dexterity excited, occasioned his destruction.[43]

Although the more favourable views of Argyll by his contemporaries, notably Baillie and Patrick Gordon, were coming into general circulation, Laing's judicious summation was not wholly accepted among historians at home and abroad. George Brodie questioned why Charles I would have plotted to ruin Argyll, and was willing to charge the Marquess with 'pusillanimity'. However, he did commend Argyll for his prudent refusal to countenance another invasion of England in 1651. The insistence of Charles II on pressing on to defeat at Worcester that September opened up Scotland to occupation, when opting for another winter campaign within the country could well have proved fatal to the Cromwellian forces.[44] For the eminent French historian François Guizot, Argyll was 'firmer in the council than in the field'. His reputed cowardice when faced by Montrose became a standard Royalist insult in both Scotland and England.

42 James Macpherson, *The History of Great Britain from the Restoration, to the Accession of the House of Hannover*, 2vols (London, 1775), I, pp. 23–4

43 Malcolm Laing, *The History of Scotland, from the Union of the Crowns on the Accession of James VI to the Throne of England to the Union of the Kingdoms in the Reign of Queen Anne*, 2 vols (London, 1800), II, p. 16.

44 George Brodie, *History of the British Empire, from the Accession of Charles I to the Restoration*, 4 vols (Edinburgh, 1822), II, pp. 433, 536; and IV, pp. 304–5.

But these insults were deemed to have fuelled Argyll's 'vindictive pleasure' in bringing about the complete ruin of the Royalists. Guizot did acknowledge that the Marquess had 'a deep and subtle mind' and was a person of 'vigilant activity'. He drew particularly close to Cromwell and the English Independents; although 'a presbyter in his religion, he was inclined to bolder notions in politics'.[45]

Steeped in Whig historiography based on Protestantism, property and progress, J. Hill Burton mounted a defence of Argyll which also drew on the scepticism of the Enlightenment. Burton considered the Marquess to have been 'an ambitious man, and inscrutable in his projects and policies' but rejected any notion that Argyll was intent on the deposition, far less the execution, of Charles I. Rather than stigmatise Argyll with cowardice, Burton stressed the difficulties faced by the Marquess as a political leader. His great managerial ability in controlling men 'was in civil policy, not in war'. Burton was also at pains to point out that Argyll died a hero after being made a political scape-goat in a trial governed more by political expediency than due process of law. As the foremost clan chief, Argyll was an 'absolute sovereign' in his Highland territory, which led to him being executed 'for what he might and could do, than for what he had done'.[46] Burton's exaggerated view of Argyll's power as a clan chief was repeated by another prominent Whig practitioner in Scotland, P. Hume Brown, who considered the Marquess as 'his country's sagest statesman in the time when it needed most guidance'. He was the one Scotsman in the mid-seventeenth century who could be regarded as a British statesman. But Argyll, like Montrose, fell short of the standard of greatness required to lead a revolution. Although 'lacking in moral as well as physical courage' during his lifetime, Argyll was sustained by his Presbyterianism, based on his genuine Calvinist convictions and by his 'sense of personal dignity' at his death.[47]

However, the doyen of British Whig historians of the mid-seventeenth century was less convinced. For S.R. Gardiner, Argyll's statesmanship was highly questionable. A man of 'subtle intelligence', Argyll was undoubtedly 'the real leader' of the Covenanting Movement. Although he was a 'miserable soldier', he had 'a keen eye for political tendencies'. Whereas Hamilton sought to preserve monarchy, Argyll sought its termination. The Marquess by nature was inclined 'to follow the multitude in order that he might appear to lead it'.[48]

---

45 M. François Guizot, *History of the English Revolution from the Accession of Charles I*, 2 vols (Oxford, 1838), I, p. 96.

46 J. Hill Burton, *The History of Scotland*, 8 vols (Edinburgh and London, 1876), VI, pp. 333–4, 370; and VII, pp. 149–50

47 P. Hume Brown, *History of Scotland*, 3 vols (Cambridge, 1912), II, pp. 309, 385–6.

48 S.R. Gardiner, *History of the Great Civil War, 1642–1649*, 3 vols (London, 1886–91), II, pp. 493, 522, 570 and *The History of the Commonwealth and Protectorate, 1649–1656*, 3 vols (London, 1903), I, p. 15

T.F. Henderson, in his entry for Argyll in the original *DNB*, was adamant that the Marquess consistently demonstrated 'masterly and triumphant' statesmanship until the patriotic accommodation in favour of Charles II, which sundered all prospect of closer parliamentary union with England under Cromwell. In particular, Argyll's penchant for political purges broke with his past record of 'safe and prudent policy' and rendered him no longer in control of events. Henderson went so far to claim that Argyll, in the wake of the regicide, became like Charles II, a 'puppet in the hands of contending factions'.[49]

Henderson's line with respect to the impact of political purging and the regicide on Argyll's political standing was taken up by W.L. Mathieson, who viewed the Marquess as pandering to the worst instincts of the Presbyterian zealots in the Kirk, as his support from Cromwell and the English Independents crumbled. Argyll and his party had outmanoeuvred both the 'half-hearted and time-serving' Hamilton and the 'man of genius' Montrose. Nevertheless, Mathieson deemed Argyll as an 'instrumental rather than a creative statesman' in that he manipulated the Covenanting Movement as much for his own interest as for the public good. Following on from Gardiner's doubts, Mathieson questioned the reputed British statesmanship of Argyll during the patriotic accommodation when he made one concession after another in a 'vain attempt to surrender his principles without relinquishing his power'.[50]

The contemporaneous Whig historian of the Covenanting Movement, J.K. Hewison, took a more charitable view of the Marquess, though he contended that neither Argyll nor his great rival Montrose had the 'supereminent qualities of a great statesman' in being able to match victories in the field with more lasting gains from the council chamber. Hewison was notably influenced by the portraiture of the Marquess as the stern Calvinist of the Scougall school:

> In person small, in appearance unprepossessing, in visage course and sinister, in vision oblique, in action dubious, in council often suspected, in ignominious defeats a craven fugitive.

But Argyll was also 'a politician of breadth and foresight' who had a firm grasp of the revolutionary situation in 1638, a grasp which he retained until he was convicted by a 'gross miscarriage of justice' in 1661. He had a masterly capacity to gauge the substance, merit and menace of his political opponents. Deft polemical thrusts in his country's defence were delivered 'from a hand that trembled to wield a claymore'. Rather than being a puppet of religious zealots,

49 T.F. Henderson, 'Campbell, Archibald, Marquis of Argyll and eighth Earl (1598–1661)' in L. Stephen ed., *DNB*, VIII (London, 1886), pp. 319–29.
50 W.L. Mathieson, *Church and Reform in Scotland*, 2 vols (Glasgow, 1906), II, 65, 77, 79, 147–50.

he had a 'modern instinct' in promoting British unity by his efforts to influence the English Independents to restrain licentious sectarianism on the one hand, and to uphold the conscientious scruples of the pious towards dogmatic uniformity on the other. His 'unwavering fidelity' contributed immensely to the cohesion of the Covenanting Movement. His 'wise counsels' gave direction to its aims and resolutions. Notwithstanding his penchant for intrigue, Argyll offered resolute leadership during the patriotic accommodation, where he viewed the threat to Scotland from English Independents as greater than that from indigenous Royalists. His conformity to the Cromwellian Occupation was a matter of political expediency, accomplished once he had protected his own power base in Argyllshire and had patriotically reserved his religious commitment to the Covenants of 1638 and 1643.[51]

As an Anglican Bishop of St Asaphs, David Mathew was not a ready sympathiser with the staunch Presbyterianism of Argyll. Nevertheless, he provided a perceptive if quixotic character sketch that challenged rather than ran counter to Whig historiography. Mathew was perceptive in recognising that Argyll, as a 'pillar of the Covenant', was a statesman of unrivalled stature in Scotland, and of impressive British significance – for his shrewdness, his calculating nature, his astute and lucid mind, his exceptional piety and, above all, for his determination to attain power in pursuit of a godly commonwealth. But Mathew was also quixotic in asserting rather than substantiating that Argyll favoured 'a theocratic polity over which he might bear viceregal rule'. Moreover, while Scotland, and especially his headship of ClanCampbell, was his greatest source of influence, his political horizons were not limited to territorial ambitions, extreme Presbyterianism and a solitary sense of providential mission.[52] In narrowing the political stage on which Argyll operated, Mathew was uncritically accepting of the views of a discredited French Ambassador who had failed to understand Argyll's British motivation in promoting the Solemn League and Covenant in 1643. He claimed that the Marquess held absolute power and was 'in the highest degree intelligent in all that relates to Scotland, but knows nothing of anything beyond his own country'.[53]

Notwithstanding the sundering of Whig historiography in the course of the last century, the concomitant introversion and introspection of Scottish history have given free rein to anglocentric historians to ignore, gloss over or seriously underplay Argyll's contribution to the British revolution of the

---

51 J.K. Hewison, *The Covenanters: History of the Church of Scotland*, 2 vols (Glasgow, 1908), I, pp. 319–21, 446, 449, 460, 469–70; II, pp. 42, 83, 87–8.
52 D. Mathew, *Scotland Under Charles I* (London, 1955), pp. 58, 81, 223–31, 254, 270, 290, 295, 305.
53 *Montereul*, II, p. 556.

mid-seventeenth century.[54] This negligence has been addressed in part in the wake of the New British History that has emerged from the 1990s.[55] For Scottish historians, Argyll has remained a problematic figure as clan chief, magnate and statesman. As Gordon Donaldson noted, the Marquess was to the fore among leading Covenanters in putting his 'private aims before the general good of the cause'. His record 'had all along been a curious one'.[56] In fleshing out this analysis, David Stevenson found Argyll to be both 'dour' and 'devious', while making the pertinent point that the Marquess, like Cromwell, preferred to wait upon events in times of crisis until the providential will of God became clear to him. However, Stevenson, like Mathieson and Mathew before him, was unable to break free from reliance on post-Restoration commentators, who deemed Hamilton a moderate for his conservatism and Argyll an extremist for his radicalism. In turn, Argyll's unrivalled capacity to control general assemblies as well as parliaments has been grossly understated by depicting him as in thrall to the Kirk, or merely as leader of the Kirk Party.[57] In like manner, Walter Makey has contended fancifully that Argyll emerged from the Scottish civil war of 1644–45 as no more than 'the hangman of a revolutionary church which he had once contrived to dominate'.[58]

In revisiting the Marquess for his entry in the *Oxford DNB*, Stevenson adheres to the Henderson thesis that Argyll's penchant for political purges directed against the nobility, and his preference to ally with the gentry, burgesses and clergy, reduced him from master to victim by the time of the patriotic accommodation. It is rather difficult to reconcile with victim history a man noted for his manipulative abilities, his craftiness, his cleverness, his dissembling, his single-mindedness, his cruelty and his financial oppression, especially as 'Argyll was driven rather by principle and ambition, compelled to push himself into a dominant position in Scotland through conviction that his status (as representing a great noble family) justified it and the will of God required it'.[59] It has

54 Cf. C. Hill, *The Century of Revolution, 1603–1714* (London, 1961); R. Ashton, *The English Civil War: Conservatism and Revolution 1603–1649* (London, 1978); J. Morrill, *The Nature of the English Revolution* (Harlow, 1993).

55 Cf. A. Woolrych, *Britain in Revolution, 1625–1660* (Oxford, 2002); D. Scott, *Politics and War in the Three Stuart Kingdoms, 1637–49* (Basingstoke, 2004); R. Armstrong, *Protestant War: The 'British' of Ireland and the War of the Three Kingdoms* (Manchester, 2005); J. Adamson, *The Noble Revolt: The Overthrow of Charles I* (London, 2007).

56 G. Donaldson, *Scotland: James V–James VII* (Edinburgh, 1965), p. 328

57 D. Stevenson, *The Scottish Revolution, 1637–44* (Newton Abbot, 1973), pp. 128, 200, 206, 224, 264, 266 and *Revolution and Counter-Revolution in Scotland, 1644–1651* (London, 1977), pp. 86, 109, 124, 138, 164, 213.

58 W. Makey, *The Church of the Covenant, 1637–1651* (Edinburgh, 1979), pp. 180–1.

59 D. Stevenson, 'Campbell, Archibald, Marquess of Argyll (1605x7–1661)' in *Oxford DNB*, http.www.oxforddnb.com/articles/4/4472-article.html

been left to the meticulously painstaking analysis of John Young to demonstrate how Argyll controlled the constitutional assemblies of the Covenanting Movement. He worked an elaborate system of committees in parliaments and general assemblies to his advantage. In the Scottish Estates, his trusted agents in each of the three constituent estates of the nobility, gentry and burgesses played prominent roles, which they replicated in general assemblies in their capacity as ruling elders to support Argyll's clerical agents and backers among the ministry of the Kirk. In this manner, the Marquess was usually able to prevail, even if absent or not actually a member of any executive, judicial, diplomatic, or financial committee.[60]

A Force for Modernity?

The limited rehabilitation of Argyll mounted by Whig historians and their successors can only in part be attributed to Enlightened scepticism. No less powerful an influence was the enduring Romanticism associated with the legendary mystique surrounding the Marquess of Montrose. This mystique was historically grounded in the highly partial editions of the correspondence and memorials of Montrose edited and published in the mid-nineteenth century by his descendant, Mark Napier.[61] These sources served to corroborate and reinforce the Romantic genre of historical novel, most notably by Sir Walter Scott and John Buchan, Lord Tweedsmuir, which glorified the epic heroism of Montrose.[62] Scott, in his seminal *Tales of a Grandfather* (1827), furthered his highly favourable biography of Montrose as a man of high genius, glowing ambition, indomitable courage and scholarly talents by disparaging references to his political rivals. Hamilton, though praised for being 'a moderate man', was dismissed as having 'little decision of character, and less military skill'. Argyll was reputedly 'dark, close and crafty', bent on forwarding his own interests while seemingly devoted to public service. He 'stooped lower to court popularity, and was more successful in gaining it'. Scott nevertheless exonerated Argyll, who 'was bold in council though timid in battle', from any hand in the regicide. After a protracted and politically expedient trial, he faced execution 'with a courage which other passages of his life had not prepared men to expect'.[63]

This traducing of Argyll as a Machiavellian schemer, who lacked personal

---

60 J.R. Young, *The Scottish Parliament, 1639-1661: A Political and Constitutional Analysis* (Edinburgh, 1996), *passim*.

61 *Memorials of Montrose and His Times*, M. Napier ed., 2 vols (Edinburgh, 1848-50); and *Memoirs of the Marquis of Montrose*, M. Napier ed., 2 vols (Edinburgh, 1856).

62 Sir Walter Scott, *A Legend of Montrose* (London, 1819), recently republished as *A Legend of the Wars of Montrose*, J.H. Alexander ed. (Edinburgh, 1995); John Buchan, *The Marquis of Montrose* (London, 1913).

63 Sir Walter Scott, *Tales of a Grandfather* (London, 1898), pp. 453-4, 479, 507-8, 579-80.

warmth and put a higher premium on his own survival than on engaging coura-
geously in combat, was checked in the historical novel by Neil Munro. Although
Argyll was not the central character in *John Splendid*, Munro – alias the distin-
guished journalist Hugh Foullis – did offer a more rounded and perceptive
characterisation, as befitting an author sprung from Inveraray, the seat of the
house of Argyll.[64] The Marquess, though ill-fitted to fulfil his traditional chiefly
role as a war-leader, was above all a statesman of magnitude and vision. His
preference for the sensible and prudent over the heroic, even at the cost of his
pride and reputation, ensured that he managed rather than just symbolised
changing values and attitudes in times of revolutionary upheaval.[65] In essence,
both in terms of history and literature, Montrose and Argyll seem to tap into
antithetical aspects of the Scottish psyche, which can perhaps best be explained
in football parlance. Montrose is associated with a certain style marked by pace,
daring and invention. But ultimately he is cast as the gallant loser who snatches
defeat from the jaws of victory. Conversely, Argyll was a winner who ground out
results remorselessly, relentlessly and ruthlessly. His win-at-all-costs attitude
ensured that he won in an ugly manner rather than with grace, flair and imagin-
ation. Historians continue to be bemused by the Romantic image of Montrose,
and pay but grudging respect to the prosaically purposeful Argyll. However,
this perspective tends to be more historicist than historical.[66]

Apart from grinding out results, Argyll has a more enduring political legacy
that tends to be masked by his seemingly universal reputation for craftiness.
In his robust defence of Argyll, particularly in relation to the impulsiveness,
chivalry, military brilliance and political levity of Montrose, John Willcock
considered the Marquess as greater and more worthy for his piety, shrewd
judgement and tenacity of purpose. Willcock eulogised the 'astonishing intellectual gifts' and the steadfast religious commitment of Argyll, whose virtues
'vastly outweighed' his faults. Although Argyll had an implacable memory for
perceived wrongs that could not go unavenged, he was selfless in his daring
political plans, in which he too freely 'employed his own private fortune and
credit'. Given to a sober and sparing lifestyle, his 'bountiful and princely gener-
osity' together with his 'genial pliability' masked a fixed and unyielding sense
of purpose. Indeed, such was his vast range of mental ability that he not only
guided and controlled the Covenanting Movement with 'moderate counsels',

---

64 Neil Munro, *John Splendid: The Tale of a Poor Gentleman, and the Little Wars of Lorne*
   (Edinburgh 1994, first published 1898).
65 D. Gifford, 'John Splendids and Jaunty Jocks: Neil Munro, the Highlands and Scottish Fiction',
   and E.J. Cowan, '*John Splendid* and Scottish History' in R.W. Renton and B.D. Osborne eds,
   Exploring New Roads: Essays on Neil Munro (Colonsay, 2007), pp. 37–67 and pp. 79–94
66 Cf. E.J. Cowan, 'Montrose and Argyll' in G. Menzies ed., *The Scottish Nation: A History of the
   Scots from Independence to Union* (London, 1972), pp. 118–32.

but also made a deep British impression 'in offering resistance to the arbitrary government of Charles I and in breaking down the military power by which he would have maintained it'. For Willcock, there were two lasting images of the Great Marquess. On the one hand, Argyll could be represented biblically as a Hebrew patriarch, if not as an Old Testament prophet. On the other, he was in advance of his time for his political opinions:

> Largely through his influence Democracy in Scotland succeeded to a considerable measure of the power which had been wrested from the King.

However, Willcock went a step too far in suggesting that Argyll, in checkmating the power of the monarchy and the aristocracy, was a harbinger of democracy.[67]

Nevertheless, in the course of outmanoeuvring Hamilton as well as Montrose, Argyll did come to realise that he had to reach out beyond aristocratic republicanism to attain the godly commonwealth. Simultaneously, Argyll demonstrated that British State formation was neither an exclusive nor singular baronial pursuit, and that Scotland in the seventeenth century was not a static society dominated by perennial power struggles between Crown, nobility and Kirk.[68] As a clan chief and Scottish magnate, Argyll certainly drew extensively on ties of kinship, local association and clientage within and beyond the Scottish Estates to shape political allegiances and opinions. However, as a British statesman, he was notably responsive to changes wrought by inflation, price instability, expanding trade and demographic shifts. He realised that the gentry, more so than the nobility and no less than the burgesses, were distinctive participants in the expansion of landownership, in the commercialising of estate management and in developing manufactures. The gentry also took the lead in colonial enterprises to the Americas and the Indies, and in military adventuring on the European continent, through Scandinavia to Russia. In association with the burgesses, the gentry were also to the fore in integrating cities and towns with their rural hinterlands.[69]

Accordingly, Argyll not only consolidated his political power base outwith the

---

67 Willcock, *The Great Marquess*, pp. 335–8

68 J. Wormald, 'Confidence and Perplexity: The Seventeenth Century' in J. Wormald ed., *Scotland a History* (Oxford, 2005), pp. 143–77; K.M. Brown, *Noble Society in Scotland: Wealth, Family and Culture from Reformation to Revolution* (Edinburgh, 2004), pp. 8–14.

69 Macinnes, *Union and Empire*, pp. 102–03, 138–47, 201–05, 227–8; I.D. Whyte, ' Poverty or Prosperity? Rural Society in Lowland Scotland in the Late Sixteenth and Early Seventeenth Centuries', *Scottish Economic and Social History*, 18 (1998), pp. 19–31; G. Marshall, *Presbyteries and Profits: Calvinism and the development of capitalism in Scotland, 1560–1707* (Oxford, 1980), pp. 284–92.

ranks of the nobility among the gentry and the burgesses, he also expanded the boundaries of the political nation in countenancing rights of resistance exercised by the lesser landowners (the bonnet lairds) and the leading peasant farmers, who together constituted the Scottish yeomanry. By 1648, he was prepared to overthrow the nobility's dominance of what had become a centralised oligarchy to effect internal revolution on behalf of the Covenanting grass-roots. Argyll's radical aspirations were frustrated by the Cromwellian Occupation, and he was eventually executed at the Restoration. Yet the Marquess, in his pursuit of a more progressive polity, can be represented as not so much a disappointed revolutionary as a force for modernity, the case for which has now to be established in the succeeding chapters.

THREE

The Formative Years, 1607–1628

On accomplishing regal union in 1603, James VI and I envisaged ruling as an imperial monarch empowered by an incorporating union of Scotland and England (with Ireland as a dependent kingdom). Four years of fitful negotiations by commissioners drawn from the Scottish Estates and the English Parliament foundered on the back of English concepts of political hegemony and parliamentary sovereignty. The Scottish Estates, who had conditionally accepted integration out of deference to James, were more than relieved that the projected union was terminated by a wrecking motion in the House of Commons in 1607.[1] Nonetheless, as flag-bearers for the first encompassing British dynasty, the Stuarts sought to give tangible effect to imperial monarchy in order to demonstrate the sovereign independence and interdependence of Scotland, England and Ireland. Accordingly James, and from 1625 his son Charles I, successively promoted their exclusive sovereignty as kings of Great Britain, their *ius imperium* by land and sea. Abroad, they promoted an international British agenda as manifest in foreign policy through espionage, embassies and military intervention in the Thirty Years War. The projection of the Stuarts as a British dynasty also impacted on colonial policy. Spanish dominion in the New World was challenged by ventures for trade and plantation which, though authorised separately from the three kingdoms, created a British presence in North America and the West Indies through acquisition and settlement.[2]

The Scots were foremost amongst the peoples of the three kingdoms in accepting the British internationalism of their native dynasty. They played

---

1 B. Galloway, *The Union of England and Scotland 1606–1608* (Edinburgh, 1986), pp. 59–130; G. Burgess, *The Politics of the Ancient Constitution: An Introduction to English Political Thought 1603–1642* (University Park, PA, 1993), pp. 25–8, 102–5, 126–30, 162–7; J.H. Burns, *The True Law of Kingship: Concepts of Monarchy in Early Modern Scotland* (Oxford, 1996), pp. 255–81.

2 A.H. Williamson, 'Scots, Indians and Empire: The Scottish Politics of Civilization, 1519–1609', *Past & Present*, 150 (1996), pp. 46–83; J. Robertson, 'Empire and Union: Two Concepts of the Early Modern European Political Order' in J. Robertson ed., *A Union for Empire: Political Thought and the Union of 1707* (Cambridge, 1995), pp. 3–37; S. Murdoch, *Britain, Denmark-Norway and the House of Stuart, 1603–1660* (East Linton, 2000), pp. 44–63.

significant roles in the military, diplomatic and colonial affairs concerted from the royal court. In addition to foreign and colonial policies, the Stuarts promoted a British frontier policy which received a more problematic reception. The early Stuarts endeavoured to civilise frontiers through concerted action in Edinburgh, London and Dublin. Thus, James implemented projects designed to bring order to his Britannic Empire through the cross-border policing of the Middle Shires, the plantation of Ulster, and the military and legislative offensive against the West Highlands and Islands. The annexation of Orkney and Shetland was partly an extension of such a policy, but primarily it was the consolidation of the territorial waters around the British Isles into the Stuart's *ius imperium*. The ClanCampbell was the approved role model at Court for the implementation of frontier policy in the *Gàidhealtachd*. The elite of the clan were to the fore from 1607 in using the term 'North British' for Scotland and 'British' for settlers in Ulster.[3] However, the participation of the ClanCampbell under the leadership of the house of Argyll was far from disinterested. Before examining how the formative years of the future Marquess were shaped by this British frontier policy, we must scrutinise the standing of the house of Argyll with respect to its composition, its structure and its territorial influence.

ClanCampbell and the House of Argyll

The chief of the ClanCampbell was traditionally addressed by his Gaelic patronymic, *MacChailein Mor* (literally, the great son of Colin) after the eponymous founder of the house of Argyll in the thirteenth century. The movement of the Campbells from the Lowland peripheries in central Scotland into the West Highlands, originally around Lochaweside, coincided with the rise to prominence of the ClanDonald as Lords of the Isles. Both clans capitalised on their support for Robert the Bruce in his reassertion of Scottish kingship during the Wars of Independence, to expand their territorial influence. The Lords of the Isles, who tended to expand north and westwards, developed a primarily Gaelic identity that straddled the North Channel. The Lordship of the Isles, which became the Hebridean focal point of the classical culture common to the Irish and Scottish Gael, maintained an abrasive relationship with the Scottish Crown. Internal divisions within the ClanDonald facilitated the forfeiture of the Lordship in 1493. By the outset of the sixteenth century, the Lordship of the Isles had effectively split into eight autonomous branches. In addition to the ClanDonald South, who held lands in Kintyre, Islay and Jura as well as Antrim, seniority was contested by the MacDonalds of Clanranald, the MacDonalds of

3 ICA, Argyll Transcripts, VIII (1600–10), nos 114, 256 and IX (1611–20), no.163; NAS, Breadalbane Collection, GD 112/1/393a; A.I. Macinnes, *Clanship, Commerce and the House of Stuart, 1603–1788* (East Linton, 1996), pp. 56–75.

Glengarry and the MacDonalds of Sleat; while the MacIains of Ardnamurchan, the MacDonalds of Glencoe, the MacDonalds of Keppoch and the MacAllisters of Knapdale remained disruptive kinsmen.

In marked contrast to the ClanDonald, the ClanCampbell, which had also branched into Ayrshire from the late thirteenth century, continued to enjoy relatively favourable relations with the Scottish Crown. The house of Argyll concentrated on expansion to the south and east across the cultural divide between Highlands and Lowlands, between the *Gael* and the *Gall*. The chiefs of ClanCampbell essentially pursued a twin-track approach. They maintained their Gaelic identity while establishing themselves as Scottish magnates through the substantial acquisition of estates in the central Lowlands, in the shires of Dumbarton, Stirling, Clackmannan, Perth, Angus, Fife and Midlothian. Crown favour for the ClanCampbell was underscored when their chiefs were ennobled, first as lords in 1445, then as earls in 1457, and then further honoured when the office of justice-general of Scotland, initially bestowed in 1514, was confirmed as hereditary within the house of Argyll in 1528. Campbell chiefs also served intermittently in place of the Crown as royal lieutenants in the West Highland and Islands in the course of the sixteenth century.[4]

Nonetheless, the house of Argyll was not the only magnate family which enjoyed particular royal favour in Scottish Gaeldom following the termination of the Lordship of the Isles. The Scottish Crown also authorised the expansion of Gordon interests as represented by the house of Huntly. Ennobled as earls at the same time as the house of Argyll and then given precedence as marquesses from 1599, the house of Huntly expanded their territorial influence from the north-eastern shires of Aberdeen, Banff and Moray into the extensive Highland shire of Inverness. Apart from expanding in a reverse direction to the house of Argyll, the Gordons were neither a recognised Gaelic clan nor a coherent territorial interest in both Highlands and Lowlands. In contrast to *MacChailein Mor*, the earls and marquesses of Huntly had no patronymic and were not recognised among the chiefs of the Gael at the outset of the War for the Three

---

4 D. Gregory, *The History of the Western Highlands and Isles of Scotland 1493–1625* (Edinburgh, 1836 reprinted 1975) pp. 9–68; J.E. Dawson, *Scotland Reformed 1488–1587* (Edinburgh, 2007), pp. 100–5; *The Scots Peerage*, 9 vols, J.B. Paul ed. (Edinburgh, 1904–14), I, pp. 316–68; *Letters at the Instance of Sir George McKenzie of Rosehaugh, His Majesties Advocat for His Highness Interest* (Edinburgh, 1681). The Campbells and the MacDonalds were both of Celtic origin, their rivalry being traced to the mythical Fingalian heroes Diarmaid and Cu-Chulainn. In reality, the ClanDonald were derived from the Norse-Gaels who dominated both sides of the North Channel from the ninth to the thirteenth centuries, while the ClanCampbell (literally 'the children of the twisted mouth') were of contemporaneous British stock, most probably from the Lennox in central Scotland (W.D.H. Sellar, 'The Earliest Campbells: Normans, Britons or Gael?', *Scottish Studies*, 17 (1973), pp. 109–24).

Kingdoms. Furthermore, while the house of Argyll had taken Protestantism in its stride at the Reformation, the house of Huntly remained politically compromised by its prominent association with Catholic recusancy.[5]Although they were not immune to rivalries between chiefs and leading gentry who constituted the *fine* or clan elite, the ClanCampbell under the house of Argyll had unrivalled cohesion. This cohesion was based on a sustained ethos of territorial acquisitiveness, legalistic pragmatism and the complementary association of personal and institutional authority since the Middle Ages. At the same time, the Campbells were also to the fore in having their *fine* limit their individual liabilities by standing surety for each other whether dealing with central government or in negotiating financial contracts with third parties in Highlands and Lowlands.

As manifest by these sureties, clanship in Scottish Gaeldom operated within the framework of Scots law as an amalgam of kinship, local association and feudalism. This situation stood in marked contrast to the Irish Gaels, whose social structures were largely antipathetic to the legal codification afforded by English common law.[6] At the territorial level, ClanCampbell was a confederation bonded by kinship and local association that had three distinctive components. First were the house of Argyll and its numerous cadet lines, such as the Campbells of Inverawe, of Ardkinglas, of Lochnell and of Auchinbreck. Second were families of the same origin, such as the MacTavishes, the MacIvors and the MacArthurs, who may even have had genealogical precedence but deferred to the chiefship of *MacChailein Mor*. Third were the satellite families absorbed within the house of Argyll's sphere of influence such as the MacCallums, the MacMillans and the MacVicars. These families also included professional specialists such as the MacEwans, the hereditary bards to the house of Argyll. The professional specialists included families detached from other clans. Thus, the MacLachlans of Inchconnel served as hereditary keepers of the original Campbell stronghold on Lochawe, and the MacLachlans of Kilbride served as hereditary medicinars. The diverse heads of these cadet lines, original associates and satellite families were designated the leading gentry of the ClanCampbell, whose chiefship had been vested heritably in the house of Argyll since the fourteenth century. All able-bodied, adult males affiliated to the ClanCampbell were expected to participate in hosts whether mobilised by the fiery cross to

---

5 *Reliquiae Celticae*, A. MacBain and J. Kennedy eds, 2 vols (Inverness, 1894), II, pp. 174–5; NLS, Antique Papers, MS 1915, fo.35; A. Cathcart , *Kinship and Clientage: Highland Clanship 1451–1609* (Leiden and Boston, 2006), pp. 159–209; B.G. Robertson, 'Continuity and Change in the Scottish Nobility: The House of Huntly, 1603–1690' (University of Aberdeen, PhD thesis, 2007), pp. 16–79.

6 Macinnes, *Clanship, Commerce and the House of Stuart*, pp. 1–29.

guard and gain territory or turned out on formal occasions, such as marriages and funerals, to affirm demonstrably the social standing of their chief.[7]

The right as well as the obligation of the chief and leading gentry, individually and collectively as the *fine*, to protect and administer justice to their clan constituted their *duthchas*: their personal, but hereditary, authority to exercise trusteeship throughout the territory of the Campbells within the *Gàidhealtachd*. Complementing territorial trusteeship was the *oighreachd* of the *fine*; that is, their individual, but hereditary, title to their estates and jurisdictions as recorded in charters. The acquisition of charters gave heritable definition to the role of the *fine* as landlords. Indeed, from the fourteenth century, the house of Argyll was to the fore not only in acquiring titles from the Crown for estates held as property, but in promoting feudal conveyancing within and beyond the clan elite to ensure that personal ties of trusteeship were consolidated by the institutional warrant of charters. Lands conveyed feudally to members of the ClanCampbell as property were normally retained within the feudal superiority of the house of Argyll rather than held directly from the Crown. The Campbell chiefs had also attained regalian privileges as hereditary justiciars. Thereby the Crown had devolved competence for all civil and criminal cases, bar treason, over not just the Campbells but all clans and Lowland families living within territorial spheres of influence. On the one hand, the house of Argyll had the power to repledge any case affecting its interest, whether this concerned central government or judges from the central courts on circuit or from any sheriff or burgh courts in Scotland. On the other hand, the exercise of regalian privileges, equivalent to palatine jurisdictions in England, required the house of Argyll to develop a judicial hierarchy of courts with sophisticated procedures. These courts, in turn, were serviced by bailies, notaries, writers and other legal administrators.

Individual members of the *fine* tended to have responsibility for baronial courts, whose main concern was estate management, administering and interpreting customary practices, with summary privileges to respectively execute and mutilate murderers and thieves caught red-handed. Conflicts within and between baronial courts were harmonised initially by sheriff-deputes and subsequently by bailies of regality. The house of Argyll generally exercised its unrivalled privileges responsibly. Nonetheless, the Campbell chiefs became adept at deploying their heritable jurisdictions to exploit legal technicalities in charters and other contracts in order to expand their feudal superiority over neighbouring clans, such as the MacLachlans and the Lamonts in Cowal, the MacNaughtons in Mid-Argyll, the MacAllisters in Knapdale, the MacNeills in Kintyre and the Camerons in Lochaber. Although any baronial courts held by

---

7 A. Campbell of Airds, *A History of ClanCampbell*, 3 vols (Edinburgh, 2000–04), I, pp. 70–90.

the chiefs and leading gentry of clans obliged to accept overlordship were incorporated within its judicial hierarchy, the house of Argyll remained the final arbiter of appeals from all subordinate courts. Successive chiefs rarely used this power impartially.[8]

Complementary to the house of Argyll's hierarchy of courts was the office of *mair-taighe*. This household office, effectively that of a factor, was primarily financial rather than judicial, to secure the managerial interest in districts or officiaries where the house of Argyll both held estates directly as property and exercised feudal superiority over the estates of other landlords. This office, which was entrusted to leading clan gentry, was associated heritably with the keeperships of such strongholds as Dunstaffnage, Kilchurn, Inchconnel, Dunoon, Skipness and Carrick, which were traditionally used to detain prisoners and political hostages; the latter castle also served as the repository for charters acquired or issued by the Campbell chiefs. But by the outset of the seventeenth century, this office was primarily responsible for the collation of rents, feu duties and other financial obligations; the redistribution of provender rents for hospitality; and the marketing of cattle and other surplus produce in Lowland towns. The accounts of each *mair-taighe* were centrally scrutinised by the chamberlain of Argyll, who reported biennially to the chiefs at Inveraray Castle on Lochfyneside. Presents, twice yearly provender payments and calps – death duties paid by families living outwith the Argyll estates who were bound by contracts of manrent to serve in the clan host in return for protection – were paid directly to Inveraray. These customary payments were made in recognition of chiefship, albeit central government disapproved of calps, as they took priority over the allegiance due by tenants to their landlords.[9]

8 NLS, Register of title deeds produced by landowners in Argyll c.1688, Adv.MS 31.2.3. The house of Argyll was particularly adept at having anachronistic clauses irritant inserted in charters. By the outset of the seventeenth century, growing commercialism in estate management had led to a marked preference for feu-ferme over traditional feudal tenures by ward and relief. In effect, an entry fine and a fixed annual payment in money and kind replaced periodic military obligations and occasional reliefs or fines for delayed succession, minorities and marriages However, in order to leave grounds to revoke charters by default, the house of Argyll insisted on retaining token military obligations, such as the provision of ships with up to 16 oars for fixed periods of service on the western seaboard and the maintenance of rooms in castles and tower houses for its exclusive use. These clauses were particular irritants to the *fine* of other clans brought within its overlordship.

9 ICA, Miscellaneous 17th Century Papers, bundles 60/1, 62/5, 74/3, 184/1 and Argyll Letters (1602–38), A36/64 and Argyll Transcripts, VIII, nos 74, 124; IX, nos 163, 184; X (1621–28), no. 2; *Inveraray Papers*, D.C. MacTavish ed. (Oban, 1939), pp. 83–4; *BBT*, pp. 254–61; NAS, Breadalbane Collection, GD 112/1/564a, /597, /600–1, /611–13. Rents were paid to the house of Argyll from the townships within the respective district of the *mair-taighe*. Some provender rents were redistributed for hospitality, especially feasting at weddings and funerals, and for assessing steelbow requirements – loans of seed corn, livestock, tools and occasionally money

By the regal union, the *fine* of ClanCampbell was in the enviable position – if not unique, it was certainly unrivalled within Scottish Gaeldom – that their *oighreachd* was actually greater than their *duthchas*: that is, the estates that they retained as property or over which they exercised feudal superiority were more extensive than the territories settled by their clan. The Gaelic heartlands of the Campbells stretched from the districts of Lorne, Mid-Argyll, Knapdale and Cowal in Argyllshire, south to the Rosneath peninsula in Dunbarton-shire and east to Breadalbane in Perthshire. The entrepreneurial acquisition of charters directly from the Crown or other landed families had also facili-tated opportunities for cadet lines to establish power bases that were virtually autonomous of the house of Argyll; in so doing, following the Campbells of Loudoun in Ayrshire who were autonomous from their inception. Thus, the Campbells of Glenorchy independently expanded in the Perthshire Highlands in the later sixteenth century. Simultaneously, the cadet line that had acquired the secularised property of Ardchattan Priory in Lorne was separately estab-lished as the Campbells of Cawdor, through a judicious marriage that brought in an estate straddling the shires of Inverness and Nairn. Despite the threat its own acquisitive ethos posed to the clan's cohesion, personal contacts among the *fine* were not only retained but reinforced by marriages and, more enduringly, by fostering. The house of Argyll astutely determined that the latter practice, which usually extended for seven years and amounted to formative schooling, created customary and commercial obligations which continued long after the period of fosterage.[10]

Central government was long supportive of the commercial adaptation which marked out the Campbell *fine* as innovators within Scottish Gaeldom. They had pioneered and rigorously pursued the practice of written leases on their estates since the mid-sixteenth century. Leasing gave written defini-tion to the conditions of landholding which had customarily been conveyed orally to the tacksmen. As the lesser clan gentry, the tacksmen managed the townships which, as multiple-tenanted farms, constituted the basic unit of

---

necessary to support families commencing farming or bringing wastelands back into produc-tion. The marketing of surplus produce twice yearly was vital to realise income that underwrote the intricate involvement of the Campbell chiefs in Scottish politics.

10 *BBT*, pp. 84, 254; *Collectanea de Rebus Albanicis*, W.F. Skene ed. (Iona Club, Edinburgh, 1847), pp. 19–21; NAS, Breadalbane Collection GD 112/1/496, GD 112/39/961, /979; ICA, Argyll Letters (1602–38), A36/123 and Argyll Transcripts, IX, nos 251, 398. Not only were the foster parents specifically contracted to provide the necessary education and maintenance of the chief's children at their own expense, but they were subsequently called upon to contribute to marriage settlements and set aside a proportion of livestock and other moveable property equivalent to that bequeathed to their own children. Competitive bidding among the *fine* for the privilege of fostering demonstrated their ready acceptance of the commercial adaptation of customary relationships.

land settlement within Scotland prior to the eighteenth century. But defini-
tion through leasing served also to emphasise the finite and revocable terms
of landholding. Tacksmen continued to enjoy customary security of possession as lesser clan gentry. However, ties of kinship and local association did
not prevent the Campbell *fine* shortening leases or raising rents. Although the
removal of tenantry cannot be viewed as a common occurrence, tacksmen were
empowered to evict farmers and labourers from the townships if obligations
specified in leases were endangered or unfulfilled. The Campbell *fine* was also
to the fore in using English, or more accurately the Scots language, to promote
the commercial re-orientation of estate management. In part, Scots usage was
necessary for legal security in recording contracts, such as transfers of land or
loans of money involving the *fine* as proprietors. Nevertheless, the deliberate
avoidance of Gaelic in written leases to tacksmen that specified the rents and
work services required from their clansmen as farmers and labourers indelibly
associated material progress with Scots and incrementally, after the regal union,
with English. In furtherance of this association, the house of Argyll, by the birth
of the future Marquess, had vested the key commercial role as chamberlain of
its extensive estates throughout Scotland in a laird from the central Lowlands,
William Stirling of Auchmyle.[11]

Although the dearth of towns remained a marked feature of Scottish
Gaeldom, the house of Argyll was instrumental in promoting the development
of Inveraray in Mid-Argyll and Dunoon in Cowal as market centres settled
primarily by clansmen prepared to diversify into trade. At the same time, the
Campbell chiefs assiduously developed commercial contacts with Stirling and
the burghs on the River and Firth of Clyde directly involved in continental trade,
notably Glasgow, Dumbarton and Irvine. Of particular significance was the clan
elite's steady acquisition of commercial agents in Glasgow to complement the
legal agents whom they retained in Edinburgh to ensure a watching brief over
their dealings with central government. Increasingly, these agents were drawn
from within the clan, by the entry of younger sons from cadet lines and satellite families into the merchant and craft guilds as well as the legal profession.
Contacts with Glasgow, which were further fructified by the *fine* sending their
sons to that city's grammar school from the outset of the seventeenth century,
became a vital means of mobilising credit to finance both territorial expansion
and commercial diversification from agriculture into fishing and the extractive
industries.[12]

---

11 *BBT*, pp. 408–25; ICA, Argyll Letters (1602–38), A36/20, /22–3, /35, /71 and Argyll Transcripts,
    VIII, nos 13, 130; XI, nos 300, 322, 373, 577, 611–12; C.W.J. Withers, *Scottish Gaeldom: The Trans-
    formation of a Culture Region* (London, 1988), pp. 110–14.
12 ICA, Argyll Transcripts, VIII, nos 310, 356; IX, nos 190, 239; XI, nos 73, 283, 292; XII, no. 359;

Commercial opportunity as well as the austere appeal of Calvinism facilitated the ready adherence of ClanCampbell and the house of Argyll to Protestantism at the Reformation in the mid-sixteenth century. John Carswell, as the first Protestant Bishop of the Isles who served also as superintendent (ecclesiastical overseer) for the diocese of Argyll, translated the Book of Common Order into common classical Gaelic around 1567. His primary task, however, was not necessarily to spread Protestantism within the *Gàidhealtachd*. He was particularly adept at mobilising funding for the house of Argyll from the landed resources which the Reformed Kirk had theoretically inherited from the medieval Church. The secularisation of monastic property, which transformed patterns of landownership and land-use in the Lowlands during the sixteenth century, carried considerably less social significance in the Highlands. Nonetheless, secularisation did increase the amount of marketable land against which credit could be secured and mobilised through wadsets and other forms of mortgage. Credit facilities were further augmented by lay appropriation of the teinds (tenths), the parochial funds designated as the spirituality of the Kirk. The portion available to the Protestant bishops on the western seaboard by the early seventeenth century nominally ranged from a third of the teinds in each parish in the diocese of the Isles, to a quarter of the teinds in the diocese of Argyll. The Campbells were the most prominent among the clans who acquired the teinds from their estates that had been assigned to bishoprics. These teinds were held from the bishops of Argyll and the Isles in tack – that is, by long leases usually renewable after nineteen years. Prior to the regal union, the placement of bishops and other leading clergy on both sides of the North Channel was integral to the expansion of the house of Argyll's commercial networking within and beyond the *Gàidhealtachd*. Parochial supply to preach the word and administer the sacraments was secondary.[13]

Undoubtedly, its proprietorial approach to Protestantism compounded the logistical difficulties of establishing the Kirk within the large parishes of

---

The Book of the Thanes of Cawdor, 1236–1742, C. Innes ed. (Spalding Club, Edinburgh, 1859), pp. 251, 278–9; F.J. Shaw, *The Northern and Western Islands of Scotland: Their Economy and Society in the Seventeenth Century* (Edinburgh, 1980), pp. 154–5.

13 ABDA, Valuation Roll for the Presbytery of Argyll, 1629; ICA, Argyll Transcripts, VIII, nos 74, 124; IX, nos 176, 178, 186, 189, 202–3, 250–1; X, nos 169, 232; XI (1629–37), nos 9, 44, 46, 58, 70, 75, 93, 315, 322, 373, 479, 665, 684–5, 694–5; J. Kirk and D. Meek, 'John Carswell, Superintendent of Argyll: A Reassessment', *RSCHS*, 19 (1975), pp. 1–22. No more than a third of the 48 parishes in the Inner Hebrides and adjacent mainland districts dominated by the Campbell heartlands were supplied with a Protestant minister by the regal union, and even that figure was often only sustained by amalgamating such extensive charges. Thereafter, under episcopal direction, two-thirds of the parishes of mainland Argyll and the Inner Hebrides, but only a further two charges in Skye and the Outer Hebrides were regularly supplied with ministers prior to 1638 (*Fasti Ecclesiae Scoticanae*, H. Scott ed., 8 vols (Edinburgh, 1915–50), IV, pp. 1–139; VII, pp. 166–209).

Scottish Gaeldom, which were characterised by dispersed rather than nucle-ated settlements reached as much by sea as by land. These difficulties, in turn, provoked repeated ecclesiastical complaints about the indiscipline and even barbarity of the clans, particularly in the Hebrides. Nonetheless, in the eyes of central government, the house of Argyll was deemed a progressive influence for being in the van of those chiefs and leading gentry who accorded their role as commercial landlords no less priority than that as traditional trustees. Indeed, the concerted British action after the regal union to civilise frontiers made particular effort to have the clan *fine* in the Hebrides emulate the Campbells in terms of commercial adaptation of customary practices. At the same time, the Crown's willingness to reinforce its legislative reforms with selective military action opened up political opportunities for the ClanCampbell, then headed by *Gilleasbuig Gruamach* alias Archibald the Grim, the cold, calculating and vindictive 7th Earl of Argyll.[14]

Gilleasbuig Gruamach and Frontier Policy

Gilleasbuig Gruamach had a rather chequered political career both before and after the regal union. Archibald Campbell of Lochnell reputedly sought to celebrate his chief's propitious marriage to Lady Anna Douglas, daughter of William, 8th Earl of Morton, by having him poisoned in 1592. Campbell of Lochnell had been one of the leading clan gentry charged to direct the affairs of the house of Argyll when Gilleasbuig had succeeded, barely aged nine, in 1584. Dissension among the leading gentry, particularly over the influence exerted by Sir John Campbell of Cawdor, led to assassination plots fomented by Sir Duncan Campbell of Glenorchy and Sir John Campbell of Ardkinglas. Their intent to fracture the power of the house of Argyll was covertly supported across the North Channel and at the royal court, particularly by James Gordon, 9th Earl (later 1st Marquess) of Huntly. Cawdor was actually assassinated prior to the purported poisoning of Argyll. He was killed at Knipoch in Lorne on 4 February. Three days later, his northern neighbour and the implacable rival of Huntly, James Stewart, 2nd Earl of Moray, was murdered at Donibristle on the Firth of Forth. Although Glenorchy and Ardkinglas were arrested, and the latter actually confessed to having contracted the killing of Cawdor, no charges were pressed at court. Instead, the 7th Earl of Argyll was eventually commis-sioned to mobilise his clansmen and associates to bring summary justice to bear on Huntly in 1594. However, the superior Campbell forces were emphati-cally defeated by the Gordons on the Braes of Glenlivet, a defeat facilitated by Lochnell who betrayed the disposition of his chief's forces – albeit Lochnell

14 Macinnes, *Clanship, Commerce and the House of Stuart*, pp. 56–87.

was subsequently and inadvertently killed by the Gordons. On bringing news of his defeat to the court, Argyll was actually imprisoned in Edinburgh Castle pending his payment of judicial reparations for his followers' reputed excesses after the battle. Only direct royal intervention prevented any renewal of the conflict between the Campbells and the Gordons. Reconciliation between both noble houses was effected by James VI as a preamble to regal union, when Argyll's eldest daughter Anna was contracted to marry Huntly's son George, the future 2nd Marquess. This marriage was eventually accomplished in 1607 as a mark of the commitment of both noble houses to root out clans on the western seaboard deemed uncivilised by the new British monarchy.[15]

In the interim, the 7th Earl of Argyll had enjoyed considerable success in fomenting dissent among ClanDonald. The forfeiture of the Lordship of the Isles had not only shattered their fragile unity, it also left a political vacuum in which rival clans accorded priority to military might over order and stability throughout the sixteenth century. Political disruption was further compounded by the prospects for mercenary employment opened up by the Tudor monarchy's endeavours to assert English hegemony over Ireland. The chiefs and leading clan gentry of the western seaboard developed a lucrative trade in the seasonal provision of fighting men both to aid and contain the military ambitions of the Irish Gaels. The seasonal mercenaries from the West Highlands and Islands, who were supported by bounties and food levies, became known as the redshanks or *buannachan*. The major contractors for their deployment in Ireland were the *fine* of ClanDonald South. The ClanDonald South had used their base as the principal landowners in Islay, Jura and Kintyre to build up and sustain their presence in Antrim where contingents of the clan had settled since the early fifteenth century. Their territorial spheres of influence made them the most prominent branch of the MacDonalds at the regal union. But their mercenary activities across the North Channel exemplified the whole problem of divided sovereignty within the British Isles prior to 1603.[16]

The house of Argyll's operations in these frontier areas gained *Gilleasbuig Gruamach* notoriety for his ruthlessness as much as for his 'fishing in drumlie waters'. As well as continuing his clan's role as rival contractors to ClanDonald South, he assiduously stirred up the latter's rivalry with the Macleans of Duart over disputed territories in Islay and Jura. Simultaneously, the 7th Earl profitably deployed his kinsmen as intelligence gatherers for the English as well as the

15 Gregory, *History of the Western Highlands*, pp. 244–61; Balfour, *HW*, I, pp. 406–7, 411.

16 J.E.A. Dawson, 'Two Kingdoms or Three?: Ireland in Anglo-Scottish Relations in the Middle of the Sixteenth Century', R.A. Mason ed., *Scotland and England 1286–1815* (Edinburgh, 1987), pp. 113–38; G.A. Hayes-McCoy, *Scots Mercenary Forces in Ireland* (Dublin and London, 1937), pp. 12–3, 37–40, 57–8, 61.

Scottish Crown. According to estimates of the English espionage network in the 1590s, well over 6,600 men were reputedly ready for war in the Western Isles. However in 1595, Dioness Campbell, an expatriate cleric from the cadet line of Kilmun in Cowal then serving as Dean of Limerick, attested that the reported number of fighting men in the Hebrides did not take into account the reserves of mercenaries throughout the western seaboard. These reserves all but doubled *buannachan* numbers. The capacity of indigenous chiefs to mobilise a military force on a permanent war-footing excluded clansmen who were charged 'to remayne at home for labouring of the ground'. The retinues of redshanks formed a distinct parasitic class who, when not profiteering in Ireland, were billeted on townships as a ready reservoir of manpower to perpetuate feuds instigated by the territorial ambitions of rival *fine*.[17]

James VI had usually maintained a discrete but distanced interest in *buannachan* ventures in Ireland prior to 1603. Although he sought the English succession, he was also intent on demonstrating that he was not a supplicating client, and his native kingdom not a satellite state. Only with the impending demise of Elizabeth Tudor had James begun to treat the Irish Gaels as rebels. In order to restrain their redshank accomplices, James escalated a series of royal expeditions to pacify the western seaboard; a strategy of military containment made easier by the forces of the English government routing the rebellion led by Hugh O'Neil, Earl of Tyrone at Kinsale in December 1601. At a stroke, the employment prospects for redshanks in Ulster were drastically reduced. Following the regal union, concerted action in Edinburgh, London and Dublin against frontier disruption was particularly evident in support of the king's endeavours to plant Ulster as a permanent wedge between the Gaels of Ireland and Scotland. However, sharp distinction must be drawn between polemical rhetoric and political reality when assessing the efficacy of royal strategy towards the Gael. Indeed, the propaganda which castigated the Gael for barbarity and incivility cannot be dissociated from projected financial gains to the English and Scottish Exchequers – gains which proved more fictitious than factual and which tended to be written by speculators rather than planters. Notwithstanding episodic fears of concerted Gaelic rebellion, which required continuous policing of the North Channel in the opening decades of the seventeenth century, the Crown lacked the political commitment as well as the financial resources to effect the wholesale transformation of rural society within the *Gàidhealtachd*.[18]

17 *CSP, Scotland*, XI (1593–95), pp. 253–5; XII (1595–97), pp. 201–11; Balfour, HW, I, p. 414, and II, p. 60; E.J. Cowan, 'Fishers in Drumlie Waters: Clanship and Campbell Expansion in the time of Gilleasbuig Gruamach', *TGSI*, 54 (1984–86), pp. 269–312.
18 *Advertisements for Ireland*, G. O'Brien ed. (Dublin, 1923); Gregory, *History of the Western Highlands*, pp. 275–7, 286–7, 293–4, 313–5, 330–3; BL, Letters and Papers, 1602–c.1711, Add.MSS

Moreover, regal priorities differed critically with respect to civilising influences. James I regarded Ulster as a province which, until planted with colonists, was not an acceptable part of his British dominions. Scottish Gaeldom was held not to require such drastic political surgery. *Basilikon Doron*, the king's manual for monarchy completed before the regal union, first drew distinction between the virtually irredeemable Islanders and the redeemable Highlanders. James VI subsequently demarcated the western seaboard of Scottish Gaeldom as an 'almost rotten and decayed' member of the body politic which was, nonetheless, capable of recovery through the inculcation of 'civilitie, obedyence and religoun' among the clans. The Scottish Privy Council also exerted a moderating influence by playing on the extravagance and impracticality of colonising along Ulster lines. No less significantly, faced with the prospect of a more fertile area for colonisation in Ulster, Lowlanders were reluctant to participate in, or to finance, the successive military expeditions required to uproot the feuding clans on the western seaboard.[19]

The imperial Britannic context of frontier policy has been a neglected facet in introverted Scottish perspectives of state formation, which have been founded on highly questionable assumptions. The military and legislative programme

---

32,476 ff.9–11; R. Gillespie, 'Explorers, Exploiters and Entrepreneurs: Early Modern Ireland and its Context, 1500–1700' in B.J. Graham and L.J. Proudfoot eds, *An Historical Geography of Ireland* (London, 1993), pp. 123–57; N. Canny, *Kingdom and Colony: Ireland in the Atlantic World* (Baltimore and London, 1988), pp. 44–59.

19　*Source Book of Scottish History, vol. III, 1567–1707*, p. 261; *RPCS*, first series, VIII, pp. 737–61; M. Lee, jnr, 'James VI's Government of Scotland after 1603', *SHR*, 55 (1976), pp. 49–53; J. Ohlmeyer, '"Civilising of those Rude Partes": Colonization within Britain and Ireland, 1580s–1640s' in N. Canny ed., *The Oxford History of the British Empire, vol. 1: The Origins of Empire: British Overseas Empire to the Close of the Seventeenth Century* (Oxford, 1998), pp. 124–46. Scottish undertakers and planters were able to capitalise on growing domestic prosperity which, in turn, attracted settlers of considerably higher calibre than the disruptive elements distilled from the Borders and other frontier areas. For it was only by the prior acquisition of funds in Scotland that settlers were provided with the necessary stake to develop the devastated tracts of Ulster. While the need for venture capital gave an undoubted advantage to migrants from commercially developed areas, planting by Scots in Ulster should not be regarded as the preserve of Lowlanders. Indeed, the conditions for British undertakers that were issued in 1610 specified inland Scottish as well as English planters. As borne out by the muster-rolls for the 1630s, Gaelic-speaking tenants in Ulster were neither exclusively Irish nor exclusively migrants displaced from the western seaboard as a result of the Crown's associated policy of civilising Scottish Gaeldom. The imposition of punitive tariffs on grain imports by the Scottish Privy Council during the 1620s adversely affected the profitability of farming in Ulster and tangibly reduced immigration. But two bad harvests in successive years in 1635–6 brought a renewed flood of emigrants, mainly from north of the Tay. By the outbreak of the Covenanting Movement, Scottish settlers in the province amounted to no less than a third and probably nearer to half of the 100,000 reputed immigrants (HL, Bridgewater and Ellesmere MSS, EL 7048–9, 7051, 7058; M. Perceval-Maxwell, *The Scottish Migration to Ulster in the Reign of James I* (London, 1973), pp. 8–10, 29–67, 154–6; P. Robinson, *The Plantation of Ulster* (Belfast, 2000), pp. 108–28).

pursued by the early Stuarts after 1603 was essentially a continuation of a centralising programme pursued before the regal union. Clans and families not directly engaging with the central government in Edinburgh cannot be deemed Scottish. Central government was the sole arbiter of the process of civility propagated as the rational for the Crown's frontier policy.[20] If we accept these assumptions, and if we further shift the focus from the legislative packaging of measures to civilise Gaeldom (in 1609 and 1616) to the individual processing of constituent clauses, we move away from historical contextualisation towards didactic antiquarianism.[21]

Britannic frontier policy strove to re-channel disruptive energies into productive settlement, to re-orientate estate management commercially and to inculcate both social and religious Reformation. This policy was implemented with the assistance of the royal navy around all three kingdoms and with the support of the episcopate in all frontier dioceses.[22] At the same time, the 'de facto' role of chiefs and heads of families as local governors required Scottish central government to seek pragmatic working accommodations. Clan elites ostracised and, indeed, victimised by central government before 1603 could subsequently win political favour at the British court. Despite repeated endeavours to demilitarise, to give surety for their good conduct and to insure their landed titles by avoiding rent arrears, successive Mackintosh chiefs of the ClanChattan fell prey to the territorial acquisitiveness of the noble house of Huntly. This acquisitiveness was checked not by central government, but by the protection afforded by *Gilleasbuig Gruamach*, chief of ClanCampbell; protection that enabled the Mackintosh chiefs to sustain their Gaelic cultural identity and, simultaneously, present themselves as orderly and loyal subjects of the Crown by 1609. As a result of this political clientage, Sir Lachlan Mackintosh of Dunnachton, until his untimely death in 1622, combined his role as chief of ClanChattan with that as a gentleman of the bedchamber and companion to Prince Charles, the heir to James VI and I.[23]

20 J. Goodare, *State and Society in Early Modern Scotland* (Oxford, 1999), pp. 254–85; J. Goodare and M. Lynch, 'The Scottish State and its Borderlands, 1567–1625', and M. Lynch, 'James VI and the Highland Problem' in M. Lynch and J. Goodare eds, *The Reign of James VI* (East Linton, 1999), pp. 186–227.

21 J. Goodare, 'The Statutes of Iona in Context', *SHR*, 77 (1998), pp. 31–57; M. MacGregor, 'The Statutes of Iona: text and context', *Innes Review*, 57 (2006), pp. 111–81.

22 M. Lee, jnr, *Great Britain's Solomon: King James VI and I in his Three Kingdoms* (Urbana IL, 1990), pp. 167–71; K. Fincham, *Prelate as Pastor: The Episcopate of James I* (Oxford, 1990), pp. 36–41, 96–111; BL, Letters and Papers, 1602–c.1711, Add.MSS 32,476 ff.9–11.

23 A. Cathcart, 'Crisis of Identity? Clan Chattan's Response to Government Policy in the Scottish Highlands, c.1580–1609' in S. Murdoch and A. Mackillop eds, *Fighting for Identity: Scottish Military Experience, c.1500–1900* (Leiden and Boston, 2002), pp. 163–84; Macinnes, *Clanship, Commerce and the House of Stuart*, pp. 11, 59.

The records of central government should not be accepted uncritically as reliable indicators of the situation within frontier localities. The political counsellors at Edinburgh were as adept at playing down continuous disruptions on the Anglo-Scottish borders as in overstating the impact of disorderly elements within the ClanDonald and their associates. Furthermore, their retention of Gaelic, as against Scottish or Irish, priorities on either side of the North Channel was not shared by all the clans on the western seaboard, far less those in the southern, central, eastern and northern Highlands.[24] Concerted British action did not require a uniform policy for the Gael, albeit the screening of suitable colonists for Ulster was among the supplementary duties bestowed on the judicial commissions charged with civilising the western seaboard of Scottish Gaeldom from 1608. Despite a shared cultural heritage, Gaelic society in Scotland had differed socially and legally from that in Ireland since the Middle Ages and religiously since the Reformation. As already noted, Gaelic society in Ireland lacked a corresponding feudal dimension to clanship among the Scottish Gaels. Accordingly, expropriation of the clan elite, which threatened their clans' continuity of settlement on their ancestral territories, served as an established check to rebellion not commonplace among the Irish Gaels. Roman Catholicism, which was largely revived after the regal union through Franciscan missions from Ireland as much as from inroads by Jesuits and secular clergy based in landed households on the Lowland peripheries, posed no substantive threat to the gradual spread of Protestantism throughout Scotland since the Reformation in 1560.[25]

Notwithstanding the official bluster about restoring order to the western seaboard, the first comprehensive subjugation of feuding clans was not accomplished until the launching of the expedition of Andrew Stewart, Lord Ochiltree, with English and Irish assistance, in 1608. Ochiltree, who had previously operated judicial commissions to police the Anglo-Scottish Borders, summarily incarcerated leading Island chiefs, with the notable exception of Angus MacDonald of Dunyveg, chief of ClanDonald South (who subsequently surrendered) and Sir Rory Mor MacLeod of Dunvegan and Harris (who evaded capture). The chiefs were conveyed from the Hebrides in August 1608 and warded in the castles of Dumbarton, Blackness and Stirling for ten months.

24 A. MacCoinnich, "'His spirit was given only to warre": Conflict and Identity in the Scottish *Gàidhealtachd* c.1580–c.1630' in Murdoch and Mackillop eds, *Fighting for Identity*, pp. 133–61; J. MacInnes, 'The Gaelic Perception of the Lowlands' in W. Gilles ed., *Gaelic and Scotland, Alba agus A'Ghàidhlig* (Edinburgh, 1989), pp. 89–100.

25 J. Dawson, 'Calvinism and the Gaidhealtachd in Scotland' in A. Pettegree, A. Duke and G. Lewis eds, *Calvinism in Europe, 1540–1620* (Cambridge, 1994), pp. 231–53; K.W. Nicholls, *Gaelic and Gaelicised Ireland in the Middle Ages* (Dublin, 1972), pp 21–44, 57–65; S.G. Ellis, 'The Collapse of the Gaelic World, 1450–1650', *IHS*, 31 (1999), pp. 449–69.

Another judicial expedition to the Isles, headed by Andrew Knox, Bishop of the Isles was despatched in the autumn of 1609. The choice of Bishop Knox – who advised and assisted Ochiltree in 1608, and came to hold the Ulster diocese of Raphoe in conjunction with the Isles from 1611 to 1618 – marked an official shift towards a less aggressive posture in favour of gradual social reform through legislation rather than wholesale social displacement through plantation.[26]

Chiefs and leading gentry responded positively to the Crown's pursuit of reforming legislation. The guidelines for reform, established in the course of Bishop Knox's judicial expedition in 1609, materialised as the Statutes of Iona, which were revised pragmatically and reissued piecemeal in 1616. Imbued with the cultural values of the Lowlands, the Statutes commenced a sustained offensive to modify, if not terminate, the disruptive aspects of clanship. Central government's main priority was to educate the *fine* about their civic duties as members of the Scottish landed classes, not to denigrate their status. Their privileged position was upheld and defined at the expense of their clansmen by discriminatory controls over the wearing and use of arms, by lowered expectations for hospitality, by curbs on vagrancy and military retinues, and by their annual accountability before the Privy Council. Legislation concentrated on the redundancy and redeployment of the *buannachan*, on the commercial reorientation of customary relationships within the clans, and on the imposition of bands of surety to hold the clan elite responsible for the conduct of their followers. The abolition of calps – an enactment appended to the programme in 1617 – the promotion of English schooling and the establishment of a Protestant ministry were less accommodating measures designed to expedite if not enforce the pace at which the clan elite on the western seaboard would become assimilated, like the *fine* elsewhere in the *Gàidhealtachd*, into Scottish landed society.[27]

The era of the foraging Hebridean galley had been eclipsed by the superior forces of the English navy now at the disposal of the Scottish central government. Nevertheless, the redeployment of the *buannachan* in order to promote the commercial re-orientation of estate management was a gradual process, as is evident from the upsurge of banditry in maritime districts between 1609 and 1615 and occasional lapses into piracy by Island clans during the 1620s and 1630s. A partial remedy was provided by the commitment of Charles I to a policy of direct intervention in the Thirty Years War. From 1626, the recruitment of

26 *RPCS*, first series, V (1592–99), pp. 260–1, 265, 279–80, 289, 296–7, 306–10, 312–14, 321, 324; VI (1599–1604), pp. 4–5, 8–10, 20, 24–5, 45–6, 50, 69–70, 72–3, 78, 80–1, 84, 87, 89–93, 99–101, 105, 108–9, 111–3, 127, 130–1, 837–8; VII (1604–07), pp. 59–60, 68–76, 91–2, 115–7, 229; VIII (1607–10), pp. 59–61, 72–3, 93–5, 113–4, 162, 166, 173–5, 181, 185, 211, 281, 502–3, 506–8, 514–6, 521–6, 533–4, 737–61, 766.

27 Gregory, *History of the Western Highlands*, pp. 318–30; *RPCS*, first series, IX, pp. 25–30; X, pp. 773–80; *APS*, IV, p. 548, c.21.

clansmen for military service abroad was linked systematically to the removal of disruptive elements.[28] In the West Highlands and Islands, as in all other frontier regions deemed problematic by the Stuart monarchy, the process of civilising relied primarily on initiatives taken by leading local landowners to commercialise estate management at the expense of the customary practices and of relationships based on kinship and local association. Marketing of produce and labour took priority over the redistribution of surpluses through feasting and feuding [29]

Notwithstanding the generally positive response to reforming legislation on the western seaboard, the military strategy of expropriation was not abandoned. Instead, it was privatised to the benefit of the MacKenzies in the Isle of Lewis[30] and, above all, the Campbells in the western and southern Highlands. The elite of ClanCampbell, opportunely reconciled under *Gilleasbuig Gruamach*, adroitly maintained their Gaelic identity while projecting themselves in the first rank of Scottish landowners prepared to acclimatise to the changing British political situation in the wake of regal union.[31]

Given that Ulster was planted as a loyalist buffer between the Gaels of Ireland and Scotland, the most significant aspect of the military offensive authorised by the Crown was the expropriation of the ClanDonald South from the western seaboard. By the close of the sixteenth century, the Irish branch – the MacDon-

---

28 *SRRL*, I, pp. 195–6, 386; *Collectanea de Rebus Albanicis*, pp. 156–7; *RPCS*, first series, VIII, pp. 745–6; X, pp. 13–14; NLS, Morton Papers, MS 82, fo.55.

29 R. Gillespie, 'Plantation and Profit: Richard Spert's Tract on Ireland, 1608', *Irish Economic and Social History*, 20 (1993), pp. 62–71; R.T. Spence, 'The Backward North Modernized? The Cliffords, Earls of Cumberland and the Socage Manor of Carlisle, 1611–43', *Northern History*, 20 (1984), pp. 64–87; R. Dodgshon, *From Chiefs to Landlords: Social and Economic Change in the Western Highlands and Islands, c.1493–1820* (Edinburgh, 1998), pp. 84–111.

30 The selective expropriation of clans considered incorrigibly delinquent, which had actually been initiated by James VI prior to the regal union, was greatly facilitated by internal and, indeed, internecine divisions among their *fine*. Between 1598 and 1609, sporadic efforts to colonise Lewis by Lowland adventurers drawn mainly from Fife proved unsuccessful. Not only did the island's ClanLeod unremittingly oppose their expropriation, but other island chiefs who had a vested interest in the failure of plantation offered no assistance to the adventurers whose holding in Lewis was eventually bought out by Kenneth MacKenzie, Lord Kintail. Having helped foment fratricide within the ClanLeod, the MacKenzie chief covertly supported their opposition to plantation. Once central government switched support in favour of Kintail, the surviving *fine* of the ClanLeod were summarily evicted from Lewis in 1611, albeit a further five years elapsed before the island was in the undisputed possession of the MacKenzies. The Crown formally sanctioned their acquisitiveness when their new chief, Colin, was created earl of Seaforth in 1623 (W.C. MacKenzie, *History of the Outer Hebrides* (Edinburgh, reprinted 1974), pp. 171–265; Gregory, *History of the Western Highlands*, pp. 270–2, 278–80, 290–2, 309–10, 315–6, 334–8).

31 ICA, Letters of the 7th Earl's Period, 1600–29, bundle 62/3 and Argyll Transcripts, VIII, nos 114, 256; IX, no. 163; NAS, Breadalbane MSS, GD 112/1/378.

nells of Antrim – had effectively separated from their Scottish kinsmen and wrested control of the Route and the Glens. As Randal MacDonnell, the leader of the Irish branch, had refrained from making an irrevocable commitment to the native resistance in Ulster, the English Crown rewarded him with a knighthood and landed title, a status confirmed by King James after the regal union. As the sole Gaelic chief in Ulster untainted by treason, Sir Randal was empowered to plant his estates once colonisation commenced in 1606. Subsequently elevated to the peerage – first as Viscount Dunluce in 1618, then as earl of Antrim two years later – Randal, notwithstanding his avowed Roman Catholicism, was noted for his diligence in recruiting Protestant farmers from Lowland Scotland to further his commercial approach to estate management.[32]

Angus MacDonald of Dunyveg not only had to endure the secession of the MacDonnells of Antrim, he also had to contend with a more immediate challenge to his chiefship. His inability to resolve his clan's feud with the Macleans of Duart had led his son, Sir James MacDonald of Knockramsay, to attempt his usurpation. Sir James had triggered internecine conflict from 1597 by his unsuccessful endeavours to immolate his parents in their house of Askomull in Kintyre. Accordingly, *Gilleasbuig Gruamach* required little political invention to persuade central government that the expropriation of the *fine* of the Scottish branch of ClanDonald South was a necessity. In 1607, MacDonald of Dunyveg was stripped of his control over Kintyre and Jura to the advantage of the Campbell chief, ostensibly for services against the ClanGregor (see below). Two years later, Sir James MacDonald, who had been apprehended in 1603, was tried and convicted of treason by an assize of Lowland nobles and gentry over which Lord Ochiltree presided. The conviction of Sir James impressed upon the *fine* of other clans on the western seaboard the Crown's intent to promote order and civility. Instead of being executed, Sir James was detained in prison. On escaping in 1615, he conducted a desperate, but forlorn, resistance to the annexation of Islay accomplished in the previous year by Sir John Campbell of Cawdor, his wife's brother.

Eloquent appeals against the acquisitive ClanCampbell were made to influential nobles and officials by both Angus and Sir James MacDonald. Nonetheless, the estates of the ClanDonald South were already devastated by feuding prior to the rebellion of 1615. The extent of this wastage in Kintyre meant that both Angus and Sir James were effectively dispossessed two years before *Gilleasbuig*

---

32 Perceval-Maxwell, *The Scottish Migration to Ulster*, pp. 8–10, 29–67, 154–6, 231; Ohlmeyer, *Civil War and Restoration in the Three Stuart Kingdoms*, pp. 24–41, 281–2; G. Hill, *The Macdonnells of Antrim* (Belfast, 1893), pp. 48, 195, 225–6, 229–30; N. Canny, 'The Marginal Kingdom: Ireland as a Problem in the First British Empire' in B. Bailyn and P.D. Morgan eds, *Strangers within the Realm: Cultural Margins of the First British Empire* (Chapel Hill, 1991), pp. 35–66.

Gruamach acquired title to their estates in 1607. According to his royal charter, the Campbell chief was prohibited from granting lands to any MacDonald or MacLean, or any ally or associate of these clans. Within two years, the 7th Earl had instituted proceedings to evict fifty-three principal tenants in Kintyre. Yet no systematic effort was made to colonise Kintyre, far less Jura. Although a few Lowlanders from adjacent western districts in the shires of Renfrew and Ayr were induced to settle, their holdings were confined to the domains of MacDonald of Dunyveg and his immediate family. Even after the rebellion of 1615, a few cadets of the ClanDonald South survived as tacksmen of the Campbell chief in Kintyre – albeit gentry of the Campbells and their allied clans were encouraged to resettle Kintyre and Jura from the adjacent district of Knapdale.[33]

Likewise in Islay, no plantation on the Ulster model was carried out. Following the death of Angus MacDonald of Dunyveg, his estranged cousin, Sir Randal MacDonnell, had been granted a temporary lease of Islay in 1613. Negotiations for heritable title were cut short when the island tenantry successfully petitioned the Privy Council to prevent the oppressive imposition of unaccustomed dues by their new landlord, according 'to the formes and lawis of Yreland'. Sir Randal was in effect ordered to desist from pursuing his activities as a planter outside of Ulster. In 1614, Sir John Campbell of Cawdor, with the backing of *Gilleas-buig Gruamach*, offered a yearly feu-duty of £6,000 Scots for a royal charter to Islay; a feu-duty which, though fixed in perpetuity, considerably augmented the previous rental last set in 1541 at the equivalent of £1,200. Acceptance of this bid did not signal wholesale clearance. Indeed, after it became clear that the Crown was forcibly committed to expelling the *fine* of ClanDonald South from Islay as well as Kintyre and Jura, the heads of formerly affiliated local families changed their allegiance. By 1618, they had bound themselves to become 'dewtiful kinsmen and obedient tennentis' to the Campbells of Cawdor.[34]

To a far greater extent than the ClanDonald South, the ClanGregor were subjected to prolonged prosecution that demonstrated unequivocally the

---

33 Gregory, *History of the Western Highlands*, pp. 272–3, 280–2, 288–9, 305–6, 310–2, 326–8, 366–86; *Highland Papers*, vol. *III*, J.R.N. Macphail ed. (Edinburgh, 1920), pp. 73–84, 262–3, 268–9; *APS*, IV, pp. 379–80, c.17; *RPCS*, first series, XII (1619–22), pp. 340–1; ICA, Argyll Transcripts, VIII, no. 131; IX, nos 54, 297, 306, 314; X, nos 190, 198–200, 213, 267; XI, nos 18, 199–201, 227, 251, 268–71, 279, 283, 286–7, 290–3, 300–7, 338–42, 363, 371, 393, 395–6, 412, 415, 445, 496, 536, 577.

34 *RPCS*, first series, X (1613–16), pp. 13–4; *The Book of Islay*, G.G. Smith ed. (Edinburgh, 1895), pp. 227–8; *Thanes of Cawdor*, pp. 226–34, 242–3; A. Campbell, 'The Manuscript History of Craignish', H. Campbell ed., in *Miscellany of the Scottish History Society*, vol. IV (Edinburgh, 1926), pp. 248–9; E.J. Cowan, 'Clanship, Kinship and the Campbell Acquisition of Islay', *SHR*, 58 (1979), pp. 132–57. The piecemeal, if covert, decanting of MacDonalds from Islay to the Rathlin Isles cannot be documented convincingly until the political troubles occasioned by the emergence of the Covenanting Movement in 1638.

acquisitiveness of the ClanCampbell. Because of their own notoriety as caterans or bandits in the southern Highlands, and their decimation of the Colquhouns of Luss and their Dunbartonshire allies at the battle of Glenfruin in 1603, the MacGregors were outlawed and their name proscribed in 1606. Their proscription, however, merely legitimised and extended the policy of victimisation that had been pursued since 1570, most notably by the house of Argyll and Sir Duncan Campbell of Glenorchy, the self-confessed 'blackest laird in all the land'. Outlawry and eviction aggravated their banditry. The MacGregors devastated large tracts of the estates of their former landlords and generally terrorised the Lowland peripheries of Gaeldom. In 1611, *Gilleasbuig Gruamach* had been granted a commission plenipotentiary, 'to lay mercie asyed, and by justice and the sword ruit oute and extirpat all of that race'. Yet the ClanGregor was by no means eradicated. Central government remained concerned that moderation should be exercised. Fines levied on landlords sympathetic to the clan were not excessive, and most were still outstanding when final accounts were drawn up in 1624. Over the previous seven years, the surviving *fine* of ClanGregor were able to exact compensatory payments ranging from £400 to £10,000 from the Campbells of Glenorchy to secure the peaceful resettlement of their former territories straddling the shires of Argyll and Perth.[35]

Campbell triumphalism at the expropriation of ClanDonald South and the ClanGregor was short-lived, however. During 1618, the clan was plunged into a crisis of leadership following the flight of *Gilleasbuig Gruamach* into exile in the Spanish Netherlands. The finances of the house of Argyll, already taut through its integral involvement in Scottish politics under James VI, were overstretched by the 7th Earl's pursuit of British influence at court after the regal union. Simultaneously, he had come under sustained political pressure within the Scottish Privy Council for the severity of his far from disinterested suppression of the ClanDonald South rebellion in 1615. Most damagingly, having been expeditiously granted leave by the Crown in order to recuperate his health at Spa in the Spanish Netherlands, *Gilleasbuig Gruamach* abjured Protestantism. The revelation of his conversion to Roman Catholicism – a gradual development following his second marriage in 1610 to an English heiress, Anna Cornwallis of the noted Suffolk recusant family of Brome – led to his public denunciation as a traitor in February 1619. In the early years of his exile, the alliance

---

35 *RPCS*, first series, IV, p. 558; VII, pp. 11, 68, 287–8, 463; IX (1610–13), pp. 166–8, 302, 328–9, 644; XII, pp. 47–53, 56, 593–4; second series, VI (1635–37), pp. 95–6, 142–3; *Collectanea de Rebus Albanicis*, pp. 128–36; *BBT*, pp. 33, 37–8, 61, 65, 416–7; NAS, Breadalbane Collection GD 112/1/393a , 22/2.As a result of persecution, MacGregors had migrated from the southern to the central and eastern Highlands, boosting settlements established by their clansmen in Speyside and Strathavon since the sixteenth century.

of Spanish and Austrian Habsburgs was sweeping aside the resistance of the German princes led by Frederick, the Elector Palatine and son-in-law of James VI and I. The inopportune endeavours of *Gilleasbuig Gruamach* to find favourable employment with the Spanish Crown – ironically in a troubled association with a fellow political refugee, Sir James MacDonald of Knockramsay – were tracked assiduously from Brussels by the British espionage network.[36]

The 7th Earl was eventually pardoned in 1621. Surveillance and the accompanying diplomatic tarnishing in the Spanish Netherlands seem to have gone into abeyance with the prospect of the future Charles I marrying the Spanish Infanta. The Countess of Argyll was reportedly on good terms with the Infanta. By the time all prospects for this Spanish match had failed, the 7th Earl was racking up his campaign for political rehabilitation through associates at the British court. When Charles I declared war against Spain in 1625, the posturing of *Gilleasbuig Gruamach* again came under hostile diplomatic scrutiny. However, this was relaxed when he offered his services to Charles after the king had peremptorily declared war against France in 1626. Although this offer did work in the 7th Earl's favour, King Charles was not amused to learn that Alexander MacNaughton of Dundarrow, one of the gentlemen of his bedchamber and another clan chief from Argyllshire, had covertly lobbied the royal favourite, George Villiers, Duke of Buckingham. *Gilleasbuig Gruamach* was eventually allowed to return to London by the autumn of 1628. His rehabilitation coincided with the assassination of Buckingham and the ending of hostilities with Spain and France.[37]

36 BL, James Hay, Earl of Carlisle. Correspondence, vol. I 1602–1619, Egerton MS 2592 ff.28, 37, 107–8, 127, 132, 195 and vol. II 1619–20, Egerton MS 2593 ff.59, 69 and Correspondence of Sir W. Aston, vol. I, 1619–20, Add.MSS 36,446 ff.94–5; *CSP, Venetian (1617–19)*, p. 485 and *(1621–23)*, pp. 233, 237; ABDA, Argyll Papers, 40.1303–4, 2135–6. The 7th Earl and his second wife moved between Brussels, Antwerp and Louvain where they associated with English Jesuits. *Gilleasbuig Gruamach* did make a brief sojourn to Spain in 1625 to take his leave from his patron, Philip IV, once his rehabilitation at the British court became feasible (TNA, Secretaries of State: State Papers Foreign; Flanders (1627–28), SP 77/19, ff.63–5, 187, 198–9). His raising of Scottish Infantry Company for Spanish service – albeit the majority appear to have deserted – led to Arnold Florents van Langen, cosmographer to the King of Spain, dedicating a tract on the movement of heavenly bodies to the 7th Earl (BL, Sloane MS 651, ff.2–36; *CSP, Venetian (1621–23)*, pp. 380, 386 and *(1623–25)*, p. 396; *CSP, Domestic (1619–23)*, pp. 365–6, 378; *RPCS*, first series, XII, 730–1, 739–40, 755–6; XIII (1622–25), pp. 182, 739.

37 *CSP, Domestic (1625–26)*, p. 392 and *(1627–28)*, pp. 389, 453, 576 and *(1628–29)*, pp. 276, 341, 350, 593; *CSP, Venetian (1625–26)*, pp. 89–90, 447, 586, 592 and *(1628–29)*, pp. 198, 216, 296; TNA, Secretaries of State: State Papers, Foreign; Holland (1625), SP 84/127 ff.109–10, 217–8, 272 and SP 84/128, fo.29. The 7th Earl settled in Drury Lane, a favoured habitat of Scottish courtiers. Although a measure of royal patronage and the wealth of his wife enabled him to acquire landed interests in Lincolnshire and Surrey, he was faced with a barrage of legal suits in the English Exchequer from creditors, including prominent Scots resident in London. He

Political Schooling

Following the peremptory departure of *Gilleasbuig Gruamach* into exile, the leading gentry of ClanCampbell were summoned to Edinburgh to maintain the accountability of the house of Argyll. The 7th Earl's younger brother, Sir Colin Campbell of Lundie, was duly elected by the clan elite to assume managerial oversight, with particular responsibility for the Lorne district being assigned to Alexander Campbell of Lochnell, for Mid-Argyll to Sir Dougall Campbell of Auchinbreck, for Cowal to Sir Colin Campbell of Ardkinglas, and for the recently acquired Kintyre to John Campbell of Kilberry. Sir Duncan Campbell of Glenorchy and Sir John Campbell of Cawdor were subsequently associated with this managerial commission, which was instigated in 1618 and continued until the rightful heir Archibald Campbell, Lord Lorne, came of age ten years later. Although Lord Lorne was probably no more than eleven years old, effective title to the extensive estates of the house of Argyll had been propitiously conveyed to him before his father's second marriage in 1610. Accordingly, his inheritance was not forfeited when the attainter of *Gilleasbuig Gruamach* was proclaimed in 1619. Lorne became an active participant in the work of this managerial commission from 1624, after he completed his formal education at St Andrews University.[38]

Lorne's schooling as a clan chief and Scottish magnate was of necessity diverse, especially as his father was a persistent absentee from Scotland after his second marriage. In addition to the support of the Campbell *fine*, Lorne's maternal cousin, William Douglas, 9th Earl of Morton exercised a protective and guiding influence throughout his boyhood and adolescence. This influence was reflected in their correspondence and personal relationship, which remained warm until the establishment of the Covenanting Movement in power.[39] In March 1622, Lorne concurred with his estranged father that Morton should head the prestigious list of nobles, gentry and clan elite that the 7th Earl had selected as curators five months earlier. In practice, Morton chaired a small executive grouping that included Andrew Boyd as Bishop of Argyll, William Stirling of Auchmyle as chamberlain of the Argyll estates, and Mr

---

sought to enhance his standing at the British court by acting as a lobbyist for entrepreneurs and speculators, notably in the brewing trade. As he could not resist engaging in intrigues, however preposterous or peripheral, his rehabilitation was limited prior to his death in 1638 (City of Westminster Archives Centre, St Martin-in-the-Field Parish Records and Overseers Accounts 1633, F.360; TNA, Exchequer Papers, E 133/13/44–45 and E 134 and E 192/17/8/2; ICA, Letters of 7th Earl's Period 1600–38, bundles 1/11, 3/60, 62/4; ABDA, Argyll Papers, 40.299/1–31).

38 *RPCS*, first series, XI, 487–8; Willcock, *The Great Marquess*, pp. 9–11, 21–3; ICA, Miscellaneous 17th Century Papers, bundle 183 and Argyll Letters (1602–38), A36/22–3.

39 Willcock, *The Great Marquess*, pp. 11–13, 354–67; Walker, *Relations and Observations*, Appendix, pp. 3, 7; Balfour, *HW*, III, pp. 69–71.

Andrew Colvill as itinerant legal agent and political lobbyist at Edinburgh and the British court, and principal liaison officer at Brussels during the exile of the 7th Earl. Lorne solidified the family connection across the generations when he duly married Morton's daughter, Margaret, in August 1626. Morton, whose family seat was at Dalkeith in Midlothian, was a notably well connected politician at the British court as well as within the Scottish Privy Council, where he sat as Treasurer from 1630 to 1635. Lorne also benefited from the alliance of his house to those of the noble families of Huntly and Lothian through the respective marriages of his elder sisters. The marriage of Anna to George Gordon, the future 2nd Marquess of Huntly, in 1607 has already been noted. Four years later, Annabella Campbell married Robert Ker, 2nd Earl of Lothian and commenced a process of inter-marriage between both houses that continued into the next generation.[40] While these marital connections, as well as Morton's influence, were notably useful to Lorne's schooling as a Scottish magnate, his training as a clan chief had not been sacrificed – albeit the evidence for this training is primarily circumstantial.

That Lorne, notwithstanding a squint-eye, should win the archery contest while a student at St Andrews University in 1623, may suggest that he received some of the traditional training given to sons of the clan elite, who were schooled from their youth in athleticism and military expertise, including seamanship, under the auspices of their chief's household. Of particular relevance in this respect was his youthful reliance on Sir Donald Campbell, initially of Barbreck-Lochawe, subsequently of Ardnamurchan, the illegitimate son of the assassinated Campbell of Cawdor. Lorne retained Sir Donald as his enforcer to continue the muscular, murky operations that he had performed for the house of Argyll since his father's assassination in 1592. Campbell of Ardnamurchan married Anne, the illegitimate daughter of *Gilleasbuig Gruamach* and half-sister of Lorne, in 1629. Subsequently, Sir Donald was reputed in 1641 to be the foster-father of Lorne's younger son Neil. While no contract of fosterage for Neil is extant, the arrangements Lorne made for the formative schooling of his elder son, Archibald, the future 9th Earl of Argyll, are revealing. During the latter's fostering with Sir Colin Campbell of Glenorchy between September 1633 and June 1639, Lorne was adamant that his elder son should be tutored by an appropriate scholar to attain fluency in vernacular Gaelic as well as English, which presumes an existing competence in Scots. Lorne was adamant that his son should not be attended by a bard.[41]

40 NAS, Morton Papers, GD150/2291 and Breadalbane Collection, GD 112/1/451; *The Scots Peerage*, I, pp. 349, 359; ICA, Argyll Letters (1602–38), A36/94 and Argyll Transcripts, X, nos 7, 21.
41 Martin Martin, *A Description of the Western Islands of Scotland* (London, 1703), pp. 103–4; A. Campbell of Airds, *The Life and Troubled Times of Sir Donald Campbell of Ardnamurchan* (Isle

Lorne may have been instructed in common classical Gaelic. However, this literary dialect of the bards, rooted in the educated speech of medieval Gaeldom, had become far removed from the local spoken dialects which evolved divergently as vernacular Gaelic in Scotland and Ireland. By the time of regal union, vernacular divergence between Scottish and Irish Gaelic was as great as that between Scots and English. Bardic schooling has purportedly influenced the political thought of Lorne, by transferring notions of elective chiefship onto kingship. But this is no more than fanciful conjecture. The allegedly instructive eulogy that shaped Lorne's politics was actually delivered by Arne MacEwan in 1641, eleven years after his family had been dismissed as hereditary bards to the ClanCampbell. As Lorne carried out this dismissal, the eulogy recalling the Celtic pedigree of the house of Argyll was not so much a political lesson as a forlorn plea to be restored to favour. In any event, strict adherence to the feudal principle of primogeniture since the fourteenth century had long made the traditional practice of elective chiefship redundant within the ClanCampbell.[42]

Despite the redundancy of the MacEwan bardic family, Lorne's schooling conformed neither to the requirements for formal teaching made by the Crown's legislative programme for frontier reform nor to the anti-Gaelic tenor of its educational aspects. He was the prescribed age when the Education Act of 1616 obliged the clan elite to send all children over nine years of age 'to Lowland or inland schools'. Nevertheless, Lorne was taught privately at Inveraray (and probably Dalkeith), where Robert Barclay was retained as his personal tutor and chaplain. As well as learning to read and write English, he received a basic instruction in Latin and a thorough grounding in Calvinist orthodoxy. He may also have received his formative schooling on the relationship of political powers in Kirk and State. Barclay's family connections were rooted in the town of Irvine, which had long enjoyed the protection of the house of Argyll. Its Ayrshire location was more noted for sympathising with Presbyterian claims for the autonomy of the Kirk than with the Episcopalian polity deemed vital by the Stuart monarchy to uphold their royal supremacy in both Kirk and State. Like Campbell of Ardnamurchan, Barclay remained a confidant and advisor to Lorne when he came to play a leading role in public affairs. Lorne's links

---

of Coll, 1999); *BBT*, pp. xviii–xxiii. A Mr John Maclean was duly retained as a pedagogue for the duration of the fostering, but by 1638 serious doubts had arisen to his suitability and Sir Colin Campbell was actively considering replacing him with another scholar who could speak 'both Inglishe and Erse' (NAS, Breadalbane Collection, GD 112/1/496; ICA, Argyll Letters (1602–38), A36/36).

42 E.J. Cowan, 'The Political Ideas of a Covenanting Leader, Archibald Campbell, 1607–1661' in R.A. Mason ed., *Scots and Britons: Scottish Political Thought and the Union of 1603* (Cambridge, 1994), pp. 241–61; W.J. Watson, 'Unpublished Gaelic Poetry', *Scottish Gaelic Studies*, 3 (1931), pp. 152–6.

with the Presbyterian south-west of Scotland were further reinforced when his sister Mary married Sir Robert Montgomery of Skelmorlie in 1617. Eleven years later, his sister Jean married Sir Robert Gordon of Lochinvar who, as Viscount Kenmure, became a prominent Presbyterian nonconformist under Charles I.[43]

Lorne's appreciation of political structures was undoubtedly refined by his advanced classical and philosophical studies at St Andrews, after he matriculated in St Leonard's College in January 1622. He left in less than three years without graduating, as was the custom for students not intent on entering the clerical, legal or medical professions. Among the twenty-eight students who matriculated with him were his cousin and future brother-in-law Robert Douglas, Lord Dalkeith (later 10th Earl of Morton). St Andrews afforded Lorne his first major opportunity to network on his own volition among future shire and burgh commissioners to the Scottish Estates, ministers of the Kirk and lawyers capable of moving and securing credit.[44] Lorne's networking capabilities were put to the test both at the British court and within the Scottish Privy Council immediately after he came down from university. Indeed, he faced a test-piece for his political graduation as both a clan chief and a Scottish magnate.

Political Testing

The expropriation of the MacIains of Ardnamurchan, the fourth clan to be targeted since the regal union, served both as a test-piece for Lorne and as a touchstone for the general receptiveness of the *fine* on the western seaboard towards civilising rather than colonising. Internal dissension among the MacIains, which had commenced in 1596, afforded *Gilleasbuig Gruamach* the opportunity to effect his feudal superiority over Ardnamurchan by 1602. Nine years later, he installed Sir Donald Campbell of Barbreck-Lochawe as manager over the territories of the MacIains during the minority of their chief. Campbell of Barbreck-Lochawe ignored advice that he should attempt to win over the people of Ardnamurchan with kindness. An uneasy period of co-existence, punctuated by continuous friction over payment of rents and obedience to the house of Argyll, ended in September 1624. Under their young chief Alasdair, the MacIains took to a life of piracy, which they conducted with 'no schott bot with musketts and bowes'. By April 1625, not only were they molesting continental shipping between Islay and Skye, but they had captured three ships: one

43 Willcock, *The Great Marquess*, pp. 14–15; *RPCS*, first series, IX, pp. 25–6, 28–9; X, pp. 672, 761–2, 777–8; *APS*, V, p. 21, c.5; ICA, Letters of the 7th Earl's Period 1630–37, bundle 2/25; *The Scots Peerage*, I, 349–50; *The Parliaments of Scotland: Burgh and Shire Commissioners*, M.D. Young ed., 2vols (Edinburgh, 1992–93), I, pp. 64, 158–9, 315–6, 365, 384, and II, pp. 426–7, 431, 728.
44 St Andrews University Archives, Acta Rectorum 4, p. 181; ICA, Miscellaneous 17th Century Papers, bundle 67/4.

English, one Flemish and another from Glasgow. However, their insurrection hardly proffered grounds for official apprehensions that 'ane universall defectioun and rebellion in the Illis' was imminent.

Because the insurrection of the MacIains straddled the accession of Charles I, central government was determined to respond positively to mercantile pleas that a speedy course be taken to root out 'these barbarous pirates and murthereris'. *Gilleasbuig Gruamach*, having made his title to Ardnamurchan over to his son in late 1623, Lord Lorne, as acting chief of ClanCampbell, was duly commissioned to mobilise the clans on the western seaboard. The burgh of Ayr was ordered to provide a warship with appropriate naval support and supply. The ships captured by the MacIains were liberated by the end of May. The insurrection was brought to a final conclusion in July. Lorne, who worked with his managerial commission for the duration of the campaign, won favourable notices for executing ten MacIains, slaying six and bringing fourteen to Edinburgh for trial and punishment. Crown favour was further assured, since Lorne had maintained 1,500 clansmen out of his own resources and sought reimbursement of only £4,000 for naval expenses.

In contrast to Lorne's commendation, two chiefs – Sir Rory Mor MacLeod of Dunvegan and Harris, and his son-in-law, John MacDonald of Moidart – were officially rebuked for their dilatoriness in pursuing the MacIains. Intemperate strictures against Sir Rory Mor were premature. His initial endeavours to end the insurrection had been frustrated by the assistance that the MacIains received from neighbouring Macleans in Morvern. However, the MacLeod chief hastened the end of the insurrection by discovering the rebels at sea and pursuing them on land once they had abandoned their galleys. There was considerable justification for the official rebuke for John MacDonald, whose estate of Moidart bordered Ardnamurchan. Since 1618, when he became captain of Clanranald, he had taken the ClanIain under his protection. Accordingly, he was open to censure for his failure both to purge MacIains from his lands and to apprehend their leaders. Despite the threat of ruin to himself and his estates, MacDonald of Moidart allowed around 100 warriors and their families who survived the insurrection to merge with the Clanranald. Yet, MacDonald of Moidart had never actively opposed Lorne's commission. He ultimately acquiesced in the expropriation of the ClanIain and the acquisition of Ardnamurchan by Campbell of Barbreck-Lochawe.[45]

45 Gregory, *History of the Western Highlands*, pp. 405–12; *RPCS*, first series, XIII (1622–25), pp. 604–6, 684–6; second series, I (1625–27), pp. 18–24, 26–9, 31–40, 42–4, 88–9, 97, 109–10; NLS, Yule Collection, MS 3134, ff.102, 104; ICA, Argyll Transcripts, VIII, no.84: IX, nos 161, 233, X, no. 92 and Argyll Letters (1602–38), A36/20–1. Members of the Privy Council feared in November 1625 that Sorley MacDonald, an exiled member of the *fine* of ClanDonald South, would attempt

Following the vanquishing of ClanIain, Lorne made his first appearance at the British court in the spring of 1626. Initial impressions seem to have been favourable. Charles I was adamant that Lorne should not be punished 'for his father's failures'. The king duly consolidated Lorne's jurisdictional powers by land and sea before appointing him to the Scottish Privy Council with effect from June 1628. Charles also removed all legal impediments arising from the forfeiture of the 7th Earl to allow Lorne full financial control over the Argyll estates. For his part, Lorne had become sufficiently independent to take over the direct management of his estates and wider clan affairs from August 1627, several months before he came of age and formally attained his majority.[46] Although Lorne had passed the political test posed by the expropriation of the ClanIain of Ardnamurchan, his father's return from Brussels to London posed a new test for the retention of the recently acquired estates in Kintyre and Jura; a test which took almost a decade to resolve. At the same time, Lorne, though a dutiful councillor, was becoming increasingly disaffected by Charles I's reinterpretation of the Britannic mission of the Stuarts through his pursuit of administrative, social, economic and, above all, religious uniformity.

---

a seaborne invasion from Dunkirk in support of the MacIains of Ardnamurchan. Their fears proved groundless.

46 ICA, Letters of the 7th Earl's Period 1600–29, bundle 1/11 and Argyll Letters (1602–38), A36/26–8; *RPCS*, second series, I, pp. 82–3, 371; II, pp. 331–2; *Dumbarton Common Good Accounts 1614–60*, F. Roberts and I.M.M. McPhail eds (Dumbarton, 1972), pp. 44–5.

FOUR

The Subversive Councillor, 1628–1637

Within a British context, the key feature of the reign of Charles I from his accession in 1625 until the emergence of the Covenanting Movement was his authoritarian reliance on his royal prerogative to enforce his will over Scotland, England and Ireland. In the process, the Scots, who had been foremost in upholding James VI and I's projection of Britannic monarchy through foreign, colonial and, to a lesser extent, frontier policies, were the first to revolt against Charles I's Britannic reprogramming to push for administrative, social, economic and religious uniformity.[1] Although he was energetically intent on changing the style, pace and direction of Britannic monarchy, Charles exhibited patent and ultimately potent weaknesses from the outset of his reign. He was incapable of acknowledging that political manoeuvring within constitutional assemblies was not necessarily intended to obstruct or reverse royal initiatives. Despite an express directive to the contrary from his father in 1620 when heir apparent,[2] Charles consistently pushed his prerogative to the limit without convincingly demonstrating the present necessity for authoritarian rule. Charles tended to view critics as subversive and even seditious. Yet he was not impervious to informed criticism and he was certainly a capable political propagandist. He consistently claimed that he had acted uprightly, according to his own conscience. Nonetheless, he preferred to rule by proclamation rather than by acclamation, by private counsel rather than by parliamentary consensus, and by judicial decree rather than due process. Historical apologists notwithstanding, Charles I was a micromanager of limited intellect and contestable probity in politics.[3]

From 1628, the Britannic perspective of the Stuart monarchy was facing a far more committed challenge from Scotland than from England or Ireland; a

---

1 C. Russell, *The Fall of the British Monarchies, 1637–1642* (Oxford, 1991), pp. 27–205, 303–29; Woolrych, *Britain in Revolution*, pp. 189–233.

2 Burns, *The True Law of Kingship*, pp 278–81.

3 J. Richards, '"His Nowe Majestie" and the English Monarchy: The Kingship of Charles I before 1640', *Past & Present*, 113 (1986), pp. 70–96; T. Cogswell, 'The Politics of Propaganda: Charles I and the People in the 1620s', *Journal of British Studies*, 29 (1990), pp. 187–215; M. Kishlansky, 'Charles I: A Case of Mistaken Identity', *Past & Present*, 189 (2005), pp. 41–80.

situation seriously underplayed by the historiographic convention of the personal rule to describe the 1630s when Charles ruled without recourse to parliaments in England, but not in Scotland or Ireland.[4] In Scotland, the prospect of wholesale appropriation through an ill-conceived, technically complex, ineptly executed and financially unproductive Revocation Scheme permeated a climate of distrust throughout the political nation. This Scheme was subsequently compounded by a regressive fiscal policy and liturgical innovations that challenged the received Reformed tradition. The studied neglect of Charles I to arrange his coronation in his 'ancient and native kingdom' before 1633 further aroused Scottish antagonism and did little to allay concerns that the Britannic perspective of the Stuarts was becoming distinctively anglocentric.[5] As acting chief of ClanCampbell and as a privy councillor, Lord Lorne sought first to mitigate and then to subvert royal policy, particularly as it impacted on the house of Argyll. His ambivalence became less equivocal as the bishops came to the fore as political agents of the British court, and his disaffection became more pronounced as they instigated prosecutions against Presbyterian nonconformists. By 1637, Lorne was moving cautiously towards outright disaffection without giving any public hint that he was preparing to lead a revolution against Charles I.

Finessing Frontier Policy

Lorne's immediate concern on becoming a privy councillor in 1628 was not to question royal policy towards Scotland but to fend off an insidious threat to the territorial integrity of the house of Argyll, instigated by his estranged father, *Gilleasbuig Gruamach*. In Ardnamurchan, Lorne had effectively accomplished the expropriation instigated by his father. However, the 7th Earl had sought to herald his return from continental exile by conveying Kintyre and Jura to James Campbell, the eldest son of his second marriage. As recent acquisitions, Kintyre and Jura had not been incorporated within the house of Argyll's judicial framework when the 7th Earl made over his estates to Lorne while reserving a liferent for himself in 1610. Indeed, the parliamentary ratification of both acquisitions in 1617 gave the 7th Earl, much to the displeasure of the Campbell *fine*, scope to advance the interests not of Lorne but of the half-brother four years his junior. However, the parliamentary settlement of 1621 for the repayment of the accumulated debts of the house of Argyll had assigned a proportional share to be paid out of the rents of Kintyre and Jura. In 1624, the free rent on the Argyll estates – that is, rent unencumbered with debt repayments – amounted to no

---

4 Macinnes, *The British Revolution*, 74–110; K. Sharpe, *The Personal Rule of Charles I* (New Haven and London, 1992), pp. 3–62.
5 A.I. Macinnes, *Charles I and the Making of the Covenanting Movement, 1625–1641* (Edinburgh, 1991), pp. 26–48, 103–4.

more than £17,130, of which £13,287 (77.6%) came from Kintyre and Jura. Nevertheless, *Gilleasbuig Gruamach* was adamant that his son James, who had been created Lord Kintyre in February 1626, should have Kintyre and Jura assigned to him without any liability to meet the burden of debts with which the 7th Earl had encumbered his house.

By September 1627, Lorne had taken such umbrage at his father's apparent endorsement of his half-brother's refusal to seek an accommodation over inherited financial liabilities that he was prepared to quit Scotland: 'I will rather chose to be free abroad than ane sleave at hom.' In return for Kintyre agreeing to pay £20,000, a third of the total debt encumbering the house of Argyll, Lorne was prepared to treble their father's current pension to £8,000 annually. Lorne's subsequent correspondence with Morton, as a mediator acceptable to both sides, ostensibly bears out his abiding impetuosity, his pride and his polarised interpretation of events that set supportive friends against conspiratorial enemies. Conversely, his ensuing actions demonstrate the composure, tactical awareness and strategic mastery that became his hallmarks as a political player. From his initial feints for position until the unequivocal conclusion he achieved in 1636, he steadily shored up his support within ClanCampbell while discreetly networking at the royal court and in Edinburgh not just to counter but to wholly outmanoeuvre his father and half-brother. Overtly and covertly he exploited the impecunious 7th Earl and the prodigal Lord Kintyre, who was intent on using the recently acquired estates to finance his increasingly extravagant lifestyle as an absentee landlord.[6]

Accordingly, Lorne devised a threefold strategy which reduced his half-brother from substantial landowner to dependent pensioner. In the first place, Lorne questioned the validity of Lord Kintyre's title by using as a stalking-horse Iain MacDonald of Erraset, the grandson and designated heir of Angus MacDonald of Dunyveg through his natural son Archibald, a status first recognised by the Crown but only confirmed with Lorne's backing in 1627. Over the next four years, MacDonald of Erraset was persuaded to resign title to former ClanDonald South lands in Knapdale and Gigha in favour of gentry and landed associates of the ClanCampbell. They, in turn, were prepared to accept the feudal superiority of the house of Argyll. Kintyre and Jura were made over directly to Lord Lorne once he persuaded his father, now partially rehabilitated at court but permanently exiled from Scotland, to resign all claims to the former estates

6 Willcock, *The Great Marquess*, pp. 19–23, 353–65; *APS*, V, 1610, 1617, 1621, 1633 and 1661; *RPCS*, first series, XIII, pp. 626–7; ICA, Miscellaneous 17th Century Papers, bundle 138 and Argyll Letters (1602–38), A 36/31–3, /69; ABDA, Argyll Papers, 40.282; DH, Loudoun Deeds, bundle 2/3;TNA, Secretaries of State: State Papers Foreign, Holland (1625), SP 84/128, ff.110, 217–8; *CSP, Domestic (1625–49)*, pp. 298–9 and *(1628–29)*, pp. 358, 498.

of the ClanDonald South in return for a pension of £500 sterling (£6,000 – less than half the rents of Kintyre and Jura) should Lord Kintyre agree to sell out. Although this pension was £2,000 less than was offered by Lorne in 1627, it was to be free from the accumulated debt that had hitherto encumbered his liferent. In the second place, Lorne was securing an independent landed presence in Kintyre by purchasing kirklands with the assistance of the foremost Scottish courtier, James, 3rd Marquess of Hamilton. Third, Lorne used his own factors and agents to buy up the mortgages Kintyre had contracted on his estates. Faced with a demand for a payment of £24,000 that would need to be met within three months of the 7th Earl's death, Lord Kintyre was obliged in 1634 to recognise that Lorne had not only effective control over his financial affairs but had also assumed direct management of his estates in Kintyre and Jura.[7]

The proposed sale of Kintyre and Jura to Randal MacDonnell, 1st Earl of Antrim and his son, Randal, Lord Dunluce, the Irish pretenders to the Scottish territories of the ClanDonald South, was no more than a belated attempt by *Gilleasbuig Gruamach* and Lord Kintyre to extricate themselves from Lorne's strait-jacket of financial controls. The 7th Earl, during his exile in the Spanish Netherlands, had certainly become embroiled in reported Habsburg backing for the placing of Ireland under Spanish control and the deposition of Charles I as King of Scots. But this was no more than Gaelic posturing, primarily by native Irish earls exiled from Ulster. This posturing, in the wake of Charles I's declaration of war against Spain in 1625, was fanned by Antrim. As political opportunists with extremely limited backing among the other Scottish branches of the ClanDonald, Antrim and his son were indulging themselves with the notion that they could recreate Gaelic solidarity across the North Channel.[8] Lorne's political muscle ensured that the sale was first blocked then rescinded by the Scottish Privy Council in July 1635. Thereafter, an increasingly indebted Lord Kintyre and a still impecunious 7th Earl were obliged first to mortgage then to sell Kintyre and Jura to Lorne's son Archibald, Master of Lorne, during 1636. Lorne even had trusted kinsmen raise actions for recovery of debts in English courts, which imperilled his father's hold over recently acquired estates in Lincolnshire. The 7th Earl was also obliged to make over his house in Drury Lane to Lorne who subsequently used it as his base in London. Having been obliged to assign 112,500 merks (£75,000) for unpaid debts to Lorne, Lord

---

7 ICA, Letters – 7th Earl's Period (1630–37), bundle 3/60, /67; bundle 7/148; ICA, Argyll Transcripts, VIII, nos 129, 217; IX, nos 3, 78, 101, 190, 297, 314; X, nos 190, 195, 198–200, 213, 267, 281–3; XI, nos 20, 24, 44, 225–6, 239, 243, 264, 266, 351–2, 419, 514, 526–7, 556, 558, 560–1, 571, 577, 580, 632–3, 637, 643, 653, 664, 666, 695, 697, 712, 714, 722–5, 731, 763.

8 Ohlmeyer, *Civil War and Restoration in the Three Stuart Kingdoms*, pp. 24–41; CSP, Venetian (1625–26), pp. 89–90, 447, 586, 592.

Kintyre was granted an annuity of £6,000, and the 7th Earl's annual pension was settled at £12,000, double that of the settlement of 1634, but an increase of no more than a third from that offered in 1627. The assignment for unpaid debts was equivalent to half the accumulated rental over the past eleven years and effectively exonerated Lorne for retaining the rents of Kintyre and Jura to offset his father's debts. Albeit the annuity and pension were greater than the rental prescribed in 1624, they were absorbed by the ongoing process of estate re-orientation and debt exploitation that were the managerial hallmarks of Lorne's personal stewardship of the house of Argyll during the 1630s.⁹

As central government recognised in backing Lorne over the retention of Kintyre and Jura, the house of Argyll was providing exemplary leadership on the western seaboard for the commercial re-orientation of estate management.¹⁰ But this exemplary leadership did not extend to all aspects of frontier policy. Lorne used the British recruitment of disruptive frontiersmen into expeditionary forces to the main German theatre of the Thirty Years War – first in support of the Danish monarchy in 1627, and then of the Swedish in 1631– to shed neighbouring clansmen who could check his territorial ambitions. Contingents from Clan Campbell were notable by their absence. The general prescription of the ClanGregor for their cateran activities was reaffirmed in 1633. Lorne was instrumental in apprehending the celebrated bandit Gilderoy, alias Patrick MacGregor, who was duly tried and executed in 1636. Nevertheless, Lorne did

9 ICA, Letters – 7th Earl's Period (1630–37), bundle 3/60, /367 and Letters of Marquess's Period (1635–45) bundle 7/8, 148 and Argyll Transcripts, XI, nos 654, 662, 671,673, 723; DH, Loudoun Deeds, bundle 3/67; RPCS, 2nd series, V, p. 464; Hill, *The Macdonnells of Antrim*, pp. 229–30, 237–46; D. Stevenson, *Alasdair MacColla and the Highland problem in the Seventeenth Century* (Edinburgh, 1980), pp. 49–50. After the settlement of October 1636, Lorne was obliged to pay his father's pension for no more than two years and, in March 1643, he informed Kintyre (now the Earl of Irvine) that his annuity was rescinded, as all past debts of their father were now paid off (ICA, Argyll Transcripts, XII (1638–49), no.180).

10 Venture capital in the form of steelbow was selectively targeted through loans of seed and livestock to tenantry. The building and reconstruction of mills was promoted, while the use of querns (hand-mills) was discouraged as regressive. The reclamation of lands and the creation of new townships were sponsored through leases with incremental duties. Forests were developed commercially for their timber resources. Despite the territorial disputes within his family that limited the impact of commercial landlordism in Kintyre and Jura, Lorne played a prominent role in promoting the town of Lochhead, later Campbeltown, as an outpost of 'civilitie'. Selective migration from adjacent Lowland districts served to promote liming to improve crop yields in the peninsula by the 1630s. Lorne was also prepared to import skilled entrepreneurs from Ulster to diversify the economy of his estates. Thus in 1637, salt-pans fuelled by indigenous coal supplies were constructed in Kintyre (*RPCS*, second series, VI, pp. 251–3, 256–7; ICA, Miscellaneous 17th Century Papers, bundle 135/1 and Argyll Letters (1602–38), A 36/61 and Argyll Transcripts, VIII, nos 130, 310, 356; IX, nos 10, 190, 239; XI, nos 283, 292; XII, no. 359; *Inveraray Papers*, pp. 83–4; NAS, Breadalbane MSS, GD 112/9/3/1/2; *BBT*, pp. 268–95, 361, 380–1).

not cease the practice he had commenced four years earlier of renewing bonds of maintenance that offered selective protection to MacGregor gentry.[11]

At the same time as Lorne was rehabilitating the house of Argyll as a progressive force within Gaeldom, he was exploiting to the full the statutory requirement that designated *fine* of the Hebridean clans were annually held to account before the Privy Council under sureties that ranged from 5,000 merks (£3,333) to £10,000. Central government's insistence on annual accountability from 1616, which was enforced with particular rigour in the decade prior to the emergence of the Covenanting Movement, led chiefs and leading gentry to spend prolonged and expensive sojourns in the Lowlands. Their accumulating debts severely strained and, in some cases, outstripped their financial resources despite increased rents. Notwithstanding the threat of legal action by creditors, sojourns to the Lowlands increased their appetite for conspicuous expenditure to enhance their status as Scottish proprietors, a path already trodden ruinously by Gaelic chiefs outwith the western seaboard.[12]

The social cost of annual accountability initially provoked muted criticisms from vernacular poets – criticisms which ran contrary to Gaelic tradition but nonetheless gathered force as the *fine* were obliged to mortgage their estates to pay off debts. Sir Lachlan Maclean of Duart, during his occasional but lingering sojourns in Edinburgh, was reputedly able to win more at the gaming table than could be derived from the rents of his estate. Undoubtedly, Sir Lachlan's personal extravagance compounded the financial difficulties inherited from his clan's desperate feud with ClanDonald South over Islay and Jura at the outset of the seventeenth century. By 1631, he had surrendered feudal superiority over the small isles of the Garvellachs, Luing and Shuna, as well as his estate of Torosay in Mull. Three years later, he ceded feudal superiority over Aros and Brolos in Mull and his holdings in the isles of Jura and Scarba. He was also required to secure the major part of his remaining estates against a loan from Lorne. By 1637, Sir Lachlan was reliant on the support of his leading gentry and sympathetic neighbours to stave off further acquisitive overtures from Lorne.[13]

11 ICA, Argyll Letters (1602–38), A36/55, /63 and Argyll Transcripts, VIII, nos 85, 91, 100; IX, nos 25, 34, 68–9; IX, no. 398;Willcock, *The Great Marquess*, pp. 28, 347–8, 357–9; *APS*, IV, p. 548, c.21; NAS, Breadalbane MSS, GD 112/1/393a; GD 112/22/2 and GD 112/9/3/1/1; NAS, Campbell of Stonefield Papers, GD 14/5. The response of the Campbell *fine* to the general proscription of calps from 1617 was not altered by Lorne. Instead of terminating contracts of manrent, bonding by satellite families was rendered discretely rather than demonstratively. Calps continued to be collected as customary payments but were not specified as contractual obligations.

12 *CSP, Scotland*, XII, p. 203; *RPCS*, first series, XIII, 744–5; second series, I, pp. 75, 376; VI, pp. 300–1; VII, pp. 22, 26; *SRRL*, I, pp. 279, 284; II, p. 787; NAS, Commissariat of Edinburgh, Register of Testaments, CC 8/8/43; F.J. Shaw, 'Landownership in the Western Isles in the Seventeenth Century', *SHR*, 56 (1977), pp. 34–47.

13 *Bardachd Chloinn Ghill-Eathain: Eachann Bacach and Other Maclean Poets*, C.O. O'Baoill ed.

Under Lord Lorne, the house of Argyll adroitly manipulated the legal requirement that all financial loans to proprietors had to be secured against their estates.
Expenditure arising from annual accountability ensured that opportunities to
exploit insolvency occurred with increasing frequency, particularly when the
immediate financial needs of the Hebridean *fine* could not readily be met from
the resources of their clansmen or from sufficient advances by Lowland creditors. By November 1633, Lorne had taken over debts in excess of £21,000 which
John MacDonald of Moidart, Captain of Clanranald, owed to his kinsman Sir
Donald MacDonald of Sleat and sundry Edinburgh burgesses. Six months later,
the mainland estates of the Clanranald chief in Arisaig, Morar and Moidart
had been incorporated within the feudal superiority of the house of Argyll.
Within the decade, the bulk of his island estates in South Uist and Benbecula
had followed suit.[14]

A constant backdrop to the Crown's endeavours to 'civilise' the western
seaboard was the pressure on the *fine* of most clans, including those not bound
by the Statutes of Iona, to accept the feudal superiority of the house of Argyll.
Indeed, lack of 'civility' became a touchstone for Lorne, as previously for *Gilleasbuig Gruamach*, to use his feudal superiority to engineer the partial expropriation of the MacDougalls of Dunnolly and the Stewarts of Appin and to deny
proprietary status, other than as occasional wadsetters (mortgage holders),
to the MacDonalds of Glencoe. On a positive level, the acquisition of feudal
superiority did lead the house of Argyll to promote the extensive realignment of
the *duthchas* of other clans with the *oighreachd* of their *fine*. A negative adjunct,
however, was its insistence on reserving rights to timber, coal and other extract-
able resources when renegotiating the charters of chiefs and leading gentry
brought within its feudal superiority. Lorne sought to prevent the diminution
of Campbell territory by legal actions to sequestrate, apprise or reduce titles.
At the same time, he promoted financial discipline among his clan gentry by
restricting the amount of debt that could be contracted on estates held of the
house of Argyll.[15]

(Edinburgh, 1979), pp. 6–7; *Highland Papers, vol. I*, J.R.N. Macphail ed. (Edinburgh, 1914), pp.
245, 320–3; ICA, Argyll Transcripts, VIII, nos. 154, 233, 236; X, nos 94, 285; X, no. 211; XI, nos
121, 205, 313, 605, 616, 629, 667, 781.

14 NAS, Clanranald Papers, GD 201/5/902–05; ICA, Transcripts, X, nos 214–5, 219, 223, 252,
269–70; XI, nos 3, 17, 75, 88, 314, 443, 461, 464–5, 493, 533, 550–4, 570, 590–1, 601, 603, 613–4,
686; XII, nos 11, 15; Macinnes, *Clanship, Commerce and the House of Stuart*, pp. 72–6.

15 NLS, Register of title deeds produced by landowners in Argyll c.1688, Adv.MS 31.2.3; ICA,
Argyll Transcripts, VIII, nos 130, 217, 306, 307, 317, 312–3, 390; IX, nos 53, 167; X, nos 170, 286;
XI, nos 63, 73, 107, 308–9, 358, 380–2, 430, 467–8, 480, 483–4, 486, 543, 549, 559, 562, 569, 576,
585–6, 609, 617–8, 659, 661, 713, 717, 727–8, 743–4, 754–5, 757, 782, 787; XII, nos 1, 20.

Revocable Commitments

Lorne's equivocal approach to frontier policy must be placed within the wider context of Scottish aversion to the Revocation Scheme of Charles I, particularly as the Scheme appeared to be the harbinger for the king's attempted imposition of uniformity within the British Isles. Ostensibly, Charles designed his Revocation to liberate the gentry from their traditional deference to the nobility. This was to be achieved in three ways. First, they were granted the right to buy out their feudal superiorities in order that they might hold their estates directly from the Crown. Second, following the abolition of heritable jurisdictions, they were expected to attend assiduously on circuit courts for the hearing of capital pleas and to participate as justices of the peace to maintain order in the shires. Third, the gentry were to be able to purchase for their own use a fifth of all teinds collected from their estates. In essence, the teinds were deemed traditionally as ecclesiastical spirituality for the support of religious life in every parish. Through a long process of appropriation in the Middle Ages, teinds were usually paid to the Crown and to other lay patrons who appointed the clergy and guaranteed their stipends, as to bishops and to the temporal lords who had acquired monastic estates in the course of the sixteenth century. This concession to the gentry was part of a wider programme of comprehensive teind redistribution to raise the stipends of parish ministers, to promote pious uses – notably in relation to education and poor relief – and, last but not least, to secure an annuity for the Crown. However, the gentry were not the stated beneficiaries of the final aspect of the Revocation Scheme: the reversion of feudal tenures converted since 1540 from incidental payments as ward, and relief into annual payments as taxed ward. The conversion of tenures had actually benefited the gentry through the payment of annual monetary compositions to regularise financial demands on their estates in place of incidental payments. The primary reason for reversion, which ran against the grain of the increasingly commercial approach to estate management in Scotland since the sixteenth century, was to restore a major source of patronage to the Crown.[16]

The grounds on which Charles promoted the Revocation Scheme were even more meretricious. On account of the minorities which had bedevilled Scottish kingship since the fourteenth century, it had become accepted that a sover-

---

16 Macinnes, *Charles I and the Making of the Covenanting Movement*, pp. 49–101. Once an estate held by ward and relief passed into royal custody during a minority, the king could raise, retain or gift out the rents until the heir came of age; likewise the king could sell or gift the relief for the marriage of an heir. However, gifts of wardship exposed estates to detrimental management for the duration of minorities, an eventuality which had enhanced the conversion of ward and relief into taxed ward.

eign, between his twenty-first and twenty-fifth year, could annul all grants of royal property, pensions and offices made by any regency government prior to his majority. No regency government had acted in Scotland for Charles I, who was in his twenty-fifth year at his accession. However, he was a minor when proclaimed Prince of Scotland in succession to his late brother Henry in 1612. Accordingly, Charles claimed a revocation as Prince and maintained that the patrimony of the principality was indivisible from that of the Crown. Since grants hurtful to the principality were generally inimical to the Crown, he was entitled to a general revocation of all grants of property and revenue from the Crown patrimony for an indeterminate duration! Charles had discreetly served notice of his intent in October 1625, without reference to a Convention of the Scottish Estates then sitting in Edinburgh. He remained impervious to the subsequent warning from John Erskine, 7th Earl of Mar, then his Scottish Treasurer. If landed titles and jurisdiction could be revoked solely by the royal prerogative, no landowner could be sure of any inheritance within Scotland done 'be any of his Majesties predicessors sen King Fergus the First' (from whom Charles was reputed to be 147th in succession).[17] Charles compounded his spurious reasoning for his Revocation Scheme by wilfully misreading his father's act of annexation, which followed on from James VI's own revocation when he came of age in 1587. Charles claimed that the act of annexation had incorporated teinds as spiritualities, as well as church lands as temporalities, within the patrimony of the Crown. No reading of the act can support this contention. Its main purpose was to create the legal basis for the erection of temporal lordships, with which James VI rewarded royal officials and counsellors for the remainder of his reign in Scotland.

In a bid to allay mounting concerns as news of the Revocation Scheme leaked out from Edinburgh, Charles had refined his scheme in February and again in July 1626. Despite specifying that the surrender of feudal superiorities was now to apply solely to kirklands, this still left over two-fifths of all Scottish estates liable to revocation. Indeed, over a quarter of the Scottish Privy Council, which Charles had reconstituted with forty-eight members in March 1626, stood to be among the foremost victims of his Revocation Scheme. There were wider social ramifications. The secularisation of kirklands in the sixteenth century was the catalyst for the transformation of the Scottish economy from being a net importer to a net exporter of grain. This transformation was further evident through the intensification of fishing in deep-sea as well as inshore waters and the expansion of ports and markets by the early seventeenth century. The temporal lordships were to the fore not only in the

17 HMC, *Manuscripts of the Earls of Mar and Kellie* (London, 1904), pp. 135–6, 139.

acquisition of kirklands but in the implanting of commercial estate management by land and sea.[18]

In order to enforce compliance from the temporal lords in particular and
the political nation in general, Charles suspended his father's act of prescription of 1617. Under this act, the thirteen-year period for questioning heritable
rights to property possessed continuously for forty years was due to lapse in
June 1630. Charles sought confirmation of his prerogative right to suspend from
the College of Justice, as the supreme civil court in Scotland, in March 1630. In
giving their assent, however, the senators of the College added the proviso that
the suspension applied to property claimed by the Crown as far back as 1455, but
no further! This terminal date now applied to the main elements of the Revocation Scheme, and not 1540, the date for the reversal of feudal tenures, which
has been repeated erroneously and consistently in British historiography as the
starting point for the whole revocation.[19]

Charles could initially claim support from a group of entrepreneurial gentry,
prompted by Sir John Scot of Scotstarvit, an acerbic director of chancery in
Scotland and occasional dabbler in overseas ventures. But there was no ringing
endorsement for his Revocation at the Convention of Scottish Estates in July
1630. The gentry attending as commissioners from the shires led the call that the
king be petitioned to take account of 'the great feare' aroused by his efforts to
compel compliance. Charles remained reluctant to convene a plenary meeting
of the Scottish Estates despite the continuing apprehensions of the nobility that
the implementation of his Revocation would result in 'irreperable ruin to an
infinite number of families of all qualities in every region of the land'. When the
whole Scheme was eventually brought before the coronation parliament in 1633,
Charles was only prepared to countenance minor amendments to decisions
determined by his prerogative.[20] The general unease within the Privy Council,
the judiciary and the political nation was compounded as Charles continued to
promote Revocation as an aspect of his prerogative rule. This was particularly
evident in relation to the key processes for the implementation of his Scheme. In
January 1627, he had established the Commission for Surrenders and Teinds as a
prerogative court empowered to offer compensation for surrendered superiori-

---

18 *RPCS*, second series, I, pp. 352, 509–16; A.I. Macinnes, 'Making the Plantations British, 1603–38'
    in S.G. Ellis and R. Esser eds, *Frontiers and the Writing of History, 1500–1800* (Hannover-
    Laatzen, 2006), pp. 95–125.

19 1455 (for the bulk of the Scheme) dates to the revocation of James II, while 1540 (for feudal
    tenures only) dates to the revocation of James V.

20 NAS, Cunninghame-Grahame MSS, GD 22/2/518 and /781; Balfour, *HW*, II, pp. 151–4. These
    minor amendments restricted the right of heritors to purchase their own teinds on lands held
    in feu from bishops, burghs, universities and hospitals. All purchases had to be completed
    within two years of the teinds being valued.

ties and to quantify and cost teinds liable for redistribution. Initially scheduled to run for six months, the Commission lasted over a decade before being wound up in July 1637, just before rioting against religious innovations commenced in Edinburgh. As Charles belatedly came to realise, its divisive operations and its increasing reliance on bishops for routine administration was second only to his Revocation in 'sowing seeds of sedition and discontent'.[21]

All executive decisions concerning the surrender of superiorities, the abolition of heritable jurisdictions and teind redistribution were determined solely by Charles, who wholly underestimated the technical complexities involved. Most critically, redistribution could not be effected until the teinds in every parish were evaluated, a protracted and thankless task. From the act of annexation in 1587, temporal lords had become known prescriptively as titulars of teinds and were empowered to collect the teinds of the gentry and other landlords designated as heritors.[22] In order to ensure the compliance of all titulars and lay patrons as teind sellers, and heritors as teind buyers, Charles demanded that they respectively and collectively subscribe a general submission issued as a legal decreet from the royal court in January 1628. In effect, this promise to comply with rates of compensation and valuation that were still to be determined was a blank cheque for the king. Charles eventually issued another legal decreet in September 1629, which specified the rates of compensation for the surrender of superiorities; the rates at which teinds were to be quantified and costed for purchase by heritors; and restrictions on purchases to ensure adequate redistribution for pious uses. The rates of compensation to be offered for the abolition of heritable jurisdictions remained open.

---

21 [Walter Balcanqual], *A Declaration Concerning the Late Tumults in Scotland* (Edinburgh, 1639), p. 15.

22 In Scotland, the distinction between a feuar, who held property of another landowner, and a freeholder, who held directly from the Crown, was not synonymous with the distinction between a laird, or member of the gentry, and a noble. Both gentry and nobles could hold property from other landholders and simultaneously hold estates directly from the Crown. As feuars frequently paid teinds and feu duties in a combined package, the task of disentangling the one from the other was not easily determined. Where a temporal lordship was dispersed geographically and titularship was not exercised over a consolidated group of parishes, a considerable portion of heritors were neither bound to the titular as feudal superior nor even tied by kinship and local association. As a measure of appeasement, titulars farmed the collection of their parochial teinds to prominent local landowners designated as tacksmen. Since the rights of the titulars and tacksmen took priority over those of the heritors, the process of uplifting crops designated as teind at harvest time was prone to fractious delays. Claims that the uplifting or leading of teinds were a perennial cause of civil disturbance and occasional blood-letting must be treated with caution, however (M. Lee jnr, *The Road to Revolution: Scotland under Charles I, 1625-37* (Urbana and Chicago, 1985), p. 34). The commutation of teinds from kind into money through the mechanism of fiars prices set annually in the wake of the harvest was beginning to offset delays in uplifting teinds.

The protracted and demanding task of evaluating teinds was devolved to sub-commissions operating with the civil bounds of every presbytery. Sub-commissions included not only members of the national Commission for Surrenders and Teinds, but also co-opted gentry of local influence to expedite the actual process of valuation in every parish within the civil presbytery. Persuading sub-commissioners to serve was certainly not facilitated by the prospects of a technically exacting workload and anomalous as well as contentious valuations. Although sub-commissions were authorised for fifty-nine presbyteries in July 1628, only fifteen were operative in February 1629. Albeit every sub-commission was functioning by the end of that year, few bothered to submit regular reports of their diligence over the next five years. Instead of expediting valuations, the sub-commissions actively colluded with local vested interests to restrict the amount of teind redistributable for ministers' stipends, pious uses and the king's annuity. Collusion had become such a community enterprise that Charles censured the Commission for Surrenders and Teinds in July 1635. It was routinely accepting parochial valuations in which the amount of teind eligible for redistribution had been diminished by as much as a third. The Commission admitted in December 1636, that teinds had not yet been valued in most parishes.[23] Undoubtedly, social deference and a reluctance to become entangled in legal confrontations with obstructive titulars and lay patrons contributed to the widespread aversion among heritors to secure their own teinds by compulsory purchase. Few sales proceeded by voluntary agreement. Despite vociferous overtures from clergy intent on securing augmented stipends, ministers were more concerned to appease than confront titulars, lay patrons and heritors. Indeed, ministers actually colluded in the deliberate undervaluing of teinds. Inaccurate and incomplete valuations particularly prejudiced the exaction of the king's annuity, which proved a negligible source of royal revenue prior to the emergence of the Covenanting Movement.

Other aspects of his Revocation Scheme were no more remunerative. In the case of superiorities and heritable jurisdictions, their respective surrender and abolition proved a financial drain on the Crown, especially as the supplies voted in the Conventions of Estates in 1625 and 1630 were not readily available to meet the costs of compensation. Instead, the revenues raised from taxes – £1,172,276, equivalent to £9,687sterling – were earmarked primarily for British expeditionary forces on the continent and the maintenance of the Scottish civil establishment at court and in Edinburgh. Charles was obliged to suspend payments of compensation negotiated for heritable jurisdictions in October 1634. By then, however, Charles had substantially increased his revenues from imposts and

23 NAS, Sederunt Book of the High Commission of Teinds 1633–50, TE 1/2, ff.17, 23, 28, 31, 35.

customs, primarily under the auspices of John Stewart, 1st Earl of Traquair. William Dick of Braid, a leading Edinburgh merchant and financier, was induced to take over the farming of the imposts of wines and subsequently the customs; his cumulative annual payments of £134,667 promised an additional £80,667 (£6,722 sterling) directly to the Scottish Treasury. At the same time, the increase from four to six years in the taxes awarded by the coronation parliament realised £733,674 (£61,140 sterling) by August 1636. Nevertheless, expenditure continued to outstrip income, a situation not aided by lavish expenditure for the king's coronation visit. In 1634, recurrent expenditure stood at £335,159 and accumulated debts at £922,087 (£76,840 sterling), which was serviced at an annual cost of £78,648. Notwithstanding Traquair's programme of cutting back on pensions, fees and allowances to officeholders and increased supply from taxes, customs and imposts, expenditure continued to outstrip income by £7,468 over the next two years. Charles still carried an accumulating deficit of almost £930,000 (£77,500 sterling) as the Revocation Scheme ground to a halt.[24]

Only eleven temporal lords, less than a third of the total number, made any meaningful effort to negotiate with the Crown. No more than five made a comprehensive surrender of superiorities. Although nine nobles and four gentry contracted for the abolition of heritable jurisdictions, the Crown's lack of ready cash led to payments by protracted instalment or the retention or regalities and other heritable offices under mortgage. In essence, local government remained a matter of hereditary private enterprise in Scotland, particularly after Charles sought to use circuit courts not so much for judicial purposes as for fiscal opportunism, a move which led to local rioting.[25] When Charles

---

24 Macinnes, *Charles I and the Making of the Covenanting Movement*, pp. 104–6, 115–6. The increase in customs of £41,773 between 1629 and 1634 was all but wiped out by the expenditure of £41,497 on the coronation visit (BL, Papers of the Loch Family, Add.MSS 40,885 pp. 1–31). When Charles decreed in February 1634 that his annuity from the teinds should become a composition rather than a direct tax, no more than 88 landowners took up his offer to be quit of his annuity for the payment of a lump sum equivalent to seven years exaction. By July 1635, Charles had resorted more in hope than expectation to the farming of his annuity, which yielded no perceptible financial benefit.

25 In the spring of 1628, Charles was induced to forego reversing of feudal tenures in return for an evasion tax proposed by Sir Alexander Strachan of Thornton, a courtier of dubious repute. As part of project rather optimistically promoted to treble the revenues available to the Crown from feudal casualties, at least £24,000 was to be exacted annually in compositions from landlords who had defaulted on payments of reliefs or converted feudal tenures without royal approval. Almost ten times this sum further was to be realised by compositions for unpaid feudal dues, escheated goods of outlaws, rent arrears, renegotiated titles and breaches of penal statutes. Charles simultaneously reinvigorated the justice-ayres. Four, geographically distinct, circuit courts were to be operated by the senators of the College of Justice twice yearly to try all capital cases, all transgressions of penal statutes and oversee the competence of local government officers. Plans to hold biannual circuits were never implemented and rarely were the

attempted to reinvigorate the peace commissions in September 1634 along English lines, the willingness of the gentry to serve as justices was prejudiced by their onerous and politically thankless experience on the sub-commissions for the valuation of teinds. By July 1637, the Scottish Privy Council was prepared to admit, notwithstanding frequent citations of justices for negligence and dereliction of duty, that service of the peace commissions was 'in effect cassin louse'.[26]

Lorne's stance to the Revocation Scheme was similar to that of frontier policy: studied ambivalence. He supported Charles I to further but not to compromise the territorial ambitions of the house of Argyll. On attaining his majority in 1628, he surrendered his hereditary claim to be Justice-General of Scotland, an office which had been held by his house since 1514. But, in return, he negotiated with the king to retain the heritable office of Justiciar of Argyll and the Western Isles. The Crown retained specific rights to half the profits of justice from the justiciarship, to direct justice-ayres on circuit twice yearly within its bounds, and to nominate the serving justice-general or a depute to sit as an auxiliary justice. In practice, Lorne ensured that the house of Argyll retained jurisdictional competence over all civil and criminal cases, except treason in Argyll and the Western Isles by working co-operatively with central government and making judicious concessions to other leading nobles affected by this grant, which was ratified in the coronation parliament of 1633.[27]

The next year, having procured Hamilton's support for building up his landed

---

shires within each judicial circuit visited more than once over the next three years. The lack of specification in the formal indictment of offenders immediately proved contentious. For the indictments did not inform reputed offenders whether they faced capital charges or merely breaches of penal statutes. The justice-ayres were reminded in September 1629 that circuit courts were to be held at Strachan of Thornton's convenience. He was empowered to dispense with prosecutions and exact compositions for breaches of penal statutes, half of which he was to retain for his own profit. Such was the outcry from the localities that Thornton's patent was first suspended unilaterally by leading officials and then set aside in the wake of protests at the Convention of Estates in 1630. The circuit courts were also suspended. Their revival in 1631 proved no more than fitful. After deducting legal charges, compositions yielded just over £1,068: its aggravation of political dissent had more than outweighed anticipated financial benefits (Hull University Library, Maxwell-Constable of Everingham MSS, DDEV/79/D; Macinnes, *Charles I and the Making of the Covenanting Movement*, pp. 92–6).

26 *RPCS*, second series, V, pp. 409, 424–30; VI, pp. 21, 36, 56–7, 78, 175–6, 378, 426, 453, 472, 481.

27 *APS*, V, pp. 77–80 c.69–70; *Selected Justiciary Cases, 1624–50*, S.A. Gillon ed., 2 vols (Edinburgh, 1953), I, pp. 267–76; *RPCS*, 2nd series, II, pp. 330, 45–7, 364, 373–4, 405, 420–1, 424, 535, 632–4; V, pp. 121–2, 132, 195, 404, 560–1; VI (1635–37), pp. 94–5, 103–4, 114, 145, 165, 207–9, 219–21, 231–4, 253–4, 363, 397; *Inveraray Papers*, p. 13; ICA, Argyll Letters (1602–38), A36/41, /55. As a councillor, Lorne's judicial expertise was deepened by his participation in a variety of special commissions to investigate and resolve a variety of cases that ranged from witchcraft and counterfeiting to marital and shipping disputes (*RPCS*, second series, II, p. 336; V, pp. 625–6, VI, pp. 212, 264, 313–4, 347).

interest in Kintyre, Lorne conceded that the estates of the 3rd Marquess on the island of Arran should be exempt from his justiciarship. However, it took another two years for Lorne to agree that the estates of George MacKenzie, 2nd Earl of Seaforth on the islands of Lewis and Raasay, should also be exempt. This concession was made largely to ensure that Lorne was able to have free rein to prosecute clan chiefs, such as Sir Donald MacDonald of Sleat and John MacDonald of Moidart, captain of Clanranald. They had been supported by Seaforth in their endeavours to resist Lorne holding courts in the Western Isles to recover their debts to the house of Argyll. Lorne generally ensured that the unrivalled jurisdictional privileges he retained, notwithstanding the Revocation Scheme, were exercised responsibly through a sophisticated system of hierarchical courts (see Chapter 3). However, Lorne remained the final arbiter of appeals from subordinate courts of non-Campbell landowners, a power exercised partially over chiefs and leading gentry of other clans obliged to accept the feudal superiority of the house of Argyll. At the same time, the redrawing of the jurisdictional competence of the house of Argyll in 1628 extended its criminal and civil powers to all estates in Highlands and Lowlands that came within its feudal superiority. Thus, the acquisitive policy pursued consistently by Lorne from his majority until his death in 1661 was enhanced as well as sanctioned by his guarantee of a legal monopoly – other than for cases of treason – without any appeal to royal courts.[28]

28 NAS, Breadalbane MSS, GD 112/1/378; ICA, Letters of the 7th Earl's Period 1630–37, bundle 2/22, /31, bundle 3/59 and Memorandum and Scheme of Differences of bounds in Justiciary of Argyle 1628 and 1702, bundle 143/3 and Argyll Transcripts, XI, nos 526, 558,560–1, 574, 593, 686; XII, nos 11, 15, 150, 155, 289. The office of Justice-General held not for life but at the pleasure of the Crown was granted to William Graham, 7th Earl of Menteith, who also served as Lord President of the Scottish Privy Council. He revived effective liaison between Scotland and the Court from 1628 until his dismissal from office in 1633. Menteith's energy ensured that royal government in Scotland continued to function despite growing unrest over Revocation and ongoing taxation, which had surfaced at the Convention of Estates in July 1630. Menteith welded the majority of councillors, bishops, courtiers and officials then attending into a cohesive Court party which backed his resolve to debate only the relevance, not the substance, of contentious aspects of the Revocation Scheme raised by the nobility and itemised grievances from the gentry over the conduct of central and local government. Once assent had been given to the renewal of ordinary and extraordinary taxation for four years, all proposals to redress grievances and improve government were deferred to the consideration of the coronation parliament. However, a lack of prudence, notably his questioning of the Scottish pedigree of the Stuarts when in his cups, triggered Menteith's downfall and eventual withdrawal from public life in 1633. The failure of Charles to maintain Menteith in office beyond his coronation parliament demonstrated his manifest lack of understanding about the importance of political management. His capacity to govern Scotland for the rest of his prerogative rule certainly suffered from his failure to find a successor willing to undertake a similar style of shuttle diplomacy on behalf of absentee monarchy (Lee jnr, *The Road to Revolution*, pp 46–8, 69–71, 126; Macinnes, *Charles I and the Making of the Covenanting Movement*, pp. 82–6).

Rather than selling kirklands, Lorne was more intent on their purchase and consolidation, especially in Kintyre, given the contested holding of that peninsula. Lorne secured a firm grip over the disposal of kirklands in Argyll and the Western Isles by ensuring that clerical appointments, particularly to bishoprics, were geared to advance the territorial interests of his house. Andrew Boyd, Bishop of Argyll had served as curator to Lorne during his minority and continued as an adviser and client when he extolled Charles I on his coronation visit to Scotland in 1633 as the heroic protector of Great Britain. In the same year, Lorne secured the appointment of his kinsman, Neil Campbell of Glassary, as Bishop of the Isles, 'notwithstanding great oppositione maid by both noblemen and clergie in favour of others'. Within two years, the kirklands and teinds of Iona Abbey, which had been conveyed by the Crown to the bishopric of the Isles in 1617, were wrested from the control of the Macleans of Duart. As had long been the practice among Bishops of Argyll, the new episcopal incumbent for the Isles deliberately and discriminately pursued the interests of the house of Argyll rather than the Crown when granting kirklands and teinds by charter or by lease.[29]

Once the demanding task of evaluating teinds was devolved to sub-commissions, Lorne was adamant that he, not the bishops of Argyll and the Isles, should control the appointment of the sub-commissioners. Lorne had already positioned himself in the Privy Council to take the subscription of any landowner in Argyll and the Isles who wished to sell their right to the teinds. At the same time, as an assiduous attendee at Council, he exercised oversight over any landowner in Argyll and the Isles who claimed that he wished to purchase his own teinds. In the event, full valuations of teinds in preparation for their redistribution was only effected from 1629 in mainland districts where the house of Argyll was the dominant territorial influence, or in parishes where Lorne was attempting to bring the estates of the *fine* of other clans within his feudal superiority. The process of evaluation was less protracted but no less given to collusion than in most other Scottish presbyteries. No significant teind redistribution was attempted. Lorne did support the consolidation of Protestantism in the *Gàidhealtachd*. He made resources available to rebuild or resite a few parish churches, and to realign parish boundaries in order to facilitate the preaching of word and the administration of the sacraments. He also backed royal and ecclesiastical endeavours to ensure the continuity of Protestant ministers in all parishes on the western seaboard. But he was considerably less diligent in

29 Andrew Boyd, *Ad Augustissimum Monarcham Carolum Majori Britanniae* (Edinburgh, 1633); *SRRL*, II, pp. 564, 840, 842, 851; *RPCS*, second series, V, pp. 286–7, 563–4;*Collectanea de Rebus Albanicis*, pp. 161–86; ICA, Argyll Letters (1602–38), A 36/38 andArgyll Transcripts, VIII, nos 74, 124; IX, nos 178, 189, 202; X, nos 169, 232; XI, nos 44, 46, 58, 70, 93, 315, 322, 351–2, 373, 419, 479, 514, 604, 665, 684–5, 693–5.

securing the operation of kirk sessions deemed necessary for the active stimula-
tion of Christian congregations.[30]

The Disaffected Element

From its promulgation until its winding down in 1637, Lorne did not associate
himself publicly with the dissent voiced against the Revocation Scheme or the
political influence of bishops on the Commission for Surrenders and Teinds.
Lorne, who attended the Convention of Estates in July 1630, was conspicu-
ously silent when James Elphinstone, Lord Balmerino, targeted the bishops and
their clerical associates for the promotion of prerogative rule in civil as well
as ecclesiastical affairs. Nevertheless, the climate of dissent generated by the
Revocation Scheme brought Lorne into close contact with another prominent
leader of the disaffected: his kinsman John Campbell, Lord Loudoun, who had
acted supportively when brought onto the commission to aid Lorne manage
his estates prior to his majority. Loudon also backed Lorne to wrest control of
Kintyre and Jura from his father and half-brother. Loudoun, who was nine years
older, continued to assist Lorne when fending off the acquisitive ambitions of
the house of Antrim in 1635–36. As Lorne was a privy councillor, he did not
maintain direct lines of communication with Loudoun on issues of public policy,
only on matters of estate management and landownership. Instead Lorne used
as his intermediary Archibald Campbell of Glencarradale, brother to Sir James
Campbell of Lawers, another supportive adviser of Lorne.

Lawers was actually the father of Loudoun, who succeeded to the Ayrshire
estates of the lordship in 1622 through his marriage to the heiress Lady Margaret

---

30 *RPCS*, second series, II, pp. 245–6, 249, 309, 474–5; ABDA, Valuation Roll for the Presbytery of
Argyll, 1629; NAS, Sederunt Book for the High Commission of Teinds, 1630–33, TE 1/1, ff.60–1;
ICA, Argyll Letters (1602–38), A 36/38, /75 and Argyll Transcripts, XI, nos 639, 700–6; J. Kirk,
'The Jacobean Church in the Highlands, 1567–1625' in L. Maclean ed., *The Seventeenth Century
Highlands* (Inverness, 1985) pp. 24–51. At the same time, Lorne partially assisted the collective endeavours of the Scottish bishops to enforce the penal laws against priest and recusants
in 1629–30. Though applicable to all Roman Catholics, these laws were designed primarily
to curtail Jesuit missions in the Lowlands and Franciscan missions to the Highlands. In the
same way that the Scottish bishops had promoted the reimposition of the penal laws to deflect
attention from their active compliance with the Revocation Scheme, Lorne had ulterior political motives. His collaboration with the bishops was selective rather than comprehensive. He
ensured that the estates in the shires of Argyll and Inverness of his kinsman, Sir John Campbell
of Cawdor, who had converted to Roman Catholicism in the 1620s, were not forfeited. In
particular, neither the apostasy of Cawdor nor his purported insanity was to provide grounds
for returning the island of Islay to the remnants of ClanDonald South on either side of the
North Channel. At the same time, the imposition of the penal laws was an additional tool
to compromise heavily indebted *fine* of other branches of the ClanDonald who happened to
be Catholic (A.I. Macinnes, 'Catholic Recusancy and the Penal Laws, 1603–1707', *RSCHS*, 33
(1987), pp. 27–63; ICA, Argyll Transcripts, XI, no. 517).

Campbell. Archibald Campbell, who was rewarded with the small estate of Glencarradale in Kintyre by Lorne, retained close links with his nephew Loudoun. At the same time, as he became the principal clan contact with the 7th Earl of Argyll, Glencarradale built up his contacts at the royal court. Glencarradale fronted Lorne's offensive against his father in the English courts by putting pressure on the 7th Earl's estates in Lincolnshire to meet the spiralling debts of Lorne's spendthrift half-brother, Lord Kintyre. In short, Glencarradale kept Lorne fully briefed of affairs at court and from within the ranks of the disaffected in Scotland. Lorne, in turn, would appear to have exercised a discreet but subversive influence in favour of the disaffected element in the coronation parliament of 1633, when a concerted constitutional attack on the episcopal role in church and state was prepared but prudently not delivered by Loudoun. Ostensibly Loudoun held fire because he was liable to punitive reprisals, given the absence of a defined privilege of free speech in the Scottish Estates. But he also took soundings from friends attending in Edinburgh, who included Lorne and other leading Campbell clansmen.[31]

As an assiduous councillor, Lorne was well aware that Charles I was intent on managerial overkill with respect to the composition, agenda and proceedings in the coronation parliament. Determined not to encounter a constitutional breakdown in Scotland four years after he had dissolved parliament and embarked upon his prerogative rule in England, Charles devised various stratagems to limit expressions of dissent in the Scottish Estates. He transcended similar techniques used by his father to secure the passage of the liturgical innovations known as the Five Articles of Perth and the taxes on land and annualrents (financial resources) in 1621.[32] All those seeking to be excused

---

31 *LJB*, I, pp. 476–8; John Row, *The History of the Kirk of Scotland 1558–1637*, D. Laing ed. (Edinburgh, 1842), pp. 350–1; *APS*, V, pp. 230–1; ICA, Argyll Letters (1602–38), A 36/ 35–6, /44, /56, /59, /77, /83 and Letters of 7th Earl's Period (1630–37), bundle 3/60 and Transcripts, XI, no. 670; DH, Loudoun Deeds, bundle 1/3–4, /16; bundle 2/3, /11; bundle 3/60, /67. In order to ensure the integrity of his estates in Argyllshire, Lorne was prepared to take court action with his father against Loudoun in 1628. Nevertheless, as the Campbells of Lawers were cadets of the Campbells of Glenorchy, both Loudoun and his father played important conciliatory roles in easing Lorne's difficult relationship with the aged Sir Duncan Campbell of Glenorchy (NAS, Breadalbane MSS, GD 112/1/477; ICA, Argyll Letters (1602–38), A 36/29–31, /33, /65 and Transcripts, XI, no.598).

32 J. Goodare, 'The Scottish Parliament of 1621', *HJ*, 38 (1995), pp. 29–51. In return for a guarantee that James VI and I would attempt no further liturgical innovations, the Scottish Estates in 1621 had ratified the Five Articles which had been intruded at a managed assembly of the Kirk at Perth in 1618. This liturgical programme laid stress on the observation of holy days, episcopal confirmation and private ceremonies for both baptism and communion. Undoubtedly the programme's most controversially requirement was that all members of congregations were to kneel when participating in communion. The ensuing reluctance of the bishops to publicise nonconformity by prosecution had enabled Presbyterian laity, with the connivance of

from the coronation parliament, including four of the five Englishmen who held Scottish honours but no Scottish estates, were encouraged to place their proxies at the disposal of the Court. As the proxy of the 7th Earl was duly held by Morton, Lorne did not take his seat as a member of the nobility. During the seven weeks of the coronation visit, fifty-four gentry were dubbed knights and nine were created peers; ten existing peers were elevated in rank. But Charles's award of honours was conditional on the beneficiaries supporting his legislative programme. Loudoun had his offer of an earldom withdrawn.

The committee of articles was the most crucial vehicle for management once the parliament commenced on 20 June. The bishops were the lynchpins of royal control for the nomination of eight members from each Estate. As added surety, Charles designated that the chancellor, John Hay, 1st Earl of Kinnoul, preside over the committee on which eight other officers of state attended and voted.[33] During the eight days in which the committee met to compile the full legislative programme, all separate conventions of Estates were banned. A meeting of the gentry to draw up a remedial programme for royal government was interrupted and dispersed. Despite the support of sympathetic nobles, a petition from nonconforming clergy was suppressed, as was a supplication by commissioners from the shires and burghs, attacking the rumoured agenda drawn up by the committee of articles as inimical 'both to Kirk and countrey'. The main thrust of the extensive debates in the committee was leaked to the leadership of the disaffected element before the Crown's legislative programme was presented for the approval of the Scottish Estates on 28 June. Although Lorne was not a member of the committee, as a trusted councillor who had helped plan the coronation visit and who attended the king when in Edinburgh, he was almost certainly privy to their discussions.[34]

Only one day was set aside for the plenary approval of the legislative programme. The composite agenda of 168 measures was presented for accept-

---

sympathetic ministers, either to absent themselves from communion or refrain from kneeling (P.H.R. Mackay, 'The Reception Given to the Five Articles of Perth', *RSCHS*, 19 (1977), pp. 255–98).

33 J.R. Young, 'Charles I and the 1633 Parliament' in K.M. Brown and A.J. Mann eds, *Parliament and Politics in Scotland, 1567–1707* (Edinburgh, 2005), pp. 101–37; Macinnes, *Charles I and the Making of the Covenanting Movement*, pp. 86–9; *APS*, V, pp. 8, 11. On the recommendation of the king, the bishops chose eight nobles who, in turn, chose eight bishops. All the bishops owed their position to royal patronage. The eight nobles selected were predominantly, but not exclusively, courtiers. The eight nobles and eight bishops then chose commissioners from eight shires and eight burghs; preference was accorded to those with a track record of support for the court.

34 Row, *History of the Kirk*, pp. 366–7; *Memoirs of the Maxwells of Pollock*, 2 vols, W. Fraser ed. (Edinburgh, 1863), II, pp. 232–40; *RPCS*, second series, II, p. 385; V, pp. 45, 49; ICA, Argyll Letters (1602–38), A 36/42, /44–5, /47, /70

ance or rejection as a whole, with no distinction for voting purposes observed between public enactments and private bills. Votes were collected at random, not recorded systematically from each Estate. Debate was not encouraged. Charles attended in person to reproach dissenters and note their names. The block passage of legislation was further secured by dubious tallying. John Leslie, 6th Earl of Rothes challenged the result favouring the court, but retracted on being threatened with prosecution for treason. Public rumour soon reversed the final outcome on the grounds that the tally of individual votes cast by persons actually present went against the court. Rothes, Balmerino and Loudoun, as leaders of the disaffected, were not yet prepared to criticise the Crown directly. However, Charles's reliance on bishops to secure control of the committee of the articles, to enforce rigorous vetting of the composite agenda, and to collude in voting practices enabled the disaffected in each Estate to concert their protests against parliamentary direction 'by the Episcopall and courte faction'.[35]

In the aftermath of the coronation parliament, a distinctive Scottish critique of Britannic monarchy emerged when William Haig, a former Crown solicitor, penned a supplication to justify the conduct of the disaffected element in voting against the block passage of the legislative programme. Reputedly endorsed by thirty-five out of the forty-five peers who attended, Haig's Supplication criticised Charles I for not being as attuned to Scottish sensibilities as his father, for seeking both Revocation and relatively high taxation, and for favouring parasites and prelates at court. Above all, the lack of constitutional limitations on his prerogative gave rise of 'a generall feare of some innovations intended in essential points of religion'.[36] Implicated in the covert production of Haig's Supplication, Balmerino was duly tried for treason two years later (see below). Lorne for his part continued to serve diligently as a councillor while promoting greater dialogue between lay councillors and the leaders of the disaffected element. This dialogue was designed both to isolate the bishops politically and to restrict the British endeavours of Charles I to impose economic uniformity.

Nationwide opposition to economic uniformity had first arisen over the king's proposal for a common fishing raised formally in the Convention of Estates in

---

35 Balfour, *HW*, II, p. 200; Clarendon, *The History of the Rebellion*, I, pp. 138–43, 184; William Scott, *An Apologetical Narration of the State and Government of the Kirk of Scotland since the Reformation*, D. Laing ed. (Edinburgh, 1846), pp. 293–5, 336–8.

36 Row, *History of the Kirk*, 376–81. The coronation parliament had increased the levies for both the taxes on land and on financial transactions from four to six years. The former practice of levying taxes over four years had been in place since 1621 and had been renewed by subsequent Conventions of Estates in 1625 and 1630. Although interest rates were reduced from 10% to 8%, Charles suspended this reduction for three years, during which time the 2% reduction was requisitioned as a benevolence to the Crown (Macinnes, *Charles I and the Making of the Covenanting Movement*, pp. 133–4).

1630. This grandiose initiative was fashioned according to English mercantilist aspirations. It was intended to open a window of opportunity into Scottish territorial waters at the expense of the native fishing industry as much as that of the Dutch fleet who dominated deep-sea fishing around the British Isles. On being presented with this proposal in 1630, the Scottish Estates could assert no more than a watching brief over negotiations at the royal court between commissioners appointed by the Scottish Privy Council and their English counterparts, who were exclusively courtiers and officials appointed by and answerable only to Charles. Determined to promote the common fishing to sustain the king's claim to sovereignty around the British Isles, the English commissioners were prepared to rely on the king's prerogative to secure the associated British adventurers unrestricted and exclusive access to inshore as well as deep-sea fishing off the Scottish coasts. While reluctantly accepting the implementation of the common fishing, the Privy Council, fortified by Lorne and the other Scottish commissioners, vigorously rebuffed its Britannic promotion. The suppression of the name of Scotland in all authorising warrants was found to be particularly prejudicial. Especially confusing was the generic use of 'the name of great Britane altho ther be no unioun as yit with England'. The Council thus articulated widespread concerns that the common fishing was the thin edge of a wedge designed to relegate Scotland to the provincial status of Ireland, which was not represented at the negotiations. Irish interests were encompassed with the remit of the English commissioners, who exhibited little concern for their advancement.[37]

The lack of Scottish commitment to the common fishing was especially notable in the ongoing forum for discussions on economic policy established' by the Privy Council. Plenary sessions involved not only leading royal burghs but also the committee of review for the common fishing established by the Convention of Estates in 1630, whose membership included Rothes, Loudoun and Balmerino. These sessions, which were initiated at Perth in September 1631 and continued at Edinburgh in October 1632, were accompanied by a vigorous propaganda campaign that equated the vitality of the native fishing industry with the national interest. Since the prime fishing grounds around the British Isles were off the Scottish coasts, the plenary sessions tapped into a general antipathy to English adventurers being conceded any greater privileges than Dutch, French or Spanish fishermen. No attempt was made to amend or reject the charter of incorporation for the associated adventurers drawn up at court

---

37 *RPCS*, second series, IV, pp. 56–7; Macinnes, *Charles I and the Making of the Covenanting Movement*, pp. 108–14. Notwithstanding commercial rivalry with the United Provinces, the common fishing, as a confederation of self-financing provincial associations regulated by a council of prominent adventurers from all three kingdoms, was modelled on the corporate structure of the College of Herring Fishing that met yearly to regulate the operations of the Dutch fleet.

after two years of negotiation by the commissioners for both kingdoms. Nevertheless, the contents of the charter did afford specific guidance on the imposition of constitutional checks on Britannic monarchy. For Charles conceded that the Crown must ratify all ordinances passed by the governing council to ensure that they be not derogatory 'to the statutes, Laws, Liberties or acts of parliament of his Majesties kingdoms'. In turn, the governing council was to review the decisions of the common fishing's provincial associations to ensure that they be not repugnant 'to the lawes, acts of parliament nor statutes of his Majesties kingdomes'. This emphasis on safeguards resurfaced as an integral component of the National Covenant of 1638. Initially as a Scottish negotiator and subsequently as a founding fellow of the company promoting the common fishing, Lorne was highly influential in shaping the Scottish standpoint. As well as his principled commitment to the national interest, he was also intent on preserving the house of Argyll's considerable interest in the herring fishery on the western seaboard of Scotland.[38]

The main political legacy of the common fishing was the continuance, on the initiative of Lorne and other lay members of the Scottish Privy Council, of the plenary sessions on economic policy. Lorne was viewed within the Council as having particular expertise in relation to fishing, trade and fiscal matters, albeit his expertise in the latter was secondary to that the Earl of Traquair. Committed to fiscal retrenchment but not averse to using his control over Crown finances in Scotland for his own personal aggrandisement, Traquair had put aside his past association with the disaffected element opposed to the Revocation Scheme to become the foremost Scottish-based administrator, second only to the Marquess of Hamilton at Court in counselling Charles I on Scottish affairs. Traquair was a noted anti-cleric intent on limiting the influence of the bishops in the shaping of public policy. Lorne learned much from Traquair about pragmatism but little about scruples.[39]

---

38 *RPCS*, second series, IV, pp. 181, 208, 308–9, 541–2, 546–8, 551–2, 554–6; V, pp. 177, 185; *APS*, V, pp. 230–1, 239–43; ICA, Argyll Transcripts, XI, no. 392. In the event, no more than three provincial associations were formed, all headed by leading English officials. These associations were on the brink of bankruptcy by August 1638, seventeen months after their fishing activities around the Western Isles had been abandoned following systematic disruption by inhospitable landlords and clan chiefs. Sporadic preying by pirates from Dunkirk as well as Dutch warships also took its toll. Lorne and other members of the Scottish Privy Council made no effort to hold landlords and chiefs to account, nor to implement the licensing of foreign fleets once Charles decided that his *ius imperium* could better be served by fines and compositions than by naval broadsides. All three provincial associations were defunct by 1641 (W.R. Scott, *The Constitution and Finance of English, Scottish and Irish Joint-Stock Companies to 1720*, 3 vols (Cambridge, 1911–12) II, pp. 365–71; *RPCS*, second series, VI, pp. 279–80, 292, 335, 346, 457).

39 Macinnes, *Charles I and the Making of the Covenanting Movement*, pp. 61, 81, 87, 91,114–16; *RPCS*, second series, V, pp. 305–10, 408414–16; VI, p. 312, 464–5, 517.

The plenary sessions on economic policy made pertinent and constructive criticisms of the king's prerogative rule. With respect to apprehensions about unsound money, restraining imports of foreign dollars and augmenting stocks of native coin with minimum disruption to the country's commerce was duly recommended in January 1633. Having proscribed all discussion on the coinage in the coronation parliament, Charles was eventually obliged to devalue the country's silver coin not once but twice in 1636 in a despairing endeavour to check the excessive circulation of foreign dollars in Scotland.[40] Further mobilising of lay councillors and leaders of the disaffected element against the imposition of tariff reform, which would erode the cost advantage Scottish goods enjoyed in continental markets, did lead to a further significant concession in December 1636. Despite opposition from bishops on the Council, Charles agreed that tariffs on the export of Scottish staple products should not be increased from 5% to 7% of their rated value. However, Charles was already inflicting considerable damage to the country's main currency earner, the export trade in coal and salt.

Having increased imposts on English coals, Charles decreed that the custom on bulk exports from Scotland should be doubled in February 1634. Not only did this reduce the Scottish cost advantage from nine- to five-fold over English coal in the lucrative Dutch markets, but the greater risk from the pirates of Dunkirk on the longer sea voyage to the Firth of Forth induced Dutch convoys to switch back to the coal depots on the River Tyne. Trade was also severely damaged by Charles's licensing of associations in both Scotland and England for the production and wholesale distribution of salt throughout the British Isles by April 1636. The proposed Scottish association was subordinated to the English, with a strict quota imposed on bulk exports to England and tariffs equalised between both countries. There was little scope left for redirecting exports of salt from Dutch to English markets by January 1637. Ten months later, Traquair reported that the export trade in both coal and salt had undergone 'very great decay'. The plenary sessions had proved powerless to prevent an economic recession induced by the Court. Widespread redundancies among the native workforce coincided with the spread of plague from England and followed on from two years of agricultural dearth during 1635–36. Notwithstanding fears of social disorder, the manufacturing of political disorder was already on the Scottish agenda. The pursuit of religious uniformity by Charles I and his anglocentric Archbishop of Canterbury, William Laud, further politicised nonconformity.[41]

40 Spalding, *Troubles*, I, pp. 40, 44; Macinnes, *Charles I and the Making of the Covenanting Movement*, pp. 119–23. The value of Scottish silver coin, set against the Dutch *riksdaller* as the international standard, was reduced initially from 58 to 56 shillings, then to 54 shillings. This maladroit devaluation was tantamount to an indirect tax of 7% on all commercial transactions.
41 HMC, *Ninth Report*, part ii, appendix, *Traquhair Muniments* (London, 1887) pp. 247, 253;

Politicising Nonconformity

The most contentious piece of legislation in the coronation parliament was the reaffirmation of the enactment of 1606 acknowledging the royal prerogative in Church and State, in association with that of 1609 empowering James VI and I to prescribe the apparel of all legal officers as well as clergy. Thus, Charles was claiming that the right to regulate apparel – a personal concession which his father never used – was vested inherently in the Crown. Charles further ensured that the relatively innocuous issue of clerical dress remained a matter of constitutional controversy when he ordered the wearing of 'whytes', that is surplices, by the clergy from October 1633. At the behest of Laud who had stage-managed the king's coronation ceremonial on 18 July, John Spottiswood, Archbishop of St Andrews, and the five other Scottish bishops officiating had worn rochets, a practice not witnessed since the Reformation. Bishops were now to continue wearing rochets when attending affairs of State or officiating in the Kirk. Notice was duly served that a British drive for religious uniformity would be unstinting when Charles accompanied this directive with a further order that daily prayers in the chapel royal, cathedrals and universities were to be conducted according to the English liturgy, until some course be taken to devise a Scottish complement to the Book of Common Prayer.[42]

The association of clerical dress with liturgical standards and the promotion of religious conformity in England pre-dated Charles I. However, this association was given added bite with Laud's translation from the bishopric of London to the Archbishopric of Canterbury in September 1633, especially when news leaked through to Scotland about his clampdown on nonconformity in England and his threatened dissolution of the churches of foreign nations. Established in London since the 1540s, they were viewed as bastions of the Reformed tradition as received from and now under considerable threat in continental Europe on account of the Thirty Years War. Scottish Presbyterians, committed to the attainment of a godly commonwealth through the preaching of the word, inspired prayer and disciplined religious observance, remained wary of being called Puritans by their Episcopalian opponents, not least because of the schismatic tendencies associated with label in England. Nonetheless, they were increasingly prepared to make common cause as Pastors in their steadfast opposition to Catholicism and Arminianism as to prelacy and profanity.[43]

NAS, Hamilton Papers, GD 406/1/357, /1000, /8165; Macinnes, *Charles I and the Making of the Covenanting Movement*, pp. 116–9, 141.

42 Spalding, *Troubles*, I, 17–20; Row, *History of the Kirk*, 351–2, 362–3, 368–70, 376–8. Ministers were to continue to wear black gowns when preaching, but surplices were to be worn when administering the sacraments, reading divine service or carrying out burials.

43 HL, Stowe Collection: Temple Papers. STT: Religious Papers (10–11); David Calderwood,

Arminianism, which believed in universal salvation through the exercise of free will, was more a perceived than an actual threat to the Calvinist orthodoxy of the Kirk, which predestined salvation for a godly elite as the elect. The emotive association of Arminianism with Catholicism was intended primarily to highlight the danger to the Kirk from the wholesale importation of the religious standards currently in favour at the royal court. The coronation ceremonial, particularly the seeming deference of the Scottish bishops to the altar and crucifix when conducting divine service, had brought home to Scottish Calvinists that the Court rather than Rome posed the immediate threat to their Reformed tradition.[44] Nonconformity was further politicised in Scotland by the reconstitution of the Court of High Commission in October 1634, with sweeping powers to impose civil censures for ecclesiastical transgressions. The Court exercised considerable restraint in attempting to get militant Presbyterians to recognise its jurisdiction. Nevertheless, episcopal dominance of its proceedings and demarcation disputes with the Scottish Privy Council coupled fears for Presbyterianism with antipathy to the bishops, an antipathy further fuelled by the determination of Laud to promote Scottish acolytes, such as James Maxwell, Bishop of Ross and Thomas Sydserf, Bishop of Galloway. These acolytes, though never a majority of the episcopate, constituted his 'Canterburian' vanguard in Scotland, committed to the promotion of religious and political congruence at the behest of the royal court.[45]

Spurred on by the Canterburians, Archbishop Spottiswood was instrumental in bringing Haig's Supplication, which articulated the grievances of the disaffected element in the wake of the coronation parliament, to the attention of the British Court in May 1634. The Canterburians were also the prime players in the inves-

---

The Pastor and the Prelate, or Reformation and Conformitie (Edinburgh, 1636); D.G. Mullan, *Scottish Puritanism* (Oxford, 1999), pp. 13–44; M. Todd, *The Culture of Protestantism in Early Modern Scotland* (New Haven, 2002), pp. 24–83, 402–13.

44 J. MacLeod, *Scottish Theology* (Edinburgh, 1974), pp. 28–9, 85, 219; Marshall, *Presbyteries and Profits*, pp. 74–7, 103–12. Notwithstanding differences in polity between Episcopalianism and Presbyterianism, the Protestant doctrine of the Kirk of Scotland had remained staunchly Calvinist since the Reformation. The Arminian challenge, first aroused within the Dutch Reformed Kirk before spreading to the Church of England, had gained no foothold in Scotland before 1633. Arminianism accepted Calvinist orthodoxy with regard to original sin and justification by faith, but rejected its absolute belief in predestination, which offered salvation only for the elect and eternal damnation for the reprobate. Hence, the Calvinist teaching that the grace of God was irresistible for the elect, who as the true believers could not fall from grace, was renounced in favour of universal atonement. This precept offered salvation to every individual prepared to repent his or her sins. For the Arminian, therefore, the assurance of salvation was freely available for all believers but conditional on human endeavour. For the Calvinist, who believed in absolute and exclusive salvation for the elect, belief in free will was an unwarrantable limitation on the sovereignty of God.

45 *LJB*, I, pp. 424–36; Scot of Scotstarvit, *The Staggering State of Scottish Statesmen*, p. 61.

tigate commission established in July that tied Balmerino to the publication and distribution of what Charles had predetermined was a 'scandalous and seditious lybell'. They were especially vehement in seeking a treasonable indictment when Balmerino was arraigned before a judicial commission held in December. After this commission determined that the charges of leasing-making – stirring up enmity between the king and his subjects by false and malicious writing – were relevant, they attempted to influence the final selection of the assize of fifteen laymen drawn from the forty-five nobles and gentry summoned to Edinburgh to determine the extent of Balmerino's guilt for concealing, condoning and revising Haig's Supplication. Their intrusive behaviour not only aggravated tensions within the Scottish Privy Council but also alienated moderate opinion among nobles and gentry not yet aligned with the disaffected element.

Following the eventual empanelling of the assize in March 1635, the conduct of its proceedings was marked by legal chicanery as well as farce. Traquair was elected to preside even though he had served on the investigative committee that had formulated the treasonable charges. On his casting vote, Balmerino was found guilty on only one charge: that of failing to reveal that the Supplication's author was William Haig, now safely ensconced in the United Provinces. The threat of political reprisals moved Traquair to persuade Charles personally that although the guilty verdict was just, the execution of Balmerino was impolitic. Ironically, his most influential supporter at Court was Archbishop Laud, who looked to English precedent in deciding that the imposition of the death penalty by such a narrow margin was inequitable. However, the full pardon granted to Balmerino in June could not undo the crucial damage his trial had inflicted on Britannic monarchy. From its initial diet in December 1634 until its conclusion in March 1635, the trial was held against a continuous backdrop of prayer meetings for the comfort of Balmerino, reinforced by political agitation that exposed Charles I's lack of effective forces of coercion, never mind persuasion, in Scotland.[46]

The demonstrable polarity between the bishops and the lay councillors was exploited by Traquair to project himself as the main check to the political

---

46 *State Trials*, W. Cobbet ed., 33 vols (London, 1809–28), III, pp. 593–603, 689–712; [Burnet], *History of My Own Times*, I, pp. 12–4; Balfour, *HW*, II, pp. 216–9. Notwithstanding the objections of the defence counsel, the discredited fiscal entrepreneur and courtier Strachan of Thornton was not obliged to stand down. William Keith, 6th Earl Marischal subsequently claimed that he had been filed in favour of a conviction because he was asleep when the vote to acquit was taken. In May 1634, a plenary session of councillors, burgesses and members of the disaffected element broke off from their discussions on economic policy to reject the king's appointment of Alexander Lindsay, Lord Spynie, as muster-master and colonel of the trained bands in Scotland. This initiative, which was a blatant attempt to import the English practice of financing an elite militia, would have created a standing army at no cost to the monarchy.

ambitions of the Canterburians. However, Traquair's strategy depended upon his retention of substantial support from the middle ground in Scottish politics. This support could no longer be guaranteed in the wake of Balmerino's trial. Antipathy toward the appointment of the aged Spottiswood as chancellor in December 1634, the first bishop to hold the office since the Reformation, and the aggressive posturing of the Canterburians, persuaded more discontented lay officials to give covert counselling to the disaffected. In effect, the bishops were politically isolated and, simultaneously, public disillusionment spread about the capacity of the Privy Council to prevent Scotland being treated as a province. By the time Charles's plans for further liturgical innovation were clarified in the autumn of 1635, the divisions within his Scottish administration stood in stark contrast to the cohesiveness of the disaffected element in defence of the national interest. At this critical juncture, Lorne made a pre-emptive strike.[47]

Lorne's target was the Canterburian Bishop of Galloway, Thomas Sydserf who, in July 1636, decided that the prosecution of noted nonconformists by the Court of High Commission should be renewed within his diocese. The refusal of Alexander Gordon of Earlston to appear before that Court was met by a fine of 500 merks (£333) and his banishment to Montrose in Angus. Samuel Rutherford, minister in the parish of Anwoth and a noted critic of episcopacy, the Five Articles of Perth and Arminianism, was duly banished to Aberdeen. Lorne exploited the general outcry in Galloway to widen the breach between the bishops and the lay councillors. Concerned that the Court of High Commission was being deployed against lay as well as clerical nonconformists, the Privy Council intervened in favour of Earlston, dispensing with his banishment on condition he paid his fine. Lay councillors were 'highly offended' by Bishop Sydserf's querulous acceptance of this decision, particularly as his offensive against nonconformists in Galloway had coincided with the harvest, which had ensured that the High Commission depended on episcopal adherents for its quorum.[48]

Lorne was not certainly demonstrating that he was no less anti-clerical than Traquair in relation to the Canterburians. But his targeting of Sydserf cannot be dismissed as an act of pique because he was reputedly passed over for the chancellorship in favour of Archbishop Spottiswood. Lorne claimed to be acting

47 *Diary of Sir Thomas Hope of Craighall, 1634–45*, T. Thomson ed. (Edinburgh, 1843), pp. 45–6, 51, 58; Row, *History of the Kirk*, pp. 385–6, 392–406. Forewarned by Laud's securing of the appointment of William Juxon, Bishop of London as treasurer in England, Traquhair outmanoeuvred Bishop Maxwell of Ross for this office when it became vacant in 1636.

48 *Letters of Samuel Rutherford*, A.A. Bonar ed., 2 vols (Edinburgh, 1863), I, pp. 39, 148–9, 157–62, 164; *LJB*, I, pp. 8–9, 16; *RPCS*, second series, VI, p. 359. The Court of High Commission also suspended Robert Glendinning from his ministry in Kirkcudbright. When the magistrates of the burgh refused to enforce the warrant of the High Commission, they were placed in custody in Wigtown.

on behalf of his nephew and ward John Gordon, 2nd Viscount Kenmure, patron of the parish of Earlston. Indeed, Lorne and Gordon of Earlston were both creditors and trustees for the heavily indebted Kenmure estates that were facing legal action instigated by the Bishop of Galloway to reclaim kirklands.[49] Yet, territorial interests cannot be isolated from religious principles. Both Samuel Rutherford and Lorne's late brother-in-law Robert, 1st Viscount Kenmure were not only Presbyterian nonconformists, but conventiclers. Grouped covertly in praying societies, conventiclers saw themselves as guardians of Scotland's Covenanting tradition. Private meetings for collective devotion sustained the purity of the Kirk. Periodic fasting maintained collective as well as personal discipline. Their militant sense of righteousness reinforced their assurance that they were God's elect on earth. Revitalised by the imposition of the Five Articles of Perth, conventicling circuits established for preaching and administering nonconforming communions had spread from Edinburgh to Fife, to west-central and south-west Scotland, and on into Ulster. The conventiclers were also supported by Anna Cunningham, Dowager Marchioness of Hamilton and mother of the 3rd Marquess, Margaret Campbell, Lady Loudoun, the Edinburgh lawyer Archibald Johnston of Wariston, and a leavening of leading burgesses and their wives in Scotland's capital city. Lorne became partial to their cause through religious conviction as much as by family association or political pragmatism.[50]

William Lithgow from Lanark, much travelled throughout Europe, Asia and Africa, penned an admonition to Charles I that the coronation parliament had not addressed the grievances of the commonwealth. At the same time, he eulogised the Scottish nobility, extolling the Marquess of Hamilton and highly commending the future Marquess of Montrose. Lorne was merely mentioned as an also-ran rather than as a future statesman. When Sir William Brereton, the English traveller and future Parliamentarian commander, had conversations with disaffected gentry and ministers in Edinburgh during June 1635, Lorne was not cited as either a sympathiser or a politician to watch.[51] Yet the Galloway

---

49 *MHG*, p. 14; Spalding, *Troubles*, I, p. 46; RPCS, second series, V, pp. 563–4; ICA, Argyll Letters (1602–38), A 36/58 and Argyll Transcripts, XI, nos 354, 419, 445; ABDA, Argyll Papers, 40.215, .294; HL, Loudoun Scottish Collection, box 5/ LO 8054–5. Lorne had also been involved in litigation to secure kirklands in Kintyre that had belonged to the Priory of Whithorn and were claimed by the bishopric of Galloway.

50 D. Stevenson, 'Conventicles in the Kirk, 1619–1637', *RSCHS*, 18 (1972–74), pp. 99–114; A.I. Macinnes, *Charles I and the Making of the Covenanting Movement*, pp. 155–8. Their eclectic image, not dissimilar to that of the Puritans in New England, subsequently exposed them to charges of separatism from within the Covenanting Movement.

51 William Lithgow, *Scotlands Welcome to her Native Sonne, and Soveraigne Lord, King Charles* (Edinburgh, 1633); Sir William Brereton, *Travels in Holland, the United Provinces, England, Scotland and Ireland 1634–35*, E. Hawkins ed. (London, 1844), pp. 100–1.

affair demonstrated to the political nation that Lorne was not thirled to imperial British monarchy under the Stuarts. But there was no indication by 1637 that he would seek to counter imperialism by promoting constitutional limitations in Kirk and State; that he would seek to redefine regal union as confederal; or, indeed, that he would favour Presbyterianism over episcopacy for the visionary fulfilment of the Protestant Reformation. Conversely, his partial exploitation of frontier policy and the Revocation Scheme to suit the interests of the house of Argyll, and his subversion of economic and religious uniformity, confirmed that his standpoint towards the Crown, both as a Gaelic chief and a Scottish magnate, was at best equivocal, verging on confrontational.

FIVE

The Covenanting Leader, 1637–1640

The outbreak of rebellion in Ireland in October 1641 built up the momentum initiated by the Covenanting Movement in Scotland for resistance towards Charles I in England. This has long been recognised.[1] However, Ireland had an understated significance not only in shaping the Scottish revolution against Charles I but also in Lorne's emergence as the radical leader of the Covenanting Movement. Promotion of religious uniformity in Ireland in 1634–35 served as an exemplary warning for Scots opposed to the liturgical innovations at which Charles hinted in October 1633. Nonconformity was further politicised when the Canterburian vanguard among the Irish bishops attempted to root out conventiclers from Ulster. Their exodus strengthened the common cause of conventicling with the disaffected in Scotland. Randal, 2nd Earl of Antrim, who had married the widow of the royal favourite Buckingham, was a well connected if peripheral figure at the royal court, just like Archibald, 7th Earl of Argyll. Both were antipathetic to Lorne. Both knew from first-hand experience that the territorial acquisitiveness of Lorne would be a particularly potent factor in ensuring a ready reservoir of support for Charles I among the clans. For the Crown possessed the only legitimate authority to check the house of Argyll. Of the fifty major clans within the *Gàidhealtachd*, thirty-three came within the ClanCampbell's spheres of influence. Of this cohort, sixteen were incorporated wholly or in part within Campbell overlordship; five were being threatened with their loss of feudal superiority; and the remainder, with various degrees of reluctance, operated effectively as clients.[2] In 1639, Thomas Wentworth (later Earl of Strafford), as Lord-Deputy of Ireland and a close ally of Archbishop Laud, imposed the 'black oath' that required political as well as religious conformity from Scottish settlers in Ulster after the emergence of the Covenanting Movement. In the process, Wentworth signalled to the Scottish

---

1 Russell, *The Fall of the British Monarchies*, pp. 27–205, 305–9; D. Hirst, *England in Conflict, 1603–60: Kingdom, Community, Commonwealth* (London, 1999), pp. 156–90; Woolrych, *Britain in Revolution*, pp. 189–233.
2 Macinnes, *Clanship, Commerce and the House of Stuart*, pp. 247–9.

settlers that their participation in frontier policy and other British endeavours could not be relied upon.

Religious Rioting

At the Convocation of Protestant clergy in 1634–35, James Ussher, Archbishop of Armagh and primate of the Church of Ireland, fought a valiant rearguard action to uphold Calvinist orthodoxy. Nevertheless, James Bramhall, Bishop of Derry and Laud's principal acolyte in Ireland, moved the Convocation to impose religious uniformity. The Canons that were duly prescribed for the Church of Ireland, with the backing of Wentworth, signposted the fact that religious uniformity was not to be just Anglican but distinctly Arminian. This aggressive, Canterburian imposition was particularly unfavourable to Scottish Presbyterians in the Ulster plantations. By upholding royal supremacy in ecclesiastical affairs, the Canons abrogated disciplinary powers to bishops, who were held accountable only to the Crown not to church courts. The resultant clampdown on nonconformity was accompanied by a distinctive Scotophobia among the Canterburians, who viewed the Irish Canons as an improvement on current English practice.[3]

A small, but zealous, band of Scottish Presbyterians composed less than a tenth of the Protestant ministry in Ulster. Their vulnerability to a concerted attack by Irish and Scottish bishops had been demonstrated in 1631. Robert Blair and John Livingstone, ministers in the diocese of Down, were suspended for participating in revivalist meetings organised as communions for conventiclers on both sides of the North Channel. Ulster conventiclers were acutely exposed by the Episcopalian offensive co-ordinated by Laud and Bramhall in the wake of the passage of the Irish Canons. Blair and Livingstone were excommunicated. Their Presbyterian associates were deposed for nonconformity. In September 1636, around 140 nonconformists from Ulster and Scotland seeking release 'from the bondage of prelates' embarked for New England. Although their ship neared Newfoundland, tempestuous weather forced their return to Scotland by November, a reversal interpreted as divine intervention.[4]

The influx of Ulster nonconformists hardened the resolve of Scottish

---

3 J. McCafferty, '"God bless your free Church of Ireland": Wentworth, Laud, Bramhall and the Irish Convocation of 1634' in J.F. Merritt ed., *The Political World of Thomas Wentworth, Earl of Strafford, 1621–1641* (Cambridge, 1996) pp. 187–208; A.L. Capern, 'The Caroline Church: James Ussher and the Irish Dimension', *HJ*, 39 (1996), pp. 57–85; HL, Hastings Irish Papers, box 7/HA 15162–3, 15165, 15168.

4 *Autobiography of the Life of Mr Robert Blair*, T. McCrie ed. (Edinburgh, 1848), pp. 57–148; *Select Biographies*, W.K. Tweedie ed., 2 vols (Edinburgh, 1845–7), I, pp. 134–57, 344; Patrick Adair, *A True Narrative of the Rise and Progress of the Presbyterian Church in Ireland (1623–1670)*, W.D. Killen ed. (Belfast, 1866), pp. 16–51.

conventiclers to resist further liturgical innovations. The Scottish *Canons and Constitutions Ecclesiastical*, known colloquially as the Book of Canons, was published in Aberdeen in January 1636. The *Book of Common Prayer and Administration of the Sacraments* became known as the Service Book after its first appearance in draft in Edinburgh in April 1637. The Book of Canons made no commitment to general assemblies as the supreme national court in the Kirk. All clergy and laity who refused to acknowledge the royal supremacy in ecclesiastical affairs, episcopal government unfettered by presbyteries, or future liturgical innovations faced excommunication. The Service Book's proposed liturgical innovations had accommodated Scottish sensibilities, however. Lessons from the Apocrypha in the English Book of Common Prayer favoured by Laud were removed for scriptural unsoundness. Nevertheless, the fifteen months that elapsed between both publications afforded the disaffected ample time to plan a concerted attack. As both books were introduced solely on the strength of the royal prerogative, they were deemed unconstitutional. They were both held to suborn the received Reformed tradition, especially for according precedence to the altar for observance of the sacraments over the pulpit for the preaching of the word. The religious association of liturgical innovation with British uniformity was a step too far in the relegation of Scotland from a kingdom to a province. The deliberate targeting of Laud for his malicious influence allowed the disaffected to portray themselves as the defenders of the national interest without launching an outright attack on Charles I. [5] Contemporary accusations of popery against Laud, which were damaging because of the close association of Protestantism and patriotism in England, were made the more heinous in Scotland by the imposition of sacerdotalism as a provincial exercise. The Canterburians were castigated as the 'English faction'.[6]

---

5 Row, *History of the Kirk*, pp. 392–406; Gordon, *HSA*, I, pp. 3–7; Macinnes, *Charles I and the Making of the Covenanting Movement*, pp. 147–9, 158–61. The contents of the Service Book became known in advance of publication through a combination of impolitic delays in drafting, deliberate leakage of episcopal intentions from within the Privy Council and wanton incompetence on the part of the principal printer. Robert Young had allowed discarded sheets from his printing house to be recycled as wrapping paper for tobacco and spices purchased from Edinburgh shops.

6 *LJB*, I, pp. 30, 113; Sharpe, *The Personal Rule of Charles I*, pp. 285–6, 305–8, 837–9; C. Hibbert, *Charles I and the Popish Plot* Chapel Hill NC, 1983), pp. 38–71; P. Lake, 'The Laudian Style: Order, Uniformity and the Pursuit of Holiness in the 1630s' in K. Fincham ed., *The Early Stuart Church,1603–1642* (Basingstoke, 1993) pp. 161–85. Laud consistently deplored the fashionable Catholicism of the Court clique associated with Queen Henrietta Maria. He was notably resistant to their lobbying of the papacy for a cardinal's hat for George Con, an expatriate Scot within the Vatican bureaucracy who had arrived at Court as papal envoy to the queen in 1636.

The most critical error of Charles I, Archbishop Laud and the Canterburians was their collective failure to realise that liturgical innovations could not be isolated from a patently inhospitable, political setting. Although Laud had never challenged the Marquess of Hamilton's paramount responsibility at Court for managing civil affairs, he was prepared to defer only to the king in the conduct of ecclesiastical affairs in Scotland. He demanded and was given editorial control for both text and copy over the liturgical innovations planned by Charles to meet the want of uniformity in discipline and worship between Scotland and the other two kingdoms. Notwithstanding Laud's claims that he was upholding Reformed tradition, charges from the Calvinist mainstream in both Scotland and England that the king and Laud were innovators in the pursuit of religious uniformity were irrefutable. Liturgical innovations that favoured sacerdotalism and Arminianism were received in Scotland as little better than a divisive exercise insinuating not Anglicanism but Catholicism – a deliberate subterfuge by a Romanised court in conjunction with 'popishlie affected Bishops'.[7]

The conviction of Scottish Calvinists that direct action was necessary to defend Reformed tradition of the Kirk and to counteract ungodly monarchy in the State led to premeditated rioting in 1637 and the issue of the National Covenant in 1638. But resistance was not the preserve of the conventiclers who, as a pressure group, acted as catalysts for rather than instigators of revolution. The conventiclers were not convinced that the nobles who led the disaffected element were intent on the pursuit of godliness. Nonetheless, the disaffected leadership came to appreciate the ideological advantage of such an association. The conventiclers were foremost among nonconforming Presbyterians advocating communal banding in covenants as the alternative religious standard to the liturgical innovations promoted by Charles and Archbishop Laud. Combining the covenant of grace with that of works not only assured the righteous of their temporal as well as their spiritual calling, it also affirmed the special relationship between God and Scotland, whose people were heirs to ancient Israel as a covenanted nation. Covenanting in Scotland was a means of communicating symbolically a fundamental ideological message: opposition to the royal prerogative in defence of religious and civil liberty was divinely warranted.[8]

The rioting that greeted readings from the Service Book in Edinburgh on 23 July merely appeared spontaneous. Although Rothes, Loudoun and Balmerino

---

7 *The Works of William Laud D.D.*, J. Bliss ed., 5 vols (Oxford, 1853), III, pp. 278, 310–5, 372–6, 427–8; *LJB*, I, pp. 4–8.

8 J.B. Torrance, 'The Covenant Concept in Scottish Theology and Politics and its Legacy', *Scottish Journal of Theology*, 34 (1981), pp. 225–43; Macinnes, *Charles I and the Emergence of the Covenanting Movement*, pp. 156–8.

were ever wary of attracting official surveillance, the covert discipline of the conventiclers enabled the disaffected leadership to prepare discreetly.[9] There is a contemporaneous presumption when reviewing the revolutionary troubles in Scotland that Lorne was present at the initial planning of public demonstrations against the Service Book at the end of April. This cannot be established and is highly unlikely, as he was corresponding from the royal court to Loudoun on 8 May. Indeed, the leading lay councillor who met with Balmerino and two prominent nonconforming ministers, Alexander Henderson from Leuchars in Fife and David Dickson from Irvine in Ayrshire, was not Lorne but Sir Thomas Hope of Craighall. As the Lord Advocate, he was the king's chief prosecutor in Scotland. Dickson was sympathetic to conventicling, Henderson was not. The riots were set up by Canterburian pressure on the Privy Council on 13 June to reissue the king's order of 20 December 1636 that every parish must be provided with two copies of the Service Book within fifteen days. When this order was generally ignored, David Lindsay, Bishop of Edinburgh persuaded his colleagues to issue an episcopal edict, independent of the Privy Council on 16 July, that the Service Book would be read in all churches in and around Edinburgh on Sunday 23 June. Charles I concurred. Laud was less sanguine. While not opposed to exemplary readings from the Service Book, he was apprehensive that the issuing of one week's formal notice would encourage the disaffected to stage public demonstrations. His apprehensions were duly borne out by the hostile reception accorded in the capital, particularly in St Giles Cathedral. These demonstrations, however, were the culmination of three months' planning, not one week's notice.[10]

Planning for protest had actually been finalised by 6 July 1637, ten days before the episcopal edict for exemplary readings was actually issued. A meeting in Edinburgh convened by Henderson and Dickson was attended by at least ten other nonconforming ministers from west and central Scotland as well as Fife and the Lothians. The main business of the meeting was to identify all 'corruptions' contained in the Service Book that would prepare the ground for a reasoned case to be made by nonconforming ministers against its imposition by the bishops. In turn, the Privy Council was to be petitioned to suspend use of the Service Book as lacking constitutional warrant from a general assembly, as importing Anglican usages against the national interest and, above all, as

---

9 *Letters of Samuel Rutherford*, I, pp. 59, 69, 102–5, 107, 111, 117, 134, 148–9, 159, 163, 167, 214, 274, 277; *Wariston Diary* I, pp. 206, 250, 256–9, 262; HL, Loudoun Scottish Collection, box 5/ LO 8054.

10 Spalding, *Troubles*, I, pp. 47, 55–6; Rothes, *Relation*, pp. 1–3; *LJB*, I, pp. 1–2, 16–18, 445; Gordon, *HSA*, I, pp. 3–7; *MHG*, pp. 19–24; *RPCS*, second series, VI, pp. 352–5, 448–9; *Diary of Sir Thomas Hope*, pp. 57, 60–1.

its popish leanings were inimical to the Reformed tradition of the Kirk. In the event of the bishops ordering exemplary readings, the 'weill affected' in Edinburgh were to protest by walking out of divine services and absenting themselves from church until the Service Book was withdrawn. On the day following this meeting, prominent conventiclers were placed on stand-by to lead public demonstrations. Lorne had already arrived in Edinburgh to resume attending the Privy Council.[11]

Clerical endeavours to read the Service Book in three churches in the capital on the morning of 23 July duly encountered public demonstrations. However, rumbustious behaviour went far beyond the premeditated protests. The political impact of the demonstration in St Giles was particularly significant: less on account of the celebrated stool-throwing by matrons from the mercantile community associated with conventicling, or even for the attempts of the rioters to strip the Bishop and the Dean of Edinburgh of more than their ecclesiastical garments. The rioting was conducted in the presence of the Archbishop of St Andrews, numerous bishops and lay councillors, as well as the magistrates and town council of Edinburgh. Lorne was almost certainly present at the morning rioting and later at the afternoon reading ordered by the Archbishop of St Andrews to be conducted behind closed doors. Rioting continued in the streets on the Sunday afternoon. When Bishop Lindsay left the afternoon service at St Giles and was bound for Holyroodhouse, where the Privy Council usually sat, the coach in which he was travelling was attacked by a mob throwing stones, counterfeit and debased coins, and any other missiles readily to hand. A report prepared for Lorne, almost certainly by Archibald Campbell of Glencarradale, and circulated among the Covenanting leadership, highlighted the acute discomfort of Bishop Lindsay, who never in his lifetime 'got such a laxative purgation; for requytal of the paines of his open-handed apothecaries he franklie bestowed upon them all the gold of his Low Countries'.[12]

Partly because of the violence of hostile mobs, and partly because of the reluctance of the Scottish administration (Lorne included) to investigate the social standing of those who instigated the public demonstrations, official accounts from Edinburgh blamed the riots on 'the meaner sort of people', especially serving women and apprentice boys. By having the political sagacity to adopt a low profile during the public demonstrations, and by remaining in the background until the rioting in Edinburgh had abated, the disaffected

11 J.M. Henderson, '"An Advertisement" about the Service Book, 1637', *SHR*, 32 (1925–26), pp. 199–204; *Wariston Diary* I, p. 262; *RPCS*, second series, VI, pp. 476–7.
12 Rothes, *Relation*, pp. 195–201; *RPCS*, second series, VI, 445–6, 483–4; [Balcanqual], *A Declaration Concerning the Late Tumults in Scotland*, pp. 21–6; Row, *History of the Kirk*, pp. 407–10; Gordon, *HSA*, I, 7–14.

leadership was well placed to capitalise on the populist reaction against the Service Book. Indeed, such was the scale of violent protest that the disaffected leadership could pose as defenders of the Crown, 'by whose authority abused', the bishops had imposed the Service Book. Maximum political capital was also extracted over the next month from the buck-passing between the Privy Council and the town council of Edinburgh for apprehending the instigators and perpetrators of the riots. Lorne was party to this buck-passing, but he diplomatically absented himself from the session on 29 July when the Council suspended the use of the Service Book.[13]

By this juncture, bishops and lay officials were more intent on blackening each other at the royal court than on upholding the monarchical position within Scotland. Lorne would appear to have engaged in neither practice. On 10 August, the bishops again acted unilaterally to enforce the order of 13 July requiring the purchase of two Service Books for every parish in Scotland. On this occasion, it was not the Canterburians but the two archbishops, John Spottiswood of St Andrews and Patrick Lindsay of Glasgow, who took the initiative. Their directive was duly challenged by Henderson and Dickson as representatives of the nonconforming clergy in the respective archdiocese, who concerted a formal protest to the Privy Council against this measure on 23 August. The substance of their complaints against the episcopal edict followed the guidelines drawn up on 6 July castigating the Service Book for its unconstitutional introduction, its insinuation of popery and its subverting of the doctrine and worship practised in the Kirk since the Reformation.[14]

The danger of public demonstrations made the prosecution of Henderson, Dickson and their nonconforming associates politically inexpedient, a situation appreciated by the disaffected leadership when restricting the scale of protest against the episcopal edict of 10 August. Physical support from the disaffected outwith the west and Fife was not encouraged. The alternative strategy of briefing sympathetic nobles and gentry to write or lobby lay councillors struck a responsive chord. Assertion of lay influence on 24 August moved the Council to set aside a royal letter calling for the prompt apprehension of the instigators of the demonstrations in Edinburgh and the expeditious promotion of the Service Book throughout Scotland. Instead, the Council at last chose to inform Charles I officially that the political state of affairs in his northern kingdom was now critical. The Council was not prepared to countenance the compulsory imposition of the Service Book until further consultations were held at Court. The

---

13 *RPCS*, second series, VI, pp. 486–90, 508–16; *BLJ*, I, pp. 18–19; *Wariston Diary* I, pp. 265–6; Rothes, *Relation*, 3–5; *Historical Collections*, J. Rushworth ed., vols I–III (London, 1680–91), II, pp. 387–90, 393–5. The alternative use of the English liturgy was also suspended.

14 *LJB*, I, pp. 12–13, 19, 32, 449–51; Balfour, *HW*, II, pp. 227–31; Row, *History of the Kirk*, p. 484.

response from the king was not anticipated until 20 September. This crisis was further compounded by rioting in Glasgow on Thursday 30 August, following rumours that a sermon favourable to liturgical innovations had been preached to the diocesan synod the previous day. This rioting was no less violent than in Edinburgh and again involved women associated with conventicling. The magistrates and town council of Glasgow also made no meaningful effort to investigate or apprehend those responsible for the rioting. The stage was now set for the nationwide mobilisation of the disaffected, a mobilisation whose gathering momentum has been described perceptively as 'crisis by monthly instalments'. Lorne was to play no public part for three months. Having taken his leave from Edinburgh on 10 August, he did not return to active service on the Privy Council until 15 November.[15]

Rights of Resistance

In the interim, the disaffected leadership broadened their strategy of resistance. Orderly lobbying in Edinburgh by nobles, gentry, burgesses and ministers was bolstered by sixty-eight standardised, but not stereotyped, petitions from burghs, parishes and presbyteries. Protests were synthesised into the National Petition of 20 September, which called for an end to liturgical innovations. With no offer of constructive dialogue from the royal court, petitioning reinforced by mass lobbying then attacked the prerogative rule of Charles I, but not the office of monarchy. David Dickson drafted the National Supplication of 17 October, which first served notice that the disaffected must suffer ruination or endure divine retribution for 'breach of our covenant with God, and forsaking the way of true religion'. Their divine obligation to supplicate was thus elevated above their duty to obey royal orders to disperse. The leadership's controlled militancy was underscored the next day. At the request of Traquair and other lay councillors, they dispersed the mobbing of Bishop Sydserf, which was not as long as but was of greater intensity than the rioting against the Service Book on 23 July.[16]

Grass-roots petitioning and mass lobbying in Edinburgh were initially organised on an informal basis. From November, co-ordination was directed effectively by Tables of the nobles, gentry, burgesses and clergy. Each political estate composed a Table, with representatives from the other three joining the nobles to form a revolutionary executive that was acclaimed as the fifth Table at the outset of December. Lorne had returned to public affairs by this juncture.

15 NLS, Morton Cartulary and Letters, MS 79, fo.56; Gordon, *HSA*, I, pp. 14–16; *LJB*, I, 19–21, 451–2; *MHG*, pp. 24–5; *RPCS*, second series, VI, pp. 521, 694; Stevenson, *The Scottish Revolution*, p. 74.
16 Rothes, *Relation*, pp. 5–23, 47–50; Macinnes, *Charles I and the Making of the Covenanting Movement*, pp. 166–73.

Successive orders from the king that the Privy Council remove from Edinburgh to Linlithgow, then on to Dalkeith and Stirling, allowed the Tables to assume political responsibility for the state of the nation from 15 November 1637. On its own initiative, the Council chose Traquair and a few others, including Lorne, to journey to the capital in order to confer privately with the disaffected leadership. Although Traquair was intent on temporising, Lorne advised against reliance on mass lobbying and encouraged the Tables to act responsibly as a properly constituted body. Lord Advocate Hope went further in affirming that the disaffected were legally entitled 'to choose Commissioners for Parliament, for Conventions of Estates, or for any Public business'. As a result of these discussions, the disaffected leadership claimed warrant from the Council to extend their representation on the basis of every noble prepared to identify with their cause, two gentry from every shire, at least one commissioner from every burgh, and one minister from every presbytery. The composition of all five Tables was altered constantly, but deliberately, over the next three months, in order to spread the burden of political responsibility and financial commitment.[17]

Charles was determined to make no concessions to the Tables that could only offer encouragement to the Puritans and other disaffected in England. He had the full backing of Laud, but not of his Scottish Privy Council. The Tables were now scaling up their protests, not only against liturgical innovations but also against the Court of High Commission as a prerogative court. They were also ready to decline the authority of the bishops in civil and religious affairs. Prior to their dispersal from Edinburgh on 22 December, the Tables elected a holding committee dominated by Rothes, Loudoun and Balmerino, whose principal remit was to monitor the movement of leading officials and councillors to and from the royal court. This task was facilitated by Lorne's offer of 29 December to act as 'ane intelligencer for the Tables'. Duly forewarned of an unfavourable response from the court, the holding committee summoned the Tables back to Edinburgh on 6 February 1638. In the course of a mass protest against the continuing intransigence of Charles I, the fifth Table was acknowledged publicly as leaders of a provisional government for Scotland on 22 February. Six days later, it authorised the National Covenant. Johnston of Wariston,

---

17 *LJB*, I, pp. 40–2, 46–51, 54–62; Spalding, *Troubles*, I, pp. 48–50; Row, *History of the Kirk*, pp. 485–6, 488–9; NLS, Salt and Coal: Events, 1635–62, MS 2263, ff.89–92; *The Government of Scotland under the Covenanters, 1637–51*, D. Stevenson ed. (Edinburgh, 1982), pp. xii–xvi. The use of the term 'Tables' allowed the disaffected to draw upon established administrative practice to convey the image of acting in the national interest without claiming official status. In turn, the recourse of the Estates to separate meetings – a practice in place since September 1637 – rather than a unicameral convention meant that the four Tables did not abrogate the formal standing of a parliament for Scotland. Nevertheless, the Tables were installed in the Parliament House by 6 December.

an Edinburgh lawyer of undoubted personal piety, and also a conventicler zealously committed to the triumph of Presbyterianism, drew up this revolutionary manifesto. An insomniac of prodigious energy, Wariston had readily penned rebuttals to royal proclamations against the disaffected: rebuttals that called for fundamental checks on the prerogative rule by drawing selectively on biblical sources, Roman law commentaries and parliamentary precedents. In pressing for free constituent assemblies to redress past and prevent future excesses of royal authoritarianism, he was assisted by Alexander Henderson. Having masterminded the riots against the Service Book, Henderson went on to co-ordinate appeals from the pulpit for nationwide commitment to the Tables.[18]

The National Covenant was a revolutionary enterprise, a social compact that bound the Scottish people to justify and consolidate revolt against Britannic monarchy. Its conservative format and appeal to precedents has belied its radical intent. All four Tables having approved the finalised version before subscriptions commenced, its appearance of unanimity was not deceptive. It deliberately maintained a studied ambiguity not just to attract support from all classes and from every locality, but primarily to avoid specific imputations of treason. The National Covenant was not concerned with the details of how power should be exercised or who should fill offices and places on council and committees. Nevertheless, by prescribing broad principles of governance, it established a written constitution for Scotland that asserted the independence of a sovereign people under God.

Its first component rehearsed the Negative Confession of 1581 which denied all religion and doctrine, especially all forms of popery, inimical to orthodox Calvinism as received at the Reformation. Loyalty to the Crown was made conditional on expunging idolatrous, superstitious and popish practices from the Kirk; protecting the purity of the reformed tradition; and upholding the rights of the Scots people to be governed according to the common laws of the realm as grounded in statute. Precedents for the removal of erroneous doctrines and prejudicial practices culminated with the codification of the penal laws against Catholic recusants in 1609. An uncompromising Protestant crusade to ward off the unabated threat from the Counter-Reformation was thus pressed. The attack on Episcopacy was contained within the resolve of the Tables to sweep away all innovations, not just religious, which had threatened national independence and the subjects' liberties since the regal union.

18 *RPCS*, second series, VI, pp. 545–54; *CSP, Venetian* (1636–39), pp. 362, 370, 379–80, 387, 394–5; Gordon, *HSA*, I, pp. 27–36, 38–42; *Wariston Diary* I, pp. 282, 288–90, 292–7, 302–4, 307–12, 316–19; EUL, Laing MSS, La.I.291. D. Stevenson, *King or Covenant? Voices from the Civil War* (East Linton, 1996), pp. 151–73, has postulated that Wariston was a manic depressive. The jury remains out.

Its second component elaborated the concept of a twofold contract, which encapsulated the dual imperatives of covenanting by drawing on historical and political as well as biblical precepts. Opposition to prerogative rule was inspired principally by the monarchomach ideology of French Huguenots, and to a lesser extent of Dutch Calvinists, then by the legacy of resistance to ungodly monarch espoused by John Knox at the Reformation and rationalised in its aftermath by George Buchanan. The religious covenant was a tripartite compact between the king and people to God to uphold religious purity that replaced the Israelites with the Scots in the role of chosen people. Whereas obedience to God was unconditional and irresistible, the people's obligations to the king were limited. If the king betrayed his people to God, the people had a positive duty to resist. Operating within this religious framework was a constitutional covenant between the king and the people for maintenance of good and lawful government and a just political order. If the king failed to uphold the fundamental laws and liberties of the kingdom, or sought to subvert his subjects' privileges or estates, the people were entitled to take appropriate remedial action. Final determination of all religious and civil issues was to be left to general assemblies and parliaments free from the censorious royal management evident during the coronation visit.[19]

Its third and most revolutionary component was the oath of allegiance and mutual association. Subscribers were required to swear that they would 'stand to the defence of our dread Soveraigne, the Kings Majesty, his Person and Authority, in the defence and preservation of the foresaid true Religion, Liberties and Lawes of the Kingdome'. This commitment was conditional. Loyalty was reserved for a covenanted king. In so far as he accepted the religious and constitutional imperatives of the National Covenant, the king was to be defended. There was no necessary incompatibility in promising to defend royal authority while simultaneously promoting policies contrary to the professed interests of Charles I. Resistance to Charles I was in the long-term interests of monarchy and people if the kingdom was to be restored to godly rule. The revolutionary oath upheld the corporate right of the people to resist a lawful king who threatened to become tyrannical. Such resistance was to be exercised by the natural leaders of society, not the nobles exclusively but the Tables as the corporate embodiment of the inferior magistrates imbued with civic virtue.[20]

---

19 *A Source Book of Scottish History*, III, pp. 95–104; *APS*, V (1626–40), pp. 272–6; Burns, *The True Law of Kingship*, pp. 122–52, 185–221.

20 Rothes, *Relation*, pp. 90–2, 96–8, 100–2, 211; D. Stevenson, *The Covenanters: The National Covenant and Scotland* (Edinburgh, 1988), pp. 35–44; A.I. Macinnes, 'Covenanting Ideology in the Seventeenth Century Scotland' in J.H. Ohlmeyer ed., *Political Thought in Seventeenth Century Ireland* (Cambridge, 2000), pp. 191–220.

As well as equipping the Tables with the rhetoric of defiance, the National Covenant provided the political will to effect revolution. In the week following its issue in Edinburgh, copies of the National Covenant were prepared for subscription in all leading towns and cities, universities and rural parishes. Initially, subscription was to be confined to communicants. But, carried along by popular enthusiasm and concerted propaganda spearheaded by Henderson, stress was laid on covenanting as the manifestation of the willingness, the holiness and the multiplication of the Scots as a chosen people. Communion became available only to the covenanted. Earthly vengeance as well as divine retribution awaited those not moved to covenant with God. Notwithstanding this implacable resolve, a committee for Scottish affairs was not instituted at the royal court for another five months.[21]

Constitutional Defiance

In the three months prior to the promulgation of the National Covenant, Lorne had established himself as the political broker within the Privy Council notably sympathetic to the Tables. In the immediate aftermath of the National Covenant, Lorne was duly invited to court with Treasurer-Depute Traquair for discussions on the deteriorating political situation within Scotland. Although Lorne's membership of this delegation was welcomed by the Covenanting leadership, they were also apprehensive that he would either be won over by Charles I or detained at court, as was in fact recommended by his father, the 7th Earl of Argyll and some of the bishops. Whereas Traquair cautioned against the use of force, he did not rule it out. He joined with Lorne in pressing for the Marquess of Hamilton to be sent north as the king's commissioner to treat with the Covenanting leadership.[22] The month Lorne spent at court in the spring of 1638 was primarily for information gathering. Among the inner advisers of Charles I, Hamilton was the foremost advocate of a negotiated solution. But, Lorne became acutely aware of the coercive faction led by Archbishop Laud and egged on from Ireland by Lord-Deputy Wentworth. At the outset of May, Charles had allowed Lorne to travel back to Scotland in a coach with Traquair and, rather quixotically, with his episcopal *bête noir*, Bishop Sydserf. In the following week, Hamilton was commissioned formally to act on the king's behalf in Scotland. Lorne was fully cognisant this was no more than a stalling measure. Charles I was buying time to mobilise support at home and abroad. He was anticipating

21 Alexander Henderson, *Sermons, Prayers and Pulpit Addresses*, R.T. Martin ed. (Edinburgh, 1867), pp. 9–30; P. Donald, *An Uncounselled King: Charles I and the Scottish troubles, 1637–1641* (Cambridge, 1990), pp. 68–88.

22 *LJB*, I, pp. 50, 65, 70; *MHG*, p. 36; ICA, Argyll Letters (1602–38), A 36/86–9; Willcock, *The Great Marquess*, pp. 46–7. The Lord Privy Seal, Robert Ker, 1st Earl of Roxburgh, was also invited to court. He, like Traquair, cautioned against the use of force.

assistance not only from his loyal subjects in his three kingdoms, but also from the Spanish Habsburgs to help suppress the Covenanting Movement.[23]

In the initial months of disaffected lobbying and petitioning in Edinburgh in 1637, Lorne had removed himself from the evolving crisis. He again demonstrated publicly his mastery of political inactivity. He had made no attempt to subscribe the National Covenant when it was promulgated in February 1638, nor did he make any effort to do so for another fifteen months. However, he had encouraged his clansmen to subscribe, which they did *en masse* and with apparent enthusiasm while Lorne was preparing to depart for court. At the same time, he had not condemned the coercive behaviour of the Covenanting leadership in enforcing subscriptions to the National Covenant in St Andrews, Glasgow and Aberdeen, the latter task being carried out with relish by the young Earl (and future Marquess) of Montrose. He had neither contributed nor objected to the Tables organising a fighting fund based on a voluntary land tax to further their aim of securing free constitutional assemblies in Kirk and State. Accordingly, when he returned from court, he continued to sit in the Privy Council and served as an intermediary for the king's commissioner in his dealings with the Covenanting leadership. He had already apprised them of the true situation at court in favour of coercion.[24]

Covenanting negotiations with Hamilton were conducted against a background of mass lobbying at the behest of the Tables, who were able to mobilise tens of thousands. No more than 300 Royalist adherents met Hamilton when he arrived in June, by which time the lay councillors were broadly in sympathy with the Covenanters. Lorne was notably adamant in insisting upon meaningful discussions and concessions. His discreet but firm lobbying for the Covenanters upheld the refusal of the Tables, particularly that of the gentry, to compromise the National Covenant. Hamilton duly returned to court twice, in July and August, before conceding unconditionally that a general assembly would be summoned at Glasgow in November. In the interim, Covenanting ideologues faced a formidable intellectual challenge from the six Aberdeen Doctors. Not only did they stand out against subscription to the National Covenant, but they also maintained that any resort to arms against the lawful Prince was on no account warranted. In public debates with Henderson and Dickson, they argued convincingly that neither episcopal government nor the Five Articles were inimical to the Reformed tradition; nor were they necessarily abjured by the Negative Confession of 1581.[25]

23 Sharpe, *The Personal Rule of Charles I*, pp. 825–30; Stevenson, *The Scottish Revolution*, pp. 88–90.

24 *LJB*, I, pp. 79–87, 92–3, 99–101; DH, Loudoun Deeds, bundle 1/13.

25 Rothes, *Relation*, pp. 100–86; *Wariston Diary* I, pp. 349–404; Gordon, *HSA*, I, pp. 64–134; HL,

However, the Aberdeen Doctors were not convinced of sufficient political backing for an episcopal counter-attack at the Glasgow Assembly. Their defence of Episcopalianism did inspire Hamilton to formulate a tangible alternative to the National Covenant. The Negative Confession of 1581 was associated with a bond of 1589, designed specifically to counter Roman Catholicism, that generally committed subscribers to aid the king in withstanding internal as well as foreign foes. This King's Covenant was presented for subscription to the Privy Council on 22 September 1638. Hamilton sought to discredit the Movement throughout the British Isles by having leading Covenanters named in the commissions for collecting subscriptions. However, the King's Covenant neither regained the political initiative for the Charles I nor expedited the formation of a cohesive Royalist party.[26] The most positive responses came from the north-east and the central Highlands, where George Gordon, 2nd Marquess of Huntly and his associates were not averse to coercion. An initial degree of success in west, central and eastern Scotland, as in the Borders, was largely confined to the respective domains of the king's commissioner and prominent councillors. Covenanters actively opposed subscription in the south-west, Fife and the Lothians.

By this juncture, Archibald, 7th Earl of Argyll had died and Lorne had succeeded as 8th Earl. Until Hamilton was given an unequivocal commitment from the Court that he could authorise a general assembly for Glasgow on 21 November and a parliament for Edinburgh six months later, Lorne sought to restrain the radicalism of Covenanting gentry. But now, as 8th Earl, he felt less constrained to contain his own radical sympathies. Taking their lead from the new Earl, the gentry of Argyll made no effort to encourage subscription to the King's Covenant, pending full determination of ecclesiastical affairs in the forthcoming general assembly. Lorne had already put Argyllshire in a posture of defence in the summer of 1638, having learned from Court about a potential plot by the 2nd Earl of Antrim. Exiled remnants of the ClanDonald South embedded within a contingent of 5,000 Irishmen were to be released from Habsburg service to help Hamilton enforce a settlement in Scotland. While he shared Wentworth's conviction that there was no real substance to Antrim's posturing, Lorne had moved covertly from a defensive to an offensive position that August. He asked the shire gentry not only to assess the number

Stowe Collection: Temple Papers, STT Personal box 9 (21).

26 *The Confession of the Kirk of Scotland Subscribed by the King's Majesty and his Household in the Year of God 1580. With a Designation of Such Acts of Parliament as are Expedient, for Justifying the Union, after Mentioned. And Subscribed by the Nobles, Barrons, Gentlemen, Burgesses, Ministers and Commons, in the Year of God, 1638* (Edinburgh, 1638); [Balcanqual], *A Declaration Concerning the Late Tumults in Scotland* , pp. 186–205; RPCS, second series, VII, pp. 32–3, 82–3, 89–94.

of fighting men, available weapons and ships in Argyll but also to make provision for supplying arms, training troops and financing all necessary martial endeavours by land and sea.[27] In effect, Lorne was already in the van of the Covenanting leadership in establishing shire committees of war. These committees served as prototypes for military engagement several months in advance of the blueprint for raising a national army by conscription that was drawn up prior to the Glasgow Assembly (see below).

Notwithstanding open intimidation and covert preparations by the Covenanters, Royalist prospects were dealt a further debilitating blow at the outset of November. Lord Advocate Hope made public his opinion that episcopal government was both illegal and inconsistent with the Negative Confession, an opinion that accorded with the radical interpretation favoured by the fifth Table. The Covenanting leadership opportunely switched tack. Subscription to the King's Covenant was no longer prejudicial but complementary to the National Covenant. Subscribers to both were committed to the repudiation of episcopacy, the Five Articles and liturgical innovations. Glasgow was selected as the venue for the general assembly on the grounds that the city's proximity to Hamilton's principal domain would allow him to bring his considerable landed influence into play against the Tables. Hamilton has undoubtedly been underestimated as a subtle, conciliatory and effective politician who had the unenviable task of coping with the intransigence of Charles I and his aversion to a negotiated solution with the Covenanting Movement.[28] But on this occasion Hamilton had miscalculated badly. His formidable mother, Anna Cunningham, the Dowager Marchioness and a committed Covenanter, exercised political and financial control over his estates. Though obliged to move from Edinburgh, the Tables effectively controlled the composition, remit and proceedings of the Glasgow Assembly in a more rigorous manner than Charles I had managed his coronation parliament of 1633.[29]

The presbyteries were the managerial key to the general assembly. Well in advance of the Glasgow Assembly, the fifth Table had issued guidelines for the election of commissioners from presbyteries, as from royal burghs. The general assembly should be composed primarily of clerical and lay commissioners,

---

27 ICA, Argyll Letters (1602–38), A 36/90, /92–3, /95; NAS, Breadalbane MSS, GD 112/1/510, /514–16, /555–6; *The Earl of Strafforde's Letters and Dispatches*, W. Knowler ed., 2 vols (London, 1739), II, pp. 187, 210, 220, 277–9, 281, 289, 300–6, 321–5, 353–9; *LBJ*, I, pp. 107–8.

28 Scott, *Politics and War in the Three Stuart Kingdoms*, pp. 17–18; J. Scally, "'Counsel in Crisis": James, Third Marquis of Hamilton and the Bishops' Wars, 1638–1640' in J.R. Young ed. *Celtic Dimensions of the British Civil Wars* (Edinburgh, 1997), pp. 18–34; Rubinstein, *Captain Luckless*, pp. 244–5.

29 *The Hamilton Papers*, S.R. Gardiner ed. (London, 1880), pp. 26–37, 42–7; *LJB*, I, pp. 103–8, 112, 115–6. Hope's opinion was endorsed by four senators of the College of Justice.

with up to three ministers, one noble or gentry and one burgess from every presbytery. Members of the Tables serving in kirk sessions as parochial elders were intruded onto presbyteries as ruling elders in August and September. In presbyteries sympathetic to episcopacy or where bishops could rely on powerful local backing, the endeavours of the well affected ruling elders were directed towards restricting the number of commissioners elected. In thirty-nine out of the sixty-two designated presbyteries, the guidelines of the Tables were followed by October.[30]

By summoning all nobles who had subscribed the National Covenant, by having four gentry from every presbytery accompany the commissioners as assessors, and by likewise reinforcing each burgh with up to six assessors, the fifth Table ensured that the Glasgow Assembly was effectively a plenary meeting of the Tables. Proceedings were conducted in an intimidating atmosphere. Charges cataloguing the pastoral and personal failings of the bishops were submitted from the presbyteries by members of the Tables not chosen as commissioners. The Covenanting leadership successfully promoted the selection of Henderson as moderator and Johnston of Wariston as clerk. Control over proceedings was further enhanced by Covenanting dominance in the membership of the committees for preparing and transacting business. The bishops, who had prudently absented themselves, had lodged a declaration against the usurped authority of the Tables in controlling the composition and remit of the assembly. As this was not read until six days after the assembly commenced, its content had been rendered meaningless. The assembly's response, asserting its right to try the bishops on 28 November, prompted a walkout by Hamilton. Next day, his command to dissolve was upstaged by the assembly continuing to sit: the first open act of constitutional defiance of the prerogative rule of Charles I. No less dramatically, the 8th Earl of Argyll made a public declaration for the Covenanting cause as proceedings recommenced.

The Covenanting Movement gained immense political benefit from its acquisition of the 8th Earl, who was attending as an assessor to the king's commissioner. In private meetings, the eloquence of Johnston of Wariston had resolved Argyll's doubts about the unscriptural nature of episcopacy; doubts which Wentworth had attempted to exploit when beseeching Argyll to treat issues of ecclesiastical polity as matters indifferent rather than of confessional substance. Notwithstanding his staged conversion to the Covenanting cause, the 8th Earl was welcomed as a substantive and inspirational statesman. Although he was not an elected commissioner, Argyll was allowed and encouraged to play a full part in

---

30 NLS, Wodrow MSS, folio lxii, ff.22, 25–6; Rothes, *Relation*, pp. 29, 128,135–78; *LBJ*, I, pp. 99–176, 469–72. Merely three presbyteries failed to send any commissioner. Hamilton received solid backing for only six presbyteries and three royal burghs – all from the north-east.

the assembly's proceedings as it swept away all vestiges of episcopacy, the Court of High Commission, the Five Articles and other liturgical innovations from the Kirk before dissolving itself on 20 December. He was not averse to rebuking intemperate speeches by ministers that could be construed as disrespectful to the king. His continuing importance to the Covenanting Movement was made manifest by his inclusion on interim committees for visiting universities, for transplanting ministers between parishes and for trying all clergy who held to episcopacy and declined the authority of the Glasgow Assembly.[31]

Argyll's strategic importance to the Movement was recognised not only by the encomiums of committed Covenanters. Wentworth made sustained but fruitless endeavours of to reclaim him for Britannic monarchy. Hamilton perceptively warned the royal court that Argyll, above all other Scottish politicians, had to be watched as a potential revolutionary.[32] War had become inevitable. The final enactment at Glasgow had asserted the inherent right of the Kirk, not the king, to warrant general assemblies at least once a year. The next was designated for Edinburgh in July 1639. This constituted a second, blatant attack on the royal prerogative. The Bishops' Wars of 1639–40 duly take their name from the armed conflict that followed from the replacement of an Episcopalian with a Presbyterian polity in the Kirk.

The Bishops' Wars

Initially, in the wake of the Glasgow Assembly, Argyll sought publicly to appear as a broker between the Court and the Covenanting leadership while privately steering the centralised restructuring of the Tables and the placing Scotland on a war footing.[33] Prior to the advent of war, he assumed the position of political prominence in Covenanting affairs that he was to hold throughout the 1640s. In the eyes of Argyll, limited monarchy remained a non-negotiable objective. Under his leadership, the radical mainstream interpreted the role of the Scottish

---

31 *Wariston Diary* I, pp. 374–402; Gordon, *HSA*, II, pp. 3–187; D.G. Mullan, *Episcopacy in Scotland: The History of an Idea, 1560–1638* (Edinburgh, 1986), pp. 190–3. Although the Glasgow Assembly had effected a Presbyterian reformation, it made no claims to clerical autonomy. Certainly, the prohibition on ministers exercising civil office had widespread constitutional ramifications, notably the abolition of the clerical estate in parliament (duly effected in June 1640). However, provision was also made for commissioners not to sit in, but to represent the interests of the Kirk to the next parliament. This committee served as a precedent for the Commission of the Kirk established in 1641 as a pressure group on parliament. With its composition made up of committed Presbyterian ministers led by Henderson supported by the elder sons of peers not eligible for parliament and gentry not chosen to represent the shires in the forthcoming parliament, the committee was designed to replace the clerical Table, now effectively redundant.

32 NAS, Hamilton Papers, GD 406/1/326, /1010; NAS, Breadalbane MSS, GD 112/1/516, /525; *The Earl of Strafforde's Letters and Dispatches*, II, pp. 246–8, 290–1, 299–300.

33 NAS, Hamilton Papers, GD 406/1/1315.

Estates as not just participating in but controlling central government.

The course of the Bishops' Wars provided a practical demonstration of the coactive power that held monarchy to account. According to Samuel Rutherford, the Tables were obliged to hold the Crown to the dual imperatives of the National Covenant in the interest of the monarchy, if not Charles personally: that is, the king *in abstracto* if not *in concreto*.[34] This coactive power was maintained consistently by the radical mainstream to justify resistance in both the First and Second Bishops' Wars. In the spring of 1639, ministers advocated recourse to arms from the pulpit following precepts drawn up by Alexander Henderson. An essential distinction was maintained. On the one hand, subjects rising or standing out against law and reason that they may be free from their obedience to their king were not justified in their actions. On the other hand, the Scottish people, 'holding fast their alledgence to their soveraine and in all humilitie supplicating for Religioun and justice', were obliged 'to defend themselves against extreame violence and oppression bringing utter ruin and desolation upon the kirk and kingdome, upon themselves and their posteritie'. These arguments to defend Scotland in 1639 were reiterated in 1640 to vindicate the Covenanting Army's invasion of England, now propagated as an offensive posture for defensive purposes.[35]

The Scottish resistance to Charles I had a European, not just a Britannic, significance. Whereas contemporaneous revolts in Portugal and Catalonia against a centralising Spanish monarchy were protesting about the costs of continuing engagement in the Thirty Years War, the Covenanting Movement brought this European war to the British Isles.[36]

Prior to the Bishops' Wars, Charles had been prepared to assist Spain against the Dutch with Irish troops and English ships, ostensibly to secure the restoration of his nephew, Charles Louis, to the Palatinate. In return for landing facilities for troops in transit through the Channel, the Spaniards became the best hope of Charles securing external assistance against the Covenanters. However, the Dutch Admiral Tromp decisively defeated the Spanish fleet in the Downs in the autumn of 1639. This defeat demonstrated that Charles was of limited assistance to the Habsburgs. It also ensured that the Covenanters continued to be supplied with men and munitions through Holland and Zealand.[37] Indeed,

---

34 Samuel Rutherford, *Lex Rex: The Law and the Prince* (Edinburgh, 1848), pp. 56, 98–9, 143–8, 199, 222–3; J. Coffey, 'Samuel Rutherford and the Political Thought of the Scottish Covenanters' in Young ed., *Celtic Dimensions of the British Civil Wars*, pp. 75–95.

35 NLS, Wodrow MSS, quarto xxiv, fo.165; EUL, Instructions of the Committee of Estates of Scotland 1640–1, Dc.4.16. pp. 1–3.

36 Macinnes, *The British Revolution*, pp. 119–25.

37 C. Russell, *The Causes of the English Civil Wars* (Oxford, 1990), pp. 28–9; K. Sharpe, *The Personal Rule of Charles I*, pp. 827–31, 895–9.

the Covenanting Movement drew on diplomatic, military and material support from the reconstituted alliance of France, Sweden and the United Provinces that had continued the Thirty Years War in the aftermath of the Peace of Prague between the Austrian Habsburgs and the German princes in 1635.

The Covenanters had established their own Dutch press outlets by 1639, when they, rather than the court of Charles I, were the first to receive embassies openly from Sweden and Denmark, as well as covertly from France.[38] Abbé Chambre alias Thomas Chalmers, a Scottish Jesuit, first made contact with the disaffected leadership in the autumn of 1637 under the guise of boosting recruitment for the Scottish regiment in French service since 1633. Rewarded by becoming almoner to Cardinal Richelieu, Chambers returned to Scotland to report on Covenanting affairs prior to the Bishops' Wars. Despite his religious affiliations, the Covenanters expediently used him as their chief contact with Richelieu, who seems to have confirmed the commercial privileges of the 'auld alliance' that allowed all Scots living in France, and their descendants, to be free of all taxes levied upon strangers. In the course of the Bishops' Wars, Chambers became the unofficial Scottish Ambassador to the French Court. At the same time, Sir Robert Moray, active with the Scottish troops in French service, was despatched by Richelieu to firm up covert links with Argyll.[39]

Covenanting intelligence from the continent updated information supplied from the court to Argyll in 1638 regarding the imminent release of Irish forces from Spanish service, but was now to effect further rebellion against Charles I. Albeit the release of Irish forces was delayed two years, it can be viewed as

38 A.J Mann, *The Scottish Book Trade, 1500–1720: Print Commerce and Print Control in Early Modern Scotland* (East Linton 2000), 83–4; [Archibald Johnston of Warriston], *Remonstrantie vande edelen, baronnen, state, kercken-dienaers, ende gemeente in het Coningryck van Schotland: Verclarende dat sy onschuldigh sy;n van de crimen daer mede sy in't laetste Engelsche Placcaet (vanden 27 february) beswaert werden. Gevisiteert na de Ordonnantie vande Generale Vergaderinge van den Raedt van Staten in Schotland* (Edinburgh and Amsterdam, 1639); *Informatie, aen alle oprechte christenen in het coningrijcke van Engelandt. Door de edelen, baronnen, staten, leeraers, ende gemeente in het coninckrijcke van Schotlandt. Waer in zy hare onschuldt te kennen gheven . . .* (Edinburgh, 1639); [Alexander Henderson], *Vertoog van de vvettelyckheyt van onsen tocht in Engelant* (Edinburgh, 1640); DR, TKUA, A II, no.14, Akter og Dokumenter nedr. Det politiske Forhold til England, 'Korfit Ulfelds or Gregers Krabbes Sendelse til England, 1640'; S. Murdoch, *Britain, Denmark-Norway and the House of Stuart*, pp. 90–116.

39 Stevenson, *The Scottish Revolution*, pp. 184–7; Sanderson, *A Compleat History of the Life and Raigne of King Charles I*, pp. 208, 286–7, 293; Gordon, *Distemper*, p. 6; BL, Misc. Correspondence, vol. VIII, Sep–Dec.1663, Add.MSS 23,120 ff.46–7. Grotius, the celebrated Dutch jurist in exile, who then served as the Swedish ambassador to France, also monitored the Bishops' Wars; albeit his editors and translators have frequently confused Argyll with Airlie (*Briefwisseling van Hugo Grotius (1583–1645)*, P.C. Molhugsen, B.L. Meulenbroek, P.P. Witkam, H.J.M. Nellen and C.M. Ridderikhoff eds, 17 vols ('S-Gravenhage and Den Haag, 1928–2001), X (1639) pp. 422–7; XI (1640) pp. 200–9, 251–3, 273–82, 303–4)

belated Spanish intervention in the British theatre.[40] However, the immediate threat of external intervention in 1639 came neither from the French nor the Spanish but from Sweden, which gave unstinting diplomatic, military and material support to the Covenanting Movement. Chancellor Axel Oxenstierna, deeply concerned that the growing rapprochement between Charles I and the Habsburgs would inflame the perennial antipathies of Denmark-Norway and Poland-Lithuania, was notably receptive to Covenanting pleas for assistance made by Alexander Leslie, Field-Marshal and thirty-year veteran in Swedish service, who had actually returned to Scotland under a safe-conduct from Charles I. Leslie, a longstanding associate and correspondent with Hamilton, had attended the Marquess when he was despatched from the Court to Scotland to negotiate with the Covenanters in June 1638. However, his family ties to Rothes and Argyll had prevailed.

Leslie's Covenanting commitment was communicated that same month to Oxenstierna. Hamilton's ineptitude as king's commissioner was exposed not only by his failure to secure the services of Leslie for the Royalist cause, but in allowing the Field-Marshal to return to Sweden in July to secure political and military backing. Leslie arrived back in Scotland in advance of the Glasgow Assembly, equipped with arms and ammunition as a retirement present from Swedish service. Leslie was undoubtedly the prime mover in securing not only his own release but that of leading Scottish officers in Swedish and Dutch service, most notably the foremost military tactician Colonel Robert Munro, and the artillery genius Colonel Alexander Hamilton. By maintaining a regular correspondence with Oxenstierna, he paved the way for the further release of Scottish officers, such as Colonel David Leslie, in advance of the Second Bishops' War. Diplomatic backing for an invasion of England was announced during the Covenanting embassy of another military veteran, Colonel John Cochrane, in July–August 1640, when the Riksråd (Swedish Council) authorised further supplies of munitions and copper via Holland. At the same time, Charles was continuing to flounder in his search for overseas military backing, in his attempts to prevent the release of Scottish officers from Swedish and Dutch service, and in his reluctance to admit to foreign powers that the revolution in Scotland was outwith his control.[41]

40 *The Earl of Strafforde's Letters and Dispatches*, II, pp. 187, 287.
41 A. Grosjean, 'General Alexander Leslie, the Scottish Covenanters and the Riksråd Debates, 1638–40' in A.I. Macinnes, T. Riis and F.G. Pedersen eds, *Ships, Guns and Bibles in the North Sea and Baltic States* (East Linton, 2000), pp. 115–38; Gordon, *Distemper*, pp. 6–16; BL, Trumbull Papers, vol. CLXXXXVII, Add. MSS 72,428, ff.61, 108–11, 121–2, 151, 165–7, DR, TKUA, Skotland, A II, no. 4a, Akter og Dokumenter nedr. det politiske Forhold til Skotland, 1572–1640; *Kancelliets Brevbøger: Vedrørende Danmarks Indre Forhold* (1637–39), E. Marquard ed. (Copenhagen, 1944), pp. 171, 213, 348, 672–3, 722. However, Swedish sympathies for the

Well in advance of the Bishops' Wars, the fifth Table, as the Covenanting executive, had restructured links with the localities which had hitherto depended on local initiatives by Argyll and leading Covenanters. Restructuring, based on a blueprint drawn up prior to the Glasgow Assembly, was underway by January 1639. The gentry were to the fore in establishing committees of war within the shires to liaise with and carry out directives from Edinburgh. Each committee of war had a permanent convener, in order to levy, equip and train troops; to assess and uplift a compulsory contribution based on landed and commercial rents; and to propagate commitment to the cause in every presbytery and parish. The immediate purpose of the Covenanting leadership in centrally re-orientating local government was to mobilise and provision a national army. The returning veterans secured a professional backbone for the Covenanting Army. They filled every alternate position of command among commissioned and non-commissioned officers, albeit the colonel of each regiment 'may be some nobleman or gentleman of quality'. Likewise all artillery officers, gunners and engineers were veterans, as were the muster-masters recruited by the shire committees of war to pass on the basic skills of drilling and exercising with muskets and pikes.[42]

Covenanting Movement could not guarantee the passage of soldiers, arms and ammunition through the Baltic Sound and across the North Sea. Diplomats from the Covenanting Movement worked to counter the family ties of Christian IV of Denmark-Norway by encouraging him to mediate during the Bishops' Wars, overtures that his nephew rejected in both 1639 and 1640. Effectively neutralised by Covenanting diplomacy, Christian IV opted to allow the passage of arms and ammunition to all three kingdoms – so long as English, Scottish and Irish procurers paid higher tolls, particularly exorbitant in the case of saltpetre, through the Sound (S. Murdoch, 'Scotland, Scandinavia and the Bishops' Wars, 1638–40' in A.I. Macinnes and J. Ohlmeyer eds, *The Stuart Kingdoms in the Seventeenth Century: Awkward Neighbours* (Dublin, 2002), pp. 113–34; BL, Trumbull Papers, vol. CXC, Add. MSS 72,431 fo.123; *Kong Christian Den Fjerdes Egenhaendige Breve*, C.F. Bricka and J.A. Frederica eds, 8 vols (Copenhagen, 1969–70), IV (1636–40), pp. 195–6, 272–6, 304–5, 359–60, 364–9, 378–9; DR, TKUA, England A II, no.14, Akter of Dokumenter til England, 1631–40). The monumental significance of formal Swedish backing has in part been disguised by the shipments of men, arms and ammunition through the Hanse ports of Hamburg, Bremen and Lübeck as well as the United Provinces. However, Hamilton was becoming wary of Swedish involvement as early as June 1638. Notwithstanding the stop on Scottish trade imposed by Charles I at the outset of the Bishops' Wars, the Covenanters' continuing ability to gain supplies from Sweden was noted apprehensively in England during the 'Short Parliament' of April 1640 (NAS, Hamilton Papers, GD 406/1/10491, /10816; *Proceedings of the Short Parliament*, E.S. Cope and W.H. Coates eds (London, 1977), p. 77).

42 NLS, Salt and Coal: Events 1635–62, MS 2263, ff.73–84; NAS, Breadalbane MSS, GD 112/1/510, /514, /520; Macinnes, *Charles I and the Making of the Covenanting Movement*, pp. 190–2. Every able-bodied man between 16 and 60 was eligible for military service. Every shire committee of war was expected to raise and maintain at least one regiment of foot and a troop of cavalry. The shire regiments of foot were organised into quarterly brigades of eight to ten regiments. Sufficient cavalry were mobilised in every shire to form at least one regiment from each quarter. Regional mobilisation facilitated the formation of a Covenanting vanguard, selected from the

The returning veterans ensured that the Covenanters adopted the main advances in the methodology of warfare pioneered by the Dutch and carried on by the Swedes. Armed service was regarded as a national endeavour that was reinforced by ecclesiastical as well as military discipline. Logistical difficulties did hinder the expeditious mobilisation of levies, supplies and funds from the shires during the First Bishops' War. Desertions from the armed forces were continuous. Nonetheless, the relative efficiency of restructured local government was attested by the military supremacy the Covenanting Army consistently enjoyed in the field. The Royalist forces relied predominantly on family obligation and political clientage to raise forces to supplement the trained bands from the English shires. Usually a third more troops were on active service for the Covenanting cause. Wentworth's raising of Irish levies never got off the ground in 1639, and remained no more than a potential threat in 1640.[43]

The Movement was faced with engagements on four fronts during the first campaign in 1639. Antrim's invasion of the western seaboard failed to materialise through a lack of effective leadership, planning and finance. Hamilton's naval assault on the east coast proved no more than a fitful stop to trade. However, Huntly, his son James, Lord Aboyne, their kindred, and local associates the house of Gordon maintained a five-month resistance in the northeast that was not quashed until the Covenanters concluded the Pacification of Berwick in June. During the second campaign of 1640, the Covenanters

---

ablest men in the shires, to resist invasion by land or sea and quell Royalist discontent within Scotland. Recruitment for the shire levies, though less rigorous than selection for the vanguard, was based on conscription; the landed class were preferred as volunteers for the cavalry after their enlistment as fighting men. The development of rapid-fire musketry, the linear phalanxing of pikemen by musketeers and heavy artillery, and the deployment of cavalry troops supported by mobile field artillery on the flanks improved the manoeuvrability of battle formations. The vulnerability of unwieldy infantry regiments to close-quarter skirmishing was simultaneously minimised.

43 DH, Loudoun Deeds, bundle 2/10; HL, Bridgewater and Ellesmere MSS, EL 7734 7798; NAS, Breadalbane MSS, GD 112/1/520, /523, /536; *Minute Book kept by the War Committee of the Covenanters in the Stewartry of Kirkcudbright in the Years 1640 and 1641* (Kirkcudbright, 1855), pp. 50–1, 103–8; *Unpublished Papers of John, Seventh Lord Sinclair, Covenanter and Royalist*, J.A. Fairley ed. (Peterhead, 1905), pp. 25–6, 30, 42–3; Henderson, *Sermons, Prayers and Pulpit Addresses*, pp. 144–70; *The Earl of Strafforde's Letters and Dispatches*, II, pp. 396, 399–407. The hopes of Charles to mobilise at least 30,000 men at the outset of the Bishops' Wars failed to materialise. His troops in 1639 were at least a third less than the anticipated number. Although Wentworth had established garrisons on the Irish side of the North Channel, he sent no more than 500 Irish troops to protect Carlisle. The Covenanting Army was superior not just in numbers along the Borders in July, but in the additional forces raised to suppress dissent in the north-east as a supplement to the vanguard of 2,400 men first raised in February 1639. The 25,000 troops the Covenanters assembled on the Borders in August 1640, considerably outnumbered the forces raised by Charles to resist invasion, and represented no less than 14% of eligible fighting Scots.

maintained both an invasion force in England and also a home guard capable of rapid movement from the north-east to the south-west of Scotland. The switch from defence to offence being justified by reported Royalist mobilisation in England and Ireland, the Covenanting Army crossed the Tweed and routed the Royalist forces at Newburn on 28 August, and then moved vigorously into the counties of Northumberland and Durham. Newcastle was occupied by 30 August. Covenanting control of the coal supply to London pressurised Charles I into suing for peace. As recognised by the commanders of the Royalist forces in England, the supremacy of the Covenanting Army was not just numerical. The Covenanting Movement was second only to the Swedish Crown – and the first revolutionary force in the British Isles – in possessing a standing army conscripted for national service and sustained by centralised government.[44]

Prior to the outbreak of the Bishops' Wars, supreme command of the Covenanting forces was bestowed on Leslie who, as general, was to be advised by a Council of War of twelve nobles headed by Argyll. In turn, the 8th Earl was determined that the pursuit of war to achieve the public ends of the Covenanting Movement would also serve the private interests of the house of Argyll, both defensively on the western seaboard and offensively in facilitating Campbell expansionism in northern Scotland. Because initial military preparations proved tardy north of the Tay, Argyll was granted a commission to convene a meeting of the nobles and gentry from the northern shires in Perth on 14 March 1639. Ostensibly, this meeting was called to establish a border patrol to prevent incursions of bandits from the Highlands into the Lowlands. In reality, it was a test of allegiance to the Covenanting Movement to which Huntly, the foremost Roman Catholic and Royalist magnate in Scotland, was invited to attend. His failure to appear served as the excuse for Montrose to lead 6,000 men from Perth, Fife, Angus and the Mearns, subsequently supplement by 500 from Argyllshire, to suppress the armed posturing of Royalists in the north of Scotland. The 8th Earl had used the meeting at Perth to warn Sir Alexander Menzies of Weem, chief of a clan that enjoyed amicable relations with the Campbells, to refrain from associating with suspect Royalists, who, in the absence of Huntly, seemed to be coalescing around John Murray, 28th Earl of Atholl.[45]

44 E.M. Furgol, 'Scotland Turned Sweden: The Scottish Covenanters and the Military Revolution, 1638–1651' in J. Morrill ed., *The Scottish National Covenant in its British Context* (Edinburgh, 1990), pp. 134–55; M.C. Fissel, *The Bishops' Wars: Charles I's Campaigns against Scotland, 1638–40* (Cambridge, 1994), pp. 26–9, 39–53, 195–214; M. Bennet, *The Civil Wars in Britain and Ireland, 1638–1651* (Oxford, 1997), pp. 41–8, 64–8; HL, Bridgewater and Ellesmere MSS, EL 7851, 7857, 7859; NAS, Breadalbane MSS, GD 112/1/523, /536, /556 and /9/5/16/5; DH, Loudoun Deeds, bundles 1/6/ 22 and 2/10, /14. B. Robertson, 'The House of Huntly and the First Bishops' War', *Northern Scotland*, 24 (2004), pp. 1–15.

45 NLS, Salt and Coal: Events 1635–62, MS 2263, ff.81–4 and Campbell Papers, MS 1672, fo.2; ICA,

Argyll turned Antrim's posturing about an invasion of the western seaboard to his advantage by having the last leading gentry of ClanDonald South forcibly evicted from the island of Colonsay during the First Bishops' War. Colonsay had been seized from the Macphees in 1623 by Coll Ciotach *alias* Colkitto MacDonald, whose presence on the island the 8th Earl had tolerated as Lord Lorne. However, the predatory behaviour on either side of the North Channel of Colkitto and his sons, who included the future Royalist commander, Alasdair MacColla, had become a persistent irritant to the Campbell chief. Remnants of the ClanDonald South were also purged from Jura. Argyll encouraged the Campbells of Cawdor to effect the same policy on Islay. Nevertheless, Argyll did not lose sight of his primary military duty to guard the western approaches. He secured Dumbarton Castle on the River Clyde, fortified the Kintyre peninsula against invasion and seized Brodick Castle on the island of Arran. He thereby nullified any prospect that Hamilton, as principal proprietor, could use Arran to provision an invasion fleet from Ireland. Thereafter, he mobilised his clan to join the march of the Covenanting forces to the Borders, where their presence apparently filled the English soldiers in the Royalist ranks with a mixture of shock and awe.[46]

During the Second Bishops' War, Argyll's persistent encouragement to the city of Aberdeen to distance itself from past associations with Huntly and adhere to the Covenanting cause, stood in sharp contrast to his deployment of a commission to contain Royalism in the central and eastern Highlands. Although the 8th Earl was ever vigilant about the activities of the MacKenzies and the Macleans of Duart on the western seaboard, his licence by the Covenanting executive on 12 June 1640 to harry the disaffected was targeted primarily against the associates of John, Earl of Atholl and James, Lord Ogilvie. Argyll deployed his 4,000 troops, extensively drawn from the ClanCampbell, not only to lay waste the estates of suspected Royalists in Atholl and Rannoch, the Braes of Angus and Deeside, but also to press his own territorial claims to the lordship of Badenoch and Lochaber as the foremost creditor of his beleaguered brother-in-law, the Marquess of Huntly. His two-month campaign has gained deserved, if not always accurate, notoriety for its depredations (see Chapter 2). No less significant was the political fallout. Atholl was captured and briefly detained in Edinburgh, having been ambushed on his way to make peace with

Argyll Letters (1638–85) A 36/99–100, /102, /112; Gordon, *Distemper*, pp. 12–15; Gordon, *HSA*, II, pp. 251–3; *ACL*, II, pp. 130–2; *The Government of Scotland under the Covenanters*, pp. xix–xx.

46 ICA, Argyll Transcripts, IX, nos 627, 684–5, 694; XI, nos 332, 373; XII, nos 36, 55, 59, 113, 146, 154, and Letters – Marquess's Period, bundles 11/1–2 and 12/11, and Argyll Letters (1638–85), A 36/116–18; NAS, Hamilton Papers, GD 405/1/412, /652–3, /759, /1356; BL, Registers of the Secretaries of State of Scotland, vol. III, Add.MSS 23,112, fo. 97; *LJB*, I, pp. 193–6; Hill, *The Macdonnells of Antrim*, pp. 57–62, 73–4, 241–5, 267–73; Willcock, *The Great Marquess*, pp. 74, 77.

Argyll. The 8th Earl's promise of a safe-conduct was no more than a subterfuge which did little to advance his standing as a man of honour. On marching into Angus, Argyll peremptorily dismissed the soldiers Montrose had already put in place as the Covenanting garrison of Airlie Castle. On finding that Montrose had allowed Lord Ogilvie to remove most articles of value, Argyll permitted his men to sack the Airlie estates and set fire to the castle. Lord Ogilvie's own seat at Forther in the Braes of Angus met the same fate. Again, reprisals added to the accumulating debts of the house of Airlie and made it vulnerable to a takeover by Argyll.[47]

When a further projected invasion from Ireland again failed and Royalist dissent throughout Scotland had been quelled, General Leslie summoned Argyll to come south with a regiment of volunteer horse-troopers on 17 October. Argyll's cavalry duly added a mobile presence to the Scottish occupation of the northern English counties. No less importantly, Argyll now joined the ongoing peace negotiations between the Covenanters, Charles I and leading English lords at Ripon in Yorkshire. He was now recognised by those seeking the recall of the English Parliament as the 'foremost man of business' in Scotland, a reputation earned for his political abilities rather than his territorial acquisitiveness and vindictiveness during the Bishops' Wars.[48]

Constitutional Settlement

Along with General Leslie and seventeen other leading Covenanters, Argyll was excluded from the general indemnity Charles I offered to his Scottish opponents prior to his march to the Borders in 1639. Although his presence was deemed necessary for the Covenanters to treat with the king, Argyll did not feature among the principal Scottish negotiators when the Pacification of Berwick concluded the First Bishops' War on 18 June. But the 8th Earl exerted his influence in the Council of War not to endorse without equivocation a truce negotiated with as much deference as resolve. The Council's stance was duly followed by the fifth Table, now the general committee, which staged a public

---

47 Spalding, *Troubles*, I, pp. 201, 208–32, 237–52; Gordon, *HSA*, III, pp. 163–9, 251–55; *ACL*, II, pp. 169–73, 180, 187–8, 212–17, 227, 273; NAS, Ogilvyof Inverquharity Papers, GD 205/1/27, /33–4 and /21/5/1–3 and Breadalbane MSS, GD 112/1/525; NLS, Campbell Papers, MS 1672, fo.2; ICA, Argyll Letters (1638–85) A 36/114–15, /119–21 and Argyll Transipts, XII, nos 15, 64–6; Willcock, *The Great Marquess*, pp. 102–10.

48 EUL, Instructions of the Committee of Estates of Scotland 1640–1, Dc.4.16. p. 74; NAS, Bread-albane MSS, GD 112/1/529; ICA, Argyll Letters (1638–85), A 36/122–3 and Letters – Marquess's Period, 1638–45, bundle 12/11; *The Argyle Papers, 1640–1723*, J. Maidment ed. (Edinburgh, 1834), pp. 29–30; *LJB*, I, pp. 261–3; *CSP, Domestic* (1640–41), pp. 42, 50. Having retaken Dumbarton Castle with subterfuge, Argyll was rewarded with its governorship and safe keeping by the Covenanting executive on 16 September 1640.

demonstration when the full text was published in Edinburgh on 24 June. The king's condemnation of the past proceedings of the Tables as 'disorders and disobedient courses' was not accepted. The committee was adamant that the Pacification did not contradict the religious and constitutional imperatives of Covenanting. As Charles attempted to sow divisions among the Covenanting leadership, Argyll was foremost among those who refused to return to Berwick in mid-July to resolve differences over demilitarisation.[49]

Under the terms of the Pacification, Charles I had been obliged to concede to a general assembly in Edinburgh to determine all outstanding ecclesiastical matters, with a parliament to follow for the resolution of civil affairs. When the general assembly met in August, Argyll was the moving spirit in ensuring that the entire programme at Glasgow was endorsed without any notable dissent. However, the parliament that was summoned in September did not follow the Tables' prescribed script. Traquair, who had replaced the demoralised Hamilton as king's commissioner, was intent on frustrating radical initiatives to limit the royal prerogative by focusing debate on procedural deliberations, notably the election and regulation of the committee of the articles to oversee parliamentary business. In the absence of clerical commissioners, Argyll had argued that each estate should elect its own members onto the committee rather than leave nomination to the king's commissioner. Nevertheless, Traquair prevailed to the extent that he was allowed to nominate the nobles, who, in turn, selected eight each from the gentry and burgesses to serve with the four leading officials in attendance. In the event, the only two members selected, who were not associated with the Tables, were the Marquess of Huntly and David Carnegie, 1st Earl of Southesk. Itemised programmes from the gentry and burgesses for the redress of constitutional, economic and administrative grievances arising from the prerogative rule were held up for seven weeks in this committee. Nevertheless, Charles I's heavy-handed management of the coronation parliament in 1633 (see Chapter 4) was not to be repeated. The Tables were determined to enhance the constitutional supremacy of parliament. The Estates, not the Crown or royal officials, must decide their own proceedings. The overwhelming Covenanting majority in the committee of the articles ensured a recommendation to ratify the Presbyterian Reformation and, as a corollary, the abolition of the clerical estate in parliament.

Enthusiasm for Argyll's radical leadership was by no means universal. But Traquair was unable to heal divisions to the king's advantage; divisions that

49 Row, *History of the Kirk*, pp. 521–4; *LJB*, pp. 184–224, 449–50; *Wariston Diary* II, pp. 95–7; *RPCS*, second series, VII, 119–23; NLS, Wodrow MSS, folio lxiii, ff.22, 32, 44; ICA, Argyll Letters (1638–85), A 36/104; DH, Loudoun Deeds, bundle 1/5; HL, Loudoun Scottish Collection, box 443/ LO 12565, 12870.

were particularly evident among the nobility, with Montrose coming to the fore among a conservative element. At the instigation of Charles I, parliament was prorogued on 14 November. Ostensibly this was to allow the king to receive, on the prompting of Hamilton, commissioners from the Covenanting Movement headed by Loudoun. As the king's had prorogued the Scottish Estates for seven months, he was patently intent on buying time to mobilise forces in England and Ireland. In the interim, the Tables, meeting as general conventions in January, March and again in April 1640, concentrated on financial supply and military recruitment. The first national tax levied on behalf of the Covenanting Movement bound the political nation to pay a tenth of landed and commercial rents according to valuations commenced in presbyteries and burghs during 1639. Argyll was ever willing to persuade leading cities such as Glasgow and Aberdeen not to stall over payments. Nevertheless, the raising of standing regiments was also warranted to intimidate refractory taxpayers and offer employment to the veterans of the Thirty Years War retained since the Pacification of Berwick. The fifth Table was reconstituted as a committee of estates that rejected the attempt of Charles to prorogue for another month the Scottish parliament summoned for Edinburgh on 2 June 1640.[50]

The resolve of Argyll and his radical associates to fulfil the constitutional as well as the religious imperatives of Covenanting was furthered by three key developments between November 1639 and June 1640. First, Wentworth, now created Earl of Strafford, was brought back from Ireland to become the principal exponent for a coercive settlement with the Covenanters. Having broken off all communication with Argyll on the outbreak of the Bishops' Wars, Wentworth had proceeded to impose a loyalty test on Scottish settlers from May 1639. This took the form of an oath that was imposed without exception on Ulster Scots. It clearly demonstrated that they were not trusted at the royal court and not regarded as equal partners in the frontier projects of Britannic monarchy. Strafford was unconcerned that this 'black oath' drove some settlers back to Scotland. His heavy-handed action, coupled to his recruitment of Irish Catholics into the army that he was building up for Charles in anticipation of renewed war, had forced those settlers who remained to identify with the Covenanting Movement in order to preserve their plantations. Presbyterian solidarity across the North Channel enhanced these prospects, particularly as complaints about 'hard usage'

---

50 Young, *The Scottish Parliament*, pp. 1–18; Macinnes, *Charles I and the Making of the Covenanting Movement*, pp. 194–7; ACL, II, pp. 133–7, 140–8, 180, 227; BL, Scotland, Rents and Tenths 1639, Add.MSS 33,262, ff.1–65; NAS, Breadalbane MSS, GD 112/1/523, /536; HL, Loudoun Scottish Collection, box 43/LO 12565, 12870; HL, Bridgewater and Ellesmere MSS, EL 7737, 7809, 7813. These rental valuations were based on the valuations conducted in presbyteries for the purposes of teind redistribution from 1629 to 1634.

in Ireland, which filtered through to Argyll and other leading Covenanters, continued for the duration of the Bishops' Wars. Strafford's persistent advocacy of war caused him to be identified as the 'chief incendiary' in Covenanting eyes. He encouraged Charles to garrison royal castles in Scotland and on the English Border, and to have the royal navy impose a stop on Scottish trade.[51]

Second, Charles I directly threatened Argyll with the loss of his extensive heritable jurisdictions by a proclamation, which he commanded the magistrates of Edinburgh to read at the city's market cross in March 1640. This proclamation threatened to hold Argyll to account before the English Parliament rather than the Scottish Estates. Taking advice from the Privy Council, as from the Tables, the magistrates refused to comply. They claimed that it was impolitic, unconstitutional and inappropriate for Argyll to go to England to be censured: 'No nobleman could be assured of his life, lands or goods, if this past as a practice.'[52] Third, Charles had summoned a parliament in England for 13 April 1640 in order to secure financial backing against the Covenanters. Instead of voting supply, anticipated to be £100,000 sterling per month, the parliament provided a national forum for the English disaffected to air common religious and secular grievances, and uphold parliamentary liberties and privileges disregarded during the past eleven years of the king's prerogative rule. As Argyll had anticipated, the English Houses of the Lords and Commons were not 'so prodigal of their wealth and ease as to ingadge rashlie in any business'. The 'Short Parliament' was dissolved after twenty days.[53]

The reluctance of both sides to make concessions was compounded by the detention of the Scottish commissioners, who had been attending the king since the beginning of 1640. The grounds for their detention, two days before the 'Short Parliament' commenced, was the revelation of a letter drafted, but never delivered, to the French court. This letter justified recourse to arms by the Covenanting Movement and upheld free constitutional assemblies to

---

51 BL, Original Documents relating to Scotland, the Borders and Ireland, 16th and 17th centuries, Add.MSS 5754, fo.40; BL, Nicholas Papers, Egerton MS 2533, ff.89–92; DH, Loudoun Papers, bundle 1/5; EUL, Instructions of the Committee of Estates of Scotland 1640–41, Dc.4.16. pp. 5, 16, 29; HL, Bridgewater and Ellesmere MSS, 7430; NAS, Maxwell of Orchardton MSS, RH 15/19/20/1, /4–5, /11; *The Earl of Strafforde's Letters and Dispatches*, II, pp. 324, 328, 382–5. The oath had actually been welcomed by leading Scottish planters in Ulster, such as James Hamilton, 1st Viscount Clandeboye, who were keen to rid themselves of aspersions of being disloyal subjects. It followed closely the one that Charles had attempted to impose on Scottish sojourners and traders in England and Wales from February and had demanded from March 1639, as a test of fidelity, for his troops engaged against the Covenanting Army.

52 Spalding, *Troubles*, I, 218–19; Willcock, *The Great Marquess*, pp. 96–7.

53 ICA, Argyll Letters (1638–85), A 36/109; HL, Huntington Manuscripts, HM 1554, Anon. Diary of the Long Parliament, pp. 109–22; *The Short Parliament (1640) Diary of Sir Thomas Aston*, J.D. Maltby ed. (London, 1988), pp. 3, 6–7, 63–4, 124–5, 131–2, 145.

prevent Scotland becoming 'a conquered province, as Ireland, under subjection to England'. There was certainly no intent to renounce the Stuarts. Nor were the Covenanters seeking to transfer their allegiance to France – an option exercised by the Catalans at the outset of 1641 after their revolt against the Spanish monarchy. The letter did allow Charles to taunt the Scottish commissioners about whether they came to negotiate 'as ambassadors or as subjects'. Loudoun, the leading Scottish commissioner as well as a signatory to the letter, was incarcerated in the Tower of London for two months. He was only released, again at the behest of Hamilton, to secure his attendance at the Scottish Estates in the forlorn hope that he would work for a peaceful accommodation between the Crown and the Covenanters.[54]

The Estates declared themselves to be a legally constituted assembly on 2 June 1640. Traquair was removed as king's commissioner. Robert Balfour, Lord Balfour of Burleigh, a longstanding opponent of the unfettered exercise of the prerogative, was elected in his place. Having validated past proceedings of the Tables, the Estates instigated a constitutional revolution which, in a comparative European context, demonstrated their political vitality. The clerical estate in parliament was abolished. The gentry, in recognition of their stalwart service on the Tables, had their voting powers doubled. Instead of one composite vote being cast for each shire, gentry summoned as shire commissioners were accorded the same individual voting rights enjoyed by the nobles and burgesses. Subscription of the National Covenant was made compulsory for all holding public office in Kirk and State. The committee of articles was declared an optional procedure and, if deployed, was to be elected by and answerable to the reconstituted three Estates. A triennial act specified that parliament should meet every three years regardless of a royal summons. On account of the imminent danger of invasion by Royalist forces, a Committee of Estates was constituted formally with comprehensive powers to govern the whole kingdom. The Committee, which consisted of forty members drawn from the nobility, gentry and burgesses, was split into two sections. Equal numbers of each Estate either remained in Edinburgh to sustain central government or accompanied the army, whose movements were not restricted to Scotland – a clear indication that the Covenanters were to wage renewed war in England. Argyll was not named in either section. Partly, this can be explained by his parliamentary commission to contain Royalism in the central and eastern Highlands. But with both sections dominated by his radical associates, he was afforded scope to act as a supernumerary, guiding influence.[55]

54 NLS, Wodrow MSS, folio lxiv, fo.82; HL, Bridgewater and Ellesmere MSS, EL 7811, 7819–21, 7823–30, 7836; ABDA, Argyll Papers, 40.534;Gordon, *HSA*, III, pp. 7–9, 32–6, 125, 133–46, 148–53; Burnet, *Memoirs*, pp. 162, 168–73.
55 J.R. Young, 'The Scottish Parliament in the Seventeenth Century: European Perspectives' in

The establishment of the Committee of Estates represented a classical, if corporate, alternative to the vesting of executive power in a monarch who was patently untrustworthy, palpably reluctant to make lasting concessions, and resolutely intent on reversing all constraints on his prerogative. Argyll and the Covenanting leadership were resolved to legitimise not only their past but also their future exercise of executive power. Restructured local government was affirmed as the principal agency for the nationwide imposition of ideological conformity, financial supply and military recruitment. In addition to ratifying the exaction of the tenth, a compulsory loan of a twentieth of valued rents was imposed to meet the anticipated shortfall in borrowing required to cover expenditure in the First Bishops' War and the increased payments and allowances to the Covenanting Army for the Second. The scope of treason was extended to all that advised or assisted policies destructive to Covenanting. Waging war for the Movement became patriotic; waging war against it was now treasonable.[56]

The religious and constitutional imperatives of Covenanting were pursued through constitutional defiance and waging war. As the revolutionary embodiment of the Covenanting Movement, the Tables were accomplishing a thorough transformation of government within Scotland by persuasion and coercion. Their radicalism was evident in their oligarchic centralising of state power. Committees of nobles, gentry and burgesses with clerical reinforcement by pulpit and pen imposed unprecedented demands on the Scottish localities for ideological, financial and military commitment. Argyll had gained a reputation as a highly partial force for good in mitigating demands on those he deemed deserving. By 1640, he and the radical mainstream of the Covenanting Movement were ready to serve as a radical exemplar for terminating the prerogative rule of Charles I in England and Ireland.[57]

Macinnes, Riis and Pederson eds, *Ships, Guns and Bibles in North Sea and the Baltic States*, pp. 139–72; *Government under the Covenanters*, pp. xvii–xxvii. Each section of the Committee of Estates governed autonomously, save for the declaration of war and the conclusion of peace, which required the assent of the whole Committee.

56 *APS*, V, pp. 264; 280–2, c.23–4; 285–90, c.26–33, 39, 41; NAS, Supplementary Parliamentary Papers: Army. Account of Money disbursed to the Forces, 1639–40, PA 15/1, fo.14; *Unpublished Papers of John, Seventh Lord Sinclair*, pp. 44–9.

57 Macinnes, *Charles I and the Making of the Covenanting Movement*, pp. 183–213; Morrill, *The Nature of the English Revolution*, pp. 252–7; T. ó hAnnracháin, 'Rebels and Confederates: The Stance of the Irish Clergy in the 1640s' in Young ed., *Celtic Dimensions of the British Civil War*, pp. 96–115; NAS, Maxwell of Orchardton MSS, RH 15/91/20/1, /6, /8–10.

SIX

British Intervention, 1641–1643

From their issue of articles of war on 10 August until negotiations for a cessation of arms commenced at Ripon in Yorkshire on 2 October 1641, the Covenanting leadership proactively encouraged support not only from sympathetic nobles and gentry in England, but also from the city of London, frequently the butt of criticism at the royal court for its reluctance to finance the Royalist army. As well as justifying their move to an offensive posture to maintain their constitutional gains within Scotland, the Covenanting leadership promised that their army would observe strict military discipline in England pending the conclusion of a settlement. To this end, the removal of the negotiations to London and the recall of the English Parliament were deemed indispensable. The Covenanting Movement was thus able to assert and retain the political initiative in Britain from the outset of the peace negotiations; an initiative consolidated by the promulgation of the Solemn League and Covenant in August 1643.[1] Argyll was paramount in furthering a British agenda. As he crossed the border in September 1641, to meet up with the victorious Covenanting forces under General Alexander Leslie, Argyll was convinced of Scotland's providential mission:

> As never anie poore nation hath done and ventured more for ther religioune and libertie with greater encouragement for assurance of success from God's dealings with us than this kingdom.

He was recognised throughout the British Isles as the moving radical spirit among the Covenanters, one who 'rules all the rest' in promoting a revolutionary programme that advocated the federative reconfiguration of regal union.[2]

---

1 HL, Bridgewater and Ellesmere MSS, EL 7810, 7838, 7842–7849, 7869, 7872; *LJB*, I, pp. 255–61; II, pp. 470–1; *The Intentions of the Army of the Kingdom of Scotland Declared to their Brethren in England* (Edinburgh, 1640); Sir John Borough, *Notes on the Treaty Carried on at Ripon between King Charles and the Covenanters of Scotland, A.D. 1640*, J. Bruce ed. (London, 1869), pp. 70–7.

2 ICA, Argyll Letters (1638–85), A 36/122 and Letters – Marquess's Period, 1638–1645, bundles 6/90, 12/10; DH, Loudoun Deeds, bundles 1/10; BL, Original Letters of State and Warrants etc., 1559–1593, Harley MS 7004, fo.16.

The Scottish revolt was not the cause of confrontation between Crown and parliament in England. But only the northern presence of the Covenanting Army obliged Charles to summon parliament after an eleven-year lapse. Only the security afforded by this army allowed the English disaffected sufficient scope to press for constitutional checks on monarchy. The Covenanting Movement provided not just military security but a constitutional model for revolt. A triennial act and an act continuing the current assembly enabled the 'Long Parliament' (that continued from November 1640 to the Restoration) to resist dissolution by royal fiat and, in the longer term, secure control over the apparatus of government in Church and State. The Scottish exemplar justified recourse to arms in England by the Parliamentarians in 1642. Conversely, the pressure to redress grievances generated by the Long Parliament meant that Charles was amenable to buying off the Scots to concentrate on English problems prior to the outbreak of the Irish rebellion in October 1641 where, again, the Scottish exemplar justified the Catholic Confederates taking up arms.[3]

Treaty of London

In the six months that elapsed between the dissolution of the Short and the summoning of the Long Parliament, the Covenanters and the English disaffected liaised closely. Contacts between the opponents of prerogative rule in Scotland and England, authorised initially by the Covenanting leadership in February 1639, were stepped up following reports that English noblemen were reluctant to support the king's invasion during the First Bishops' War.[4]

---

3 J. Peacey, 'The Outbreak of the Civil Wars in the Three Kingdoms' in B. Coward ed., *A Companion to Stuart Britain* (Oxford, 2003), pp. 290–308; N. Canny, 'What Really Happened in Ireland in 1641?' in J. Ohlmeyer ed., *Ireland: From Independence to Occupation 1641–1660* (Cambridge, 1995), pp. 24–42.

4 N. Canny, *Making Ireland British, 1580–1650* (Oxford, 2001), pp. 237, 295–8; Donald, *An Uncounselled King*, pp. 191–6, 218–20, 245–50. Sir John Clotworthy (later 1st Viscount Masserene) – the Ulster planter with Presbyterian sympathies who was to sit in both the Irish and English parliaments during 1640 – had actually instigated such British liaison. Clotworthy visited Edinburgh in the summer of 1638. He conversed and subsequently corresponded with Johnston of Wariston. The two most secure English conduits were seemingly Robert Greville, Lord Brooke and William Fiennes, 1st Viscount Saye and Seal, whose son Nathaniel was among a group of Englishmen attending the general assembly and parliaments in Edinburgh that autumn. Since the promulgation of the National Covenant, the Covenanting leadership had received regular, but not always reliable, intelligence from English sympathisers and Scottish courtiers, usually channelled through Eleazar Borthwick, formerly chaplain to the Scottish forces in Sweden. From the initial Scottish defiance of Charles, newsletters, often with the tacit support of disaffected government officials in England, were able to breach English licensed monopolies to print foreign news, a breach that enabled the Covenanting Movement to make their case publicly as well as covertly during the Bishops' Wars (BL, Trumbull Papers, vol. CXCI Add MSS, 72432, ff.87–8, 108–9).

Appreciation of the superiority of the Covenanting Army on the eve of the Second Bishops' War led to growing English hopes for deliverance. On the promptings of Wariston and Loudoun, Thomas Saville, Lord Saville unilaterally invited the Covenanters into England on behalf of the disaffected English nobility. His letter served as an expedient justification for the Covenanters going on to the offensive. Nonetheless, Covenanting demands that the English Parliament be recalled to participate in the peace negotiations that commenced at Ripon in October, before transferring to London in December 1640, harmonised with a supplication in the name of twelve peers headed by Francis Russell, 4th Earl of Bedford. The supplication, which was submitted to Charles I on 28 August, also requested the immediate recall of parliament to conclude a settlement with the Scots as well as resolve indigenous grievances.[5] Charles was obliged to treat with the Covenanting Movement after a council of peers, summoned to York on 24 September, affirmed that continuing English support for Britannic monarchy could no longer be relied on. Once Charles issued writs summoning a parliament at Westminster on 3 November, the council of peers assumed responsibility for the English side of the negotiations, from which Charles I was excluded at the insistence of the Covenanting leadership. This responsibility was retained by the Lords until the peace negotiations were eventually brought to a conclusion in August 1641. Having agreed not to advance beyond the Tees, the Committee of Estates with the Covenanting Army secured a daily allowance of £850 sterling, which was apportioned weekly from Northumberland and Durham as well as Newcastle. The English peers had already agreed to lend the king £200,000 sterling for the upkeep of the Royalist army. They, not Charles, underwrote this daily allowance pending a full settlement of reparations in the forthcoming Long Parliament.[6]

In his opening address on 3 November, Charles I hoped that parliament, under the guidance of the Lords, would see off the demands of the Covenanters, whom he continued to view as traitors. Playing on the complaints made from Berwick to Yorkshire about occupation by the Covenanting Army, he desired that parliament sustain his army and prevent its disbanding until the conclusion of the treaty. In return, he was prepared to satisfy grievances, anticipating that parliament would seek no more than moderate measures of reform in Church and State. While the Commons were supportive of the need to prevent

---

5 Stevenson, *The Scottish Revolution*, pp. 205–6, 213; EUL, Instructions of the Committee of Estates of Scotland 1640–1, Dc.4.16. pp. 4–5; DH, Loudoun Papers, bundle 1/8; John Selden, *A Briefe Discourse Concerning the Power of the Peeres and Comons of Parliament, in point of Judicature* (London, 1640).

6 Adamson, *The Noble Revolt*, pp. 36–52; DH, Loudoun Deeds, bundles 1/8, 2/14; HL, Loudoun Scottish Collection, box 5, LO 8053; HL, Bridgewater and Ellesmere MSS, EL 7740–1, 7743, 7862–4, 7871; Balfour, *HW*, II, 383–424.

demobilised troops preying on the English localities, the primary concern of English MPs was to continue unfinished business from the Short Parliament. The Scottish occupation of the north-east of England had raised some apprehensiveness among them. However, there was no prospect of the Commons voting sufficient funds to enable the king to renew war.[7]

The most incisive rebuttal of Charles I's intemperate opening address came in a 'root and branch petition' presented to the Commons by Isaac Pennington on behalf of the city of London on 11 December. This related to British, not just English, concerns about misgovernance from the royal court. A composite secular grievance against fiscal opportunism was sandwiched between a plethora of religious complaints that not only attacked Arminianism, but also called for the abolition of episcopacy. This latter call eventually emerged as a parliamentary bill on 10 May, albeit with the emphasis more on the replacement than the abolition of episcopacy. Attempts to exclude the bishops from parliament foundered in the Lords on 8 June. A more radical call to abolish episcopacy root and branch, which passed its first reading in the Commons on 27 June, proved too divisive to effect. Clearly, this assault on the religious establishment in England was not thirled to a Covenanting agenda. On the one hand, reform was not necessarily going to stop at the replacement of Anglicanism with Presbyterianism. On the other, the defence of Anglicanism became a defining issue for those prepared to seek an accommodation rather than confrontation with Charles I.[8]

In Scotland, the Tables had effectively and cohesively taken over the apparatus of government with a common commitment to Presbyterianism and limited monarchy several months before the National Covenant was promulgated in February 1638. But in England, the detention or flight of leading councillors in advance of the Long Parliament had left the effective levers of government in the hands of the two rival, but far from homogenous, factions who were not always consistent either in their conservatism or radicalism. The radical element was distinctively more pro-Scottish. Led initially in the House of Lords by the Earl of Bedford and in the House of Commons by John Pym, the radicals were concerned with a thorough reformation in both church and state to achieve a

---

7 HL, Bridgewater and Ellesmere MSS, 7757, 7874; Northumbria Archives, Berwick-upon-Tweed, Guild Book 1627–43, B1/9, ff.194, 197–8; EUL, Instructions of the Committee of Estates of Scotland 1640–41, Dc.4.16. pp. 11, 30–1; ICA, Letters – Marquess's Period, 1638–1645, bundle 4/70.

8 EUL, Instructions of the Committee of Estates of Scotland 1640–1, Dc.4.16. pp. 31–2, 81–3, 94, 98; NAS, Hamilton Papers, GD 406/1/1397; *Verney Papers. Sir Ralph Verney's Notes of Proceedings in the Long Parliament, temp. Chrles I*, J. Bruce ed. (London, 1845), p. 78; Morrill, *The Nature of the English Revolution*, pp. 45–90; Russell, *The Fall of the British Monarchies*, pp. 83–6, 139–42, 150, 187, 195, 198, 200, 218, 334–5.

godly commonwealth; hence their designation as 'the Commonwealth's men' by the Covenanting leadership. Not all radicals were pro-Scottish, however. For those distrustful of monarchy, the issue of how sovereignty was exercised reinvigorated the Gothic perspective. In turn, this perspective developed a distinctive Puritan spin as the defenders of Anglicanism rallied to Charles I. [9]

The Long Parliament certainly provided a national forum for the airing of local and regional grievances.[10] However, the presence of Scottish and Irish commissioners was of international significance. The Covenanting executive with the army sent eleven commissioners to the negotiations in London, with Argyll as a supernumerary. The Scots commissioners had made their priorities clear on 16 December 1640 when they sought the prosecution of both Archbishop Laud and Strafford (now Lord Lieutenant of Ireland). Clotworthy and another twelve commissioners from the Irish Parliament had made themselves available to assist in the prosecution of Strafford.[11] Given English resistance to the abolition of episcopacy, the prosecution of Laud as well as Strafford was deemed politically inexpedient. Nevertheless, the international significance of the initial session of the Long Parliament was picked up by Erik Rosenkrantz, a junior Danish legate, who witnessed the proceedings. Although Rosenkrantz noted the implementation, workings and recommendation of committees for general grievances in the Commons, his main concern was the treasonable charges pressed against Strafford, in the Lords. These charges, instigated by the Scottish commissioners, led first to Strafford's impeachment and theatrical trial at Westminster Hall, then his attainder and eventually his execution on 12 May for subverting 'the Fundamentall lawes of the Kingdome of England and Ireland'. Apart from the fate of Strafford, Rosenkrantz gave priority to the fractious negotiations which the commissioners for the Scottish Covenanters were conducting with the English Parliamentarians and Charles I. [12]

9 EUL, Instructions of the Committee of Estates of Scotland 1640–1, Dc.4.16.pp.101, 105; D.L. Smith, *Constitutional Royalism and the Search for Settlement, c.1640–1649* (Cambridge, 1994), pp. 39–80, 91–106; Woolrych, *Britain in Revolution*, pp. 170–3, 183–6; Hirst, *England in Conflict*, pp. 165–7, 173–5.

10 *Proceedings in the Opening Session of the Long Parliament, 1640–41*, 3 vols, M. Jannson ed. (Rochester, 1999–2000); T. Cogswell, *Home Divisions: Aristocracy, the State and Provincial Conflict* (Manchester, 1998), pp. 276–82; I. Roots, *The Great Rebellion* (Stroud, 1995), pp. 32–42.

11 ABDA, Argyll Papers, 40.05; M. Perceval-Maxwell, *The Outbreak of the Irish Rebellion of 1641* (Montreal, 1994), pp. 82–91; P. Little, 'The Earl of Cork and the Fall of the Earl of Strafford, 1638–41', *HJ*, 39 (1996), pp. 619–35. The Scottish commissioners included Loudoun, Wariston and Henderson.

12 *Kong Christian Den Fjerdes Egenhaendige Breve*, IV, pp. 395–6; DR, TKUA, England A II, no. 14, Akter og Dokumenter vedrgrende det politiske Forhold til England, 1631–40, 'E. Rosenkrantz, Diurnall Occurances of the Parliament Holden at Westminster 1640 from the Beginnings to the Present Time'.

John Digby, 1st Earl of Bristol, who presided over the negotiations at London, considered the pressure exerted by the Covenanting Army as 'a National Dishonour'. Nevertheless, Covenanting claims for reparations were not received unsympathetically. On 6 February 1641, the English negotiators offered £300,000 sterling; that is, more than half the sum claimed (£514,128), but less than two-fifths of the Covenanters' estimated expenditure (£785,628) during the Bishops' Wars. The willingness of the Committee of Estates accompanying the army to accept this settlement was compromised when an advance instalment of £80,000 sterling, promised as 'brotherly assistance', failed to materialise. Simultaneously, the cess money exacted for daily maintenance fell seriously in arrears.[13]

As well as securing adequate reparations, the main thrust of the Scottish commissioners' remit was to strengthen the bond of union between both kingdoms professed since the first sustained appeal to British public opinion in the prelude to the Bishops' Wars; an appeal that proved notably attractive to English Puritans. Union would vindicate 'the Religion, Liberties and Lawes of both kingdoms'. However, Covenanting efforts to have episcopacy abolished in England in favour of unity in religion and uniformity in church government was secondary to 'a firme and well grounded peace' through a defensive and offensive league between Scotland and England; that is, by confederation not parliamentary incorporation. Nevertheless, the English negotiators were extremely wary of Scottish pressures to import Presbyterianism. Claims by émigré French Huguenots that the Scottish model of Presbyterian uniformity should be resisted bolstered these apprehensions.[14] The English negotiators were adamant that the Long Parliament would decide on the nature of the Church of England. It was not fitting for ambassadors of foreign princes, far less commissioners who were also subjects of Charles I, 'to insist upon anything distinctive to government settled and established'. The only institutional innovation agreed upon was the appointment of parliamentary commissioners in both kingdoms to conserve the peace and redress any breaches in the intervals between parliaments.

13 EUL, Instructions of the Committee of Estates of Scotland 1640–41, Dc.4.16.pp.57, 60–3, 88–91; BL, Speeches in Parliament, 1558–1695, Stowe MS 361, ff.90–1; HL, Bridgewater and Ellesmere MSS, EL 7752–3, 7760; *The Great Account Delivered to the English Lords by the Scottish Commissioners* (London, 1641). The Scottish commissioners felt sufficiently emboldened by 25 May to demand equality of treatment with the English and Irish in conducting free trade throughout the Stuart dominions, securing access to colonial commerce and gaining admission to mercantile companies. The Scots were also to benefit equally from the lobbying of Christian IV by king and parliament for a reduction in the exorbitant Sound tolls.

14 BL, State Letters and Papers, Add.MSS 4155, ff.196–201; Anon., *The Beast is Wounded, or Information from Scotland, Concerning their Reformation* (1638); Peter du Moulin, *A Letter of a French Protestant to a Scotishman of the Covenant* (London, 1640).

In ratifying the Treaty of London on 7 August 1641, the English Parliament reserved its right to determine the nature of the English Reformation, but duly conceded that the waging of war and the stopping of trade within the king's dominions required parliamentary approval in both countries. The sovereign and independent power of the Scottish Estates as a 'free parliament' was now formally recognised by the Long Parliament.[15] But the Treaty did not eliminate tensions about the predominantly Catholic army that Strafford had assembled in Ireland, a force that remained restless if leaderless. Nervousness in the Long Parliament was aggravated by Charles I's decision to attend the autumn session of the reconvened Scottish Estates. Hamilton had impressed upon Charles that timely concessions to the Covenanters, coupled with a royal visit to ratify their constitutional gains in Kirk and State, could fend off pressure on monarchical authority in England. While there was no serious prospect of an alliance between Charles and the Covenanters, the king's intended visit concentrated minds in the Long Parliament to expedite approval of the Treaty of London.[16]

For the nine months of negotiations in London, which commenced on November 1640 and concluded formally on 10 August 1641, the Committee of Estates accompanying the army required and received in the camp at Newcastle regular accounts of the diligence of the Scottish commissioners. As well as routinely maintaining correspondence with the Committee of Estates at Edinburgh, members of the Committee accompanying the army were despatched occasionally from Newcastle to the Scottish capital, when progress of the negotiations at London was subject to critical appraisal. Confident that his wife, Margaret Douglas, could manage not only his estates but also the Covenanting cause in Argyllshire, the 8th Earl flitted between Newcastle and Edinburgh after the negotiations with the English commissioners shifted from Ripon to London. From the beginning of January 1641, Argyll was on stand-by to go to London once the treaty was concluded between the Scottish and English commissioners; his presence was particularly requested by the latter as vital to the Covenanting Movement's adherence to the terms negotiated. Nevertheless, as negotiations dragged on, Argyll became a vociferous critic of the Scottish commissioners, particularly during plenary sessions of the Tables at Edinburgh, held during continuations of the Scottish Estates on 14 January, 12 April and 24 May. These sessions lasted up to fourteen days. The

15 EUL, Instructions of the Committee of Estates of Scotland 1640–1, Dc.4.16.pp.79–83, 86, 94, 100–1, 105–7; DH, Loudoun Papers, bundle 1/6, /15; BL, Keyboard Music: XVI–XVII Centuries, Add.MSS 29,996 fo.184; HL, Bridgewater and Ellesmere MSS, EL 7755–6; [Archibald Campbell], *An Honourable Speech Made in the Parlament of Scotland by the Earle of Argile . . . the Thirtieth of September 1641* (London, 1641). B.P. Levack, *The Formation of the British State: England, Scotland and the Union, 1603–1707* (Oxford, 1987), pp. 110, 130–1.
16 NAS, Hamilton Papers, GD 406/1/1322, /1378, /1386; Burnet, *Memoirs*, pp. 81–8.

prolonged stay of the Scottish commissioners in London and their regular contacts with the Court were deemed to have blunted their radical edge. Argyll remained ever watchful, so as not to alienate support from the gentry and the burgesses by blanket condemnation of all commissioners. At the same time, he smoothed out financial difficulties by ensuring that farmers of the customs from the north-east to the Clyde collaborated with William Dick, the leading Scottish fiscal entrepreneur who had put his extensive resources behind the Covenanting Movement. Again, the 8th Earl's actions were not wholly disinterested, as he laid claim to the bishops' rents for Argyll and the Isles once the Covenanters appropriated not only the customs but also the rents from the royal estates and the bishoprics.[17]

Prior to negotiations commencing at Ripon, General Leslie and the Committee with the army had expressed their dissatisfaction that the royal garrison at Edinburgh Castle had been allowed to depart from Leith after their capitulation to Argyll, with their colours displayed and with their arms and baggage intact. Nevertheless, both Argyll and General Leslie stood together in rebutting charges that the Covenanters acted insensitively and rapaciously as an occupying army in exacting their allotted daily maintenance from the north-east of England. Argyll and Leslie were especially adamant that the Scottish commissioners should on no account agree that Traquair and his Scottish associates were to be included in the general indemnity for the Bishops' Wars. For their active encouragement of the king's belligerent stance towards Scotland they were deemed 'Incendiaries'. They were only to be allowed back to Scotland under armed guard to await trial before the forthcoming Scottish Estates. Argyll and Leslie also pursued their own complementary diplomatic initiatives. As the Scottish commissioners were presenting their proposals for union to their English counterparts, the Committee of Estates at Edinburgh was actively, but fruitlessly, promoting a tripartite confederation that would involve the States General of the United Provinces. Once the Treaty of London was concluded, General Leslie initiated from Newcastle repeated, but unrequited, approaches to Oxenstierna, the Swedish Regent, for an alternative confederation involving Sweden, the Scottish Covenanters and the English Parliamentarians.[18]

---

17 *LJB*, I, pp. 260–3, 266–7, 303–4, 306; NAS, Breadalbane MSS, GD 112/1/529; DH, Loudoun Deeds, bundle 1/10; ICA, Letters – Marquess's Period, 1638–1645, bundle 6/90, /108 and Argyll Letters (1638–85), A 36/126–7; *ACL*, II, p. 311; HL, Loudoun Scottish Collection, box 5/ LO 8053.
18 EUL, Instructions of the Committee of Estates of Scotland 1640–41, Dc.4.16. pp. 34–107; *Rikskanseleren Axel Oxenstiernas Skrifter och Brefvexling*, II, 9 (Stockholm, 1898), pp. 486–8; *Kong Christian den Fjerdes Egenhaendige Breve*, V, pp. 142–4; BL, John Dury, Epistolae Pace Ecclesiastica, Sloane MS 654, ff.216–7.

Plotting Treason

General Leslie's support for Argyll was particularly vital when the 8th Earl faced charges of treason prior to the resumption of the Scottish Estates, charges which delayed proceedings against the Incendiaries but flushed out Montrose as not so much a conservative as a subversive influence within the Covenanting Movement. The charges against Argyll were preferred by John Stewart, younger of Ladywell, one of the gentry in the clans and families that gave their territorial allegiance to the Earl of Atholl. According to Ladywell, Argyll conducted himself treasonably in the course of both the First and Second Bishops' Wars (see Chapter 5). When carrying out his commission to test allegiance of the nobles and gentry in the northern shires in March 1639, Argyll allegedly demanded subscriptions to two sorts of band at Logierait in Perthshire. One required subscribers to be accountable to the Covenanting executive, the other their absolute obedience to Argyll. In the following year, when Argyll was licensed to harry the disaffected in the central and eastern Highlands, he initiated a discourse at the Ford of Lyon in Perthshire after his abduction of Atholl. This discourse among his followers in June 1640 related to the grounds for deposing a king, which were deemed to be threefold: first, desertion by leaving the kingdom without good government; second, prodition (or vendition) betraying the kingdom by attempting the destruction of its laws and liberties; third, invasion by raising armed forces against his loyal subjects. Ladywell claimed to have been an eye-witness to proceedings at Logierait and the Ford of Lyon; and also that Atholl had also heard the discourse on deposition. Both Atholl and Ladywell subsequently made their concerns known to Montrose. Indeed, Atholl became a signatory to the Cumbernauld Band of August 1640, a covert protest drawn up by Montrose and his conservative associates against the Covenanting decision to invade England. This decision was attributed not so much to the settled will of the radical mainstream under the leadership of Argyll, but to 'the particular and indirect practicing of a few', a clear inference to the purportedly seditious activities of the 8th Earl during the Bishops' Wars.[19]

The allegations of treason against Argyll had subsequently been embellished by Montrose and his associates and sustained by his apologists.[20] There is no supporting evidence that Argyll was actively considering a dictatorship during the Bishops' Wars, or that he was to form part of a ruling triumvirate in which General Leslie controlled the Covenanting Army, Hamilton the south

19 ICA, Letters – Marquess's Period, 1638–1645, bundle 6/101–2, /104–6; *MM*, I, pp. 254–5. The Band was named after the Dumbartonshire domain of John Fleming, 5th Earl of Wigton, in which it was subscribed.

20 Wishart, *Memoirs*, pp. 18–19, 21–2; *MHG*, pp. 73, 76, 92–5; *MMM*, I, pp. 264–316; Spalding, *Troubles*, I, pp. 236–8; Cowan, *Montrose*, pp. 108–121.

of Scotland and the 8th Earl the north. Undoubtedly, the Bishops' Wars instigated febrile debate on how Scotland was and should be governed.[21] But Argyll's
banding and reported discourse in Perthshire were not necessarily treasonable.
In 1639 Argyll was manifestly imposing a general band of surety on nobles and
gentry, a practice not uncommon in the Highlands, but now applied specifically
as a test of loyalty to the Covenanting Movement. The particular band of loyalty
to himself was not so much a demand for despotic powers as a pressurised
offer of political clientage, through customary bands of manrent that offered
protection to those whose loyalty was suspect. When Argyll returned to Perthshire in 1640, he was actually holding the subscribers of 1639 to account on
behalf of the Committee of Estates.[22] The discourse on deposition was rooted in
classical political thought and can be deemed more academic than political, for
Covenanting rights of resistance drew primarily on the duty of the commonwealth to oppose ungodly monarchy, not on desertion, vendition or invasion
(see Chapter 5). Transmission of evidence was also problematic: Ladywell
accounts were based as much on hearsay as on direct witness.[23]

In the ongoing debate on political governance during the Bishops' Wars,
Montrose was greatly influenced by his brother-in-law Archibald Napier, Lord
Napier of Merchiston, in advocating the maintenance of a constitutional equilib-
rium. Parliament was a safeguard, not a permanent check on the monarchy.
Undoubtedly there was conservative disquiet about the radical direction of the
Covenanting Movement under Argyll, and a growing sense of public unease

---

21 Willcock, *The Great Marquess*, pp. 111–14; Stevenson, *The Scottish Revolution*, pp. 223–8.

22 Macinnes, *Clanship, Commerce and the House of Stuart*, pp. 11, 50–2; J. Wormald, 'Bloodfeud,
Kindred and Government in Early Modern Scotland', *Past & Present*, 87 (1980), pp. 54–97.
A general band requiring commitment to the Covenanting Movement had been pressed on
Orkney in April 1640 and was made mandatory for all the northern counties by the Scottish
Estates in July 1640. Argyll actually produced six bands before the Committee of Estates. Five
gave commitment to the Covenanting Movement from Atholl, the Braes of Mar and Badenoch;
a sixth was exacted from feuars and tenants of the Earl of Huntly in Badenoch, who were now
obliged to pay their duties and rents to the 8th Earl as principal creditor and mortgage holder
over the Huntly estates (ABDA, 40. 357; *Unpublished Papers of John, Seventh Lord Sinclair*, pp.
24, 37–8).

23 ICA, Letters – Marquess's Period, 1638–1645, bundle 6/101–2, /104–6. Ladywell, who was
commissary clerk of Dunkeld and presumably a lawyer trained in the classics, did converse
discreetly with Atholl in Latin at the Ford of Lyon. But neither he nor the Earl were in close
proximity to Argyll's discussions with his followers and associates, all clansmen, who included
his political enforcer Sir Duncan Campbell of Ardnamurchan and his man of business,
Archibald Campbell of Glencarradale. It can be inferred from Ladywell's testimony before the
Committee of Estates between 31 May and 6 July that this discourse on deposition was not in
Latin. But, it is not certain whether Gaelic or Scots was used. While Ladywell and Atholl could
probably understand both, Montrose was dependent not only on hearsay, but on translated
hearsay if Argyll and his associates conversed in Gaelic.

in the strict subordination of the localities to the centralist demands of the Committee of Estates. Yet Montrose's limited political ability, his overriding ambition and his consuming jealousy towards Argyll had left him all but isolated. At the outset of the peace negotiations at Ripon, his support was reduced to Napier and a small circle of friends and relatives. He was unable to carry influential fellow banders, such as James Livingstone, Lord Almond (later 1st Earl of Callendar), the Covenanting lieutenant-general formerly in Dutch service. Nor was Montrose able to cultivate Rothes who, as a Scottish commissioner, was prepared to work for the effective restoration of royal authority, having been won over by Charles I during the negotiations in London. He could not rely on the supporting testimony of Atholl when he and his few associates were imprisoned as Plotters in May 1641. No less critically, Montrose alienated not only General Leslie but also Hamilton, who remained a powerful influence at the royal court. He thus left himself exposed to the superior political manoeuvrings of Argyll.[24]

While attending the Committee of Estates with the army at Newcastle, Montrose was regularly upbraided by General Leslie for his attempts to maintain correspondence with the king in London. The Committee at Edinburgh having been made aware of the Cumbernauld Band in November 1640, a plenary meeting of the Tables in January 1641 was moved by Argyll to a vociferous condemnation. The 8th Earl also used his considerable influence to have the original draft of the Band burned publicly at the gallows in Edinburgh. Montrose and his associates having issued a disclaimer that their Band was prejudicial to the National Covenant, no further disciplinary action was taken against them until the king announced his intention to come to Scotland once the Treaty of London was concluded. Covenanting suspicions about the motives of the king were not appeased by further evidence coming to light about Montrose's covert contacts with the royal court. Proceedings against Montrose and his close associates were duly instigated through the Committee of Estates in Edinburgh by Argyll on 24 May. Montrose denounced rumours that the Covenanting leadership was intent upon the overthrow of monarchical government as a 'calumnie'. But, he was inexorably compromised by evidence delivered in his presence to the Committee by Mr John Graham, minister of Auchterarder in Perthshire. Indeed, Montrose admitted that he had claimed Argyll had received legal counsel on the means to depose Charles I. Montrose's discomfort was compounded by the evidence presented and then retracted under duress by Ladywell about Argyll's alleged treasonable activities in Perthshire during the Bishops' Wars.[25]

24 NAS, Hamilton Papers, GD 406/1/1378, /1386; *MHG*, pp. 65, 87–98; Cowan, *Montrose*, pp. 96–101, 108–18; Donald, *An Uncounselled King*, pp. 292–7. Rothes' death in August 1641 prevented his further participation in the Scottish Estates.
25 NAS, Hamilton Papers, GD 406/1/1315; *LJB*, I, pp. 262, 356; *MHG*, pp. 92–4; *MM*, I, pp. 293–349.

Ladywell went on to reveal that Lieutenant-Colonel Walter Stuart, a relative of Traquair, acted as a regular courier for Montrose and his associates to the court. When Colonel Stuart was subsequently intercepted and his bags searched on returning from England, sundry coded papers were found in his possession, which Argyll duly presented to the Committee of Estates. Although the papers were encrypted ambiguously, they appeared to suggest that Montrose was warning the king not to attend the Scottish Estates until the Covenanting Army was disbanded. In addition, Montrose and his associates sought to remove Argyll from the proceedings to ensure a free hand for Traquair and the leading Anglo-Scottish courtier James Stewart, 4th Duke of Lennox in Scotland and recently created Earl of Richmond in England. Lennox was closely linked to the defenders of Anglicanism in the English Parliament who were prepared to seek an accommodation with Charles I. Hamilton was palpably distrusted as a serpentine influence at court.[26] Montrose and his fellow Plotters could now be associated with Traquair and the Incendiaries. More importantly, the growing accord between Hamilton and Argyll to work out the intentions of Charles I in coming to Scotland was cemented. It was Hamilton who had confirmed that Montrose was still attempting to correspond with the court prior to his citation before the Committee of Estates in May 1641. Indeed, Hamilton revealed that Montrose had maintained an occasional correspondence with the king since October 1639. Hamilton was convinced that the cause of Britannic monarchy in Scotland could best be served through an accommodation with Argyll and the radical mainstream. He had long been wary of the political posturing of Montrose, whom he considered, among leading Covenanters, as 'none more verilie foolish'.[27]

With Montrose and his associates confined to Edinburgh Castle well before the Scottish Estates were due to resume on 15 July 1641, the Committee of Estates decided to appoint two judicial committees, headed respectively by Argyll and Balmerino, to determine whether both Incendiaries and Plotters should face charges of leasing-making as extended in 1640 to include activity inimical to the Covenanting Movement. When the Scottish Estates duly ratified these commissions on 23 July, the extended charge of leasing-making was actually brought

26 Adamson, *The Noble Revolt*, pp. 306–45; Cowan, *Montrose*, pp. 117–18; Spalding, *Troubles*, I, pp. 323–4, 329–30; *Certain Instructions Given by the L. Montrose, L. Napier, Lairds of Keir and Blackhall, with a True Report of the Committee for this New Treason* (London, 1641).

27 ICA, Letters – Marquess's Period, 1638–1645, bundle 4/70 and Argyll Transcripts, XII, no.118; NAS, Hamilton Papers, GD 406/2/326, /1472, /1759; Burnet, *Memoirs*, pp. 178–80. Talk of a marriage alliance between the houses of Argyll and Hamilton, which Loudoun was prepared to broker, never came to fruition. Argyll, who had drawn up a provisional contract in January 1642, still held out hope for three more months for a marriage between his son and heir, Archibald, now Lord Lorne, and Anna, the eldest daughter of the Marquess of Hamilton.

against Ladywell and upheld by a Covenanting assize. Although Argyll had been prepared to argue for clemency, the execution of Ladywell was deemed necessary as a deterrent to others prepared to fabricate 'false, wicked and odious calumnies' against the Covenanting leadership. Nevertheless, Ladywell's expeditious execution on 28 July removed the one witness able to give a measure of credence to the Plotters' aspersions against Argyll, who subsequently used his command of the parliamentary agenda to secure a complete and irredeemable exoneration for his conduct in enforcing Covenanting allegiance in 1639–40.[28]

Despite its mandate having technically expired with the summoning of the Scottish parliament for 15 July 1641, the Committee of Estates continued to control proceedings for the radical mainstream. The weeks prior to the king's opening address on 17 August were taken up not only with judicial matters relating to the Plotters and the Incendiaries, but also to ensuring that the remit and composition was purposely ordered to prevent Montrose using the Scottish Estates to galvanise a Royalist revival in Scotland. Accordingly, Montrose was conceded a judicial hearing, but not until 24 August, fourteen days after the promulgation of an oath committing every member of the Estates to uphold the National Covenant, to bring the Plotters and Incendiaries to trial, and to work for a permanent peace and union with England. This latter proposal was accepted in principle but not resolved in practice by the Treaty of London. With the tacit consent of Charles I, a group of pragmatic Royalists led by Hamilton took the parliamentary oath to secure their attendance at the Scottish Estates. Hamilton, not Montrose, now forged an alliance with conservative Covenanters, which concurred with the radical mainstream and Charles I that a judicial hearing would be politically inexpedient. This alliance posed no immediate threat to the radical mainstream.[29]

---

28 ICA, Letters – Marquess's Period, 1638–1645, bundle 6/104–6; *APS*, V, p. 399; *HMG*, p. 94; Balfour, *HW*, III, pp. 10–29, 34–8; *Selected Justiciary Cases*, II, pp. 423–42.

29 *MMM*, I, 349–57; *Diary of Sir Thomas Hope*, pp. 140–3; ICA, Argyll Letters (1638–85), A 36/128; *APS*, V, pp. 318, 323–4, 328–9, 330–58; Young, *The Scottish Parliament*, pp. 30–42. Argyll and the radicals were now bolstered by the individual voting rights accorded to the gentry as shire commissioners in 1640. Each Estate met separately as a Table to discuss bills and overtures referred from the floor of the house or from relevant committees. The endorsement of one Table, particularly that of the nobility over which Argyll was elected to preside on 13 August, was deemed vital before a bill or overture could be approved by the whole house. Actual control over proceedings on the floor of the house continued to be vested in a president elected by the Scottish Estates, not a commissioner elected by the king. Burleigh, who had presided from June 1640, now gave way to the more assertive Balmerino, the longstanding opponent as well as the victim of the unfettered exercise of the royal prerogative. At the same time, Argyll and the Committee of Estates were determined to uphold parliamentary dominance over the general assembly meeting in Edinburgh. Argyll, attending as an elder, had played a leading role in ensuring that the assembly had no truck with Brownism and other religious strains of

Monarchy Limited

Charles had assented to the Treaty of London primarily in the hope of detaching the Covenanting Movement from its alliance with the English Parliamentarians – a forlorn mission. Despite the attention given in English newsletters to the proposed trial of the Plotters and Incendiaries, the main objective of Argyll and the radical mainstream was to perpetuate revolution. Priority was accorded to retaining a military presence within Scotland; to securing parliamentary control over the executive and judiciary; and to replacing the Committee of Estates by diverse commissions to govern Scotland in the interval between parliaments.

The phased withdrawal of the Covenanting Army from England had been concluded and the disbandment of the shire levies was well underway by 30 August, when commissioners from the English Parliament arrived in Edinburgh to conserve the peace as well as observe the proceedings of the Scottish Estates. The Treaty of London had been fulfilled financially to the extent that all arrears of daily cess (totalling £254,575 sterling) and the initial instalment of the brotherly assistance (£80,000) had been paid. However, the Covenanting leadership was not contemplating total disbandment, having instigated a motion in the Scottish Estates on 20 August that three standing regiments of foot were to be retained. Infantry numbers were to be augmented by up to 4,500 men and reinforced by a cavalry troop of 400. The Covenanters thus retained the services of the professional soldiers who had returned from the continent for the Bishops' Wars. Friction arising from the disbandment of troops with pay still substantially in arrears was thereby reduced. This retention of a professional corps to enforce Covenanting conformity was justified on 28 August not in terms of internal order, but on account of the continuing presence of armed forces elsewhere in the British Isles. The continuance of garrisons at Berwick and Carlisle and the menacing presence of predominantly Catholic forces in Ireland questioned the inclination and the capacity of the English Parliament to expedite its own commitment to total disbandment.[30]

Independency migrating north from England. Conventicling was reined in, being licensed as no more than prayer meetings auxiliary to the public worship of congregations and the private worship of families. The assembly had conveniently pronouncement that the Cumbernauld Band was illegal. However, no direct or unsolicited interference by the assembly in political affairs was to be tolerated. (*LJB*, I, pp. 362–79, 469; NLS, Yester Papers, MS 7032, ff.49; Balfour, *HW*, III, pp. 30–2).

30 NAS, Supplementary Parliamentary Papers, 1606–42, PA 7/2/74 and PA 14/1, fo.7 and PA 16/3/5/3; *APS*, V, pp. 334–5, 346–50, 364, 369, 400; *The Nicholas Papers, Correspondence of Sir Edward Nicholas, Secretary of State*, G.F. Warner ed., 2 vols (London, 1886), I, pp. 25, 33–4; Anon., *Questions Exhibited by the Parliament now in Scotland Assembled Concerning the Earl of Montrose his Plot* (London, 1641).

Reserves of goodwill within the Scottish Estates to Charles I were soon dissipated by his rearguard action to reserve as 'a special part of his prerogative' the appointment and removal of officers of state, councillors and senators of the College of Justice. Charles was particularly concerned lest his concession of a veto to the Scottish Estates would serve as a precedent to limit monarchical power in England. Nevertheless, the Estates did secure an effective veto over the executive and judiciary when Charles eventually conceded on 16 September that he would chose officials, councillors and senators with their 'advyse and approbatione'. This concession, which had been on the Covenanting agenda since 1639, was seemingly made more palatable for Charles on the grounds that, as an absentee monarch, he was not always or adequately informed about the best qualified candidates for office. Nevertheless, the Covenanting leadership did not have a clear run with their preferred candidates for the two senior offices of state – the chancellorship and the treasury – which they had hoped would be filled by Argyll and Loudoun respectively.

The reluctance of the king to accept Argyll has been attributed to the vehemence with which the 8th Earl opposed the king's nomination of the heavily indebted Morton as chancellor. Albeit Argyll had broken with Morton, who had remained at Court during the Bishops' Wars, his berating of his father-in-law and former guardian was received as extremely ungracious and ungrateful. However, Charles was primarily incensed by the 8th Earl's speech to the Scottish Estates on 30 September, when he claimed that the absence of parliaments in both Scotland and England had allowed evil councillors to attempt religious innovations and favour monopolists. He went on to commend the English Parliament for its dealings with those who broke the indissoluble bonds of protection and allegiance between the king and his subjects in all of his three kingdoms. This unsubtle reference to the attainter of Strafford and the imprisonment of Archbishop Laud concluded with a rallying cry for the parliaments in both Scotland and England to reconcile national differences and follow up the Treaty of London by perpetuating 'the happy Peace and Union of both nations'. The British confederate had talked himself out of becoming the king's chief official in Scotland. Nevertheless, Charles was obliged to accept Loudoun as chancellor. He also had to concede that the treasury should be run by a five-man commission that included Argyll and Loudoun.[31]

---

31 [Archibald Campbell], *An Honourable Speech Made in the Parlament of Scotland by the Earle of Argile (being now Competitor with Earl Morton for the Chancellorship) the Thirtieth of September 1641* (London, 1641); Anon., *A Declaration of the Proceedings of the Parliament of Scotland* (London, 1641); APS, V, pp. 354–5 c.21, 356–7, 368, 655–6, 666; *LJB*, I, pp. 389–98; Balfour, *HW*, III, pp. 58–9, 64–9; Walker, *Relations and Observations*, II, appendix, p. 7. Morton was also named on the treasury commission.

The king's limited capacity to influence parliamentary proceedings was critically undermined when he appeared to condone tumultuous lobbying of parliament on 12 October. The rumoured assassination of Argyll, Hamilton and his brother William, Earl of Lanark (later 2nd Duke of Hamilton) became known as 'The Incident'. Their assassination or their forcible abduction by ship to London was allegedly a prelude to the public rupture of the Scottish Estates by an armed force sympathetic to Montrose and reinforced by disgruntled war veterans. Although reprisals may also have been planned against Loudoun and General Leslie, 'The Incident' was forestalled by the flight of the intended victims from Edinburgh to Hamilton's residence at Kinneil on the Firth of Forth. Charles interpreted this action as a personal affront; likewise the arrest of the reputed ringleaders with the militant Royalist and impecunious courtier, Ludovic Lindsay, 6th Earl of Crawford to the fore. The king's insistence upon a public investigation to embarrass the Covenanting leadership rebounded. A secret investigation conducted by a twelve-man committee of Covenanting activists invited Argyll, Hamilton and Lanark to return to parliament on 1 November.[32] 'The Incident' hastened the political rapport between Covenanters and pragmatic Royalists, which obliged Charles to accept the constitutional dictates of the radical mainstream. At the same time, all prospects of the king securing Covenanting support against the English Parliamentarians were severed.[33]

Charles I's formal acceptance of the realities of political power in Scotland was manifested in his liberal bestowal of honours and pensions in the wake of 'The Incident'. Thus, Argyll was promoted to Marquess and Loudoun to Earl. General Leslie became Earl of Leven. Johnston of Wariston was knighted and Alexander Henderson given charge of the chapel royal in Scotland.[34] The dominance of the radical mainstream has tended to be masked by the reconstitution of the Privy Council, a reconstitution certainly dominated by the nobility,

---

32 NAS, Hamilton Papers, GD 406/1/1440–1, /1544; BL, Political and State Papers, 16th–17th Centuries. Ramsey Papers, vol. XXV, Add.MSS 33,469, ff.49–50; HL, Loudoun Scottish Collection, box 29/ LO 10271; APS, V, pp. 407–9; Anon., *The Truth of the Proceedings in Scotland Containing the Discovery of the Late Conspiracie* (Edinburgh, 1641); Anon., *A Great Discoverie of a Plot in Scotland, by a Miraculous Meanes* (London, 1641); [Charles I], *King Charles his Resolution Concerning the Church of England, Being Contrary to that of Scotland. With a Speech Spoken by the Lord Car, in the Parliament of Scotland, Being a Little before his Examination Concerning the Plot which was Found out in Scotland* (London, 1641). Lanark had played a significant role as a facilitator for the truce at Ripon when serving the king as Secretary of State for Scottish Affairs (EUL, Instructions of the Committee of Estates of Scotland 1640–41, Dc.4.16. pp. 5–10).

33 Whitelock, *Memorials*, I, pp. 147–8; Donald, *An Uncounselled King*, pp. 313–6; Cowan, *Montrose*, pp. 122–8.

34 *MHG*, pp. 99–111; *LJB*, I, pp. 395–7; Anon., *The Dissolution of the Parliament in Scotland* (London, 1641).

but strictly within the terms of their parliamentary accountability. Compromise with Hamilton and the pragmatic Royalists in the composition of the Council was no more than a cosmetic exercise.[35] All councillors, like all members of the Scottish Estates, were bound by oath to sustain not only the National Covenant but to acknowledge that the parliamentary session of 1641 was free and lawful. They were also bound to promote its enactments.

The radical mainstream was intent on maintaining revolutionary momentum through executive commissions composed of all leading Covenanters. Although the Committee of Estates was not resuscitated at this juncture, its past role as the national government was continued financially, judicially and diplomatically. Financial affairs were devolved to two commissions with a shared membership. The commission for regulating the common burdens of the kingdom was to bring order to the financial chaos left by the Bishops' Wars. The commission for receiving the brotherly assistance from the English Parliament was charged to collate and disburse the chief source of income (£220,000 sterling) still outstanding and due in equal instalments over the next two years. Judicial matters were assigned to separate commissions for the prosecution of Plotters and Incendiaries. Their principal task was to determine the relevance of treasonable charges against the four Plotters led by Montrose and the five Incendiaries headed by Traquair. Diplomatic affairs were entrusted to the commission for the Articles of the Treaty, with special responsibility for conserving the peace within the king's British dominions. The interests of the Kirk were represented by a procurator, Johnston of Wariston who, as a close confidant of Argyll, was also included among the inner core of the conservators of the peace charged to continue negotiations with the English Parliament to resolve all outstanding issues from the Treaty of London. Argyll featured on all financial and diplomatic commissions either as an elected member or as a supernumerary. As an interested party who had faced fabricated charges of treason and attempted assassination, he did not feature on the judicial commissions. Pragmatic Royalists appointed to the Privy Council were denied membership of the commissions for financial affairs. They were also excluded from the commissions for trying the Plotters and Incendiaries. While some were nominated along with Hamilton as conservators of the peace, none were admitted to the inner diplomatic core whose negotiating remit, in the aftermath of rebellion in Ireland, was extended to establishing the assistance required from Scotland to suppress Catholic insurgency.[36]

35 Makey, *The Church of the Covenant*, pp. 56–8; *Government under the Covenanters*, pp. xxvii–xxxix.

36 *APS*, V, pp. 505–7 c.89, 391–6 c.76–7, 400–3 c.85, 404–5 c.87–88, 408–9, c.92; HL, Loudoun Scottish collection, box 43/ LO 7014; SPT, I, pp. 1516; A.I. Macinnes, 'The Scottish Constitution, 1638–1651'.

Irish Rebellion

The menacing presence of an armed Catholic force under Sir Phelim O'Neill forcibly brought the Irish perspective to the centre stage of British politics following the outbreak of rebellion in Ulster on 22 October 1641. Although the rebels failed to seize Dublin Castle, the insurrection spread to Connacht by November and to Munster by December – albeit its full extent was not apparent until the following spring. Its immediate political impact in Scotland was to change the international priorities of the Covenanting Movement.

Speaking on behalf of the nobility to the gentry and burgesses on 19 August, Argyll had affirmed that the promotion of religious uniformity with England must be held in abeyance. Nevertheless, there was still scope to develop projects which would advance unity and brotherly love between both kingdoms. A speech by Loudoun to the Scottish Estates on 9 September suggested that the Treaty of London could be consolidated through joint action by Scottish Covenanters and English Parliamentarians to recover the Palatinate for the family of the Winter Queen. This project appealed not only to Covenanting radicals but also to the conservatives and pragmatic Royalists grouped around Hamilton who had a long track record of support for Elizabeth of Bohemia. Support for the recovery of the Palatinate was a notable defining feature of the Commonwealth grouping among English Parliamentarians. When Charles I invited his nephew to accompany him to Scotland, Elector Charles Louis was accorded an honoured place by the Scottish Estates. Mobilising of military support for the restoration of the Elector was given a serious hearing, not least because it allowed the Covenanters to retain a military presence within Scotland rather than disband all their forces. Loudoun returned to this theme on 24 September, when he rebutted objections that Scotland had been so ruined and depopulated by the Bishops' Wars that the country was in no position to undertake a military venture overseas. An expedition to recover the Palatinate, with their English brethren in tow, would secure gainful employment for those professional troops deemed superfluous since the conclusion of the Bishops' Wars, and would also provide relief for former conscripts now obliged to find alternative subsistence pending economic recovery.[37]

The Rise and Fall of Oligarchic Centralism' in J. Morrill ed., *The Scottish National Covenant in its British Context, 1638–51* (Edinburgh, 1990), pp. 106–33); Young, *The Scottish Parliament*, pp. 44–6. There was one other commission to dispose of episcopal rights of patronage as well as the titularship of the teinds. Its concerns were the parochial ramifications arising from the abolition of episcopacy, which served as the primary grounds for resurrecting the work of teind valuation and redistribution. No ministers were included to represent the Kirk.

37 Balfour, *HW*, III, pp. 4–45; NAS, Hamilton Papers, GD 406/1/1378; Sir Simonds D'Ewes, *Speech Delivered in the House of Commons 7 July 1641, Being Resolved into a Committee . . . in the Palatine Case* (London, 1641); [Archibald Campbell], *A True Copy of a Speech Delivered in*

Six days after its outbreak, news of the Irish rebellion was conveyed by Charles I to the Scottish Estates, along with an invitation for armed intervention to protect the plantations. However, the Covenanting leadership was not prepared to intervene without the consent of the English Parliament. Nonetheless, the Irish rebellion afforded a more plausible guise than the recovery of the Palatinate for the retention and, indeed, the escalation of their military forces. Argyll had wanted to open up a second Irish front to complement General Leslie's march into England in August 1640, and he received a commission to levy 10,000 men for this purpose. Although this commission was not implemented, the Scottish Estates duly offered the services of 10,000 troops to the Long Parliament on 2 November. The Scottish expeditionary force was to be made up of eight regiments and include 2,500 Highlanders drawn primarily from territories affiliated to the ClanCampbell. Alexander Montgomery, 6th Earl of Eglinton, a radical noble from the west of Scotland with extensive family and landed interests in Ulster, chaired a committee to ascertain the availability of transport on the Firth of Clyde to ship Covenanting volunteers to Ireland. With Argyll to the fore as a political facilitator, military preparations for Ireland were continued by the Privy Council after the Scottish Estates concluded on 17 November.[38]

The Covenanters had a profound constitutional as well as political impact in shaping Irish affairs between the outbreak of the rebellion in October 1641 and the formation of the Confederation of Irish Catholics at Kilkenny in May 1642. Economic recession following a run of poor harvests from 1636, the pace of commercial re-orientation of estate management, and the growing indebtedness of native Irish landowners such as Sir Phelim O'Neill certainly contributed to the rapid spread of rebellion within and beyond Ulster. Recession had also hit Scotland from 1636, where poor harvests were compounded by the king's pursuit of economic uniformity (see Chapter 4). However, the resultant migration of Scots to Ulster had further diminished the prospects of native Irish being retained rather than displaced by plantations. Reversal of plantations was of particular significance to the native Irish. But rebellion to achieve this end and, in the process, offer the security for Roman Catholicism which Strafford

---

the Parliament in Scotland, by the Earle of Argile, Concerning the Government of the Church (London, 1641); [John Campbell], *The Lord Lowden his Learned and Wise Speech in the Upper House of Parliament in Scotland, September 9, 1641* (London, 1641); [John Campbell], *A Second Speech Made by the Lord Lowden, in the Parliament of Scotland the 24 of Septemb. 1641* (London, 1641). Overseas service was also an attractive means of ridding Scotland of militant Royalists (ICA, Letters – Marquess's Period, 1638–1645, bundle 6/110).

38 *LJB*, I, pp. 254, 396–7; Balfour, *HW*, III, pp. 64, 92, 125, 128–30, 134–5, 143–6; *APS*, V, pp. 376–8, 429–30; *RPCS*, VII, pp. 149, 171–2, 199, 227, 245–6, 260, 287, 480; *ACL*, II, pp. 311, 316, 320; NAS, Hamilton Papers, GD 406/1/1708.

had been intent on undermining, only became feasible with the belated return of veterans in Spanish service, such as Owen Roe O'Neill, in the summer of 1642.

The capacity of the native Irish to reach out to the Old English was facilitated not just by their common Catholicism, but by their joint determination to prevent direct rule by the English Parliament. This distinctly Irish perspective, which was first articulated by Geoffrey Keating (Séathrún Céitinn) around 1634, asserted that Ireland was not a barbaric backwater that required civilising through conquest, plantation and the imposition of the English common law. Keating, as befitting a descendant of an Old English family, was concerned to ensure that due place was given to the contribution of the *Sean-Gallaibh* as well as the Irish Gael in sustaining Roman Catholicism. Both groups should be designated *Éireannaigh*, that is the Catholic Irish, in contrast to the *Nua-Gallaibh*, effectively the Protestant settlers who arrived in Munster under the Tudors and in Ulster under the Stuarts. Keating was primarily concerned to validate Irish acceptance of the Stuart dynasty through such traditional mechanisms as providence, prophecy and legitimacy. Ireland should be accorded constitutional equality with England and Scotland as a free not a dependent Stuart kingdom.[39]

These same mechanisms ensured that the Irish rebels sought rapprochement with Charles I as the rightful king of Ireland, not just to resolve factional and territorial differences but to counter pressure from the Scottish Covenanters that Ireland be reduced to a parliamentary dependency. The right of the Irish parliament to wage war was subsumed within the remit of the English Parliament when the Treaty of London was ratified with the Scottish Covenanters in August 1641: a situation that stood in stark contrast to the Treaty's formal recognition of the sovereign and independent power of the Scottish Estates. Moreover, the Scottish commissioners had not only insisted that the English Parliament sanction the king's future raising of forces in England and Ireland, but also wanted the Irish parliament to ratify its acceptance of this dependency. This standpoint was supported by Pym's associates among the radical Commonwealthmen who were intent on enforcing Irish dependency in order to limit monarchical power in England. The Irish response was articulated by Patrick Darcy, an Old English lawyer, who moved the Irish parliament of 1641 to impose permanent checks on the exercise of executive power through Dublin and to secure direct access to monarchy at Court. Although Ireland was to be governed by the common law and general customs of England, all statutes were to be made and approved by the Irish parliament. The annexation

---

39 B. Ó Buachalla, *Foras Feasa ar Éirinn, History of Ireland: Foreword* (Dublin, 1987); pp. 1–8; B. Cunningham, *The World of Geoffrey Keating* (Dublin, 2000), pp. 31–40, 83–101; Perceval-Maxwell, *The Outbreak of the Irish Rebellion*, pp. 129–239.

of Ireland to the English Crown was accepted; the subordination of the Irish to the English parliament was not. This doctrine was subsequently endorsed by the Confederate Catholics. Nevertheless, Irish opposition should not be overstated as a principled parliamentary critique of arbitrary rule. Recourse to a military option was more potent.[40]

Despite appealing to Covenanting precedents for their recourse to arms, the rebels had no coherent constitutional programme to implement prior to the landed elite and the clergy imposing a confederal structure of government in May 1642. The resultant Catholic confederation was designed to legitimise rebellion, restrain the excesses of reprisals against Protestant settlers, and bring about a measure of political stability among factional Irish interests. In essence, both the native Irish and the Old English were not so much opposed to the prerogative powers of monarchy as to the pretensions of the English parliament to legislate for Ireland. Furthermore, any confederal union between Scottish Covenanters and English Parliamentarians carried the inherent threat of reducing Ireland to the profession of Protestantism, not Roman Catholicism, as the true religion.[41]

Notwithstanding the marked hostility of English Parliamentarians and Scottish Covenanters, the Irish Catholics were reluctant rebels. Their ideological standpoint in favour of autonomy under the Stuarts made them anxious for reconciliation with Charles I. When the Confederation of Irish Catholics was established at Kilkenny in May 1642, Ireland was proclaimed to have the same freedom as that enjoyed by the subjects of the Stuart monarchy in both England and Scotland. Despite a similar rhetoric of resistance, the Confederate perspective was markedly different from that of the Covenanters. Their oath of association pledged allegiance to Charles I, and their promise to act in his defence made no distinction between his person and his office; a theme reiterated by their official seal affirming unconditional loyalty to God, king and country. When the Confederates held their first general assembly at Kilkenny

---

40 A. Clarke, 'Patrick Darcy and the Constitutional Relationship between Ireland and Britain' in Ohlmeyer ed., *Irish Political Thought in the Seventeenth Century*, pp. 35–55; M. Perceval-Maxwell, 'Ireland and the Monarchy in the Early Stuart Multiple Kingdom', *HJ*, 34 (1991), pp. 279–95; M. Ó Siochrú, *Confederate Ireland, 1642–9: A Constitutional and Political Analysis* (Dublin, 1999), pp. 21–6, 237–40.

41 T. Ó h-Annráchain, 'Rebels and Confederates: The Stance of the Irish Clergy in the 1640s' in Young ed., *Celtic Dimensions of the British Civil Wars*, pp. 96–115; M. Ó Siochrú, 'Catholic Confederates and the Constitutional Relationship between Ireland and England, 1641–1649' in C. Brady and J. Ohlmeyer eds, *British Interventions in Early Modern Ireland* (Cambridge, 2005), pp. 207–29; Canny, *Making Ireland British*, pp. 404–8, 553–6, 561. The rebels had become increasingly alarmed not just at the prospect of the full panoply of the penal laws being deployed against recusancy, but at the language of extirpation used by Pym and his associates in relation to Catholicism.

five months later, they elected a supreme council of twenty-four members, six from each province. Although twelve were to sit permanently between assemblies in the manner of the Committee of Estates, the assembly increasingly circumscribed independent action by the executive. The Irish Catholics never developed centralised agencies of government. Their cause remained that of a confederation of provincial associations riven by faction, underfinanced yet militarily capable by land and sea.[42]

Radical Consolidation

The Irish rebellion had consolidated the growing rapport between the Covenanting radicals and the pro-Scottish radical faction among English Parliamentarians, which was based on their shared distrust of Charles I. Nevertheless, tripartite negotiations with the English Parliament and Charles I to suppress rebellion, which again involved the despatch of Scottish commissioners to London, became protracted. The Covenanters sought guarantees that the English Parliament would meet the operational costs of their forces in Ireland; that the Ulster ports of Londonderry, Coleraine and Carrickfergus would be ceded to them for the duration of their intervention; and that Scots as well as English settlers would benefit from plantations created from confiscated Irish lands. The commissioners, drawn from the inner diplomatic core of the conservators of the peace, were led by Argyll's close ally, William Ker, 3rd Earl of Lothian and by the more conservatively inclined John Lindsay, 1st Earl of Lindsay (later Crawford-Lindsay). The endeavours of Charles to commit Covenanting forces without waiting for the consent of the English Parliament blatantly disregarded the Treaty of London, much to the chagrin of Scottish Covenanters. Indiscriminate reports of outrageous Irish atrocities and the pitiful condition of the British in Ireland gave Charles the excuse to return to England on 17 November, to secure backing for armed intervention. However, his blatant equivocation on the Irish issue accelerated the descent to civil war in England.[43]

Nine days before the king's return to London, the Commons at Pym's behest had taken responsibility for suppressing the Irish rebellion. At the same time, the Commons drew up and debated the Grand Remonstrance, which had been

42 BL, Turnbull Papers vol. CXCI, Add.MSS 72,432 fo.151; M. Ó Siochrú, *Confederate Ireland, 1642–9*, pp. 205–15; J.H. Ohlmeyer, 'The Civil Wars in Ireland' in J. Kenyon and J.H. Ohlmeyer eds, *The Civil Wars: A Military History of England, Scotland and Ireland 1638–1660* (Oxford, 1998), pp. 73–102; Russell, *The Fall of the British Monarchies*, pp. 373–94.

43 *The Nicholas Papers*, I, pp. 25, 33–4; 58–9; D. Stevenson, *Scottish Covenanters and Irish Confederates* (Belfast, 1981), pp. 43–60. A cavalry troop of the Marquess of Argyll actually escorted Charles out of Scotland (*RPCS*, VII, p. 504).

in preparation by Pym and his associates since the opening of the Long Parliament. This contentious indictment of prerogative rule, which secured only a narrow majority in the House, was duly presented to Charles on 1 December. Again Scottish precedent was evident in its demand that the king should only employ officials, councillors and judges with parliamentary approval. But Scottish influence on the religious establishment was diluted when all issues of doctrine, worship and discipline were referred to a synod of divines drawn from England and the other Protestant communities of Europe. Charles sought to pre-empt radical action by attempting to arrest Pym and four associates in the Commons on 4 January 1642. Forewarned, the five MPs escaped. Having lost face, the king ceded control of the capital to the Parliamentarians.

By 5 March, both the Commons and the Lords had agreed on the Militia Ordinance, which put the raising, command and supply of forces, whether they were sent to Ireland or not, under parliamentary control. Hostilities were initially opened through a prolonged propaganda war. On 1 June, the Long Parliament published the Nineteen Propositions with the intention of dictating terms. Charles was required to have his executive and judiciary subject to parliamentary approval. He was also to consent to the reform of the Church of England by an international synod and to accept the Militia Ordinance. Henry Parker, the foremost polemicist for the Parliamentarians, claimed that Charles was more solicitous of the interests of the Irish Confederates than of the many Protestants murdered daily at their hands. Parker saw the need for a British resolution. It was better that 'the State of Scotland were intreated to mediate and adjudicate' than civil war break out in England. [44]

Three months earlier, the Scottish Privy Council's offer of Argyll as mediator between the king and the Parliamentarians was actually rejected by the latter, on the grounds that the Irish rebels would 'take great advantage' of his absence from Scotland. Argyll had actually encouraged Hamilton to approach Charles I about the desirability of mediation in late December 1641. By 20 January 1642, Argyll was convinced that the king would be the inevitable loser should his dispute with the English Parliament lead to armed conflict. As supreme magistrate, Charles I was facing 'the loss of the Commonwealth'. He stood to gain more by allowing the Parliament to play a full part in government rather than 'by making them Jealous of his power by the offer of violence'. Argyll wrote to Charles regretting the lost opportunity of his parliamentary rejection of 22 February. Although the king wanted to separate Argyll from the Parliamentarians, the king was no more agreeable than the Lords or the Commons to his mediation. By the

---

44 Woolrych, *Britain in Revolution*, pp. 199–230; Smith, *Constitutional Royalism and the Search for Settlement*, pp. 80–91; Henry Parker, *The Danger to England Observed, upon its Deserting the High Court of Parliament* (London, 1642).

beginning of April, the Scottish commissioners were prepared to withdraw from the tripartite negotiations as English concerns about Ireland were being overtaken by the growing constitutional impasse between king and Parliament. Their presence was retained after a concerted endeavour by the negotiators for the English Parliament, who had constituted themselves into the committee 'for preserving the union betwixt the two nations'. In effect, this committee was the English parliamentary delegation sent to Scotland to observe the proceedings of the Scottish Estates in 1641. In Edinburgh, they had developed particularly good personal relationships with Argyll, the Earl of Leven and John Kennedy, 6th Earl of Cassillis, a noble from the south-west of Scotland noted for his radicalism.[45]

Although rumours of the king's going to Ireland caused palpitations among Scottish Covenanters and English Parliamentarians, Charles I was primarily concerned to make Royalism a cause worth fighting for. The Irish rebellion had ruled out any prospect of his ability to dissolve the Long Parliament. Accordingly, his response to the Nineteen Propositions on 18 June did not stress his prerogative. Instead he argued, as Montrose had done earlier in Scotland, for constitutional equilibrium. Monarchy should be respectful of, but not subordinated to, the Lords and Commons. Tilting this equilibrium to favour Parliament in general and the Commons in particular threatened chaos in Church and State. The king's rallying cry proved effective in drawing support from both houses once the royal standard was raised at Nottingham on 22 August. Royalism was not confined to England. Montrose had committed to the cause on his release from captivity and his inconclusive trial in Scotland. James Butler, 12th Earl (later Marquess and Duke of) Ormond, was stirred from the lethargy that had afflicted him as Royalist commander in Ireland during the Bishops' Wars.[46]

Despite the British political dimension, there was no clear solidarity on the Protestant side beyond a shared aversion towards Catholicism and outrage at such humiliations as the stripping and forced marching of surviving settlers. On the outbreak of rebellion, Irish fears of Covenanting military prowess meant

---

45 Anon., *Certaine Reasons Presented to the Kings Most Excellent Maiestie, Feb. 24. 1641. By the Lords and Commons in Parliament Touching the Princes Stay at Hampton Court* (London, 1642); NAS, Hamilton Papers, GD 406/1/3106, /1757, /1759, /1769, /8267; HL, Loudoun Scottish Collection, box 29/ LO 10503; *Letters to the Argyll Family*, A. Macdonald ed. (Edinburgh, 1839), p. 37; *RPCS*, second series, VII, pp. 198, 211, 217, 224.

46 HL, Bridgewater and Ellesmere MSS, EL 7763–4, 7803 and Stowe Collection: Temple Papers, STT Ship Money L8C10; Scott, *Politics and War in the Three Stuart Kingdoms*, pp. 33–6; W. Kelly, 'James Butler, Twelfth Earl of Ormond, the Irish Government and the Bishops' Wars, 1638–1640' in Young ed., *Celtic Dimensions of the British Civil Wars*, pp. 35–54. The commission for the trial of the Plotters held the case against Montrose in camera at the end of February 1642. He was found guilty of breaching the Covenant and acting to divide the Movement. However, he was given a royal pardon (Cowan, *Montrose*, pp. 131–2).

that Scottish settlers were subject to relatively fewer reprisals and depredations than the English. In turn, the English clergy in Dublin, who compiled the grossly exaggerated depositions on the extent of atrocities against the Protestant plantations, differentiated between Scottish, Irish and Welsh victims and tended to appropriate the designation of 'British' for settlers born in England. The term British became a synonym for the English interest in Ireland.[47] Sir John Clotworthy, who viewed the abolition of episcopacy as the first step towards reducing Ireland to the profession of Protestantism, was nevertheless wary of encouraging Covenanting intervention. Indeed, he actively worked to frustrate Scottish demands for terms of engagement that conflicted with the territorial ambitions of his fellow English planters. Clotworthy promoted the Adventurers Act through the Long Parliament in March 1642. The recovery of Ireland was duly tied to further plantation. This combination of religious and speculative interests attracted considerable support from the Protestant elite in Ireland, as from London merchants and English Parliamentarians. Scottish subscribers were neither excluded nor encouraged.[48]

However, the Covenanting leadership had already made a distinctive response. Up to 4,000 impoverished refugees, at least 13% of the Scottish population in Ulster prior to the rebellion, fled across the North Channel. Around 500 of these refugees had arrived in Cowal and the Kyles of Bute by December 1641. The burden of supporting widows and orphans became a national concern.[49] This concern sustained voluntary financial contributions from February and compulsory troop mobilisation from March 1642, under Major-General Robert Munro, a veteran of the Thirty Years War and a Covenanting stalwart of the Bishops' Wars. Munro led an expeditionary force of 2,500 Scottish troops into Ulster on 3 April. At the same time, Argyll exploited reports that the Irish branch of the ClanDonald South and its Scottish remnants had joined with the rebels in order to revive their territorial claims to Kintyre, Islay and Jura. To head off this threat, Argyll was licensed by both Charles I and the English

47 BL, Observations of the State of Ireland, April 1640, Stowe MS 29, fo.2; R. Gillespie, 'Destabilising Ulster' in B. MacCuarta ed., *Ulster 1641: Aspects of the Rising* (Belfast, 1997), pp. 107–22; Canny, *Making Ireland British*, pp. 461–534.

48 A. Clarke, 'The 1641 Rebellion and Anti-Popery in England' in Mac Cuarta ed., *Ulster 1641*, pp. 139–57; Canny, *Making Ireland British*, pp. 404–8, 541–50, 553–6, 561; M. Perceval-Maxwell, 'Ireland and Scotland' in Morrill ed., *The Scottish National Covenant in its British Context*, pp. 193–211.

49 J.R. Young, '"Escaping Massacre": Refugees in Scotland in the aftermath of the 1641 Ulster Rebellion' in D. Edwards, P. Lenihan and C. Tait eds, *Age of Atrocity: Violence and Political Conflict in Early Modern Ireland* (Dublin, 2007), pp. 219–41. An unintended cultural consequence of this exodus was the Marquess of Argyll making provision for English schooling at Dunoon in Cowal from October 1642 (ICA, Letters – Marquess's Period, 1638–1645, bundle 6/115).

Parliament to raise 1,500 men to launch an offensive against the Antrim estates. Not only was this additional force to be maintained by the English Parliament, but Argyll was made governor of the Rathlin Isles as the Highland bridgehead into Ulster. Covenanting hopes for reimbursement from the English Parliament for mobilising troops, transport and munitions remained uncertain, however. Accordingly, Argyll and Loudoun insisted that Leven's commission as general should be authorised by the king and the Scottish Privy Council. Thus, an army of 4,000 volunteers was despatched 'from the kingdome of Scotland for his maties service to assist the kingdome of England against the rebels in Ireland'.[50]

By 7 July, the English Parliament had agreed to pay the Scottish forces at the higher rates allowed to English troops. The Covenanting Army was also ceded control of Coleraine and Carrickfergus for use as magazines and garrisons. Initial engagements between the Catholic Confederates and the Scottish Covenanters were confined to skirmishes, guerrilla campaigning and reciprocal massacres from May 1642, instigated by the British forces under Edward Conway, 2nd Viscount (later 1st Earl of) Conway at Newry, then continued by the Irish forces under Phelim O'Neill at Armagh and concluding with the Argyll regiment in the Rathlin Isles. Subsequently, the professionalism of the respective Ulster commanders Robert Munro and Owen Roe O'Neill ensured that restraint was exercised on both sides. Although confessionalism remained a bitterly and brutally divisive issue, both the Covenanting and Confederate forces had a backbone of veterans from the Thirty Years War who were wary of exchanging atrocities. Such experienced and orderly influences were not so evident in England once civil war broke out between Royalists and Parliamentarians.[51]

Counting officers, artillery and cavalry detachments as well as ten regiments of infantry, the Covenanters had over 11,350 troops in Ulster by August 1642. Although the Earl of Leven was the designated supreme commander of the Scottish forces, he only spent three months in Ireland, departing in November of that year. The war against the Catholic Confederation, if not the antithesis of

---

50 NAS, Hamilton Papers, GD 406/1/1488, /1580, /1602, /1610, /1635; ICA, Argyll Transcripts, XII, nos 111, 141, 123–33 and Letters – Marquess's Period, 1638–1645, bundle 6/124 and Argyll Letters (1638–85), A 36/121–4, /129; *RPCS*, second series, VII, p. 185, 191, 221, 225, 233; Stevenson, *Scottish Covenanters and Irish Confederates*, pp. 61–80. Loudoun's brother, Sir Mungo Campbell, younger of Lawers was a colonel in Argyll's advance guard. Although Argyll raised a regiment for service in Ireland and was duly named a colonel in the Scottish expeditionary force, he had already effectively resigned his charge on 21 March when he appointed his kinsman, Sir Duncan Campbell of Auchinbreck, to take command as lieutenant-colonel and as governor of the Rathlin Isles.

51 *Unpublished Letters of John, Seventh Lord Sinclair*, pp. 49, 51–2; [Alexander Leslie, Earl of Leven], *Camp Discipline, or the Souldier's Duty* (London, 1642); B. Donagan, 'Codes of Conduct in the English Civil War', *Past & Present*, 118 (1988), pp. 64–95.

his intervention in England in 1640–41, had limited success. The most substantive achievement of the first sixteen months of campaigning in 1642–43 was
the regaining of great swathes of Ulster by Munro, albeit his effective exercise
of command over the British as well as the Scottish forces was continually
challenged by Viscount Conway. Published despatches to the Commons from
Ireland, which reported the factual and providential success of the English army
in the spring and summer of 1642, made no mention of joint British endeavours
to secure redress for Protestant settlers.[52]

Munro also had a measure of success in preventing the Catholic Confederacy
giving meaningful support to the Royalists in England. Nevertheless, with the
outbreak of civil war in England, spasmodic supplies from the Parliamentarians
dried up. The Covenanting Army in Ulster was forced to live a hand-to-mouth
existence, dependent on foraging and occasional loans from Scotland. At the
same time, respect for England's claims on Ireland as a dependent kingdom
inhibited the Covenanting Army from annexing Ulster and establishing the
equivalent of Scottish shire committees of war in the reclaimed counties to
supply money and provisions. An element of ideological commitment was
promoted through the establishment of the presbytery of Ulster, drawn initially
from the chaplains and elders of the ten Scottish regiments, and then expanded
to include Scottish contingents among the British forces as well as Scottish
settlers in Antrim and Down. However, Munro refused persistently to move the
Covenanting Army out of Ulster. His total disregard to overtures for assistance
from Ormond in Dublin eventually drove the Irish Royalists, with encouragement from Charles I, to negotiate a cessation of hostilities with the Catholic
Confederates by September 1643.[53]

Argyll did not actively participate in the initial campaigns in Ulster. Therefore, he cannot be directly held to account for the massacre carried out by his
regiment in the Rathlin Isles. Nevertheless, he again used the Covenanting

---

52 Sir Simon Harcourt, *March 18. A Letter Sent from Sr. Simon Harcourt, to a Worthy Member of
   the House of Commons. With a True Relation of the Proceedings of the English Army, under his
   Command to this Present March* (London, 1641); Edward Conway, 2nd Viscount Conway, *A
   Relation from the Right Honourable the Lord Viscount Conway, of the Proceedings of the English
   Army in Ulster from June 17 to July 30* (London, 1642). In part, this bickering can be attributed
   to Conway's defeat as commander of the king's forces at Newburn during the Second Bishops'
   War.
53 Stevenson, *Scottish Covenanters and Irish Confederates*, pp. 103–44; Adair, *A True Narrative*, pp.
   69–134; BOU, Carte Papers, 1636–52. Ireland, MS Carte 65, ff.61–2; ICA, Letters – Marquess's
   Period, 1638–1645, bundle 61/1. When the Presbytery of Ulster took in civil parishes occupied
   by the Covenanting Army, local ministers and gentry eligible for eldership were obliged to
   purge themselves of past acceptance of Strafford's 'black oath'. However, it was only with an
   injection of young and unplaced ministers from Scotland that Presbyterianism was able to
   expand into the counties of Derry, Donegal and Tyrone in the course of 1644.

cause for his own private ends. In the same way that Munro would not lead the Covenanting Army out of Ulster, the Argyll Regiment, once it had occupied the Antrim estates, would not accept any order that took it away from the Rathlin Isles, the Antrim Glens and the Route. In effect, Argyll and his regiment carried on a clan feud in Ulster under Covenanting colours. But Argyll cannot be written off as pursuing clannish interests in Ireland any more than in his northern campaigns during the Bishops' Wars. On both occasions he bore campaigning costs in excess of £135,815 (£12,316 sterling), with no immediate prospect of remuneration from the public purse. Having expended over £54,437 on the northern campaigns, he personally spent over £81,377 financing the first two years of Scottish intervention in Ulster. An English newsletter report of 19 October 1642 also suggests wider concerns. A punitive raid against the Isle of Man by Argyll was viewed as a singular contribution to the Parliamentary war effort. The overlord of Man was James Stanley, 7th Earl of Derby, a Roman Catholic and prominent Royalist. Argyll, who had been building up his naval resources on the western seaboard from 1639, had the shipping capacity to attack the Isle of Man. However, his motivation was almost certainly to clear the island of pirates, who were interrupting supplies from both England and Scotland to the Covenanting forces in Ulster. The association of Argyll with the Parliamentary cause, nonetheless, was not too wide of the mark as the rival sides in the English theatre of the Wars for the Three Kingdoms sought to secure Covenanting backing.[54]

The Solemn League and Covenant

At the outset of the civil war in England, the Parliamentarians had distinct military advantages. The royal navy deserted the king; accordingly his overseas aid, as anticipated from Christian IV of Denmark-Norway, remained deficient. London supplied recruits by the thousand, the ready money to secure arms and ammunition, and the customs gleaned from global commerce. Nevertheless, Charles mobilised support in towns and counties through commissions of array, supplemented by individual summons to the landed elite, in the north, the south-west and Wales. The reluctance of the Parliamentary forces, in contrast to the Scottish Covenanters, to seek outright victory ceded Charles the day at Edgehill in Warwickshire on 23 October 1642. Charles moved his headquarters from York to Oxford, where he established an alternative parliament as

54 Macinnes, *Clanship, Commerce and the House of Stuart*, p. 96; ICA, Argyll Transcripts, XII, nos 94, 112, 178, 199 and Letters – Marquess's Period, 1638–1645, bundles 6/118, 7/138; ABDA, Argyll Papers, 40.09, 352; Dundee City Archives, Council Book Dundee, IV (1613–1653), fo.46; *RPCS*, second series, VII, pp. 222, 228, 230–1, 321–2, 400, 403, 413, 423, 425, 444; Anon., *Exceedingly Joyfull Newes from Coventry* (London, 1642).

well as his court. But he was unable to mount a frontal assault on London. His forces, particularly the cavalry under Prince Rupert, the younger brother of the Elector Charles Louis, earned a bad press for their atrocities in the Midlands during the spring of 1643. By this juncture, the Parliamentary forces had regrouped into regional associations in the Midlands, East Anglia and the West Country. Following Scottish precedent, commissions of peace were turned into committees of war for the constituent shires. Finances were also overhauled to pay these forces.[55]

Acutely conscious that a substantive majority of the Lords and a significant minority of the Commons had become Royalists, Viscount Saye and Seal supported Pym's push for a military and religious alliance with the Scottish Covenanters that opened up the prospect of confederal union. However negotiations, which commenced in September 1642, took almost eleven months. The main stumbling block was not so much the hesitancy in the Long Parliament about another round of Scottish assistance, but the regrouping of conservative Covenanters and pragmatic Royalists under Hamilton within the Scottish Privy Council. Since its reconstitution in November 1641, the Council had remained susceptible to overtures from the king, particularly after Hamilton's brother Lanark was re-established at court as Secretary of State for Scottish affairs.[56] There were also alternative Covenanting priorities. Argyll, Loudoun and the other radical leaders had determined that the Privy Council must be

---

55 Bennett, *The Civil Wars in Britain and Ireland*, pp. 150–5; R. Hutton, *The Royalist War Effort, 1642-1646* (London, 1999), pp. 22–48; *Declaration of the Lords and Commons Assembled in Parliament Concerning His Majesties Advancing with his Army toward London: With Direction that all Trained Bands and Volunteers be Put into a Readinesse* (London, 1642); Anon., *The King of Denmark's Resolution Concerning Charles King of Great Britain, Wherein is Declared the Determination for the Setting Forth of a Fleet towards England* (London, 1642). An act passed in March to raise £4 million sterling in two instalments by December supplemented the weekly assessment or cess imposed on shires under English Parliamentary control from February. To counteract adverse publicity from levies on landed property, an ordinance of July instituted a new impost, effectively an excise tax, on imports. Notorious delinquents contributing money to or appearing for the Royalist cause faced the sequestration of their estates.

56 John Pym, *A Most Learned and Religious Speech Spoken by Mr. Pym, at a Conference of both Houses of Parliament the 23 of . . . September* (London, 1642); *The Scots Resolution Declared in a Message Sent from the Privie Councell of the Kingdome of Scotland, to His Majestie at Yorke . . . wherein is Expressed their Earnest Desires both to his Maiestie and Parliament, That They Would be Pleased to Joyne in a Perfect Unione, it Being the Chiefe Meanes to Give an Overthrow to the Enemies of the Three Kingdoms* (Edinburgh, 1642); NAS, Hamilton Papers, GD 406/1/1688, /1742–3, /1751, /1775, 1782; *LJB*, II, pp. 45–8, 53–5; Scott, *Politics and War in the Three Stuart Kingdoms*, pp. 40–3. Following overtures from the Parliamentarians to the general assembly in July 1642, Argyll was determined that the Kirk was not to meddle in diplomatic affairs with respect to the king, religion and peace, albeit the commission for the public affairs of the Kirk – constituted formally as the interval committee for the general assembly in August 1642 with an in-built radical majority – promoted Covenanting solidarity with the Parliamentarians.

consulted on foreign as well as domestic affairs. Scottish independence would be prejudiced if the king, as an absentee monarch, relied only on English advice when treating with foreign states in matters affecting Britain. Common British concerns about rebellion in Ireland masked the Covenanting leadership's determination to maintain its own diplomatic channels, particularly with France. Queen Henrietta Maria had already been despatched to her homeland to lobby for the Royalist cause. The Earl of Lothian was entrusted with the Covenanters' diplomatic counter-mission in early December (see Chapter 7). Ongoing negotiations for Covenanting support obliged Charles to concur.[57]

With majority backing from the nobility, Hamilton persuaded the Privy Council on 20 December to publish a letter from the king justifying his stance towards the Parliamentarians, but not the declaration of the latter espousing religious unity and uniformity in church government. Lanark had been sent north by the king to denounce Parliament's misrepresentation of events in England. He clashed bitterly with Argyll on the king's intentions. However, Argyll drew on overwhelming support from the gentry and burgesses who constituted the in-built radical majority on the Council. The Parliamentarians' letter was published on 10 January 1643. At the same time, Argyll mobilised the Kirk to counter Hamilton's surreptitious manoeuvre of a Cross-Petition which prioritised the maintenance of peace in Britain over religious unity. Conservative Covenanters were also wary of becoming involved in a power play for control of the Movement, especially as Argyll was able to mobilise committed Covenanters in Fife and the Lothians to lobby *en masse* in Edinburgh. Both conservative and radical Covenanters, supported by the commission which ran the affairs of the Kirk between general assemblies, issued a warning to Royalists on the English border not to link up with émigrés attempting to foment a rising in Scotland. This declaration was clearly aimed at Montrose, who was plotting with Queen Henrietta Maria to this end after her return from France. Indeed, Hamilton was moved to travel to York in February to dissuade the king from backing Montrose's plans for a rising. Hamilton gained a dukedom from the king and permanent enmity from Montrose. The Royalist cause could manifestly not accommodate both Scottish nobles; advantage Argyll.[58]

The Privy Council was not the only agency for the discussion of issues of war and peace in Scotland. The conservators of the peace were more than capable of mounting diplomatic initiatives. Dominated by Argyll and the radicals, the

57 BL, Nicholas Papers, Egerton MS 2533, fo.365; DH, Loudoun Deeds, bundle 1/6; *RPCS*, second series, VII, pp. 346, 355; NAS, Hamilton Papers, GD 406/1/1716, /1784.
58 NAS, Hamilton Papers, GD 406/1/1808, /1869; *LJB*, II, pp. 35, 41–3, 58–9, 63–4; *MHG*, pp. 118–9, 127–8; Anon., *The Scots Declaration to the Earl of Cumberland* (London, 1642/3); Stevenson, *The Scottish Revolution*, pp. 255–61; Cowan, *Montrose*, pp. 137–9.

conservators contacted their English counterparts, effectively Saye and Seal and Pym's supporters. Simultaneously, the commission for common burdens, also under radical control, intermittently supplied the Covenanting Army in Ireland. At a joint meeting of the Privy Council, the conservators of the peace and the commission for common burdens on 12 May 1643, Argyll and the radicals pressed for a Convention of Estates to be summoned as an effective substitute for the parliament that Charles I was resolutely refusing to call. As Hamilton regretfully informed the Court, the radicals' institutional dominance resulted in the firm resolution of the Scottish Covenanters 'to be actors and no longer spectators in the English civil war'.[59]

Ostensibly required to supply the Covenanting Army in Ireland and review the arrears of brotherly assistance, the Convention was managed adroitly by Argyll and the radicals from 22 June to 28 August. Papers recovered fortuitously from the Earl of Antrim, following his capture in Ulster by the Covenanting Army, implicated prominent Scottish Royalists, including Montrose. Robert Maxwell, 1st Earl of Nithsdale and James, Lord Aboyne, both Catholic nobles and militantly anti-Covenanters, were duly indicted for fomenting insurrection at home in anticipation of an Irish Catholic force coming over to aid the king against the English Parliamentarians. A general assembly was summoned in Edinburgh to coincide with the Convention. On 19 August, with strong prompting from Henderson as moderator and Argyll as the foremost ruling elder, the assembly accepted an invitation from the Long Parliament to observe, advise and direct discussions on the Presbyterian reformation of the Church of England. Suitably conditioned, the Convention on 26 August concluded a formal alliance with commissioners from the English Parliament, led by Sir Henry Vane junior, for armed assistance on the basis of the Solemn League and Covenant.[60]

This alliance, drawn up by Wariston and Henderson, affirmed that the Covenanting Movement was in the driving seat in British politics. Ireland had been included within the remit of the Solemn League and Covenant, but only at the insistence of the English commissioners, the Scots being reluctant

59 NAS, Hamilton Papers, GD 406/1/1828, /1840, /1846, /1887; HL, Loudoun Scottish Papers, box 29, LO 10503; *The Proceedings of the Commissioners, Appointed by the Kings Maiesty and Parliament of Scotland, for Conserving the Articles of the Treaty and Peace betwixt the Kingdomes of Scotland and England* (London, 1643).

60 Young, *The Scottish Parliament*, pp. 54–70; BL, Historical Papers, Egerton MS 2884, fo.19; NAS, Maxwell of Orchardton MSS, RH 15/91/20/16; *LJB*, II, pp. 67–9, 72–5, 84–5, 90–6; *A Declaration of the Lords of His Majesties Privie-Councell in Scotland and Commissioners for the Conserving the Articles of the Treaty: For the Information of His Majesties Good Subjects of this Kingdom. Together with a Treacherous and Damnable Plot* (Edinburgh, 1643); Robert Munro, *A Letter of Great Consequence Sent . . . out of the Kingdom of Ireland, to the Honorable, the Committee for the Irish Affairs in England, Concerning the State of Rebellion There* (London, 1643).

to accord equal standing to a satellite kingdom whose dominant confession was Roman Catholic. In effect, the Solemn League represented an extension of confessional confederation to achieve common spiritual and material aims while maintaining distinctive national structures in church and state. Confederal union was to replace regal union. In terms of ecumenical congruence, the Solemn League and Covenant was propagated as the necessary application of the covenant of works to that of grace in order to achieve religious reformation in all three kingdoms. In terms of political congruence, the coactive power to resist the Crown was specifically exported in clause three, which incorporated the oath of allegiance and mutual association from the National Covenant.[61]

The inspiration for this federative realignment of the three kingdoms came from two distinctive traditions that soon proved far from compatible. On the one hand, the Scottish Covenanters looked to continental Europe. The Protestant Estates had reinvigorated confederation for confessional and constitutional purposes first in Moravia, Austria and Hungary against imperial power in 1608, then in Bohemia, Moravia, Silesia and the two Lusatias against territorial integration in 1619. Like federal theology, this tradition was viewed by the Covenanters as favouring Presbyterianism, which they promoted as the basis for religious uniformity in the British Isles. On the other hand, the English Parliamentarians looked to North America. The association of a solemn league with a perpetual confederacy had been laid out explicitly in the incorporating articles of the United Colonies of New England, subscribed by four Puritan plantations for common defence against the Dutch, the French and the Indians in May 1643 – three months before the Anglo-Scottish treaty. This confederal formulation drew on a long tradition of providential banding by English Puritans which, like that followed by Scottish Presbyterians, went back to the sixteenth century. But in England, as in America, this form of covenanting was deemed favourable to the Independency of gathered churches rather than to a single denominational establishment, Presbyterian or Anglican, within the Stuart dominions.[62]

The Solemn League and Covenant was of fundamental significance in consummating 'the Scottish moment': the brief period from 1638 to 1645, when the Covenanters set the political agenda within the British Isles. Although the

---

61 *APS*, VI (i) (1641–47), pp. 41–3, 47–9.
62 G. Schramm, 'Armed Conflict in East-Central Europe: Protestant Noble Opposition and Catholic Royalist Factions, 1604–20', and I. Auerbach, 'The Bohemian Opposition, Poland-Lithuania, and the Outbreak of the Thirty Years War' successively in R.J.W. Evans and T.V. Thomas eds, *Crown, Church and Estates: Central European Politics in the Sixteenth and Seventeenth Centuries* (London, 1991), pp. 176–225; *The Journal of John Winthrop, 1630–1649*, R.S. Dunn, J. Savage and L. Yeandle eds (Cambridge, Mass, 1996), pp. 429–40; E. Vallance, *Revolutionary England and the National Covenant: State Oaths, Protestantism and the Political Nation, 1553–1682* (Woodbrige, 2005), pp. 51–129.

export of Covenanting ideology was characterised by the language of religious revelation, negotiations were founded primarily on political pragmatism and military experience, a combination initially welcomed by Parliamentary polemicists as the effective counter to an untrustworthy king who had been continuously plotting against the Long Parliament since its inception; and who had also been seeking Habsburg aid from Flanders and an accommodation with the Irish Confederates. The Protestants of Zealand, the Dutch province entrusted with oversight of British affairs, endorsed the alliance as 'a seasonable engagement'.[63]

The immediate response of Charles I to the Solemn League and Covenant was his conclusion of a twelve-month truce with the Irish Confederates on 15 September 1643. Loudoun, as Scottish Chancellor, issued a stinging rebuke to Charles on 19 October about importing troops to aid the Royalist cause. For the Confederates, who had massacred many Protestants, were now authorised to secure arms and ammunitions not only in the Stuart dominions, but in all kingdoms allied to the Stuart monarchy, in order to prosecute all of the king's Protestant subjects not prepared to embrace the cessation. These subjects included Scottish Covenanters and English Parliamentarians. Giving force to this rebuke was the restoration of the Committee of Estates. Authorised on 26 August, on the same day that the Solemn League was issued, its primary task was to oversee military assistance to the English Parliamentarians. Having reconstituted shire committees of war, the central committee was divided into two sections by 1 December: one to remain in Edinburgh, the other to accompany the army into England. Loudoun and Argyll dominated the respective sections. The Earl of Leven was confirmed as supreme commander of the Covenanting Army.[64]

63 E.J. Cowan, 'The Solemn League and Covenant' in Mason ed., *Scotland and England 1286–1815*, pp. 182–202; Edward Bowles, *The Mysterie of Iniquity, Yet Working in the Kingdomes of England, Scotland, and Ireland, for the Destruction of Religion Truly Protestant* (London, 1643).

64 NAS, Hamilton Papers, GD 406/1/1916; HL, Loudoun Scottish Collection, box 30/ LO 10337; BOU, Carte Papers, 1636–52. Ireland, MS Carte 65, ff.112–13; Young, *The Scottish Parliament*, 70–8.

SEVEN

Confederal Britain, 1643–1646

The institution of the Committee of Both Kingdoms in February 1644 was the culmination of an alternative Scottish agenda for the British Isles. This agenda had commenced confrontationally with constitutional defiance of Charles I in 1638 and had reached a British accord through the Solemn League and Covenant in 1643. But this agenda was subsumed gradually by the splits among English Parliamentarians into the factions known as the Presbyterians and Independents from 1645, and was ultimately sundered after Charles I placed himself in the custody of the Covenanting Army in 1646. Having intervened militarily in England and Ireland, the Covenanting Movement was intent on a programme of confessional confederation to establish godly monarchy in association with godly commonwealths in all three Stuart kingdoms. The Covenanters offered a radical vision of Britain that was federative and constitutional, confessional but not sectarian. At the same time Argyll, as the driving force for British confederation, realised long before Oliver Cromwell that Charles I had to be defeated if this radical vision was to be fulfilled.

The Scottish alternative to both Britannic monarchy and Gothic Parliamentarianism had considerable international resonance. Hugh Mowatt, a Swedish diplomat of Scottish extraction was despatched as senior envoy to both Scotland and England in the spring of 1644. Like most diplomats from Scandinavia since the Bishops' Wars of 1639–40, Mowatt chose to visit Scotland initially before moving south to England. This was not simply a demonstration of solidarity with his compatriots but a clear recognition that the Covenanting Movement had a British position of leadership in shaping the political agenda throughout England and Ireland as well as Scotland. In seeking a defensive and offensive alliance against Denmark-Norway, Mowatt was concerned initially to obtain Covenanting backing and then secure the assent of both Scotland and England through the Committee of Both Kingdoms.[1] The international importance of

---

1 SR, Hugh Mowatt's Letters to Sweden, AOSB ser B. E583; Grosjean, *An Unofficial Alliance*, pp. 197, 202–5. I would like to thank Dr Alexia Grosjean for providing me with her translation of Mowatt's letters, 1645–47.

Scottish participation on this British Committee is understated historiographi-
cally. Yet this was a feature recognised immediately by other diplomats. The
Dutch jurist, Hugo Grotius, then Swedish agent to France, viewed the Committee as a council of war (*een crijsraidt opgerechd*) for Covenanters and Parliamentarians that served as trustees for the implementation of the Solemn League
and Covenant of 1643. Despatched as an emissary from the French Court in
August 1645 to broker peace between the Covenanters, the Parliamentarians and
Charles I, Jean de Montereul accorded the Committee international standing as
the *comité des deux nations*.[2] Émigrés resident in England also recognised the
diplomatic standing of this Committee. Indeed, Samuel Hartlib, pre-eminent as
an educational reformer, intellectual and entrepreneur, thanked the Committee
in January 1645 for sponsoring his endeavours to promote 'the Publicke Religion,
Justice and Liberty of the Three Kingdoms' overseas. The Committee embodied
the confidence of the Covenanters and Parliamentarians that they were fighting
a godly war in the field and through the pulpit to secure Britain's divine deliverance from utter ruin and devastation and, especially, from the king's eradication
of true religion, law and civil liberties.[3]

Heightened Expectations

The Scottish Presbyterian Robert Baillie had claimed that 'the English were for a
civil league, we for a religious Covenant'. Nevertheless, the Solemn League and
Covenant carried not just religious but apocalyptic connotations for English
Puritans as well as Scottish Presbyterians. The Solemn League was projected
as providing British comfort to the Reformed churches on the continent and,
as the Thirty Years War still raged, to the Protestant powers fighting against
the forces of Anti-Christ; namely the papacy backed up by the Spanish and
Austrian Habsburgs on the continent and the Catholic Confederacy in Ireland.
In this context, the Solemn League was preparing the ground not just for the
political reconstruction of Britain but also for a fundamental world reordering
that would mark the triumph of Protestantism in anticipation of the second
coming of Christ.[4]

2 *Briefwisseling van Hugo Grotius* (XIV (1643), pp. 555, 591–2, 728; XV (1644), *passim* and p. 652;
   XVI (1645) *passim* Montereul, I, pp. 29, 34, 77, 164, 169.
3 The Hartlib Papers (Sheffield University. HROnline. Humanities Research Institute, 2002),
   HP9/4/1A–2B; *Memoirs of Master John Shawe, sometime Vicar of Rotherham, Minister of St
   Mary's, Lecturer of Holy Trinity Church, and Master of the Charterhouse at Kingston-upon-
   Hull. Written by himself in the Year 1663–64*, J. R. Boyle ed. (Hull, 1882), pp. 36, 193; Stephen
   Marshall, *A Sacred Panegyrick* (London, 1644); Thomas Mocket, *A View of the Solemn League
   and Covenant* (London, 1644).
4 *LJB*, II, p. 90; Hezekiah Woodward, *Three Kingdoms Made One, by Entering Covenant with One
   God* (London, 1643); Williamson, *Apocalypse Then*, pp. 145–8; C. Hill, *Antichrist in Seventeenth-
   Century England* (Oxford, 1971), pp. 78–88.

Religious revelation made the prospects of Scottish intervention appealing both to Presbyterians and Independents among English Puritans. The former had been campaigning since 1642 for unity in religion and uniformity in church government; the latter supported a thorough reformation of the Church of England with more emphasis on congregational autonomy than a Presbyterian hierarchy of courts. Stephen Marshall and Philip Nye, as the respective representatives of these interests, had accompanied the English Parliamentary commissioners who negotiated the Solemn League and Covenant in 1643. Both concurred on the fundamental importance of the Covenant to Scotland, 'the whole body of the Nation looking upon it as the cause of God'. Both saw the Solemn League as the arm of Lord being extended to England. Nye subsequently commended the Covenanting oath of allegiance to the Westminster Assembly of Divines as worthy not only of the three kingdoms, but 'of all the Kingdoms of the world'. His Independent colleague, Jeremiah Burroughs, asserted that Scotland, as a chosen nation, was 'united the most firmly under heaven, we may truly call it a Philadelphia'. England should rejoice to have godly union with the Scots in a commonwealth of brotherly love. However, there were more pressing, if prosaic, military and political considerations that Parliamentarians had to address to effect their alliance with the Covenanters. Thus, Burroughs strongly urged the Parliamentary treasury at the Goldsmith's Hall in London to advance £100,000 sterling to facilitate Covenanting intervention.

Oliver St John, as the solicitor general for England, had taken up this theme of financial obligation in October 1643. The Long Parliament had failed to supply the Covenanting Army in Ireland for the past fourteen months; starvation had only been fended off by the Scottish Estates, which supplied over £80,000 sterling from its hard-pressed resources (see Chapter 6). A significant portion of the brotherly assistance promised by the Treaty of London remained unpaid. Nonetheless, Covenanting intervention opened up the twin prospect of assuring a Parliamentary victory and expediting the sequestration of Royalist estates to meet the cost of war. On the death of Pym, two months later, St John was to take over leadership of the pro-Scottish interest in the Commons and consolidate the power block built up in association with Viscount Saye and Seal, the longstanding Covenanting ally in the Lords. Notwithstanding his determination that the religious and political imperatives of the Solemn League and Covenant should not proscribe liberty of conscience, Sir Henry Vane, the younger, was the other politician in whom the Covenanters placed particular trust. He reported to the city of London that the Scots were so sensible of the dangers to religion if the Parliamentary cause should fail that they were ready to break through all military and financial difficulties in return for the advance of £100,000 sterling. In the formal terms negotiated for Covenanting intervention in November, the Scots accepted this advance, which was to be discounted against the first monthly allowance for the 21,000 troops brought over the Border.[5] Among Parliamentarians, Argyll was viewed as the key to expediting the intervention of Covenanting forces. He duly secured £5,000 sterling from the English advance: reimbursement for three-quarters of his personal outlay on the Covenanting Army in Ireland. The Marquess was also prepared to exploit Parliamentary urgings that the Covenanters hasten their march into England before Charles received military aid from Ireland. He insisted on diplomatic concessions. The Parliamentarians were obliged to accept that no pacification or peace treaty should be made by either kingdom with Charles I or with other foreign states, 'without the mutuall advice and consent of both Kingdoms'.[6]

This point, like the Covenanters' anti-Catholic rhetoric, was somewhat disingenuous. As in the Bishops' Wars, the Covenanters were intent on securing covert support from France, the foremost European power in the continuing fight against the Habsburgs. As early as January 1643, the Earl of Lothian had been despatched to France, ostensibly to reinvigorate the reciprocal civic, military and commercial privileges of the 'auld alliance', but also to sound out the prospects of French backing for Charles I and the Catholic Confederates of Ireland. In the course of this mission Louis XIII died. The task of governing France on behalf of his infant son Louis XIV passed to a regency government headed by the Queen Mother, Anne of Austria, but dominated by Cardinal Jules Mazarin as first minister. During the nine months that Lothian remained in France, he ingratiated himself at the French Court by facilitating recruitment of Scottish troops to bolster the French presence in Germany and Italy. The fresh contingents sent from Scotland, the first authorised by the

5 Anon., *The Love and Faithfulnes of the Scottish Nation, The Excellency of the Covenant, The Union between England and Scotland cleared, by Collections, from the Declarations of Parliament and Speeches of Severall Independent Brethren* (London, 1646); M.A. Judson, *The Political Thought of Sir Henry Vane the Younger* (Philadelphia, 1969), pp. 6–10; Scott, *Politics and War in the Three Stuart Kingdoms*, pp. 68–70. The Covenanters were committed to sending 18,000 foot and 2,100 horse; around 300 Scottish officers were also infiltrated into the Parliamentary forces. Covenanting intervention was to be maintained at £30,000 sterling per month from the revenues of papists and other malignants. However, the Covenanting leadership was also committed to negotiating a loan of £200,000 sterling jointly with the English Parliamentarians in continental money markets.

6 HL, Loudoun Scottish Collection, box 16, LO 9998; ICA, Letters – Marquess's Period, 1638–1645, bundle 7/1; ABDA, Argyll Papers, 40.2196. Argyll's principal parliamentary informant at this juncture was John Carey or Carew or Crewe, who seems to have been the chairman of the committee on religion in the Commons and had presided over the initial committee of the Long Parliament that had supported Covenanting overtures for uniformity of church government as the prerequisite for confessional confederation on 17 May 1641 (*Verney Papers*, p. 78). I should like to thank Dr Kirsteen MacKenzie for this information.

Covenanting Movement, were led briefly by Argyll's half-brother James, Earl of Irvine (formerly Lord Kintyre). Diplomatic ties from the Bishops' Wars were also revitalised by Lothian's meeting with Abbé Chambre, almoner to the late Cardinal Richelieu, who set up contact between the Queen Mother and Argyll. Lothian's principal achievement was to convince Mazarin not to give military assistance to Charles I, on the grounds that the combined forces of Scottish Covenanters and English Parliamentarians would be too strong for the Royalists and Irish Confederates, with or without French reinforcements.[7]

During his time in France, Lothian had informed Charles I of his diplomatic activities through Lanark, Secretary of State for Scottish Affairs. On his return in October, he made a courtesy visit to the king at Oxford. He was promptly arrested and incarcerated in Bristol Castle for six months. Ostensibly, he was imprisoned following reports that he was to serve as lieutenant-colonel in the Covenanting Army coming to the aid of the English Parliamentarians. But his close confinement also served to deny the Covenanting leadership accurate information about the situation at the French Court while an envoy, a certain Monsieur de Boisivon, was despatched to Scotland at the behest of Charles I. He was accredited not by Mazarin or the Queen Mother, but by the king's uncle, Gaston, Duc d'Orléans. The king's action against Lothian was also indicative of a renewed Royalist militancy in the wake of the Solemn League and Covenant. When Hamilton, who had refused to sign the Solemn League, arrived at Oxford in December to report on the Scottish situation, he was denounced by Montrose and thrown into prison. His brother, Lanark, was dismissed as Secretary of State.[8]

7 *CAL*, I, pp. 142–3, 147–9; NAS, Clerk of Penicuik Papers, GD 18/2429–30, /2432, /2434 and Lothian MSS, GD 40/2/2/11, /17; BL, Trumbull Papers vol. CXCIII, Add.MSS 72,434 ff.1–2, 5–8; ICA, Argyll Transcripts, XII, no.198. Existing Scottish forces in French service consisted of the Guarde de Corps, Gens d'Arms and the Regiment of Guards, The senior Scottish officer was Lord James Douglas, son to William, 1st Marquess of Douglas, a prominent Catholic but a rather low profile Royalist. Lord Douglas, along with other Scottish officers in French service, had been lobbying for Scottish reinforcements without success since 1640 (NAS, Hamilton Papers, GD 406/1/1255; BL, Turnbull Papers, vol. CLXXXVII, Add.MSS 72,428 fo.167). Despite the general assembly's insistence that the reinforcements all had to be Presbyterian, the presence of Irvine indicates that the Covenanting leadership was primarily concerned to move political misfits, adventurers averse to ideological conformity and other disruptive elements overseas. Seriously wounded in Germany, Irvine returned to London to die in the autumn of 1644.

8 *CAL*, I, pp. 146–7, 152–9, 162–70; NAS Lothian MSS, GD 40/12/5; Scott, *Politics and War in the Three Stuart Kingdoms*, pp. 61, 80. The Duc d'Orléans was the brother of Henrietta Maria, wife of Charles I. He was a longstanding enemy of Richelieu but was squeezed out of the regency government by Anne of Austria to become the maladroit governor of Languedoc in 1644. He subsequently opposed Mazarin during the Frondes which convulsed France between 1648 and 1653. His accreditation of de Boisivon to Argyll and Hamilton can be viewed essentially as a freelance diplomatic venture on behalf of his sister, not of the regency government

The French envoy turned out to be a rather quixotic, self-serving diplomat with a penchant for exaggeration and distortion that wholly undermined his credibility in France as well as Scotland. He claimed that Lothian had really been sent to France to treat with the Huguenots. The only evidence of Lothian being engaged outwith his official remit was when he used his stay to boost his library, furnishings and art collection. Argyll was correctly identified by de Boisivon as the controlling influence in Scotland. His alleged absolutism (*Le Marquis d'Argueil est icy absolu*) was pursued without any semblance of knowledge about foreign affairs, which were left to the messianic inclinations of Leven, who pressed for a Protestant Crusade that would soon extend from England to France and on to Rome to vanquish the Anti-Christ. These claims had the same ring of authenticity as the purported attempts of the Covenanting leadership to have him assassinated; claims belatedly made after he had retired from Edinburgh, heavily indebted from gambling throughout his November stay, to pursue hunting and other leisurely pursuits around Manchester.[9] His protracted posturing, along with that of Montrose among the Royalists at Oxford, enabled the Covenanting leadership to spin reports on current affairs in order to heighten the sense of anticipation in England about the arrival of their army, once adequately funded, to implement the Solemn League and Covenant.

The Scots had stated their militant intent by re-occupying Berwick-upon-Tweed on 20 September. But another four months were to elapse before the Covenanting Army began its push into England on 19 January 1644. In the interim, news management became a particular concern of Argyll and the radical leadership. Notwithstanding the disparity in news outlets between Scotland and England, the Covenanting Movement had been notably adept at exploiting the British press to its advantage since the outset of the Bishops' Wars. Accordingly, on 6 November 1643, the Covenanters had a statement published in London on *The Readinesse of the Scots to Advance into England*, which dealt with military preparations, with limited resistance to the confessional and military alliance, and with the last-ditch but futile attempts by the French envoy (now elevated to

---

(J.B. Collins, *The State in Early Modern France* (Cambridge, 1995), pp. 23, 52, 56–7, 65–8; M. Vergé-Franceschi, Colbert: *La politique du bons sens* (Paris, 2005), pp. 70–1, 91–2).

9　*Montereul*, II, pp. 539–63; NAS, Clerk of Penicuik Papers, GD 18/2424, /2426, /2440, /2444 and Lothian MSS, GD 40/2/2/13. Charles had attempted to counter Lothian's mission to France by despatching a Scottish courtier, Sir Thomas Dishington, to propose the reinvigoration of the 'auld alliance' from a Royalist rather than a Covenanting perspective. His mission signally failed. Dishington subsequently returned to Paris in February 1645 claiming to be an envoy for the two kingdoms. His mission was again a Royalist front having no warrant from either the Parliamentarians or the Covenanters, but he did gain the ear of the Queen Mother and was viewed as supportive to Swedish interests in Britain (BL, Turnbull Papers, vol. CXCIII, Add.MSS 72,434, fo.20; *Montereul*, I, p. 3 and II, pp. 564–5; SR, Hugh Mowatt's Letters, AOSB ser B. E583).

the status of ambassador) to prevent Scottish aid to the Parliamentarians. Three newsletters immediately picked up this report. *The True Informer* accepted the Covenanting line uncritically if not verbatim. *The Kingdomes Weekly Intelligencer* embellished and editorialised the role of the French Ambassador, taking this as a warning to the Parliamentarians to be wary of dealing with the French Crown. Since Charles I was expecting reinforcements from Ireland, Scottish assistance was particularly welcomed. However, the most supportive editorialising came from *The Scottish Dove*, which was dismissive of the endeavours of the French Ambassador and focused more on the advanced state of Scottish military preparations. The Covenanters' manifest commitment, in turn, necessitated prompt payment of the funds promised by the English Parliament for military assistance.[10]

---

10 Anon., *The Readinesse of the Scots to Advance into England: The Policie and Practice of the French Agent there to Hinder it* (London, 1643); *The True Informer*, no.10 (18–25 November, 1643); *The Kingdomes Weekly Intelligencer* no.34 (28 November–5 December, 1643); *The Scottish Dove* no.7 (24 November–1 December, 1643). At this juncture, there were 17 newsletters covering British current affairs from England. Three had a specified Scottish provenance. *The Scotch Counsellor*, like *The Scottish Dove*, was supportive of the Solemn League and Covenant, while *The Scotch Intelligencer* took a more circumspect line between Parliamentarians and Royalists. Two Royalist newsletters were manifestly hostile to the Scottish Covenanters, and another four (two with Welsh titles) were sceptical about the proposed Covenanting intervention in England, for which the remaining 11 were generally favourable. The most enduring of newsletters with a Scottish provenance was *The Scottish Dove*, which ran from 13 October 1643 until 26 November 1646, basically covering the implementation of the Solemn League until the Covenanting withdrawal from England, when relations with the Parliamentarians had been strained to breaking point. *The Scottish Dove* initially viewed itself as an ally of the aggressively Parliamentarian *Mercurius Britannicus* in its war of words with the stridently Royalist *Mercurius Aulicus*. However, *The Scottish Dove* under its London editor George Smith was less prone to factual distortion or partial editorialising. Certainly it was a consistent apologist for the Covenanting Movement. But its enduring concerns were with the wider British and international context, with the ongoing threats posed by the Counter-Reformation to Protestantism and with military atrocities, especially those of the Royalists which it compared to the reported brutalities of the Thirty Years War. *The Scottish Dove*, though run as an English enterprise, was almost certainly initiated by the much-travelled Scot, William Lithgow, the self-styled 'Bonaventure of Europe, Asia and Africa' who had been in London as part of a cohort of Scottish military advisers to the Parliamentarians when the paper was launched. William Lithgow can be deemed the founder of embedded journalism from his published reports of the siege of Breda in 1637, where he attached himself to the Scottish forces in Dutch service (*A True and Experimentall Discourse, upon the Beginning, Proceeding and Victorious Event of this Last Siege of Breda* (London, 1637)). His last military assignment was to cover the Covenanting siege of Newcastle in 1644 (*The Siege of Newcastle* (Edinburgh, 1645)). Somewhat discomfited by the lack of respect from English Parliamentarians for the Scottish veterans once their programme of military training was complete, he contented himself with the provision of a detailed blueprint of fortifications and other defensive topographical features that would allow the Scottish Covenanters to seize the metropolis should the need arise (*The Present Survey of London and England's State* (London, 1643)).

Winning the War

The reconvened Convention of Estates issued a declaration on behalf of both kingdoms on 6 January 1644, which was ratified by the Long Parliament thirteen days later. It vindicated joint action against the Royalists who were to be held to account for the 'troubles and sufferings' of Scotland, the 'desolation of Ireland' and the 'many unnatural Tragedies' in England. Public warning was given that neutrality and indifference would not be tolerated. All those refusing to subscribe the Solemn League and Covenant in England, as in Scotland, were threatened with fines for delinquency. But punitive fines were partially offset by the willingness of Covenanting apologists to accommodate English consciences. While little truck was had with papists, separatists or those claiming neutrality to avoid military commitments outwith their own localities, every effort was made to comprehend a range of beliefs from Anglicanism to Congregationalism, provided their adherents upheld the reform of the Church of England purged of the Laudian bishops. Presbyterianism remained the stated ideal, but not necessarily that according to the Scottish model, a tolerance of diversity not inconsistent with confessional confederation. Every effort was made to encourage subscription to the Solemn League and Covenant, even if subscribers had no track record as committed Presbyterians.[11]

Although its intervention did not enjoy the swift and spectacular success of the Second Bishops' War, the Covenanting Army consolidated the turning of hostilities in favour of the Parliamentary forces. Hitherto, the Royalists had the edge in fighting regional campaigns, especially in the north and south-west, if less convincingly in the Midlands. The Covenanters under the firm direction of Leven immediately made their presence felt throughout the north of England. Argyll, who was in the van of the Covenanting intervention, was cited frequently in military despatches from the north of England until he was obliged to return to Scotland in April to attend a Convention of Estates at Edinburgh intent on dealing with a Royalist resurgence. His departure carried more political than military resonance as the Covenanting Army moved from intervention to occupation, albeit Royalists were more successful in distracting rather than confronting its military presence. At the same time, Lanark rejoined the Covenanters, acknowledging his past errors as a Royalist and offering to undergo censure by the Kirk. His despatch back to Scotland by the Committee of Estates with the army boosted conservative support for the war effort at home

---

11 *The Declaration of the Kingdomes of Scotland and England* (Edinburgh, 1644); HL, Bridgewater and Ellesmere MSS, EL 7732, 7773–4; BL, Family of Pitt. Official Papers, 17th Century, Add. MSS, 29,975, ff.88–9; E. Vallance, 'Protestations, Vow, Covenant and Engagement: Swearing Allegiance in the English Civil War', *Historical Research*, 75 (2002), pp. 408–24.

now being masterminded by Argyll.[12]

The Covenanting Army was unable to take Newcastle until October 1644, after a siege of almost three months. The Parliamentarians, therefore, did not gain an immediate dividend from the freeing of coal supplies from the Tyne. In the interim, Royalists under the command of William Cavendish, 1st Earl (later Duke) of Newcastle, continued to use Newcastle as the port of entry for arms and ammunition from Denmark and the Netherlands. In terms of set battles, the Covenanting Army made little contribution to the Parliamentarian war effort after the combined victory at Marston Moor in Yorkshire on 2 July 1644. Its three-year stay in England led to no meaningful Presbyterian establishment within the Church of England. Accordingly, Covenanting intervention has tended to be written off as a naive and fruitless endeavour to shape the outcome of the civil war. The Scots demonstrated a limited capacity to control events and tended to become the tools of rival Parliamentary interests.[13] The Covenanting Army has also been viewed as ancillary to the English military narrative of the civil war that culminated in the creation of the New Model Army and its crushing victory over the Royalist forces at Naseby in Northamptonshire on 14 June 1645.[14] The three-year presence of the Covenanting Army in the north of England has been deemed particularly counter-productive, as anti-Scottish sentiment even led to former Royalists siding with the Independents to effect its removal by January 1647.[15]

12 *A Letter from the Marques of Argile and Sir W. Armyn, in name of themselves and their Confederates to Sir Thomas Glenham*, dated at Barqicke, January 20. With the Answer of Sir Thomas Glemham and the Commanders and Gentry of Northumberland, dated at Newcastle, January 23 (York, 1643/4); *The Copy of a Letter from Colonell Francis Anderson to Sir Thomas Glemham, January 20 1643, touching the Invasion of Scotland* (Oxford, 1643/4); Anon., *A True Relation of the late Proceedings of the Scottish Army, sent from his Excellency the Lord Generall Lesley's Quarters before Newcastle, the 8th of February 1643* (London, 1643/4); Anon., *The Last Proceedings of the Scots, being a report by a messenger sent from the English Commissioners at Sunderland* (London, 1644); Anon., *Intelligence from the South borders of Scotland written from Edinburgh, April 24, 1644* (London, 1644); *LJB*, II, p. 164; *Diary of Sir Thomas Hope*, pp. 201, 204; *MHG*, p. 149; ICA, Argyll Letters (1638–85), A 36/131; DH, Loudoun Deeds bundle 1/4; HL, Loudoun Scottish Collection, box 33/LO 9073, /LO 10598, /LO 10600.

13 L. Kaplan, *Politics and Religion during the English Revolution: The Scots and the Long Parliament, 1643–1645* (New York, 1976), *passim*; Stevenson, *Revolution and Counter-Revolution*, pp. 1–81; Smith, *Constitutional Royalism and the Search for Settlement*, pp. 109–218.

14 M. Kishlansky, *The Creation of the New Model Army* (Cambridge, 1979), pp. 22–102; I. Gentles, *The New Model Army in England, Ireland and Scotland, 1645–1653* (Oxford, 1992), pp. 1–86; Bennett, *The Civil Wars in Britain and Ireland*, pp. 169–229; J.S. Wheeler, *The Irish and British Wars 1637–1654: Triumph, Tragedy and Failure* (London, 2002), pp. 94–157.

15 D. Scott, 'The "Northern Gentlemen", the Parliamentary Independents and Anglo-Saxon Relations in the Long Parliament', *HJ*, 42 (1999), pp. 347–75; S. Barber, 'The People of Northern England and Attitudes towards the Scots, 1639–1651: "The Lamb and the Dragon cannot be Reconciled"', *Northern History*, 35 (1999), pp. 93–118; BL, Turnbull Papers, vol. CXCIII,

However, the interests of the Covenanting Movement were British, not just English, and were maintained with ideological consistency tempered by political pragmatism. Notwithstanding the civil war raging within Scotland from the autumn of 1644 (see Chapter 8), the Covenanting Army remained the largest in the field in Parliamentary service until the spring of 1645. Furthermore, Scotland effectively expanded its territorial bounds to an unprecedented extent through the Covenanting armies of intervention, south from the Tweed to the Tees and on the Humber and west from the Solway Firth to Lough Neagh. This expansion, which was the greatest by any army prior to the Cromwellian occupations of Ireland and Scotland in 1650-1, provoked genuine if unfounded fears of Scottish imperialism in both England and Ireland throughout the 1640s.[16]

Imperialism was impossible without adequate funding. Notwithstanding treaty arrangements, the Covenanting armies of intervention in England and Ireland continued to have major problems of supply; problems that remained substantive in England and never less than chronic in Ireland. The Parliamentary treasury in London juggled with funds raised specifically for the Irish campaigns through subscription to the Adventurers Act of 1642. Fines imposed on Royalists and others deemed notorious delinquents were spread to pay for the British and Scottish armies in Ireland as well as the Parliamentary forces in England. As Argyll was acutely aware, problems of subsistence in Ireland were

---

Add.MSS 72,432 ff.111–12 and vol. CXCVIII, Add.MSS 72,439 ff.119–22. At least, the Scottish Covenanters had a more disciplined military record in terms of massacres and atrocities than either the Royalists or the Parliamentarians in England. Of the 18 attested massacres during the first phase of the civil war in England, the Scots were only held responsible for two – following the siege of Newcastle in October 1644 and after the skirmish at Canon Frome, Herefordshire in June 1645. The Royalists, who instigated the atrocities at Barthomley, Cheshire on Christmas Day 1643, were involved in nine incidents, the most notorious being the massacre at Bolton, Lancashire in May 1644, when estimates of the number of victims ran from three to four figures. The Scots, despite persistent problems with their funding, were also considerably more professional in their restraint in comparison to the Parliamentary forces before and after the creation of the New Model Army. In only one of the four incidents cited prior to 1645, that at Cheriton, Hampshire instigated under Sir William Waller in March 1644, did casualties run into three figures. But victims did run into the hundreds in two out of the three incidents following the creation of the New Model Army, notably after Sir Thomas Fairfax's victory at Naseby and Oliver Cromwell's capture of Basing House, Hampshire in October 1645 (W. Coster, 'Massacre and Codes of Conduct in the English Civil War' in M. Levene and P. Roberts eds, *The Massacre in History* (Oxford, 1999), pp. 89–105; C. Carlton, *Going to the Wars: The Experience of the British Civil Wars, 1638–1651* (London, 1994), pp. 34–7, 257–60).

16 *The Journal of Sir Simonds D'Ewes from the Beginning of the Long Parliament to the Opening of the Trial of the Earl of Strafford*, W. Notestein ed. (London, 1923), p. 9; George Wither, *The British Appeals with Gods Mercifull Replies on the behalfe of the Commonwealth of England* (London, 1650), pp. 12–3; M. Perceval-Maxwell, 'Ireland and Scotland 1638–1648' in Morrill ed., *The Scottish National Covenant in its British Context*, pp. 193–211.

compounded by inadequate arrangements for shipping troops. But at least the command structure seemed resolved in March 1644. As part of a package to ensure sufficient regular supplies to fend off destitution among the troops in Ulster, the Long Parliament agreed that the commander of the Scottish forces should also command the British forces. Although the conduct of the war in Ireland came under the remit of the Committee of Both Kingdoms, supplies remained sporadic and unreliable. In England, fines were replaced by national taxes and monthly assessments levied in the counties. Continuing difficulties of financial supply by the Parliamentarians were compounded when a further 10,000 Covenanting troops were despatched to England in the summer of 1644.[17]

The Parliamentary revenue base did expand as Royalist forces were vanquished. But the Covenanting forces continued to be denied ready access to monies raised in the counties. In the aftermath of Naseby, the Covenanting forces relied as much on supplies from Scotland, raised usually on credit, as from London or latterly York. Obliged to take free quarters or impose their own levies, which were usually higher than comparable Parliamentary exactions, the Covenanters were confronted by revolts in Cumberland and Westmoreland and had to face down the threat of local uprisings in Yorkshire.[18] However, antipathies

---

17 BL, Ordinances of Parliament 1642–49, Add.MSS 5492, ff.11, 54–5, 115–6, 167–8; DH, Loudoun Deeds, bundle 1/2; HL, Loudoun Scottish Collection, box 30/LO 10335, box 41/LO 10067, box 43/LO 7601, /LO 12561; DH, Loudoun Papers, A15/6; TFA, Papers, TD 4666; BOU, Carte Papers, 1636–1652. Ireland, MS Carte 65 ff.112–13; *CAL*, I, pp. 175–6, 179; *LJB*, II, p. 176; *Memoirs of Master John Shawe*, pp. 34–6; *SPT*, I, pp. 32–3; *Die Sabbati 30 December 1643. Ordered that the Adventurers of this House for lands in Ireland, and the body of Adventurers in London, doe meete at Grocers-Hall on Thursday in the afternoon at two of the clock, and take into their serious consideration by what wayes and meanes the British Army in Ulster, opposing the cessation may be maintained and encouraged to process in prosecution of that warre of Ireland against the Rebels, and to prepare some propositions to be presented to the House* (London, 1643).

18 TNA, State Papers Domestic, Supplementary: Orders, Warrants and Receipts for payment of the Scots Army in England 1643–48, SP 46/106, ff.129–32, 134, 22, 268, 314–5; DH, Loudoun Papers, A525/1; *CSCL*, pp. 21, 35–8, 54–7, 72–3, 89–93, 124–30, 144–5, 160–1, 166–7; *An Ordinance of the Lords and Commons assembled in Parliament for the Further Supply of the British Army in Ireland* (London, 1645); *The Journal of Thomas Juxon, 1644–47*, K. Lindley and D. Scott eds (Cambridge, 1999), pp. 27–9, 61–2, 75, 78, 81–7, 114–7; Bennett, *The Civil Wars in Britain and Ireland*, pp. 182–4; Wheeler, *The Irish and British Wars*, pp. 129–31. Unlike the Second Bishops' War, when the Covenanting forces instigated the occupation of northern England, Scottish intervention into England at the outset of 1644 came fifteen months after the inception of civil war and when territories had already been devastated. Accordingly, the Covenanting Army had never achieved the same productive relationships with the county committees as that which pertained in 1640–41. Advances on sums raised for their monthly maintenance made by the city of London were underwritten by the customs. However, these payments of cess, like monies raised from sequestrated rents, gifts and forced loans, continued to be fitful. Most of the £200,000 sterling loaned to pay for Scottish intervention was recouped from the 14 counties under Parliamentary control at the outset of 1644 that were situated in the south-east

towards the Covenanting Army must be balanced by a continuing willingness in Yorkshire and the north to see the Covenanters as forces for deliverance from Royalism and for the godly reconfiguration of Britain.[19]

No less problematic than finances were coastal defences, since the Covenanters prioritised commercial over naval shipping. As a condition of intervention in England, the Covenanting leadership had insisted that eight ships be deployed at Parliamentary expense to protect Scottish coastal waters. The initial allocation of six to the east coast reflected Scottish concerns for their trading activities on the North Sea and the Baltic, which were especially vulnerable to the pirates operating out of Dunkirk. However, Robert Rich, 2nd Earl of Warwick, as naval commander for the Parliamentarians, did not fulfil this commitment until the summer of 1644, and then only on the east coast. As Argyll was demonstrably aware when chartering three privateers, one from Glasgow and two from London, the west coast remained exposed to Dunkirkers that had relocated to Ireland. With the outbreak of civil war in England, Scottish ships had been seized and detained in both Newcastle and Berwick, to the detriment of Scottish trade and in breach of the Treaty of London. By October 1644, however, the Covenanters had added Newcastle and Sunderland, with a twenty-fifth part share of the coal and excise on the Tyne and Wear, to their acquisition of Berwick as the initial price of intervention in September 1643. Nevertheless, the Long Parliament subsequently reduced the tariff on coal exported from the Tyne and Wear under Covenanting oversight, ostensibly to encourage trade. The Scottish Covenanters remained vulnerable

---

around London and its commercial hinterland. However, the first four months' assessment from March 1644 encountered significant arrears for an assessment of almost £69,000 sterling that ran to just under £18,000 sterling (a shortfall in excess of 16%). A second four-monthly assessment, which commenced in August 1645 from the same 17 counties, led to further arrears close to £26,000 (a shortfall above 37%). In addition to these defaults, the first four months' assessment failed by the sum of £55,000 sterling to meet the agreed rate of £31,000 per month that the Covenanting Army was to receive. Although the monthly rate for 1645 was reduced to £21,000 sterling following the withdrawal of troops to engage in the Scottish civil war, the sums assessed for the second four months still failed to meet this rate by £15,000. For a comprehensive account of monies received from the Parliamentarians by the Covenanters see L. Stewart, 'English Funding of the Scottish Armies in England and Ireland, 1640–48', *HJ*, 53 (2009), pp. 573–93. Two points must be borne in mind, however: this funding was not the cause of Scottish intervention; and the monies accounted for in Scotland do not necessarily tally with the sums actually dispatched from England.

19 John Shawe, *Brittains Remembrancer: Or, The National Covenant, As it was laid out in a sermon preached in the minster at Yorke . . . upon Friday Sept. 20 1644* (London, 1644) and *The Three Kingdomes Case: or, Their sad calamities, together with their causes and cure. Laid down in a sermon preached at a publique fast at Kingston upon Hull* (London, 1646); *Records of the Committees for Compounding with Delinquent Royalists in Durham and Northumberland*, R. Welford ed. (Durham, 1905), p. 111.

by sea as well as overstretched on land.[20]

Ongoing problems of supply and coastal defence notwithstanding, the major difficulty confronting the alliance of Scottish Covenanters and English Parliamentarians were fundamental differences over the conduct of war and the attainment of religious uniformity. The Covenanting position, which was consistently maintained by the Scottish commissioners from their arrival in London at the outset of 1644, was to effect the Solemn League and Covenant as a written constitution for Britain in the same way as the National Covenant had served for Scotland (see Chapter 5). The ideal was the permanent establishment of a Covenanted, Stuart monarchy. The Covenanters, taking their lead from Argyll, realised that Charles I had to be defeated to accomplish this. Thus, they differed from the peace grouping led by Edward Montague, 2nd Earl of Manchester, Robert Devereux, 3rd Earl of Essex, and Warwick in the Lords; and by Denzil Holles, Bulstrode Whitelocke, and Sir William Waller in the Commons. This group pursued war to bring Charles to the negotiating table without necessarily requiring outright victory. The Covenanters' desire to win was shared by the war grouping around Algernon Percy, 10th Earl of Northumberland, and Saye and Seal in the Lords; and Vane the younger, St John, and especially Oliver Cromwell in the Commons. The peace grouping was not unsympathetic to Presbyterianism. Essex had even claimed to Loudoun in October 1644 that he was ready to serve Scottish interests with his life. But they did not support the ecclesiastical autonomy enjoyed by the Kirk of Scotland. Although they became known as the Presbyterian interest, they preferred an erastian version in which the religious establishment in England would be wholly subordinated to Parliament. Conversely, the war grouping favoured congregationalism and the independence of gathered churches rather than a national establishment. Consequently they became associated with the Independent interest that favoured toleration for the godly rather than the replacement of Anglicanism by Presbyterianism. More importantly, differences of war and religion wholly coloured the political situation and left the Covenanters as a distinctive, third force to Parliamentarians and Royalists in the English civil war.[21]

---

20 BL, Naval Papers, 1643–1677, Add.MSS 22,546 ff.5, 7 and Political and Miscellaneous Papers. XVII and XVIII centuries, Add.MSS 25,277 fo.84; TWA, Hostmen's Company, Old Book 1600–c.1690, GU/HO/1/1, ff.206–8, 242–4; DH, Loudoun Deeds, bundle 1/2; ICA, Letters – Marquess's Period, 1638–1645, bundles 6/118, 7/695; ABDA, Argyll Papers, 40.20, .391; CSCL, pp. 31, 39–41; *Extracts from the Records of the Merchant Adventurers of Newcastle-upon-Tyne*, vol. 1, F.W. Dendy ed. (Durham, 1895), p. 140. Argyll, through the intermediacy of an Edinburgh merchant, David Jenkin, had already purchased a frigate in Ireland (for £13,333) to help protect the western seaboard from 1639.

21 HL, Loudoun Scottish Collection box 21, LO 11367; *LJB*, II, p. 226; *Making the News: An Anthology of the Newsbooks of Revolutionary England, 1641–1660*, J. Raymond ed. (Moreton-

Confederation by Committee

Within days of the arrival of Scottish commissioners to attend on Parliament and sustain good relations with the city of London, the Committee of Both Kingdoms was established to oversee the conduct of civil war in England and Ireland; to maximise diplomatic support for the Covenanters and Parliamentarians; and to minimise foreign intervention in support of the beleaguered Charles I. In strategic terms, British unity as negotiated in 1643 entailed convergence of public policy rather than institutional incorporation. However, the Committee of Both Kingdoms, the one institutional development that did arise out of the Solemn League and Covenant, opened up the fault lines between Parliamentarians and Covenanters. Operating from February 1644 until October 1646, the Committee also became the focus of rival antagonisms among Parliamentarians.

Initially there were four Scottish commissioners on the committee: Loudoun, John Maitland, Lord Maitland (later 2nd Earl and 1st Duke of Lauderdale), Johnston of Wariston and Mr Robert Barclay. Another six commissioners headed by Argyll were added in July 1644. The Committee by this juncture consisted of twenty-six Parliamentarians, with representation loaded in favour of the Commons. Domestic upheavals, as well as his own shuttling between Scotland north of the Tay, Edinburgh and the north of England, kept Argyll away from the Committee until 1646. Nevertheless, his radical associates dominated the Scottish membership. He also made sure that the Scottish commissioners were held to account by the Committees of Estates in Edinburgh and the army in England, as by the plenary sessions of the Scottish Estates at Edinburgh in June–July 1644, in January–March and in July 1645, at Perth in July–August 1645, and at St Andrews from November 1645 to February 1646. While the Scots were decidedly in the minority, they enjoyed a disproportionate influence. Johnson of Wariston usually managed business. The Committee, which met at Derby House in London, undoubtedly served as the official channel for dealings between the Covenanters and the Parliamentarians. However, to effectively carry out its diplomatic functions and oversee the war effort by land and sea, the Committee would have required to function as a federal executive. But the Long Parliament

---

in-Marsh, 1993), pp. 110–2; Alexander Henderson, *A Sermon Preached to the Honourable House of Commons, At their Late Solemne Fast, Wednesday, December 27, 1643* (London, 1644); [Robert Devereux], *A Letter from his Excellency, Robert Earl of Essex, to the Honourable House of Commons Concerning the Sending of a Commission forthwith to Sir William Waller* (London, 1644). This substantive divide on religious issues made participation by commissioners for the Kirk in the Westminster Assembly of Divines a less than rewarding experience. In addition to Henderson, the other Scottish clerics attending the Westminster Assembly were Robert Baillie, Robert Douglas, George Gillespie and Samuel Rutherford, all powerful preachers and polemicists linked in vary degrees of closeness to Argyll.

was palpably not prepared to concede final decisions on war and peace.[22]

For their part, the Covenanting leadership viewed the Committee as a co-ordinating confederal council, the prime but not the sole agency for preserving the interests of Scotland in managing the affairs of both kingdoms. Its British roots lay with the commission for the Conservators of the Peace established by the Treaty of London in 1641, which evolved into the commission for negotiating the Solemn League and Covenant on behalf of the Long Parliament and the Scottish Estates. This same body, now constituted as a temporary committee of both kingdoms, had also facilitated the Scottish re-occupation of Berwick, on terms favourable to the continuing autonomy of the frontier town in September 1643 and, subsequently, had laid the groundwork for regularising Parliamentary contributions towards the expenses of the Covenanting Army in Ireland. English commissioners had been attached to the Covenanting Army of intervention but were seemingly not accorded the equivalent consultation within the Committee of Estates as that accorded to the Scottish commissioners in London. The English commissioners, especially those with northern connections, became the most vociferous critics of the deleterious impact of the Scottish presence in the north of England. In the aftermath of Marston Moor, when the Covenanting Army became increasingly reluctant to move south as civil war broke out within Scotland, their vitriol became a feature of the anti-Scottish sentiment that was coming to characterise the Parliamentary war grouping.[23]

22 J. Adamson, 'The Triumph of Oligarchy: the Management of War and the Committee of Both Kingdoms, 1644–1645' in C.R. Kyle and J. Peacey eds, *Parliament at Work: Parliamentary Committees, Political Power and Public Access in Early Modern England* (Woodbridge, 2002), pp. 101–27; Young, *The Scottish Parliament*, pp. 73, 85–6, 90–154; M. Kishlansky, *A Monarchy Transformed: Britain 1603–1714* (London, 1996), pp. 155–6, 163–4; TNA, Committee of Both Kingdoms. Entry Book: letters received 1644 September – 1645 February, SP 21/7, pp. 75–9, 112–3, 153, 194–6, and Committee of the House of Commons for Scottish Affairs: Order Book 1643 October – 1645 December, SP 23/1A, pp. 18–21, 48, 50, 58, 63, 71, 77, 102. Developed on the English side from the committee of safety, the Committee of Both Kingdoms, though viewed as an executive committee of the Long Parliament, was obliged to share direction of the war effort, initially with the Committee to reform the Lord General Essex's Army, which dealt with the compositions of regiment, and then with the Army Committee, which was primarily concerned with supply. Meeting the costs of the Covenanting armies in England and Ireland remained the responsibility of the Committee at Goldsmith's Hall for Scottish Affairs. The Committee of Both Kingdoms was entrusted to promote treaties for free trade with France, Spain and the United Provinces on behalf of England and Scotland. The Committee also had responsibility for resolving trade disputes among British communities overseas that had been referred to the Long Parliament. Moreover, it had primary responsibility for intelligence and counter-intelligence on behalf of the Parliamentarians and the Covenanters (BL, Turnbull Papers, vol. CVCVI, Add.MSS 72,433 ff.29, 34–8, 41, 48–9, 56–9, 89, 91, 103–5, 120 and vol. CXCVII, Add.MSS 72,438 ff.5–6, 24).

23 Northumbria Archives, Berwick-upon-Tweed, Guild Book, 1627–1643, B 1/9, ff.258, 261 and Guild Book, 1643–1651, B1/10, ff.2–4; TNA, State Papers Domestic, Supplementary: Orders,

The first hint of discord between Covenanters and the war grouping came in the immediate aftermath of Marston Moor in July 1644, when Cromwell claimed that the English forces of godliness had triumphed. The victory, which secured the north and fragmented the Royalist forces, could not have been achieved without the resolute military presence of the Covenanting Army under Leven. In the short term, any potential fissure was covered up by the triumphant generals – Manchester; Sir Thomas Fairfax; his father, Ferdinando, Lord Fairfax of Cameron; and Leven – writing to the Committee of Both Kingdoms to affirm their commitment to the Solemn League and Covenant. However, Essex's campaign in Cornwall and the west country in July and August were characterised by ineptitude. Manchester's campaigns in Gloucestershire were marked by inconclusive sieges and indecisiveness in the field. Cromwell resumed his offensive, which was particularly directed against Manchester and his Scottish second-in-command, Major-General Lawrence Crawford. The outcome of this bickering, which Cromwell broadened into an attack on all generals inclined to the peace grouping, was a decisive parliamentary debate in late November. In his response, Manchester attacked Cromwell as a radical intent on war, antipathetic to the Lords and contemptuous of the Westminster Assembly of Divines. Cromwell reputedly disdained the Covenanters, against whom he 'would als soon draw his sword as against these who ar declared enemies to both kingdoms'.

The initial reaction of the Scottish commissioners was not to promote reconciliation but to contemplate, in association with Essex and the peace grouping, the indictment of Cromwell as an incendiary. However, the Covenanting leadership were intent on setting the agenda for negotiations with the king at Uxbridge. They also shared the concerns of the war grouping about the lack of professionalism among the Parliamentary forces. Accordingly, the Scottish commissioners endorsed the Self-Denying Ordinance promoted in the Commons on 9 December to remove all MPs from holding civil or military commands.[24] The

---

Warrants and Receipts for payment of the Scots Army in England 1643–48, SP 46/106, ff.150, 255, 257; DH, Loudoun Deeds, bundle 1/9; HL, Loudoun Scottish Collection, box 16/LO 9998; BOU, Carte Papers, 1636–1652. Ireland, MS Carte 65 ff.114–5; *CSCL*, pp. 2–4, 39, 46–8, 68–9, 82–3, 88–9, 93, 102, 107, 141 202; D. Scott, 'The Barwis Affair: Political Allegiance and the Scots during the British Civil Wars, *EHR*, 115 (2000), pp. 843–63. When English commissioners were sent north to attend the Scottish Estates in 1645 and 1646, they constituted committees of both kingdoms in their dealings with the Committee of Estates at Edinburgh. A like committee was mooted, but never implemented, for the actual conduct of the war in Ireland on behalf of both kingdoms.

24 TNA, Committee of Both Kingdoms. Entry Book: letters received 1644, June–September, SP 21/16, pp. 145–7; HL, Loudoun Scottish Collection, box 21, LO 11367; *The Quarrel between the Earl of Manchester and Oliver Cromwell: An Episode of the English Civil Wars*, D. Mason ed. (London, 1875), pp. 62–70, 78–95;*CSCL*, pp. 50–3; Kaplan, *Politics and Religion during the English Revolution*, pp. 55–96.

British commitment of the Scots was of vital significance in persuading peers who felt particularly threatened by the anti-aristocratic thrust of Cromwell's criticisms to accept this Ordinance. Their apprehensions signalled the growing significance of party divisions formulated in the course of the Uxbridge negotiations. The passage of the Ordinance through both houses in April 1645 formalised these divisions. The Presbyterians wished to use the Scottish commissioners as a counter to the radicalism of the Independents, who had established an alternative power base to Parliament with the formation of the New Model Army, notwithstanding the appointment of Sir Thomas Fairfax, a comrade in arms of General Leven, as its commander-in-chief. Commanders associated formerly with the peace group and now with the Presbyterian interest – Essex, Manchester, Warwick and Sir William Waller – were purged, as were Scottish officers serving with the Parliamentary forces. Cromwell alone was granted a temporary exemption, made permanent after the decisive victory attained at Naseby, where he brilliantly commanded the cavalry and proclaimed a further unalloyed triumph of the godly English.[25]

The Presbyterians led by Essex hoped the Covenanters would support their desires for an accommodation with Charles I. Accordingly, they ensured that the Solemn League and Covenant had to be subscribed by all officers in the New Model Army twenty days after the Long Parliament confirmed their appointment. The Independents were intent on outright victory rather than an accommodation with Charles I. The Scots were no longer deemed essential to this objective after Naseby. The Independents were able to insist that ordinary soldiers enlisted in the New Model Army should only 'take ye Covenant' at the discretion of both houses. English considerations were thus given priority over the British reconfiguration espoused by the Covenanters. Nonetheless, the position of the Covenanters as the third force in the English civil war was reinforced by their continuing good relations with the City of London; relations that remained an irritant to the Independents.[26]

Argyll and the Covenanting leadership used their accord with the Presbyterians to secure Scottish representation on the delegation sent from the Committee of Both Kingdoms to take stock of the war in Ireland in March 1645. Political

25 HL, Bridgewater and Ellesmere MSS, EL 7778; DH, Loudoun Papers, A15/4 and Loudoun Deeds, bundles 1/16, 44/1; [Robert Devereux], *A Paper Delivered in the Lord's House by the Earle of Essex, Lord Generall, at the Offering up of his Commission* (London, 1645).

26 DH, Loudoun Papers, A15/4, /14–15; Whitelock, *Memorials*, I, pp. 460–7; *The Journal of Thomas Juxon*, pp. 94–5, 102–5; W.M. Lamont, 'The Puritan Revolution: A Historiographical Essay' in J.G.A. Pocock ed., *The Varieties of British Political Thought, 1500–1800* (Cambridge, 1996), pp. 119–45; E. Vallance, '"An Holy and Sacramental Paction": Federal Theology and the Solemn League and Covenant in England', *EHR*, 116 (2000), pp. 50–75.

distancing from the Independents, however, led to Robert Munro being stripped of his overall command of the Scottish and British forces in Ireland. Further embroiled in controversy for the Covenanters' refusal to give up their Belfast garrison, the Scottish commissioners at London were effectively removed from executive discussions on Irish affairs by December. The Independents moved onto the offensive with charges that the Scots were actually breaching their treaty obligations under the Solemn League and Covenant by their preference to remain in the north and unilaterally establish garrisons between the Tees and Carlisle. Having conducted a lacklustre, short campaign along the Welsh marches in the summer of 1645, the Covenanting Army remained resistant to overtures to venture south of the Humber until the civil war then raging in Scotland was resolved, particularly as they were ordered to liaise with Cromwell rather than the more supportive Sir Thomas Fairfax. The Covenanting leadership in Edinburgh concurred in seeking to prevent any conjunction with Royalist forces in England and Scotland. When they did eventually agree to participate in the siege of Newark-upon-Trent in November, the Committee of Estates insisted that General Leven be made supreme commander of the Covenanting and Parliamentary forces for a blockade that dragged on until May 1646.[27]

In the meantime, the Scots were buoyed up then let down by the Long Parliament's dealings on religious issues. Five years after the Covenanters had first pressed charges Archbishop Laud was eventually attainted and duly executed in January 1645. But, nine months later, the Long Parliament opted for an erastian Presbyterian settlement in the Church of England. The endeavours of the Scottish clerical commissioners to the Westminster Assembly of Divines had certainly been directed towards the replication in England of the relative autonomy enjoyed by their Kirk. Robert Baillie was particularly articulate in expressing Scottish disappointment about the malign influence of the Independents in Parliament and of sectaries within the New Model Army. Nevertheless, the congregational influence exerted by Robert Nye and his associates in the Westminster Assembly was by no means the sole cause of its protracted proceedings. Argyll and his radical associates in the Kirk, in what they viewed as the true spirit of confessional confederation, were to accept unreservedly the standards prescribed at Westminster for faith, worship and even church government, though the familiar Scottish terminology for Presbyterian courts was replaced by the continental preference for classical assemblies. However, the

---

27 DH, Loudoun Papers, A15/5, /7–11, /16 and bundle 1/25; *CSCL*, pp. 82–3, 97–8, 109–11, 118–23, 133–4, 137–9, 147; Whitelock, *Memorials*, I, pp. 542–3; [John Chiesly] *A Manifesto of the Commissioners of Scotland Delivered to the Honourable Houses of Parliament the 24 of May 1645* (London, 1645); Wheeler, *The Irish and British Wars*, pp. 148–50; Stevenson, *Revolution and Counter-Revolution in Scotland*, pp. 61–3.

Scottish commissioners and the Committees of Estates took a more pragmatic approach to the erastian nature of English Presbyterianism as implemented by the Long Parliament in March 1646, when all church courts were subordinated to parliament and their powers of ecclesiastical censure strictly limited; a situation which differed in degree rather than in kind from the actual situation which prevailed in Scotland under the Covenanting Movement.[28]

Internationally, the divisions played out between Presbyterians and Independents in the Westminster Assembly, as in parliament, carried a religious resonance. However, the key to these divisions, which emerged before victory over Charles I was assured, was polarised political attitudes to continuing Covenanting intervention in England. Accordingly, the view that the New Model Army was simply a conservative restructuring of existing Parliamentary forces can only be sustained from a narrow, military, anglocentric perspective.[29] But from a broader, political and religious, British perspective, it was a radical creation. Essentially it was a Gothic construct, being based on, but without acknowledgement to, the national armies created initially in Sweden then in Scotland as products of the Thirty Years War. Under Fairfax and Cromwell it was fashioned to attain an English victory for the Parliamentarians, not a British triumph for the Solemn League and Covenant.[30]

Despite growing tensions with the Covenanters on the conduct of the war and the failure to implement Presbyterian uniformity, the Parliamentarians had been anxious to involve Scottish expertise in international relations through the Committee of Both Kingdoms. In February 1644, the Parliamentarians had invited the Covenanters to appoint an agent to work with Walter Strickland, their resident in the United Provinces. Thomas Cunningham, the leading fundraiser and financial facilitator for the Covenanting Movement, who was based at Campvere in Zeeland, was duly nominated the following month.

28 DH, Loudoun Deeds, bundles 1/7, 1/21, 1700/1; BL, Turnbull Papers, vol. CXCVIII, Add.MSS 72,439 ff.77–80; *LJB*, II, pp. 103, 195, 211, 229–30, 234, 242, 250, 265–6, 270, 286, 299, 317–20, 326, 335–41, 357, 360–2, 485; III, pp. 10–11; *CSCL*, pp. 43, 71, 155; *CAL*, I, pp. 176–7; Kaplan, *Politics and Religion during the English Revolution*, pp. 128–44. The National Covenant of 1638 had affirmed that matters of faith, worship and government in Scotland required to be grounded in parliamentary statutes. The committees of war established subsequently in the Scottish shires also not only carried out the civil sanctions required for ecclesiastical transgressions, but also determined the ideological soundness of those suspected of being antipathetic to the godliness of the Covenanting cause.

29 M. Kishlansky, 'The Case of the Army Truly Stated: The Creation of the New Model Army', *Past & Present*, 81 (1978), pp. 51–74; I. Gentles, 'The Choosing of the Officers for the New Model Army', *Historical Research*, 67 (1994), pp. 264–85.

30 BL, Historical Autographs, 16th–18th Centuries, Add.MSS 28,103, fo.41;Bennet, *The Civil Wars in Britain and Ireland*, pp. 220–9; Wheeler, *The Irish and British Wars*, pp. 125–9; Hirst, *England in Conflict*, pp. 220–4, 229–30.

Unlike Strickland, whose appointment had been the subject of protest by Queen Henrietta Maria, Cunningham was an uncontested and fully accredited envoy, which actually gave him seniority at The Hague. His remit, as prescribed by the Committee of Estates at Edinburgh, was not only to promote the joint cause before the States General, but also to extend the Solemn League and Covenant to the Dutch Republic. Thus, the prospect of reviving confessional confederation in defence of European Protestantism was undertaken as a joint endeavour for both kingdoms. The States General, however, preferred to maintain a mediating position between Charles I and his British opponents while continuing to license shipments of arms and ammunition to all sides.[31]

The Parliamentarians again took the initiative in seeking a joint undertaking to promote confessional confederation with Sweden in the wake of Hugh Mowatt's embassy in the spring of 1644. Whereas the Scots felt inhibited by the Solemn League and Covenant from concluding a bilateral treaty with Sweden, the English Parliamentarians were less scrupulous, even though the issue had been referred to the Committee of Both Kingdoms in January 1645. However, the pro-Scottish influence of Oxenstierna was waning in Swedish affairs once Queen Kristina came of age to embark upon her personal rule. The British envoy who was sent to Sweden in May, Colonel Christopher Potley, a veteran recently released from Swedish service, duly took advantage of this situation to promote a bilateral alliance with the English Parliamentarians that marginalised Scottish interests.[32] In order to counter any revived inclination of Christian IV to assist Charles I, Saye and Seal and Wariston had written to the Danish king in June 1645 on behalf of the Committee, which was now projected as *Concilium Amborum Magnae Britanniae*. Restricting shipments of arms from Denmark-Norway remained a particular concern of both kingdoms. The Long Parliament

31 Young, 'The Scottish Parliament and European Diplomacy' in Murdoch ed., *Scotland and the Thirty Years' War*, pp. 87–92; *The Journal of Thomas Cunningham of Campvere*, E.J. Courthope ed. (Edinburgh, 1928), pp. 5–7, 14–6, 82–8, 109–17, 251; BL, Turnbull Papers, vol. CXCIV, Add.MSS 72,435, ff.21–109 and vol. CXCVI, Add.MSS 72,437, ff.50–3, 85–6. By May 1645, the States General preferred to deal directly with the Long Parliament rather than through the Committee of Both Kingdoms. Nevertheless, Cunningham and Strickland worked together to downplay claims of Royalist successes in Scotland in the spring and summer of 1645 and subsequently to prevent shipments of arms to the defeated Royalists in the spring of 1646. In the interim, they had to counter claims by Anglo-Irish Protestants that Ulster was benefiting disproportionately from relief raised for Ireland in the United Provinces. They also had to contend with the partiality of the house of Orange for the Stuarts; a partiality which led to attempts to restrict compulsory subscription to the Solemn League and Covenant by English and Scottish regiments in Dutch service as by the English Merchant Company in Rotterdam.
32 SR, Anglica 521 and Hugh Mowatt's Letters to Sweden, AOSB ser B. E583; BL, Turnbull Papers, vol. CXCIV, Add.MSS 72,435 ff.64–5 and vol. CXCVI, Add.MSS 72,437 ff.44–6, 61–2; Grosjean, *An Unofficial Alliance*, pp. 206–13.

had commissioned the translation of the Solemn League and Covenant into French, German and Latin to broadcast British commitment to the Protestant cause. But its diplomatic missions to Hamburg, Denmark and Sweden were primarily to serve English commercial interests. [33]

The Scottish commissioners tended to take a back seat whenever business relating to the American colonies, especially to competition with the Portuguese and Spanish, passed through the Committee of Both Kingdoms. But they did retain international influence in two key areas: the Palatinate and France. In 1642, Lothian had persuaded Elector Charles Louis not to become embroiled in the Royalist cause. Instead he should place his hopes on regaining the Palatinate through the joint endeavours of the Scottish Estates and the English Parliament. Lothian, in turn, was receptive to overtures from the Elector in 1643 to lobby on his behalf at the French court. The Elector in the course of 1644, and again in 1645, pushed the Scots on the Committee for assistance in the recovery of the Palatinate, even stating on the former occasion that he would come to London to lobby in person. But he had to be content with a statement endorsed by Saye and Seal and Wariston that his restoration would be a British priority once issues of war and peace were resolved with Charles I. The Scottish commissioners in London, as well as the Committee of Estates in Edinburgh, were also intent on maintaining their own distinctive as well as joint British links to France following the failure of tripartite peace negotiations with the king at Uxbridge in February 1645.[34]

Losing the Peace

As shaped by Argyll and his radical associates, the key features of Covenanting policy during the period of English intervention were a demonstrable concern with confederal union, a pragmatic willingness to temper military force with peace negotiations, and an international commitment to Protestantism, not just Presbyterianism. From their arrival in London in February 1644, the Scottish commissioners were intent on pursuing war against the Royalists. But they did

---

33 DR, TKUA, England, A I, no.3, Breve, til Vels med Bilag fra Medlemmer af det Engelske Kongehus til medlemmer af det danske, 1613–89 and TKUA, England, A II, no. 15, Akter og Dokumenter vedr. det politiske Forhold til England, 1641–48; *Kong Christian Den Fjerdes Egenhaendige Breve*, IV, pp. 423–5, 513–5; BL, Turnbull Papers, vol. CXCV, Add.MSS 72,436, ff.1–4, 29–30, 53–8, 73–7, 116–21, 128–31, 146–52, 155–64, 170–3, 177–8, 181, 184–5, 190–1 and vol. CXCVI, Add.MSS 72,437 ff.80–4; Murdoch, *Britain, Denmark-Norway and the House of Stuart*, pp. 124–38. Indeed, the Parliament had only temporarily set aside its endeavours since December 1643 to take over Sound toll negotiations without reference to the Covenanting leadership or Scottish interests. This endeavour was effectively achieved in March 1646, albeit the treaty for relief from exorbitant tolls was not concluded until June 1647.

34 *CAL*, II, p. 491; BL, Turnbull Papers, vol. CXCIV, Add.MSS 72,435, ff.27–8 and vol. CXCVI, Add.MSS 72,437, ff.17–18, 20–9, 54–5, 84, 86–8 and vol. CXCVIII, Add.MSS 72,439, fo.87.

not rule out brokering a negotiated peace with the king and the Parliamentarians that would be consistent with the British aspirations of the Covenanting Movement. The Scottish commissioners were well aware that an embassy had been sent from the United Provinces to effect a meaningful reconciliation. They were determined to be represented separately as the third force in any peace negotiations. [35]

Accordingly, the Covenanting leadership was not content that peace negotiations, which opened at Uxbridge in November 1644, should simply tighten up on the bilateral propositions between Parliamentarians and Royalists that had failed to secure agreement at Oxford in February 1643. The Scottish commissioners certainly respected issues of mutual concern raised by the Parliamentarians such as control over the militia, executive and judiciary; effecting religious reformation; the removal of delinquent counsellors; and the exemption of named 'malignants' from pardon. In order to secure a lasting peace between the king and the Parliamentarians, the commissioners were instructed to negotiate with a degree of flexibility even on the promotion of Presbyterian uniformity according to a Scottish prescription. The Scottish commissioners were especially determined that funding for the Covenanting forces in Ireland should be regularised and that the British in Ireland were to be obliged to subscribe the Solemn League and Covenant. The Covenanters were also determined that no Scottish peer should be held to account in England for transgressions in Scotland in the same way that Strafford, in 1641, had been tried for his malpractices in Ireland. The Committee of Estates had strenuously petitioned the king in January 1644 that Lothian's close confinement was a breach of international law, and that diplomatic convention required that 'he be judged at home' if he had negotiated in France against the interests of the king or country. Hamilton's desire 'more to serve the king than God' had attracted radical opprobrium. Nevertheless, the Scottish commissioners complained that he was currently being kept prisoner in Oxford contrary to Scots law, which required that all subjects who committed wrongs in Scotland were tried there. [36]

However, this Scottish package was not attractive to the king and did not enjoy unequivocal support from the Parliamentarians. Charles I remained

---

35 BL, Nicholas Papers, Egerton MS 2533, fo.365 and Turnbull Papers, vol. CXCIV, Add.MSS 72,435, ff.112–29; ICA, Letters – Marquess's Period, 1638–1645, bundle 7/161; Whitelock, *Memorials*, I, pp. 263, 370.
36 DH, Loudoun Papers, bundles 1/26–7 and Loudoun Deeds, bundle 1700/2; NAS, Hamilton Papers, GD 406/1/1940; *CAL*, I, pp. 160–1; *CSCL*, pp. 6, 10–3, 22–7, 33–4, 45, 50, 53, 57–8. When the Scottish Privy Council was purged at the behest of Argyll and the radical in June 1645, eight English councillors, including four serving on the Committee of Both Kingdoms, were given honorary appointments. The main losers were the Royalist nobility, who were replaced by Argyll's radical associates, predominantly from the gentry (TFA, Papers, TD 3751).

adamantly opposed to a Covenanted monarchy or to making any meaningful concessions in England that would diminish his power to the level secured by the Covenanters in Scotland by 1641. Charles's resolve not to compromise was stiffened by support from Queen Henrietta Maria and George Digby, Lord Digby. The king was also hoping to firm up the cessation between Confederates and Royalists in Ireland into a treaty whereby substantive reinforcements for his war effort in England would be secured through a comprehensive toleration for Irish Catholics. Committed to the Stuart monarchy, the Covenanters had no real alternative to Charles I. Elector Charles Louis was reported to have subscribed the Solemn League and Covenant while in the United Provinces in March 1644. There were continuing but unfounded fears within Royalist circles that he was being lined up to replace his uncle. However, his restoration to the Palatinate appeared more likely with French assistance than his intrusion to the British succession. His two younger brothers, Princes Rupert and Maurice, were tainted through their martial association with the Royalist cause. A regency government appeared out of the question, as the queen stood solidly with Charles, and both the Prince of Wales (the future Charles II) and James, Duke of York enjoyed the protection of France and the United Provinces. Outright republicanism remained a distinctive minority pursuit in England. Nonetheless, there were growing concerns within the Covenanting Movement that the Parliamentary war grouping was becoming less committed to a Stuart monarchy when the peace negotiations at Uxbridge broke up in February 1645; concerns compounded by the subsequent emergence of the New Model Army. The Covenanters also suffered from a piece of Royalist mischief-making in publishing intercepted letters which revealed that the civil war in Scotland was not running in their favour. At the same time, renewed solidarity between radicals and conservatives brokered between Argyll and Lanark suggested that the Covenanters were prepared to exploit divisions among Parliamentarians to reach an accommodation with Charles I. [37]

The Scots had actually entered the peace negotiations with alternative fields of engagement beckoning, a situation that remained open following Uxbridge. In

---

37 *Letters from the Marquesse of Argyle, the Earl of Lanerick, Lord Wariston, and others now at Edinburgh to their friends in London. Intercepted by Sir Richard Willys, Governour of Newarke, and Printed truthfully by the Originals* (Oxford, 1645); HL, Ellesmere and Bridgewater MSS, EL 7776; BL, Turnbull Papers, vol. CXCVII, Add.MSS 72,438, ff.5–6; CSCL, pp. 9, 29, 59–63; CAL, II, pp. 490–1; D.L. Smith "'The More Posed and Wised Advice": The Fourth Earl of Dorset and the English Civil Wars', *HJ*, 34 (1991), pp. 797–829. Digby (later 2nd Earl of Bristol) had expected that Hamilton, though languishing in prison without being brought to trial, would encourage his friends and dependents to act vigorously on behalf of the king within Covenanting circles in Scotland and with the army of intervention, to promote peace at Uxbridge (NAS, Hamilton Papers, GD 401/1/1932).

the aftermath of Marston Moor, the Covenanters had actively debated the revival of confederation with Sweden to facilitate wresting the provinces to the east of the Øresund from Christian IV of Denmark. The acquisition of these provinces by Sweden would eradicate the tolls crippling the Scottish trade to and from the Baltic. The Swedes were intent on renewing the recruitment of *hjaelptrupperne* from Scotland, and Mowatt, the émigré Scot, stepped up his hitherto unsuccessful recruitment efforts. Chancellor Oxenstierna also wrote to the same effect to his Scottish counterpart, Loudoun, just before negotiations commenced at Uxbridge. Notwithstanding the warm reception accorded to Mowatt by leading Covenanters in both London and Edinburgh, neither he nor Oxenstierna were promised troops. While stating his intent to lay the issue before the Committee of Both Kingdoms, Loudoun was adamant that no assistance could be forthcoming until a lasting peace was secured with the king and Presbyterianism established in England. Nevertheless, Swedish overtures added to the tensions between the Covenanters and Parliamentarians at Uxbridge.[38] Scandinavian-induced tensions were further evident after this. The Covenanting leadership had monitored Danish attempts to secure Scottish assistance against Sweden through an embassy despatched under Colonel John Henderson, another émigré with longstanding ties to the house of Argyll. Although they were not receptive to raising forces for Danish service, other than to decant Royalist sympathisers from Scotland, they took umbrage when the Parliamentarians incarcerated Henderson when he passed through London in June 1645.[39]

The withdrawal of Swedish troops from the German theatre to fight in the Northern War of 1643–45 against Denmark-Norway made the French determined to step up recruitment from the British Isles, which Mazarin and the Queen Mother felt could best be achieved by the promotion of peace between Charles I, the Covenanters and the Parliamentarians. Building on the foundations laid by Richelieu, Mazarin sought to wrest from Spain the mantle of universal monarchy for France. But, by Uxbridge, French forces were not only committed in Germany but also lined up against Spain, with varying degrees of success, in Italy, Catalonia and Flanders. Their presence in the latter theatre was of concern to the Dutch as well as the Parliamentarians. France sought Irish as well as Scottish recruits. However, French diplomatic links with the Catholic Confederates was relatively low-key. Certainly, Mazarin was aware that the putative conversion of the cessation into a peace treaty between Royalists

---

38 DH, Loudoun Deeds, bundles 1/1, 2/2; SR, Hugh Mowat's Letters to Sweden, AOSB ser B. E583; A. Grosjean, *An Unofficial Alliance*, pp. 195–206.

39 DR, TKUA, Alm.Del I Indtil 1670, 'Latina' vol. 11, ff.272–4, 310–5, 335–7 and TKUA, England, A II, no. 15, Akter og Dokumenter vedr. det politiske Forhold til England, 1641–48; BL, Turnbull Papers, vol. CXCV, Add.MSS 72,436, ff.176, 182–3, 190–1.

and Confederates had the potential not only to transform Charles I's military prospects in England, but also to release Irish forces for French service. Yet there was a tacit recognition at the French Court that Spanish influence over the Irish carried more weight.[40]

At the same time, where the French were studiously vague in their promises to the Irish, Mazarin and the Queen Mother, in the name of Louis XIV, had actually despatched a statement of intent to Chancellor Loudoun that they were prepared to reinvigorate the 'auld alliance'. This statement coincided with the breakdown of negotiations at Uxbridge in February 1645. In the following month, Loudoun accredited Sir Robert Moray as colonel of the Scottish regiment formerly commanded by the late Earl of Irvine. Moray, in turn, was to become the principal diplomatic agent to negotiate further Scottish forces in return for a firm alliance. To this end, Mazarin, notwithstanding papal overtures to provide armed assistance to Charles I, was also willing to promote peace between the Royalists and Parliamentarians that would facilitate the withdrawal of the Covenanting Army from England. Once in Paris, Moray encouraged Henrietta Maria to become more flexible. But the exiled Queen, like Charles I, had been heartened by Royalist successes in Scotland and was still insistent that the Covenanters would have to abandon the imposition of Presbyterianism on England if there was to be any prospect of a meaningful peace.[41]

Undoubtedly, the rise of the New Model Army and triumphal intransigence among Independents were negative influences on such a prospect from the Parliamentary side. Charles I discounted any suggestion of replacing an Anglican with a Presbyterian establishment, as this shift would imperil his immortal soul. Indeed, he was incapable of making meaningful concessions on the religious issue. The Covenanters' resolve to reach an accommodation with the king suffered critically when Charles's secret correspondence regarding a negotiated peace was intercepted and published in part by the Parliamentarians in the wake of Naseby; a correspondence that laid bare the king's untrustworthiness, as well as the straightened financial circumstances of the Royalist cause.[42]

40 BL, Turnbull Papers, vol. CXCIII, Add.MSS 72,434, ff.15–16 and vol. CXCVI, Add.MSS 72,437, ff.15–16, 37; J-F. Schaub, *La France Espagnole: Les raciness hispaniques d l'absolutisme français* (Paris, 2003), pp. 14–16, 90–1, 263–4, 281–2; J. Ohlmeyer, 'Ireland Independent: Confederate Foreign Policy and International Relations during the Mid-Seventeenth Century' in Ohlmeyer ed., *Ireland: from Independence to Occupation*, pp. 89–111. Manoeuvres of French troops in Brittany and Normandy during the Uxbridge negotiations were no more than sabre rattling, not a serious threat to deploy forces either against the Covenanters and Parliamentarians or in support of the Irish Confederation of Catholics.

41 NAS, Bute Papers, RH 1/7/20–21; BL, Trumbull Papers vol. CXCIII, Add.MSS 72,434, ff.1–2 and Historical Letters and Papers, Add.MSS 33,596, ff.7–8.

42 *Making the News*, pp. 339–48; Henry Parker, John Sadler and Thomas May, *The King's Cabinet Opened* (London, 1645); BL. Turnbull Papers, vol. CXCIII, Add.MSS 72,434 ff.1–10 and vol.

The Covenanters, while immoveable on Presbyterian uniformity, were prepared to negotiate with latitude on the other key issues discussed at Uxbridge, notably the militia and Ireland. This greater flexibility was a sign of the revival of pragmatic conservatism brought about by the rehabilitation of Lanark in Edinburgh and by the growing prominence of Lauderdale among the Scottish commissioners at London. Preoccupied with civil war raging in Scotland north of the Tay, and with protecting his estates from the devastation by Royalist clans, Argyll was in danger of taking his eye off the diplomatic ball. The Parliamentary triumph at Naseby had, however, regalvanised French diplomacy with respect to the British situation and encouraged the more conservatively inclined Covenanters to contemplate a bilateral peace with Charles I. In turn, the reluctance of the Covenanting Army to leave their northern garrisons made Charles I more susceptible to French overtures for peace, especially as he felt Royalist success in Scotland was strengthening his hand against Argyll and the radicals who could not be induced to disown a tripartite British solution. Indeed, Charles was proposing to summon the Scottish Estates to Glasgow in October 1645 to reassert his control over Scotland and secure reparations for his supporters from the Covenanting Movement.[43]

Two months after Naseby, Jean de Montereul arrived in London as the French envoy empowered by Mazarin to pursue peace. Considerably less subtle than Mazarin in the promotion of French politique, Montereul prioritised Royalist and Covenanter interests. In the process, he was prepared to work against Swedish endeavours to promote confederation and recruit troops, leading the under-resourced and under-instructed Mowatt to complain to Oxenstierna that the French no less than the Danes were hostile diplomatic influences in London (if not yet in Edinburgh). From August 1645 until May 1646, Montereul worked in association with Sir Robert Moray in London and Paris to secure a bilateral if not a tripartite peace. Montereul and Moray were able to draw on the increasing prominence of Lauderdale, who was eclipsing Balmerino, the nominal leader of the Scottish commissioners in London in the absence of Loudoun and Argyll. Montereul was also working assiduously with Henry Rich, 1st Earl of Holland, a pragmatic Royalist more at home in London than in Oxford and well connected to the Presbyterian faction in Parliament. Holland was also a longstanding

---

CXCVII, Add.MSS 72,438, ff.1–99. Letters from the king's principal agent in Paris, George Goring, 2nd Earl of Norwich, also highlighted the embarrassment of Henrietta Maria attempting to pawn her jewelry in Amsterdam and other Dutch markets.

43 BL, Miscellaneous Letters etc., 1566–1804, Add.MSS 36,540, ff.16–17; *LJB*, II, p. 345; Stevenson, *Revolution and Counter-Revolution*, pp. 54–8. Argyll and Loudoun were both liable to reimburse the French for £400–500 sterling advanced to the late Earl of Irvine and for which they had stood surety. Although Mazarin and the Queen Mother were prepared to waive this sum as an inducement to win them over, both stood firm for a tripartite peace (*Montereul*, I, p. 42).

associate of the still imprisoned Hamilton and his brother Lanark.[44]

Montereul and Holland originally hoped that Charles I would come to London and push for peace with the assistance of Essex and the Presbyterian faction. However, hard-liners within the Royalist camp, led by Lord Digby, were more prepared to countenance an accommodation with the Independents. Their belief in gathered churches of the godly nationwide, rather than a single ecclesiastical establishment for England, opened up the prospect of toleration rather than eradication for Anglicanism; a position from which Charles I also derived hope. Nevertheless, Montereul and Mazarin pressed for the alternative of the king seeking safe custody with the Scots, who were repelled by rampant sectarianism and the growing strain of republicanism among the Independents, albeit the termination of the Stuart dynasty was still a measure of last resort for Parliamentarians. Military relations between the Independents and the Scots were close to breaking point. The Scottish commissioners as well as the Committees of Estates complained persistently about the continuing shortages of money and supplies for their army from Parliament. The Independents were outraged by the Scots' unilateral resort to local assessments, free quarters and occasional depredations in the north of England. They also harboured exaggerated fears that France and Scotland would formulate an international alliance involving Sweden and Denmark to restore Charles I to power in England. Both radical and conservative Covenanters were contemplating war between the two kingdoms following Leven's eventual move to lay siege to Newark in Northamptonshire.[45]

---

44 SR, Hugh Mowatt's Letters to Sweden, AOSB ser B. E583; *Montereul*, I, pp. 1–78 and II, pp. 669–75; Macinnes, *The British Revolution*, p. 140. Montereul's seeming partiality to the Covenanters over the Parliamentarians was particularly welcomed by the Scottish commissioners even though they were working on the surface towards the same diplomatic ends through the Committee of Both Kingdoms, which was in receipt of regular reports from the French court through its Parisian agent Rene Augier, a former courtier in Paris now reinstated as British resident. In giving notice of Montereul's departure from London, Augier claimed that he was coming ostensibly to resolve commercial disputes. In fact, this was the province of Monsieur de Sabran, already resident in London as secretary to the French embassy for commercial affairs. Montereul operated out of separate premises from de Sabran. Augier also asserted that Montereul's dispatch reflected dissatisfaction at the French court with the directory established to maintain a watching brief over the three kingdoms, particularly as this directory had failed to pick up growing tensions among the Parliamentarians between the Presbyterians and Independents. Augier provided regular despatches from the French court until December 1646, albeit his credentials had come under question by the Committee of the Lords and Commons for Foreign Affairs seven months earlier (BL, Turnbull Papers, vol. CXCIII, Add.MSS 72,434, ff.21–178 and vol. CXCVI, Add.MSS 72,437, ff.87,91).

45 BL, Historical Letters and Papers 1633–1655, Add.MSS 33,596, ff.7–8; ICA, Letters – Marquess's Period, 1646–1649, bundle 8/192; *Montereul*, I, pp. 79–162 and II, pp. 575–83; *CSCL*, pp. 150, 153, 160, 163, 19–80. The adversarial nature of the divisions between Presbyterians and Independ-

The ending of the Scottish civil war in favour of the Covenanting Movement, which left Charles I 'in deep melancholy and despair', as well as the growing political hostility between Presbyterians and Independents, allowed Montereul and Mazarin additional scope to press for the option of Scottish custody. Henrietta Maria, now lodged at St Germain outside Paris, was encouraged to put pressure on her husband to come to some conscientious accommodation over the Solemn League and Covenant and the establishment of Presbyterianism in England. An increasingly exasperated Montereul eventually persuaded Charles I to abandon his court at Oxford and throw in his lot with the Covenanters. Two months after the formal capitulation of Royalist forces in England – at Stow-on-the-Wold in Gloucestershire – the king surrendered to General Leven at Newark on 5 May 1646. But this was only after Charles had attempted a feint towards London in a forlorn hope of rapprochement with the Independents. Montereul was less than enthused by the Covenanting response to the arrival of the king. This response, led by Lothian into whose custody the king was entrusted, was a reassertion of radical control over proceedings. Charles was required to order the surrender of the besieged Royalist garrison in Newark, to disband the Royalist forces in Scotland, and to sign the Solemn League and Covenant. His refusal to undertake the latter or even to signify his acceptance of its validity ensured that he was taken into protective custody rather than welcomed as a peacemaker as the Covenanting Army promptly withdrew to Newcastle.[46]

Retreat from England

Although the Covenanters had actively been considering a further round of talks with the king since autumn 1645, the Parliamentarians only seem to have given renewed impetus to peace proposals at the outset of 1646. The Scottish commissioners were originally excluded from these discussions, which commenced not in the full Committee of Both Kingdoms but in a sub-committee, and resulted in the drawing up of what became the Newcastle Propositions in July. But as the king was then in Scottish custody, the Covenanters remained the third force to be accommodated in any negotiations.

---

ents was laid bare in the summer of 1645, when Thomas, Lord Saville, at the prompting of Saye and Seal for the latter party, attempted to implicate Denzil Holles and Bulstroke Whitelock in secret dealings with the Scots to negotiate terms of peace with Charles I (M. Mahoney, 'The Saville Affair and the Politics of the Long Parliament', *Parliamentary History*, 7 (1988), pp. 212–27).

46 *Montereul*, I, pp. 163–208; *CAL*, I, pp. 181–6; NAS, Lothian MSS, GD 40/2/2; ICA, Letters – Marquess's Period, 1646–1649, bundle 8/192. William Moray, a cousin of Sir Robert and a member of the queen's household, was despatched from St Germain with the queen's overtures for the king's compliance. However, his mission was aborted on his capture by Parliamentary forces while making his way to Oxford.

The Covenanters were unconvinced that any meaningful Parliamentary pressure was exerted on Charles to take the Solemn League and Covenant, even though the Presbyterians had secured agreement in the Long Parliament that its religious imperatives were to be sustained. The Covenanters did not regard control over the militia as solely an English issue, as the Independents were insisting. The king's effective exclusion from control for life was too long, fundamentally inconsistent with the Solemn League, and a further disincentive to Charles to covenant. The issue of command over the forces in Ireland was in danger of going by default if the Parliamentarians took no account of Scottish interests. Although the Scottish forces were decisively defeated by the Catholic Confederates at Benburb in County Tyrone on 5 June 1646, Ulster did not fall. The major casualty was the Covenanters' working accommodation with the Parliamentarians in Ireland. The exclusion of Scots from ongoing discussions on Irish affairs was again viewed as a breach in the spirit of the Solemn League and contrary to the understanding upon which the Covenanting Army had intervened in England. While there was little doubt that Scottish participation on the Committee of Both Kingdoms had run its course, the Covenanting leadership was insistent that the making of peace and war remained common issues for Scotland and England.[47]

Argyll, the driving force behind British confederation, had attempted to transcend divisions between Parliamentarians and Covenanters, and within the ranks of both. English intransigence towards an accommodation had grown now that the king was in Covenanting custody. The Lords still exercised a restraining influence on the Scotophobia then rampant in the Commons, which maintained that the disposal of the king was a purely English, not a British, matter. Nonetheless, internal divisions between Presbyterians and Independents were a further complication, especially as the New Model Army inclined towards the latter in terms of restricting royal authority and promoting religious toleration. The Scottish Estates were increasingly restless about the continuing cost of military intervention in England and Ireland. Argyll was also

---

47 DH, Loudoun Papers, A15/5, A213/4 and Loudoun Deeds, bundles 1/20, /23–5, 2/7; BOU, Carte Papers, 1636–1652. Ireland, MS Carte 65, ff.343–5; *CSCL*, pp. 104–5, 148–52, 173–7, 181–2, 186–200, 219, 222–3; Whitelock, *Memorials*, I, pp. 548–9, 557, 564, 578; Smith, *Constitutional Royalism and the Search for a Settlement*, pp. 128–31, 149–50, 183–7; P. Little, 'The English Parliament and the Irish Constitution' in M. Ó Siochrú ed., *Kingdoms in Crisis: Ireland in the 1640s* (Dublin, 2000), pp. 106–21. In pushing amendments to the Newcastle propositions, the Scots claimed half, but were prepared to settle for a third, of all places of trust in the royal household to counter the impact of absentee monarchy, which had been deemed prejudicial to Scotland since 1603. Equal number of Scots and English were to be employed on foreign embassies of concern to both kingdoms and the Covenanters claimed a share of the royal navy to guard the Scottish coasts and for convoys to protect Scottish ships engaged in overseas trade.

experiencing increasing difficulty in holding together the radical Covenanting mainstream. The purging of public offices in the wake of the Scottish civil war had witnessed the emergence of a distinctive grouping of gentry and burgesses intent on the political exclusion of all nobles, their clients and associates tainted by association with Royalism. An act of proscription, which passed through the Scottish Estates in January, had imposed swingeing fines equivalent to as much as six years rents on all deemed delinquent or malignant.[48]

In these trying circumstances, Argyll joined with Loudoun and Leven to issue a robust defence of the Scottish position at the outset of June 1646. They called for the Committee of Both Kingdoms to be re-convened at Newcastle to resolve a unified approach to peace and in handling the king. Argyll used his stay in Newcastle to reacquaint himself personally with Charles I, the first time they had met since the Covenanting triumph in the Scottish Estates of 1641. It was not a meeting of minds. Argyll was hoping Charles would moderate his position sufficiently to take stock of the Newcastle Propositions from the Long Parliament. He also stated his willingness to deal with Royalists in London who inclined towards a negotiated settlement, most notably the Anglo-Scot James Stewart who, as 4th Duke of Lennox in Scotland and 1st Duke of Richmond in England, had long been inclined towards peace rather than war. Charles was prepared neither to trust Argyll nor to compromise on religious issues. A further irritant to Charles was the pressure exerted on him at Newcastle by the Committee of Estates to discharge Ormond from attempting any further treaties between Royalists and Catholic Confederates, especially as the French Queen Mother was receptive to such a firm peace in Ireland. However, she was still not prepared to commit French forces to re-establish the king's position in England and Scotland. The king remained irritated that Argyll continued to push for Ormond to surrender to forces loyal to the Long Parliament.[49]

---

48 ICA, Letters – Marquess's Period, 1646–1649, bundle 8/192; Thomas Chalmer, *An Answer to the Scotch Papers Delivered in the House of Commons in Reply to the Votes of both Houses of Parliament of England, Concerning the Disposal of the King* (London, 1646); J.R. Young, 'The Scottish Parliament and the Covenanting Revolution: The Emergence of a Scottish Commons' in Young ed., *Celtic Dimensions of the British Civil Wars*, pp. 164–84; Stevenson, *Revolution and Counter-Revolution in Scotland*, pp. 63–72. The Lords declined to accept the vote of the Commons on 19 May to dispense with the services of the Covenanting Army, having determined twelve days earlier that no move should be made by the New Model Army to interpose itself between the Scottish forces and the Borders. The monthly maintenance for the Scots had been reduced to £15,000 sterling at the outset of 1646.

49 BL, Royal and Noble Autographs, 1646–1768, Add.MSS 19,399, fo.4; BOU, Carte Papers, 1636–1652. Ireland, MS Carte 65, ff.313–4; *Letters from the Committee of Estates at Newcastle and the Commissioners of the Kingdom of Scotland to both Houses of Parliament* (London, 1646); *A Declaration of the Commissioners of the Parliament of Scotland Concerning the Paper Sent to the Marquess of Ormond in his Majesties Name Presented to the Rt. Hon. the House of Peers,*

In the interim, Argyll continued on to London, to make a celebrated speech to the Grand Committee of Both Houses on 25 June that reaffirmed his credentials as the foremost British confederate in the three kingdoms. In signifying Covenanting consent to the Newcastle Propositions without amendment, the Marquess steadfastly maintained the imperative of confederal action while affirming that the move from regal to complete union remained a visionary ideal. Argyll stated that the Scots had a natural affection towards their monarch, 'whereby they wish he may be rather Reformed than Ruined'. Yet he added that this personal regard had never made them forget the common rule: 'The Safety of the People is the Supreme Law'. The Stuart monarchy as an institution should be 'rather regulated than destroyed'. Accordingly, the Parliamentarians should not negotiate unilaterally with Charles I; the Covenanting forces in England and Ireland should be promptly supplied; and tensions between the New Model Army and the Covenanting Army of intervention should be headed off. Argyll was wholly dismissive that any settlement with the king would serve to unite Irish and Scottish Royalists with the Presbyterians in England. Argyll, however, was not wholly idealistic. He had journeyed to Ireland in March, both to appraise himself of the deplorable state of the under-funded and under-supplied forces, but also to arrange for three regiments of 2,100 men to be brought over to Scotland under Major-General George Munro. Originally the Covenanting leadership had set aside £80,000 (£6,667 sterling) for these forces, to be used to mop up lingering Royalist resistance on the western seaboard of Scotland, but Argyll and his radical associates were prepared to redeploy them to England in the event of war breaking out between Covenanters and Parliamentarians.[50]

The king's aversion to the Newcastle Propositions left the Covenanting leadership with little alternative but to negotiate an honourable withdrawal from England. Nevertheless, their retention of the king until satisfactory recompense for past services was agreed increased the ire of the Independents, detached the Presbyterians and led to a marked decline in support from their most steadfast constituency, the city of London. Vane, the younger, regretted that an unresolved peace would tie up English and Scottish forces, and leave

Monday 8 June 1646 (London, 1646); *Charles I in 1646: Letters of King Charles the First to Queen Henrietta Maria*, J. Bruce ed. (London, 1856), pp. 47, 70; Whitelock, *Memorials*, II, pp. 42–3; Willcock, *The Great Marquess*, pp. 190–4; Smith, *Constitutional Royalism*, pp. 4–5, 150.

50 [Archibald Campbell], *The Lord Marquess of Argyle's Speech to A Grand Committee of Both Houses of Parliament* (London, 1646); *Making the News*, pp. 349–50; *LJB*, II, p. 357; *MHG*, pp. 213, 220; ADBA, Argyll Papers, 40.21; BOU, Carte Papers, 1636–1652. Ireland, MS Carte 65, fo.266; ICA, Argyll Letters (1638–85), A 36/150 and 17th Century Papers – Mostly Accounts, bundle 53/3 and Letters – Marquess's Period, 1646–1649, bundle 8/198; Armstrong, *Protestant War*, pp. 164–5, 173, 178–9. The British forces in Ireland had declined to part of the contingent brought over to Scotland (HL, Loudoun Scottish Papers, box 30/LO 10336).

Ireland under the unfettered control of the papacy, to the detriment of Protestant kingdoms throughout Europe. Siren voices in the Long Parliament sought to deny the Covenanting Army any recompense and even pressed for reparations for the Scottish occupation of the north of England. Following the demise at Newcastle of Alexander Henderson, who had been attempting diligently, but fruitlessly, to convince Charles I about the godly merits of Presbyterianism, the Kirk in September gave voice to widespread concerns among radicals about the intransigence of the king, his continuing encouragement of disaffected forces in Scotland and his suspect dealings with the French court. At the beginning of October, Loudoun declared to the Grand Committee of Both Houses that the Covenanters had behaved with candour and integrity in their proceedings 'towards the King and our Brethren of England'. The Covenanting leadership, though wary of any toleration that threatened unity in religion, remained resolute that the disposal of the king was to be effected by joint action to preserve 'the Unity between the Kingdomes'.[51]

Initiative in negotiating final terms for the withdrawal of the Covenanting Army and the handing over of the king was taken by the Presbyterians, who saw a satisfactory resolution without recourse to the war threatened by the Independents as a means to consolidate their control over the Long Parliament. Denzill Holles played a key role in securing £400,000 sterling as compensation and getting the Covenanters to agree that this sum should be paid in equal instalments: the initial two payments when the Covenanting Army withdrew from England, with the third and fourth to follow when funds became available. This sum was equivalent to the money the Covenanters had actually received from the Parliamentarians since January 1644; yet it still offered scant reward to their hard pressed forces in Ulster, who were now more inclined to receive prayers than payment. With Montereul temporarily recalled, Pompone

---

51 [John Campbell], *The Lord Chancellor of Scotland his First Speech: At a Conference in the Painted Chamber with a Committee of Both Houses, Octob. 1. 1646* (London, 1646); [William Pyrnne], *Scotland's ancient obligation to England and publicke acknowledgement thereof, for their brotherly assistance to, and deliverance of them, with the expence of their blood, and hazard of the state and tranquility of their realm, from the bondage of the French, in the time of their greatest extremity, 1560* (London, 1646); *A Remonstrance from the Kirk of Scotland* (London, 1646); Anon., *Papers from the Scottish Quarters, Containing the Substance of Two Votes Made by the Estates at Edinburgh at their General Meeting this Present Septemb. 1646* (London, 1646); CAL, I, pp. 188–92; LJB, II, pp. 376, 379, 383, 386–7, 402; DH, Loudoun Deeds, bundle 1/2; BL, Royal and Noble Autographs 1646–1768, Add.MSS 19,399, fo.4; D. Scott, '"Particular Businesses" in the Long Parliament: The Hull Letters, 1644–1648' in C.R. Kyle ed., *Parliament, Politics and Elections, 1604–1648* (Cambridge, 2001), pp. 321–4, 329–31. The Kirk also voiced concerns that Scottish soldiers withdrawing from England and preparing to serve in France, Holland or Flanders must have their arrears of pay promptly met, in the interests of public order.

de Bellièvre, the president of the Paris Parlement, had been dispatched as an ambassador from France to mediate between the king and the Parliamentarians in July 1646. Ambassador de Bellièvre was instructed that Mazarin would prefer a tripartite peace. But he was to keep open the option of a bilateral deal, notwithstanding growing doubts at the French court about Scottish intentions towards the king. Although de Bellièvre attended assiduously on Charles I, and Montereul shuttled between Paris, London, Newcastle and Edinburgh, the king remained as obstinate to French as to Scottish overtures to negotiate. Lingering hopes that Charles would take stock of his grave situation and accept the Newcastle Propositions were dashed on 20 December.[52]

Now freed from captivity and restored to the Scottish Estates that reconvened on 3 November 1646, Hamilton took over the leadership of the conservative Covenanters whose strength had been built up discreetly by Lanark with covert assistance from Lauderdale. Hamilton had intruded himself into the peace negotiations in an attempt to delay giving up the king until his safety was firmly assured. Despite Hamilton's sterling endeavours, which were commended by Henrietta Maria, Argyll with the aid of Wariston reasserted radical control over Covenanting negotiations with the king and Parliamentarians. Argyll had also secured solid backing from the Kirk which, on 19 December, issued a powerful condemnation of all clandestine diplomatic dealings and compared the activities of Royalist sympathisers to that of locusts. Notwithstanding the proliferation of sectaries in the New Model Army, chastised as 'Dunghill Warriors', Scotland must stand by the Solemn League and Covenant with England; for only concerted action in the two kingdoms could demonstrate 'that Great Brittane is the most renowned and famous Isle in the World'. Argyll's managerial dominance of the Scottish Estates was duly affirmed when a radical motion that an unconvenanted king should not be brought to Scotland was carried by 25 votes in a highly charged parliamentary debate. This vote among the 154 members on 16 January 1647 ensured that Charles was left at Newcastle.[53]

52 *Montereul*, I, pp. 231–426 and II, pp. 583–95; *CSCL*, pp. 201–6; ICA, Letters – Marquess's Period, 1646–1649, bundles 4/68, 14/68; DH, Loudoun Papers, A 213/2; SR, Hugh Mowatt's Letters to Sweden, AOSB ser B. E583. Two instalments amounting to £200,000 sterling were actually paid between 30 January and 3 February 1647, on the surrender of the northern garrisons but prior to the Covenanting forces crossing the border; the remainder went by default. The French diplomatic mission was not entirely fruitless, as the Covenanting leadership did agree in principle to the release of Scottish forces to serve in France once its army had withdrawn from England (NAS, Hamilton Papers, GD 406/1/2101, /2114, /2107).

53 Young, *The Scottish Parliament*, pp. 162–75; DH, Loudoun Papers, A213/1, /3 and Loudoun Deeds, bundles 1/15, /17, /20 and 2/9 ; HL, Loudoun Scottish Collection, box 5/LO 8056; ABDA, Argyll Papers, 40.428; ICA, Letters – Marquess's Period 1646–1649, bundle 8/209; NAS, Hamilton Papers, GD 406/1/1953, /2024, /2044, /2104, /2108, /2145, /9611; *SPT*, I, pp. 73–4; NLS,

Whereas Hamilton claimed to Sir Robert Moray on 19 January that his sorrow over the surrender of the king was 'inexpressible', Argyll had been somewhat disingenuous when he told Loudoun, ten days earlier:

> Yet I pray God, non wisched the king wors nor I doe and so he might be weall I should be content never to see his dominions always Gods will be doune.

Nevertheless, Argyll had countenanced a last-ditch manoeuvre to win over Charles I. At his instigation, John Stewart, Earl of Traquair, removed from public life as an Incendiary during the Bishops' Wars, was rehabilitated and despatched to Newcastle to persuade the king to accept the Covenants and Presbyterianism. But Charles remained intractable and was duly handed over to the Parliamentarians on 30 January. The Covenanters received no guarantees for his safety or for the future of the Stuart monarchy in England, save a vague promise from the Long Parliament to sustain British confederation in terms of the Solemn League and Covenant.[54]

Halkett of Pitfirrane Papers, MS 6408, fo.82; *Letters of Charles I*, pp. 48–9, 65; [Commissioners of the Kirk], *A Solemn and Seasonable Warning to all Estates and Degrees of Persons throughout the Land* (Edinburgh, 1646).

54 HL, Loudoun Scottish Collection, box 5/LO 8057; ICA, Letters – Marquess's Period, 1646–1649, bundle 8/209; NAS, Hamilton Papers, GD 406/1/2114; *Montereul*, I, p. 406.

EIGHT

Scottish Civil War, 1644–1647

Domestically, the political price of Covenanting intervention in Ireland and England was the spread of civil war from both these kingdoms into Scotland. Compulsory subscription of the Solemn League and Covenant throughout the British Isles compounded division and thereby created a paradox. Argyll and his radical associates in the Covenanting Movement exercised a political control that appeared to be unrivalled in the three kingdoms during the 'Scottish Moment' from 1638 to 1645. Yet Scotland was the one kingdom that the Royalists came closest to reclaiming. This situation was brought about by the brilliant northern campaign of 1644–45 mounted by Montrose in association with Alasdair MacColla, an exiled member of the ClanDonald South, who brought assistance from the Catholic Confederates in Ireland. Their campaign was particularly directed against Argyll and the ClanCampbell. They not only challenged Argyll's standing as a clan chief and a Scottish magnate, but undermined his position as the foremost statesman pushing British confederation as the antidote to war.

The Royalist campaign of Montrose and MacColla had a particular appeal within the *Gàidhealtachd*. The centralist demands exerted by the Covenanting Movement for ideological conformity, military recruitment and financial supply promoted a polemical reaction that associated the traditional values of clanship with the Royalist cause. The vernacular poets and poetesses who assumed the mantle of cultural leadership from the exclusively male bardic orders within the *Gàidhealtachd* were drawn predominantly from the fringes of the clan gentry. They did not abandon the celebration of the clan elite which had hitherto been a bardic preserve through eulogies and elegies. But vernacular poetry accorded priority to political propaganda and social comment over stereotyped artistic standards. Topical information was disseminated and public opinion shaped through the *ceilidh*, the spontaneous folk session, which became the alternative to the literary evening in the great halls of the *fine* as well as the rival to the Covenanting pulpits. Grass-roots criticism of national leadership was most vociferously and deliberately targeted against Argyll. At the same time, political polarisation became as pronounced a feature as resistance to centralism as clans either volunteered for or were forced into rival Covenanting and Royalist camps during the Scottish civil war of 1644–47. The intensity of the fighting, particularly between 1644–45, occasioned widespread social dislocation throughout the *Gàidhealtachd*, which was the main, but by no means the sole, Scottish theatre for military operations. Social dislocation was aggravated by the ravages of the plague in the wake of the avenging Covenanting Army.[1]

Conflicting Allegiances

Scotland underwent a period of cathartic change after the promulgation of the National Covenant on 28 February 1638. The revolutionary impetus of the Covenanting Movement was sustained by oligarchic centralism, which ensured that directives issued by in Edinburgh would be carried out uniformly in the localities. Ideologically, the Movement entrenched itself by making subscription to the National Covenant compulsory for all holding or aspiring to hold public office, whether civil, military or ecclesiastical. This requirement was expanded to compulsory subscription in every burgh and parish when the Covenanters sought to export revolution through their alliance with the English Parliamentarians in the Solemn League and Covenant of 1643. Public subscription of the Covenants became the prerequisite for anyone seeking a voice, nationally or locally, in the conduct of Scottish affairs. Disaffected members of the landed classes deemed delinquents were liable to have their rents uplifted for use in the Covenanting cause, and even faced sequestration of their estates. All delinquents were subject to the ecclesiastical censure of the Kirk which, as a truly Reformed and Presbyterian institution, regarded itself as the moral guardian of the Covenants. The *Gàidhealtachd* was not exempt from these pressures. However, compulsory subscription to the National Covenant had not always been observed on its western seaboard by 1643. Even though ministers were instructed by the Scottish Estates as well as the general assembly to ensure that all inhabitants swore obedience to the Solemn League and Covenant, some areas remained refractory. In April 1644, all inhabitants of Badenoch were reputed to 'absolutlie refuse obedience'. Parishioners in Skye and the Outer Hebrides still remained negligent in May 1650.[2]

---

1 Hutton, *The Royalist War Effort*, pp. 86–109; A.I. Macinnes, 'Scottish Gaeldom, 1638–1661: The Vernacular Response to the Covenanting Dynamic' in J. Dwyer, R.A. Mason and A. Murdoch eds, *New Perspectives on the Politics and Culture of Early Modern Scotland* (Edinburgh, 1982), pp. 59–94. The bards were schooled and wrote in classical common Gaelic. This literary dialect, rooted in the educated speech of medieval Gaeldom, had become far removed from the local spoken dialects that had subsequently evolved in Scotland, as in Ireland.
2 NLS, Sea Laws etc, MS. 2263, ff.73–9; NAS, Breadalbane MSS, GD 112/1/510, /520, /523 and Synod Records of Moray, 1623–44, CH 2/27/1, fo.278; *APS*, V, pp. 270 c. 18, 276 c.19, 329, 605;

Finance was no less problematic than conformity. The Covenanting Movement was forced to revise its national basis for taxation in 1639 and in 1643 (as again in 1649). Simultaneously, the Covenanting leadership resorted to a variety of fiscal expedients in order to spread the burden of taxation from landed wealth to personal income. Among these expedients were two innovatory taxes: the excise, imposed on commercial transactions from January 1643, and the monthly maintenance (later cess), initially levied from February 1645 for the upkeep of the army to oppose Montrose and MacColla. The British commitments of the Movement were always to outstrip its financial resources, however. From the Covenanters' first involvement in the Bishops' Wars I in 1639–40, there was a continual state of financial emergency featuring a mounting burden of public debt. Misplaced confidence that they would be fully compensated by brotherly assistance from the Parliamentarians had induced the Covenanters not only to maintain an army in Ireland from 1642 but also to intervene in the English civil war from 1644. Escalating expenditure was compounded by delays between the assessing and the actual levying of taxes. Within the *Gàidhealtachd*, rates of exaction were no less severe than in the rest of Scotland, though geographic inaccessibility and family solidarity did afford a measure of immunity for those reluctant to contribute. Increasing recourse to private loans from prominent Covenanters had to be supplemented by local contributions of money, silver and other valuables from the well affected.[3]

Military commitments proved no less demanding. From the summer of 1638, the progress of the Covenanting Movement was marked by regular musters of able-bodied males between the ages of sixteen and sixty. The *Gàidhealtachd* could not ignore recruiting calls on tenants and labourers; calls which frequently disrupted seasonal demands for sowing, manuring and harvesting. Grievances occasioned by frequent levies were secondary to the complaints provoked from localities obliged to provide quarters, victuals and livestock for troops; complaints that endured notwithstanding the inauguration of the monthly maintenance in 1645 that was intended to free the country of quartering. Transient quartering had a less devastating impact than the ferocious and unrestrained waging of civil war. However, the campaigns of Montrose and MacColla, characterised by constantly moving guerrilla warfare, unleashed inordinate family, racial and religious tensions throughout Scotland. The intensity of their campaigning

---

VI (1) (1643–47), pp. 11, 41–2, 61, 92, 152, 503 c. 102; *Records of the Kirk of Scotland*, A. Peterkin ed. (Edinburgh, 1843), pp. 279, 346, 398; *Minutes of the Synod of Argyll, 1639–61*, 2 vols, D.C. Mactavish ed. (Edinburgh, 1943), I, pp. 43, 88, 91, 150, 176; 100–1, 120–2, 144–5, 163–7; *Records of the Presbyteries of Inverness and Dingwall, 1643–88*, W. Mackay ed. (Edinburgh, 1896), pp. 157–74.
3 HL, Loudoun Scottish Papers, box 30/ LO 10335–7; D. Stevenson, 'The Financing of the Cause of the Covenants, 1638–51', *SHR*, 51 (1972), pp. 89–123.

in the central Lowlands, as on the north-eastern peripheries of the *Gàidheal-tachd*, can be considered the signal contemporary influence which widened the cultural rift between the *Gall* and the *Gael*. Yet the devastation and barbarism which particularly characterised the waging of civil war within Gaeldom cannot be attributed solely to traditional feuding between the clans. Moreover, events in Scotland pale into insignificance when compared to the high incidence of violent death during the Thirty Years War.[4]

Covenanting commitment must also be set against the prevailing belief within Scotland that Protestantism in Europe was endangered by the forces of the Counter-Reformation. The *Gàidhealtachd* was no less prone to religious intolerance than any other war-torn European community. On the one hand, Presbyterian chaplains instigated and justified the zealous excesses of the Covenanting Army. On the other hand, the Jesuit priests who accompanied the Irish regiments fighting under Alasdair MacColla propagated the same crusading fanaticism which was inspiring the efforts of the Catholic Confederation to purge Ireland of Protestants. Religious affiliations notably promoted support for the Covenanting cause in Argyllshire, the Perthshire Highlands and in districts bordering the Lowland peripheries in Ross, Sutherland and Caithness. In these areas, where a Protestant tradition stretched back to the Reformation, clans such as the Campbells, the Rosses and Munroes were in broad sympathy with the Presbyterianism of the Covenanters. Most clans, however, had been exposed to more than a semblance of Protestantism during the Episcopal direction of the Kirk prior to 1638. Indeed, the Royalist cause during the civil war of 1644–47 attracted majority support from the clans who, in turn, mainly adhered to Episcopalianism. Their aversion to Presbyterianism cannot be equated with support for Roman Catholicism.[5]

Although the propagation of both Catholicism and Protestantism were essentially missionary endeavours within the *Gàidhealtachd* prior to the emergence of the Covenanting Movement, the latter faith was undoubtedly better resourced and on the ascendant. Catholicism continued to thrive only within scattered pockets. Indeed, despite the endeavours of the Jesuits, as earlier of the Irish Franciscans, Catholicism was not sustained among all clans initially receptive to missionary priests. By the outbreak of the Scottish civil war, the Catholicism of the Irish *Gael* was only shared by a minority of the clans. The ClanDonald was

---

4 *APS*, VI (1), pp. 351, 447, 534 c. 127, 583 c. 220, 646 c. 89, 684–5; ICA, Miscellaneous 17th Century Papers, bundle 97/16; GCA, Hamilton of Barns Papers, TD 589/953; NAS, Breadalbane MSS, GD 112/1/551–4 and /9/5/16/5; H. Kamen, *The Iron Century: Social Change in Europe, 1550–1660* (London, 1971), pp. 38–44; Cowan, *Montrose*, p. 234.

5 Stevenson, *Revolution and Counter-Revolution in Scotland*, p. 24; Cowan, *Montrose*, p. 181; Macinnes, *Clanship, Commerce and the House of Stuart*, pp. 93–4.

reputed by the vernacular poets as well as the priests to be the bedrock of the Royalist cause within Scottish Gaeldom. Yet Catholicism was not sustained with the same vitality among its various branches. Certainly, the initial success of Montrose as the Royalist commander was in no way hindered by the tolerance which he, as a former Covenanter and committed Protestant, extended to the Catholic priests within his army. Nevertheless, his forces, as those of MacColla, were also attended by Protestant ministers.

The stridently anti-popish tenor of the National Covenant, which was more than reiterated by the Solemn League and Covenant, had threatened to place Catholic recusants in the *Gàidhealtachd* as elsewhere in Scotland in a sustained state of siege. Undoubtedly, Catholics were readily identifiable targets for punitive sanctions because of their tendency to associate actively with the Royalist cause and the presumption within the Covenanting leadership that anyone suspected of recusancy was a Royalist sympathiser. Catholics were classified automatically as delinquents and excluded absolutely from public office. Of greater significance, however, was the fact that the financial sanctions encoded in the penal laws against recusants were extended to all deemed delinquent to the Covenanting cause.[6]

The most important polarising factor within the *Gàidhealtachd* prior to the outbreak of the Scottish civil war was not so much religious differences as the territorial ambitions of ClanCampbell, and especially of their chief, Archibald, Marquess of Argyll. Regardless of Charles I's demerits as an absentee monarch, only the Crown had the legitimate authority to check their acquisitive instincts. Thus, the Royalist cause attracted the support of clans threatened, if not already victimised, by the Campbell *fine*. When the Marquess of Hamilton was still courting the assistance of Argyll (then Lord Lorne) to curtail the revolutionary activities of the Covenanting Movement, he advised Charles I in June 1638 that clans on the western seaboard would join the Royalist cause, 'not say for anie greatt affection they cayrie to your Majestie bot because of ther splen to Lorne'.[7] Antipathy to Lorne was motivated largely by his habitual practice of turning public policy to private advantage; a practice that was not checked by his meteoric rise to prominence within the Covenanting Movement.

---

6 *Memoirs of Scottish Catholics in the Seventeenth and Eighteenth Centuries*, W.F. Leith ed., 2 vols (London, 1909), I, pp. 221–5, 263–358; Minutes of the Synod of Argyll, I, pp. 119–23, 184, 216; *Records of the Presbyteries of Inverness and Dingwall*, pp. 160, 162; Stevenson, *Alasdair MacColla*, pp. 210, 229–30, 236–7, 240. Only the Keppoch, Glengarry and Clanranald branches of the ClanDonald can be deemed unequivocally Catholic within Scotland.
7 NAS, Hamilton Papers, GD 406/1/10775; ICA, Letters – 7th Earl's Period, 1630–1637, bundle 4/69; *The Hamilton Papers*, pp. 11–3.

Territorial Partiality

Hamilton, as the principal landowner on the isle of Arran, soon realised that Lorne was in the process of fortifying the adjacent peninsula of Kintyre to guard against invasion from across the North Channel. Indeed, the *fine* of ClanCampbell and of their associated clans in Argyll and the Perthshire Highlands had already established shire committees of war well before Lorne (as 8th Earl of Argyll) publicly declared for the Covenanting Movement at the Glasgow Assembly. In making advance military preparations, Argyll was primarily concerned with the threat posed to his estates by Randall MacDonnell, 2nd Earl of Antrim, a threat which failed to materialise during the Bishops' Wars. However, Lorne did use the First Bishops' War to impose punitive fines on the remnant gentry of ClanDonald South in Kintyre; to purge members of that clan from Jura; to encourage the Campbells of Cawdor to do the same from Islay; and to evict Coll Ciotach MacDonald alias Colkitto and his family (including his son, Alasdair MacColla) from Colonsay. During the Second Bishops' War, Argyll had suppressed dissent in the north not only by laying waste the estates of suspected Royalists in Atholl and the Braes of Angus, but also by pressing home his claims to the lordships of Badenoch and Lochaber as the foremost creditor of George Gordon, 2nd Marquess of Huntly. The spoiling of the lordships by 4,000 Campbells caused rents to fall in arrears, compounded the financial embarrassment of Huntly and paved the way for the absorption of Badenoch and Lochaber into Argyll's territorial spheres of influence from the outset of 1642 (see Chapter 5).

On the former estates of ClanDonald South, Argyll intruded leading kinsmen as a managerial interest charged only to lease, mortgage or sell lands to fellow Campbells; a policy which he extended to lands acquired from the Stewarts of Appin in Lorne and the MacLachlans in Cowal and in Mid-Argyll.[8] Argyll also gained a series of concessions from the Covenanting executive that were subsequently ratified by the Scottish Estates in the course of the constitutional settlement of 1640–41.[9] By the time he was elevated to Marquess, Argyll had already been conceded the right to uplift Crown rents, the taxes of the tenth and twentieth penny on all rents, and other public dues, including punitive fines on delinquents, claimed by the Covenanters within his judicial bounds of Argyll and the Isles. The feu duties, rents, teinds and other revenues of the terminated bishoprics of Argyll and the Isles were also placed at his disposal. His public position enabled him to tighten the ongoing credit squeeze that further compromised the territorial integrity of the estates of heavily indebted chiefs and clan

---

8 ICA, Argyll Transcripts, XII, nos 20, 37, 48–53, 55, 59, 104, 113, 146, 182.
9 Spalding, *Troubles*, I, pp. 202, 217–18 and II, pp. 59, 98, 128–34, 317–18; Cowan, *Montrose*, pp. 94–6.

gentry – most notably, Sir Lachlan Maclean of Duart and John MacDonald of Moidart, captain of Clanranald. Others, such as Murdoch Maclaine of Lochbuie, were obliged to resign estates in Mull, Morvern and Kingairloch held of the Crown and have them regranted from Argyll as their feudal superior. Prior to the issue of the Solemn League and Covenant, Argyll's public commissions also allowed him to expand his territorial influence on Bute, Lismore and Luing in the Inner Hebrides. He also secured his hold over Lochaber and Badenoch in the central Highlands once his nephew, James Gordon (the future 3rd Marquess of Huntly), became his assiduous ally and estate manager in defiance of his father.[10] At the same time, he built up his position as a counterpoint to the house of Huntly in Aberdeenshire by counselling the family and friends of the house of Forbes to stand together during the absence overseas of Alexander, Lord Forbes. In April 1643, Lord Forbes had accepted a freelance commission from Louis Comte d'Egmont, Duke of Gueldres-Juilliers to drive out the Spaniards from his small principality that bordered France and the Netherlands.[11]

Yet three pleas can be lodged in defence of Argyll who, as a consummate politician, was easily able to outmanoeuvre and remove from the Covenanting ruling oligarchy detractors such as Montrose (see Chapter 6). First, the territorial ambitions of the 2nd Earl of Antrim, which attracted polemical support from vernacular poets sympathetic to the ClanDonald, posed a real threat to ClanCampbell interests on the western seaboard.[12] Second, while Argyll was undoubtedly the most ruthlessly successful political operator in the *Gàidhealtachd* as in Scotland, he was not alone in using his public position within the Covenanting Movement to private advantage. The acquisitive overtures of John Gordon, 14th Earl of Sutherland encouraged the Mackays to take up the Royalist mantle to defend their patrimony of Strathnaver. Conversely, aversion to the hitherto pervasive influence of the Royalist magnate George, Marquess of Huntly in the central Highlands persuaded the Frasers and originally the Grants to declare for the Covenanters and for the Mackintoshes among the ClanChattan to remain neutral. The territorial ambitions of the MacKenzies remained not so much unstated as unfulfilled, primarily because their vacillating chief, George, 2nd Earl of Seaforth, demonstrated an unparalleled lack of touch in switching adversely whenever Royalist or Covenanting forces enjoyed

---

10 ICA, Letters – Marquess's Period, 1638–1645, bundles 6/115, /122; 7/143 andArgyll Transcripts XII, nos 64–6, 70, 88–90, 101, 106, 109–10, 147, 159, 161, 183, 206–7, 209, 224, 242, 261, 267, 274, 299; ABDA, Argyll Papers, 40.358, .533; NAS, Gordon Castle MSS, GD 44/27/3.

11 ICA, Argyll Letters (1638–85), A 36/130; BL, Turnbull Papers, vol. CXCVI, Add.MSS 72,437, ff.1–6, 9–10.

12 *The MacDonald Collection of Gaelic Poetry*, A. and A. MacDonald eds (Inverness, 1911), pp. 46–7; R. Flower, 'An Irish-Gaelic Poem on the Montrose Wars', *Scottish Gaelic Studies*, I (1926), pp. 113–8; Ohlmeyer, *Civil War and Restoration in the Three Stuart Kingdoms*, pp. 6–10, 172–83.

ascendancy in the civil war.[13]

Third, although Argyll was remunerated for his public services on behalf of the Covenanting Movement, reimbursement was a slow process that was more than outweighed by his ongoing public expenditure. By June 1644, Argyll had received just over £19,167 from the Scottish Estates but had laid out more than £69,337 to fortify Kintyre, to patrol the North Channel, to suppress dissent in the north of Scotland, and to advance taxation, silver and public loans due from Argyll and the Isles. He had also committed to more than £81,377 to outfit the Covenanting expeditionary force into Ireland. Albeit this latter expenditure was partially redeemed by the £5,000 sterling (£60,000) advanced to him by the Parliamentarians (see Chapter 7), Covenanting intervention in England as in Ireland was a continuing commitment. Running a deficit in excess of £50,170 for his Covenanting expenditure, Argyll preferred to be reimbursed not in ready cash but from fines to be imposed on Royalists and all others deemed delinquent in the north of Scotland. Judicial processes, like public policies authorised by the Covenanting Movement, were now to be privatised to his advantage.[14]

Argyll's territorial acquisitiveness, his privatisation of public policy and judicial process and his Covenanting prominence demonised him among Gaelic polemicists inclined to Royalism. He became the single most divisive influence in the *Gàidhealtachd*. Thus Iain Lom (John MacDonald) from Keppoch in Lochaber, the pre-eminent vernacular poet whose vitriolic outpourings as a war correspondent were inspired by a personal antipathy to the ClanCampbell, rejoiced when the Royalists carried the war into Argyll's country:

> Gum bi'm feachd so dol thairis
> Gu dùthaich Mhic Cailein,
> 'S gum be smùdan is deannal 'nan deidh.

[This host will make its way over to Argyll's country, and the smoke of conflict will follow in its train.]

Iain Lom also condemned the ruthless acquisitiveness of Argyll in using his Covenanting position to have the Marquess of Huntly expropriated for Royalist activities:

---

13 E.M. Furgol, 'The Northern Highland Covenanting Clans, 1639–51', *Northern Scotland*, 7 (1987), pp. 119–31; R. King, *The Covenanters in the North* (Aberdeen, 1846), pp. 261–96.

14 ICA, Letters – Marquess's Period, 1638–1645, bundles 6/101–2, /104–6, /118, /127 and 7/138–41, /166 and Argyll Transcripts, XII, nos 90, 94, 111, 178, 199, 244–5, 255, 259, 267, 269–73, 275–6, 279–80, 287–8, 294; ABDA, Argyll Papers, 40.09, .352, .409; DCA, Dundee Council Book IV (1613–1653), fo.183; A.I. Macinnes, 'The Impact of Civil Wars and Interregnum: Political Disruption and Social Change within Scottish Gaeldom' in R. Mitchison and P. Roebuck eds, *Economy and Society in Scotland and Ireland, 1500–1939* (Edinburgh, 1988), pp. 58–69.

Ach do thùrbhailte móra
Bhith gun chòir aig MacCailein

[But your large tower houses were unjustly given to Argyll.]

Diorbhail Nic a'Bhriuthainn (Dorothy Brown) from the isle of Luing sought compensation for the eventual defeat of the Royalist cause in a novel cure for insomnia at Argyll's expense:

'S truagh nach eil mi mar a b'àite leam,
Ceann Mhic-Caileinn ann am achlais, . . .
Bu shunndach a ghelbinn cadal,
Ged a b'i chreag chruaidh mo leabaidh.[15]

[It is sad that I am not as I might wish, with Argyle's head under my armpit, then I would happily be able to sleep, even if my bed was a hard rock.]

Antipathies towards Argyll and ClanCampbell were undoubtedly the most pronounced of the negative factors provoked by the Covenanting Movement's favouring of powerful magnates whose public espousal of its cause cloaked private territorial ambition. When the unrelenting demands of their central-ised oligarchy and their imposition of Presbyterianism were thrown into this mix, the Covenanters provoked a hostile reaction from the majority of clans. However, there were also positive considerations in favour of Royalism, notably the traditional values of clanship, especially paternalism, protection and inclu-sive kinship, which were projected nationally onto the political stage. As the *fine* were the protectors of the clan patrimony, their collective *duthchas*, so were the Stuart kings trustees for Scotland; their hereditary entitlement to rule, their *oighreachd*, provided the roots of justice and legitimised the social order. In the *Gàidhealtachd*, as elsewhere in the British Isles, the Royalist cause was dependent primarily on family connections, a dependency that accentuated the importance of the clan hosts as territorial levies that could be mobilised expedi-tiously through the passing round of the fiery cross. Nevertheless, while the

---

15 *Orain Iain Luim*, pp. 40–1, 50–1; *Sar-Obair nam Bard Gaeleach: The Beauties of Gaelic Poetry*, J. Mackenzie ed. (Edinburgh, 1872), pp. 56–7. Iain Lom's repeated sentiment that the civil war was ultimately a racial and cultural struggle between the *Gael* and the *Gall* for supremacy in Scotland was echoed not just by fellow vernacular poets but also by the professional bards. Most notably Niall MacMhuirich, an active combatant with the MacDonalds of Clanranald, later left a corrective chronicle – albeit recorded esoterically in common classical Gaelic – in order to redress the balance of contemporaneous Lowland sources, which 'made no mention at all of the Gael' (*Reliquiae Celticae*, II, pp. 174–205).

clans provided a distinctive Royalist momentum, clan support was not sufficient to launch the king's cause in Scotland. External assistance was required.[16]

The Irish Dimension

Following the outbreak of rebellion in Ulster and exaggerated reporting of the
massacre of indigenous Protestants by Irish Catholics in the autumn of 1641,
Argyll was to the fore in pressing for Covenanting intervention (see Chapter 6).
When a Scottish expeditionary force was duly launched with the backing of the
Long Parliament in the spring of 1642, Argyll mobilised 1,500 clansmen under
the command of Sir Duncan Campbell of Auchinbreck. The Marquess exploited
his own appointment as governor of the Rathlin Isles to have reprisals exacted
on the Antrim estates; reprisals which soon permeated from the Rathlins to
the mainland of Northern Ireland. His reprisals, albeit an integral aspect of
the British suppression of the Irish rebellion, were instrumental in provoking
freelance raids by exiled members of the ClanDonald South with at least tacit
support from their kinsman, Randal, Earl of Antrim, with whom they had taken
refuge. Alasdair MacColla led a raid on the western seaboard at the close of
1643. By this juncture, MacColla and many of his associates had sided with the
Irish rebels now incorporated as the Catholic Confederation. Commissioned to
suppress this incursion, Argyll had deputed James Campbell of Ardkinglass to
raise 600 clansmen, who took over four months to repulse the raiders. Having
initially sought shelter in Mull before returning to the Rathlin Isles, MacColla's
party was forced back across the North Channel and harried through Islay and
Jura. Around 150 were killed. Few were taken prisoner. Despite its freelance
nature, this raid and the association of MacColla with the Catholic Confederation gave further credence to the 'Antrim Plot', which had followed on from
the capture of the Earl by the Covenanting Army in Ireland that June. Publication of Antrim's edited correspondence had served to authenticate reports
that Royalist forces in England, featuring substantial contingents of Catholics, were mobilising on the Borders and preparing to act in collusion with the
Irish Confederates against the Covenanters. Argyll and his radical allies had
systematically deployed these revelations to drive through the Solemn League
and Covenant in August 1643. But this British alliance expedited the cessation
between Royalists and Confederates in Ireland which, in turn, facilitated civil
war in all three kingdoms.[17]

16 Macinnes, *Clanship, Commerce and the House of Stuart*, pp. 88–121.
17 ICA, Letters – Marquess's Period, 1638–1645, bundles 6/121, /123–4 and bundle 7/154 and Argyll
   Transcripts, XII, nos 123–32, 141, 228, 244–5, 256, 262; NAS, Hamilton Papers TD 76/100/5/1635;
   RPCS, second series, VII, p. 185; Stevenson, *Scottish Covenanters and Irish Confederates*, pp.
   110–5; B. Fitzpatrick, *Seventeenth Century Ireland: The War of Religions* (Dublin, 1988), pp. 70–6.

A military appraisal on the state of Ireland, seemingly commissioned for the English Parliamentarians in the wake of the cessation agreed between the Royalists and the Confederates on 15 September 1643, was far from pessimistic about Protestant prospects, even though disparate claims to represent the Protestant interest were made by the Scots army, the British forces and even the Royalists. Although only three counties in Leinster were in Protestant hands, as against the eight dominated by the Confederation, one county was disputed and the Protestants had strongholds in three others. In Munster, the Protestants held no counties, but contested control of two, and had strongholds in two of the four counties under Catholic control. In Connacht, the Protestants claimed to hold one county and have strongholds in two of the four counties held by the Catholics. In Ulster, five counties were under Protestant control, but only one (Down) was undisputed; the Confederate forces dominated in only two of the remaining four counties. In sum, the Confederation had a controlling interest in twenty out of the thirty-two Irish counties. Far from Ireland being a 'free state', the Confederate writ was neither accepted nor unchallenged in over a third of counties in 1643 and, despite further territorial advances, never extended to the whole island prior to the dissolution of the Confederation six years later.[18]

The twelve-month cessation also posed an enduring, strategic problem of conflicting interests for the Catholic Confederation. The insular or Irish perspective required the pursuit of total victory before reaching an accommodation with the king to secure the recovery of all of Ireland for Catholicism. The alternative Royalist or Britannic perspective encouraged the Confederation to seek an expeditious settlement with the king and the release of Irish forces to counter the threat posed by the Parliamentarians. A compromise between those positions was offered by the refusal of the Scottish and British forces to accept the cessation as leading to 'the destruction of all the Protestants & subversion of the British plantations'. A direct assault on Ulster was not entrusted to Owen Roe O'Neill, however, but to the far less capable James Tuchet, 3rd Earl of Castlehaven, who was intent on avoiding battle. Lack of supplies and the favouring of Scottish over British forces in the allocation of quarters had produced internal tensions that even led to a unilateral decision by the Scottish commanders to return three of their ten regiments to Scotland in February 1644. However, Robert Munro's counter-offensive, which carried the fight into Leinster, provided the cover necessary for the Covenanting Army to take over Belfast and other Royalist garrisons. Reforged solidarity with the British forces was underscored by the resolute imposition of the Solemn League

18 HL, Hastings Irish Papers, box 8/HA 14987 and box 9/HA 15009; BOU, Carte Papers, 1636–1652. Ireland, MS Carte 65, ff.343–5; S. Wheeler, 'Four Armies in Ireland' in Ohlmeyer ed., *Ireland from Independence to Occupation*, pp. 43–65.

and Covenant on Ulster from the spring of 1644. Moved by apprehensions that the Confederates were intent upon 'the extirpation of the British nation' and the Protestant religion in Ireland, Protestant forces in Munster hitherto aligned with the Royalists threw in their lot with the Parliamentary backed forces. At the same time, Ormond's refusal to aid the Confederates in Ulster severely strained the prospects of converting the cessation into a lasting peace and thereby denied Charles hopes of meaningful reinforcements for his English campaign.[19]

Nevertheless, as a complement to the assault on Ulster, the Confederates determined that intervention in Scotland rather than England would prove a more productive strategy. A defensive withdrawal of Covenanting forces from Ulster would restrict further mobilisation of Scottish troops to aid both the English Parliamentarians and the British forces in Ulster. The main architect of this strategy was Antrim, who secured the support of both the king and the Supreme Council at Kilkenny to ship three regiments of less than 2,000 Irish troops recruited almost exclusively from his estates to the western seaboard in June 1644. These troops were led by his charismatic kinsman Alasdair MacColla, who was charged to link up with Montrose as supreme Royalist commander in Scotland. Undoubtedly, this was a far from disinterested scheme by Antrim to run the expeditionary force rebuffed by Strafford in 1639. But only the logistical and financial support afforded by the Supreme Council made this endeavour feasible. Montrose had been operating intermittently on both sides of the Borders without any appreciable degree of military success in the spring of 1644. He had not linked up with the guerrilla resistance being pursued in north-east Scotland by the Marquess of Huntly. Irish Catholic intervention ensured meaningful conjunction between divergent Royalist forces, which the Covenanting Movement had not hitherto regarded as a serious threat.[20]

Although his relationship with the noble house of Huntly remained problematic, Montrose provided the political credibility necessary to convince clans throughout the *Gàidhealtachd* to come out for the Royalist cause. Notwithstanding MacColla's charismatic appeal as an epic hero of the *Gael*, his personal following, even within the ClanDonald, was limited. Sir James MacDonald of Sleat refused outright appeals to recruit among his clan, which maintained a neutral stance throughout the civil war. Angus MacDonald of Glengarry was initially reluctant to associate with MacColla. The captain of Clanranald, John

---

19 HL, Hastings Irish Papers, box 7/HA 15051 and box 8/HA 14929, 1500–1, 15030, 15904; TNA, Committee of Both Kingdoms, Entry Books, letters received 1644, SP21/16, fo.144; P. Lenihan, 'Confederate Military Strategy, 1643–7' in Ó Siochrú ed., *Kingdoms in Crisis*, pp. 158–75; Wheeler, *The Irish and British Wars*, pp. 99–102, 121–3; Stevenson, *Scottish Covenanters and Irish Confederates*, pp. 139–63.

20 DH, Loudoun Papers, bundle 1/2; *CSCL*, pp. 5–7, 16, 37–8; D. Stevenson, *Alasdair MacColla and the Highland Problem in the Seventeenth Century* (Edinburgh, 1980), pp. 69–70, 73, 99–101.

MacDonald of Moidart, adopted a more subtle approach, confining his own Royalist activities to the western seaboard while sending his son and heir, Donald, on MacColla's campaigns. Other clan chiefs on the western seaboard shunned the recruiting drive begun by MacColla and the Irish troops after their arrival on the Ardnamurchan peninsula that July. His chequered record of commitment to the Royalists and Confederates in Ireland provoked aversion rather than admiration in the Highlands as well as the Lowlands. Notwithstanding pleas for Gaelic solidarity from the vernacular poets, affinity with the Irish was not immediately evident among Argyllshire clans antipathetic to the Campbells and was totally lacking among the clans of the central Highlands, who blocked MacColla's passage into Speyside. Clans with Royalist inclinations were prepared to resist MacColla's advance into Atholl, where his eventual rendezvous with Montrose ensured the military viability of the Royalist cause. While the training, discipline and resolution of the Irish regiments provided the profession backbone of the Royalist army, it was the leadership of Montrose, a *Gall* but a Scot, which ensured legitimacy and respectability for the cause among the Scottish *Gael*.[21]

By mixing guerrilla warfare with pitched battles after they joined forces in August 1644, the Royalist commanders ran up a series of bloody victories which commenced at Tippermuir in Perthshire on 1 September and culminated in the defeat of the Covenanting forces at Kilsyth in Stirlingshire on 15 August 1645. The brilliance of their campaigning wholly outmanoeuvred and exposed the ineptitude of the Covenanting commanders, such as Argyll, who were originally charged to eradicate the Royalist threat in Scotland. For his part, Argyll conceded in the immediate aftermath of Kilsyth that the Royalist rebellion had 'risen beyond all men's expectation'. He viewed the disaster of Kilsyth as a providential day of reckoning for those who put their trust more in military than divine might. Another radical Covenanter, Alexander, 6th Earl of Eglinton, lamented that the religion and liberties of the country were now 'in hazart be ane pack of base raskalles'. Certainly, widespread acquiescence in and resignation about the achievements of Montrose meant there was a meaningful prospect of Charles I summoning the Scottish Estates to Glasgow in October 1645, to reassert the king's control over Scotland and secure reparations for his supporters from the Covenanting Movement. However, the Royalists made no tangible territorial acquisitions in the Lowlands in the wake of Kilsyth.

Undoubtedly, the departure of MacColla and most of the clan levies after Kilsyth proved critical for Montrose. While Royalist commentators uncharitably attributed this departure to Montrose's refusal to let the clans sack Glasgow,

21 *Reliquiae Celticae*, II, pp. 176–9, 182–3; ICA, Letters – Marquess's period, 1638–1645, bundle 14/60; Hill, *The Macdonnells of Antrim*, pp. 61, 85.

MacColla was intent of fulfilling Antrim's commission to secure the western seaboard and maintain a bridgehead with Ireland. MacColla's return to the western seaboard also demonstrated that the ultimate strategic priority of the clans, whether Royalist or Covenanter, was to protect their own patrimonies. In the meantime, troops withdrawn from England under Lieutenant-General Sir David Leslie, reasserted Covenanting dominance by defeating Montrose at Philiphaugh in Selkirkshire on 13 September; a victory that Argyll proclaimed unequivocally as divine deliverance, the Lord having that day 'appeared gloriously for his people'.[22]

The Royalist defeat at Philiphaugh led to the English ordinance of October 1644 for no quarter to the Irish being extended to Scotland. The Irish troops had taken the lead in the sacking of Scottish towns, most notably Aberdeen. As reprisals against Scottish Royalists continued well into 1647, the process of law tended to be applied even to Catholic clans. But all Irish troops were summarily executed on capture or surrender. Irish soldiers and their camp followers were slaughtered, 'with such savage and inhumane crueltie, as nether Turke nor Scithean was ever hard to have done the lyke'. Even in Royalist eyes, this conduct was partially mitigated by the total lack of compassion the Irish troops had exhibited in their ubiquitous killing 'without any motion of pitie, or any consideration of humanity'.[23]

MacColla's maintenance of a bridgehead with Ireland did lead to his temporary reinforcement by Antrim in July 1646. However, Antrim's Scottish sojourn was pre-empted by instructions from Charles I, then in the custody of the Covenanting Army in England, that the Royalist forces in Scotland should surrender. Nonetheless, MacColla continued to maintain his bridgehead for another fourteen months in the forlorn hope that Antrim would be able to secure renewed assistance from the Catholic Confederation. But the increasingly fractious and financially stretched Confederation had become destabilised after the arrival of the papal agent, Giovanni Battista Rinuccini, Bishop of Fermo, in October 1645. Rinuccini was averse to a peace with the Royalists and worked to steer the Confederation off its purported allegiance to Charles I in favour of the papacy. Catholic Ireland could only be restored through a military

---

22 ICA, Argyll Letters (1638–85), A 36/144; HL, Loudoun Scottish Collection, box 38/ 10371; NAS, Hamilton Papers GD 406/1/1635; BL, Miscellaneous Letters etc. 1566–1804, Add.MSS 36,450 ff.16–7; Archibald Campbell, Marquess of Argyll, *Right Honourable, the Lord hath this Day, here at Philiphauch, neer Selkirk, Appeared Gloriously for his People* (London, 1645).

23 Gordon, *Distemper*, pp. 152–4, 160–61, 168–72; Turner, *Memoirs*, pp. 48–9; M. Ó Siochru, 'Atrocity, Codes of Conduct and the Irish in the British Civil Wars 1641–1653', *Past & Present*, 195 (2007), pp. 55–86. When the Covenanting Army began mopping up Royalist resistance on the western seaboard, chiefs such as Sir Lachlan Maclean of Duart abjectly acceded to demands that Irish soldiers be handed over for summary execution.

not a diplomatic solution. Rinuccini effectively split the Confederation into peace and war groupings, which enabled recently reinvigorated Parliamentary forces to make substantive inroads into both Munster and Ulster.[24]

Many among the Scottish *Gael* were not in favour of continuing the campaign in Ireland once MacColla had been forced to retreat there by the Covenanting Army in the summer of 1647; albeit contingents from some clans on the western seaboard did follow him in order to continue the Royalist alliance with the Irish Catholics. Few MacDonalds of Glengarry had been willing to follow their chief, Angus, who had departed with Antrim the previous summer. Solidarity among the *Gael* was effectively laid to rest when MacColla was killed in battle against Parliamentary forces at Knocknanuss, County Cork, on 13 November 1647. In the interim, Montrose and his political entourage had acquiesced in the king's order to disband their forces and go into exile. Departing in the summer of 1646 as unrepentant and committed Royalists, they left their followers to fend for themselves.[25]

Although he had defied Charles I, MacColla can be viewed as a more successful Royalist commander than Montrose, whose star waned on their parting. MacColla's military prowess was based not just on his battlefield valour, but on his sound tactical knowledge. If not the inventor, MacColla was certainly the most innovative exponent of the 'Highland charge' which he had used in the services of the Irish Catholics prior to his campaigns with Montrose. The Highland charge was a superb tactic for irregular infantry that made optimum use of Highland terrain, the technology the clans could afford, and the effectiveness of the sword and targe at close quarters after the discharge of firearms prior to engaging in hand to hand combat. MacColla had demonstrated his strategic abilities at the outset of his campaign in the summer of 1644, when he caught both the Campbells and the Covenanting establishment off-balance. Instead of launching the expected frontal assault on Kintyre, Islay and Jura, the former territories of ClanDonald South, he landed his Irish contingents in Morvern and began recruiting on the former territories of the MacIains of Ardnamurchan. MacColla also fulfilled his strategic remit from the Confederates. His invasion of the western seaboard not only prevented reinforcements being sent to existing Scottish forces in Ulster, but led to the withdrawal of Covenanting troops from Ireland as well as England to counter Royalist resistance. However, the tactical ineptitude of his withdrawal from Scotland in 1647

---

24 Macinnes, *The British Revolution*, pp. 180–3; R. Armstrong, 'Ormond, the Confederate Peace Talks and Protestant Royalism' in Ó Siochru ed., *Kingdoms in Crisis*, pp. 122–40; Ó Siochru, *Confederate Ireland*, pp. 122–40.

25 NAS, Breadalbane MSS, GD 112/1/551, /553 and Hamilton Papers, GD 406/1/1972, /2002; Stevenson, *Alasdair MacColla*, pp. 240, 245–52: *Orain Iain Lom*, pp. 36–9.

was to cast doubts on his abilities as a general. Having underestimated the speed of the Covenanting Army's advance into Kintyre, MacColla had to rely on the stubborn resistance of his aged father within the garrison of Dunyveg to buy time for his retreat from Islay. Coll Ciotach paid with his life. After he had been forced to surrender a garrison which was deficient in supplies, especially of water, his execution was engineered by Argyll.[26]

From his defeat at Philiphaugh until his departure into exile in September 1646, Montrose was a spent force in Scotland. His recruiting ability in the Lowlands was severely restricted by his close identification with the clans. His access to towns was barred by the spread of plague in the wake of the avenging Covenanting Army withdrawing from England. His tetchy relationship with Huntly dissolved in acrimony, and the Gordons reverted to their freelance campaigning, which continued sporadically until November 1647. While MacColla was not obliged to lay siege to large towns, his continuing pursuit of guerrilla warfare was distinctively less naïve and more constructive. MacColla had built up a ready reservoir of support among the clans opposed the territorial ambitions of the ClanCampbell. His prolonged occupation of Kintyre and Islay continued to detract from Argyll's standing within the Covenanting Movement: this situation was appreciated by the more discerning of the vernacular poets, such as Eachann Bacach (Hector Maclean) from Mull, who commended MacColla's unbending stance towards Argyll and the Covenanting leadership.

> 'S cha b'e mala na réit e
> Do dh'fhearaibh Dhùn Éideann,
> Na do Mhac Cailein cha ghéilleadh r'a bheò.[27]

[His countenance was not one for compromise with the men of Edinburgh, nor would he ever submit to Argyll.]

Politics versus Valour

Argyll was a more adroit, audacious and accomplished political operator than either Montrose or MacColla. However, Argyll could not match either Montrose's brilliance as a general or MacColla's charisma and valour on the battlefield. These deficiencies, which were amplified by Royalist polemicists as well as the vernacular poets, not only queried Argyll's historical reputation as a

26 Turner, *Memoirs*, pp. 45–8; *Montereul*, II, pp. 126, 15; Stevenson, *Alasdair MacColla*, pp. 73, 76–84, 99–101, 260–2; Ohlmeyer, *Civil War and Restoration in the Three Stuart Kingdoms*, pp. 6–10, 172–83.

27 *Bardachd Chloinn Ghill-Eathain*, pp. 20–1; ICA, Letters – Marquess's Period, 1645–48, bundles 7/136 and 8/91, /198, /200 and Argyll Transcripts XII, nos 194, 309; NAS, Hamilton Papers GD 406/1/1972; Cowan, *Montrose*, pp. 154, 232–4.

statesman of calibre (see Chapter 2), but also raised contemporaneous doubts, nationally and internationally, about Argyll's political and military capabilities.[28]

Argyll had left the Covenanting Army in England to return to Scotland in April 1644 following rumours of a three-pronged Royalist assault: MacColla from the west and Montrose from the south were to join up with Huntly in the north. In the event, Argyll faced down Huntly by a campaign of attrition. Huntly was not captured – but he was forced to retreat from Aberdeen and to seek refuge in the far north, in Strathnaver. Although Argyll did harry the countryside, he treated the town of Aberdeen with courtesy and respect, in marked contrast to Huntly and especially to Montrose. Having defeated makeshift forces at Tippermuir, Montrose moved against Aberdeen, which he took from ill-positioned Covenanters on 13 September. But he allowed the Irish troops and clansmen to run amok. Thereby the Royalist cause was readily associated with the atrocities of the Irish Catholics in the rebellion of 1641. Until Tippermuir, the Committee of Estates in Edinburgh had not taken the threat from Montrose and MacColla seriously. The defence of Scotland was left to Argyll assisted by Lothian. Argyll was still preparing to mobilise his forces, secure adequate provisions and instil military discipline into poorly armed irregulars as Aberdeen was being sacked.[29]

Notwithstanding expectations among Covenanters and Parliamentarians that Argyll would soon defeat and disperse the Royalist threat, his subsequent campaign in the north of Scotland was again marked by pursuit rather than engagement. Apologists for Montrose and MacColla have attributed this tactic to cowardice.[30] In essence, Argyll was buying time for the recall of his own regiment from Ireland. He did persistently seek opportunities to ambush enemy contingents and was ever watchful that MacColla did not make a break for the west to assault the territories of the ClanCampbell. When Argyll did catch up with Montrose at Fyvie in Aberdeenshire on 10 November, he failed to make his superior military numbers count in the skirmish. Montrose retreated without serious losses to Atholl. Nevertheless, Argyll did succeed in diminishing Royalist numbers by offering financial inducements for desertions.

28 SR, Hugh Mowatt's Letters to Sweden, AOSB ser B. E583; *Montereul*, I, pp. 60, 295, 350; and II, pp. 41, 51, 71–2, 82–3, 95, 126, 151, 157, 175, 189, 217; Whitelock, *Memorials*, I, pp. 391, 515 and II, pp. 42–3; Walker, *The History of Independency: Appendix*, pp. 5–6, 10; *LJB*, II, pp. 232–4, 251, 262–4, 376; Willcock, *The Great Marquess*, pp. 158–89, 201–5.

29 Anon., *A Polt (sic) Discovered in Ireland and Prevented without the Shedding of Blood* (London, 1644); ICA, Argyll Letters (1638–85), A 36/132, /135–6, /139 and Letters – Marquess's Period, 1638–1645, bundle 14/60; NAS, Breadalbane MSS, GD 112/1/552, /554, /556/1–2; NLS, Halkett of Pitfirrane Papers, MS 6408, fo.81; ACA, Aberdeen Council Register, vol. LII (1630–44), p. 837 and vol. LIII (1644–58), pp. 7–8; *ACL*, II, pp. 85–9, 381, 383; Stevenson, *Revolution and Counter-Revolution*, pp. 6–9. Argyll's clan contingents lacked guns and still relied on swords and targes, bows and arrows.

30 Wishart, *Memoirs*, pp. 71–7; *MHG*, p. 172.

His covert and repeated offer of bounties for the assassination of Montrose has been asserted but never proven. In the event, Argyll, against his wishes, was replaced as commander of the Covenanting forces by Lieutenant-General William Baillie, who was specifically recalled from England to defend Scotland against Montrose and MacColla. Argyll had to be content with the subordinate command over the West Highlands and Islands; that is, the contingents of Campbell and allied clans mobilised for the Covenanting cause.[31]

However, it was Argyll, not Baillie, who was next pressed into action when MacColla persuaded Montrose to ravage the territories of the Campbells and their allies in Argyllshire and the Perthshire Highlands. This ravaging was wanton but systematic. It drew upon the specialist knowledge of the notorious bandit family of MacInnes in Laroch, who were affiliated to the MacDonalds of Glencoe. On receiving news that the Royalists were approaching his family seat at Inveraray, Argyll was castigated for taking flight by fishing boat and abandoning his clansmen and allies to their own devices.[32] But Argyll did have a more reputable reason in coming to Dumbarton on the Clyde. He sought and successfully secured additional forces from Baillie and got confirmation that his own regiment, under the command of Sir Duncan Campbell of Auchinbreck, would return from Ireland by the outset of 1645. Nevertheless, townships in every district of Argyll were despoiled; 895 of the ClanCampbell were killed. Colonel James MacDonald, an Irish officer accompanying MacColla, was content to record that 'throughout all Argyll were left neither house nor hold unburned, nor corn, nor cattle that belonged to the whole name of Campbell'. The Scottish Estates subsequently confirmed that the Royalist forces from November 1644 to January 1645 had devastated eighteen parishes in Argyll and the neighbouring district of Breadalbane. The winter ravaging of the south-western Highlands not only carried territorial devastation to the back door of the Marquess of Argyll, but encouraged clans hitherto contained within Campbell spheres of influence to cut loose in support of the Royalist cause.[33]

Reinforced by Lowland troops and his regiment from Ireland, Argyll marched into Lochaber hoping to sandwich Montrose and MacColla with the aid of the forces raised by George, Earl of Seaforth at Inverness. Instead,

---

31 Anon., *Intelligence from the South Borders of Scotland* (Edinburgh, 1644); Anon., *Extracts of Letters Dated at Edinburgh 14, 16 and 17 April 1644* (London, 1644); NAS, Breadalbane MSS, GD 112/1/551, /553–4; ICA, Argyll Letters (1638–85), A 36/133–4.

32 Gordon, *Distemper*, pp. 94–9; *Reliquiae Celticae*, II, pp. 180–3, 202–3; Wishart, *Memoirs*, pp. 79–82; *MHG*, pp. 173–4; A. I. Macinnes, 'Lochaber – The Last Bandit County, c.1600–c.1750', *TGSI* 64 (2004–06), pp. 1–21.

33 Hill, *The Macdonnells of Antrim*, p. 90; *APS*, VI (2), pp. 460–3 c. 187, 544–7 c. 398; ICA, Letters – Marquess's Period, 1646–1649, bundle 8/198 and Argyll Transcripts, XIII (1650–59), nos 5, 63; NAS, Breadalbane MSS, GD 112/1/557–8; Stevenson, *Alasdair MacColla*, pp. 260–1.

Montrose brilliantly outmanoeuvred Argyll and slaughtered the Covenanting forces at Inverlochy on 2 February 1645. Argyll observed the battle from the safety of his galley in Loch Linne and made his escape before the carnage was concluded. On this occasion, the counter to the charges of cowardice was that he was actually incapacitated from partaking in active combat by a shoulder dislocated as a result of a fall in mid-January. His flight along with some from the Committee of Estates was viewed as a political necessity and it was only undertaken after he was compelled by leading clansmen and associates to retire to his galley. Argyll certainly played upon his temporary disability when he appeared in Edinburgh ten days after the battle, with his arm still in a sling, to receive a sympathetic hearing and an official exoneration of his conduct. The Scottish Estates commended the Marquess for the painstaking way in which he 'wyselie and diligentlie behaved himself'.[34] Nevertheless, the mortification of ClanCampbell was especially evident in the triumphalist vitriol of Iain Lom when celebrating the Royalist victory:

> 'S lionmhor claidheamh claisghorm còmhnard
> Bha bualadh 'n lamhan Chlann Dòmhnaill
> 'N uair chruinnich mór dhragh na falachd,
> 'N am rùsgadh nan greidlean tana,
> Bha iongnan Dhuibneach ri talamh
> An déidh an luithean a ghearradh.[35]

[Numerous are the blue-fluted, well balanced swords that were wielded in the hands of ClanDonald. When the great work of blood-letting came to a height at the time of unsheathing of slender swords, the claws of the Campbells lay on the ground with sinews severed.]

A no less passionate but more focused riposte was provided by Florence, sister of Sir Duncan Campbell of Auchinbreck and wife of John Maclean of Coll. Although she lamented her fallen brother, she primarily composed a hymn for vengeance against the Royalist forces, including her husband's clan.

> N' an robh mis' an Inbhir-Lochaidh,
> Is claidheamh da-fhaobair am dhòrnaibh,
> Is neart agam gu'm mhiann, is eolas,
> Dheanainn fuil ann, dheanainn stròiceadh,

---

34 ABDA, Argyll Papers, 40.401; Willcock, *The Great Marquess*, pp. 173–7; *LJB*, II, pp. 262–3; Balfour, *HW*, II, pp. 272–3; Gordon, *Distemper*, p. 102; *MHG*, pp. 178–9, Wishart, *Memoirs*, pp. 83–5; Menteith of Salmonet, *The History of the Troubles of Great Britain*, p. 197.

35 *Orain Iain Luim*, pp, 22–5.

Air na Leathanaich 's Clann Dòmhnaill;
Bhiodh na h-Eireannaich gun deò annt,
Is na Duibhnich bheirinn beò as.

[Were I at Inverlochy, with a two-edged sword in my hand, all the strength
and skill I could desire, I would draw blood there, and I would tear
asunder the Macleans and ClanDonald. The Irish would be without life,
and I would bring the Campbells back alive.]

However, the widow of Campbell of Glenfeochan derived little consolation
from Argyll's escape by galley while her husband, her father, her three sons, her
four brothers and her nine foster-brothers did not survive:

Thug MacCailein Mór an linn' air,
'S leig e'n sgrìob ud air a chinneadh. [36]

[Argyll took to the loch and let that calamity come upon his kindred.]

As Argyll had been removed from the military command, he was not directly
responsible for the subsequent Covenanting defeats at Auldearn in Nairnshire
on 9 May or at Alford in Aberdeenshire on 2 July. However, he was not entirely
blameless, as he used his dominant influence on the Committee of Estates in
Edinburgh and its devolved Committee with the army in the north of Scotland
to question Baillie's judgement. So persistent was this criticism that Baillie
had actually resigned his command before the Covenanters again met up with
Montrose at Kilsyth. Baillie remained in nominal charge on sufferance. But
he allowed Argyll and his close associates to pick an inappropriate site from
which to give battle. Argyll again fled the field, this time by horse, travelling over
twenty miles to South Queensferry, allegedly without ever looking back. [37] But
again there was a political intent. Argyll embarked from the Firth of Forth to
Newcastle, where he was instrumental in persuading Leven and the Committee
of Estates with the army in England to return overwhelming forces to Scotland
to join up with additional Covenanting troops from Ireland in order to crush
Montrose. Over 6,000 troops duly returned from England under the command
of Sir David Leslie (later Lord Newark) to reinforce home troops and the 1,400
brought over from Ulster in the wake of the decimation of the Argyll Regiment
at Inverlochy. Ill-prepared and overconfident, despite vastly inferior numbers of

36 A.M. Sinclair, 'A Collection of Gaelic Poems', *TGSI*, 26 (1904–07), pp. 237–9; *Na Baird Leatha-nach: The Maclean Bards*, A.M. Sinclair ed., 2 vols (Charlottetown, PEI, 1898), I, p. 57.
37 *LJB*, II, pp. 417–25; Wishart, *Memoirs*, p. 125; *MHG*, pp. 193–5; Stevenson, *Revolution and Counter-Revolution*, pp. 28–35.

around 1,500 foot and horse, Montrose and the Royalist cause were annihilated at Philiphaugh near the town of Selkirk. Argyll made no attempt to interfere in Leslie's command and disposition of troops. When Montrose fled the field he did so to no purpose other than to blame his loss on defections by Highlanders and the Gordons, and on the betrayal of the Royalist cause by Borderers unwilling to oppose Leslie.[38]

Argyll's presence at Philiphaugh certainly did not contain the slaughter after the battle. But Argyll cannot be indicted for an inordinate blood-lust in first countering then mopping up Royalist resistance. Certainly, Argyll was intent on revenge when MacColla compounded his ravaging of the winter of 1644 with a second ravaging of Argyllshire in the winter of 1645, after he had separated from Montrose. Again his depredations encouraged former Covenanting clans to switch sides and plunder. MacColla concentrated his destructive energies on the Campbell heartlands in the districts of Lorne, Mid-Argyll and Cowal before asserting control over Kintyre and Islay. Other contingents of clansmen used the Royalist mantle to despoil the estates of Campbell cadets and associates in Bute, Ardnamurchan, Breadalbane and Lochtayside. The distress inflicted in the name of the Royalist cause was at least matched by the reprisals exacted by the Covenanters. Especially victimised were two clans, the Lamonts and the MacDougalls, who had fought as allies of the Campbells until 1645, but changed sides to participate in the devastations of MacColla. The first incident occurred one month after Charles I had instructed all Royalist commanders to disband their forces by land or sea. The second reprisal came eleven months later and eight months after the king had actually mandated Argyll to effect the compulsory withdrawal of Antrim, MacColla and their followers to Ireland. Argyll and the radical leadership interpreted this directive uncompromisingly, as a licence to pursue 'without mercie' all refusing to comply.[39]

38 Cowan, *Montrose*, pp. 233–41; BL, Trumbull Papers vol. CXCVII, Add.MSS 72,438, fo.24; Wishart, *Memoirs*, p. 193.

39 ICA, Letters – Marquess's Period, 1638–1649, bundles 7/136, 8/191 and Argyll Transcripts, XII, nos 269–73, 275–6, 279–80, 287–8, 292, 309, 313, 348, 357, 423; Wishart, *Memoirs*, pp. 155–8, 193; *Highland Papers, vol. II*, J.R.N. Macphail ed. (Edinburgh, 1916), pp. 248–60; Stevenson, *Alasdair MacColla*, pp. 214–5, 217, 226. Sir Lachlan Maclean of Duart fared relatively better as a committed Royalist. Having failed to pay public dues to the Covenanting Movement since the outset of the civil war and having run up private debts in excess of £31,015 on his estates by 1647, Sir Lachlan was brought before the Marquess as hereditary justiciar of Argyll and the Isles and duly imprisoned within the Campbell stronghold of Carrick in Cowal. Because Argyll had taken over Sir Lachlan's public debts and bought out his creditors, the Maclean chief was only liberated after a year's imprisonment once he signed a bond on 5 May 1648, acknowledging accumulated debts of £6,490 to the Marquess. In the meantime, Argyll had accorded himself the legal pretext of reallocating townships on the Duart estates in Mull to the disadvantage of ClanGillean (*Highland Papers*, I, pp. 244–5, 320–3; ICA Argyll Transcripts XII, nos 106, 147, 274, 377).

In June 1646, a contingent of Covenanting irregulars, mainly Campbells, under the command of James Campbell of Ardkinglass, laid siege to the Lamont strongholds in Cowal. The chief, Sir James Lamont of Inveryne, was spared under the terms agreed for the capitulation of his clan. But 36 of his gentry and possibly another 100 clansmen were massacred in the confusion that followed the surrender of the castles of Ascog and Toward. Lamont prisoners taken to the town of Dunoon were summarily hanged in the course of a week following exhortations from the local Presbyterian minister, Colin MacLachlan. In the following June, 300 clansmen, mainly MacDougalls, were massacred several days after surrendering Dunaverty Castle to the Covenanting forces recalled from England under Sir David Leslie. This slaughter on the Kintyre peninsula was instigated by two Presbyterian zealots accompanying the army: John Nevoy, a chaplain; and Thomas Henderson, a clerk. Argyll, who then held the rank of colonel, was in attendance as a more than interested onlooker. He subsequently instigated legal proceedings in his own heritable jurisdiction to strip the surviving *fine* of the Lamonts and the MacDougalls of title to their estates on account of excessive debts owed to the house of Argyll and other Campbell creditors. Arrears of public dues to the Covenanting Movement compounded their delinquency.

The massacre of the Lamonts was the culmination of acts of retaliation perpetrated on both sides of the North Channel by the Campbells. In the course of the massacres in June 1646, damages in excess of £600,000 were reputedly inflicted on Toward, Ascog and other Lamont estates. Some of those hanged at Dunoon only died after being suffocated by earth heaped upon them when cast into graves. Reprisals after the massacre at Dunaverty were no less vicious and were not restricted to the MacDougalls, whose estates in Lorne and on the island of Kerrera were laid waste as the Covenanting Army swept north from Kintyre. Their chief, Dougall MacDougall of Dunnolly, was imprisoned for eighteen months in the Campbell stronghold of Inchconnel on Loch Awe. While Dunaverty was being besieged, the neighbouring Royalist fortification of Lochhead was allowed to surrender. This garrison, mainly of MacAllisters, who had also switched from their alliance with the Campbells to become followers of MacColla, were initially allowed to disperse. The clansmen paroled at Lochhead, together with the minority of the garrison who had survived the massacre at Dunaverty, were pressed into the French army. However, sixteen of the leading MacAllister gentry were recalled from parole and hanged, their estates being forfeited to the house of Argyll.

Undoubtedly, the vindictive but successful combination of reprisals and territorial acquisitiveness were the hallmarks of Argyll's deliberate confusion of public and private advantage as a leading Covenanter. However, Argyll was actually absent from the slaughter in Cowal and was present in a subordinate military capacity during the killing in Kintyre. Indeed, Argyll was making his celebrated speech promoting British confederation to the English Parliament (see Chapter 7) when the Lamonts were being massacred. The garrison at Dunaverty had been offered unconditional surrender, with their fate to be left to the discretion or mercy of the Covenanting Army's council of war. Sir James Turner, a veteran of the Thirty Years War who was present at Dunaverty, was to affirm that Leslie's decision to authorise the massacre, though against prevailing European practice, was a breach of neither law nor custom. But he also added that Argyll sided with Nevoy and Henderson in being 'horribly delighted in blood' and in persuading Leslie not to spare the Royalist clansmen. In like manner, the French envoy Jean de Montereul, monitoring the mopping up of Royalist resistance from Edinburgh, concurred that Argyll was vengeful and brutal, much given to subterfuge and intent on no compromise with MacColla and his Irish contingents. Indeed, Argyll had reportedly claimed that the only meaningful negotiations with MacColla would be whether to shorten or lengthen him: that is, to behead or hang him. Nevertheless, Montereul did not attribute the atrocities at Dunaverty directly to Argyll.[40]

Protective Reparations

Argyll's vindictive behaviour is mitigated but not excused by the personal costs he bore in opposing the Royalist campaigns during the civil war. From the suppression of MacColla's freelance raid until his retiral to Argyllshire from pursuing Montrose and MacColla in the north of Scotland, the Marquess expended over £98,259 of his own money in raising and sustaining three regiments of over 2,881 officers and men in the course of 1644. Some of this expenditure was to be recovered in the course of the next five years, principally from Crown rents in Argyll and the Isles and from the appropriation of

---

40 A.I. Macinnes, 'Slaughter under Trust: Clan Massacres and British State Formation' in Levene and Roberts eds, *The Massacre in History*, pp. 127–48; Duke University N.C., Special Collections. Sir James Turner, Papers, Seventeenth Century: Some Animadversions on Bishop Guthries Memoirs, pp. 7–10; *Montereul*, II, pp. 126, 140, 151, 157, 169. Sir James Lamont of Inveryne had held a Royalist commission since March 1644, although he did not activate it until the following year (ICA, Argyll Transcripts, XII, no. 194). Albeit he was spared from slaughter in 1646, he was held in various Campbell strongholds before being brought to Stirling Castle in 1651 to answer for his participation with MaColla in the devastations of Argyllshire. Although he was released on the occupation of Scotland by Oliver Cromwell, Argyll continued to raise actions for the recovery of debts and to claim in excess of £2,900 for the entertainment and lodging of Sir James Lamont as his prisoner! At least one of the clan gentry executed at Dunaverty, Angus Mac Eachairn of Killellan, purportedly gave his title deeds to Argyll in the forlorn expectation that his estates would be passed on to his children (ABDA, Argyll Papers, 40.1235).

Covenanting taxation levied in 1643 on the shires of Argyll, Dumbarton and Bute. But Argyll did not gain a commitment to reclaim more than £71,172 from public funds, leaving a shortfall of £27,087 (£2,257 sterling). Argyll continued to be the principal financier of Covenanting endeavours by land and sea until the last vestiges of Royalist resistance had been mopped up. With scant prospect of prompt or full remuneration from the public purse, his civil war debts in Covenanting service stood in March 1649 at more than £145,403, in addition to the £54,438 he had expended during the Bishops' Wars and the £79,864 he supplied to the Scottish forces in Ireland. In all, he laid out around £279,706 (£23,309 sterling) for the Covenanting cause in Scotland and Ireland. By this juncture he was still awaiting remuneration from the English Parliament for the £15,000 sterling (£180,000) he had expended on Covenanting intervention in the wake of the Solemn League and Covenant. On his own reckoning, the cumulative impact of both winter ravagings by MacColla denied the Marquess any rents from his Argyllshire estates between 1644 and 1647 and inflicted damages in excess of £3 million (£250,000 sterling).[41]

The leading branches of the Clan Campbell fared little, if it at all, better. The yearly rents on the estates of Sir John Campbell of Cawdor in Lorne and on Islay were decimated, falling from around £22,000 in 1643 to under £2,217 in 1651, the first year it was thought worthwhile to draw up accounts since the civil war, the townships 'being almost altogidder waist'. Their northern estates in the shires of Inverness and Nairn were not immune from the spoliation wreaked by Montrose and MacColla, particularly in their spring campaign of 1645. Clans in the central and eastern Highlands previously reluctant to join their banner declared for the Royalist cause in order to exact reprisals against Covenanting neighbours. Of the damages totalling £11,728 inflicted by Royalist forces, over £4,226 worth was attributable to the plundering of James Grant of Freuchie, his kinsmen and associates in Strathspey after the threat of having their own territories despoiled persuaded the Grants to join Montrose and MacColla. Damages in excess of £800,000 were incurred on the estates of Sir Robert Campbell of Glenorchy in Lorne and Breadalbane. The inordinate devastation in the latter district moved the Covenanting leadership to establish a relief fund for widows and orphans by January 1647. Their estates having been torched, their livestock and other moveable property carried off and their rents reduced to a pittance, the Campbells of Glenorchy were advanced £10,000 and promised a further

---

41 ICA, Letters – Marquess's Period, 1638–1649, bundles 7/135, /139–44, 8/ 130/140, /146, /220 and Argyll Transcripts, XII, nos 292, 304; ABDA, Argyll Papers, 40.386, .391, .397, .417, .430, .536, .674, .805; *APS*, VI (1), pp. 642–3 c. 80. The award of the Dunbartonshire estate of Mugdock, forfeited from the marquis of Montrose and computed to be worth £40,000 with an annual rental of under £6,122, had offset no more than a third of Argyll's public debts.

£5,000 sterling (£60,000) in reparations.[42]

Devastations were by no means confined to ClanCampbell and their allies. The Royalist campaigns inflicted damages totalling almost £93,960 on the hinterlands around the town of Inverness, which was to suffer further when Montrose attempted to revive his flagging fortunes with a renewed guerrilla campaign through the winter of 1645. Damages already running in excess of £10,000 on the estates of the Frasers of Lovat had extended to more than £14,255 by the time of Montrose's unsuccessful siege of Inverness in April 1646. According to James Fraser, Presbyterian minister of Wardlaw parish, 'betwixt the bridge end of Inverness and Gusachan, 26 miles, there was not left in my country a sheep to bleet, or a cock to crow day, nor a house unruffled'.[43] The continuing Royalist endeavours of the Marquess of Huntly served to prolong the ruination of his extensive Highland estates until his capture at the close of 1647. The principal beneficiary of Huntly's eventual trial, forfeiture and execution after fourteen months' imprisonment was Argyll, who received undisputed title to the lordships of Lochaber and Badenoch, which he had managed directly, but not productively, since 1643. Such was the spoliation wreaked by Covenanting forces as well as their Royalist rivals during the civil war that the Campbell chief, despite receiving armed assistance from the garrisons on the Huntly estates, obtained no meaningful rents from Lochaber until 1651.[44]

In the meantime, further suffering followed the avenging Covenanting Army which, in keeping with contemporary European experience, spread

42 *APS*, VI (1), 713–4 c.224; *The Book of the Thanes of Cawdor*, pp. 302–3; *BBT*, pp. 99–102; NAS, Breadalbane MSS, GD 112/1/560–1, /567and Supplementary Parliamentary Papers: Report to the Committee on Horses, 1646–47, PA 16/4/30; *The Red and White Book of Menzies*, D.P. Menzies ed. (Glasgow, 1894), pp. 275–6, 290, 292–3; *The Chiefs of Grant*, W. Fraser ed., 3 vols (Edinburgh, 1883), II, pp. 237–8 and III, pp. 236–9; *Reliquiae Celticae*, II, pp. 178–9; Cowan, *Montrose*, pp. 176–7, 252–3. Glenorchy's neighbour on Lochtayside, Sir Alexander Menzies of Weem, was mortally wounded resisting the winter ravaging of 1644. His son Duncan inherited material losses in excess of £2,666 13s 4d prior to the winter ravaging of 1645. Both the Campbells of Glenorchy and the Menzies were exempt from the levies of troops for the Engagement of 1648 in order that their devastated estates 'be not laid waste by lack of tenants'. Breadalbane was to be further afflicted by an outbreak of bubonic plague in December 1647.

43 James Fraser, *The Wardlaw Manuscript: Chronicles of the Frasers, 916–1674*, W. Mackay ed. (Edinburgh, 1905), pp. 289–90, 294–7, 313–5, 323–4; *Culloden Papers, 1625–1748*, H.R. Duff ed. (London, 1815), pp. 5–6; *More Culloden Papers*, D. Warrand ed., 5 vols (Inverness, 1923–30), I, pp. 43–78; NAS, Supplementary Parliamentary Papers: Report to the Committee on Horses, 1646–47, PA 16/4/31.

44 NAS, Gordon Castle MSS, GD 44/27/3/28; ICA, Letters – Marquis Period, 1638–1649, bundles 7/143, 8/190 and Argyll Transcripts XII, nos 109–10, 395, 421; XIII, no. 70; ABDA, Argyll Papers, 40.24; Spalding, *Troubles*, II, pp. 276, 284; Gordon, *Distemper*, pp. 198–200, 204–5; *APS*, VI (1), pp. 402–3 c. 203, 786–7 c. 388. Argyll was forced to rebate over a sixth (£3,431) of the Badenoch rents in July 1651 in order to prevent that estate, on which arrears had accumulated markedly from 1644–47, becoming totally waste and altogether unprofitable.

epidemic disease while eradicating the last vestiges of Royalist resistance on the western seaboard and in the north of Scotland. Notwithstanding the brutality and plunder that marked the civil wars in Scotland, as in Ireland, by far the leading cause of civilian death was the spread of the bubonic plague. Two years of plague after three years of intermittent warfare restricted the capacity of the Covenanting leadership to raise revenues, devastated rent rolls and depopulated towns. For their involvement with Montrose and MacColla, sixteen MacKenzie gentry from Easter and Wester Ross were fined almost £28,667 in 1646; but the Covenanting leadership soon wrote off these penalties as unobtainable. Aberdeen was probably the most occupied city in all of the three kingdoms, having been unwilling host to troops seeking free quarter on fifteen occasions between 1638 and 1646. Even before it was afflicted by plague, the magistrates were claiming that most of the city's inhabitants were 'so exhaustit and depaupered' that commerce was in disarray and leading merchants had taken refuge in France, Poland, Norway and Flanders. By this juncture, damages from warfare were estimated at £221,036; this sum subsequently increased to nearly £1.6 million when all losses by land and sea were taken into account. This period of 'more than Egyptian bondage and slavery' culminated in the long-dreaded plague striking the town in May 1647 at an estimated loss of £30,000 and sixty-five civilian lives.[45]

Because of the political clout of Argyll within the Covenanting Movement, relief for Argyllshire was more immediate than anywhere else on the western seaboard or in the north of Scotland. The central oligarchy in Edinburgh despatched substantial quantities of malt and meal from the Lowlands, at a cost of £18,500, to provide basic subsistence for the displaced and destitute at the outset of 1646. All public dues from the shire were suspended in the following month pending the award of reparations, which was eventually resolved at the outset of 1647 when £15,000 sterling (£180,000) was assigned to the Campbell chief and £30,000 sterling (£360,000) to the other landowners in the shire. However, this money was essentially assigned as the first claim on the £200,000 sterling still due from the Long Parliament from the transfer of the king. But this money promised to the Covenanters remained unpaid. Accordingly, for the next two years the *fine* of the Campbells and associated clans in Argyll still required relief from public dues, notwithstanding their collective promotion of a recovery programme 'to procure God's blessing' from September 1647. Godli-

---

45 C. Fraser-Mackintosh, *Antiquarian Notes* (Inverness, 1865), pp. 307–9; *ACL*, III (1645–1660), pp. 43–52,69–70, 85–90, 117–24, 227–30; ACA, Aberdeen Council Register, vol. LIII (1644–58), pp. 75, 1202–4, 1271, 1392; DCA, Dundee Council Book IV, fo.190; C. Carlton, 'Civilians' in Kenyon and Ohlmeyer eds, *The Civil Wars*, pp. 272–305; Stevenson, *Revolution and Counter-Revolution*, pp. 41–2.

ness was to be pursued not only by securing ministers' stipends to encourage them to instruct and keep their congregations 'in the feare of God', but also by restoring social order, by bringing lands back into production, and by regulating prices for goods and livestock. Argyll took his protective responsibilities as a chief extremely seriously, being particularly considerate that Campbell widows and orphans were given basic sustenance. Dunstaffnage Castle in Lorne, whose captain, Alistair Campbell of Dunstaffnage, had acted as quarter-master general for the Marquess when combating the Royalists, became the centre of the clan's relief operations.[46]

In supplicating the Scottish Estates at St Andrews on 4 February 1646 for relief for himself and his distressed clan, Argyll maintained that his personal setbacks in the civil war had made him acutely aware 'of God's love for honouring me to be an instrument', charged to perfect the work of reformation in both Scotland and England through British confederation. However, Argyll's partial approach to reparations and reimbursements weakened his political influence both as a clan chief and as a Scottish magnate. He and his radical associates were notably castigated for seeking to benefit financially from the transfer of the king at the outset of 1647. Thus, Murchadh MacMhurchaidh alias Murdo MacKenzie from Wester Ross unequivocally lambasted the principal negotiators who sold Charles I to the Parliamentarians:

> Gu'm be'n t-Judas fallsa
> Is ùghdar do na ghniomhsa;
> Bhuail e ploc 'san uaisle,
> Is dògh gur olc a dhìol-sa.

[It was the false Judas who is the perpetrator of this deed; he threw a sod in the face of nobility because evil is his close associate.]

Royalist polemicists also had a field day, vilifying the Scots as beasts from a northern wilderness, and as serial regicides and apostates. As pestilential rebels, the Scots were comparable to the Jews as 'a Nation Epidemical' in the wake of the king's transfer. Such English invective tarnished the Covenanters well beyond

---

46 ICA, Letters – Marquess's Period, 1638–1649, bundles 7/135, /165, 8/193, /198, /204, /220, /223, /226, 15/44, 16/41 and Argyll Letters (1638–85), A 36/137–8, /140–3, /145–8, /150–1 and Argyll Transcripts XII, nos 356, 360–1, 385, 418–20, 372, 376; *APS*, VI (1), pp. 498–9 c. 87, 591–2 c. 247, 642–3 c. 80, 702; VI (2), pp. 155, 448. In the aftermath of civil war, costs of garrisoning Covenanting forces in the *Gàidhealtachd* were generally passed on to less afflicted areas in the Lowlands. Such subventions, however, were designed to spread rather than alleviate the mounting burden of public debt (NLS, Campbell Papers, 1639–1837, MS. 1672, ff.10–1, 15, 32, 37).

the reach of Gaelic verse at home and abroad.[47] For the remainder of the year, Argyll became more reliant on support from the radical elements in the gentry and burgess, as the nobility were increasingly attracted to the conservative programme being built up assiduously by Hamilton, Lanark and Lauderdale. They sought both to restore aristocratic dominance in Scotland and to uphold the monarchical position in England. Support for Charles I, which duly materialised as the Britannic Engagement when Loudoun temporarily switched to the conservatives, was to further test Argyll's standing, nationally and internationally, as a British statesman of substance.

---

47 ABDA, Argyll Papers, 40.424; *Lamh Sgriobhainn Mhic Rath: The Fernaig Manuscript*, M. Macfarlane ed. (Dundee, 1923), pp. 119–21; John Cleveland, *The Character of a London-diurnall with Severall Poems* (London, 1647); *The Poems of John Cleveland*, B. Morris and E. Withington eds (Oxford, 1967), pp. 30–1, 116; *Montereul*, I, p. 445; Young, *The Scottish Parliament*, pp. 162–88.

NINE

Frustrated Radical, 1647–1649

By the outset of 1647, Argyll was sufficiently confident about his radical leadership in Scotland and his continuing British influence with the Parliamentarians to allow his eldest son and heir, Archibald, Lord Lorne (the future 9th Earl of Argyll) to undertake the grand tour which had been denied him by his own troublesome succession. For almost three years, the Marquess made subventions well in excess of £1,750 sterling to sustain the continental travels of his son, principally in France, Switzerland and Italy.[1] In the interim, however, the political situation within the British Isles changed drastically, and not always to Argyll's advantage. The Britannic Engagement saw him temporarily lose leadership of the Covenanting Movement to Hamilton and the conservatives. Argyll became increasingly reliant on the support of the Kirk, now effectively led by Robert Douglas following the death of Alexander Henderson at the close of 1646. The use of the commission of the Kirk by Argyll and the radicals to counter their declining influence in the Scottish Estates has led them to be misrepresented as 'the Kirk party'. Yet Hamilton, in his diary for the first parliamentary session in 1648, was scrupulous in differentiating the principled but pragmatic interests of Argyll and the radicals from the implacable ideological opposition he encountered from the Presbyterian clergy.[2] Indeed, Argyll should not be viewed as a politician tied to the Kirk, but rather as a pioneer Whig willing to take direct action to uphold the revolutionary principles of the Covenanting Movement and to maintain contractual limitations on the monarchy in both Kirk and State. Although the radicals, following an accommodation between Argyll and Cromwell, regained political power by the close of 1648, the regicide at the outset of 1649 caused an irreparable breach between Covenanters and

---

1 ICA, Argyll Transcripts, XII, nos 321, 414; ABDA, Argyll Papers, 40.450. Lorne may have been sent abroad to broaden his experience of Presbyterians, particularly at Geneva and in France, but he was there to broaden his education, not simply maintain religious contacts for his father (Lord Archibald Campbell, *Records of Argyll* (Edinburgh, 1885), p. 23).

2 Stevenson, *Revolution and Counter-Revolution*, pp. 115–232; NLS, Scottish Parliament 1648, MS 8482. I am indebted to Dr John Scally, Librarian of Edinburgh University, for providing me with a transcript of this manuscript.

Parliamentarians. At the same time, this breach frustrated the endeavours of Argyll's radical associates among the gentry and burgesses to accomplish an internal revolution that would curtail the political and social dominance hitherto enjoyed by the nobles within a centralised oligarchy since 1638.

Shifting Perspectives

With the transfer of Charles I from the Covenanters to the Parliamentarians and his lodging in Holmby Castle, Northamptonshire, political initiative appeared to pass to the Presbyterians, who were still committed to a negotiated peace with the king, if not the Scots. Following the completed withdrawal of the Covenanting Army from England at the outset of February 1647, the commissioners of the Kirk had extolled the Scottish Estates to maintain negotiations with the Parliamentarians, 'to hold fast the Union with our brethren in England' and uphold the British commitment to Presbyterianism enshrined in the Solemn League and Covenant. However, Argyll was not confident that the Presbyterians in England could reach a binding accommodation with the king that would satisfy both Parliamentarians and Covenanters; albeit the endeavours of Charles I to divide the kingdoms 'forces them to nearer union'. Rather than engage in another round of fruitless negotiations in London, Argyll was more intent on terminating Royalist resistance in the north of Scotland and on providing relief but not additional troops for the hard pressed Scottish forces in Ireland. His downgrading of peace negotiations with Charles I gave substance to the opinions of the French diplomats, Bellièvre in London and Montereul in Edinburgh, that the Covenanters, having removed themselves from the centre stage of British politics, were struggling to stay in the wings.

Indeed, Bellièvre was keen that both the Presbyterians and the city of London distance themselves from the Covenanters. To this end, he supported the Presbyterians' proposals that the king be brought to London without being obliged to subscribe the Solemn League and Covenant, and that Presbyterianism be established for a trial period of three years in the Church of England. However, Bellièvre was wary of any backlash from Independents that would afford leverage to Spain to propose a triple alliance with them and the Dutch to prevent further French incursions in the Spanish Netherlands. Accordingly, he backed an English resolution between Parliamentarians and the king. Montereul was more circumspect. While he remained deeply sceptical that either conservative or radical Covenanters would seriously promote the restoration of the king's authority in all three kingdoms, he saw immediate advantage to France if Scotland continued to be supported as an irritant to both the Presbyterians and Independents in England. Moreover, the withdrawal of the Covenanting Army from England opened up the prospect of recruiting far more troops for French service. Notwithstanding the redeployment of Covenanting forces to mop up Royalist resistance and the plague that still ravaged the country, Montereul was optimistic that at least three regiments could be raised in Scotland. Not only would the regiments already recruiting for Sir Robert Moray and the Marquess of Douglas be brought up to strength, but Robin Leslie, the brother of the Covenanting commander Sir David Leslie, was sanguine about recruiting another from Royalists in the north-east. Montereul was also hopeful that Argyll and Hamilton would at least facilitate this recruitment if not raise regiments on their own account to cement their standing at the French court and, in the process, demonstrate to both Parliamentarians and Independents that the Covenanters still had an international profile.[3]

British politics did not follow the French script, however. Notwithstanding continuing support from the city of London, the Presbyterians' determination to stand down most of the infantry units within the New Model Army, other than those designated to assist the Parliamentary war effort in Ireland, provoked a twin reaction in the country and the Army, which ceded advantage to the Independents. Attempts to recover arrears in monthly maintenance and impose a new levy to supply the troops in Ireland were extensively resisted in fourteen counties as well as the city of London; that is, more than a third of English counties though the north, like Wales, remained quiescent. Simultaneously, extensive arrears of pay, a lack of indemnity for past acts of war and the Presbyterian mobilisation of disbanded troops of dubious provenance to reinforce the trained bands of London provoked agitation in the New Model Army. With retrospective approval from Cromwell, Coronet George Joyce and his cavalry escorted Charles I from Holmby at the beginning of June, moving him through the Home Counties until he was secured in familiar surroundings at Hampton Court.[4]

Both radical and conservative Covenanters viewed this seizure of the king as a hostile act. Despite strident calls from the clergy for armed reprisals, Argyll was still able to hold the line in favour of British confederation within the Committee of Estates, which determined that this abduction of the king was insufficient grounds for war between the two kingdoms. Nevertheless, the political balance within the Covenanting leadership was tilting away from Argyll and the radicals in favour of Hamilton and the conservatives. In part, this

---

3 *The Humble Remonstrance of the Commissioners of the General Assembly to the Honourable and High Court of Parliament now Assembled* (Edinburgh, 1647); *CAL*, I, pp. 203–4, 207–10; *Montereul*, I, pp. 430–52 and II, pp. 9–75.
4 TNA, Derby House Committee for Irish Affairs, Letters Sent 1647–48, SP21/27, ff.14, 24, 123–9, 132–3; BL, Miscellaneous Letters and Papers, Add.MSS 33,506, fo.26; Sir Thomas Adams, *Plain Dealing or a Fair Warning to the Gentlemen of the Committee for Union* (London, 1647).

can be attributed to Robin Leslie working assiduously with Hamilton, Lanark and Lauderdale to encourage the greater attendance of gentry and burgesses disinclined towards radicalism in the parliamentary session that lasted from 3 November 1646 until 27 March 1647. At the same time, the nobility were discomfited by radical agitation from a group of gentry and burgesses led by Sir John Scot of Scotstarvit, who revisited the issue of feudal superiorities exercised over kirklands by temporal lords. The surrender of these superiorities had been an integral aspect of the Revocation Scheme which had foundered on the authoritarianism of Charles I (see Chapter 4). Conscious that some of his leading associates would lose out should superiorities of kirklands be surrendered, Argyll supported postponing discussion of this issue until the next parliament, which was not due until March 1648. However, when the Committee of Estates was recast as the Covenanting executive on 20 March 1647, with a membership expanded from fifty-two to seventy-six, Argyll was no longer sure of a working majority. Hamilton could certainly rely on support from the bulk of the nobility. The gentry appeared evenly split, with only the burgesses showing strongly for Argyll.[5]

In the meantime, political discussions within the New Model Army over the redress of grievances were broadened into the formulation of peace proposals in tandem with the Independents. Introduced to the Lords as the Heads of Proposals on 1 August, their formal ratification was furthered when the New Model Army occupied London five days later and began intimidating the Long Parliament. The Heads of Proposals were probably the least restrictive terms offered to Charles I in England. Prominent Royalists were only to be barred from office for five years rather than for life, and no more than seven were to be denied an indemnity. The king was to surrender control of the militia for ten rather than twenty years. Taking the Covenant was no longer to be compulsory. Independent congregations were to be tolerated outside an erastian Presbyterian structure, and Anglicanism was even to be permitted shorn of the bishops' coercive powers. While Charles was prepared to contemplate replacing the Privy Council by a Council of State, he was not prepared to compromise either on an episcopal establishment or on the militia. The king was acutely aware of deep divisions among the Anglican clergy about the merits of reducing the power of the bishops in return for toleration.[6] Negotiations were rendered

---

5 DH, Loudoun Papers, A 15/1; ICA, Miscellaneous Seventeenth Century Papers, bundle 126/34; NAS, Hamilton Papers, GD 406/1/2104, /2108; *CAL*, I, pp. 210–16; *Montereul*, II, pp. 76–211. Scotstarvit and a few associates among the gentry had supported this aspect of the Scheme from its inception in 1626. But they could now draw on wider support forged on the strength of common radical action since the emergence of the Covenanting Movement.

6 Whitelock, *Memorials*, II, pp. 182–93; [Walker], *The History of Independency*, pp. 31, 75,78–9; ABDA, Argyll Papers, 40.22; J.S.A. Adamson, 'The English Nobility and the Projected

redundant not only by the customary truculence of Charles I, but by an upsurge of agitation inspired by London radicals that was not restricted to the rank and file in the New Model Army. An innovative, democratic polity for England marked the debates conducted at Putney from 28 October to 11 November 1647, when an uneasy truce was maintained with the Presbyterians and the city of London.[7]

The radical case made by the Levellers, as specified in their *Agreement of the People*, presented a serious challenge to the prevailing Gothic perspective in the Long Parliament that was especially favoured by the Independents, as it was by the officers in the New Model Army. This perspective saw Parliament as the supreme maintainer and the Army as the guardian of English religious and civil liberties. Cromwell's son-in-law, Henry Ireton, spoke principally for the officers intent on maintaining unity with the rank and file. Without doubting the integrity of his protagonists, he stood by the tradition of social cohesion sustained by constitutional law, particularly as the Leveller emphasis on natural rather than civic rights appeared subversive of private property. The Levellers, however, stood neither for communism nor unchecked individualism, but for the collective interests of the freeborn in a secular covenant of natural rights that promoted religious toleration. The confessional covenant of works and grace under which Puritans and Presbyterians required the limitation of monarchy through the Solemn League and Covenant of 1643 was now superseded. Sovereignty was vested in the people not in Parliament.[8]

The Leveller-inspired turmoil in the New Model Army afforded Charles I the opportunity in November to escape from Hampton Court and seek refuge in Carisbrooke Castle on the Isle of Wight. Having succeeded in ending the Putney debates without a show of force, Sir Thomas Fairfax assisted by Cromwell

---

Settlement of 1647', *HJ*, 30 (1987), pp. 567–602; A. Milton, 'Anglicanism and Royalism in the 1640s' in Adamson ed., *The English Civil Wars*, pp. 61–81.

7 Smith, *Constitutional Royalism and the Search for Settlement*, pp. 132–6, 195–6; M. Kishlansky, 'The Army and the Levellers: The Roads to Putney', *HJ*, 22 (1979), pp. 795–824; A. Woolrych, *Soldiers and Statesmen: The General Council of the Army and its Debates, 1647–48* (Oxford, 1987), pp. 214–99; I. Gentles, 'The Politics of Fairfax's Army, 1645–9' in Adamson ed., *The English Civil Wars*, pp. 175–201.

8 S. Kliger, *The Goths in England: A Study in Seventeenth and Eighteenth Century Thought* (New York, 1952), pp. 260–86; P. Baker, '"A Despicable Contemptible Generation of Men"?: Cromwell and the Levellers' in P. Little ed., *Oliver Cromwell: New Perspectives* (Basingstoke, 2009), pp. 90–115; *The Clarke Papers*, C.H. Firth ed., 4 vols (London, 1891–1901), I, pp. 226–418. The Levellers argued that English liberty was not a continuous development since the incursion of the Anglo-Saxons. Liberty had been abrogated by the Norman Conquest. Accordingly, the Levellers sought a more proactive role for Parliament, supported by the Army, to throw off the Norman Yoke and meaningfully restore to all freeborn the religious and civil liberties subordinated by both the monarchy and the propertied interest since 1066.

moved swiftly to disperse the agitators. Nevertheless, Leveller influence within the New Model Army and on British revolutionary politics was by no means eradicated. The Levellers played an integral role in the pressure generated from within the Army to break off negotiations between the Parliamentarians and the king in January 1648, and subsequently to secure the parliamentary prosecution of Charles I as 'that man of blood' from November and to justify the regicide on 30 January 1649.[9] More immediately, Leveller agitation cannot be divorced from the reluctance among officers as well as the rank and file of the New Model Army to countenance their redeployment to Ireland. The continuing centrality of Ireland to British politics had been reflected in Committee for Irish Affairs, hitherto a sub-committee, taking over from the Committee of Both Kingdoms at Derby House in October 1646. The Committee, however, proved a battleground for competing Presbyterian and Independent interests until the latter secured undisputed control with the help of the New Model Army in August 1647. Thereafter, the abbreviated Derby House Committee became a forum to reappraise Ireland's constitutional relationship as a dependency of the English Parliament, not the Crown.[10]

Largely as the result of the dogmatic direction of the papal nuncio, Rinuccini, Irish revolutionary politics were imploding. The Confederates in Ulster under Owen Roe O' Neill were looking south to aid Rinuccini rather than press home the advantage gained at Benburb in June 1646. Within the space of three months in 1647, the Confederates faced defeat in Leinster and Munster. Parliamentary forces under Michael Jones won decisively at Dungan's Hill, County Meath on 8 August. The former Royalist Murrough O'Brien, Lord Inchiquinn claimed another Parliamentary victory at Knocknanuss, Co. Cork on 13 November (with MacColla a prominent casualty on the Confederate side). Ormond's earlier surrender of Dublin to the Parliamentarians that July had not helped the Royalists make common cause with Confederates alienated by Rinuccini, or with the Scottish and British forces in Ulster.[11]

---

9 S. Barber, *Regicide and Republicanism: Politics and Ethics in the English Revolution, 1646–1659* (Edinburgh, 1998), pp. 40–65, 157–8, 177–8; A. Sharp, 'The Levellers and the End of Charles I' in Peacey ed., *The Regicides and the Execution of Charles I*, pp. 181–201; N. Carlin, 'The Levellers and the Conquest of Ireland in 1649', *HJ*, 39 (1987), pp. 269–88.

10 J. Adamson, 'Strafford's Ghost: The British Context of Viscount Lisle's Lieutenancy of Ireland' in Ohlmeyer ed., *Ireland From Independence to Occupation*, pp. 128–60; R. Armstrong, 'Ireland at Westminster: The Long Parliament's Irish Committee, 1641–1647' in Kyle and Peacey eds, *Parliament at Work*, pp. 79–99; Anon, *A Warning to the Parliament of England* (London, 1647); TNA, Derby House Committee for Irish Affairs, Letters Sent 2 Mar. 1647 to 1 Aug. 1648, SP21/27, ff.8, 11, 49, 57, 79–80, 89.

11 Wheeler, *The Irish and British Wars*, pp. 175–8, 195–8; T. Ó hAnnracháin, 'The Strategic Involvement of Confederate Powers in Ireland 1596–1691' in P. Lenihan ed., *Conquest and Resistance: War in Seventeenth Century Ireland* (Leiden, 2001), pp. 25–52.

Now outnumbered by the British forces, the Covenanters under Robert Munro were engaged in a political stand-off with the English Parliament, a stand-off which brought to the fore his nephew Sir George Munro, if not the most irascible, certainly the least conciliatory of the Scottish commanders in Ulster. In a bid to expedite the departure of the Scottish forces from Ireland, the Commons had voted to withdraw funding in March and the Lords had further undermined Robert Munro's command in July, when control over the British forces was reassigned unilaterally, with the former Royalist turned Parliamentarian commander, George Monck, now coming to prominence. Never averse to exaggerating the continuing threat to the Covenanting Movement from the Catholic Confederates, the Scottish forces refused to withdraw from Ireland until arrears of pay were fully met. Indeed, the Scottish commanders in Ulster emphatically prioritised securing arrears over having their numbers reinforced by Covenanting veterans withdrawn from England. For their part, these veterans had already demonstrated in the Scottish Borders and in Galloway that they were not just reluctant to be redeployed but prone to mutiny if shipped across the North Channel.[12] As the French diplomats soon realised, well in advance of the self-deluding Charles I, his prospects of receiving aid from Ireland were rapidly receding, and what external assistance the king could expect from Scotland was also afflicted by party interests.[13]

The Britannic Engagement

Notwithstanding the withdrawal of their forces from England by February 1647, the Covenanting leadership retained commissioners in London, albeit their numbers were refreshed to reflect changing party fortunes, with Lanark prominent for the conservatives and Lothian for the radicals. Despite the noted aversion of Cromwell to any further Covenanting participation in peace negotiations, the Independents were marginally more amenable than the Presbyterians so that the Scottish commissioners, who retained close ties to the city of London, continued to be consulted on foreign and domestic matters of British significance.[14] However, Lauderdale was now prepared to distance himself openly from Argyll, and Loudoun was courted assiduously by Lanark. Thus, Argyll had to contend with a substantive challenge to his hitherto dominant influence over Scottish affairs in both Edinburgh and London. Nevertheless, Argyll had a more considered British position than Hamilton, in terms of collaboration between

12 Stevenson, *Scottish Covenanters and Irish Confederates*, pp. 237–53; Armstrong, *Protestant War*, pp. 189–90. *CAL*, I, pp. 204–6, 208–9, 213–14, 217–21; HL, Hastings Irish Papers, box 8/HA 14116, 14667, 15355; box 9/HA 14345, 14998.
13 *Montereul*, II, pp. 213–417.
14 NAS, Hamilton Papers, GD 406/1/10806.

Covenanters and Parliamentarians. He diligently maintained his contacts among Presbyterians and Independents in both the Lords and the Commons. In part, this was because he remained highly motivated to secure the £15,000 sterling promised him from the second tranche of £200,000 that the Parliamentarians were due to pay the Covenanters for transferring custody of Charles I. Argyll was also less concerned than Hamilton or indeed the Kirk, as represented by its commissioners, by the growing dominance of the Independents in association with the New Model Army. He was not opposed to the Heads of Proposals to the extent that if subscription of the Solemn League and Covenant was no longer to be compulsory, it should still be undertaken as a public attestation of fitness for office. Toleration for Independent congregations was not anathema to him so long as Presbyterianism became the established polity of the Church of England. But he would have preferred an autonomous version along the lines of the Kirk, rather than an erastian establishment. He was less than accommodating towards any rehabilitation of episcopacy.

In keeping with his depiction by Montereul in June 1647 as 'one of the subjects of this island that has done most harm to the king', Argyll's stance towards rapprochement with Charles I remained that of an uncompromising British confederate. Covenanting attainments in Kirk and State could not be secured until the king subscribed both Covenants and accepted unconditionally the establishment of Presbyterianism throughout his three kingdoms. Montereul appeared to reverse his opinion of the Marquess in the following month, when he informed Mazarin: 'I know no Scotsman here more sincere and more faithful to his prince.' But Montereul was indulging heavily in irony. He remained adamant that the Covenanting leadership, notwithstanding any 'sham disagreement' between Argyll and Hamilton, was far more committed to securing the £200,000 sterling still owed by the Parliamentarians for the transferred custody of the king than in restoring monarchical authority.[15]

Montereul had originally found Argyll cautious and reserved. He soon discovered that the Marquess was a much more volatile character, given to theatrical plays in the Scottish Estates. Argyll certainly was concerned about longstanding claims that 'he sought his own private interest in the public cause' and more recent aspersions that 'he thought rather of establishing his own authority with the help of the army than of preserving the liberties of the people'. At the same time, he was not averse to subterfuge to flush out Hamilton's comparative standing with the French court. Lanark was then pursuing a pension from France to complement that paid to his brother, albeit Hamilton's was unpaid for six years. It continued so, as the French remained uncertain about the Duke's

---

15 *Montereul*, II, pp. 95, 164, 183, 212; *LJB*, III, p. 18.

commitment to restoring Charles I either by negotiation or by force. Montereul was inclined to favour Hamilton over Argyll, as the former was viewed as a more exploitable in the interests of France.[16]

Indeed, Hamilton was more reliant on French backing than was Argyll. His British contacts lay primarily with the House of Lords, former courtiers, Royalists and the household in exile of Queen Henrietta Maria, where Argyll also had discreet representation through William Moray, the brother of Sir Robert.[17] Montereul also reported to Mazarin that Hamilton's credibility with the king, as within Scotland, was undermined by suspicions –wholly unsubstantiated – that he harboured designs on the Scottish throne should the Stuarts cease to be a British dynasty. No such suspicions afflicted Argyll. Nevertheless, Hamilton was more pragmatic and tenacious than Argyll in pursuing an accommodation with Charles I. At the same time, he was more able to capitalise on the conservative reaction against Leveller radicalism. Its spread to Scotland was especially feared given the continuing uncertainty over the state of the Covenanting forces withdrawn from England. They were as reluctant to be redeployed to Ireland as to disband unpaid after the suppression of Royalist resistance.

By mid-September, Hamilton was able to carry the vote within the Committee of Estates to disband the Army in Scotland. However, this was not a clear-cut victory over Argyll and the radicals, merely a power play to transfer control of the Covenanting forces, whose £250,000 arrears of pay was to be met by an extraordinary maintenance levied over three months. Argyll and Hamilton had actively colluded to secure this levy as a payment to demobilise because of the mounting public outcry against free and forced quartering by the troops nationwide. Hamilton's intent was to disband the existing army but then reform both the infantry and cavalry and reconstitute the command structure under himself. Not surprisingly, Argyll was determined to keep the army under his

---

16 *Montereul*, II, pp. 71, 140, 280–1, 337. Even when the last vestiges of Royalist resistance had been snuffed out, Argyll was not prepared to countenance large-scale levies for French service. Covenanting forces may have been required for the defence of the country in the face of Parliamentary aggression from England. Nonetheless, he not only held out the prospect that the regiment of his ally, Sir Robert Moray, would be made up from contingents released from Argyll's own regiment in Scotland and Ireland. But he also postulated that he would enlist as second-in-command if Moray's regiment became the royal guard for Louis XIV. Montereul interpreted this offer as Argyll attempting to secure protection from the French court should his British political machinations turn against him. For his part, Argyll, though he lacked fluency in French, had already established that the French court was open to patronising Scottish politicians. He asked Montereul to convey his thanks to Mazarin for confirming in late November 1647 the pension of his cousin, Sir Colin Campbell of Lundie, who had been in French service since 1633.

17 Argyll also maintained discreet links to the leading Anglo-Scottish courtier, James Stewart, Duke of Lennox and Richmond (*Ibid.*, pp. 83, 374).

control. In this he was supported by the leading commanders Leven and Sir David Leslie. Only Lieutenant General William Baillie was an implacable opponent. However, the artillery commander had strong family connections to the house of Hamilton, and the Scottish forces in Ireland were collectively no better than a wild card. Argyll had managed to overturn the vote in the Committee in less than a month. But he did so by only one vote after stirring up fears, which he later recanted, that the French, who actually lacked accurate or updated maps of Scotland, were prepared to invade on behalf of Charles I if Scotland was left defenceless. Argyll's dramatic exaggerations, which his close ally Cassillis found embarrassing, did not prevent the officers having their wages cut by a third and the rank and file reduced to basic subsistence pending final determination of the fate of the Army when the Scottish Estates reconvened in March 1648. Argyll was also on the defensive in terms of the remit allowed to the Scottish commissioners in London. His determination that nothing should be undertaken that would occasion a rupture with England was increasingly viewed as supine by the conservatives and did lead to Loudoun becoming more receptive to Hamilton.

Nevertheless, the collusion of Argyll and Hamilton over maintaining the Covenanting Army had served to confirm the opinion of Montereul that they were as liable to work with as against each other, notwithstanding the manifest antipathies between their respective followers. Montereul never came to terms with the possibility that Argyll, 'who will not brook having a master', and Hamilton, who 'does not want a companion', actually enjoyed good personal relations while the former operated as a radical and the latter as a conservative. They did not conspire to bring about the ruin of the Stuart monarchy. Indeed, while they disagreed over the prospects of reaching a satisfactory accommodation with a monarch whom Montereul held to be afflicted by 'his natural irresolution', they both agreed that the key to any British settlement for the meaningful restoration of the Stuart monarchy was to bring the Prince of Wales (the future Charles II) to Scotland. However, there was no prospect that this would be accomplished as a joint endeavour. In any case, bringing the Prince to Scotland was staunchly resisted by Montereul as by Pierre de Bellièvre, who had replaced his brother Pompone as French Ambassador in London in October 1647. Montereul was particularly adamant that Mazarin caution Queen Henrietta Maria against allowing the Prince of Wales to fall into the clutches of Hamilton or Argyll. The acquisition of the Prince of Wales would not necessarily assist Charles I, as both Hamilton and Argyll were liable to use his arrival in Scotland as a means of raising their bargaining position with the Independents and the New Model Army. If France was seen to countenance the departure of the Prince of Wales for Scotland it would compromise her room for diplomatic manoeuvre with the Parliamentarians and facilitate Spanish overtures for an alliance, especially with the Independents.[18]

Although the coming of the Prince of Wales to Scotland was stalled, Hamilton had made discreet approaches to Charles I on the Isle of Wight. His key intermediary was Traquair, who was now acting independently of Argyll. A covert accommodation with the Covenanters, proposed by Lauderdale, Loudoun and Lanark in their capacity as Scottish commissioners, was accepted by Charles I in Carisbrooke Castle on 26 December 1647. But this Engagement to defend and restore the authority of Britannic monarchy was concluded by conservative Covenanters without any guarantee of commitment from Argyll and the radicals. Hamilton did concede that war could not be declared until the recall of the Scottish Estates in March 1648. Nevertheless, he was confident of his capacity to mobilise troops and of parliamentary backing for the Britannic Engagement, especially as he built up the conservative position within the Scottish Estates by assiduously deploying patronage and surreptitiously promoting carpet-bagging among the shire and burgh commissioners when elections were held in October 1647. Thus Hamilton, in association with Lanark and Lauderdale, had facilitated the intrusion of gentry and burgesses who had no more than a nominal interest in the constituencies they were elected to represent. In the interim, Argyll and his associates were intent on delaying tactics. There was 'not a step to which they could not proceed too slowly' pending the return of the Scottish commissioners to clarify their dealings with the king on the Isle of Wight. Argyll also took every opportunity to cast up the untrustworthiness of the king. However, despite clandestine meetings with Sir David Leslie and their trusted lieutenants, Argyll held back from following the English example of having the Army intimidate the Estates: a precedent deemed inopportune not inappropriate.[19]

Weakened by the defection of Traquair and Loudoun, Argyll could call nevertheless on the persuasive support of the Kirk. Its commissioners had

---

18 *Ibid.*, pp. 51, 213, 240, 247, 275, 294–5, 299; *MHG*, pp. 240, 248–9; NAS, Lothian Papers, GD 40/2/2/57. Montereul was concerned that France could be compromised over the Prince of Wales, as Rene Augier, the former resident at the French Court who had reported to the Committee of Both Kingdoms, had recently been accredited as the Parliamentary resident in Paris. Augier was not averse to spinning reports that French plans to recruit troops from Ireland and Scotland served as cover for their shipments of arms and ammunition to aid Charles I (*Montereul*, II, pp. 59–60, 70, 74, 98–9, 106, 111, 196–7, 205).

19 *Ibid.*, pp. 362–3, 370, 383, *MHG*, pp. 252–3. As part of his defence against charges of treason following his capture and imprisonment in November 1647, Huntly let it be known that he had letters from the king instructing him to continue in arms despite the royal command to the contrary after Charles I had handed himself over to the Covenanting Army at Newark in May 1646. Hamilton succeeded in having only a brief note taken of these letters in the Committee of Estates at the outset of January 1648, whereas Argyll, who was pressing for the execution of his Royalist brother-in-law, wished them to be read in full to discredit Charles I.

reaffirmed its commitment to tripartite negotiations between Covenanters, Parliamentarians and the monarchy nine days before the conclusion of the Britannic Engagement. Their public strictures were certainly directed against the Parliamentarians, especially the Independents and the New Model Army, whose maltreatment of the king since his transfer from Covenanting custody was compounded by their recent unilateral refusal of an offer to mediate with the king from the States General of the United Provinces. But, any backsliding from the express conditions of the Solemn League and Covenant and its imperative to uphold the union and joint interests of both kingdoms breached 'the very Law of Nations and the rule of common equity'. [20]

The Britannic Engagement, which came into force in 1648, was the first Scottish-instigated effort to promote incorporating union as prescribed by James VI and I in the wake of the regal union. Charles I was not obliged to subscribe the Covenants. Ideological imperatives were further diluted by the stipulation that Presbyterianism would be imposed on England for no more than a trial period of three years. Both of these concessions were taken over from the proposals by the English Presbyterians to the king after he was lodged in Holmby Castle in February 1647; proposals which did not then attract the support of Charles. Even when endorsing Covenanting intervention in England on his behalf, he made no mention of any future commitment to take the Covenants. The conservative Covenanters had neither sought nor secured English backing from the Presbyterians; neither had they pursued assistance from the more receptive city of London. Their abrogation of the Covenanters' power to compel monarchy was intolerable to Argyll and the radicals who, for the duration of this 'tragicomediall' adventure, enjoyed the vociferous but not unalloyed support of the Kirk. On the return of the Scottish commissioners from London to clarify their negotiations and concentrate their fire on the Independents, Lauderdale was able to make a witty aside in the Committee of Estates on 15 February 1648: 'There were four things Englishmen could not tolerate, the Covenant, Presbyterianism, monarchical government, and Scotsmen.' However, the Engagement effectively conceded that the Covenanters had lost the political initiative within the British Isles. It was a reactionary effort to reassert aristocratic dominance over Scotland and, simultaneously, promote a conservative resurgence in all three kingdoms. [21]

20 *The Answers of the Commissioners of the Kingdom of Scotland to Both Houses of Parliament, upon the now Propositions of Peace, and the Foure Bills to be sent to his Majestie* (Edinburgh, 1647); Anon., *The Scots-Mans Remonstrance* (London, 1647); SR, Anglica 521; Burnet, *Memoirs*, pp. 365–78; J. Scally, 'Constitutional Revolution, Party and Faction in the Scottish Parliaments of Charles I' in C. Jones ed., *The Scots and Parliament* (Edinburgh, 1996), pp. 54–73.

21 *Montereul*, II, p. 407; *A Source Book of Scottish History*, III, pp. 134–9; *LJB*, III, pp. 44–50; NAS, Hamilton Papers, GD 406/1/2156, /2212, /2368; BL, Miscellaneous Autograph Letters, Add.MSS 24,422, fo.1.

Tories and Whigs

When the Scottish Estates reconvened on 2 March 1648, the political balance was manifestly loaded in Hamilton's favour. Not only had he engaged in extensive carpet-bagging to boost his support among the gentry and burgesses, he had also brought in Royalist backwoodsmen who had maintained a low profile during the civil wars, such as his kinsman, James Hamilton, 2nd Earl of Abercorn and William Crichton, 1st Earl of Dumfries. Considerable numbers of other gentry and younger sons of the nobility were also present in Edinburgh notwithstanding the imminent threat of plague. Argyll and the radicals were not averse to carpet-bagging, but they were comprehensively outmanoeuvred both in terms of representation and in the subsequent control of business.[22]

The alleged threat from England led to the formation of the Committee for Dangers on 10 March, albeit the main threat to the Border garrisons of Berwick and Carlisle came from Royalists in contact with Hamilton and the conservatives. The need both to contain and counter the sustained, ideological opposition from the Kirk led on 22 March to the formation of the Committee of 18, subsequently expanded into the Committee of 24. All three committees were dominated by the conservatives and presided over by Hamilton, rather than Loudoun, who had been elected formally as president of the Scottish Estates and had expected to chair all parliamentary proceedings. A nominal presence was accorded to Argyll and the radicals who rarely moderated the fulminations of the Kirk and were unable to secure anything more than a courtesy hearing for commissioners from the Parliamentarians, mainly Independents. They had arrived in Edinburgh in February but had been denied access to the Committee of Estates. For their part, the English commissioners were manifestly stalling in making unspecified promises to pay the remaining tranche of £200,000 sterling for the transfer of the king should the Covenanters not move onto a war footing. Argyll marked this parliamentary session, which lasted until 11 May, by tactical gestures that were dramatic but ultimately fruitless.[23]

His first dramatic gesture was a duel with Crawford-Lindsay that was more simulated than serious. Argyll had sought to remove Hamilton's brother-in-

---

22 *LJB*, III, pp. 33–6; Burnet, *Memoirs*, pp. 336, 341–2; *MHG*, pp. 257, 259–60; William Rosse, *Papers from Scotland of the Transactions of the Scots Commissioners, Concerning the King and the Parliament of England* (London 1647/48). The most striking case of carpet-bagging by the radicals was Argyll's placing of Johnston of Wariston as a shire commissioner for Argyll after he was dislodged by Hamilton's associates from Mid-Lothian (*The Parliaments of Scotland*, I, pp. 381–2 and II, pp. 812–13).

23 *Montereul*, II, pp. 417–88; *SPT*, I, p. 93; NLS, Scottish Parliament 1648, MS 8482, ff.1–82; NAS, Hamilton Papers, 406/1/2389, /2403; *Mercurius Caledonius* (Edinburgh, 1648); Young, *The Scottish Parliament*, pp. 189–214.

law as treasurer. At the same time, Crawford-Lindsay used his office to delay reimbursement to Argyll for his extensive expenditure on behalf of the Covenanting cause. The contest on the links at Musselburgh was arranged on 8 March, after it became clear that Hamilton and the conservatives were to control the parliamentary agenda. Argyll had anticipated that the duel would be broken up by a party despatched by Chancellor Loudoun. In the event, the intervention was delayed for two hours. Argyll refrained from stripping off warm clothing in inclement weather, but he had to be restrained from attacking when Loudoun's party were about to intervene. Differences were resolved by the pen rather than the sword, even though their eventual reconciliation was neither heartfelt nor free from ecclesiastical censure.[24] Argyll subsequently reissued his speech to both Houses of Parliament of July 1646 to reaffirm his credentials as a statesman who espoused British confederation and would have no truck with malignants intent on war with England. He also continued to reassure Presbyterians and Independents privately that he was opposed to further armed conflict which would set Covenanter against Parliamentarian.[25] However, his reputation for cowardice was trumpeted among Parliamentarians as well as Royalists in England, where he was denounced as the Independents' confederate:

> His Nature is more suspect than his Reason, and though that be not so great, but that many men are wiser: Yet his qualities are so bad, that few men are worse.[26]

Thereafter, his parliamentary conduct underscored his reluctance to pursue inexpedient confrontation. His next tactical ploy was to walk out of the Scottish Estates with forty radical associates on 17 March, in protest at Hamilton's procedural manipulations for military intervention in England. But they

---

24 *Montereul*, II, pp. 30–3, 82, 93, 427–28, 599–600; *LJB*, III, pp. 35–6; *MHG*, p. 261; Balfour, *HW*, pp. 395–6; NAS, Hamilton papers, GD 406/1/2408. While Crawford-Lindsay was supported by Lanark, Argyll was seconded by Sir James Innes of Sandsyde, who had been prominent among the military forces deployed not only to quell Royalist resistance in the north, but also to secure the Marquess's control over the Huntly estates (ICA, Miscellaneous Seventeenth Century Papers, bundle 97/16). Innes of Sandsyde make a long speech which more than hinted at reconciliation and simultaneously protracted the preliminaries to duelling. The candour with which the Marquess made his repentance did raise his standing with the commission of the Kirk. But the practice of duelling was not actually condemned outright by the Kirk until August when the general assembly was in session.

25 [Archibald Campbell], *The Marquess of Argyle his Speech Concerning the King, the Covenant and Peace or War between Both kingdoms* (London, 1648); Willcock, *The Great Marquess*, pp. 208–9.

26 Anon., *Certain Considerations Touching the Present Faction in the King's Dominion of Scotland* (London, 1648).

meekly accepted Hamilton's invitation to return within a week rather than face parliamentary censure. Indeed, Argyll was all but isolated when the Scottish Estates on 24 March conceded that military intervention would be necessary unless Presbyterianism was implanted in England, the king restored to London and the New Model Army disbanded. However, Hamilton's own position was not watertight. He had secured control over the reconstituted Covenanting Army, but could not retain the services of the leading commanders, the Earl of Leven and Sir David Leslie, though he did have the support of James, 1st Earl of Callander, a veteran of the Thirty Years War and a longstanding conservative. Also siding with Hamilton was the less heralded Lieutenant-General John Middleton (later 1st Earl of Middleton) who had been charged to mop up the Royalist resistance in the north-east that concluded with the capture of Huntly in November 1647. Middleton was a key player in winning over a sufficient cohort of officers to make the Britannic Engagement a viable military undertaking.[27]

Argyll's final tactic was born out of political frustration when Hamilton was empowered to recruit troops from the localities through the imposition of martial law. This initiated a further walkout by the Marquess and the radicals on 11 April. The conservatives' forcible conscription of an army had led to a recrudescence of petitioning on a scale unprecedented since 1637, against ungodly deviations from religious and constitutional fundamentals. God's wrath would undoubtedly be provoked 'if the land should be involved in a bloodie warre'. While the majority of the radicals soon returned and were boosted by the defection of Loudoun from the conservatives, Argyll, as in 1637, withdrew from Edinburgh both to reflect on proceedings and refine his own opposition. He certainly condoned but did not directly involve himself in grass-roots resistance to recruitment, which mainly occurred in Scotland south of the Tay, particularly in the shires of Fife, Mid-Lothian, Renfrew and Lanark, throughout the south-west and in the cities of Glasgow and Edinburgh. Argyll also absented himself from the brief parliamentary session at the outset of June and from the Committee of Estates re-established to implement the Engagement. The Marquess remained determined to ensure that his support for recalcitrant localities did not bring him within the revised law of treason, whose scope had been expanded for party advantage. All who resisted or traduced the Britannic Engagement now faced prosecution as traitors.[28]

27 NLS, Scottish Parliament 1648, MS 8482, fo.45; HMC, *Report on the Laing Manuscripts Preserved in the University of Edinburgh*, vol. I, H. Paton ed. (London, 1914), pp. 241–3; *MHG*, pp. 262, 265–6, 269–72; Whitelock, *Memorials*, II, pp. 334–5.
28 BL, Maitland and Lauderdale Papers 1532–1688, Add.MSS 35,125, fo.54; DCA, Council Book Dundee, IV, fo.209; NAS, Hamilton Papers, GD 406/1/2284, /2291, /2320, /2324, /2442; Edinburgh

Argyll was conspicuous by a profile that was not so much low as subliminal at the most violent expression of grass-roots resistance to the Britannic Engagement: the disturbance at Mauchline Moor in Ayrshire, which involved radical contingents from Hamilton's own estates in neighbouring Lanarkshire on 12 June. This predominantly peasant rising was only suppressed by Callander after he brought in reinforcements to relieve a beleaguered Middleton. Perhaps no more than 150 out of the 2,000 insurgents were killed, injured or imprisoned. The majority made good their escape along with a handful of Presbyterian clergy who had ministered to their militancy which, though now bloodied, was not vanquished.[29]

As Argyll continued to lie low, Jean de Montereul, the French envoy, took his leave from Scotland in July, in advance of the Engagers crossing the Border into England. Over the course of the seventeen months he was stationed in the Scottish capital, Montereul complained frequently about his inadequate diplomatic funding. However, he had acted supportively for Scottish merchants who were aggrieved by diverse requirements to pay levies on strangers trading in France; levies that they deemed contrary to the 'auld alliance'. The French envoy was also sympathetic to political overtures, notably from Argyll, to deny Dunkirkers, licensed to privateer by the Prince of Wales, access to their home port after its capture by the French from the Spanish. But in a valedictory address from Edinburgh, Montereul made clear to Mazarin that Franco-Scottish relations were but 'the shadow of an old alliance'. Nevertheless, in response to entreaties from radicals as well as conservatives, his brother Mathieu, who had arrived that June, was left as a resident French presence in Edinburgh. Still not convinced that the Engagers prioritised the restoration of Charles I over improving their negotiating position with the Independents and the New Model Army, Montereul strenuously exhorted Mazarin to ensure that the French court offered no more than good wishes along with limited supplies of arms and ammunition. On no account was France to be compromised in England to the advantage of Spain. He made no meaningful effort to contact Charles I on the Isle of Wight

---

University Library, Laing MS, I.308; TFA, Papers, TD 3758–9; *LJB*, III, pp. 53, 64. Argyll excused his absence on the grounds that there was a fresh incursion of Catholic Confederates in the Western Isles. Although he mobilised contingents from his own regiment and organised shipping to police the North Channel, the threat supposedly from Wexford seems to have been no more than the return of surviving clansmen, predominantly from the MacDonalds of Clanranald, who had left to support MacColla in September 1647 but were now redundant as the Irish Confederacy imploded. Their presence was also used by Argyll's allies in Ayrshire to defer mobilisation for the Engagement (ICA, Argyll transcripts, XII, no.376; *Reliquiae Celticae*, II, pp. 204–7; NLS, NLS, Scottish Parliament 1648, MS 848, ff.60, 62, 74, 78)

29 *Montereul*, II, pp. 507–8, 511; *MHG*, pp. 277–9; Turner, *Memoirs*, p. 242; *LJB*, III, pp. 47–9; Anon., *Two Letters from Penrith Another from Northumberland* (London, 1648).

once he arrived in London en route for Paris.[30]

By the time Montereul departed for Paris, the Engagers under Hamilton had been emphatically defeated by Cromwell at Preston in Lancashire on 17 August. Argyll may not have been able to prevent the Engagers crossing the Border. But his delaying tactics in the Scottish Estates and the commission of the Kirk, together with that fact that he condoned resistance to recruitment in the country, had certainly hindered mobilisation, discouraged diplomatic backing and made redundant any prospect of co-ordinated action between Engagers, Royalists, Presbyterians and other disaffected interests in England. His spoiling role was recognised by both Houses of Parliament in June, when they voted that the first claim on the residual monies owed to the Covenanters for the transfer of Charles I was the £35,000 sterling due to the Marquess and the shire of Argyll, with 8% interest added.[31]

Although Royalists and military adventurers of varying hues had been congregating in Edinburgh since February 1648, Scottish armed intervention in a renewed phase of civil war only briefly raised hopes of the king's restoration. Instead of the anticipated force of 30,000 blue bonneted Covenanters crossing the Border, which would have all but matched Covenanting intervention in 1644, only half of that number marched into England on 18 July. The Engagers' invasion was not co-ordinated with localised resistance in Wales, Kent and Essex; nor with the brief Royalist resurgence on the English Border under Sir Marmaduke Langdale, which had led to the capture of Berwick and Carlisle; nor with the Parliamentary naval mutiny in the Downs.[32] The Engagers did not make common cause with the Royalist coalition led by Ormond and Inchiquinn in Ireland, nor did the latter's offer to bring over 6,000 troops materialise. A like number was expected from the Scottish forces in Ulster, but only a third belatedly came over under Sir George Munro on 29 July after receiving a contribution of £8,000 sterling towards arrears of pay from the Engagers. Soldiers of the Argyll Regiment stationed in Ireland refused to participate, preferring to garrison Dunluce Castle, County Antrim,

30 *Montereul*, II, pp. 74, 127, 241, 286–7, 377, 394, 489–538. Montereul had cautioned Mazarin against enforcing Scottish privileges by decree – as had happened under Richelieu in 1639 (BL, Misc. Correspondence, vol. VIII, Sep.–Dec. 1663, ADD.MSS 23,120, ff.46–7) – as he wished to keep the Scots as supplicants rather than grant them permanent exemptions. Although the French did clear out the privateers licensed by the Prince of Wales from Dunkirk, they made no effort to check their relocation to Irish ports or their preying on Scottish shipping in the North Sea any more than in the North Channel.

31 ICA, Letters – Marquess's Period, 1646–49, bundle 8/6.

32 Burnet, *Memoirs*, pp. 345, 348–367; *Montereul*, II, pp. 402–3, 421, 460–1, 482, 519; TNA, Derby House Committee for Irish Affairs, Letters Sent 1647–48, SP21/27, ff.129–30; NAS, Hamilton Papers, GD 406/1/2212, /2403; NLS, Scottish Parliament 1648, MS 8482, ff.29, 58, 75.

in order to intimidate the Irish branch of ClanDonald South.[33]

A substantive quantity of arms and ammunition was acquired for the Engagers through Scottish commercial networks after Hamilton had despatched Sir William Ballenden of Broughton to the United Provinces in May. But Ballenden was not able to secure diplomatic endorsement from the States General, only from the house of Orange, which had strong family ties to the Stuarts. The military supplies were brought back to Leith in July, four days after the Engagers had marched into England, by Sir William Fleming, son of John, 2nd Earl of Wigtown, a longstanding conservative. These supplies were little more than a consolation prize. Fleming had been shuttling from April between Hamilton and the household in exile of Queen Henrietta Maria, in the forlorn hope that he would return with the Prince of Wales, who would lead the Engagers' army of intervention. Minimal diplomatic endorsement for the Britannic Engagement was not changed by the late commissioning of Lauderdale to go to France and the United Provinces at the outset of August.[34]

In England, the Britannic Engagement revived Scotophobia and the desire of the Independents to be quit of the Solemn League and Covenant. Although the Independents and the New Model Army had intermittently suspected them for wishing to bring back Scottish forces during 1647, the Presbyterians remained aloof. Their residual commitment to the cause of both kingdoms took solace from the refusal of Argyll, Leven and Sir David Leslie to participate in an expeditionary force that again began to unravel under Hamilton's uncertain military leadership.[35] Instead of moving on Newcastle and cutting off the coal supply to London, the manoeuvre that had obliged Charles I to sue for peace in 1640 (see Chapter 6), Hamilton opted to aid the Royalists in the north-west. This way presented greater logistical challenges than the north-east and resulted in his infantry being detached from both the cavalry and artillery at Preston, with the forces from Ireland several days in arrears. The New Model Army, supplemented by Independent militias in Leicester, Berkshire and Somerset who were vehemently opposed to a conservative resurgence, had effectively suppressed

33 Anon., *The British Bell-man* (London, 1648); ICA, Argyll transcripts, XII, no. 385; M. Bennett, 'Dampnified Villagers: Taxation and Wales during the First Civil War', *Welsh History Review*, 19 (1998), pp. 29–43; Stevenson, *Scottish Covenanters and Irish Confederates*, pp. 256–65.

34 NAS, Hamilton Papers, GD 406/1/1193, /2389; BL, Maitland and Lauderdale Papers 1532–1688, Add.MSS 35,125, fo.52; *Montereul*, II, 439–40, 445, 465–6, 482, 493–4, 529, 531.

35 [Marchmont Nedham], *Anti-Machiavelli or, Honesty Against Policy* (London, 1647); [Walker], *The History of Independency*, pp. 80–1, 100–1, 118–20, 123–6; *A Letter from the House of Commons Assembled in the Parliament of England at Westminster, to the Right Honourable and Right Reverend, the Lords, Ministers and Others of the Present General Assemble of the Church of Scotland Sitting at Edinburgh* (London, 1648); *The Clarke Papers*, II, pp. 251–2; NAS, Hamilton Papers, GD 406/1/2284, /2368, /2454.

English dissent prior to the Engagers' invasion in July. Warwick rallied the naval forces that had remained loyal to the Parliamentarians. Without supporting the Engagers or blockading London, the mutineers were forced to seek shelter in the United Provinces by November.[36]

Scottish Royalists formerly allied to the Irish Confederates castigated the Britannic Engagement as a Tory endeavour. News of the rout of Preston, along with the capture and imprisonment of Hamilton, was received as a national humiliation throughout Scotland that was channelled by an anonymous Gaelic poet into a plea for peace, which took little solace in the impotence of the Kirk and denounced further military adventures:

> Tha masladh mòr is mi-chliuth
> Air tigh'n o'n Chrich 'nar n-uchd;
> Ar n-armaild air a striocadh
> Le seachd mile marcach trup:
> Ar ministeirin seirich
> Mar bhraighdin min-gheal mult,
> Is oighre nan'n tri rìigheachdan
> Am priosan an Eilein Uicht.[37]

[Great disgrace and humiliation has come from the border to our breast; our army has surrendered to seven thousand horse-troopers: our embittered ministers like captive soft-white wedders, and the inheritor of the three kingdoms in prison on the Isle of Wight.]

The general assembly of the Kirk wasted no time in condemning 'a most bloody and intestine war' and reaffirming its British commitment to the Solemn League and Covenant. Militants in the south-west staged a revolt, which commenced with the Whiggamore Raid on Edinburgh that was led by Cassillis, Loudoun

---

36 Turner, *Memoirs*, pp. 49–75; S. Barber, '"A bastard kind of militia", Localism, and Tactics in the Second Civil War' in I. Gentles, J. Morrill and B. Worden eds, *Soldiers, Writers and Statesmen of the English Revolution* (Cambridge, 1998), pp. 133–50; Wheeler, *The Irish and British Wars*, pp. 182–92, 200–2; Bennett, *The Civil Wars in Britain and Ireland*, pp. 284–305.

37 A.I. Macinnes, 'The First Scottish Tories?', *SHR*, 67 (1988), pp. 56–66. The anonymous poet was almost certainly a Royalist veteran of the civil wars affiliated to the MacDonalds of Glengarry. His protest song 'An Cobhernandori' can be translated as 'help to the Tories'. The label Tory, first applied abusively by planters and colonists to the native Irish dispossessed, was attached, subsequently, by Parliamentarian and Royalist forces in Ireland to the Catholic Confederacy. The direct Gaelic borrowing of the label, used as a term of reproach rather than abuse, probably derives from the military association of MacColla's Irish regiments with the Royalist clans and pre-dates its English introduction to Scotland by three years, when the rural guerrillas resisting the Cromwellian occupation within Gaeldom were termed Tories.

and Eglinton and endorsed by Argyll, Leven and Sir David Leslie. Having forced the conservative Committee of Estates to abandon the capital, the radicals regrouped around Argyll but did not immediately regain power. Nevertheless they have a greater claim to be the original Whigs than do Hamilton and the Engagers as the first Tories.[38]

Argyll and the radicals were outflanked and checked temporarily at Stirling on 12 September by Lanark's home guard backed up by Munro's troops from Ireland, who had not been involved at Preston, having moved belatedly against Newcastle. Far from securing an emphatic victory, Argyll's supporters, who numbered about 5,000, faced combined forces of 8,000 Engagers. Only armed support from Oliver Cromwell, who had crossed the Border to assist the Covenanting radicals with 9,000 troops, persuaded the Engagers to give up the reins of government and return Berwick and Carlisle to English control. Having narrowly escaped capture at Stirling, Argyll took no part in the protracted negotiations between 'Whigs' and 'Tories', as he opted instead to meet Cromwell after he crossed into Berwickshire.[39]

Although Cromwell contemplated and many Scots feared a conquest, he was content to reinstall Argyll and the radicals in power with a renewed commitment to a policy of exclusion from public office. He had entered Scotland on Argyll's invitation and promised that his troops would observe military discipline at all times, in contrast to the behavior of Munro's forces in England. The Engagers, after two weeks of heated discussions, were assured of their lives and property in return for disbanding their army.[40] Argyll and other leading radicals entertained Cromwell amicably in Edinburgh during his brief sojourn in Scotland, which seemed to consolidate a mutual respect between the future regicide and

38 Gordon, *Distemper*, pp. 210–12; Burnet, *Memoirs*, pp. 370–7; Whitelock, *Memorials*, II, pp. 403–6, 410–11; *The Clarke Papers*, II, p. 44. Both rival labels of Whig and Tory can be said to derive from the same set of political circumstances in Scotland, though their currency was not general throughout the British Isles until the 1670s (R. Willman, 'The Origins of "Whig" and "Tory" in English Political Language', *HJ*, 17 (1974), pp. 247–64.

39 Anon., *A Great Victorie Obtained in the Kingdom of Scotland by the Marquis of Argyle* (London, 1648); Stevenson, *Revolution and Counter-Revolution*, pp. 115–22. Argyll's hasty departure from Stirling to North Queensferry was not so much another flight from combat (Wishart, *Memoirs*, pp. 219–20; *MHG*, pp. 283, 286, 288, 290, 294) as an expeditious move to take ship in order to meet up with Cromwell at Mordington in Berwickshire.

40 *A Letter Sent from Lieutenant Generall Cromwell to the Marquis of Argyle and General Lesley* (London, 1648); *The Clarke Papers*, II, pp. 47–8, 52–3; *CAL*, I, pp. 224–6; TFA, Papers, TD 4667. As well as despoiling the countryside and disrupting trade, Munro's forces had revived past Covenanting practice of commandeering rents and profits from sequestered estates in Northumberland (*Records of the Committees for Compounding with Delinquent Royalists in Durham and Northumberland*, pp. 41, 82–3, 111; *Extracts from the Records of the Merchant Adventurers of Newcastle-upon-Tyne* vol. 1, p. 159).

Argyll as godly men of honour. However, there are no grounds for Cromwell apprising Argyll of anything more than future negotiations with Charles I.[41] Indeed, his fellow radicals remained adamant that the Marquess would have done nothing to compromise the maintenance of monarchy as prescribed in the Covenants. In turn Argyll, who had no wish to prolong Cromwell's stay in Scotland, issued a declaration on 16 October on behalf of his fellow radicals now in control of the Committee of Estates. Cromwell and the New Model Army were thanked for their brotherly assistance. The Parliamentarians were given a free hand to negotiate with the king in the anticipation of divine guidance bestowing sufficient wisdom on Charles I 'that he be not involved in new snares to the endangering of himself and these kingdoms'. Argyll was also adamant, on behalf of 'the Godly party' in Scotland, that the confessional grounding for British confederation was the only way 'to remove unhappie differences and quench the fire of a wasting warre between king and people'.[42]

Internal Revolution

The Scottish Estates reconvened with a membership securely managed in favour of the radicals at the start of 1649. Argyll took advantage of the diplomatic absence of all but a quarter of the eligible nobility and the influx of gentry and burgesses with extensive experience of local administration, particularly on the shire committees of war, to replace compromised Engagers. His long opening speech on 5 January 'which he called the brecking of the malignants teeth' constituted a frontal attack on the Engagers. He was determined that punitive action should be prioritised over discussions on the hazardous predicament of the king, despite the mood of the house being in favour of the latter. The rigorous application of the Act of Classes that duly passed on 23 January entrenched schism within the Covenanting Movement. In 1646, anyone who had participated over the previous two years in the Royalist campaigns of Montrose and MacColla was classified as delinquent, forfeited and purged from public office. The political prescription resorted to in 1649 was directed against not only former Royalists but all conservative Covenanters who had become embroiled in the ill-fated Britannic Engagement. While not forfeited, those deemed delinquent were subject to vigorous fines and periodic exclusion

---

41 Anon., *A Letter from Edinburgh Concerning the Differences of the Proceedings of the Well Affected in Scotland, from the Proceedings of the Army in England* (Edinburgh, 1649); Whitelock, *Memorials*, II, pp. 413, 415, 422; Gordon, *Distemper*, p. 213; *MHG*, p. 298; Wishart, *Memoirs*, p. 223.

42 *A Declaration of the Marquess of Argyle, with the rest of the Lords, and others of the Estate of that kingdome of Scotland, Concerning the Kings Majesty and the treaty; and their desires to the Parliament of England* (London, 1648); Willcock, *The Great Marquess*, pp. 212–18.

from office – from life to one year – scaled to their perceived malignancy. At the same time, they were exposed to ecclesiastical censures that ranged from outright excommunication to public repentance in sackcloth during divine services. While the Kirk gained a right of veto over office holding, Argyll and the radicals were adamant that the general assembly remained a supplicant, not a director, in the shaping of public policy. The ideological principle underlying the Act of Classes, which remained operative until 1651, was that acquiescence in the directives of the Covenanting Movement was insufficient. Those seeking public office had to demonstrate a positive commitment to radicalism. Loudoun was among the first to make public repentance for his part in formulating the Engagement.[43]

Although there was little prospect of disgruntled Engagers making common cause with Royalist clans, Argyll was ever vigilant to ensure that Campbell territories be protected and that the full rigour of the law be applied to Engagers and Royalists, especially those whose estates he coveted. Nonetheless, the imposition of punitive fines by quartering had not been implemented systematically in the *Gàidhealtachd* after the civil war, partly because delinquents remained liable to forced loans and partly because the Covenanting leadership was not unsympathetic to the resulting financial embarrassment to prominent families, the elite of Catholic clans included. The attitude of the vast majority of the indigenous chiefs and clan gentry to the Covenanting oligarchy, if not downright hostile, was distinctly lukewarm; a situation not changed when they, in contrast to the ClanCampbell, were offered comparatively little by way of reparations from the public purse. Nor were they conceded wholesale exemptions or even individual dispensations from the cess and other fiscal dues.[44]

Such discriminatory treatment, as well as an aversion to the increasingly radical direction of the Covenanting Movement, was instrumental in provoking the abortive rising in February 1649, led by Thomas MacKenzie of Pluscardine, brother of George, 2nd Earl of Seaforth. Pluscardine's rising had the backing of almost 1,200 clansmen, mainly from the MacKenzies and the MacKays, and drew support from the leading gentry in the neighbourhood of Inverness. The insurgents, who attempted to ship in arms and ammunition from Holland, gained

43 Balfour, *HW*, III, pp. 377, 385–6; *The Parliaments of Scotland*, II, p. 814–15; *APS*, VI (2) (1648–60), pp. 143 c. 30, 676; *MHG*, pp. 301–2; Young, *The Scottish Parliament*, pp. 189–227.

44 ICA, Argyll Letters (1638–85), A36/153 and Argyll transcripts, XII, no. 421 and XIII, nos 12, 18; Wishart, *Memoirs*, pp. 215–16; NAS, Supplementary Parliamentary Papers, PA 14/3, ff.501–7; *APS*, VI (2), pp. 327, 356, 400, 460–3 c. 187. The radical regime that came to power after the failure of the Britannic Engagement actually relaxed forced quartering on Catholics. Although four of the five clan chiefs forfeited belatedly in 1649 for Royalist complicity during the civil war were tainted with popery, recusancy was not specified in their indictments. Their forfeitures were justified for their prolonged failure to make peace with the Covenanting leadership.

control of Inverness, which they held for over a month before being routed by numerically inferior Covenanting forces at Balvenie in Speyside on 6 May.[45] The rising was not so much a forlorn harbinger of a Royalist revival as a protest against repeated Covenanting requisitions for men and money. Initially, this protest seemed capable of attracting support in Atholl and Badenoch, of encouraging mutiny among the Covenanting forces garrisoning Stirling Castle, and even of fomenting the assassination of Argyll in Perth. But its main impact on the radical regime was to expedite the trial and execution of Huntly, imprisoned in Edinburgh since his capture in late 1647; an outcome long desired by Argyll.[46]

Huntly's execution in March coincided with a determined push by Argyll to reclaim the extensive debts he was due from the public purse. The Scottish Estates duly established that Argyll was owed over £145,403 for expenditure incurred in the civil war against the Royalists, with another £12,000 to be added to the £79,864 he had spent on provisioning the Scots army in Ireland. While the scale of Argyll's debts was verified by parliamentary audit, no programme of remedial action was implemented immediately.[47] For the radical regime that had recently come to power was primarily intent on redressing eleven years of demand management by the Covenanting oligarchy. With full backing from the commissioners of the Kirk, the new regime promoted social restructuring, including the imposition from below of the Revocation Scheme, which had done so much to prejudice Charles I's prerogative rule.

The legislative programme of the radical mainstream in 1641 had already put a block on the award or acquisition, other by inheritance, of such heritable jurisdictions as regalities and sheriffships. This was now confirmed to prevent transfers through purchase or mortgage. The anti-aristocratic thrust of this legislation was reinforced by an enactment which affected around half the ownership of land in Scotland; namely, that the superiority over kirklands was to be phased out in favour of direct landholding from the Crown. Radical gentry had continuously pushed for this since 1647. This legislation was to apply not only to temporal lords but was extended to lands that formerly pertained to the bishops. The wholesale redistribution of teinds was not contemplated. Nor was there any parliamentary support for clerical claims that the teinds, as

---

45 *More Culloden Papers*, I, pp. 90–9; Fraser, *The Wardlaw Manuscript*, pp. 332–40; Fraser-Mackintosh, *Antiquarian Notes*, pp. 155–8; DCA, Council Book Dundee, IV, fo.224; *ACL*, III, pp. 140–1.

46 *APS*, VI (1), p. 702; VI (2), pp. 156 c. 50, 241 c. 196, 448; Whitelock, *Memorials*, III, p. 38; *MHG*, pp. 252–3, 276; Stevenson, *Revolution and Counter-Revolution*, pp. 145–8.

47 ICA, Letters – Marquess's Period, 1646–49, bundle 8/223, /226; ABDA, Argyll Papers, 40.430, .397, .445, .449, .451–3, .805. Argyll was to receive a share in the farming of the excise for wines, beer and spirits from 1 November 1651, which was anticipated to yield him £36,000 annually for five years.

spirituality, were the exclusive preserve of the Kirk. However, redistribution to augment stipends, improve schooling, support social welfare and redraw parish boundaries to promote more active Christian congregations was endorsed. No time limits were imposed on future purchases of teinds by the gentry or, indeed, burgesses. The radical intent of these estates was underscored when rights of patronage – whether held by the Crown, temporal lords, barons or freeholders – were abolished in favour of ministers being appointed by kirk sessions with oversight vested in the presbyteries. This legislation was uncomfortable not only for the conservatives but also for 'Whig grandees' such as Loudoun, Lothian, Eglinton, Cassillis and Argyll. All but the Marquess were temporal lords, and Loudoun throughout the 1640s had sought to benefit personally from an exclusive lease to collect the annuity from the teinds claimed by Charles I. Over this period, Argyll, within his own extensive territories, had steadily been consolidating his claims on all episcopal lands and teinds formerly held by the bishops of Argyll, the Isles, Dunkeld and Galloway.[48]

Notwithstanding the discomfiture of the nobility, the radical regime was undoubtedly responding to endemic exhaustion throughout Scotland after a decade of continuous demands for ideological commitment, financial supply and military recruitment, aggravated by civil war and bubonic plague between 1644 and 1647. Indeed, the radical legislative programme of 1649 was as much a reaction against unremitting centralism as it was against the aristocratic leadership of the Britannic Engagement. An act of 5 July, for 'Redress of Complaints and Grievances of the People, against Masters, Collectors, Officers and Souldiers' devolved power in local government from shire to presbytery committees, which were to liaise directly with the Committee of Estates. The presbytery committees were civil, not ecclesiastical, agencies charged to act as local commissions of grievance, taking special cognisance of complaints arising from the mustering and quartering of troops as well as fiscal levies in town and country. In the meantime, members of the shire committees were to accord priority to their collective role as justices of peace rather than as administrators of war.[49]

---

48 *APS*, V, pp. 390, 400–3, c.85, 404 c.87, 664, 679 and VI (i), pp. 199 c.202 , 266 c.266, 775 c.385, 778 c.362 and VI (ii), pp. 20 c.46, 114 c.217, 244–6 c.199, 287 c.253, 297 c.265, 300 c.274, 321 c.310, 717; ICA, Argyll Transcripts, XII, nos 360–1, 388, 390, 418–20 and XIII, nos 23–4; HL, Loudoun Scottish Collection, box 16/LO 10951; NLS, Scottish Parliament 1648, MS 8482, ff.23, 47, 54; Balfour, HW, III, pp. 391, 417–8. Although Argyll was rigidly opposed to any exclusive claims by the Kirk, he was not opposed to teind redistribution for pious uses, such as founding a new grammar school in October 1649 at Inveraray, which he had, with the consent of Charles I in Carisbrooke Castle, erected into a royal burgh in January 1648 (ICA, Argyll Transcripts, XII, nos 359, 424).

49 *APS*, VI (ii), pp. 268 c.215, 449 c.159, 464–7 c.194, 502 c.282; *ACL*, III, pp. 144–6.; J.R. Young, 'Scottish Covenanting Radicalism, the Commission of the Kirk and the Establishment of the

However, such grass-roots reform was overtaken by news of the execution of Charles I on 30 January 1649. In England, as in Scotland, there had been an effective coup d'état by radical forces in late 1648. Although the Long Parliament had effectively broken off negotiations with the Royalists at the outset of 1648, the Presbyterians had recommenced exploring the grounds for a settlement with Charles I in August. Negotiations, which dragged on until November under the guise of the Treaty of Newport, did mark a distinctive move away from the Heads of Proposals back towards the Newcastle Propositions. The king was prepared to be flexible over the control of the militia. Having already made the concession to the Engagers, he agreed that Presbyterianism should be established in the Church of England for a trial period of three years. Nonetheless, the negotiations were unable to protect the king from increasingly assertive elements within the New Model Army, which occupied London on 2 December. Within four days, Colonel Thomas Pride purged the Long Parliament.[50]

This Rump Parliament, malleable to the control of Cromwell and the Independents, redefined English government in claiming that power was vested in the people and that the Commons represented supreme power. The Gothic perspective was thus reformulated to ensure that the supremacy of the Commons overrode that of the monarchy or the Lords. Using this authority to establish a high court of justice on 6 January, Charles I was brought to London and impeached as a tyrant, implacably intent on 'the destruction of the fundamental laws and liberties' of England. After an eight-day trial from which the Lords were excluded, the king was sentenced to death on 27 January and duly executed three days later. Within a week of the regicide, the House of Lords and the monarchy were abolished.[51]

Parliamentary Radical Regime of 1648–1649', *RSCHS*, 25 (1995), pp. 342–75. This return to localism had the negative effect of provoking a witch hunt in 1649–50 in which the clergy, who were otherwise excluded from shaping public policy, figured prominently. The main charges brought against the accused, who were drawn predominantly from the more vulnerable and less productive members of communities, related not so much to their engagement in demonology as in their purported ungodly covenant with the devil. Argyll was not caught up in this mania, nor were his estates afflicted by the witch trials, which mainly concerned the Central Lowlands, especially the Lothians (P. Hughes, 'The 1649–50 Scottish Witch Hunt, with particular reference to the Synod of Lothian and Tweeddale' (University of Strathclyde, PhD thesis, 2009); Glasgow University Archives, Beith Parish MSS, P/CN, II/139/3–14).

50 [Walker], *The History of Independency*, pp. 140, 156–8, 166–74. Smith, *Constitutional Royalism and the Search for a Settlement*, pp. 138–40, 196–7. The Presbyterian shift away from the Heads of Proposals had already been signposted by the Four Bills in December 1647 but truncated by the passage through the Long Parliament of no addresses to the king in the following month.

51 Whitelock, *Memorials*, II, pp. 468–516; J. Adamson, 'The Frightened Junto: Perception of Ireland, and the Last Attempts at Settlement with Charles I' and S. Kelsey, 'Staging the Trial of Charles I' in Peacey ed., *The Regicides and the Execution of Charles I*, pp. 36–93. As a result of the purge, 317 MPs were arrested, excluded or else they walked out.

Scottish commissioners led by Lothian had protested vehemently about these extraordinary judicial proceedings. With Argyll having reconsidered the free hand in dealing with the king accorded to Cromwell in Edinburgh three months earlier, the Scottish commissioners had pushed their own agenda on 6 January. They presented proposals for both king and Parliament based on the Newcastle Propositions to sustain the Solemn League and Covenant and impose Presbyterian uniformity as eventually defined by the Westminster Assembly of Divines in terms of faith, worship and polity. However, Charles was not prepared to make any concessions to the Scots. Notwithstanding the appeals of the commissioners to past brotherly association as British confederates, Parliament was adamant that the Covenanters should play no part in their dealings with the king. To no avail the commissioners made a last-minute appeal for clemency to Fairfax as commander of the New Model Army: 'Consider what an unsettled peace it is like to prove, which should have its foundations laid on the blood of this king.' On 24 February, the Scottish commissioners conceded that Parliament had the sole right to settle religion in England, so long as this was consistent with the Solemn League and Covenant. They also pleaded that the new king, Charles II, be admitted to the government of the three kingdoms. Their overtures were dismissed as 'scandalous and reproachful'. British confederation was emphatically rejected by the Rump Parliament two days later. As they were about to embark for Holland to treat with the new king, the Scottish commissioners were arrested at Gravesend and sent back to Berwick under armed escort. Hamilton, who viewed himself as an unfortunate servant of the Scottish Estates, was executed on 9 March for his leadership of the Britannic Engagement, albeit in his capacity as an English peer.[52]

Struggling to maintain his control over the radical regime in Scotland, Argyll did not lift a finger to aid Hamilton, whom he now viewed as expendable.[53] With the Derby House Committee re-established as the Council of State from 13 February, the Gothic free state was proclaimed internationally on 14 May as the English Commonwealth (*Res Publica Anglicae*), untrammelled by any bilateral commitment to the Solemn League and Covenant, which the Scots were held to have breached by the Britannic Engagement.[54] News of the unilateral

52 *CAL*, I, pp. 227–48; Stevenson, *Revolution and Counter-Revolution*, pp. 127–33. Hamilton was Earl of Cambridge.

53 Monteith of Salmonet, *The History of the Troubles*, p. 501; Dugdale, *A Short View of the Late Troubles in England*, p. 389; [Marchmont Nedham], *Digitus Dei: or God's Justice upon Treachery and Treason, Exemplified in the Life and Death of the Late James, Duke of Hamilton* (London, 1649); NAS, Hamilton Papers, GD 406/1/2369, /5945.

54 Anon., *The Bounds & Bonds of Publique Obedience* (London, 1649); Whitelock, *Memorials*, II, pp. 532–48; DR, TKUA, England, A I, no.3, Breve, til Vels med Bilag fra Medlemmer af det Engelske Kongehus til medlemmer af det danske, 1613–89.

execution of Charles I had been greeted with outrage in Scotland. Collaboration between the radical regimes in Edinburgh and London was sundered. Argyll was instrumental in ensuring on 5 February that the Scottish Estates promptly proclaimed the Prince of Wales as Charles II, King of Great Britain and Ireland. This British affirmation reasserted the international identity of the house of Stuart within the context of confederal union. However, this proclamation and the subsequent opening up of negotiations in March with Charles II, then in exile at Breda, to return as a Covenanted monarch were also unilateral acts. They provoked profound indignation in England, where Charles II was deemed only as King of Scots.[55]

55 Young, *The Scottish Parliament*, p. 225; Anon., *A Letter from Scotland: And the Votes of the Parliament for Proclaiming Charles the Second, King of Great Britain, France & Ireland* (London, 1649); Anon., *The Vindication and Declaration of the Scots Nation* (Edinburgh, 1649); [Charles II], *The King of Scots his Message and Remonstrance to the Parliament of that Kingdome, convened at Edenburgh, for a perfect Union, and Agreement, between Prince and People and his desires to all his loving Subjects of that Nation, requiring their due obedience towards him, as their law-full King and Governor* (London, 1649).

TEN

The Partial Patriot, 1649–1654

Cromwell's military priority in the wake of the regicide was not the correction of his errant former brethren in Scotland, but the civilisation through conquest of Ireland. Cromwell was faced by an alliance of Royalists and conservative Confederates under Ormond who had been joined by disgruntled Parliamentarians under Inchiquinn. With the meddlesome Rinuccini having already departed Ireland, Ormond and Inchiquinn had driven the radical cohort of Confederates commanded by Owen Roe O'Neill deep into Ulster. There they had run into opposition from the Scottish troops under Sir George Munro, who had returned to Ireland after the failure of the Britannic Engagement. However, Munro's desultory endeavours to support the Royalist coalition in Ulster only drove a deeper wedge between Scottish and English planters. George Monck, now firmly in command of the British forces in Ulster, concluded an expedient alliance with O'Neill. Anticipation of Cromwell's invasion pushed Ormond back into Leinster and Inchiquinn to Munster. Eleven days before Cromwell's landing near Dublin, Michael Jones decisively defeated Ormond at Rathmines on the Liffey on 2 August. Cromwell's brief, but bloody, campaign in Ireland was marked less by battles than by sieges: notably at Drogheda in September and Wexford in October 1650, where his undoubted military brilliance was tarnished by his penchant for eradicating the ungodly. Notwithstanding a belated accord between Ormond and O'Neill, Cromwellian forces secured Ulster. In Munster, Inchiquinn's forces steadily mutinied and switched their allegiance to his former Parliamentary associate, Robert Boyle, Lord Broghill. By Cromwell's departure in May 1650, the Confederate capital of Kilkenny had fallen and only the province of Connacht was offering substantial resistance, which took another three years to mop up.[1]

---

1 HL, Hastings Irish Papers, box 9/HA 14167, 14954, 14992, 14999, 15308–9, 15311, 15313, 15354, 15357, 15426; *The Clarke Papers*, II, pp. 202–6; Walker, *The History of Independency*, pp. 86–7, 121–2; Gentles, *The New Model Army in England, Ireland and Scotland*, pp. 350–84; Wheeler, *The Irish and British Wars*, pp. 209–20. M. Ó Siochrú, *God's Executioner: Oliver Cromwell and the Conquest of Ireland* (London, 2008), pp. 77–105. The conquest of Ireland was only effected after a massive injection of English troops and the licensing of almost 34,000 Irish soldiers to enter Spanish service.

In the interim, Argyll used this breathing space to shape a patriotic accommodation between radicals and conservatives under Charles II. Argyll was intent on accomplishing what he had failed to achieve in 1647–48 when the king was Prince of Wales: that is, bring him to Scotland to subscribe the Covenants and promote Presbyterianism throughout his dominions. Charles eventually came to Scotland from the United Provinces in the spring of 1650 and was crowned as the Covenanted King of Great Britain and Ireland on 1 January 1651. This patriotic accommodation was duly extended to Royalists as Cromwell and the New Model Army occupied Scotland south of the Forth. Notwithstanding the apparent offer of a dukedom, Argyll distanced himself from the subsequent invasion of England that proved disastrous. Cromwell's complete occupation of Scotland was duly followed up by a negotiated incorporation within the Commonwealth in 1652. This incorporation endured a patriotic rising in Scotland, initially under the Earl of Glencairn in 1653, from which Argyll, but not his son, Lord Lorne, remained aloof. Failure to engage in this rising, which petered out in 1654, not only raised questions about Argyll's patriotism but also amplified accusations that he was a Cromwellian collaborator. More significantly, Argyll exercised a steadily diminishing British influence in the wake of the regicide, which carried over into the 1650s.

A Covenanted King

As a prelude to the negotiations with Charles II that commenced at The Hague in March 1649, Lothian had accrued intelligence from the continent. There was widespread revulsion at the regicide, deep sympathy for the political plight of Charles, but a willingness to offer only diplomatic, not military, support. German princes in particular were intent on promoting reconstruction in the wake of the debilitating Thirty Years War, which had been concluded by the Peace of Westphalia in 1648.[2] With the Commonwealth triumphant in England and Ireland, the radical regime now in power in Scotland was realistically the new king's best hope to avenge his father and hold the regicides to account. Determined to shape negotiations from Edinburgh, Argyll wrote to the new king on 25 April 1649, saying: 'No earthly thing shall be dearer to me'. Argyll also hoped that Charles II would be moved by God to satisfy the faithful and humble desires of 'this kingdom and church'. These desires were emphatically laid out within three months. In addition to removing undesirable Royalists such as Montrose from his court in exile, Charles II must subscribe the Covenants, promote Presbyterian uniformity throughout his dominions according to the standards for faith, worship and polity laid down by the

---

2 NAS, Lothian Papers, GD 40/2/16/3–18, 32; TFA, Papers, TD 3756.

Westminster Assembly of Divines, and ratify all constitutional settlements in Kirk and State formerly condescended to by his father, Charles I. In return, the Covenanters would uphold royal government over democracy or any new model of government that may take root in England. They would also aid the king to recover his rightful authority in England and bring the regicides to justice. Argyll had ensured that the negotiations at The Hague were conducted by his trusted associates, headed by Cassillis. William Moray remained his main contact with the household of Queen Henrietta Maria. He was also determined to keep the French court onside, notwithstanding the political convulsions provoked by the Frondes since 1648; likewise the States General and house of Orange, notwithstanding the internal ructions also afflicting the United Provinces in 1649.[3]

Negotiations became protracted, basically because the predominantly English courtiers with Charles II did not trust the radical Covenanters in general and Argyll in particular. For their part, the radical Covenanters and the Kirk were determined to ensure that there would be no indemnity for Montrose and his followers, and that Charles must meet in full their prescribed conditions for a Covenanted King.[4] Despite the despatch of Scottish commissioners at regular intervals, and despite the Covenanters' stance being backed by both the French court and the States General, Charles II continued to stall negotiations. In October 1649, a Scottish judge, George Winram of Libberton, was sent first to Holland then to Jersey (the Channel Islands were still not under the control of the Commonwealth) to secure the king's consent to the Covenanters' conditions for his restoration. When Libberton reported back to the Committee of Estates four months later, the decision to continue negotiations generated considerable debate. Cassillis and Wariston were pitted against Argyll and Loudoun. The latter pair, who favoured continuing, had been discreetly mobilising support in Holland through Lauderdale and other exiled Engagers. They were aided by the Duke of Lennox and Richmond within Royalist circles in the British Isles. The Marquess also enjoyed the confidence of former Royalist commander, William Cavendish, 1st Marquis of Newcastle, then exiled in the Netherlands. Even though the commissioners for the Kirk

---

3 BL, Correspondence of R. Lang, Secretary of State, 1649–61, Add.MSS 37,047, fo.22 and Royal and Noble Autographs, 1646–1768, Add.MSS 19,399, fo.70; HL, Loudoun Scottish Collection, box 38/LO 1648; Balfour, *HW*, III, p. 417; *The Proceedings of the Commissioners of the Church and Kingdom of Scotland with His Majestie at the Hague* (Edinburgh, 1649). Argyll, who had taken the honours of Scotland into temporary custody in the wake of the regicide, delivered back the Crown, sceptre and sword for safekeeping in Edinburgh Castle by 9 August (ICA, Argyll Transcripts, XII, no 413).

4 BL, Holme Hall Papers, vol. I, 1518–1773, Add.MSS 40,132, ff.1–5; Clarendon, *History*, pp. 707–11, 737–40; Whitelock, *Memorials*, III, pp. 153–4; Woolrych, *Britain in Revolution*, pp. 461–2.

opposed further deliberations, negotiations were continued by a plurality of voices on 12 February.[5]

Protracted negotiations were discomfiting Royalists as well as Covenanters in Scotland. Iain Lom, the Gaelic polemicist, reprimanded Charles II for his tardiness in returning from exile as the monarchy and the nobility were marginalised by the radical regime, while the English regicides were threatening Scotland's independence:

> Ach a Theàrlaich òig Stiùbhairt,
> 'S bochd an dùsal a th'agad,
> On is fhada gun sùnnd thu,
> 'S còir do dhùsgadh o d'chadal;
> Ma tha t'aire gu dìlinn
> Air do rìoghachd a thagradh,
> Na leig dhìot 'san droch uair i
> Ma tha cruadal air t'aignidh.[6]

[But, young Charles Stuart, deplorable is this slumber of yours; since you have long been listless you ought to be awakened from your sleep. If you have any intention whatsoever of claiming your kingdom, do not abandon it in an evil hour if there is any hardihood in your spirit.]

Charles II's tardiness can only in part be attributed to the aversion of courtiers and polemicists towards the Covenanting Movement. He persisted with the vain hope that a Royalist coalition could be reforged in Ireland, with international support from Portugal. Although he did not depart for exile in France until December 1650, Ormond had already lost credibility among the Catholic Confederates by the death of Owen Roe O'Neill in November 1649. In the meantime, Charles II effectively sacrificed an attempt by Montrose to rekindle Royalist fortunes in Scotland with Scandinavian backing through the Orkney Isles. In March 1650, Montrose replicated the unco-ordinated guerrilla campaigns mounted by himself and other Royalists in the north of Scotland after his defeat at Philiphaugh in September 1645. After a decisive victory for the Covenanters at Carbisdale in Sutherland on 27 April, Montrose was taken to Edinburgh, where he was driven to the Tolbooth in the hangman's cart, with Argyll a discreet but hardly discontented onlooker from a tenement in the High Street.[7]

5 HL, Loudoun Scottish Collection, box 45/LO 10397; Balfour, *HW*, IV, p. 2; *LJB*, III, p. 524; *CAL*, II, pp. 252–5, 258–9, 266–7, 347–8; Stevenson, *Revolution and Counter-Revolution*, pp. 148–58.

6 *Orain Iain Luim*, pp. 50–3.

7 Anon., *The Scots Remonstrance or Declaration* (London, 1650); BL, Nicholas Papers, Egerton MS 2542, ff.17–19 and T. Astle, Historical Collections, 1642–1769, Add.MSS 34,713, ff.5–6;

Argyll abstained from taking any formal part in the parliamentary proceedings that determined the fate of Montrose. Nevertheless, he took considerable satisfaction from the fatal dilemma in which his Royalist opponent was placed. If Montrose admitted that he was commissioned by Charles II, he would implicate the king in his treachery, which would imperil the negotiations about to be concluded at Breda. But if he did not seek to vindicate his campaign as a Royalist endeavour, he was giving himself up to summary justice as a failed rebel. Already declared a traitor, Montrose was hanged at the market cross on 21 May. Three days later, Argyll reported with some satisfaction to the Scottish Estates that Lothian, in his new capacity as Secretary of State, had received a letter from Charles II which stated that he was 'in no way sorry' that Montrose had been defeated.[8] Charles had not only compromised his credibility with Sweden and Denmark-Norway, but his disowning of Montrose raised huge doubts about his own trustworthiness in supporting a patriotic accommodation in Scotland.[9]

Before news of Carbisdale had reached Charles II, he acceded to the demands of the Scottish commissioners on 1 May 1650 while at Breda, at the court of his brother-in-law, William II of Orange. Charles was now committed to the radical prescriptions for a Covenanted King. The Scottish Estates insisted on an added proviso on 17 May. Help to recover his position in England and Ireland did not bind the Covenanters to wage war for him unless and until this was judged lawful and necessary by the Scottish Estates and the general assembly of the Kirk. Charles reluctantly accepted all conditions but held off subscribing the Covenants until he arrived at Garmouth on Speyside on 23 June. Returning from exile with Charles II were leading Engagers, such as Lauderdale, Traquair and Lanark, now 2nd Duke of Hamilton. Their presence, along with some English Royalists, reignited the debate among the radicals for a more thorough purge of the army to rid it of malignant influences. Argyll was readily accepted as leader of the committee which was given the responsibility of purging both

---

Wishart, *Memoirs*, pp. 277, 288; BOU, Carte papers, 1636–52. Ireland, MS Carte, 65 ff.485–6. While some of Montrose's officers followed him to the scaffold, the bulk of the captured troops were sent into French service; 40 men with families from Orkney were sent home, but 18 were pressed into indentured service – 12 as fishermen for Argyll and Sir David Leslie and the remainder as lead miners for Sir James Hope of Hopetoun .

8 Balfour, *HW*, IV, 18–19, 25, 32; *CAL*, II, pp. 262–3; Whitelock, *Memorials*, III, p. 197; Cowan, *Montrose*, pp. 276–301; Willcock, *The Great Marquess*, pp. 233–9. Having been denied a pardon for Montrose, Charles II sent him an equivocal directive to lay down his arms on 3 May. This directive was communicated to Sir William Fleming, who was probably also the courier of the letter to Lothian.

9 Murdoch, *Britain, Denmark-Norway and the House of Stuart*, pp. 150–9; Grosjean, *An Unofficial Alliance*, pp. 221–7; *CAL*, II, pp. 310–13.

the Army and the entourage of Charles II from late June. More intent on facilitating a patriotic accommodation that carried a British resonance than purging for party advantage, Argyll moved slowly. But he was unable to defer calls for the removal of malignant influences about the king. Lauderdale, Traquair and Lanark discreetly retired from public life.

On 4 July, the final round of negotiations with the king was ratified as the Treaty of Breda; his coronation was set for August. Argyll was shrewd enough to ensure that Charles II conceded an indemnity for all past actions by the Covenanting Movement over the last ten years. This complemented the indemnity that Charles I had been obliged to concede from the outbreak of the revolution in 1638 until the finalising of the constitutional settlement in 1641. With parliament prorogued, a Committee of Estates was appointed to advise Charles II on his government of Scotland. In practice, Charles was lodged at Falkland Palace in Fife, with Lord Lorne installed as his chief bodyguard. He was given no meaningful part in determining affairs of state. The radical leadership as well as the Kirk were apprehensive about his popularity, particularly if he was allowed to come to Edinburgh and, more especially, if he was given free access to an Army not yet fully purged. Plans for his coronation were shelved, however, when a belligerent Cromwell crossed the Border on 22 July.[10]

Argyll's motives in being the prime mover in bringing over Charles II became the subject of intense public scrutiny as Cromwell moved against Scotland. The Marquess was purportedly intent on preventing his punishment for compliance in the regicide. Others of a more moderate disposition considered that he acted chiefly out of ambition to be the dominant if not the sole royal advisor in Scotland. Certainly, Argyll had used his political influence within the exiled household of Queen Henrietta Maria and at the French court, through his strong personal links with Mathieu de Montereul as the Edinburgh resident, to help persuade Charles II to ally with the radical Covenanters. Most pertinently, perhaps, Argyll was commended for his determination to maintain monarchy not just within Scotland, but to sustain the Stuarts as a British dynasty, notwithstanding the faults of Charles I. Conversely, the regicides also regarded Argyll as

10 BL, Correspondence of R. Lang, Secretary of State, 1649–61, Add.MSS 37,047, ff.149, 152, 158; DH, Loudoun Deeds, bundle 1/4; Balfour, *HW*, IV, p. 86; *CAL*, II, pp. 265–6, 269–71, 280–97; Stevenson, *Revolution and Counter-Revolution*, pp. 159–72; Young, *The Scottish Parliament*, pp. 244–61. Particularly targeted for removal from the king's entourage were George Villiers, 2nd Duke of Buckingham, Sir James Montgomerie of Skelmorlie and Sir John Henderson. All three had been involved in mobilising support for the Britannic Engagement at home and abroad. Buckingham was also vilified for his name as the son of Charles I's problematic adviser assassinated in 1628. Nevertheless, as the 2nd Duke was now a favourite of Charles II, he remained in his entourage. Montgomerie of Skelmorlie and Henderson were similarly favoured as the former was Argyll's nephew and the latter his client and former foreign correspondent.

the radical least inclined to war with the English Commonwealth. In February 1650, the Marquess had been promised £10,000 sterling with interest by the Rump Parliament, as the major proportion of the £15,000 he was due from the £200,000 sterling still owed to the Covenanters for the transfer of the king at the outset of 1647; the same portion that the Long Parliament assigned him in June 1648 when he withheld support from the Britannic Engagement.[11] But Argyll's motivation transcended both power plays and financial reimbursement. He remained committed to Covenanting imperatives that required permanent checks on monarchy in Kirk and State in Scotland, which would be upheld in the Stuart's other two kingdoms through British confederation. However, the Commonwealth favoured incorporation over a federative agenda for the three kingdoms. A considerable head of steam was building up within the New Model Army to move against the Covenanters in Scotland once the conquest of Ireland was well underway.

When news of Cromwell's intent to march on Scotland first filtered through to the Scottish Estates at the outset of July, Argyll had taken considerable satisfaction that the Presbyterians in England had persuaded Fairfax to step down as commander of the New Model Army. Although hopes of British reconciliation had receded markedly in the wake of the regicide, Cromwell's offensive against the Covenants had a mixed press in England. Among Presbyterians, especially among the metropolitan core for whom Covenanting was the foundation of political authority, Cromwell was portrayed as the heir of Strafford in weakening Protestant solidarity, constitutional government and international resistance to Spanish hegemony in Europe and the Americas.[12] Among Independents, however, the Scottish Covenanters were now clearly marked out as enemies to the Commonwealth and the freeborn people of England. They rejected the published declaration that Charles II had made at Dunfermline in Fife on 16 August stating that he had acted righteously in accepting the Covenants. They likewise rejected the right of the Covenanters to deal with the king on behalf of the people of England and Ireland. The radicals around Argyll were now no better than the conservatives formerly around Hamilton in seeking to rerun

11 T. Astle, Historical Collections, 1642–1769, Add.MSS 34,713, ff.7–8; *LJB*, III, p. 99; Wishart, *Memoirs*, p. 291; Anon., *The Remonstrance or Declaration of the Levellers in Scotland* (London, 1650); ABDA, Argyll Papers, 40.481.
12 Balfour, *HW*, IV, p. 69; John Shawe, *Britannia Rediviva: of the Proper and Sovereign Remedy for the Healing and Recovering of these Three Distracted Nations* (London, 1649); Anon., *A brief narration of the mysteries of state carried on by the Spanish faction in England, since the reign of Queen Elizabeth to this day for supplanting of the magistracy and ministry, the laws of the land, and the religion of the Church of England* (London, 1651); E. Vernon, 'The Quarrel of the Covenant: The London Presbyterians and the Regicide' in Peacey ed., *The Regicides and the Execution of Charles I*, pp. 202–24.

the Britannic Engagement. Their defeat was vital to the establishment of a free state and represented the ultimate British phase of Gothic triumphalism over Royalists, Presbyterians and Levellers.[13]

Patriotic Accommodation

Having taken full advantage of the factional disarray among Royalists and Catholic Confederates to conquer Ireland, Cromwell was likewise able to exploit division within the Covenanting Movement to effect the occupation of Scotland. These divisions were immediately apparent with respect to troop levies and military strategy. Although the Covenanters had the military capacity to match and surpass the troops Cromwell brought with him to Scotland, levies were delayed by the ongoing controversy over the need to purge former Engagers and other malignants from the Army. With a chronic shortage of victuals throughout Scotland, the military command was undecided on whether the Army had the capacity to fight a pitched battle before the harvest. For Charles II, a diversionary raid into England was preferable to a lingering war in Scotland. In the event, purging was rigorously promoted by Wariston and his more radical associates in the Army and the Kirk. Carried out more thoroughly than either Argyll, Sir David Leslie or even Robert Douglas wished, purging deprived the Covenanting forces of several thousand men, albeit this was partly compensated by the return of reliable troops from Ireland and fresh recruits from Scots displaced from Ulster. When the Covenanters lined up against the New Model Army at Dunbar in East Lothian on 3 September 1650, they had almost double the forces, with 22,000 men to Cromwell's 11,000. However, aberrant leadership by Sir David Leslie, a lack of effective communication between officers and men, and political interference over troop deployment by the Committee of Estates turned military advantage into a rout. The majority of the Covenanting forces were either killed or captured. The errant capacity of the Covenanters to snatch defeat from the jaws of victory facilitated the Cromwellian occupation of a Scotland debilitated psychologically by Dunbar's seeming transference of divine favour to England.[14]

---

13 Marchmont Nedham, *The Case of the Common-Wealth of England Stated* (London, 1650); *The Answer of the Parliament of England to a Paper Entituled, A Declaration by the King's Majesty, To His Subjects of the Kingdoms of Scotland, England and Ireland* (London, 1650); Henry Parker, *Scotlands Holy War* (London, 1651); S. Kelsey, 'The Foundation of the Council of State' in Kyle and Peacey eds, *Parliament at Work*, pp. 129–48. The Independents' alliance with the Army found executive expression through the Council of State, which oversaw the military campaigns for the occupation of Scotland as of Ireland, organised a massive expansion of the Commonwealth navy, and conducted war with the Dutch from 1652 to 1654.

14 BL, T. Astle, Historical Collections, 1642–1769, Add.MSS 34,713, ff.3–4; *CAL*, II, pp. 274–7, 297–9; Stevenson, *Revolution and Counter-Revolution*, pp. 172–9.

Despite the shock of defeat and the urgency of maintaining the country upon a war footing, the Scottish predilection for ideological schism was unquenchable. The drive for radical purity in the wake of the Act of Classes had led to the internally damaging split between those that felt only the godly should fight for in Scotland and those who took the more pragmatic view that purging should not imperil national independence. Argyll, despite unfounded doubts about his commitment to Charles II, was firmly in the latter camp. The issue of purging the Army gained added force after Dunbar with the revival of the Western Association, essentially the forces that had participated in the radical protests first at Mauchline Moor then in the Whiggamore Raid. They were determined that further purging of the ungodly was necessary to win back divine favour. Their military leaders included Sir Andrew Ker and Major Archibald Strachan, associates of Argyll, who had been sent to assure Cromwell, in advance of his first sojourn to Scotland, that no treaty would be made at Stirling with the Engagers unless they relinquished power and disbanded their forces. Strachan had subsequently ambushed and captured Montrose in the spring of 1650.

The conviction of the Western Association, that Charles II was no more trustworthy than his father, was reinforced when the king removed himself from the protective custody of the Committee of Estates in Perth on 3 October. It did so in the hope of linking up with the forces of former Engagers and Royalists who were reportedly mobilising in the Highlands. Rather than pursue a military showdown, Charles returned to Covenanting custody within two days. Although the king expressed contrition to the Committee on 7 October, the episode became known as 'The Start', as he did gain access to all future dealings of the Estates. No less importantly, the former Engagers and Royalists who were prepared to mobilise on his behalf subscribed a 'Northern Band' stating their willingness to join the fight against Cromwell as a patriotic endeavour. While they affirmed their commitment to the king's person, monarchical authority and the royal prerogative, they were adamant that they would not compromise the Covenants and would uphold Presbyterianism and parliamentary privileges. These Northern Banders included former Engagers, such as Middleton (who had escaped from captivity in England), Seaforth (who had returned from exile in Holland with the king) and Sir George Munro (who had also come from Holland after giving up his command in Ireland). MacKenzie of Pluscardine, who had led the abortive rising in the spring of 1649, was also a signatory, as were two relatively youthful Royalists: John Murray, 29th Earl of Atholl and Lewis Gordon, son of Huntly and nephew of Argyll. Instead of being attacked by superior Covenanting forces, they were assured of an act of indemnity when Sir David Leslie accepted their surrender at Strathbogie in

Aberdeenshire on 4 November.[15]

Notwithstanding the endeavours of Argyll and Cassillis on behalf of the Committee of Estates, and Robert Douglas for the commission of the Kirk 'to solicit unity for the good of the kingdome', the anti-aristocratic Western Association was outraged both by 'The Start' and the subsequent leniency shown to the Northern Banders. Their gentlemen, commanders and ministers issued a Remonstrance on 17 October, which was presented to the Committee of Estates five days later. The Remonstrants, supported by such Covenanting ideologues as Wariston and Samuel Rutherford, were certainly correct in deeming Charles II unreliable. Their insistence that their duty to support a Covenanted King did not commit them unconditionally to a patently sinful Charles II was ideologically consistent with the Covenanting distinction between the person and the office of monarchy. While they were intent on expelling the New Model Army from Scotland, the Remonstrants were not prepared to invade England or meddle in the affairs of the Commonwealth to suit the ungodly purposes of Charles II. The Remonstrance provoked extensive discussions between the Committee of Estates and the commissioners of the Kirk that were not concluded until 25 November. Argyll lambasted the Remonstrants' insistence on pursuing their own campaign against Cromwell as opening up 'a breache for toleration and subversion of the government, both ecclesiastical and civil'. Although Wariston moved to distance himself from the Western Association, he along with Cassillis and Sir James Hope of Hopetoun held back from joining with Argyll, Lothian and Alexander Lindsay, Lord (soon to be 1st Earl of) Balcarres in having the conduct of the Remonstrants condemned by the Committee of Estates as divisive, scandalous and treasonable. Argyll took out his ire on Hopetoun, whom he condemned not only as a leading enemy to king and kingdom, but also as 'a maine plotter and contriver, assister and abaitter of all the mischiefee' that had happened to Scotland since the regicide.[16]

Although the commissioners of the Kirk reluctantly joined in the condemnation of the Remonstrance, the headstrong determination of the Western Association to pursue their own military campaign did not rid Scotland of the New Model Army. Instead, control of the country south of the Forth-Clyde was effectively conceded when Major-General John Lambert, who had been Cromwell's principal support in vanquishing the Engagers in 1648, crushed the Western Association at Hamilton in Lanarkshire on 1 December 1650. The

15 ICA, Argyll Letters (1638–85), A36/154; NAS, Fothringham of Murthly Castle MSS, GD 121/92/1; *CAL*, II, 300–3, 305–6, 317–18; *SPT*, I, pp. 163–4; *LJB*, III, pp. 106–9; Stevenson, *Revolution and Counter-Revolution*, pp. 117, 174–5, 180–6.
16 Balfour, *HW*, IV, pp. 92–109, 123, 141–60, 169–70, 173–8, 186; *LJB*, III, pp. 114–5, 119–22; *CAL*, II, 325–6; *A Source Book of Scottish History*, III, pp. 144–6.

response of the recalled Scottish Estates at Perth had already been predetermined when a Committee for the Affairs of the Army was constituted on 27 November. Dominated by Argyll and his closest political allies, this Committee was charged to effect a patriotic accommodation by unifying and strengthening as well as supplying the armed forces that were to reclaim and secure national independence. It was also empowered to deal with the commission of the Kirk to determine ceremonial matters for the delayed coronation of Charles II and, more controversially, the grounds for admitting or excluding troops, both officers and men, who were to participate in the impending patriotic war. After the Kirk's commissioners, with a substantial dissenting minority, had determined that all lawful means should be used to resist Cromwell and the regicides, the Scottish Estates passed a series of resolutions that readmitted leading Engagers into the Covenanting Army and left the door open for Royalists. Thus, the Act of Levy promoted by the Resolutioners 23 December led to the recall of Crawford-Lindsay, a noted target of the Act of Classes, as a colonel. The same rank was accorded to Atholl, who had been prominent in the 'Northern Band' three months earlier. Loudon took no part in the awarding of commissions once he realised that Engagers and Royalists were being favoured over Covenanting stalwarts. Nevertheless, Cassillis welcomed his brother-in-law, Hamilton, back into public life, a welcome later endorsed by Lothian after the 2nd Duke made due repentance to the Kirk for this part in the Britannic Engagement.[17]

The Resolutioners led by Argyll, and backed by Robert Douglas and Robert Baillie in the Kirk, could claim with equal validity to the Remonstrants that they too adhered to Covenanting principles. The Resolutioners, who still constituted the radical majority, countered the Remonstrants' conditional support for monarchy with the curse of Meroz: that the pursuit of radical purity carried the danger of undefiled inactivity in the face of the external threat from Cromwell. Notwithstanding the demise of the Western Association, the success of the Resolutioners in the Scottish Estates and in the commission of the Kirk provoked protests from a group of ministers, some of whom, such as Samuel Rutherford and Patrick Gillespie, had cut their radical teeth as nonconforming conventiclers in shaping the Covenanting Movement (see Chapter 5). They were zealously supported by James Guthry, who had protested against the proclamation of Charles II as King of Great Britain and Ireland in the wake of the regicide, as his fitness to govern had yet to be proved. However, not all conventiclers or their fellow travellers became Protestors. David Dickson, the prime

---

17 NAS, Hamilton Papers, GD 406/1/2501, 2505, /2507, /2512, /4044; DH, Loudoun, Deeds, bundle 2/6; BOU, Carte Papers, 1636–52. Ireland, MS Carte 65, ff.577–8; CAL, II, pp. 323–4; Young, *The Scottish Parliament*, pp. 262–75.

mover along with Alexander Henderson in the petitions of the clergy in 1637, strongly supported the Resolutioners. Such was the righteous rage of the Protestors and the vehemence of their schismatic division with the Resolutioners over the patriotic accommodation that general assemblies became partisan rather than national courts of the Kirk throughout the 1650s.[18]

Nonetheless, the patriotic accommodation of Resolutioners, former Engagers and Royalists was consolidated in fundamentalist terms by the coronation of Charles II at Scone, Perthshire, as King of Great Britain and Ireland on 1 January 1651. Robert Douglas, who preached for two hours, reminded Charles II that his compulsory subscription of the Covenants was to deny absolutism, for 'total government is not upon a king'. The religious and constitutional imperatives of Covenanting were reaffirmed, the power to compel monarchy exercised by the political nation was endorsed, and the vesting of the right of resistance in 'the estates of a land' was reasserted. Prior to his coronation, the king had ratified all Covenanting legislation since the constitutional settlement of 1641, except that implemented by the Engagers in 1648. Argyll placed the crown on the monarch's head and installed him on his throne. The triumph of the radical mainstream was seemingly complete. But this triumph, both personally and politically, was more symbolic than substantial.[19]

On 24 September, Charles II had apparently agreed to create Argyll a duke, in recognition of his political pre-eminence within Scotland, whenever it suited the Marquess. The offer of a dukedom was followed up in January 1651 by Charles II referring to his mother a proposal for his marriage to Anna, eldest of the four daughters of Argyll. He did so confident that Queen Henrietta Maria would counsel against it. He was not disappointed. In the interim, Charles II was increasingly discomfited by the sombre piety of Argyll and his penchant for extempore and protracted prayer. More importantly, the radical sheet anchors around Argyll were loosening, but were not yet entirely lost. Among his principal advisers in the Scottish Estates, only Robert Barclay, the burgess for Irvine, held firm. The support of Wariston for the gentry, Loudoun and even Lothian for the nobility could no longer be taken for granted. The radical dominance of the reconstituted Committee of Estates was diluted and no longer assured as the rehabilitation of former Engagers and Royalists was stepped up.[20]

18 NAS, Hamilton Papers, GD 406/1/515/3/2; *Records of the Commissions of the General Assemblies for the Years 1650–52*, J. Christie ed. (Edinburgh, 1909), pp. 557–62; *Register of the Consultations of the Ministers of Edinburgh, and some other Brethren of the Ministry, 1652–60*, J. Christie ed., 2vols (Edinburgh, 1921 and 30), I, pp. 292–340 and II, pp. 143–75; Stevenson, *Revolution and Counter-Revolution*, pp. 132, 187–90, 194–5, 203–4.

19 *The Covenants and the Covenanters*, J. Kerr ed. (Edinburgh, 1896), pp. 348–98; Nicoll, *Diary*, pp. 41–7; Willcock, *The Great Marquess*, pp. 253, 259–67.

20 BL, Hardwicke papers, vol.CCCXC, Historical Collections, 1567–1720, Add.MSS 35,838, fo.177

When the Scottish Estates briefly resumed proceedings at Perth in March 1651, the shifting political balance was signposted when approval was given for a new Committee for Managing the Affairs of the Army, notwithstanding vociferous and prolonged dissent led by Argyll, Loudoun, Cassillis and Lothian. They could no longer rely on wholehearted support from the gentry and burgesses who placed the patriotic interest before party politics. The dominance of former Engagers and Royalists on this Committee, which was to be distinct from the Committee of Estates, was consolidated by the effective suspension of the Acts of Classes against the Royalists in 1646 and against the Engagers in 1649. By April, the Committee of Estates had been subsumed within the Committee for Managing the Affairs of the Army. When the Scottish Estates resumed briefly at the onset of summer, their main business was the formal repeal of both Acts of Classes, which was accomplished on 2 June. The next day, the Remonstrance made by the Western Association in October 1650 was condemned with the threat that any who did not renounce it would be treated a seditious; only Argyll, Cassillis, Loudoun, Robert Barclay and two other burgesses dissented from this impolitic measure. The Kirk's permission was still required before any former Engager or Royalist could be admitted back into public life. Nevertheless, the principal commands of the army, for the recovery of Scotland south of the Forth-Clyde, had already been assigned, predominantly to former Engagers and Royalist. As clans who served under Montrose were being recruited, the New Model Army relentlessly pressed into Fife and threatened Tayside. [21]

Ongoing military preparations were complemented by overtures to France, to the United Provinces, to the Emperor and the German Princes, to Denmark and Sweden, and to Poland and even Courland, which recalled past beneficial diplomatic, military and commercial links to Scotland. Overseas aid for the restoration of Britannic monarchy was not accomplished through these channels. The only effective means of supplying arms, ammunition and other military assistance was through Scottish commercial networks, primarily in the United

and Autographs of King Charles the First and Second, Egerton MS 1533, fo.20; Balfour, *HW*, IV, pp. 223, 242, 247; *LJB*, III, pp. 128, 133–4, 140, 160, 167, 171; Clarendon, *History*, pp. 758–9. Anna, who never married, received the largest portion (£1,333) of the annual pensions amounting to £3,600 which the Marquess apportioned to his daughters from the revenues of his Argyllshire estates in March 1652. His other daughters were called Marie, Jean and Isobell. However, the financial difficulties of the Marquess led to this arrangement being shifted in October 1653 towards discretionary payments from the £60,000 owed by the late Sir Hector Maclean of Duart. Anna was to have the largest individual claim on this sum (over £25,000 with accruing interest) on her father's death. However, she was to die within two years of her father in 1663. At the same time, Robert Barclay continued to receive an annual pension of £367 from Argyll (ICA, Argyll Transcripts, XIII, nos 114, 169, 171–2, 176).

21 TFA, Papers, TD 986; *Government under the Covenanters*, pp. 105–73; Whitelock, *Memorials*, III, p. 309; Young, *The Scottish Parliament*, pp. 275–91.

Provinces and France. However, such fundraising for the patriotic accommodation was underwritten primarily by Argyll and Lothian – not by former Engagers and Royalists.[22] Moreover, Scottish resistance to the Cromwellian occupation was debilitated by sheer physical and financial exhaustion as well as territorial devastation.

The Committee for Managing the Affairs of the Army experienced particular difficulties in persuading chiefs and leading clan gentry in the *Gàidhealtachd* to support the patriotic accommodation. The pervasive influence of the Marquess had ensured that territories of ClanCampbell in Argyll and the Perthshire Highlands continued to enjoy wholesale exemptions from public burdens and relief from private debts owed to Royalists. By way of contrast, troops were regularly quartered elsewhere in the Highlands to supply victuals, money and manpower and to expedite payments of forced loans as well as the cess, 'without regard to former exemptions' given to hard-pressed localities since 1648.[23] Notwithstanding affirmative action by the radical regime from 1649 that had exempted people providing quarter from paying cess, there was still no equitable system of compensation by the patriotic accommodation. Localities and individuals burdened with quartering were still subjected to prohibitive exactions and victimised by the disorderly behaviour of soldiers. Aggravating this situation was the tendency among some members of the landed classes to pass the physical and financial burden of quartering on to their tenantry under the pain of forced recruitment. The Kirk had not let this reprehensible situation go unchallenged. In October 1650, the Synod of Moray, which covered both Highland and Lowland communities, made it clear that tenants and labourers should not endure further suffering. Particular attention was drawn to those 'who have fair estates and put the whole burden of quarters upon the poore tenants'.[24]

The patriotic campaign against the occupying forces of the Commonwealth soon provided a salutary reminder that martial involvement was an expensive drain on manpower, notably among the clans. As in the civil war, losses of manpower caused townships to fall into disuse. The Macleans were among the west Highland clans warned off assisting Montrose in the spring of 1650 at the instigation of Argyll. However, Sir Hector Maclean of Duart did raise 1,000 clansmen for the patriotic accommodation. Around 700 were killed when the patriotic forces were decisively defeated by Lambert at Inverkeithing in Fife

---

22 *CAL*, II, pp. 314–5, 330–6, 351–4, 358–60.

23 *ACL*, III, pp. 166–9; *The Records of Invercauld, 1547–1828*, J.G. Mechie ed. (Aberdeen, 1901), pp. 237–8; ICA, bundle 17/53; ABDA, Argyll papers, 40.460; NAS, Breadalbane MSS, GD 112/1/563–6.

24 *Government under the Covenanters*, pp. 116, 140, 145–8, 164–5; NAS, Synod Records of Moray, 1646–68, CH 2/217/2, fo.173; *APS*, VI (2), pp. 56, 388 c.29, 464 c.194, 264 c.208, 620, 649.

on 20 July 1651; a loss which left insufficient men to till the soil on the Duart estates on the islands of Mull and Tiree and in mainland Morvern. The clan that would appear to have suffered the greatest casualties in the conclusive defeat at Worcester on 3 September 1651 was the one led by Rory MacLeod of Dunvegan. Such was the level of casualties among the 1,000 clansmen recruited from his estates on the islands of Skye and Harris, and in mainland Glenelg, that the ClanLeod was reputedly incapable of raising a fighting force for over a generation.[25]

The crushing of the Scottish forces by Cromwell at Worcester was the brutal outcome of a flawed decision to make a diversionary raid into England rather than prolong active resistance in Scotland. This erroneous British strategy can primarily be attributed to Charles II. But it also had the hallmarks of the military ineptitude that characterised the Britannic Engagement and the Royalist campaign that came unstuck at Philiphaugh. The patriotic forces were top heavy in their command structure. Although Leven had resigned on grounds of age and Sir David Leslie's generalship had been undermined at Dunbar, there was no accomplished alternative under whom Resolutioners, Engagers and Royalists could unite. Repetitive manoeuvres against Cromwell in central Scotland that summer had no clear purpose, were morale-sapping and encouraged wholesale desertions. When the patriotic forces marched for England, they chose – like Montrose in 1645 and the 1st Duke of Hamilton in 1648 – to pursue a north-west passage rather than move on Newcastle, which Leven had accomplished brilliantly in 1640. Charles II's maladroit sacrificing of Montrose in 1650 had so damaged his international credibility that he had even less diplomatic backing than Hamilton in 1648. Like the Engagers, the Army assembled for Charles II failed to gain assurances of support from Presbyterians and Royalists disaffected with the Commonwealth. James Stanley, Earl of Derby, did bring across to Lancashire a substantive force of Royalists who had taken refuge in the Isle of Man. But they effectively fought and lost a separate campaign, having no meaningful presence among the 13,000 Scots who took on about 31,000 troops of the New Model Army at Worcester, exactly one year after the debacle at Dunbar.[26]

Argyll, though he had not withdrawn from public life as in 1637 and 1648, was less than accommodating in his dealings with the former Engagers and

---

25 Macinnes, *Clanship, Commerce and the House of Stuart*, pp. 108–9; ICA, Argyll Transcripts, XIII, nos 28–32.

26 TFA, Papers, TD 4669; BL, Collection of Historical and Parliamentary Papers, 1620–1660, Egerton MS 1048, ff.134–41; BOU, Papers Relating to the Civil War, 1603–1660, MS Don.c.184, ff.132–3; NAS, Hamilton Papers, GD 406/1/2488–9, /5956. Among the Scots seriously wounded at Worcester was the 2nd Duke of Hamilton, who died five weeks later.

Royalists on the Committee for Managing the Affairs of the Army. Operating mainly from the Firth of Clyde, he was justly suspected of hindering rather than expediting the recruitment of troops from the western seaboard. Having strengthened the fortifications at his stronghold at Rosneath in Dunbartonshire, he provided secure lodgings at Carrick Castle in Lochgoilhead, Argyllshire for the charter chests of family and friends among the landed elite as of the royal burghs of Glasgow, Dumbarton and Stirling. Implacably opposed to further English intervention, neither he nor Lord Lorne participated in the march to Worcester which fatally undermined Scottish independence. On the grounds that that his wife was seriously ill, the participation of Argyll was actually excused by Charles II.[27] The Marquess was not present at Alyth in Perthshire on 28 August, when leading members of the Committee of Estates, which had remained in Scotland, were surprised and captured by Lieutenant-General George Monck, who went on to sack Dundee three days later. This atrocity scarred the occupation of Scotland as that of Drogheda and Wexford had stigmatised the Cromwellian conquest of Ireland.[28]

Confident that the Scots would embrace the civil and religious liberties of the Commonwealth, English commentators had nevertheless anticipated that Argyll would link up with Balcarres and Lewis Gordon, who had been restored as 3rd Marquess Huntly in March, to prevent Cromwell completing his occupation of Scotland. With no prospect of relief from France or any further release of Scottish troops from Swedish and Dutch service, Argyll opted instead to open up lines of communication with Monck to secure a truce and thus prevent further bloodshed. At the same time, the Marquess supported the endeavours of Loudoun to sustain the Committee of Estates as the executive power in the north until the Scottish Estates could be reconvened. However, Monck had made clear to Argyll that he could not attain a truce unless he prevented the recall of the Scottish Estates on Lochtayside in November. In this he acquiesced, though he did continue as an active member of the commission of the Kirk, on the side of the Resolutioners until December.[29] Argyll was excluded from the peace

27 ICA, Argyll Letters (1638–85), A36/155–61 and Miscellaneous Argyll Letters, ff.12, 16, 19–20, 23, 31, 88 and Miscellaneous Seventeenth Century Papers, bundle 17/53; CAL, II, p. 359; Willcock, *The Great Marquess*, pp. 273–4. The Marchioness was actually helping with the running of the Argyll estates as the Scottish forces were being defeated at Worcester. However, Lord Neill Campbell, the second son of the Marquess, was reported to have been unwell in April.

28 DH, Loudoun Papers, A15/13; ACA, Aberdeen Council Register, vol. LIII, pp. 304, 311–12, 322–4; *Dumbarton Common Good Accounts*, p. 181; Balfour, *HW*, IV, pp. 316–17.

29 Anon., *Strange Newes from the King of Scots* (London, 1651); Anon., *The King of Scots Message to the Northern Counties, and his Sister the Princess of Orange* (London, 1651); BL, Collection of Historical and Parliamentary Papers, 1620–1660, Egerton MS 1048, fo.14; NAS, William Clark MSS. Diary, RH4/127/11/7–8; Whitelock, *Memorials*, III, pp. 343–4, 360, 362–8, 375.

negotiations. Nevertheless the Marquess, who had retired to his family seat at Inveraray Castle, did not come to terms with occupying forces for another eight months. Even then guerrilla resistance continued in the Highlands, energetically led by Ewen Cameron of Lochiel, a former ward of Argyll but an indefatigable Royalist.[30]

Negotiated Incorporation

The failure of Charles II's patriotic accommodation with the Scots deprived him of any foreseeable prospect of power in the three kingdoms and made him a dependent pensioner rather than an independent player among European states.[31] Notwithstanding Cromwell's personal vexation that Scotland remained attached to the exiled Stuart dynasty, Scotland, unlike Ireland, was not annexed to the Commonwealth. Consent was sought through the Tender of Incorporation. The Rump Parliament despatched commissioners headed by Oliver St John and Henry Vane the younger on the civil side, and Major-General John Lambert and Lieutenant-General George Monck for the military in November 1651. Charged to order the affairs of Scotland, the commissioners were in place by January 1652. They instructed the constituent shires and royal burghs of Scotland to elect two deputies to come to Dalkeith to give their assent to union prior to their formal subscription of the Tender at Edinburgh by March.[32] The Scottish deputies were certainly not negotiating from a position of equality. Yet these proceedings were not simply the imposition of an English settlement.[33]

The authorisation granted to the Scottish deputies, as 'persons of integritie and good affection to the wealfaire and peace of this Island', allowed for a measure of latitude. Archibald Campbell of Drumsynie, Argyll's main agent for his custodial operations on the Firth of Clyde, did have his commission for Argyllshire rescinded. Despite this direct rebuff to the Marquess, the remaining

---

30 ICA, Miscellaneous Argyll Letters, ff.21, 67; Whitelock, *Memorials*, III, pp. 396, 439–40, 448; *Memoirs of Sir Ewen Cameron of Lochiel*, J. Macknight ed. (Edinburgh, 1842), pp. 106–43.

31 DR, TKUA, Alm.Del I Indtil 1670, 'Latina' vol. 13 (1652–61), ff.74–5, 89, 103, 107–8, 278, 338–9; Whitelock, *Memorials*, III, pp. 207–11.

32 BL, Collection of Historical and Parliamentary Papers 1620–1660, Egerton MS 1048, ff.142–8; ACA, Aberdeen Council Register, vol. LIII, pp. 345–6, 348, 350, 353–5; DCA, Council Book Dundee, IV, ff.243–4, 246; Woolrych, *Britain in Revolution, 1625–1660*, pp. 500–1, 552–3, 567–73, 589–92; Macinnes, *The British Revolution, 1629–1660*, pp. 199–205.

33 F.D. Dow, *Cromwellian Scotland, 1651–1660* (Edinburgh, 1979), pp. 30–6; K.M. Brown, *Kingdom or Province? Scotland and the Regal Union, 1603–1715* (London, 1992), pp. 136–7. As the military balance swung in favour of the Commonwealth during the first Anglo-Dutch war of 1652–54, original English schemes for a union with the United Provinces based on a federation of equals gave way to plans for incorporation, in which the Dutch were to be offered similar terms to the Scots (S. Pincus, *Protestantism and Patriotism: Ideologies and the Making of English Foreign Policy, 1650–1668* (Cambridge, 1996), pp. 51–79).

deputies for the shires of Argyll, along with those for Midlothian and Selkirk, were instructed to 'treat, reason and debate, but not to conclude' until they reported back their proceedings at Dalkeith. This reserved consent duly affected the formal subscription of the Tender of Incorporation at Edinburgh.[34] Less than half the shires and burghs fully subscribed to Scottish incorporation into the Commonwealth. Conversely, only three shires (Renfrew, Ayr and Kirkcudbright) and three burghs (Renfrew, Ayr and Irvine) from the radical Covenanting south-west made no effort to participate in the process. For the majority of deputies who complied, their position varied from *de facto* acceptance to conditional acquiesce that reserved prior commitment to the Covenants. The twenty-one deputies (fourteen from the shires, seven from the burghs) summoned to England for further negotiations complied only after express permission had been attained from the exiled Charles II.[35]

Negotiations at Westminster lasted from October 1652 to April 1653. The Scottish deputies were made initially to feel as much supplicants as negotiators in their dealings with the English Committee on Union. Leading politicians and army officers, most notably Lord General Oliver Cromwell, supplemented this Committee, which included most of the commissioners sent to Scotland. Although they lacked the parity accorded in negotiating the Solemn League and Covenant, the Scots in the course of the negotiations duly gained a measure of recognition for their standing not as political clients from a dependent state, but as junior partners in union. The desire of the deputies to be constituted a standing committee for Scottish affairs was not conceded. Nevertheless, they did succeed in retaining Scots Law unscathed – a situation unchanged by the advent of the Protectorate in 1654; but they were not able to establish that sixty MPs should represent Scotland in the reconstituted Rump Parliament. Scotland, like Ireland, was to be represented by thirty MPs, a proportion determined by

---

34 DH, Loudoun Papers, bundle A15/2; ICA, Letters – Marquess's Period 1650–58, bundle 13/18 and Miscellaneous Argyll Letters, fo.33–9 and Argyll Transcripts, XIII, nos 89, 102; NAS, Breadalbane MSS, GD 112/1/568 and William Clarke MSS, RH 4/127/1/10; Anon., *The Antiquity of Englands Superiority over Scotland and The Equity of Incorporating Scotland or other Conquered Nations, into the Commonwealth of England* (London, 1652). Of the 31 Scottish shires, 28 sent deputies to assent to union at Dalkeith, but only 20 sent deputies to Edinburgh to subscribe the tender. No more than 15 deputies signed the commission for 21 deputies to continue detailed negotiations. Of the 58 royal burghs, 44 sent deputies to Dalkeith, but only 37 were represented at Edinburgh, where 34 deputies actually subscribed the tender. Only 25 signed the commission for the deputies to Westminster.

35 HL, Loudoun Scottish Collection, box 32, LO 9054; BL, Hardwicke Papers, vol. DXVI, Add. MSS 35,864, ff.1–12; *Scotland and the Commonwealth 1651–53*, C.H. Firth ed. (Edinburgh, 1895), pp. 15–185; Whitelock, *Memorials*, III, pp. 397, 406, 419. Charles II was now back in the United Provinces.

assessment and population. However, the actual distribution of Scottish seats was not settled until June 1654, when the Scottish shires were grouped to provide twenty constituencies and the burghs grouped into ten. There was also a similar delay in resolving associated issues on the extent of forfeitures and sequestrations, stabilising the currency, purging local government, administering justice without respect to heritable jurisdictions, and sweeping away feudal dependencies. Delay can be attributed partly to the changing political climate, but primarily to the lack of Scottish commitment to the Commonwealth.[36]

Just after the Committee on Union had concluded business, tensions with the New Model Army led to the Rump Parliament's replacement by the Nominated or Barebones Parliament in April 1653. The army was committed to the pursuit of radical reform in the interests of a godly Commonwealth. The Independent-dominated Rump Parliament was intent on conserving the propertied interest and promoting political stability in the absence of monarchy. Cromwell's inclination to side with the former yet sympathise with the latter promoted neither constitutional stability nor parity of interests. At the same time, the separate incorporations of first Ireland and then Scotland with England had not created a triple alliance of equal states. There was no place for either Ireland or Scotland when the 'Keepers of the Liberties of England' authenticated the process of government throughout the British Isles. The deliberate avoidance of Great Britain for this incorporative union denoted not only a chauvinistic disregarded for traditional Scottish defences against English overlordship, but an emphatic Gothic rejection of both the Stuart vision of Britannic Empire and Argyll's confederal conception of kingdoms united by Covenanting.[37]

Only two of the twenty-one deputies that had negotiated the Tender of Incorporation were among the five Scottish nominees to a parliament that lasted nine months before further pressure from the army led to Cromwell assuming executive power as Lord Protector. Although the union of Scotland and Ireland with England did receive legislative sanction under an ordinance of the Protectorate in April 1654, another three years were to elapse before

---

36 NAS, Anglo-Scottish Committee of Parliament appointed to confer with the deputies from Scotland: minute book, 14 October 1652– 8 April 1653, SP 25/138, pp. 3–64; BL, Letters and State Papers: Birch Collection, Add.MSS 4158, ff.101–3; TFA, Papers, TD 3760; *The Cromwellian Union 1651-52*, C.S. Terry ed. (Edinburgh, 1902), pp. 11–184. The quorum of 60 proposed for the reconstituted Rump Parliament technically allowed parliament to function without English MPs.

37 *The Clarke Papers*, III, pp. 22, 81–2, 96; IV, pp. 49–55; Whitelock, *Memorials*, III, pp. 392–3, 410, 414–5, 419; [M.H.], *The History of the Union of the Four Famous Kingdoms of England, Wales, Scotland and Ireland* (London, 1660); S. Kelsey 'Unkingship' in Coward ed., *A Companion to Stuart Britain*, pp. 331–49; B. Coward, *The Cromwellian Protectorate, 1653-59* (Manchester, 2002), pp. 155–6.

union was embedded in statute. Only twenty-one constituencies actually returned members to serve for Scotland in September 1654, of whom nine were non-Scottish military or civil administrators.[38] As evident from their refusal to serve as deputies or MPs, the vast majority of Covenanters, Protestors and Resolutioners remained as opposed to the Protectorate as they had been to the Commonwealth. Indeed, prior to the conclusion of negotiations in April 1653, the Scottish deputies had attested that there were several assemblies in Edinburgh and elsewhere of disaffected persons, intent on 'keeping off the hearts of the people of Scotland from this Union'. In essence, the Commonwealth and Protectorate were labels of convenience for the reassertion of English hegemony in the guise of republicanism.[39]

Active collaboration with the Cromwellian regime was confined to a radical handful in Scotland. Notwithstanding the appeal of sectarian pluralism in Edinburgh and Aberdeen, those of an Independent, Baptist or Quaker persuasion tended to be clustered around the garrisons of the New Model Army.[40] Presbyterian dominance in Scotland was not substantively challenged by the introduction of toleration by the Tender of Incorporation. Nor was this dominance undermined by the Resolutioner-Protestor controversy; albeit those actively prepared to collaborate, such as Johnston of Wariston, tended to be drawn from the latter grouping. Collaborators provided a minority Scottish presence on the Commission for the Administration of Justice, which had replaced the English Commissioners as the civil government of Scotland from April 1652; and, subsequently, on the devolved Scottish Council instituted under the Protectorate in May 1655. Sharing British apocalyptic visions of world reordering, some, like Sir James Hope of Hopetoun, sought Cromwellian backing to carry through the social restructuring instigated in the anti-aristocratic parliament of 1649. However, they became estranged by the occupying regime's ineffective imple-

---

38 Young, *The Scottish Parliament*, pp. 297–99; TFA, Papers, TD 3758–60; BL, Maitland and Lauderdale Papers, 1532–1688, Add.MSS 35,125, fo.54. The Scottish MPs were rigorously vetted to ensure not only their current loyalty to the Protectorate, but also that their past political activity had not been tainted by subscription to the Britannic Engagement. The process of political incorporation lacked formal parliamentary warrant other than for two years between April 1657 and May 1659.

39 TNA, Anglo-Scottish Committee of Parliament, SP 25/138, pp. 62–3; D. Hirst, 'The English Republic and the Meaning of Britain' in B. Bradshaw and J. Morrill eds, *The British Problem, c.1534–1707: State Formation in the Atlantic Archipelago* (Basingstoke, 1996), pp. 192–219.

40 DH, Loudoun Papers, bundle 1/8; G. DesBrisay, 'Catholics, Quakers and Religious Prosecution in Restoration Aberdeen', *Innes Review*, 37 (1966), pp. 136–68; R.S. Spurlock, '"Anie Gospel Way": Religious Diversity in Interregnum Scotland', *RSCHS*, 37 (2007), pp. 89–120. Scottish Presbyterians took advantage of toleration to spread significantly in Ireland during the 1650s: see K.M. MacKenzie, 'Presbyterian Church Government and the "Covenanted interest" in the Three Kingdoms, 1649–1660' (University of Aberdeen, PhD thesis, 2008).

mentation of the radical legislative programme that had been truncated by the patriotic accommodation.[41]

Notwithstanding his strained but ongoing ties to Johnson of Wariston, Argyll cannot easily be placed among the thin ranks of Cromwellian collaborators. From the outset of the Cromwellian occupation, the chief of ClanCampbell and his associates in Argyllshire had sought to buy time to promote recovery from the devastations of civil war. In delaying his consent to the incorporation of Scotland within the Commonwealth, Argyll again resorted to medical pretexts, claiming that his movements were hampered by problems with his gallstones. Nevertheless, the Marquess was intent on negotiating from a position of strength to uphold Presbyterianism in the national interest over sectarian toleration, and to affirm the British vitality of the Solemn League and Covenant.[42] Accordingly, as the negotiations for incorporation were still progressing at Westminster, Argyll summoned a meeting of ClanCampbell and their associates, along with his allies and clients in the western shires, to meet at Cardross in Dunbartonshire on 4 April 1651. There, they were reported to have drawn up 'a new League and Confederacy against the English'. The fears of the occupying forces that Argyll and his Scottish confederates were planning an armed insurrection were overstated. However, they were certainly intent on restricting the number of Cromwellian garrisons and the incidence of military quartering on their territories. In effect, Argyll had re-established a Western Association north of the Clyde that would negotiate with the Commonwealth on its own terms; terms that were not necessarily in the national interest.[43]

Having negotiated a package of concessions as early as April 1652, the Marquess and his confederates successfully resorted to arms in August to secure a favourable revision of terms from Major-General Richard Deane. While they agreed to pay their proportional share of cess, they systematically opposed Cromwellian exactions of this monthly maintenance, which took no account of past damages, and later lobbied persistently against the general revalua-

---

41 DH, Loudoun Deeds, bundle 2/6; *LJB*, III, p. 430; A.H. Williamson, 'Union with England Traditional, Union with England Radical: Sir James Hope and the Mid-Seventeenth Century British State', *EHR*, 110 (1995), pp. 303–12.

42 ICA, Argyll Letters (1638–85), A36/163–4 and Miscellaneous Argyll Papers, fo.5; ABDA, Argyll Papers, 40.173; *SPT*, I, pp. 205–6, 514–15; NLS, Halkett of Pitfirrane Papers, MS 6408/91, /93, /103; Willcock, *The Great Marquess*, pp. 281–5

43 Anon., *A Letter Sent from the Marquess of Argyle to the King of Scots* (London, 1652); Whitelock, *Memorials*, III, pp. 375, 382, 384, 407, 409–10, 419, 439, 442–3, 448, 451, 453–4, 458; Balfour, *HW*, IV, p. 350; Nicoll, *Diary*, pp. 95–6, 100. Perhaps as a complement to Argyll's endeavour, Cassillis was attempting by October 1652 to continue the meetings of the shire gentry of Ayr that had elected deputies to negotiate the Tender of Incorporation. His excuse was the need to reimburse himself and his fellow commissioners for the money expended during their negotiations with Charles II in the United Provinces (HL, Loudoun Scottish Collection, LO/9054).

tion of tax liabilities imposed in 1653. The Marquess, whose estates were to be free of sequestration or molestation by the occupying forces, was accorded a cess rebate for Argyllshire on condition that he agreed to live peaceably and quietly and 'neither directlie or indirectlie act or contrive anything' to the prejudice of the Commonwealth. He was not expected to do anything that infringed his Presbyterian conscience. The only garrisons to be permitted in Argyllshire were at Dunstaffnage and Dunolly on the Firth of Lorne. Both were to be maintained on sufferance and allowed minimum interaction with the local people. Although no specific reference was made to his regalian powers, Argyll was allowed to retain and exercise his extensive heritable jurisdiction.[44] Indeed, this accord became the subsequent model for Monck's agreements with chiefs and landlords, who had found it difficult to devise effective coping strategies to circumvent forfeitures, sequestrations and rigorous but discriminatory fines for past resistance to Cromwellian occupation. In practice, the Marquess consistently opposed gratuitous violence towards the occupying forces. Nevertheless, English commentators continued to view Argyll's commitment to the Commonwealth as that of enigmatic equivocation. Indeed, his relationship with the Cromwellian regime was more that of a political trimmer than a wholehearted collaborator.[45]

Although he had not abandoned his British ideals, the Marquess was clearly reverting to type as clan chief and Scottish magnate. This was immediately apparent in the settlement Argyll enforced on his heavily indebted nephew, Lewis Gordon, Marquess of Huntly, who had hoped for protection after he made his own accord with the Cromwellian forces at the outset of 1652.[46] Initial arbitration between friends and families on both sides having proved inconclusive,

---

44 NLS, Halkett of Pitfirrane Papers, MS 6408/92; BL, Papers of General Desborough, 1651–1660, Egerton MS 2519, ff.19, 21, 23, 25 and Miscellaneous Letters and Papers, Add.MSS 41,295, ff.129–30; ICA, Argyll Letters (1638–85), A36/166 and Letters – Marquess's Period, 1650–1658, bundle 13/29; NAS, William Clarke MSS, RH 4/127/1/12. The full extent of Argyll's military showdown with Cromwellian forces in 1652 was only admitted during the endeavours of the military command in Scotland to have him excluded from the 1659 parliament.

45 HL, Loudoun Scottish Collection, box 37/LO 9201; *Scotland and the Protectorate*, C.H. Firth ed. (Edinburgh, 1899), pp. 147–8, 226, 270, 272–6, 286, 303, 321; A. Woolrych, *Commonwealth to Protectorate* (Oxford, 1986), p. 298. The only significant difference with subsequent compacts between Monck and the landed elite was the sureties required. The landed elite were bound over for sums of money ranging from £6,000 to 10,000 sterling (£12,000–72,000), whereas Argyll and his son Lorne were expected to make themselves available as hostages in England if required. The varying success of the coping strategies of the landed elite is covered extensively in D.J. Menarry, 'The Irish and Scottish Landed Elites from Regicide to Restoration' (University of Aberdeen, PhD thesis, 2001).

46 NLS, Halkett of Pitfirrane Papers, MS 6408/83, /100; ICA, Miscellaneous Seventeenth Century Papers, bundles 17/52, 176/12 and Argyll Transcripts, XIII, nos 25, 43–5, 70, 88, 91, 196.

Argyll secured permission from the occupying forces to the principle of his reaching an agreement with Huntly through further arbitration. By July 1653, he had persuaded his nephew to meet him at Finlarig on Lochtayside, the same location designated for the unfulfilled meeting of the Scottish Estates called in November 1651. On both occasions, Finlarig was chosen for its remoteness. It lay well out of the reach of the Cromwellian garrisons. Both parties agreed to bring no more than eighty followers to the meeting. While Huntly adhered to this number, Argyll made a liberal interpretation which allowed him to place up to eighty followers in surrounding areas within easy striking distance of the meeting, and also to block off the passes through the hills. Notwithstanding their Royalist inclinations, the Camerons of Lochiel and even the MacDonalds of Keppoch were more disposed to his interests in Lochaber, and likewise the Mackintoshes and the Macphersons in Badenoch. Thus, by subterfuge and bullying, in which he outmuscled and outmanoeuvred his nephew, Argyll secured a comprehensive if coerced title to the Huntly estates from the central Highlands to the north-east of Scotland. After he had signed over his estates, Lewis Gordon managed to make his escape. But such were the privations he subsequently endured in getting back to Aberdeenshire that the young marquess died before the end of the year.[47]

Argyll's accommodation with the Cromwellian regime in 1652 had also allowed him to control the limited opening up of the land-market occasioned by forfeitures and excessive debts from the 1640s. He was particularly adept at imposing a credit squeeze on the *fine* of clans antipathetic to the Campbells, while encouraging his own clansmen to bring wastelands back into production.[48] At the same time, he became a significant promoter of an economic

47 NAS, Gordon Castle Collection, GD 44/14/1/1–3 and /22/20; AUL, David Burnet 1691, 'The Portrait of True Loyalty Exposed in the Family of Gordon, MS 658, ff.520–1; West Sussex Record Office, Goodwood/1167/77 and 1431/18–20; *The Miscellany of the Spalding Club*, vol. IV, J. Stuart ed. (Aberdeen, 1852), pp. 166–7. I am obliged to Dr Barry Robertson, Trinity College Dublin, for drawing this incident to my attention. For a comprehensive picture of the tangled relationship of the houses of Huntly and Argyll see his 'Continuity and Change in the Scottish Nobility: The House of Huntly, 1603–1690' (University of Aberdeen, PhD thesis, 2007). This episode is recalled by Gordons who accompanied the young Huntly, but they were not recorded until well after the event – up to forty years later. Accordingly, one testimony that Argyll acted in a frightened manner unless surrounded by his henchman was almost certainly influenced by the published accounts of Wishart and other Royalist propagandists. Argyll was actually more accommodating to James Graham, son and heir of Montrose, whom he allowed to repurchase the estate of Mugdock on Lochlomondside for £50,000, principally because it was yielding him no meaningful income after being given to him by the Scottish Estates for £40,000 in lieu of his public debts (NLS, Halkett of Pitfirrane Papers, MS 6408/22, /85–6, /98–9).
48 Argyll Transcripts, III, nos 6–11, 16–17, 28–32, 47–8, 50–2, 61, 63, 69, 100, 105, 111, 129, 131–4, 136, 147, 164, 176, 192, 194, 197, 209–10, 224, 226–7; NLS, Halkett of Pitfirrane Papers, MS 6408/106;

variant to his reformed Western Association, by bringing in settlers from the western shires to reclaim the Kintyre peninsula, which had been devastated by intermittent warfare and bubonic plague. In the wake of the Whiggamore Raid of 1648, Argyll had been preparing to replenish the peninsula's population not only by offering preferential leases to attract enterprising clansmen, but by drawing heavily on settlers from the Lowlands. The marquis had already instigated this process in Mid-Argyll, which was also expanded in Cowal by Sir James Lamont of Inveryne. The depletion of manpower in the civil war made the attraction of tenants from the shires of Ayr and Renfrew a necessity, even though migration from these Lowland shires threatened continuity of clan settlement and the local vitality of Gaelic culture. Over the course of the 1650s, Lowland settlers were to occupy about a third of Kintyre, as against the quarter settled by Campbells and their affiliates; the remainder was held by families traditionally affiliated to the ClanDonald South. The practice of leasing townships at preferential rates, with rents escalating over five years as lands were brought back into production, was also applied in Colonsay, Jura and Ardnamurchan. Campbell and allied gentry benefited by the specific understanding that former Royalists, particularly of the ClanDonald South, were not to be allowed to resettle as tenants. The Marquess was concerned to plant churches as well as tenants, being an enthusiastic promoter of active Christian congregations, whether Gaelic- or Scots-speaking, throughout Argyll and the Isles.[49] Nevertheless, his patriotic commitment was now confined to his unstinting partiality for Presbyterianism and did not extend to a war of liberation.

Patriotic Resistance

The emergence of the New Model Army in England in 1645 had constituted a key moment in the establishment of an assertive English national consciousness. The rank and file, as well as the officers, made no appreciable attempt to

---

NAS, Breadalbane MSS, GD 112/1/569. In his financial dealings with merchants, Argyll insisted on the fulfillment of his contractual obligations to pay back borrowed monies that all notes from himself or his agent concerning loans were to be destroyed. He commenced this action, designed to pre-empt fully scrutiny of his legal liabilities, before the Cromwellian conquest of Scotland was complete (ABDA, Argyll Papers, 40.1825).

49 ICA, Letters – Marquess's Period, 1650–1658, bundle13/17 and Argyll Transcripts XIII, nos 12, 15, 21, 34, 55, 62, 78–9, 81, 97, 106–7, 112, 115, 127–8, 142–3, 163, 170, 175, 177–9, 186–7, 198, 217, 230, 233–4; ABDA, Argyll Papers, 40.454, .457, .469, .1728, .1730–2, .1740–5; *Minutes of the Synod of Argyll*, I, pp. 95, 147–8, 176, 188, 207, 214, 252 and II, pp. 45, 70, 72; A. McKerral, *Kintyre in the 17th Century* (Edinburgh, 1948), pp. 74–9, 80–4. Immigration was also necessary to repopulate Islay. The Campbells of Cawdor were able to recruit kinsmen and associates – not so much from their mainland estates in Argyll as from their northern estates in the shires of Inverness, Nairn and Moray (NLS, Macpherson Correspondence, 'A Succinct Account of the Family of Calder', MS. 9982, ff.27–8).

publicise themselves as British. This sense of identity was enhanced through the conquest of Ireland and Scotland, conquests necessitated by the refusal of both kingdoms to accept the accomplishment of an English republic through regicide. The Irish were viewed as uncivilised and deluded, but neither subhuman nor beyond redemption. The Scots were chided as misled, even false, brethren who had strayed from the path of godliness through the uniting of Covenanters and Royalists in the patriotic accommodation to support Charles II. A sense of English superiority seems to have resonated throughout the New Model Army, particularly as the officers and soldiers viewed themselves as freeborn Englishmen who shared a common heritage of rights and liberties.[50]

Under occupation, the Scots experienced greater leniency, though the Scots Gaels, like their Irish counterparts, were to be the butt of an ethnically debasing polemic for their refusal to accept subjugation. Clans who engaged in guerrilla resistance were deemed Tories for their purported activities as bandits. They were smeared by association with cateran bands who had thrown over the social constraints of clanship and with moss-troopers, former cavalrymen from all over the British Isles who had taken refuge in the Highlands as in the Borders, where they supported themselves by racketeering. Although these mounted marauders proved a highly mobile irritant to peripheral Cromwellian garrisons, they posed no serious threat to the regime. However, the clans, particularly those from Lochaber, were the mainstays of the guerrilla resistance fought predominantly within the *Gàidhealtachd*. Guerilla activity culminated in the ill-fated patriotic rising of Royalists, former Engagers and some Resolutioners who considered the army of occupation, and especially the need to pay for it through enhanced taxation as well as fines, sequestrations and forfeitures, an affront to national independence.[51] Notwithstanding the personal difficulties for nobles, gentry and burgesses arising from punitive fiscal policies, the army of occupation was not sustained from Scottish resources. By December 1654, the cost of maintaining garrisons and troops amounted to £282,675 sterling, of which only £45,000 (the equivalent of £300,000) was raised in Scotland through cess. Another £40,000 was provided by diverting money from Ireland, but the bulk of the revenue raised (£137,260) was met by direct subvention from England.

---

50   J.S. Wheeler, 'Sense of Identity in the Army of the English Republic' in Macinnes and Ohlmeyer eds, *The Stuart Kingdoms*, pp. 151–68; Barber, *Regicide and Republicanism*, pp. 191–5; Cuthbert Sydenham, *The False Brother, or, A New Map of Scotland, Drawn by an English Pencil* (London, 1651).

51   NAS, Glencairn MSS, GD 29/2/66 and Gordon Castle MSS, GD 44/27/3; Whitelock, *Memorials*, IV, p. 42; Dow, *Cromwellian Scotland*, pp. 14, 53, 61–71, 74–160; É. Ó Ciardha, 'Tories and Moss-troopers in Scotland and Ireland in the Interregnum: A Political Dimension' in Young ed., *Celtic Dimensions of the British Civil Wars*, pp. 141–63.

However, an accumulating deficit of more than £60,415 sterling remained.[52]

The patriotic rising was initiated in August 1653 by William Cunningham, 9th Earl of Glencairn, a former participant in the Britannic Engagement. This rising soon spread throughout the *Gàidhealtachd* and the north-east of Scotland. At the behest of Charles II, another veteran of the Britannic Engagement, Lieutenant-General George Middleton, returned from continental exile in March 1654 to replace Glencairn as commander. Four months later, he issued a manifesto in the name of the king, promising to deliver Scotland from the tyranny and oppression of the Commonwealth. In particular, he cited the savage cruelty at Dundee where aged men, women and children were massacred with little evidence of 'Christian pitty'. Scottish soldiers had been sold into slavery after Dunbar and Worcester; others had faced starvation as prisoners. Mushrooming religious toleration, the appropriation of Scottish revenues and the disruption to trade were also condemned. Aiding, abetting or assisting the Cromwellian occupation was treasonable. Although this further politicising of the treason laws lacked parliamentary warrant, Argyll was again vulnerable as in 1648. However, only his kinsmen, the unfortunate Campbells of Glenorchy, had their estates in Lorne and Breadalbane despoiled by the patriotic forces. Unlike the patriotic accommodation of 1650–51, this war of liberation was confined to Scotland: 'we having no designe to invade the rights and liberties of any of our Fellow Subjects in the Kingdoms of England or Ireland'. But, Sir George Munro, the former commander of the Scottish forces in Ulster, again proved disruptive. Notwithstanding his wounding in a bout with Glencairn, he and his close associates readily resorted to duelling. By April 1654, their behaviour had occasioned a debilitating rift between Middleton and Glencairn. With the considerably more adept General George Monck having replaced Lambert as commander of the New Model Army in Scotland, Middleton was defeated at Dalnaspidal in Perthshire on 20 July. Monck then undertook systematic pillaging and burning from Lochaber to Wester Ross to persuade the clans, who had formed the bedrock of the patriotic campaign, to sue for peace.[53]

52 BL, Letters and State Papers. Birch Collection, Add.MSS 4156, fo.112 and Lauderdale Papers, Miscellaneous Correspondence, vol. 1, 1630–60, Add.MSS 23,113, fo.40; ABDA, Argyll Papers, 40.83; DH, Loudoun Deeds, bundle 2/1; *CAL*, II, pp. 371–2. This taxation is less than that levied under Charles I or the Covenanting Movement.

53 BL, Nicholas Papers, Egermont MS 2542, ff.111–14 and Letters and State Papers, Birch Collection, Add.MSS, 4156, fo.73; GCA, John Graham of Duchrie. Account of the Earl of Glencairn's expedition to the Highlands of Scotland 1653–1654, SR 163, pp. 1–21; NAS, Breadalbane MSS GD 112/1/568, /574–7, /579–80; *LJB*, III, pp. 255–6; Macinnes, *Clanship, Commerce and the House of Stuart*, pp. 110–14. Notwithstanding the presence of Sir George Munro, Ulster Scots were not prominent in the patriotic rising. Although they were more harshly treated than other Irish Protestants opposed to the regicides, Argyll's control over the bridgehead between

Endemic disaffection to the Cromwellian occupation did not exclude Argyllshire, where the payment of Cromwellian taxes was resented as the exaction of tribute. Argyll was not always able to contain dissent among his own and associated clans opposed to the Cromwellian occupation: most notably, his son Archibald, Lord Lorne, assisted by Sir Dugald Campbell of Ardkinglass, who had persistently refused to levy, collect or pay taxes for the Commonwealth, and by Archibald MacNaughton of Dundarrow, whose probity was being questioned by Argyll following reports from kinsmen that the chamberlain of Kintyre was one of 'the greatest knaves living and deserved to be hanged'. Together they raised over a 1,000 clansmen for the patriotic forces. Lorne, backed up by Balcarres, was among the minority of Resolutioners still prepared to bear arms with former Engagers and, less easily, with Royalists, who included James Graham, son and heir of Montrose.[54] Lorne, as Robert Baillie pointed out more in sorrow than in anger, was 'coarselie used' by his father. Undoubtedly, there were personal as well as ideological reasons for this rift. Argyll was particularly concerned that his son and his young wife were making unreasonable demands for their maintenance at a time of economic stringency. Lorne was also much slighted and distrusted by Glencairn, who recalled the irreconcilable discords between Argyll and Hamilton during the Britannic Engagement as he faced constant questioning of his command by Lorne and Balcarres. Although Lorne had secured Lochhead Castle in Kintyre, he gave generous terms for its surrender to the Lowland planters who constituted the garrison; terms that led to a breach with his cousin, Robert Gordon, 2nd Viscount Kenmure. By October 1653, Lorne had effectively refrained from active campaigning. He only rejoined the patriotic forces once Middleton took over command. Middleton duly commended him to Charles II, who sent a belated note from Cologne on 30 December 1654 that carried a clear threat to the Marquess of Argyll. In addition to thanking Lorne for his affection and zeal, Charles expressed the hope that he would have more credit and power over his clan than those who had seduced the Campbells and their associates from the patriotic cause. The king affirmed: 'I shall look upon all those who

---

Kintyre and Antrim may well have encouraged them to settle rather than fight (D. Menarry, 'Rebellion, Transplantation and Composition: the Ulster-Scots landed elite and the Commonwealth' in W.P. Kelly and J.R. Young eds, *Scotland and the Ulster Plantation: Explorations in the British Settlement of Stuart Ireland* (Dublin, 2009), pp. 137–59).

54 ICA, Argyll Letters (1638–85), A36/165, /167–72 and Letters – Marquess's Period, 1650–1658, bundle 13/25, /27–8; NAS, Breadalbane MSS, GD 112/1/570; NLS, Halkett of Pitfirrane Papers, MS 6408/90, /94–5; Argyll had given Lorne and his wife, Jane Stewart, his stronghold at Rosneath and a living allowance of £7,567 yearly, but they wanted their own household though Argyll reckoned this, with overheads, would not amount to £6,000 yearly.

refuse to follow yow as unworthy of any protection hereafter.'[55]

Despite his political impotency as an exile, Charles II was clearly questioning the depth of Argyll's commitment first to the Commonwealth and now to the Protectorate. Argyll's correspondence with Cromwell and his commanders during the patriotic rising of 1653–54 does not provide clear-cut evidence that he provided early and full intelligence of the movements of his son and associates, or that he co-operated energetically and zealously. These same letters were to be the principal grounds for his condemnation as a collaborator in 1661. His provision of intelligence came only at the beginning and at the end of the rising. Initially he was self-exonerating in distancing himself from his son, as he was intent on maintaining his own standing with the Cromwellian regime and his continuing exercise of hereditary privileges as a clan chief and Scottish magnate. Latterly, he was primarily concerned to prepare the ground for his son's submission without swingeing sanctions being imposed on the house of Argyll. He was certainly aggrieved by his son's disrespectful behaviour, but he retained the support of most clansmen and consistently sought to honour the terms of his revised agreement with Major-General Deane in August 1652. He did nothing directly or indirectly to undermine the army of occupation. He offered to give himself up as hostage to compensate for his son's adherence to the patriotic forces, and he did continue to levy and collect taxes. While this fiscal engagement can serve as an excuse for his mobilising forces to participate in defensive manoeuvres with the New Model Army, his primary purpose was to demonstrate the independent military capacity of his revitalised Western Association. In this he was undoubtedly successful, as neither Cromwellian nor patriotic forces nor his son infringed on his territories as Montrose and MacColla had done in 1644–45.[56]

An additional letter (never produced at Argyll's trial in 1661), reveals his ambiguous rather than collaborative relationship with Cromwell. Writing from Carrick Castle on 4 August 1654, with the patriotic cause in disarray, Argyll seeks to solicit help from the Lord Protector in settling with his creditors. Cromwell favoured executive orders to clear public debts rather than have recourse to the Barebones Parliament. But the Marquess skips around the provision of intelligence. He informs Cromwell that he doubts not he 'hes a better accompt of your affaires in the Highlands nor I can give you'. Argyll was no more trusted

55 *LJB*, III, pp. 249–51; ICA, Argyll Letters (1638–85), A36/175GCA, Hamilton of Barns Papers, TD 589/956; Whitelock, *Memorials*, IV, pp. 27, 32, 35–8, 43, 46, 79–80, 87, 150–1, 152, 155, 161.

56 Willcock, *The Great Marquess*, pp. 289–92, 378–86; *SPT*, II, pp. 359, 475, 478–9; Whitelock, *Memorials*, IV, pp. 40, 44, 109–11, 114; ICA, Argyll Letters (1638–85), A36/173 and Miscellaneous Argyll Letters, fo.100–5; NAS, Breadalbane MSS, GD 112/1/572 and William Clarke MSS, RH 4/127/1/13–14.

by Cromwell and the regicides than by the Royalist circles around Charles I in the 1640s or in exile with Charles II throughout the 1650s. Both Cromwell and Argyll believed in providence, in that they were doing the Lord's work. But Cromwell did so individually, whereas Argyll saw himself as a leading agent in a corporate endeavour. Cromwell believed himself to the personification and protector of England as an elect nation. Argyll was convinced he was acting for Kirk and nation in moving Scotland into British confederation.[57] But as his aspirations were thwarted his personal debts continued to accumulate. Even before the patriotic rising had run its course, Argyll, who was now flirting with the Protestors, was 'almost drowned in debt, in friendship with the English, but in hatred with the country'.[58]

57 Letters and State Papers. Birch Collection, Add.MSS 4156, fo.73; DH, Loudoun Papers, bundle 1/9; *SPT*, II, p. 517; K.M. MacKenzie, 'Oliver Cromwell and the Solemn League and Covenant of the Three Kingdoms', in Little ed., *Oliver Cromwell*, pp. 142–67.
58 *LJB*, III, pp. 259, 568; NLS, Halkett of Pitfirrane Papers, MS 6422/17, /21. and MS 6408/23–4, /84, /89, /96–7, /102, /105, /107–8, 110).

ELEVEN

Restoration End Game, 1655–1661

Although Lord Lorne made his peace with the Cromwellian regime in the course of 1655, reconciliation with his father took considerably longer. Argyll remained a marked man for Royalists and former Engagers. He had not only vehemently opposed the Britannic Engagement to restore the monarchical authority of Charles I in 1648, but he also pulled out of the patriotic accommodation before Charles II crossed the Border to meet defeat at Worcester in 1651. Most heinously, he had maintained a position of armed neutrality during the patriotic rising led by Glencairn and Middleton in 1653–54. No less ominously, Resolutioners, who had hitherto lauded him for his radical leadership of the Covenanting Movement, were increasingly estranged by his Western Association and by his flirtation with the Protestors. However, another six years were to elapse before the Restoration of Charles II brought about the end game for the Marquess, as represented by his incarceration, trial and eventual execution in May 1661. In the interim, Argyll's standing with the Protectorates of Oliver Cromwell and, from September 1658, with that of his son Richard Cromwell, was not that of a bosom collaborator or even a favoured associate. The Marquess played no central role in Scottish affairs. He enjoyed only limited protection from his creditors in Edinburgh, notwithstanding his excessive partiality in dealing with debtors in his own courts in Argyll and the Isles. His British activities as a lobbyist for the Protestors and as Member of Parliament at Westminster also left him vulnerable to imprisonment from legal actions raised by creditors in London. His endeavours to become an MP under Richard Cromwell were vigorously but unsuccessfully resisted by the military command in Scotland. He was deliberately excluded from General Monck's march on London from Scotland in 1659 that led to the Restoration of 1660. Monck was to cement his own elevation to the peerage as Duke of Albemarle by disclosing Argyll's letters to the military command in Scotland during the patriotic rising of 1653–54; a belated but fatal disclosure in the course of the trial of the Marquess that was engineered by the Scottish Estates, then packed with Royalists, former Engagers and even Resolutioners intent on judicial vengeance.

Compromised Lobbyist

Lord Lorne had accompanied Middleton on his wanderings in the Highlands after his defeat at Dalnaspidal in July 1654 until his departure into exile in April 1655. Only then did Lorne make any meaningful attempt to come to terms with General Monck, who allowed him to surrender at Dumbarton in May but also required him to give a bond for £5,000 sterling (£60,000) for his peaceable deportment. Lorne assiduously avoided asking his father for help to raise this money, preferring to rely on his own contacts among the friends, clients and associates of the house of Argyll. Nevertheless, the Marquess was prepared to re-engage him in the management of the Argyll estates from the autumn, albeit Lorne was imprisoned in November 1656 not so much for breaching his bond as for failing to secure the necessary financial backing.[1] Periodic bouts of imprisonment followed for the next twenty-one months. When he was finally released from Edinburgh Castle by Monck in June 1659, his bail was increased to £10,000 sterling, which was guaranteed by Lothian and Sir James Halkett of Pitfirrane, the nephew of the Marquess and his leading financial adviser based in Edinburgh. By February 1658, Argyll had ceded to Lorne his estate of Rosneath, estimated to be worth £2,000 annually with an additional yearly allowance of £6,000 from the rents of Kintyre.[2]

Nevertheless, the ongoing personal and political differences between Lorne and his father continued to vex Robert Baillie, especially as Argyll was prepared to deflect any possible charges of collusion with his son by relaxing his strictures against Cromwellian garrisons. Accordingly, he allowed the Cromwellian troops occasional access to Inveraray Castle, with the use of the local kirk and school for their stables. Their contrary conduct, no less than their accumulation of public and private debts, was reputedly a hazard to the survival of the house of Argyll, a finding endorsed by Alexander Brodie of Brodie, a judge who had served as a Scottish commissioner in the negotiations with Charles II in the United Provinces in 1649–50. Having taken over the advisory role vacated by Johnston of Wariston's collaboration with the Cromwellian regime and become a close confidant of the Marquess, Brodie was moved to attest that Lorne's

---

1 ICA, Argyll Letters (1638–85), A36/176–7, /184 and Miscellaneous Argyll Letters, bundle 15/32 and Argyll Transcripts, XIII, nos 242, 291, 330, 336, 341–2, 382, 429–31, 453, 463; NLS, Halkett of Pitfirrane Papers, MS 6408/111; *CAL*, II, 390–1.

2 NAS, William Clarke MSS, RH 4/127/2/15; DH, Loudoun Papers, bundle 15/32; TFA, Papers, TD 1013; LJB, III, p. 367. Lorne actually had a son baptised during his imprisonment in Edinburgh Castle on 15 July 1658. The rough and tumble of prison life almost led to Lorne's accidental death that summer, when a hand-bullet that ricocheted off a wall struck him a glancing blow to his head, which not only rendered him unconscious but deprived him of the power of speech for several days.

'unsubmissiveness' was compounded by Argyll's 'deep recenting' of real and imagined past injuries, and offences, and prejudices.[3]

Lorne's brother, Lord Neil Campbell, proved a more reliable estate manager as Argyll, supported strenuously by his wife Margaret Douglas, strove to make inroads into the mountain of debt that was threatening to ruin his house. By the close of 1658, he was required to pay a reputed annual interest of between £467,000 and £534,000. Yet he was 'no more drowned in debt than public hatred'. In a Scottish context, this can largely be attributed to the Marquess's endeavours to maintain intact the territorial interests of the house of Argyll by not giving needless offence to the Cromwellian regime. Argyll was not subjected to the fines, sequestration, forfeiture, house-arrest and exile that afflicted former Covenanting associates such as Loudoun, Lauderdale, Lothian and Generals Leven and Leslie. At the same time, Argyll ruthlessly used his own courts to protect himself from his Scottish creditors while rigorously pursuing his debtors, particularly among the Royalist clans. Sir Allan Maclean of Duart, the brother of Sir Hector who had fallen at Inverkeithing in July 1650, inherited debts to the Marquess of £60,000 which were serviced by rising interest payments. The new chief of the ClanGillean was obliged to cede a managerial interest to Argyll that led to the intrusion of Campbell gentry into Mull, Tiree and Morvern by the close of 1657.[4]

In an English context, loathing and disparagement were subordinated to courtesy and caution in the Cromwellian regime's dealings with Argyll. His partial judicial decisions were checked but not reversed. He had also faced personal and financial humiliation after journeying to Dalkeith to meet Monck in November 1654, in order to distance himself from his son and Middleton, whom he had driven out of Argyllshire. Notwithstanding a current moratorium on the payment of debts due to a shortage of money, the Marquess was taunted by his creditors as a 'false traitor'. His horse, clothing and household gear were impounded then sold off at the market cross of Edinburgh.[5] The capacity of Halkett of Pitfirrane, aided and abetted by Robert Balfour, Lord Burleigh, to ease repayments of the Marquess's debts by renegotiating contracts not just in Edinburgh but throughout the Lowlands, was not helped by Argyll's difficult relationship with the regime in Scotland, particularly when headed by Robert, Lord Broghill (later 1st Earl of Orrery) from September 1655 until August 1656.

3 *The Diary of Alexander Brodie of Brodie*, p. 167; *LJB*, III, pp. 287–8, 367.

4 *LJB*, III, p. 387; BL, Lauderdale Papers, Miscellaneous Correspondence, vol.I, 1630–1660, Add. MSS 23,113, fo.40; DH, Loudoun Deeds, bundle 2/1; ICA, Argyll Letters (1638–85), A36/178–83, /187 and Argyll Transcripts, XIII, nos 47, 105, 172, 176, 248, 251, 274–5, 285, 347, 370, 374, 385–6, 402, 410, 437.

5 Nicoll, *Diary*, pp. 140, 143; *SPT*, IV, p. 500; ICA, Argyll Transcripts, XIII, 318–22, 325–6, 328–9, 394, 406–7, 421–2, 425, 427, 430, 432.

The patriotic rising had not yet been suppressed when the ordinance for political incorporation was promulgated on 12 April 1654. Its associated programme for the governance of Scotland had sought to combine punitive and progressive measures. Outright confiscations were restricted to twenty-four landowners, with another seventy-three subject to rigorous fines. Commissions of the peace were to be reinvigorated in the shires, and heritable jurisdictions and feudal dependencies were to be swept away. This latter aspect won contemporaneous commendation when the Scottish Council, under Broghill's direction, commenced reforms in Kirk and State. Broghill was transferred from his duties in Ireland as Lord President of Munster to provide the civil complement to Monck's military pacification by individual treaties with Highland chiefs and Lowland landlords. He was a talented conciliator, but his brief administration was more about style than substance. The series of garrisons and citadels which littered the Highlands and Lowlands provided the means for the regime's continuing recourse to quartering troops on refractory taxpayers.[6] Initially, Broghill was willing to search for a religious accommodation. But his favouring of Patrick Gillespie from the Protestors, who was installed as Principal of Glasgow University, ensured that denominational discrimination against the Resolutioners took precedence. Not only did the Protestor–Resolutioner conflict remain intractable, but he discovered rather sooner than Charles I in the course of the Revocation Scheme that the wholesale abolition of heritable jurisdictions and feudal superiorities was time consuming, technically complex and politically disruptive.

The main thrust of Broghill's policy became the conditional retention of landed interests and feudal privileges. Fiscal rebates were tied to punitive sureties for future good conduct. Within the Highlands especially, the emphasis was on containment rather than impartial justice. Notwithstanding the forcible enlistment of moss-troopers and caterans for military service overseas by Monck, banditry remained virulent on the Lowland peripheries. Accordingly, Lieutenant-Colonel Donald MacGregor, a civil war veteran, was commissioned to eradicate all predatory raiding. A monopoly of control over protection

---

6 Whitelock, *Memorials*, IV, pp. 98–10; Dow, *Cromwellian Scotland*, pp. 17–22, 44, 53, 67–8, 107, 244–5; Woolrych, *Britain in Revolution*, pp. 567–73, 589–92. Monck had recognised through his negotiated settlements with the clan elite that the *Gàidhealtachd* could not be governed, nor disorders suppressed, without their co-operation. Chiefs like Ewen Cameron of Lochiel, who were prepared to curtail the territorial mobility of their clansmen, to restrict the size of their personal retinues, and to seek a working accommodation with the army of occupation, were accorded favoured treatment which ranged from the privilege that their clansmen could bear arms for defensive purposes to the award of lucrative contracts to supply the garrisons and citadels with timber, fuel and provisions. (Macinnes, *Clanship, Commerce and the House of Stuart*, p. 111–12.)

rackets was thus accorded to the acting chief of the ClanGregor. Rates of extortion duly rose by Cromwellian appointment to as much as £47 for every £100 of rent.[7]

Having tied in the MacFarlanes on Lochlomondside and the Menzies in Rannoch to his Western Association, racketeering and cattle lifting were not issues of significance for the Marquess of Argyll. However, another plank of his Western Association was proving more problematic, as the Lowland planters in Kintyre faced considerable hostility from retained satellite clans as well as displaced Gaels. Moreover, although Argyll sought to diversify estate management by encouraging fishing, slate quarrying and timber extraction, they offered no immediate return in revenue to offset declining rentals and accumulating debts. His desire to increase rents, if necessary by removing tenantry deemed unproductive, had to be tempered by customary obligation to maintain kindness in his relations with his kinsmen and local associates. Although rentals could be renegotiated upwards on the expiry of leases, this was a gradual and piecemeal process that was not an expeditious means of clearing his debts. The Marquess sought to ease problems of cash flow by selectively mortgaging and even selling lands in Argyll and the Isles to trusted associates among his kinsmen and clients, including Campbells established as merchants in Glasgow and Edinburgh. However, all mortgages were redeemable, and even when selling property Argyll reserved his rights as feudal superior to preserve his overlordship. In like manner, his acquisition of the Huntly estates in the central Highlands and Aberdeenshire offered another income stream from rents, mortgages and sales. But he prioritised the establishment of good working relations with the clans in Badenoch and Lochaber, as with the city and shire of Aberdeen, to consolidate his territorial influence. He was particularly assiduous in cultivating the town council as patron and benefactor, as well as the houses of the Forbes, the Frasers and the Keiths, who had longstanding strained relations with the Gordons of Huntly, Aboyne and Haddow.[8]

---

7 BL, Register of the Production of Charters of Kirklands in Scotland, Mar.–Oct. 1656, Add. MSS, ff.1–147; *Scotland and the Protectorate*, pp. 147–8, 226, 270, 272–6, 286, 303, 321; Woolrych, *Commonwealth to Protectorate*, p. 298; Macinnes, *Clanship, Commerce and the House of Stuart*, pp. 113–14. For a comprehensive and constructive exploration of Broghill's career as a Cromwellian administrator see Patrick Little, *Lord Broghill and the Cromwellian Union with Ireland and Scotland* (Woodbridge, 2004). Reform focused on the proscription of military tenures and work services exacted as rents. Feudal superiority was retained through commercial tenures and was requisite for the payment of teinds to cover the stipends of accredited ministers, schooling and social welfare in the burghs as in rural parishes. Moreover, heritable jurisdictions were discreetly continued in practice if not in name, a precedent having been set by the package of concessions negotiated by the Marquess of Argyll in August 1652.

8 ICA, Miscellaneous 17th Century Papers, bundle 133/1–2 and Argyll Letters (1638–85), A36/188, /195, /199 and Argyll Transcripts, XIII, nos 215, 247, 249–51, 266, 268–9, 271, 279, 283, 285, 307–8,

Argyll's principal strategy to relieve the debts threatening to engulf his house was to access public monies. Accordingly, he sought to uphold and continue his lucrative lease on the assize of herrings in the western seas, from the North Channel to the Hebridean Minches, which were traditionally paid by inshore and deep-sea fishermen from the royal burghs to the Crown. Having secured this lease from Charles I during the constitutional settlement of 1641, he spent considerable time and energy in having it confirmed not only in Scotland but at the court of Cromwell in London, where he also lobbied assiduously for the overdue payment of £35,000 sterling (£420,000) due to himself and the shire of Argyll under the agreement between the Covenanters and Parliamentarians for the transfer of Charles I in 1647; payments which had been promised in part in the course of the Britannic Engagement and again during the patriotic accommodation (see Chapters 9 and 10). Whereas his former Covenanting associates first lobbied Broghill, Argyll preferred to go straight to London, where he was still able to raise private funds on the strength of Lincolnshire and Suffolk estates inherited from his father, the 7th Earl. Like the 1st Duke of Hamilton, Argyll had readily used the Scots embedded in the city's commercial community, notably Sir David Cunningham, during the 1640s. However, his declining political clout, which also affected his capacity and that of other former Covenanters to raise money in Amsterdam at reasonable rates of interest, made borrowing from London Scots and other city merchants less routine and less rewarding.[9]

His Presbyterian affinities with the city of London were not enhanced when, in the course of a lobbying visit in 1656, he countered a complaint made on behalf of the Resolutioners by James Sharp, minister of Crail in Fife, against the endeavours of the Protestors to plant kirks and depose ministers. Argyll secured a hearing before Cromwell for the Protestors. His subsequent support for Patrick Gillespie effectively burned his bridges with the Resolutioners without gaining the unalloyed trust of the Protestors. Nevertheless, he gradually ingratiated himself with the latter by becoming their regular lobbyist in London over the next two years. Lobbying was not only hazardous politically but it exposed him to legal action in English courts which, even led to his temporary imprisonment for debt in November 1655. He had been sued by Elizabeth Maxwell, dowager Countess of Dirleton, who claimed for an unpaid bill for £1,000 sterling

322, 330, 334–5, 344–7, 349, 354–5, 360, 372, 387, 398, 402–4, 410, 413–14, 416, 420, 430, 435, 444–5, 448, 451–3, 463 and XIV (1660–69), nos 4–6, 19, 39, 45; *ACL*, III, pp. 298–9.

9 ICA, Miscellaneous 17th Century Papers, bundle 130/143, /147 and Argyll Letters (1638–85), A36/185 and Miscellaneous Argyll Letters, fo.17; ABDA, Argyll Papers, 40.830; NAS, Hamilton Papers, GD 406/1/10738; *CAL*, II, pp. 395–8, 403–6, 421–3, 507–8; BL, Papers of General Desborough, 1651–1660, Egerton MS 2519, fo.30.

(£12,000) due to her late husband for supplying meal to the Covenanting Army during their intervention in England in 1644–45. As this was a debt contracted in Scotland, it should have been tried before Scottish judges, as the Council of State in England recognised. The Countess was eventually gaoled for contumacy in making false representations. But her debt was repaid, even though the Marquess was not solely liable for the contract. The case did eventually win recognition for Argyll from the Barebones Parliament in September 1656 of his overdue payments from the monies due from the transfer of the king in 1647. However, he was assigned no more than £10,000 sterling (£120,000), which was set against a renewed grant of the excise of wine in Scotland, first conceded by the Scottish Estates in March 1651 and now reputedly worth £3,000 sterling a year. Again. promissory payments were not fulfilled.[10]

Argyll's regular lobbying in London, as well as the time spent consolidating his hold over the Huntly estates, necessitated considerable periods of absence from Argyllshire, during which times his clan gentry in their capacity as justices of the peace administered the county, and as commissioners of supply levied and collated taxation. Much to the consternation of the Cromwellian regime in Edinburgh, however, the administration of justice returned to the Marquess's courts, and tax was no longer paid, whenever Argyll returned to Inveraray Castle. He attended the belated proclamation of Oliver Cromwell as Lord Protector in Edinburgh, along with his son-in-law, George Sinclair, 6th Earl of Caithness and other nobles, gentry and burgesses present in the capital on 15 July 1657. He did so without enthusiasm. When Argyll secured his return to the Parliament at Westminster called to mark the new Protectorate of Richard Cromwell at the outset of 1659, his election as MP for Aberdeenshire was vigorously but unsuccessfully opposed by the Cromwellian regime in Scotland, who claimed that the Marquess owed almost £3,545 sterling (£42,540) in public dues to the Protectorate. General Deane went so far as to admit, after a seven-year silence on the issue, that Argyll had forcibly bettered him when securing the deal for his Western Association in August 1652.[11]

10 Willcock, *The Great Marquess*, pp. 296–7; *Memoirs of the Life of Mr Robert Blair, Minister of the Gospel Sometime at Bangor in Ireland, and Afterwards at St Andrews in Scotland* (Edinburgh, 1754), pp. 120–1; *LJB*, III, pp. 361, 404; ABDA, Argyll Papers, 40.805; ICA, Argyll Letters (1638–85), A36/189–91, /93–4.

11 BL, Papers of General Desborough, 1651–1660, Egerton MS 2519, ff.19, 29–30; NAS, William Clarke MSS, RH 4/127/1/17; *SPT*, V, pp. 604–5 and VI, pp. 295, 306, 405 and VII, p. 584; Nicoll, *Diary*, pp. 200, 226; *The Diary of Mr John Lamont of Newton, 1649–1671* (Edinburgh, 1830), p. 119. Although the full complement of 30 MPs was returned from Scotland to the parliament called by Richard Cromwell in 1659, Argyll was one of only 10 Scots elected. A full complement had also been returned at the election in 1656, when 14 constituencies were actually represented by Scots (Young, *The Scottish Parliament*, pp. 299–303).

The Marquess readily assumed leadership of the Scottish grouping of MPs and chaired the committee for Scottish affairs, which again left him open to charges of compliance with the Protectorate. In reality, his influence on proceedings was marginal prior to the Parliament being forcibly dissolved on 22 April 1659 at the behest of the New Model Army now commanded by Lieutenant-General Charles Fleetwood. Under constant fear of arrestment for personal debt and unpaid public dues, Argyll soon retired back to Scotland, where polemical vilification followed. His parliamentary service led him to be denounced along with other Cromwellian collaborators, with additional charges that he had used his public position for personal aggrandisement during the 1640s; that he had not been averse to affirming this by massacres of the Lamonts and MacDougalls on the conclusion of the civil war; and that he now was in denial about his leading role in bringing Charles II back to Scotland in 1650.[12] In the meantime, despite the rigid Presbyterian demeanour in his portraiture, he had actually acquired for £80 on 7 May a pleasure boat of 12 tons burden on the River Thames, the *St Lawrence of Dorft*. This should not be viewed as an uncharacteristic indulgence, but rather as forward planning to allow him yet again to escape by ship, this time across the English Channel, should the monarchy be restored. Indeed, Argyll's need for personal insurance was readily borne out when a manifesto on behalf of Charles II and his brother James, Duke of York was issued from Brussels in November to the nobility and gentry of Scotland. Clemency was offered to all former opponents, other than those deemed complicit in the regicide and the execution of Montrose, who were prepared to work through parliamentary channels for the restoration of monarchy.[13]

Deliverance from the North

By this juncture, the Cromwellian regime was imploding. Oliver Cromwell had died on 3 September 1658, the anniversaries of Dunbar and Worcester. His immediate legacy was a family power struggle that negated the constitution, threatened renewed civil war and paved the way for a Restoration of the Stuart monarchy in just over twenty months.[14] Key features of the Protectorate's

---

12 *LJB*, III, p. 430; Nicoll, *Diary*, pp. 237–8, 264–5; NAS, William Clarke MSS, RH 4/127/1/19; Woolrych, *Britain in Revolution*, pp. 707–22.

13 ICA, Argyll Transcripts, XIII, no. 436; C. Culpepper, *A Message Sent from the King of Scots and the Duke of York's Court in Flanders* (Aberdeen, 1659).

14 Hirst, *England in Conflict*, pp. 311–27; J.S. Morrill, 'Postlude: Between War and Peace, 1651–1662' in Kenyon and Ohlmeyer eds, *The Civil Wars*, pp. 306–28; *The Diary of John Evelyn*, p. 208; 'The Life of Master John Shaw' in *Yorkshire Diaries and Autobiographies in the Seventeenth and Eighteenth Centuries* (Durham, 1877), p. 152. James Fraser, the Presbyterian minister of Wardlaw in the shire of Inverness, when in London after Cromwell's death, claimed that his dissected body was found to be 'full of corruption and filth, but his name and his memory stank worse' (Fraser, *The Wardlaw Manuscript*, pp. 403, 409–10, 412–3, 417–19).

implosion were audits of public policy, both international and domestic. These audits included not only judicial and confessional concerns affecting sovereignty and godly rule, but also such issues of political economy as the advancement of free trade, commerce, manufacturing and fisheries. On all counts the Protectorate was found wanting.[15]

England's marginal capacity to be self-sufficient as a military-fiscal state through a revenue base generated principally from cess, customs and excise was terminated by the Western Design of 1655, whose primary endeavour was to take over the Panama Isthmus and divert the silver and gold bullion from the Spanish Empire into Protectorate coffers. The island of Hispaniola was to be seized to serve as a transit station. However, a divided command structure between Admiral William Penn and General Robert Venables, inadequate provisioning for the Caribbean, and greater Spanish resistance than expected in San Domingo made the assault on Hispaniola a military fiasco. The island of Jamaica was taken as a consolation prize, but the capture of the Panama Isthmus was abandoned. The costs of the Western Design exceeded the cost of royal government throughout the 1630s and added a further £500,000 sterling annually to naval expenditure. This situation was further compounded by Cromwell's estrangement from the mercantile interests in the city of London, as by the reduction in cess required by the revised Humble Petition and Advice of May 1657, when the Protectorate admitted to running an annual deficit of around £500,000 sterling.

Pay for the New Model Army was at least six months in arrears and not ameliorated by the raising of an additional 6,000 troops to fight in Flanders following an alliance with France against Spain in March 1657. By April 1659, the accumulated public debts of the Protectorate exceeded £2.2 million sterling. The annual income generated from England (£1.5 million) only fell £30,500 short of domestic expenditure. But Scotland was generating only £143,653 and was running a deficit of £163, 619, while Ireland was generating £207,790 with a deficit of £138,690. Occupation of the satellite states had entrenched the Protectorate in a financial mire. Its aggressive foreign policy ensured that it never recovered. By December 1659, Richard Cromwell was personally held accountable for the accumulated public debt, now reduced only by £706,492. A parliamentary cash advance of £600,000 to be raised through cess cut this notional deficit to £849,374. The other current sources of public revenue in England, Scotland and Ireland did not exceed £150,000 sterling. The only prospect of generating further supply was through recourse to the fiscal expedients. Fiscal exhaustion, in turn, made the assertive dominance of the

---

15 BL, Letters and State Papers: the Birch Collection, Add.MSS 4156, fo.112 and Collection of Historical and Parliamentary Papers, 1620–1660, Egerton MS 1048, ff.176–80; ACL, III, pp. 332–8; Macinnes, *The British Revolution*, pp. 213–35.

New Model Army in civil affairs less and less tenable.[16]

Richard Cromwell's uneasy relations with contending factions in the Council of State were manifest in his decision to summon a parliament in January 1659, based on the old franchise rather than that laid down at the outset of the Protectorate in 1654. The Commons were hostile to the retention of the new senate or 'Other House' established through a revised constitution in June 1657, which had become the mouthpiece of the higher command of the New Model Army. In April, the Council of Officers meeting at Wallingford House, the palatial residence of General Fleetwood in Stoke Newington, a suburb of London, had forced the new Protector to dissolve the Parliament as implacably hostile to the Army. Nonetheless, the New Model Army was not united and not beyond challenge from within. Junior officers, with the support of the rank and file, pressed for the recall of the Rump Parliament but were duly dispersed by the generals. In October, the Council of State was replaced by a Committee of Safety charged to settle the constitution without recourse to a monarch, lord protector or the House of Lords in a restored Commonwealth. However, the strains between the civil and military authorities in England were again subject to redress from Scotland. General George Monck, whose loyalty to the Wallingford House group had been questionable since the summer, called for a responsible return to parliamentary government at the outset of November. Having either imprisoned or bound over all potential troublemakers in Scotland to keep the peace, he proceeded to secure the loyalty of the Scottish garrisons and confined disaffected officers in Tantallon Castle, East Lothian. He then took over Berwick-upon-Tweed. At the same time, the presence of agents for the exiled Charles II in Scotland raised apprehensions in England about a further invasion from the north. The Rump Parliament was fully restored through regimental pressure on the high command on 27 December as the army prepared to mutiny in the north of England and rioting beset London.[17]

Having summoned a convention of shire and burgh commissioners to meet in Edinburgh on 15 November to secure the peace in Scotland, Monck called for the election of either one noble or one member of the gentry from each shire to

---

16 BL, Papers Relating to the Revenue etc, Add.MSS 11,597, ff.1–10; T. Venning, *Cromwellian Foreign Policy* (New York, 1995), pp. 238–50; K.O. Kupperman, 'Errand to the Indies: Puritan Colonization from Providence Island through the Western Design', *William and Mary Quarterly*, 45 (1988), pp. 70–99; B.S. Capp, *Cromwell's Navy: The Fleet and the English Revolution, 1648–1660* (Oxford, 1989), pp. 86–106.

17 George Monck, *General Monck's Last Letter to His Excellency the Lord Fleetwood* (London, 1659); William Pyrnne, *A brief narrative of the manner how divers Members of the House of Commons, that were illegally and unjustly imprisoned or secluded by the Armies force in December 1648 and May 7, 1659, coming upon Tuesday the 27th of December . . . were again forcibly shut out* (London, 1659); *Making the News*, pp. 435, 443; *The Clarke Papers*, IV, pp. 25–9, 41.

attend on him at Berwick on 12 December, along with burgesses from Edinburgh, Haddington and Linlithgow. Argyllshire refrained from participating other than 'to suppress all tumults, stirrings, and unlawful assemblies', on the spurious grounds that their nobles and gentry lived 'obscurelie in a remote corner of the land'. Monck's response, channelled through Argyll, was to thank them for their irenicist intentions and resolutions. Following pressure to mobilise the shire militias for his assistance, Monck issued a clarion call on 7 January 1660, stating that he was moved by God to act on behalf of the Scottish nation, that its inhabitants may enjoy equality with the English.[18] Monck duly commenced his long march south aided by former adherents of the patriotic accommodation, which included a contingent from the Royalist clans, most notably from Lochaber. In the meantime, the consultation process initiated by Monck continued, in the form of political conventions held by permit in February and without the general's permission in April. Proceedings were dominated by Glencairn and the former radical John Leslie, 7th Earl of Rothes. Four commissioners led by Glencairn were authorised to go to London to negotiate on behalf of the political nation when Charles II arrived to reclaim his kingdoms.[19]

On entering London at the outset of February 1660, Monck was instrumental in forcing through the recall of the Long Parliament through the readmission of members excluded since December 1648. The army high command under Fleetwood, staunchly supported by Lambert, had been primarily concerned to refashion the Protectorate. However, a joint rearguard action was fought on behalf of a restored Commonwealth, untainted by Covenanting, led by Sir Henry Vane the younger for the Independents. Others clamoured for a renewed patriotic accommodation between Royalists and Presbyterians, which had materialised in Scotland but not in England in 1649–51. Monck was persuaded that the recalled Long Parliament should dissolve itself and call fresh elections, which was promptly accomplished by 25 April. Three weeks earlier, at the suggestion of Monck, Charles II had issued his Declaration of Breda. A free pardon was

18 ICA, Argyll Letters (1638–85), A36/196–7; ABDA, Argyll Papers, 40.467, .2195; BL, Historical Letters and Papers 1556–1753, Egerton MS 2618, fo.57.

19 *Memoirs of Sir Ewen Cameron of Lochiel*, pp. 148–53; Dow, *Cromwellian Scotland*, pp. 254–7; Young, *The Scottish Parliament*, pp. 304–6. Ireland was not far behind Scotland in staging pre-emptive action against the army's high command. The English interest had regrouped in a military and civil alliance around the veteran Protestant planter and commander, Sir Charles Coote, and Lord Broghill, recently returned from Scotland. In December 1659, Coote had actually instigated the first military action against the restored Commonwealth outwith England in staging a coup d'état that captured Dublin. The city was retained in defiance of the military high command. A Convention of Estates summoned for 27 January 1660 continued in session for next four months, to ensure that a Restoration of the monarchy took full account of the English interest in Ireland (A. Clarke, *Prelude to Restoration in Ireland: The End of the Commonwealth, 1659–60* (Cambridge, 1999), pp. 92–168).

offered to all prepared to 'return to the loyalty and obedience of good subjects'. Military arrears were to be paid in full. A general toleration remained a possibility, not a commitment. The new, and overwhelmingly Royalist, English Parliament duly voted on 8 May for the Restoration of the Stuarts.[20]

The Restoration of Charles II produced constitutional settlements in all three kingdoms, which revived the Stuarts' *ius imperium*, but ruled out the confederal concept of Britain and Ireland united by Covenanting that was particularly associated with the Marquess of Argyll. Apart from the monarchy, episcopacy and aristocracy were restored as the twin pillars of Stuart rule. Parliaments as they had operated under the control of Charles I were restored in England, Scotland and Ireland. With regards to the initial promises made by Charles II in his Declaration of Breda in April 1660, the free pardon to loyal subjects was not extended to the regicides, living or dead. Accordingly, the body of Cromwell was exhumed, hanged in its shroud and the skull impaled in Westminster Hall. Military arrears were paid off, if not in full, certainly in sufficient amounts to ensure stability through the peaceful disbanding of the Cromwellian forces and the substantive decommissioning of naval warships. The removal of Cromwellian garrisons took longer in Scotland and Ireland, however. Charles II reclaimed Crown lands, and bishops were given back their temporal estates to complement their restored spiritual authority in all three kingdoms. Toleration remained a frustrated hope. Nevertheless, the constitutional settlements in the three kingdoms took up to five years to conclude. Their differences were as important as their similarities.[21]

Scotland, indeed, demonstrated the limits of Britannic conformity. Formally restored to independence in 1660, Scotland continued to operate as a junior political partner, albeit with the fuller participation of Scots in the process of government than in the 1650s. The Scottish Council at Whitehall, a devolved committee of the English Privy Council, initially marked Scotland's provincial standing while serving as a channel for the royal court to press for the constitutional and religious settlement in Scotland to follow English practice. The constitutional situation in England was effectively restored to the situation at the outset of the Long Parliament in 1640–41. But all vestiges of the Covenanting Movement were swept away through the Act of Recissory. Scotland was returned to its constitutional position at the coronation parliament of 1633. The oath of allegiance mandatory for all officeholders now required unreserved

20 Woolrych, *Britain in Revolution*, pp. 728–79; Anon., *A Phanatique League & Covenant, Solemnly Entered into by the Assertors of the Good Old Cause* (London, 1659); William Sprigg, *A Modest Plea for an Equal Common-wealth against Monarchy* (London, 1659).

21 R. Hutton, *Charles II: King of England, Scotland, and Ireland* (Oxford, 1989), pp. 133–65; J. Smyth, *The Making of the United Kingdom, 1660–1800* (Harlow, 2001), pp. 77–87.

commitment to the royal prerogative. The Restoration Settlement was initiated in August 1660 through the reconstituted Committee of Estates dissolved by Cromwell's forces in August 1651, but now stripped of all radical Covenanters, like Argyll, who were deemed to have remonstrated against or renounced the monarchy. All Cromwellian collaborators in central or local government were also excluded. The Settlement was ratified formally by the Scottish Estates in plenary session from 1 January to 12 July 1661.[22]

The abandonment of Presbyterianism, though not immediately required by Charles II, was effected partly by the naivety of the Resolutioners in trusting negotiations to James Sharp, and partly to this cleric's personal duplicity in securing for himself the archbishopric of St Andrews in the restored episcopate. While no effort was made to reimpose the fateful liturgical innovations of the 1630s, the restoration of episcopacy created the most sizeable element of Protestant dissent within the three kingdoms that was led by militant Protestors and sustained by conventicles in house and field. Nonetheless, the driving force behind the change of the religious establishment, as of the constitutional settlement as a whole, was the nobility led by former Britannic Engagers such as Middleton (now ennobled as Earl of Middleton), who became the king's commissioner to the Scottish Estates; Glencairn, who was made chancellor; and, above all, Lauderdale as secretary of state for Scotland. Another Engager, Crawford-Lindsay, was reaffirmed as treasurer. Their dominance in the revived Scottish Privy Council was fortified by unflinching support from the restored judiciary.[23] The only former radicals who secured high office were Cassillis as justice-general and Rothes as president of the revitalised Privy Council. Loudoun was handsomely pensioned off. Lothian, who claimed to have lost £20,000 sterling (£240,000) since the failure of the patriotic accommodation, was stripped of his office as secretary of state. But having clearly signalled that he was no longer acting in concert with Argyll, he was accepted back into royal favour. His successor as secretary lost little time in exploiting an exaggerated climate of religious dissent in the Lowlands and social disorder in the Highlands.

---

22 BL, Lauderdale Papers, Miscellaneous Correspondence, vol.II, May–Dec. 1660, Add.MSS 23,114, fo.42; DH, Loudoun Papers, bundles 1/19; TFA, Papers, TD 1171; *CAL*, II, pp. 438–40; Young, *The Scottish Parliament*, pp. 306–23. The original intent of the Scottish nobles and gentry in favour with Charles II at the Restoration was to summon the Committee of Estates as constituted by parliamentary warrant in 1650; but this would have excluded the Royalists who had served with Montrose (Rosehaugh, *Memoirs*, pp. 31–3).

23 T. Harris, *Restoration: Charles II and His Kingdoms, 1660–1685* (London, 2005), pp. 104–35; J.M. Buckroyd, 'Bridging the Gap: Scotland 1659–1660', *SHR*, 66 (1987), pp. 1–25; *LJB*, III, pp. 585–6. Cassillis, however, refused to take the oath of allegiance and was stripped on his office in April 1661 on being declared by the Scottish Estates as not capable of holding 'anie public charge within the natione' (ACL, IV (1660–69), p. 132; TFA, Papers, TD 1171).

Lauderdale did so as the dominant British politician in Scotland, to build up not just standing forces but also a militia that was empowered to quell unrest anywhere within the king's dominions.[24]

Although former Royalists regained estates forfeited in the 1640s and 1650s, arrears of taxes due to the Covenanting Movement were not written off. In effect, Scotland was recast as a military-fiscal state in deficit, with nobles and gentry pressing for army commissions in order to benefit from a share of the stringent fines imposed on religious dissenters and disorderly clans. Scotland's constitutional standing was not so much approximate to that of England as realigned to that of Ireland, where a dependent parliament was restored. Like the Irish parliaments and constitutional assemblies in Caribbean colonies, the Scottish Estates awarded Charles a substantive annuity of £480,000 (£40,000 sterling) for life raised mainly through the excise. Such awards obviated the need for regular parliaments to vote supply.[25]

Judicial Retribution

Among the revolutionary politicians who actually witnessed the Restoration, Argyll became the most prominent victim. Acting against the advice of his closest friends and kinsmen, Argyll went to London in June 1660 to seek an audience with Charles II, following notification from Lorne that the king 'took kindlie with all men'. At the end of May, Lorne had taken upon himself the composition of an obsequious letter of loyalty to Charles II on behalf of the ClanCampbell and their associates. Prior to his departure, however, Argyll placed the management of his estates firmly in the control of his wife, Margaret Douglas, and his second son, Lord Neil Campbell. He also transferred to Lord Lorne his lease on the assize herrings in the western seas, his claim on the English Parliament for £15,000 sterling and his grant of the excise on wines and strong waters that was supposed to reimburse the Scottish public debts to the house of Argyll.[26] The Marquess was summoned to meet Charles II on 8 July. Instead of being granted an audience, he was arrested and imprisoned without having time or opportunity to make his escape down the Thames on the *St*

24 *CAL*, II, pp. 431–8, 440–1, 450–1; DH, Loudoun Deeds, bundles 1/11–12 and 2/12; TFA, Papers, TD 1110; Macinnes, *Clanship, Commerce and the House of Stuart*, pp. 130–7.
25 TFA, Papers, TD 3770 and 3775; R. Lee, 'Retreat from Revolution: The Scottish Parliament and the Restored Monarchy, 1661–1663' in Young ed., *Celtic Dimensions of the British Civil Wars*, pp. 164–85.
26 ICA, Argyll Letters (1638–85), A36/200–2 and Miscellaneous 17th Century Papers, bundles 15/44, 16/41 and Argyll Transcripts, XIV, nos 45, 48. Argyll had also started the legal process to make his estates over to Lorne, to create a barony in Kintyre for his second son, Lord Neill, and to make settlements of £12,000 and £8000 respectively for his two unmarried daughters Anna and Isabella.

Lawrence of Dorft. He languished in the Tower for five months without being allowed to take supportive testimony by way of precognitions from English and Scottish associates in London, or even to receive letters of exculpation from the regicides among his fellow prisoners. He was also denied paper, pen and ink to prepare his own defences against his reputedly treacherous conduct since 1638. Although Argyll faced indictment for reputed crimes that were both Scottish and British, he had no English peerage. Accordingly, he could not be tried in London as Hamilton had been in 1649. With the Scottish Estates due to commence on New Year's Day, he was transferred by ship to Leith, arriving on a stormy night on 21 December. The next morning, strictly guarded by musketeers, he was led with his head covered from Leith past baying crowds deriding him as a traitor. Under the close supervision of the magistrates and town guard, he was imprisoned in Edinburgh Castle. Again he was offered few if any facilities for his legal defence, as Presbyterians came to realise that his head was the price of a Restoration Settlement in Scotland that renounced all past association with the Covenanting Movement.[27]

Argyll was shunned by Edinburgh's legal establishment in his endeavours to secure leading counsel and had to be content with six advocates appointed by the Scottish Estates after processes for treason were initially intimated to him on 28 January 1661 and duly led against him three days later. Of the six advocates, the burden of defence was essentially carried by Mr Robert Sinclair, Mr John Cunninghame and, above all, a relatively junior counsel, Mr George MacKenzie of Rosehaugh, later knighted and made Lord Advocate. Rosehaugh, who became a leading Scottish jurist and upholder of authoritarian monarchy in the Restoration era, was a staunch Royalist. Nevertheless, political incompatibilities actually aided Argyll's defence, as the Marquess and his counsel focused on legal issues, not political point scoring. However, their endeavours were severely compromised by the unusual legal procedures followed by the Scottish Estates for over three months from 12 February until 24 May. Argyll was not allowed to summon witnesses in his defence, nor was his counsel allowed to take supportive precognitions on his behalf. Indeed, no immunity was accorded to his counsel should they articulate statements in defence of the Marquess that

27 *LJB*, III, pp. 418, 447; Nicoll, *Diary*, pp. 295–6, 308–9, 321–2; Kirkton, *The Secret and True History of the Church of Scotland, pp. 69–70; The Diary of Mr John Lamont of Newton*, p. 149. Also sent back to Leith with Argyll was Sir John Swinton of Swinton, who had served as a judge under Cromwell and converted to Quakerism at the Restoration. As Swinton was already excommunicated and forfeited for his collaboration with Cromwell during the occupation of Scotland, he was marched through the streets with his head uncovered and deposited in the Tolbooth with the common criminals. Ironically, Argyll was lodged in the custody of former troopers of the New Model Army who still garrisoned Edinburgh Castle (TFA, Papers, TD 1103).

could be construed as treasonable; an intimidatory warning against speaking 'thing's prejudicial to his Majesty's government' that effectively meant Argyll led the pleading on his own behalf.[28]

Furthermore, the main business of pleading before the Scottish Estates was devolved to the reconstituted Committee of the Articles. Though not yet including bishops as clerical commissioners, the Committee was firmly under the managerial control of Middleton and Rothes. Intent on a conviction on all counts, they consistently refused Argyll's pleas for clemency. They made no effort to have the indemnity offered by Charles II in the Declaration of Breda extended from England to Scotland. They paid no heed to pleas from Argyll that this situation was both anomalous and lacking in mercy. The Lord Advocate, Sir John Fletcher, was allowed considerable latitude in drawing up a comprehensive but far from factually accurate dittay (indictment). His laying of charges against Argyll was not so much a forensic exercise as a discourse in legal flyting, supplemented by verbal sparring with the Marquess that was rarely checked by the presiding judge, Sir John Gilmour. The full participation of the Scottish Estates was only called upon to ratify the discriminatory proceedings in the Committee of Articles, notably to restrict the time available to the Marquess to prepare his defences, and to deny him the opportunity of making a speech or submitting a precognition before the charges laid against him were specified. Most irregularly, the Estates refused Argyll permission to question the relevancy of the fourteen detailed charges against him in the grand indictment of 31 January 1661, before he defended himself against the libel of treason. When Argyll requested that his trial be remitted to the Court of Session sitting as a High Court of Justice, because of the intricate detail and legal complexity of the charges against him, this request was construed as declining the authority of the Scottish Estates.

The fourteen detailed charges in the grand indictment against Argyll can be broken down into three chronological periods. The first period, from 1638–41, covered Argyll's emergence as a radical leader of the Covenanting Movement. Three charges related to his subscription of the National Covenant, his conduct in the central and eastern Highlands during the Bishops' Wars, and the trial for treason of Mr John Stewart of Ladywell. The second period, from 1642–51, ranged through Argyll's role in formulating the Solemn League and Covenant

---

28 No official record appears to have survived of Argyll's trial in 1661. However, the relevant material has been extensively collated by Robert Wodrow in both his published *Sufferings*, I, pp. 42–57 and appendix, pp. 22–9, and his personal papers (NLS, Wodrow MSS, folio xxvii, ff.100–26). These papers, along with the reprinted material in *State Trials*, vol. 5, pp. 1369–499 and in Rosehaugh, *Memoirs*, pp. 33–41, form the basis of this account. For Rosehaugh's subsequent activities as a jurist, political philosopher and polemicist see C. Jackson, *Restoration Scotland, 1660–1690: Royalist Politics, Religion and Ideas* (Woodbridge, 2004).

until his reputed collusion with Cromwell to undermine the patriotic accommodation. The eight charges here also concerned his involvement in the trials and executions of Huntly, Hamilton, Montrose and, above all, Charles I. He was also indicted for slaughter under trust of the Lamonts in 1646 and the MacDougalls and the MacAllisters in 1647. The third period, from 1652–59, focused on his role as a Cromwellian collaborator. Three charges claimed he had withheld support from the patriotic resistance in 1653–54, had attended Westminster as an MP in 1659, and had consistently suppressed the offering of prayers for the exiled Charles II.

The first series of charges against him were dismissed by Argyll, partly through legalistic sleight of hand and partly because his conduct had already been exonerated by Charles I and the Scottish Estates. To the charges of signing the National Covenant, Argyll claimed he did so with the approval of Charles I, as he had first signed the King's Covenant, which was found not to be inconsistent with the National Covenant, albeit this judgement was by Covenanting ideologues as ratified at the Glasgow Assembly in 1638. Argyll maintained he did not actually sign the National Covenant until the spring of 1639, up to which point he was working for an accommodation between Charles I and the Covenanting Movement. His emergence as the leading radical was consistent not only with his patriotic duties to Kirk and country, but also with his religious duty to further the Reformation in Scotland. Moreover, Charles had ratified the proceedings of the Covenanting Movement from the emergence of the Tables in 1638 to the constitutional settlement warranted by the Treaty of London and concluded in 1641. His reputed burning down of the house of Airlie was largely conjectural, its actual timing was imprecise and could not be proved by any written instruction – at least not any Argyll was prepared to release to the court (see Chapter 1). The Scottish Estates in 1641 had recognised his honourable conduct as well as his considerable expenses in pacifying the central and eastern Highlands in the previous year. The prosecution of Stewart of Ladywell for claiming that Argyll was prepared to depose Charles I involved the Marquess as the wronged party. Otherwise his participation was marginal. The case against Ladywell was conducted with all due process. Again these proceedings of the Scottish Estates were ratified by Charles I in 1641 when he implemented his commitments under the Treaty of London. As well as authenticating all past proceedings of the Covenanting Movement, all involved in the Bishops' Wars against the king were indemnified from subsequent legal actions. In short, there was no case to answer to the first series of charges specified in his grand indictment.[29]

Argyll initially took the second series of charges as the most challenging,

---

29 Argyll used the indemnity of 1641 to excuse himself from the ancillary charge of his taking possession of Dumbarton Castle and redistributing its armaments in the course of the Bishops' Wars.

partly because they involved the regicide and partly because Sir James Lamont of Inveryne was able to bring his personal quest for redress into the grand indictment. Indeed, Lamont of Inveryne had been encouraged to do so by Middleton, Rothes, Glencairn and all other members of the Restoration regime intent on securing a capital conviction against Argyll. The Marquess mounted a vigorous defence against his involvement in the trials and executions of Huntly, Hamilton, Montrose and Charles I. He steadfastly maintained, both in his public utterances and in his private correspondence, that these charges were outright calumnies with no foundation in fact. There was no paper trail to prove his complicity in any or all of these political murders or in his reputed collusion with Cromwell to undermine the patriotic accommodation. This defence was legally correct and vindicated the longstanding preference of the Marquess to rely on personal contacts and political clientage rather than on written instructions.[30] Argyll did admit to dealing with Cromwell for assistance against the Engagers in 1648. But he did so at the behest of the Committee of Estates, then restored to radical control. He denied any subsequent contact with Cromwell prior to the occupation of 1652. His defence against the charges of slaughter under trust against the Lamonts in Cowal, and the MacDougalls and MacAllisters in Kintyre, again relied on there being no incriminating paper trail.

Argyll was able to muster a selectively robust exoneration of his conduct during these massacres, a defence enhanced by his absence from the slaughter in Cowal and by his presence in the subordinate capacity as colonel in the Covenanting Army in Kintyre. He attested that he had given no special direction for the reprisals against the Lamonts. As no document could be produced proving the contrary, he contended he was not liable for the crimes committed either under statute or common law. At the same time, he challenged the existence of articles of capitulation for the garrison at Lochhead. He claimed that the offer of surrender to the garrison at Dunaverty was unconditional. In effect, Argyll argued that his indictment was not relevant in Cowal because the Covenanting irregulars were under the command of another, namely James Campbell of Ardkinglass, and not relevant in Kintyre because no assurance had been given to the surrendered garrisons that their lives would be spared. The Marquess's defence was not hindered when two of his leading co-accused in the massacre, Campbell of Ardkinglass and Dougall Campbell of Inverawe, absconded rather than testify in court. A third accused, George Campbell,

---

30 ICA, Argyll Letters (1638–85), A36/205. Argyll even turned the lack of a paper trail to his advantage in the case of Montrose claiming that he had reached an accord with the Royalist commander in 1645, presumably after Philiphaugh rather than Kilsyth, which would have prevented further bloodshed. But this reputed accord was not supported by the Covenanting leadership as a whole.

sheriff-depute of Argyll, agreed to give evidence in return for a pension and a pardon; his conduct thereby confirming that the political nature of the charges against Argyll took precedence over the integrity of the judicial process. The Marquess had already put on record that fact that witnesses were being pardoned for past crimes and misdemeanours so that they could testify against him.[31]

However, articles of capitulation, if not extant for the garrison at Ascog, certainly survived for the garrison at Toward. They were subscribed on 3 June 1644 by Inveryne on behalf of his clansmen and Ardkinglass, and six other leading gentry of the ClanCampbell for the Covenanting irregulars. Held by the house of Argyll, these articles were certainly not produced in court. While the articles of capitulation were manifestly breached by massacre, they also contained the explicit admission of the Lamonts' association with the destructive Royalist forces of Alasdair MacColla and their past military involvement against the Campbells. Indeed, Argyll was able to use a supplementary defence for reprisals against the Lamonts in Cowal, as against the MacDougalls and the MacAllisters in Kintyre. The three clans were acknowledged adherents of MacColla and the Royalist forces on the western seaboard whom he had been empowered to prosecute with fire and sword under a commission of lieutenancy authorised by the Scottish Estates in 1644, a commission that was still current throughout the summer of 1647. Argyll argued persuasively that the conduct of himself and his clansmen, as that of the Covenanting Army under David Leslie, was covered by the Act of Oblivion which accompanied the ratification of the Treaty of Breda by the Scottish Estates at Stirling following the arrival of Charles II in Scotland in July 1650, and was subsequently reaffirmed at Perth on the rescinding of the Acts of Classes in June 1651.[32]

---

31 Nicoll, *Diary*, pp. 307, 320; TFA, Papers, TD 1103; ICA, Miscellaneous Argyll Papers, fo.113. Argyll was able to ridicule two associated charges in this second series – that the people of the island of Jura had been starved to death on his instructions in 1647, and that he had personally been responsible for the sacking of Menstrie house and estates in 1645. To the first, Argyll was able to demonstrate that he was not there, and there was no paper trail. But the famine actually related to Islay and was occasioned by the devastations wreaked by MacColla's troops. People from this island were decanted to Jura as to Ulster to escape the famine. To the second, Argyll was not in the position of command at Menstrie, which was actually held by Lieutenant-General William Baillie. Albeit the Marquess conveniently glossed that he was present as a meddlesome political adviser, the Menstrie estates in Clackmannanshire actually came within the overlordship of the house of Argyll.

32 ICA, Argyll Transcripts, XII, no. 313. That the treatment of prisoners at Kintyre was not outwith the bounds of restraint has particular force in a European context with respect to reprisals against armies perceived to be in opposition to the state – in this case the Covenanting Movement in 1647. (G. Parker, 'Constraints on Warfare in the Western World', in M. Howard, G. J. Andreopolous and M. R. Shulman, eds, *The Laws of War* (New Haven and London, 1994), pp. 40–58, 233–40).

Argyll could also claim that all his actions under the second series of charges, from the formulation of the Solemn League and Covenant to the bringing over of Charles II from Holland to implement the patriotic accommodation, had all been done with the warrant and approval of the Scottish Estates, from whom he had suffered rebuffs as well as triumphs as a Covenanting leader. He had actually been in Ireland when the king placed himself in the custody of the Covenanting Army at Newark in May 1646. The subsequent transfer of the king from the Covenanters to the Parliamentarians at Newcastle at the outset of 1647 was the concerted decision of the Scottish Estates, and by no means his sole doing. That he stood to gain £15,000 sterling from this transfer was not in itself motivation but just recompense for his extensive public expenditure on behalf of the Covenanting Movement. But, above all, his actions as a Covenanting leader were also indemnified by the Treaty of Breda. His subsequent absence from the army of intervention which came to grief at Worcester in September 1651 was not an act of malevolence but one of necessity, which was excused by Charles II on compassionate grounds. Again, Argyll could claim that he had no case to answer for all charges, including the regicide, specified in the second series.

That there was no case to answer for the charges in both the first and second series was taken up at the court of Charles II by Lauderdale, who was particularly sympathetic to the fate of Lorne (who was married to his niece), should the Marquess be forfeited as well as executed for his alleged treason. In this he was supported by the presiding judge, Sir John Gilmour, who had become less and less enamoured with Sir John Fletcher's increasingly desperate endeavours to tie Argyll to the regicide. Middleton and Rothes had rushed to Court to counteract Lauderdale's discreet lobbying, which also served to undermine their own position to the secretary of state's advantage.[33] By the outset of April, the general indictment against Argyll had effectively been reduced to the charges in the third series. Argyll again mounted a selectively vigorous defence, both in principle and practice, against his purported collaboration with the Cromwellian regime. By appealing to biblical texts (mainly from the Books of Kings and of Solomon), to classical philosophers (Aristotle leavened by Plato and the Stoics) and to contemporaneous jurists, most notably Grotius, Argyll claimed that he was obliged by both necessity and prescription to work with a usurping power for the best part of a decade. However, he did so as a passive actor not an active collaborator. This position was not exceptional and could actually be said to be no more than compliance, 'which was the epidemical fault' among the Scottish nation during the 1650s.[34]

---

33 *LJB*, III, pp. 422, 465.
34 Rosehaugh, *Memoirs*, p. 48; NLS, Woodrow MSS, folio xxvii, ff.120–1; ABDA, Argyll Papers, 40.594.

His claim that he was personally ill and incapacitated when he reached his accommodation with General Deane in August 1652 conveniently glossed over his mobilisation of clansmen and clients in a reformed Western Association to exact more favourable terms. Argyll was also confident that no evidence could be produced against him that he had actively supported Monck's suppression of the patriotic rising of 1653–54. Testimony from witnesses, such as his kinsman, John Campbell, younger of Glenorchy (later 1st Earl of Breadalbane), only revealed that Argyll had met Monck while armed with a sword, not that the Marquess played an integral part in military manoeuvres. Indeed Monck (now Duke of Albemarle) had sent a certificate to Argyll in late December 1660, which affirmed that the Marquess had raised a company of 100 clansmen for the defence of Argyllshire in 1654. But this company did 'little or no service at all' during the three months they remained in arms.[35]

Charges of Argyll discouraging Presbyterian ministers from praying for the king were nebulous, lacking in specification as to time and place, and easily refuted both with regard to his purported presence and lack of written instruction or even verbal collaboration. His attendance at the proclamation of Oliver – not, as initially specified, Richard – Cromwell in Edinburgh in July 1657 was by military command, an order which Albemarle had actually confirmed in December 1660 before charges were actually finalised against Argyll. The Marquess asserted he had taken no part in the Tender of Incorporation of 1652–53. His presence at Westminster in 1659 should be taken neither as his assent to union by political incorporation nor as denoting his approval of the usurpation. He was in the English Parliament to press Scottish interests. He had not been invited to participate in Monck's march to London. There was a long history of strained relations between Argyll and Albemarle, which went back to the latter's opposition to the expansion of Presbyterianism in Ulster that the Marquess had promoted on his visit to Ireland in the spring of 1646.[36]

Undoubtedly, Albemarle was on the side of Middleton and Rothes, not the Marquess. While visiting London in the spring of 1661, Lord Neil Campbell had been rather indiscreet in suggesting that all charges against his father would soon fall. On learning this, Albemarle released letters he had received from Argyll in the course of the patriotic rising of 1653–54. These letters related primarily to Argyll's desire to protect his house from the activities of Lorne at the outset of the campaign, and to ensure that his house would not suffer from the protracted refusal of his son to make peace with Monck (see Chapter

---

35 NLS, Wodrow MSS, folio xxvii, fo.123; ICA, Argyll Letters (1638–85), A36/204.
36 *The Clarke Papers*, IV, p. 272; ICA, Argyll Letters (1638–85), A36/203; ABDA, Argyll Papers, 40.478–80. Relations with Monck were more recently strained when Argyll had seemingly made no effort to discourage guerrilla resistance by the Gordons on the former Huntly estates.

10). Argyll's associated letter to Cromwell sidestepping the issue of supplying military intelligence, and Cromwell's brief, formal and detached correspondence with the Marquess, were not admissible. Moreover, Albemarle's insidious evidence was presented to the Committee of Articles after all notified testimony from witnesses had been concluded, and in the course of the debate to determine the belated relevance of the process against Argyll, in order to establish whether any or all of the charges were proven or not proven. At the behest of Middleton, the debate was immediately broken off to hear the fresh evidence from Albemarle, which did not actually relate to any specific charge in the third series. Notwithstanding their dubious provenance, the letters were sufficient to sway the debate in the Committee in the political direction wished by Middleton and Rothes. Argyll's conviction as a Cromwellian collaborator but not as a regicide was duly upheld in the Scottish Estates by Royalists, former Engagers and even Resolutioners. Only the Protestors, as they readily broadcast, could claim no part in Argyll's conviction on Friday 24 May. Two days earlier, by order of the Lords and Commons, the Solemn League and Covenant, as the most distinctive Scottish contribution to the British confederation espoused by Argyll, was burned by the common hangman at Westminster and removed from all public places of record, as from all churches in England and Wales.[37]

After the Scottish Estates on 25 May sentenced him to be beheaded, forfeited and stripped of his titles, the Marquess made a final poignant but pointless appeal, drawing on imperial Roman precedent, for thirty days to elapse before his execution to allow time for merciful reflection. However, he was unceremoniously removed from Edinburgh Castle to the Tolbooth, to await execution by guillotine at 2 p. m. on Monday 27 May 1661. Despite repeated charges of cowardice through his political career, Argyll went to his death with fortitude, dignity and composure. Indeed, he believed firmly he was in a state of grace before the Maiden severed his head from his body.[38] In his last speech upon the scaffold erected in the High Street of Edinburgh, he firmly rejected any involvement in the regicide and vehemently denied he had acted prejudicially either to the person of the late king or to the authority of monarchy. He then went on to give a brief exposition of his Presbyterian faith, in which he affirmed Calvinist orthodoxy in determining his election to personal salvation. He castigated the reprobate who preferred profanity, swearing, drinking and whoring to the godly pursuit of grace through active participation in the Kirk. He also admonished

---

37 TFA, Papers, TD 1197; ICA, Argyll Transcripts, XIV, nos 54, 56; *ACL*, IV, pp. 142–4; Anon., *The Funeral of the Good Old Cause or a Covenant of Both Houses of Parliament against the Solemn League and Covenant* (London, 1661); Willcock, *The Great Marquess*, pp. 324–34.

38 Nicoll, *Diary*, pp. 334–5; *CAL*, II, pp. 448–9; ICA, Miscellaneous 17th Century Papers, bundle 100/101.

all members of the visible Kirk that they must adhere to the engagements God has laid upon Scotland, they being 'tyed by Covenants to Religion and Reformation' through which they must strive to attain the grace that would ensure their election. For his own part, he was convinced that he was moving on to glory in the Kirk invisible, having attainted through his devout faith sufficient grace to ensure his election as one of the 'truly Godly'. He did not repent going to London at the Restoration, as he was now convinced that 'the Lord hath pardoned me'. Having reiterated his innocence with respect to the regicide, he took his farewell of family and friends in the expectation of 'eternal Salvation and happiness'.[39]

British Legacy

Argyll's abiding temporal concern prior to his execution was the survival of his house after his title and estates were forfeited. However, assistance was again to hand from Lauderdale. He faced formidable opposition at the royal court and in Scotland to any rehabilitation of the house of Argyll, as Lorne was no less a committed Presbyterian than his father. Indeed, Lauderdale was not helped by Lorne's political impetuosity, which led to another brief spell of imprisonment in Edinburgh Castle from where he was released in June 1663.[40] Four months later, however, with staunch backing from Margaret Douglas, the Dowager Marchioness of Argyll and from the king's aunt, Elizabeth of Bohemia,

---

39 [Archibald Campbell] *My Lord Marquis of Argyle his Speech upon the Scaffold the 27 of May 1661* (Edinburgh, 1661); BL, Scottish Sermons etc, 1659–1664, Egerton MS 2215, ff.62–4; Wodrow, *Sufferings*, I, pp. 55–6 and appendix, pp. 28–9; Rosehaugh, *Memoirs*, pp. 41–7; *LJB*, III, p. 466–7. From his final confinement in the Tolbooth Argyll was attended by two ministers, David Hutcheson and John Hamilton, and was supported principally on the scaffold by his two sons-in-law, George, Earl of Caithness and Robert Ker, Lord Newbattle, whose father Lothian was also present along with Loudoun and Sir James Montgomerie of Skelmorlie. His personal chaplain Mr Traill and his physician Mr Cunningham were also in attendance. While Argyll's head replaced that of Montrose upon the west end of the Tolbooth, his body was carried by friends to the church of St Mary Magdalene in the Cowgate, and then to Lothian's home at Newbattle Abbey where it lay for a month before being conveyed back to Edinburgh at night with great pomp in a carriage of the Earl Marischal's that was drawn by six horses. Escorted by a huge company of clansmen, the carriage went to Linlithgow, then to Falkirk and Glasgow, and on to Kilpatrick on the River Clyde, where it was put on a boat for Dunoon and then carried to his ancestral burial place at Kilmun on the Holy Loch (ICA, Argyll transcripts, XIV, no.155).

40 Clarendon, *History*, pp. 1112–13; *CAL*, II, p. 449; Anon., *Some Reasons why Archibald Campbell, Sometime Lord Lorne, Ought not to be Restored to the Honour or Estate of his Late Father Archibald Sometime Marquess of Argyle* (1661). On 14 May 1661, the Scottish Estates had placed an order arresting the rents of the Argyll estates and discharging the current administrators and factors. Four days later, Lorne had rather optimistically given legal instruction for a process to reverse the impending forfeiture of his father in the misplaced hope of prompt royal clemency for himself (ICA, Miscellaneous 17th Century Papers, bundles 100/94, 110/38).

the Winter Queen, Lauderdale persuaded Charles II to restore Lorne as heir of his grandfather, Archibald, 7th Earl of Argyll. The horrendous burden of debt on his restored estates meant that the new 9th Earl of Argyll was allowed only £15,000 annually from his rents, the remainder of which was assigned to pay off creditors. The 9th Earl was fully restored as heir to his father in 1664, after the head of the Marquess was removed from the Tolbooth by royal warrant before 5 a.m. on 8 June. He was also confronted by a discriminatory financial settlement imposed by the Restoration regime in Scotland.[41]

He was obliged to honour all outstanding debts, included those contracted by his father on the Huntly estates. Thus George Gordon, restored to his estates as 4th Marquess of Huntly and later created 1st Duke of Gordon, was able to avoid liability for debts in excess of £27,752 sterling (£333,024). The 9th Earl was also denied reparations with interest in excess of £68,707 sterling (£824,484) promised to his father by the Scottish Estates and the English Parliament. He also had to pay £66,667 for the estate and rents of Mugdock awarded to his father following the forfeiture of James Graham, 1st Marquess of Montrose in 1645, even though his father had actually sold the estate back to James Graham, 2nd Marquess of Montrose, by 1653. The 9th Earl owed over £360,000 to his father's creditors in addition to debts of £232,101 which he had contracted jointly with his father. Despite being faced with debts equivalent to eighteen years' rent from the Argyll estates, and with public pressure from creditors to sell off lands, the 9th Earl did not embark on a fire sale. As his unrivalled heritable jurisdiction had also been restored along with his lands and honours, he was able to protect the territorial integrity of his house. Accordingly, the debts of the Marquess took generations to redeem and were still outstanding by the making of the United Kingdom in 1707.[42]

It is too facile to write off the Marquess of Argyll's British legacy as a horrendous burden of debts, frustrated political ideals and deep public hostility – the fate of many an ambitious Scottish politician from the Restoration to the present

---

41　BL, Lauderdale Papers, Miscellaneous Correspondence vol. III, Sep.–Dec. 1663, Add.MSS 23,120, fo.146 and Miscellaneous Autograph Letters, 1550–1833. Foreign. Add.MSS 24,024, fo.42; ICA, Miscellaneous 17th Century Papers, bundle 175/13 and Argyll Transcripts, XIV, nos116, 135–6, 138, 153, 160–2, 164. The Winter Queen sent her letter of July 1661 from Brussels following overtures for clemency towards Lorne from Argyll's half-sisters Isabella and Victoria who, along with their sister Barbara, were closeted in nunneries there.

42　Nicoll, *Diary*, pp. 384, 403, 413–14; ABDA, Argyll Papers, 40.805, .1914; ICA, Miscellaneous 17th Century Papers, bundles 16/41, 45/10, 52/3–6, 53/2, 67/1 and 4, 100/94, 147/2, 173/9, 175/1 and 3, 184 and Miscellaneous Argyll Letters, fo.1126 and Argyll Transcripts, XIV, nos 52, 58, 70, 166, 214; Anon., *Information for the Earl of Argyle and his Creditors of the Marquis of Argyle against the Duke of Gordon and Earl of Aboyne* (Edinburgh, 1700). The 9th Earl was also supported financially by a voluntary stent of £40 for every merkland held of the house of Argyll by the gentry of the Campbells and associated clans.

day. Argyll compares adversely to his two leading contemporaries, Charles I and Oliver Cromwell, only in terms of his persistent pursuit of private gain from public policy: in effect, when he acted as a clan chief and Scottish magnate rather than as a British statesman. The political abilities of Charles I as a monarch, communicator and commander are continuously subject to historical revision that can be more partial than credible.[43] Notwithstanding his Britannic pedigree, Charles I operated primarily as an English monarch in peace and war who became an Anglican martyr in the wake of the regicide. Cromwell's enduring appeal can be attributed in part to his role as a revolutionary leader who belligerently pursued peace through war. As a godly soldier he was determined to be a servant of a God who demanded sacrifices and ruled by will rather than by law or covenant. Quintessentially, Cromwell became the Gothic Emperor, the epic hero who personified and globally projected the national excellencies of England.[44] From a non-anglocentric perspective, both Charles I and Cromwell subordinated Scottish interests; the former provoking revolution which spread from Scotland to Ireland and England, and the latter forcing subjection on both Scotland and Ireland through conquest and occupation.

Argyll was a revolutionary, not an imperialist. He did not favour an organic body politic dominated by either a monarch or lord protector intent on pushing English interests, whether in the name of uniformity or godliness. Argyll believed that governance in Kirk and State should be contractual as well as godly through the consensual working of nobles, gentry, burgesses and clergy, preferably with, but if necessary against, the king. His political career was a personal affirmation of the right of resistance vested in the commonwealth, not just the aristocracy. This perspective was both Scottish and international;[45] though Argyll's favoured theatre of political operation was undoubtedly British. The sole public memorial to the Marquess – his recumbent representation in the Kirk of St Giles in Edinburgh – is near the scene of his execution but far from his last resting place in Argyllshire. Indeed, the former Cathedral Kirk established by Charles I in 1633, at the expense of the citizenry of Edinburgh,

---

43 Cf. W.J. Bulman, 'The Practice of Politics: The English Civil War and the "Resolution" of Henrietta Maria and Charles I', *Past & Present*, 206 (2010), pp. 43–80; R. Cust, *Charles I: A Political Life* (Harlow, 2005).

44 B. Worden, 'The Politics of Marvell's Horation Ode', *HJ*, 27 (1984), pp. 525–47; J. Raymond, 'Framing Liberty: Marvell's *First Anniversary* and the Instrument of Government', *Huntington Library Quarterly*, 62 (1999), pp. 313–50; J.C. Davis, *Oliver Cromwell* (London, 2001), pp. 116–70; Barber, *Regicide and Republicanism*, pp. 193–4.

45 A.I. Macinnes, 'The Hidden Commonwealth: Poland-Lithuania and Scottish Political Discourse in the Seventeenth Century' in K. Friedrich and B.M. Pendzich eds, *Citizenship and Identity in a Multi-National Commonwealth. Poland-Lithuania in Context, 1550–1750* (Leiden and Boston, 2009), pp. 233–60.

is not necessarily the most appropriate setting to commemorate an uncompromising Presbyterian and resolute Covenanter. Yet it is an iconic reminder that Argyll sought to pursue Scottish interests within a British context on the basis of confederation, not incorporation. His modernist commitment to mutual respect between both kingdoms – if not his pervasive concern for godliness in guiding human affairs – may well offer a constructive way forward for Anglo-Scottish relations in the twenty-first century. At the same time, when engaging international support for the Covenanting Movement, Argyll was conscious of Scotland's distinctiveness in a European context. This may well prove a more reliable federative future for a currently stateless nation.

Bibliography

1 PRIMARY SOURCES

1.1 Archival Material

Argyll and Bute District Archives, Lochgilphead
    Argyll Papers
    Valuation Roll for the Presbytery of Argyll, 1629
Aberdeen City Archives
    Aberdeen Council Registers, vols LII–LIII (1630–58)
Aberdeen University Library
    David Burnet 1691, 'The Portrait of True Loyalty Exposed in the Family of Gordon',
      MS 658
Bodleian Library, Oxford University
    Carte Papers, 1636–52. Ireland, MS Carte 65.
    Papers Relating to the Civil War, 1603–1660, MS Don.c.184
British Library, London
    Autographs of King Charles the First and Second, Egerton MS 1533
    Collection of Historical and Parliamentary Papers, 1620–1660, Egerton MS 1048
    Correspondence of R. Lang, Secretary of State, 1649–61, Add.MSS 37,047
    Correspondence of Sir W. Aston, vol. I, 1619–20, Add.MSS 36,446
    Family of Pitt. Official Papers, 17th Century, Add.MSS, 29,975.
    Hardwicke papers, vols DXVI and CCCXC, Historical Collections, 1567–1720, Add.
      MSS 35,864 and 35,838
    Historical Autographs, 16th–18th Centuries, Add.MSS 28,103
    Historical Letters and Papers, Add.MSS 33,596
    Historical Papers, Egerton MS 2884
    Holme Hall Papers, vol. I, 1518–1773, Add.MSS 40,132
    James Hay, Earl of Carlisle. Correspondence, vols I and II, 1602–1620, Egerton MS
      2592–3
    John Dury, Epistolae Pace Ecclesiastica, Sloane MS 654
    Keyboard Music: XVI–XVII Centuries, Add.MSS 29,996
    Letters and Papers, 1602–c.1711, Add.MSS 32,476
    Letters and State Papers: Birch Collection, Add.MSS 4158
    Lauderdale Papers, Miscellaneous Correspondence, vols I–II, 1630–60, Add.MSS.
      23,113–14 vol. III, Sep.–Dec. 1663, Add.MSS 23,120
    Maitland and Lauderdale Papers 1532–1688, Add.MSS 35,125
    Miscellaneous Autograph Letters, Add.MSS 24,422

Miscellaneous Autograph Letters, 1550–1833. Foreign. Add.MSS 24,024.
Miscellaneous Correspondence, vol. VIII, Sep–Dec. 1663, Add.MSS 23,120
Miscellaneous Letters and Papers, Add.MSS 33,506 and Add.MSS 41,295
Miscellaneous Letters etc., 1566–1804, Add.MSS 36,540
Naval Papers, 1643–1677, Add.MSS 22,546
Nicholas Papers, Egerton MS 2533 and 2542
Observations of the State of Ireland, April 1640, Stowe MS 29
Ordinances of Parliament 1642–49, Add.MSS 5492
Original Documents relating to Scotland, the Borders and Ireland, 16th and 17th centuries, Add.MSS 5754
Original Letters of State and Warrants etc., 1559–1593, Harley MS 7004
Papers of General Desborough, 1651–1660, Egerton MS 2519
Papers of the Loch Family, Add.MSS 40,885
Papers Relating to the Revenue etc, Add.MSS 11,597
Political and Miscellaneous Papers. 17th and 18th centuries, Add.MSS 25,277
Political and State Papers, 16th–17th Centuries. Ramsey Papers, vol. XXV, Add.MSS 33,469
Register of the Production of charters of Kirklands in Scotland, Mar–Oct. 1656, Add. MSS
Registers of the Secretaries of State of Scotland, vol. III, Add.MSS 23,112
Royal and Noble Autographs, 1646–1768, Add.MSS 19,399
Speeches in Parliament, 1558–1695, Stowe MS 361
Scotch Sermons etc 1659–1664, Egerton MS 2215
Scotland, Rents and Tenths 1639, Add.MSS 33,262
State Letters and Papers, Add.MSS 4155
T. Astle, Historical Collections, 1642–1769, Add.MSS 34,713
Trumbull Papers, vols CLXXXXVII–CXCVIII, Add. MSS 72,428–439
City of Westminster Archives Centre
St Martins-in-the Field Parish Records and Overseers Accounts 1633
Rigsarkivet, Copenhagen, Denmark
TKUA, Alm.Del I Indtil 1670, 'Latina' (1640–61)
TKUA, England. Akter og Dokumenter nedr. Det politiske Forhold til England, 1631–48
England. Breve, til Vels med Bilag fra Medlemmer af det Engelske Kongehus til medlemmer af det danske, 1613–89
TKUA, Skotland. Akter og Dokumenter nedr. det politiske Forhold til Skotland, 1572–1640
Duke University NC, Special Collections
Sir James Turner Papers: Tracts Critical and Historical
Dumfries House, Cumnock, Ayrshire [now relocated to Mount Stuart House, Isle of Bute]
Loudoun Deeds
Loudoun Papers
Dundee City Archives
Council Book Dundee, IV (1613–1653)
Edinburgh University Library
Instructions of the Committee of Estates of Scotland 1640–41
Laing MSS

Glasgow City Archives
  Graham of Duchrie, John. Account of the Earl of Glencairn's expedition to the High-
    lands of Scotland 1653–1654, SR 163
  Hamilton of Barns Papers, TD 589
Glasgow University Archives
  Beith Parish MSS
Hull University Library,
  Maxwell-Constable of Everingham MSS
Huntington Library, San Marino, California
  Bridgewater and Ellesmere MSS
  Hastings Irish Papers
  Huntington Manuscripts
  Loudoun Scottish Collection
  Stowe Collection: Temple Papers
Inveraray Castle Archives, Inveraray, Argyllshire
  Argyll Letters (1602–85)
  Argyll Transcripts, vols VIII–XIV (1600–69)
  Letters of the 7th Earl's Period, 1600–38
  Letters of the 8th Earl's Period, 1638–41
  Letters of the Marquess's Period, 1641–61
  Miscellaneous Argyll Letters
  Miscellaneous 17th Century Papers
National Archives of Scotland, Edinburgh
  Bute Papers, RH 1/7
  Breadalbane MSS, GD 112
  Campbell of Stonefield Papers, GD 14
  Clanranald Papers, GD 201
  Commissariat of Edinburgh, Register of Testaments, CC 8
  Cunninghame-Grahame MSS, GD 22
  Fothringham of Murthly Castle MSS, GD 121
  Glencairn MSS, GD 29
  Gordon Castle MSS, GD 44
  Hamilton Papers, GD 406
  Lothian MSS, GD 40
  Maxwell of Orchardton MSS, RH 15
  Morton Papers, GD150
  Ogilvyof Inverquharity Papers, GD 205
  Sederunt Books of the High Commission of Teinds 1630–50, TE
  Supplementary Parliamentary Papers, 1606–61, PA 7, 14 –16
  Synod Records of Moray, 1623–68, CH 2/27/1-2
  William Clark MSS. Diary, RH4
National Library of Scotland, Edinburgh
  Antique Papers, MS 1915
  Campbell Papers, MS 1672
  Clerk of Penicuik Papers, GD 18
  Halkett of Pitfirrane Papers, MS 6408
  Macpherson Correspondence, MS. 9982

Morton Letters and Papers, MS 79 and 82

Register of title deeds produced by landowners in Argyll c.1688, Adv.MS 31.2.3.

Salt and Coal: Events, 1635–62, MS 2263

Scottish Parliament 1648, MS 8482

Wodrow MSS, folios xxvii, xxxii, lxii, lxiii, lxiv; quartos xxiv, xxxv

Yester Papers, MS 7032

Yule Collection, MS 3134

Northumbria Archives, Berwick-upon-Tweed,
  Guild Books 1627–51

Riksarkivet, Stockholm, Sweden
  Anglica 521
  Hugh Mowatt's Letters to Sweden, AOSB ser B. E583

The National Archives, London
  Anglo-Scottish Committee of Parliament appointed to confer with the deputies from Scotland: minute book, 14 October 1652–8 April 1653, SP 25/138
  Committee of Both Kingdoms. Entry Books: Letters received 1644–45 February, SP 21/16–17
  Committee of the House of Commons for Scottish Affairs: Order Book 1643–45, SP 23/1A
  Derby House Committee for Irish Affairs, Letters Sent 22 Mar. 1647– 1 Aug. 1648, SP21/27
  Exchequer Papers, E 133–4 and 192
  Secretaries of State: State Papers Foreign; Flanders (1627–28), SP 77/19
  Secretaries of State: State Papers, Foreign; Holland (1625), SP 84/127–8
  State Papers Domestic, Supplementary: Orders, Warrants and Receipts for payment of the Scots Army in England 1643–48, SP 46/106

Tollemache Family Archives, Buckminster, Grantham, Lincolnshire
  Papers, TD

Tyne and Wear Archives, Newcastle
  Hostmen's Company, Old Book 1600–c.1690

University of St Andrews
  Acta Rectorum 4

West Sussex Record Office
  Goodwood/1167and 1431

1.2 Pamphlets and Tracts

Adams, Sir Thomas. *Plain Dealing or a Fair Warning to the Gentlemen of the Committee for Union* (London, 1647)

A Declaration of the Commissioners of the Parliament of Scotland Concerning the Paper sent to the Marquess of Ormond in his Majesties Name Presented to the Rt. Hon. the House of Peers, Monday 8 June 1646 (London, 1646)

A Declaration of the Lords of His Majesties Privie-Councell in Scotland and Commissioners for the Conserving the Articles of the Treaty: For the Information of His Majesties good Subjects of this Kingdom. Together with a Treacherous and Damnable Plot (Edinburgh, 1643)

A Declaration of the Marquess of Argyle, with the Rest of the Lords, and Others of the Estate of that Kingdome of Scotland, Concerning the Kings Majesty and the Treaty; and

Their Desires to the Parliament of England (London, 1648)

A Letter from the House of Commons Assembled in the Parliament of England at Westminster, To the Right Honourable and Right Reverend, the Lords, Ministers and Others of the Present General Assemble of the Church of Scotland sitting at Edinburgh (London, 1648)

A Letter from the Marques of Argile and Sir W. Armyn, in Name of themselves and their Confederates to Sir Thomas Glenham, dated at Barqicke, January 20. With the Answer of Sir Thomas Glemham and the Commanders and Gentry of Northumberland, dated at Newcastle, January 23 (York, 1643/4)

A Letter Sent from Lieutenant Generall Cromwell to the Marquis of Argyle and General Lesley (London, 1648)

Anon. *A Brief Narration of the Mysteries of State Sarried on by the Spanish Faction in England, since the Reign of Queen Elizabeth to this Day for Supplanting of the Magistracy and Ministry, the Laws of the Land, and the Religion of the Church of England* (London, 1651)

Anon. *A Declaration of the Proceedings of the Parliament of Scotland* (London, 1641)

Anon. *A Great Discoverie of a Plot in Scotland, by a Miraculous Meanes* (London, 1641)

Anon. *A Great Victorie Obtained in the Kingdom of Scotland by the Marquis of Argyle* (London, 1648)

Anon. *A Letter from Edinburgh Concerning the Differences of the Proceedings of the Well Affected in Scotland, from the Proceedings of the Army in England* (Edinburgh, 1649)

Anon. *A Letter from Scotland: And the Votes of the Parliament for Proclaiming Charles the Second, King of Great Britain, France & Ireland* (London, 1649); *The Vindication and Declaration of the Scots Nation* (Edinburgh, 1649)

Anon. *A Letter Sent from the Marquess of Argyle to the King of Scots* (London, 1652)

Anon. *A Phanatique League & Covenant, Solemnly Entered into by the Assertors of the Good Old Cause* (London, 1659)

Anon. *A Polt (sic) Discovered in Ireland and Prevented without the Shedding of Blood* (London, 1644)

Anon. *A True Relation of the Late Proceedings of the Scottish Army, Sent from his Excellency the Lord Generall Lesley's Quarters before Newcastle, the 8th of February 1643* (London, 1643/4)

Anon. *A Warning to the Parliament of England* (London, 1647)

Anon. *Certain Considerations Touching the Present Faction in the King's Dominion of Scotland* (London, 1648)

Anon. *Certaine Reasons Presented to the Kings Most Excellent Maiestie, Feb. 24. 1641. By the Lords and Commons in Parliament Touching the Princes Stay at Hampton Court* (London, 1642)

Anon. *Exceedingly Joyfull Newes from Coventry* (London, 1642)

Anon. *Extracts of Letters Dated at Edinburgh 14, 16 & 17 April 1644* (London, 1644)

Anon. *Information for the Earl of Argyle and his Creditors of the Marquis of Argyle against the Duke of Gordon and Earl of Aboyne* (Edinburgh, 1700)

Anon. *Intelligence from the South Borders of Scotland Written from Edinburgh, April 24, 1644* (London, 1644)

Anon. *Papers from the Scottish Quarters, Containing the Substance of Two Votes Made by the Estates at Edinburgh at their General Meeting this Present Septemb. 1646* (London, 1646)

Anon. *Questions Exhibited by the Parliament now in Scotland Assembled Concerning the Earl of Montrose his Plot* (London, 1641)

Anon. *Some Reasons why Archibald Campbell, Sometime Lord Lorne, Ought not to be Restored to the Honour or Estate of his Late Father Archibald Sometime Marquess of Argyle* (1661)

Anon. *Strange Newes from the King of Scots* (London, 1651)

Anon. *The Antiquity of Englands Superiority over Scotland and The Equity of Incorporating Scotland or Other Conquered Nations, into the Commonwealth of England* (London, 1652)

Anon. *The Beast is Wounded, or Information from Scotland, Concerning their Reformation* ([Amsterdam], 1638)

Anon. *The Bounds & Bonds of Publique Obedience* (London, 1649)

Anon. *The British Bell-man* (London, 1648)

Anon. *The Dissolution of the Parliament in Scotland* (London, 1641)

Anon. *The Funeral of the Good Old Cause or a Covenant of Both Houses of Parliament against the Solemn League and Covenant* (London, 1661)

Anon. *The King of Denmark's Resolution Concerning Charles King of Great Britain, Wherein is Declared the Determination for the Setting Forth of a Fleet towards England* (London, 1642)

Anon. *The King of Scots Message to the Northern Counties, and his Sister the Princess of Orange* (London, 1651)

Anon. *The Last Proceedings of the Scots, Being a Report by a Messenger Sent from the English Commissioners at Sunderland* (London, 1644)

Anon. *The Love and Faithfulnes of the Scottish Nation, the Excellency of the Covenant, the Union between England and Scotland Cleared, by Collections, from the Declarations of Parliament and Speeches of Severall Independent Brethren* (London, 1646)

Anon. *The Miraculous and Happie Union of England & Scotland* (Edinburgh, 1604)

Anon. *The Readinesse of the Scots to Advance into England: The Policie and Practice of the French Agent there to Hinder it* (London, 1643)

Anon. *The Remonstrance or Declaration of the Levellers in Scotland* (London, 1650)

Anon. *The Scots Declaration to the Earl of Cumberland* (London, 1642/43)

Anon. *The Scots-Mans Remonstrance* (London, 1647)

Anon. *The Scots Remonstrance or Declaration* (London, 1650)

Anon. *The Truth of the Proceedings in Scotland Containing the Discovery of the Late Conspiracie* (Edinburgh, 1641)

Anon. *Two Letters from Penrith Another from Northumberland* (London, 1648)

An Ordinance of the Lords and Commons Assembled in Parliament for the Further Supply of the British Army in Ireland (London, 1645)

A Remonstrance from the Kirk of Scotland (London, 1646)

Argyle, [Archibald Campbell], My Lord Marquis of. *His Speech upon the Scaffold, 27 May 1661: As it was Spoken by himself, and Written in Short-hand by One that was Present* (Edinburgh, 1661)

Argyll, Archibald Campbell, Marquess of. *Right Honourable, the Lord hath this Day, here at Philiphauch, neer Selkirk, Appeared Gloriously for his People* (London, 1645)

[Balcanqual, Walter.] *A Declaration Concerning the Late Tumults in Scotland* (Edinburgh, 1639)

Bowles, Edward. *The Mysterie of Iniquity, Yet Working in the Kingdomes of England,*

Scotland, and Ireland, for the Destruction of Religion Truly Protestant (London, 1643)

Boyd, Andrew. *Ad Augustissimum Monarcham Carolum Majori Britanniae* (Edinburgh, 1633)

[Brown, John.] *An Apologeticall Relation of the Particular Sufferings of the Faithfull Ministers & Professours of the Church of Scotland since August 1660* (Rotterdam, 1665)

[C.C.]. *Ane Brief Explanation of the Life, or A Prophicy [sic] of the Death of the Marquis of Argyle, with Diverse Verse thereupon* (Edinburgh, 1686)

[Campbell, Archibald.] *An Honourable Speech Made in the Parlament of Scotland by the Earle of Argile . . . the Thirtieth of September 1641* (London, 1641)

[Campbell, Archibald.] *An Honourable Speech made in the Parlament of Scotland by the Earle of Argile (Being now Competitor with Earl Morton for the Chancellorship) the Thirtieth of September 1641* (London, 1641)

[Campbell, Archibald.] *A Speech by the Marquesse of Argile, to the Honourable Lords and Commons in Parliament. 25 June 1646* (London, 1646)

[Campbell, Archibald.] *A True Copy of a Speech Delivered in the Parliament in Scotland, by the Earle of Argile, Concerning the Government of the Church* (London, 1641)

[Campbell, Archibald.] *My Lord Marquis of Argyle his Speech upon the Scaffold the 27 of May 1661* (Edinburgh, 1661)

[Campbell, Archibald.] *The Lord Marquess of Argyle's Speech to a Grand Committee of Both Houses of Parliament* (London, 1646)

[Campbell, Archibald.] *The Marquess of Argyle his Speech Concerning the King, the Covenant and Peace or War between both Kingdoms* (London, 1648)

Campbell, Archibald. *To the King's Most Excellent Majesty, the Humble Petition of Archibald, Marquess of Argyle* (London, 1661)

[Campbell, John.] *A Second Speech Made by the Lord Lowden, in the Parliament of Scotland the 24 of Septemb. 1641* (London, 1641)

[Campbell, John.] *The Lord Chancellor of Scotland his First Speech: At a Conference in the Painted Chamber with a Committee of Both Houses, Octob. 1. 1646* (London, 1646)

[Campbell, John.] *The Lord Lowden his Learned and Wise Speech in the Upper House of Parliament in Scotland, September 9, 1641* (London, 1641)

Calderwood, David. *The Pastor and the Prelate, or Reformation and Conformitie* (Edinburgh, 1636)

Certaine Instructions Given by the L. Montrose, L. Napier, Lairds of Keir and Blackhall, with a True Report of the Committee for this New Treason (London, 1641)

Chalmer, Thomas. *An Answer to the Scotch Papers delivered in the House of Commons in Reply to the Votes of both Houses of Parliament of England, Concerning the Disposal of the King* (London, 1646)

[Charles I.] *King Charles his Resolution Concerning the Church of England, Being Contrary to that of Scotland. With a Speech Spoken by the Lord Car, in the Parliament of Scotland, Being a Little before his Examination Concerning the Plot which was Found out in Scotland* (London, 1641)

[Charles II.] *The King of Scots his Message and Remonstrance to the Parliament of that Kingdome, Convened at Edenburgh, for a Perfect Union, and Agreement, between Prince and People and his Desires to all his Loving Subjects of that Nation, Requiring their Due Obedience towards him, as their Law-full King and Governor* (London, 1649)

[Chiesly, John.] *A Manifesto of the Commissioners of Scotland Delivered to the Honourable Houses of Parliament the 24 of May 1645* (London, 1645)

Cleveland, John. *The Character of a London-diurnall with Severall Poems* (London, 1647)

Conway, Edward Conway, 2nd Viscount. *A Relation from the Right Honourable the Lord Viscount Conway, of the Proceedings of the English Army in Ulster from June 17 to July 30* (London, 1642)

Culpepper, C. *A Message Sent from the King of Scots and the Duke of York's Court in Flanders* (Aberdeen, 1659).

Declaration of the Lords and Commons assembled in Parliament Concerning His Majesties Advancing with his Army toward London: With Direction that all Trained Bands and Volunteers be Put into a Readinesse (London, 1642)

[Devereux, Robert.] *A Letter from his Excellency, Robert Earl of Essex, to the Honourable House of Commons Concerning the Sending of a Commission Forthwith to Sir William Waller* (London, 1644)

[Devereux, Robert.] *A Paper Delivered in the Lord's House by the Earle of Essex, Lord Generall, at the Offering up of his Commission* (London, 1645)

D'Ewes, Sir Simonds. *Speech delivered in the House of Commons 7 July 1641, Being Resolved into a Committee . . . in the Palatine Case* (London, 1641)

Die Sabbati 30 December 1643. Ordered that the Adventurers of this House for lands in Ireland, and the body of Adventurers in London, doe meete at Grocers-Hall on Thursday in the afternoon at two of the clock, and take into their serious consideration by what wayes and meanes the British Army in Ulster, opposing the cessation may be maintained and encouraged to process in prosecution of that warre of Ireland against the Rebels, and to prepare some propositions to be presented to the House (London, 1643)

du Moulin, Peter. *A Letter of a French Protestant to a Scotishman of the Covenant* (London, 1640)

Dury, John. *A Summary Discourse Concerning the Work of Peace Ecclesiastical, how it may Concurre with the Aim of a Civill Confederation amongst Protestants. Presented to the Consideration of my Lord Ambassador Sir T. Row at Hamburg 1639* (Cambridge, 1641)

[Gauden, John.] *Eikon Basilike: The Portraiture of His Sacred Maiestie in his Solitudes and Sufferings* (London, 1649)

[H., M.] *The History of the Union of the Four Famous Kingdoms of England, Wales, Scotland and Ireland* (London, 1660)

Harcourt, Sir Simon. *March 18. A Letter Sent from Sr. Simon Harcourt, to a Worthy Member of the House of Commons. With a True Relation of the Proceedings of the English Army, under his Command to this Present March* (London, 1641)

Henderson, Alexander. *A Sermon Preached to the Honourable House of Commons, At their Late Solemne Fast, Wednesday, December 27, 1643* (London, 1644)

Henderson, Alexander. *Sermons, Prayers and Pulpit Addresses*, R.T. Martin ed. (Edinburgh, 1867)

[Henderson, Alexander.] *Vertoog van de vvettelyckheyt van onsen tocht in Engelant* (Edinburgh, 1640)

Heylyn, Peter. *A Short View of the Life and Reign of King Charles (the second monarch of Great Britain) from his Birth to his Burial* (London, 1658)

Informatie, aen alle oprechte christenen in het coningrijcke van Engelandt. Door de edelen, baronnen, staten, leeraers, ende gemeente in het coninckrijcke van Schotlandt. Waer in zy hare onschuldt te kennen gheven . . . (Edinburgh, 1639)

[Johnston, Archibald of Warriston.] *Remonstrantie vande edelen, baronnen, state, kercken-dienaers, ende gemeente in het Coningryck van Schotland: Verclarende dat sy onschuldigh sy;n van de crimen daer mede sy in't laetste Engelsche Placcaet (vanden 27 february) beswaert werden. Gevisiteert na de Ordonnantie vande Generale Vergaderinge van den Raedt van Staten in Schotland* (Edinburgh and Amsterdam, 1639)

[Kirk, Commissioners of the.] *A Solemn and Seasonable Warning to all Estates and Degrees of Persons throughout the Land* (Edinburgh, 1646)

Letters from the Committee of Estates at Newcastle and the Commissioners of the Kingdom of Scotland to both Houses of Parliament (London, 1646)

Letters from the Marquesse of Argyle, the Earl of Lanerick, Lord Wariston, and Others now at Edinburgh to their Friends in London. Intercepted by Sir Richard Willys, Governour of Newarke, and Printed Truthfully by the Originals (Oxford, 1645)

[Leven, Alexander Leslie, Earl of.] *Camp Discipline, or the Souldier's Duty* (London, 1642)

Lithgow, William. *A True and Experimentall Discourse, upon the Beginning, Proceeding and Victorious Event of this Last Siege of Breda* (London, 1637)

Lithgow, William. *Scotlands Welcome to her Native Sonne, and Soveraigne Lord, King Charles* (Edinburgh, 1633)

Lithgow, William. *The Present Survey of London and England's State* (London, 1643)

Lithgow, William. *The Siege of Newcastle* (Edinburgh, 1645)

Making the News: An Anthology of the Newsbooks of Revolutionary England, 1641–1660, J. Raymond ed. (Moreton-in-Marsh, 1993)

Marshall, Stephen. *A Sacred Panegyrick* (London, 1644)

Mercurius Caledonius (Edinburgh, 1648)

Mocket, Thomas. *A View of the Solemn League and Covenant* (London, 1644)

Monck, George. *General Monck's Last Letter to His Excellency the Lord Fleetwood* (London, 1659)

Munro, Robert. *A Letter of Great Consequence Sent . . . out of the Kingdom of Ireland, to the Honorable, the Committee for the Irish Affairs in England, Concerning the State of Rebellion there* (London, 1643)

[Nedham, Marchmont.] *Anti-Machiavelli or, Honesty Against Policy* (London, 1647)

[Nedham. Marchmont.] *Digitus Dei: Or God's Justice upon Treachery and Treason, Exemplified in the Life and Death of the Late James, Duke of Hamilton* (London, 1649)

Nedham, Marchmont. *The Case of the Common-Wealth of England Stated* (London, 1650)

Parker, Henry *Scotlands Holy War* (London, 1651)

Parker, Henry. *The Danger to England Observed, upon its Deserting the High Court of Parliament* (London, 1642)

Parker, Henry, Sadler, John and May, Thomas. *The King's Cabinet Opened* (London, 1645)

Pyrnne, William. *A Brief Narrative of the Manner how Divers Members of the House of Commons, that were Illegally and Unjustly Imprisoned or Secluded by the Armies Force in December 1648 and May 7, 1659, Coming upon Tuesday the 27th of December . . . were again Forcibly Shut out* (London, 1659)

[Pyrnne, William.] *Scotland's ancient obligation to England and publicke acknowledgement thereof, for their brotherly assistance to, and deliverance of them, with the expence of their blood, and hazard of the state and tranquility of their realm, from the bondage of the French, in the time of their greatest extremity, 1560* (London, 1646)

Pym, John. *A Most Learned and Religious Speech Spoken by Mr. Pym, at a Conference of both Houses of Parliament the 23 of . . . September* (London, 1642)

Rosse, William. *Papers from Scotland of the Transactions of the Scots Commissioners, concerning the King and the Parliament of England* (London 1647/48)

Selden, John. *A Briefe Discourse Concerning the Power of the Peeres and Comons of Parliament, in Point of Judicature* (London, 1640)

Shawe, John. *Britannia Rediviva: of the Proper and Sovereign Remedy for the Healing and Recovering of these Three Distracted Nations* (London, 1649)

Shawe, John. *Brittains Remembrancer: Or, The National Covenant, As it was Laid out in a Sermon Preached in the Minster at Yorke . . . upon Friday Sept. 20 1644* (London, 1644)

Shawe, John. *The Three Kingdomes Case: or, their Sad Calamities, together with their Causes and Cure. Laid down in a Sermon Preached at a Publique Fast at Kingston upon Hull* (London, 1646)

Sprigg, William. *A Modest Plea for an Equal Common-wealth against Monarchy* (London, 1659)

Sydenham, Cuthbert. *The False Brother, or, a New Map of Scotland, Drawn by an English pencil* (London, 1651)

The Answers of the Commissioners of the Kingdom of Scotland to Both Houses of Parliament, upon the now Propositions of Peace, and the Foure Bills to be sent to his Majestie (Edinburgh, 1647)

The Answer of the Parliament of England to a Paper Entituled, A Declaration by the King's Majesty, To His Subjects of the Kingdoms of Scotland, England and Ireland (London, 1650)

The Confession of the Kirk of Scotland subscribed by the King's Majesty and his Household in the year of God 1580. With a Designation of such acts of Parliament as are expedient, for justifying the Union, after mentioned. And subscribed by the Nobles, Barrons, Gentlemen, Burgesses, Ministers and Commons, in the year of God, 1638 (Edinburgh, 1638)

The Copy of a Letter from Colonell Francis Anderson to Sir Thomas Glemham, January 20 1643, Touching the Invasion of Scotland (Oxford, 1643/44)

The Declaration of the Kingdomes of Scotland and England (Edinburgh, 1644)

The Great Account Delivered to the English Lords by the Scottish Commissioners (London, 1641)

The Humble Remonstrance of the Commissioners of the General Assembly to the Honourable and High Court of Parliament now Assembled (Edinburgh, 1647)

The Intentions of the Army of the Kingdom of Scotland Declared to their Brethren in England (Edinburgh, 1640)

The Kingdomes Weekly Intelligencer no.34 (28 November–5 December, 1643)

The Proceedings of the Commissioners, Appointed by the Kings Maiesty and Parliament of Scotland, for Conserving the Articles of the Treaty and Peace betwixt the Kingdomes of Scotland and England (London, 1643)

The Proceedings of the Commissioners of the Church and Kingdom of Scotland with His Majestie at the Hague (Edinburgh, 1649)

The Scots Resolution Declared in a Message Sent from the Privie Councell of the Kingdome of Scotland, to His Majestie at Yorke . . . wherein is expressed their earnest Desires both to his Maiestie and Parliament, That they would be pleased to joyne in a perfect Unione, it being the chiefe meanes to give an overthrow to the Enemies of the three Kingdoms (Edinburgh, 1642)

The Scottish Dove no.7 (24 November–1 December, 1643)

The True Informer, no.10 (18–25 November, 1643)

The Whole Prophecies of Scotland, England, France, Ireland and Denmarke (Edinburgh, 1617)

[Walbancke, Matthew.] *Sundry Strange Prophecies of Merline, Bede, Becket and Others* (London, 1652)

Wither, George. *The British Appeals with Gods Mercifull Replies on the Behalfe of the Commonwealth of England* (London, 1650)

Woodward, Hezekiah. *Three Kingdoms Made One, by Entering Covenant with One God* (London, 1643)

1.3 Commentaries and Memoirs

A Collection of the State Papers of John Thurloe, Esq. Secretary, First to the Council of State, and Afterwards to the two Protectors, Oliver & Richard Cromwell, J. Birch ed., 7 vols (London, 1742)

Adair, Patrick. *A True Narrative of the Rise and Progress of the Presbyterian Church in Ireland (1623–1670)*, W.D. Killen ed. (Belfast, 1866)

Autobiography of the Life of Mr Robert Blair, T. McCrie ed. (Edinburgh, 1848)

Balfour, Sir James. *Historical Works*, J. Haig ed., 4 vols (Edinburgh, 1824–25)

Bardachd Chloinn Ghill-Eathain: Eachann Bacach and Other Maclean Poets, C.O. O'Baoill ed. (Edinburgh, 1979)

Brereton, Sir William. *Travels in Holland, the United Provinces, England, Scotland and Ireland 1634–35*, E. Hawkins ed. (London, 1844)

Brodie, George. *History of the British Empire, from the Accession of Charles I to the Restoration*, 4 vols (Edinburgh, 1822)

Buchan, John. *The Marquis of Montrose* (London, 1913)

Burnet, Gilbert. *The Memoirs of the Lives and Actions of James and William, Dukes of Hamilton and Castleherald* (London, 1838)

[Burnet, Gilbert.] *Bishop Burnet's History of His Own Time*, W. Legge, 1st Earl of Dartmouth, P. Yorke, 1st Earl of Hardwick and A. Onslow eds, 6 vols (Oxford, 1833)

Clarendon, Edward [Hyde], Earl of. *The History of the Rebellion and Civil Wars in England* (Oxford, 1843)

Craufurd, George. *The Lives and Characters of the Officers of the Crown, and of the State in Scotland, from the Beginning of the Reign of King David I to the Union of the Two Kingdoms* (London, 1726)

Diary of Sir Archibald Johnston of Wariston, 1632–39, J.M. Paul ed. (Edinburgh, 1911)

Diary of Sir Thomas Hope of Craighall, 1634–45, T. Thomson ed. (Edinburgh, 1843)

Dugdale, William. *A Short View of the Late Troubles in England* (London, 1681)

Fragment of the Diary of Sir Archibald Johnston of Wariston, 1639, G.M. Paul ed. (Edinburgh, 1896)

Fraser, James. *The Wardlaw Manuscript: Chronicles of the Frasers, 916–1674*, W. Mackay ed. (Edinburgh, 1905)

Gordon, James. *History of Scots Affairs from MDXXXVII to MDCXLI*, J. Robertson ed., 3 vols (Aberdeen, 1841)

Gordon, Patrick of Ruthven. *A Short Abridgement of Britane's Distemper from the Yeare of God MDCXXXIX to MDCXLIX* (Aberdeen, 1844)

Guizot, M. François. *History of the English Revolution from the Accession of Charles I*, 2 vols (Oxford, 1838)

Hume, David. *The History of Great Britain*, 2 vols (Edinburgh, 1754 and 1758)

Julius, Alexander. *In Illlustrissimam Dominam Annam Duglasiam, Comitissam Argatheliae* (Edinburgh, 1607)

Kirkton, James. *The Secret and True History of the Church of Scotland from the Restoration to the Year 1678*, C.K. Sharpe ed. (Edinburgh, 1817)

Laing, Malcolm. *The History of Scotland, from the Union of the Crowns on the Accession of James VI to the Throne of England to the Union of the Kingdoms in the Reign of Queen Anne*, 2 vols (London, 1800)

Mackenzie, Sir George of Rosehaugh. *Memoirs of the Affairs of Scotland from the Restoration of King Charles II, A.D. MDCLX* (Edinburgh, 1821)

Macpherson, James. *The History of Great Britain from the Restoration, to the Accession of the House of Hannover*, 2 vols (London, 1775)

Martin, Martin. *A Description of the Western Islands of Scotland* (London, 1703)

Memoirs of Henry Guthry, Late Bishop of Dunkeld: Containing an Impartial Relation of the Affairs of Scotland, Civil and Ecclesiastical, from the Year 1637, to the Death of King Charles (Glasgow, 1747)

Memoirs of the life of Mr Robert Blair, Minister of the Gospel Sometime at Bangor in Ireland, and afterwards at St Andrews in Scotland (Edinburgh, 1754)

Memoirs of the Marquis of Montrose, M. Napier ed., 2 vols (Edinburgh, 1856)

Memoirs of Master John Shawe, sometime Vicar of Rotherham, Minister of St Mary's, Lecturer of Holy Trinity Church, and Master of the Charterhouse at Kingston-upon-Hull. Written by himself in the Year 1663–64, J. R. Boyle ed. (Hull, 1882)

Memoirs of Sir Ewen Cameron of Lochiel, J. Macknight ed. (Edinburgh, 1842)

Memorials of English Affairs from the Beginning of the Reign of Charles the First to the Happy Restoration of King Charles the Second, 4 vols (Oxford, 1853)

Memorials of Montrose and His Times, M. Napier ed., 2 vols (Edinburgh, 1848–50)

Monteith, Robert of Salmonet, *The History of the Troubles of Great Britain* (London, 1735)

Munro, Neil. *John Splendid: The Tale of a Poor Gentleman, and the Little Wars of Lorne* (Edinburgh 1994, first published 1898)

Neilson, John. *An Impartial Collection of the Great Affairs of State, from the Beginning of the Scotch Rebellion in the Year MDCXXXIX to the Murther of King Charles I*, 2 vols (London, 1682–83)

Nicoll, John. *A Diary of Public Transactions and Other Occurrences, Chiefly in Scotland, from January 1650 to June 1667*, D Laing ed. (Edinburgh, 1836)

Orain Iain Luim: Songs of John MacDonald, Bard of Keppoch, A.M. MacKenzie ed. (Edinburgh, 1973)

Reliquiae Celticae, A. MacBain and J. Kennedy eds, 2 vols (Inverness, 1894)

Row, John. *The History of the Kirk of Scotland 1558–1637*, D. Laing ed. (Edinburgh, 1842)

Rothes, John Leslie, Earl of. *A Relation of Proceedings Concerning the Affairs of the Kirk of Scotland from August 1637 to July 1638*, J. Nairne ed. (Edinburgh, 1830)

Rutherford, Samuel. *Lex Rex: The Law and the Prince* (Edinburgh, 1848)

Sandersone, Sir William. *A Compleat History of the Life and Raigne of King Charles I* (London, 1658)

Scot, Sir John [of Scotstarvit]. *The Staggering State of the Scottish Statesmen* (1754)

Scott, Sir Walter. *A Legend of Montrose* (London, 1819), republished as *A Legend of the Wars of Montrose*, J.H. Alexander ed. (Edinburgh, 1995)

Scott, Sir Walter. *Tales of a Grandfather* (London, 1898)

Scott, William. *An Apologetical Narration of the State and Government of the Kirk of Scotland since the Reformation*, D. Laing ed. (Edinburgh, 1846)

Scottish Ballads and Songs: Historical and Traditional, J. Maidment ed., 2 vols (Edinburgh, 1868)

Select Biographies, W.K. Tweedie ed., 2 vols (Edinburgh, 1845–47)

Spalding, John. *The History of the Troubles and Memorable Transactions in Scotland and England, 1624–45*, J. Skene ed., 2 vols (Edinburgh, 1828–29)

The Diary of Alexander Brodie of Brodie, 1652–1680 & of his Son, James Brodie of Brodie, 1680–1685, D. Laing ed. (Aberdeen, 1863)

The Diary of John Evelyn, esq., F.R.S., from 1641 to 1705–6, W. Bray ed. (London, 1890)

The Journal of John Winthrop, 1630–1649, R.S. Dunn, J. Savage and L. Yeandle eds (Cambridge, Mass, 1996)

The Diary of Mr John Lamont of Newton, 1649–1671 (Edinburgh, 1830)

The Journal of Sir Simonds D'Ewes from the Beginning of the Long Parliament to the Opening of the Trial of the Earl of Strafford, W. Notestein ed. (London, 1923)

The Journal of Thomas Cunningham of Campvere, E.J. Courthope ed. (Edinburgh, 1928)

The Journal of Thomas Juxon, 1644–47, K. Lindley and D. Scott eds (Cambridge, 1999)

The Letters and Journals of Robert Baillie A.M., Principal of the University of Glasgow, 1637–1662, D. Laing ed., 3 vols (Edinburgh, 1841–42)

The Poems of John Cleveland, B. Morris and E. Withington eds (Oxford, 1967)

The Short Parliament (1640) Diary of Sir Thomas Aston, J.D. Maltby ed. (London, 1988)

Turner, Sir James. *Memoirs of His Own Life and Times, 1632–70*, T. Thomson ed. (Edinburgh, 1829)

Walker, Clement. *Relations and Observations, Historicall and Politick, upon the Parliament, Begun Anno Dom. 1640: Divided into II Books: 1. The Mystery of the Two Iunto's, Presbyterian and Independent. 2. The History of Independency, &c. Together with an Appendix, Touching the Proceedings of the Independent Faction in Scotland* (London, 1648)

Walker, Sir Edwald. *Historical Discourses upon Several Occasions* (London, 1705)

Wilson, Arthur. *The History of Great Britain Being the Life and Reign of King James the First, Relating to what Passed from his First Access to the Crown, till his Death* (London, 1653)

Winstanley, William. *The Loyall Martyrology* (London, 1665)

Wishart, George. *De Rebus Auspiciis Serenissimi, & Potentissimi Caroli Dei Gratia Magnae Britanniae, Franciae & Hiberniae Regis, &c. sub imperio illustrissimi Jacobi Montisrosarum Marchionis … Supremi Scotiae Gubernatoris anno MDCXLIV, & duobus sequentibus praeclare gestis, Commentarius* (The Hague, 1647)

Wishart, George. *The Memoirs of James, Marquis of Montrose, 1639–1650*, A.D. Murdoch & H.F.M. Simpson eds (London, 1893)

Wodrow, Robert. *The History of the Sufferings of the Church of Scotland from the Restoration to the Revolution*, 2 vols (Edinburgh, 1721–22)

Yorkshire Diaries and Autobiographies in the Seventeenth and Eighteenth Centuries (Durham, 1877)

1.4 Published Records

A Source Book of Scottish History, vol. III (1567–1707), W.C. Dickinson and G. Donaldson eds (London and Edinburgh, 1961)

Aberdeen Council Letters, 1552–1681, L.B. Taylor ed., 6 vols (Oxford, 1942–61)

Acts of the Parliament of Scotland, T. Thomson and C. Innes eds, 12 vols (Edinburgh, 1814–72)

Advertisements for Ireland, G. O'Brien ed. (Dublin, 1923)

Borough, Sir John. *Notes on the Treaty Carried on at Ripon between King Charles and the Covenanters of Scotland, A.D. 1640*, J. Bruce ed. (London, 1869)

Briefwisseling van Hugo Grotius (1583–1645), P.C. Molhugsen, B.L. Meulenbroek, P.P. Witkam, H.J.M. Nellen and C.M. Ridderikhoff eds, 17 vols ('S-Gravenhage and Den Haag, 1928–2001)

Calendar of State Papers and Manuscripts Relating to English Affairs Existing in the Archives and Collections of Venice, and in other Libraries of Northern Italy, A.B. Hinds ed. (London, 1913–23)

Calendar of State Papers Domestic Series, of the Reign of Charles I, J. Bruce and W.D. Hamilton eds, 17 vols (London, 1858–82)

Calendar of State Papers, Scotland, vols 11–12 (1593–97), A.I. Cameron and M.S. Giuseppi eds (Edinburgh, 1936 and 1952)

Campbell, Lord Archibald. *Records of Argyll* (Edinburgh, 1885)

Charles I in 1646: Letters of King Charles I to Queen Henrietta Maria, J. Bruce ed. (London, 1856)

Collectanea de Rebus Albanicis, W.F. Skene ed. (Edinburgh, 1847)

Correspondence of Sir Robert Kerr, First Earl of Ancrum and his Son William, Third Earl of Lothian, D. Laing ed., 2 vols (Edinburgh, 1875)

Correspondence of the Scots Commissioners in London, 1644–1646, H.W. Meikle ed. (Edinburgh, 1907)

Culloden Papers, 1625–1748, H.R. Duff ed. (London, 1815)

Dumbarton Common Good Accounts 1614–60, F. Roberts and I.M.M. McPhail eds (Dumbarton, 1972)

Extracts from the Records of the Merchant Adventurers of Newcastle-upon-Tyne, vol. 1, F.W. Dendy ed. (Durham, 1895)

Fraser-Mackintosh, C. *Antiquarian Notes* (Inverness, 1865)

Highland Papers, vols I–III, J.R.N. Macphail ed. (Edinburgh, 1914–20)

Historical Collections, J. Rushworth ed., vols I–III (London, 1680–91)

HMC, *Manuscripts of the Earls of Mar and Kellie* (London, 1904)

HMC, Ninth Report, part ii, appendix, *Traquhair Muniments* (London, 1887)

HMC, *Report on the Laing Manuscripts Preserved in the University of Edinburgh*, H. Paton ed., vol. I (London, 1914)

Inveraray Papers, D.C. MacTavish ed. (Oban, 1939)

Kancelliets Brevbøger: Vedrørende Danmarks Indre Forhold (1637–39) E. Marquard ed. (Copenhagen, 1944)

Kong Christian Den Fjerdes Egenhaendige Breve, C.F. Bricka and J.A. Frederica eds, 8 vols (Copenhagen, 1969–70)

Lamh Sgriobhainn Mhic Rath: The Fernaig Manuscript, M. Macfarlane ed. (Dundee, 1923)

Letters at the Instance of Sir George McKenzie of Rosehaugh, His Majesties Advocat for His Highness Interest (Edinburgh, 1681)

Letters of Samuel Rutherford, A.A. Bonar ed., 2 vols (Edinburgh, 1863)

Letters to the Argyll Family, A. Macdonald ed. (Edinburgh, 1839)

Memoirs of the Maxwells of Pollock, W. Fraser ed., 2 vols (Edinburgh, 1863)

Memoirs of Scottish Catholics in the Seventeenth and Eighteenth Centuries, W.F. Leith ed., 2 vols (London, 1909)

Minute Book Kept by the War Committee of the Covenanters in the Stewartry of Kirkcud-bright in the Years 1640 and 1641 (Kirkcudbright, 1855)

Minutes of the Synod of Argyll, 1639–61, D.C. Mactavish ed., 2 vols (Edinburgh, 1943)

Miscellany of the Scottish History Society, H. Campbell ed., vol. IV (Edinburgh, 1926)

More Culloden Papers, D. Warrand ed., 5 vols (Inverness, 1923–30)

Na Baird Leathanach: The Maclean bards, A.M. Sinclair ed., 2 vols (Charlottetown, PEI, 1898)

Proceedings of the Short Parliament, E.S. Cope and W.H. Coates eds (London, 1977)

Proceedings in the Opening Session of the Long Parliament, 1640–41, M. Jannson ed., 3 vols (Rochester, 1999–2000)

Records of the Commissions of the General Assemblies for the Years 1650–52, J. Christie ed. (Edinburgh, 1909)

Records of the Committees for Compounding with Delinquent Royalists in Durham and Northumberland during the Civil War, 1643–1660, R. Welford ed. (Durham, 1905)

Records of the Kirk of Scotland, A. Peterkin ed. (Edinburgh, 1843)

Records of the Presbyteries of Inverness and Dingwall, 1643–88, W. Mackay ed. (Edinburgh, 1896)

Register of the Consultations of the Ministers of Edinburgh, and Some Other Brethren of the Ministry, 1652–60, J. Christie ed., 2vols (Edinburgh, 1921 and 30)

Registers of the Privy Council of Scotland, first series, D. Masson ed., 14 vols (Edinburgh, 1877–98); second series, D. Masson and P.H. Brown eds, 8 vols (Edinburgh, 1899–1908)

Rikskanseleren Axel Oxenstiernas Skrifter och Brefvexling, II, 9 (Stockholm, 1898)

Sar-Obair nam Bard Gaeleach: The Beauties of Gaelic Poetry, J. Mackenzie ed. (Edinburgh, 1872)

Scotland and the Commonwealth 1651–53, C.H. Firth ed. (Edinburgh, 1895)

Scotland and the Protectorate, C.H. Firth ed. (Edinburgh, 1899)

Selected Justiciary Cases, 1624–50, S.A. Gillon ed., 2 vols (Edinburgh, 1953)

State Trials, W. Cobbet ed., 33 vols (London, 1809–28)

The Argyle Papers, 1640–1723, J. Maidment ed. (Edinburgh, 1834)

The Black Book of Taymouth, C. Innes ed. (Edinburgh, 1855)

The Book of Islay, G.G. Smith ed. (Edinburgh, 1895)

The Book of the Thanes of Cawdor, 1236–1742, C. Innes ed. (Edinburgh, 1859)

The Chiefs of Grant, W. Fraser ed., 3 vols (Edinburgh, 1883)

The Clarke Papers, C.H. Firth ed., 4 vols (London, 1891–1901)

The Covenants and the Covenanters, J. Kerr ed. (Edinburgh, 1896)

The Cromwellian Union 1651–52, C.S. Terry ed. (Edinburgh, 1902)

The Diplomatic Correspondence of Jean De Montereul and the Brothers De Bellievre, French Ambassadors in England and Scotland 1645–48, J.G. Fotheringham ed., 2 vols (Edinburgh, 1898–99)

The Earl of Stirling's Register of Royal Letters, Relative to the Affairs of Scotland and Nova Scotia from 1615 to 1635, C. Rogers ed., 2 vols (Edinburgh, 1885)

The Earl of Strafforde's Letters and Dispatches, W. Knowler ed., 2 vols (London, 1739)

The Government of Scotland under the Covenanters, 1637–51, D. Stevenson ed. (Edinburgh, 1982)

The Hamilton Papers, S.R. Gardiner ed. (London, 1880)

The MacDonald Collection of Gaelic Poetry, A. and A. MacDonald eds (Inverness, 1911)

The Miscellany of the Spalding Club, J. Stuart ed., vol. IV (Aberdeen, 1852)

The Nicholas Papers, Correspondence of Sir Edward Nicholas, Secretary of State, G.F. Warner ed., 2 vols (London, 1886)

The Quarrel between The Earl of Manchester and Oliver Cromwell: An Episode of the English Civil Wars, D. Mason ed. (London, 1875)

The Records of Invercauld, 1547–1828, J.G. Mechie ed. (Aberdeen, 1901)

The Red and White Book of Menzies, D.P. Menzies ed. (Glasgow, 1894)

The Works of William Laud D.D., J. Bliss ed., 5 vols (Oxford, 1853)

Unpublished Papers of John, Seventh Lord Sinclair, Covenanter and Royalist, J.A. Fairley ed. (Peterhead, 1905)

Verney Papers. Sir Ralph Verney's Notes of Proceedings in the Long Parliament, Temp. Chrles I, J. Bruce ed. (London, 1845)

2 WORKS OF REFERENCE

2.1 Electronic

Early English Books Online: http://eebo.chadwyck.com/home?ath

Grosjean, A. and Murdoch, S. 'Scotland, Scandinavia and Northern Europe, 1580–1707' (SSNE: computer database, University of St Andrews 2006–07): http//www.st-andrews.ac.uk/history/ssne

Oxford Dictionary of National Biography: http://www.oxforddnb.com

Internet Archive: http://www.archive.org

The Hartlib Papers (Sheffield University. HROnline. Humanities Research Institute, 2002), HP9/4/1A-2B

2.2 Hard Copy

Fasti Ecclesiae Scoticanae, H. Scott ed., 8 vols (Edinburgh, 1915–50)

Moreland, C. and Bannister, D. *Antique Maps* (London, 2000)

Scots Peerage, Sir J. Balfour-Paul ed., 9 vols (Edinburgh, 1904–14)

Stevenson, D. and W.B. *Scottish Text and Calendars: An Analytical Guide to Serial Publications* (Edinburgh, 1987)

The Parliaments of Scotland: Burgh and Shire Commissioners, M.D. Young ed., 2 vols (Edinburgh, 1993)

3 SECONDARY SOURCES

3.1 Theses

Hughes, P. 'The 1649–50 Scottish Witch Hunt, with Particular Reference to the Synod of Lothian and Tweeddale' (University of Strathclyde, PhD thesis, 2009)

MacKenzie, K.M. 'Presbyterian Church Government and the "Covenanted interest" in the Three Kingdoms, 1649–1660' (University of Aberdeen, PhD thesis, 2008)

Menarry, D.J. 'The Irish and Scottish Landed Elites from Regicide to Restoration' (University of Aberdeen, PhD thesis, 2001)

Robertson, B.G. 'Continuity and Change in the Scottish Nobility: The House of Huntly, 1603–1690' (University of Aberdeen, PhD thesis, 2007)

3.2 Monographs

Adamson, J. *The Noble Revolt: The Overthrow of Charles I* (London, 2007)

Armstrong, R. *Protestant War: The 'British' of Ireland and the Wars of the Three Kingdoms* (Manchester, 2005)

Ashton, R. *The English Civil War: Conservatism and Revolution 1603–1649* (London, 1978)

Barber, S. *Regicide and Republicanism: Politics and Ethics in the English Revolution, 1646–1659* (Edinburgh, 1998)

Bennet, M. *The Civil Wars in Britain and Ireland, 1638–1651* (Oxford, 1997)

Brown, K.M. *Kingdom or Province? Scotland and the Regal Union, 1603–1715* (London, 1992)

Brown, K.M. *Noble Society in Scotland: Wealth, Family and Culture from Reformation to Revolution* (Edinburgh, 2004)

Brown, P.H. *History of Scotland*, 3 vols (Cambridge, 1912)

Burgess, G. *The Politics of the Ancient Constitution: An Introduction to English Political Thought 1603–1642* (University Park, PA, 1993)

Burns, J.H. *The True Law of Kingship: Concepts of Monarchy in Early Modern Scotland* (Oxford, 1996)

Burton, J.H. *The History of Scotland*, 8 vols (Edinburgh and London, 1876)

Campbell, A of Airds. *A History of ClanCampbell*, 3 vols (Edinburgh, 2000–04)

Campbell, A of Airds. *The Life and Troubled Times of Sir Donald Campbell of Ardnamurchan* (Isle of Coll, 1999)

Canny, N. *Kingdom and Colony: Ireland in the Atlantic World* (Baltimore and London, 1988)

Canny, N. *Making Ireland British, 1580–1650* (Oxford, 2001)

Capp, B.S. *Cromwell's Navy: The Fleet and the English Revolution, 1648–1660* (Oxford, 1989)

Carlton, C. *Going to the Wars: The Experience of the British Civil Wars, 1638–1651* (London, 1994)

Cathcart, A. *Kinship and Clientage: Highland Clanship 1451–1609* (Leiden and Boston, 2006)

Clarke, A. *Prelude to Restoration in Ireland: The End of the Commonwealth, 1659–60* (Cambridge, 1999), pp. 92–168

Cogswell, T. *Home divisions: Aristocracy, the State and Provincial Conflict* (Manchester, 1998)

Collins, J.B. *The State in Early Modern France* (Cambridge, 1995)

Cowan, E.J. *Montrose: For Covenant and King* (London, 1977)

Coward, B. *The Cromwellian Protectorate, 1653–59* (Manchester, 2002)

Cunningham, B. *The World of Geoffrey Keating* (Dublin, 2000)

Curry, P. *Prophecy and Power: Astrology in Early Modern England* (Princeton, 1989)

Cust, R. *Charles I: A Political Life* (Harlow, 2005)

Davis, J.C. *Oliver Cromwell* (London, 2001)

Dawson, J.E. *Scotland Reformed 1488–1587* (Edinburgh, 2007)

Dodgshon, R. *From Chiefs to Landlords: Social and Economic Change in the Western Highlands and Islands, c.1493–1820* (Edinburgh, 1998)

Donald, P. *An Uncounselled King: Charles I and the Scottish Troubles, 1637–1641* (Cambridge, 1990)

Donaldson, G. *Scotland: James V–James VII* (Edinburgh, 1965)

Dow, F.D. *Cromwellian Scotland, 1651–1660* (Edinburgh, 1979)

Eisen, R. *Gersonides on Providence, Covenant, and the Chosen People: A Study in Medieval Jewish Philosophy and Biblical Commentary* (New York, 1994)

Fincham, K. *Prelate as Pastor: The Episcopate of James I* (Oxford, 1990)

Fissel, M.C. *The Bishops' Wars: Charles I's Campaigns against Scotland, 1638–40* (Cambridge, 1994)

Fitzpatrick, B. *Seventeenth Century Ireland: The War of Religions* (Dublin, 1988)

Galloway, B. *The Union of England and Scotland 1606–1608* (Edinburgh, 1986)

Gardiner, S.R. *History of the Great Civil War, 1642–1649*, 3 vols (London, 1886–91)

Gardiner, S.R. *The History of the Commonwealth and Protectorate, 1649–1656*, 3 vols (London, 1903)

Gentles, I. *The New Model Army in England, Ireland and Scotland, 1645–1653* (Oxford, 1992)

Gillespie, R. *Devoted People: Belief and Religion in Early Modern Ireland* (Manchester, 1997)

Goodare, J. *State and Society in Early Modern Scotland* (Oxford, 1999)

Gregory, D. *The History of the Western Highlands and Isles of Scotland 1493–1625* (Edinburgh, 1836 reprinted 1975)

Grosjean, A. *An Unofficial Alliance: Scotland and Sweden 1569–1654* (Leiden and Boston, 2003)

Harris, T. *Restoration: Charles II and His Kingdoms, 1660–1685* (London, 2005)

Hayes-McCoy, G.A. *Scots Mercenary Forces in Ireland* (Dublin and London, 1937)

Hewison, J.K. *The Covenanters: History of the Church of Scotland*, 2 vols (Glasgow, 1908)

Hibbert, C. *Charles I and the Popish Plot* (Chapel Hill NC, 1983)

Hill, C. *Antichrist in Seventeenth-Century England* (Oxford, 1971)

Hill, C. *The Century of Revolution, 1603–1714* (London, 1961)

Hill, G. *The Macdonnells of Antrim* (Belfast, 1893)

Hirst, D. *England in Conflict, 1603–60: Kingdom, Community, Commonwealth* (London, 1999)

Holloway, J. *Patrons and Painters: Art in Scotland 1650–1760* (Edinburgh, 1989)

Hutton, R. *Charles II: King of England, Scotland, and Ireland* (Oxford, 1989)

Hutton, R. *The Royalist War Effort, 1642–1646* (London, 1999)

Jackson, C. *Restoration Scotland, 1660–1690: Royalist Politics, Religion and Ideas* (Woodbridge, 2004)

Judson, M.A. *The Political Thought of Sir Henry Vane the Younger* (Philadelphia, 1969)

Kamen, H. *The Iron Century: Social Change in Europe, 1550–1660* (London, 1971)

Kaplan, L. *Politics and Religion during the English Revolution: The Scots and the Long Parliament, 1643–1645* (New York, 1976)

King, R. *The Covenanters in the North* (Aberdeen, 1846)

Kishlansky, M. *A Monarchy Transformed: Britain 1603–1714* (London, 1996)

Kishlansky, M. *The Creation of the New Model Army* (Cambridge, 1979)

Kliger, S. *The Goths in England: A Study in Seventeenth and Eighteenth Century Thought* (New York, 1952)

Lee jr, M. *Great Britain's Solomon: King James VI and I in his Three Kingdoms* (Urbana IL, 1990)

Lee jr, M. *The Road to Revolution: Scotland under Charles I, 1625–37* (Urbana and Chicago, 1985)

Levack, B.P. *The Formation of the British State: England, Scotland and the Union, 1603–1707* (Oxford, 1987)

Little, P. *Lord Broghill and the Cromwellian Union with Ireland and Scotland* (Woodbridge, 2004)

Macinnes, A.I. *Charles I and the Making of the Covenanting Movement, 1625–1641* (Edinburgh, 1991)

Macinnes, A.I. *Clanship, Commerce and the House of Stuart 1603–1788* (East Linton, 1996)

Macinnes, A.I. *The British Revolution, 1629–1660* (Basingstoke, 2005)

Macinnes, A.I. *Union and Empire: The Making of the United Kingdom in 1707* (Cambridge, 2007)

MacKenzie, W.C. *History of the Outer Hebrides* (Edinburgh, reprinted 1974)

MacLeod, J. *Scottish Theology* (Edinburgh, 1974)

Makey, W. *The Church of the Covenant, 1637–1651* (Edinburgh, 1979)

Mann, A.J. *The Scottish Book Trade, 1500–1720: Print Commerce and Print Control in Early Modern Scotland* (East Linton 2000)

Marshall, G. *Presbyteries and Profits: Calvinism and the Development of Capitalism in Scotland, 1560–1707* (Oxford, 1980)

Mathew, D. *Scotland Under Charles I* (London, 1955)

Mathieson, W.L. *Church and Reform in Scotland*, 2 vols (Glasgow, 1906)

McKerral, A. *Kintyre in the 17th Century* (Edinburgh, 1948)

Morrill, J. *The Nature of the English Revolution* (Harlow, 1993)

Mullan, D.G. *Episcopacy in Scotland: The History of an Idea, 1560–1638* (Edinburgh, 1986)

Mullan, D.G. *Scottish Puritanism* (Oxford, 1999)

Murdoch, S. *Britain, Denmark-Norway and the House of Stuart, 1603–1660* (East Linton, 2000)

Murdoch, S. *Network North: Scottish Kin, Commerical and Covert Associations in Northern Europe 1603–1746* (Leiden and Boston, 2006)

Nicholls, K.W. *Gaelic and Gaelicised Ireland in the Middle Ages* (Dublin, 1972)

Ó Buachalla, B. *Foras Feasa ar Éirinn, History of Ireland: Foreword* (Dublin, 1987)

Ohlmeyer, J.H. *Civil War and Restoration in the Three Stuart Kingdoms: The Career of Randal MacDonnell, Marquis of Antrim* (Cambridge, 1993)

Ó Siochrú, M. *Confederate Ireland, 1642–9: A Constitutional and Political Analysis* (Dublin, 1999)

Ó Siochrú, M. *God's Executioner: Oliver Cromwell and the Conquest of Ireland* (London, 2008)

Perceval-Maxwell, M. *The Outbreak of the Irish Rebellion of 1641* (Montreal, 1994)

Perceval-Maxwell, M. *The Scottish Migration to Ulster in the Reign of James I* (London, 1973)

Pincus, S. *Protestantism and Patriotism: Ideologies and the Making of English Foreign Policy, 1650–1668* (Cambridge, 1996)

Robinson, P. *The Plantation of Ulster* (Belfast, 2000)

Roots, I. *The Great Rebellion* (Stroud, 1995)

Rubinstein, H.L. *Captain Luckless: James, First Duke of Hamilton, 1606–1649* (Edinburgh and London, 1975)

Russell, C. *The Causes of the English Civil Wars* (Oxford, 1990)

Russell, C. *The Fall of the British Monarchies, 1637–1642* (Oxford, 1991)

Schaub, J-F. *La France Espagnole: Les raciness hispaniques d l'absolutisme français* (Paris, 2003)

Scott, D. *Politics and War in the Three Stuart Kingdoms, 1637–49* (Basingstoke, 2004)

Scott, W.R. *The Constitution and Finance of English, Scottish and Irish Joint-Stock Companies to 1720*, 3 vols (Cambridge, 1911–12)

Sharpe, K. *The Personal Rule of Charles I* (New Haven and London, 1992)

Shaw, F.J. *The Northern and Western Islands of Scotland: Their Economy and Society in the Seventeenth Century* (Edinburgh, 1980)

Smith, D.L. *Constitutional Royalism and the Search for Settlement, c.1640–1649* (Cambridge, 1994)

Smyth, J. *The Making of the United Kingdom, 1660–1800* (Harlow, 2001)

Stevenson, D. *Alasdair MacColla and the Highland Problem in the Seventeenth Century* (Edinburgh, 1980)

Stevenson, D. *King or Covenant? Voices from the Civil War* (East Linton, 1996)

Stevenson, D. *Revolution and Counter-Revolution in Scotland, 1644–1651* (London, 1977)

Stevenson, D. *Scottish Covenanters and Irish Confederates* (Belfast, 1981)

Stevenson, D. *The Covenanters: The National Covenant and Scotland* (Edinburgh, 1988)

Stevenson, D. *The Scottish Revolution, 1637–44* (Newton Abbot, 1973)

Todd, M. *The Culture of Protestantism in Early Modern Scotland* (New Haven, 2002)

Thompson, D. *The Life and Art of George Jamesone* (Oxford, 1974)

Vallance, E. *Revolutionary England and the National Covenant: State Oaths, Protestantism and the Political Nation, 1553–1682* (Woodbrige, 2005)

Venning, T. *Cromwellian Foreign Policy* (New York, 1995)

Vergé-Franceschi, M. *Colbert: La politique du bons sens* (Paris, 2005)

Walsham, A. *Providence in Early Modern England* (Oxford, 1999)

Warden, B. *Roundhead Reputations* (London, 2001)

Wheeler, J.S. *The Irish and British Wars 1637–1654: Triumph, Tragedy and Failure* (London, 2002)

Williamson, A.H. *Apocalypse Then: Prophecy and the Making of the Modern World* (Westport CT, 2008)

Willcock, J. *The Great Marquess: Life and Times of Archibald, 8th Earl, and 1st (and only) Marquess of Argyll* (Edinburgh and London, 1903)

Withers, C.W.J. *Scottish Gaeldom: The Transformation of a Culture Region* (London, 1988)

Woolrych, A. *Britain in Revolution, 1625–1660* (Oxford, 2002)

Woolrych, A. *Commonwealth to Protectorate* (Oxford, 1986)

Woolrych, A. *Soldiers and Statesmen: The General Council of the Army and its Debates, 1647–48* (Oxford, 1987)

Young, J.R. *The Scottish Parliament, 1639–1661: A Political and Constitutional Analysis* (Edinburgh, 1996)

3.3 Edited Books

Adamson, J. ed. *The English Civil War: Conflicts and Contexts, 1640–49* (London, 2009)

Bailyn, B. and Morgan, P.D. eds. *Strangers within the Realm: Cultural Margins of the First British Empire* (Chapel Hill, 1991)

Brady, C. and Ohlmeyer, J. eds. *British Interventions in Early Modern Ireland* (Cambridge, 2005)

Bradshaw, B. and Morrill, J. eds. *The British Problem, c.1534–1707: State Formation in the Atlantic Archipelago* (Basingstoke, 1996)

Brown, K.M. and Mann, A.J. eds. *Parliament and Politics in Scotland, 1567-1707* (Edinburgh, 2005)

Byrne, C., Harry, M. and O'Siadhail, P. eds. *Celtic Languages and Celtic Peoples* (Halifax, N.S., 1992)

Canny, N. ed. *The Oxford History of the British Empire, vol. 1: The Origins of Empire: British Overseas Empire to the Close of the Seventeenth Century* (Oxford, 1998)

Coward, B. ed. *A Companion to Stuart Britain* (Oxford, 2003)

Dwyer, J., Mason, R.A. and Murdoch, A. eds. *New Perspectives on the Politics and Culture of Early Modern Scotland* (Edinburgh, 1982)

Edwards, D., Lenihan, P. and Tait, C. eds. *Age of Atrocity: Violence and Political Conflict in Early Modern Ireland* (Dublin, 2007)

Ellis, S.G. and Esser, R. eds. *Frontiers and the Writing of History, 1500-1800* (Hannover-Laatzen, 2006)

Evans, R.J.W. and Thomas, T.V. eds. *Crown, Church and Estates: Central European Politics in the Sixteenth and Seventeenth Centuries* (London, 1991)

Fincham, K. ed. *The Early Stuart Church, 1603-1642* (Basingstoke, 1993)

Friedrich, K. and Pendzich, B.M. eds, *Citizenship and Identity in a Multi-National Commonwealth: Poland-Lithuania in Context, 1550-1750* (Leiden and Boston, 2009)

Gilles, W. ed. *Gaelic and Scotland, Alba agus A'Ghàidhlig* (Edinburgh, 1989)

Gentles, I., Morrill J. and Worden, B. eds. *Soldiers, Writers and Statesmen of the English Revolution* (Cambridge, 1998)

Graham, B.J. and Proudfoot, L.J. eds. *An Historical Geography of Ireland* (London, 1993)

Greengrass, M., Leslie, M., and Raylor, T. eds. *Samuel Hartlib and Universal Reformation* (Cambridge, 1994)

Howard, M., Anderson, G.J. and Shulman, M.R. eds. *The Laws of War: Constraints on Warfare in the Western World* (New Haven, 1994)

Jones, C. ed. *The Scots and Parliament* (Edinburgh, 1996)

Kelly, W.P. and Young, J.R. eds, *Scotland and the Ulster Plantation: Explorations in the Britsh Settlement of Stuart Ireland* (Dublin, 2009)

Kenyon, J. and Ohlmeyer, J.H. eds. *The Civil Wars: A Military History of England, Scotland and Ireland 1638-1660* (Oxford, 1998)

Kyle, C.R. and Peacey, J. eds. *Parliament at Work: Parliamentary Committees, Political Power and Public Access in Early Modern England* (Woodbridge, 2002)

Kyle, C.R. ed. *Parliament, Politics and Elections, 1604-1648* (Cambridge, 2001)

Lenihan, P. ed. *Conquest and Resistance: War in Seventeenth Century Ireland* (Leiden, 2001)

Levene, M. and Roberts, P. eds. *The Massacre in History* (Oxford, 1999)

Little, P. ed. *Oliver Cromwell: New Perspectives* (Basingstoke, 2009)

Lynch, M. and Goodare, J. eds. *The Reign of James VI* (East Linton, 1999)

MacCuarta, B. ed. *Ulster 1641: Aspects of the Rising* (Belfast, 1997)

Macinnes, A.I., Riis, T. and Pedersen, F.G. eds. *Ships, Guns and Bibles in the North Sea and Baltic States* (East Linton, 2000)

Macinnes, A.I. and Ohlmeyer, J. eds. *The Stuart Kingdoms in the Seventeenth Century: Awkward Neighbours* (Dublin, 2002)

Maclean, L. ed. *The Seventeenth Century Highlands* (Inverness, 1985)

Mason, R.A. ed. *Scots and Britons: Scottish Political Thought and the Union of 1603* (Cambridge, 1994)

Mason, R.A. ed. *Scotland and England 1286–1815* (Edinburgh, 1987)

Menzies, G. ed. *The Scottish Nation: A History of the Scots from Independence to Union* (London, 1972)

Merritt, J.F. ed. *The Political World of Thomas Wentworth, Earl of Strafford, 1621–1641* (Cambridge, 1996)

Mitchison, R. and Roebuck, P. eds. *Economy and Society in Scotland and Ireland, 1500–1939* (Edinburgh, 1988)

Morrill, J. ed. *The Scottish National Covenant in its British Context* (Edinburgh, 1990)

Murdoch, S. ed. *Scotland and the Thirty Years' War, 1618–1648* (Leiden and Boston, 2001)

Murdoch, S. and Mackillop, A. eds. *Fighting for Identity: Scottish Military Experience, c.1500–1900* (Leiden and Boston, 2002)

Ohlmeyer, J. ed. *Ireland: From Independence to Occupation 1641–1660* (Cambridge, 1995)

Ohlmeyer, J.H. ed. *Political Thought in Seventeenth Century Ireland* (Cambridge, 2000)

Ó Siochrú, M. ed. *Kingdoms in Crisis: Ireland in the 1640s* (Dublin, 2000)

Peacey, J. ed. *The Regicides and the Execution of Charles I* (Basingstoke 2001)

Pettegree, A., Duke, A and Lewis, G. eds. *Calvinism in Europe, 1540–1620* (Cambridge, 1994)

Pocock, J.G.A. ed. *The Varieties of British Political Thought, 1500–1800* (Cambridge, 1996)

Renton, R.W. and Osborne, B.D. eds. *Exploring New Roads: Essays on Neil Munro* (Colonsay, 2007)

Robertson, J. ed. *A Union for Empire: Political Thought and the Union of 1707* (Cambridge, 1995)

Wormald, J. ed. *Scotland: A History* (Oxford, 2005)

Young, J.R. ed. *Celtic Dimensions of the British Civil Wars* (Edinburgh, 1997)

3.4 Journal Articles

Adamson, J.S.A. 'The English Nobility and the Projected Settlement of 1647', *HJ*, 30 (1987), pp. 567–602

Barber, S. 'The People of Northern England and Attitudes towards the Scots, 1639–1651: "The Lamb and the Dragon cannot be Reconciled"', *Northern History*, 35 (1999), pp. 93–118

Bennett, M. 'Dampnified Villagers: Taxation and Wales during the First Civil War', *Welsh History Review*, 19 (1998), pp. 29–43

Buckroyd, J.M. 'Bridging the Gap: Scotland 1659–1660', *SHR*, 66 (1987), pp. 1–25

Bulman, W.J. 'The Practice of Politics: The English Civil War and the "Resolution" of Henrietta Maria and Charles I', *Past & Present*, 206 (2010), pp. 43–80

Capern, A.L. 'The Caroline Church: James Ussher and the Irish Dimension', *HJ*, 39 (1996), pp. 57–85

Carlin, N. 'The Levellers and the Conquest of Ireland in 1649', *HJ*, 39 (1987), pp. 269–88

Cogswell, T. 'The Politics of Propaganda: Charles I and the People in the 1620s', *Journal of British Studies*, 29 (1990), pp. 187–215

Cowan, E.J. 'Clanship, Kinship and the Campbell Acquisition of Islay', *SHR*, 58 (1979), pp. 132–57

Cowan, E.J. 'Fishers in Drumlie Waters: Clanship and Campbell Expansion in the Time of Gilleasbuig Gruamach', *TGSI*, 54 (1984–86), pp. 269–312

DesBrisay, G. 'Catholics, Quakers and Religious Prosecution in Restoration Aberdeen', *Innes Review*, 37 (1966), pp. 136–68

Donagan, B. 'Codes of Conduct in the English Civil War', *Past & Present*, 118 (1988), pp. 64–95

Ellis, S.G. 'The Collapse of the Gaelic World, 1450–1650', *IHS*, 31 (1999), pp. 449–69

Flower, R. 'An Irish-Gaelic Poem on the Montrose Wars', *Scottish Gaelic Studies*, I (1926), pp. 113–18

Furgol, E.M. 'The Northern Highland Covenanting Clans, 1639–51', *Northern Scotland*, 7 (1987), pp. 119–31

Gentles, I. 'The Choosing of the Officers for the New Model Army', *Historical Research*, 67 (1994), pp. 264–85

Gillespie, R. 'Plantation and Profit: Richard Spert's Tract on Ireland, 1608', *Irish Economic and Social History*, 20 (1993), pp. 62–71

Goodare, J. 'The Scottish Parliament of 1621', *HJ*, 38 (1995), pp. 29–51

Goodare, J. 'The Statutes of Iona in Context', *SHR*, 77 (1998), pp. 31–57

Henderson, J.M. '"An Advertisement" about the Service Book, 1637', *SHR*, 32 (1925–26), pp. 199–204

Kirk, J. and Meek, D. 'John Carswell, Superintendent of Argyll: A Reassessment', *RSCHS*, 19 (1975), pp. 1–22

Kishlansky, M. 'Charles I: A Case of Mistaken Identity', *Past & Present*, 189 (2005), pp. 41–80

Kishlansky, M. 'The Army and the Levellers: The Roads to Putney', *HJ*, 22 (1979), pp. 795–824

Kishlansky, M. 'The Case of the Army Truly Stated: The Creation of the New Model Army', *Past & Present*, 81 (1978), pp. 51–74

Kupperman, K.O. 'Errand to the Indies: Puritan Colonization from Providence Island through the Western Design', *William and Mary Quarterly*, 45 (1988), pp. 70–99

Lee, jnr., M. 'James VI's Government of Scotland after 1603', *SHR*, 55 (1976), pp. 49–53

Little, P. 'The Earl of Cork and the Fall of the Earl of Strafford, 1638–41', *HJ*, 39 (1996), pp. 619–35

MacGregor, M. 'The Statutes of Iona: Text and Context', *Innes Review*, 57 (2006), pp. 111–81

Macinnes, A.I. 'Catholic Recusancy and the Penal Laws, 1603–1707', *RSCHS*, 33 (1987), pp. 27–63

Macinnes, A.I. 'The First Scottish Tories?', *SHR*, 67 (1988), pp. 56–66

Macinnes, A.I. 'Lochaber – The Last Bandit County, c.1600–c.1750', *TGSI*, 64 (2004–06), pp. 1–21

Mackay, P.H.R. 'The Reception Given to the Five Articles of Perth', *RSCHS*, 19 (1977), pp. 255–98

Mahoney, M. 'The Saville Affair and the Politics of the Long Parliament', *Parliamentary History*, 7 (1988), pp. 212–27

Ó Siochru, M. 'Atrocity, Codes of Conduct and the Irish in the British Civil Wars 1641–1653', *Past & Present*, 195 (2007), pp. 55–86

Perceval-Maxwell, M. 'Ireland and the Monarchy in the Early Stuart Multiple Kingdom', *HJ*, 34 (1991), pp. 279–95

Raymond, J. 'Framing Liberty: Marvell's *First Anniversary* and the Instrument of Government', *Huntington Library Quarterly*, 62 (1999), pp. 313–50

Richards, J. '"His Nowe Majestie" and the English Monarchy: The Kingship of Charles I before 1640', *Past & Present*, 113 (1986), pp. 70–96

Robertson, B. 'The House of Huntly and the First Bishops' War', *Northern Scotland*, 24 (2004), pp. 1–15

Rusche, H. 'Prophecies and Propaganda, 1641 to 1651', *EHR*, 84 (1969), pp. 752–70

Scott, D. 'The Barwis Affair: Political Allegiance and the Scots during the British Civil Wars', *EHR*, 115 (2000), pp. 843–63

Scott, D. '"The Northern Gentlemen", the Parliamentary Independents and Anglo-Saxon Relations in the Long Parliament', *HJ*, 42 (1999), pp. 347–75

Sellar, W.D.H. 'The Earliest Campbells: Normans, Britons or Gael?', *Scottish Studies*, 17 (1973), pp. 109–24

Shaw, F.J. 'Landownership in the Western Isles in the Seventeenth Century', *SHR*, 56 (1977), pp. 34–47

Sinclair, A.M. 'A Collection of Gaelic Poems', *TGSI*, 26 (1904–07), pp. 237–9

Smith, D.L. '"The More Posed and Wised Advice": The Fourth Earl of Dorset and the English Civil Wars', *HJ*, 34 (1991), pp. 797–829

Spence, R.T. 'The Backward North Modernised? The Cliffords, Earls of Cumberland and the Socage Manor of Carlisle, 1611–43', *Northern History*, 20 (1984), pp. 64–87

Spurlock, R.S. '"Anie Gospel Way": Religious Diversity in Interregnum Scotland', *RSCHS*, 37 (2007), pp. 89–120.

Stevenson, D. 'Conventicles in the Kirk, 1619–1637', *RSCHS*, 18 (1972–74), pp. 99–114

Stevenson, D. 'The Financing of the Cause of the Covenants, 1638–51', *SHR*, 51 (1972), pp. 89–123

Stewart, L. 'English Funding of the Scottish Armies in England and Ireland, 1640–48', *HJ*, 53 (2009), pp. 573–93

Torrance, J.B. 'The Covenant Concept in Scottish Theology and Politics and its Legacy', *Scottish Journal of Theology*, 34 (1981), pp. 225–43

Vallance, E. '"An Holy and Sacramental Paction": Federal Theology and the Solemn League and Covenant in England', *EHR*, 116 (2000), pp. 50–75

Vallance, E. 'Protestations, Vow, Covenant and Engagement: Swearing Allegiance in the English Civil War', *Historical Research*, 75 (2002), pp. 408–24

Watson, W.J. 'Unpublished Gaelic Poetry', *Scottish Gaelic Studies*, 3 (1931), pp. 152–6

Whyte, I.D. 'Poverty or Prosperity? Rural Society in Lowland Scotland in the Late Sixteenth and Early Seventeenth Centuries', *Scottish Economic and Social History*, 18 (1998), pp. 19–31

Williamson, A.H. 'Scots, Indians and Empire: The Scottish Politics of Civilization, 1519–1609', *Past & Present*, 150 (1996), pp. 46–83

Williamson, A.H. 'Union with England Traditional, Union with England Radical: Sir James Hope and the Mid-Seventeenth Century British State', *EHR*, 110 (1995), pp. 303–12.

Willman, R. 'The Origins of "Whig" and "Tory" in English Political Language', *HJ*, 17 (1974), pp. 247–64

Worden, B. 'The Politics of Marvell's Horation Ode', *HJ*, 27 (1984), pp. 525–47

Wormald, J. 'Bloodfeud, Kindred and Government in Early Modern Scotland', *Past & Present*, 87 (1980), pp. 54–97

Young, J.R. 'Scottish Covenanting Radicalism, the Commission of the Kirk and the Establishment of the Parliamentary Radical Regime of 1648–1649', *RSCHS*, 25 (1995), pp. 342–75.

Index